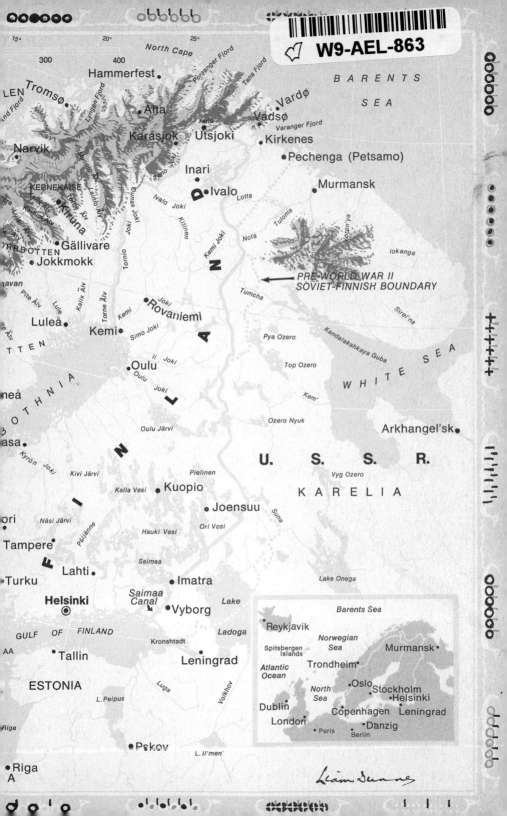

The Scandinavians

The
SCANDINAVIANS

Donald S. Connery

SIMON AND SCHUSTER · NEW YORK

For Leslie

Author's Note

There is a certain ritual about partaking in a Scandinavian *smörgåsbord*: a customary sequence of dishes. But there is nothing to restrain an adventurous diner from starting his selection with whatever whets his appetite. So too with this book. It is perhaps best read from beginning to end, but its design makes each of the five parts, and each chapter, a self-contained unit. The reader may, if he wishes, go first to whatever appeals to him most.

Contents

Part Three / Norway

Postscript/Iceland

INTRODUCTION

Scandinavia was well off the beaten path when I first went to Europe in 1948. It was a summer in which I tried to squeeze the whole continent into one long working vacation. Denmark, Norway and Sweden could easily have been left off the itinerary. They looked like small, unimportant countries filling in the space between the ruins of Germany and the Arctic Ocean. I knew almost nothing about them except that they were inhabited by honest, hard-working people who had somehow constructed modern 'middle-way' societies out of meager resources. They were people in a northern world of dark days and bright nights who read a lot of books, enjoyed good plumbing and had some problems about love and laughter in a cold climate.

The Danes by reputation were jolly, the Norwegians sturdy and the Swedes skillful but stuffy. During the war, Denmark had been conquered in two hours but had later mounted a resistance movement. Norway had been occupied after a struggle but had fought on with a Free Norwegian government in London. Sweden, miraculously untouched by war for a century and a half, had escaped attack and stayed on the sidelines. And then there were the Finns, also known to be honest and hard-working, but I was not to meet them until years later. They seemed a distant, scarcely European race, like ghostly skiers in a snow-shrouded eastern forest, yet they were said to be as progressive and enlightened as the rest of the Scandinavians. They were the people who had 'paid their debts' and had bravely battled the Russian invaders in the Winter War. But then in the larger World War their history became muddied and their survival as a free people uncertain. In those early postwar days it was said that Finland had become a Soviet satellite. It seemed hard to believe.

I wanted to visit the Scandinavian countries because I was

curious to see whether they had found a democratic way for the world to rise above communism, fascism and the primitive form of capitalism which ignores human distress. Nineteen forty-eight was a good time to be in Denmark and Norway, even if life was difficult in that gray period before the blossoming of postwar prosperity. The wartime occupation was still so fresh in mind that a visiting American was overwhelmed by the hospitality of people delighted to be free again. In Sweden, life was better— better than in all the rest of Europe—but there was no joy. The war seemed to have left the Swedes conscience-stricken. This, plus their natural reserve, made them hospitable but uncommunicative. Streetcars full of silent people rumbled through Stockholm like wheeled coffins.

I left Scandinavia a month later puzzling about the differences of national temperament but exulting in what I had seen: not a perfect society by any means, but a compelling one, where social inequalities and injustices were being attacked without loss of freedom. I had found that these were not socialist countries, as they were widely believed to be, but highly socialized communities predominantly relying on private enterprise to build their prosperity. Most of all, I went away with an impression of a 'clean, well-lighted place' where air, sea and glass combined to give a special clarity to up-to-date societies built in harmony with nature. From that radiant summer there were vivid memories of Norway's spectacular mountains and fjords, Sweden's carefully tailored beauty and the innocent delights of Denmark.

In the intervening years as a reporter in America and a foreign correspondent in Asia and Europe I had good reason to marvel at any society which was able to retain its idealism and good sense in a world scarred with brutality. 'The battle is between humanity and subhumanity,' wrote Dag Hammarskjöld, the most notable of the many Scandinavians who have gone about the globe as peacemakers. In November 1962, at the time of the Cuban crisis, I was expelled from Russia for 'unobjective' reporting. I flew from Moscow, that most cheerless of cities, into the loving arms of Copenhagen. It took only a few minutes of driving from the ultramodern airport to the downtown shops bursting with well-designed goods to see how fruitful the last fourteen years had been. Denmark, and Scandinavia as a whole, had become an affluent society, where the wealth was spread more equitably than in almost all the rest of the world.

In the several years since that first reunion with the Nordic countries, I have made repeated journeys to them all, and in all seasons. A series of magazine assignments provided the occasion to observe the northern peoples in their everyday life, to spend weeks with industrialists and artists, and to follow cross-country skiers through the winter silences of Finnish Lapland. In my last two trips immediately before beginning this book I drove ten thousand miles through the four countries (and then flew to Iceland as well) in an attempt to see everything, from the south of Jutland to that Arctic corner north of Finland where armed Norwegians and Russians face each other at the edge of Europe's last great wilderness.

It has been a deliberate exercise in self-education: first, because the Danes, Finns, Swedes and Norwegians—and the Icelanders—are people well worth knowing, and too little understood; second, to see if the higher living standard and the more rewarding life they seemed to be enjoying was a miracle or mirage. Was it too good to be true? And if it was true, was there something in it for other nations, however larger, more complex or conflict-ridden they might be?

This book is a description of contemporary Scandinavia as I have found it. While I have turned to the histories of the North, read other works on the Scandinavians and made use of official material and newspapers, I am relying primarily on my own observations and a great many conversations. This is meant to be a reporter's account of the machinery of the Scandinavian civilization and its important moving parts. It is concerned with some of the special attractions and personalities of a place too often dismissed as dull and uneventful simply because it is so eminently constructive. The opening chapters deal with the Nordic world as a whole and look into some of the prevailing misconceptions about Scandinavian sex, suicide and socialism. The succeeding chapters cover the five nations in turn, but they do not pretend to describe in detail every institution of each country. I am simply writing about what I found most interesting and think most significant. A description of the 'labor peace' techniques or the treatment of criminals in one country can serve to suggest the essence of them all. The Scandinavians, for all their individual characteristics, have similar institutions as well as a common concern for human rights and a common optimism that solutions can be found for even the most vexing of human problems.

This is not an uncritical portrait of Scandinavia. I am much too aware of its imperfections, and I would even hesitate to recommend it as a place to live in for anyone whose nervous system is attuned to the more turbulent and temperamental world outside. I respect the Nordic peoples, but I think the truth is best served by viewing their societies with a healthy skepticism. It is not paradise and it never will be. And yet the Scandinavian aim, as the Danes express it, is to achieve 'the greatest possible happiness for the greatest number of people.' The objective is worthy. The effort has been mighty, and it is continuing. The achievement is open for examination.

Part One

Scandinavia

Chapter 1

THE NEW VIKINGS

The first great thing is to find yourself and for that you need solitude and contemplation—at least sometimes. I tell you deliverance will not come from the rushing noisy centers of civilization. It will come from the lonely places.

FRIDTJOF NANSEN

We are suffused with a pale benevolence instead of the antagonism we used to know.

NORWEGIAN CLERGYMAN

A thousand years ago the Vikings slipped out of the fjords and forests of northern Europe to plunder the civilized world and colonize the uncivilized world. The Danes and Norwegians swarmed into England and Ireland, swept down the European coast, founded Normandy, attacked Paris, and plunged into the Mediterranean as far as the Byzantine Empire. In their ingeniously designed longboats they struck across the Atlantic to Iceland, Greenland and North America five hundred years before Columbus reached the Caribbean in ships half the length. By sea and land, the Swedish Vikings, known as 'the Rus', penetrated so deeply into the eastern land mass that they reached the Middle East and Central Asia, and left the name 'Russia.'

The Viking Age was a time of merchant adventurers and empire builders. It was the wonder of the world how such resourceful and well-organized people could have emerged in the harsh, forbidding North, where the iron-gray winters were interrupted only briefly by the warming sun of summer. It is a question which

3

can as well be asked today about the phenomenon of the four Scandinavian countries, the most prosperous, orderly, democratic and socially secure group of nations in the world.

Sweden pays the best wages and has the highest standard of living in Europe. In its distribution of prosperity to all its citizens it exceeds the United States. Slightly less wealthy but just as welfare-minded are Denmark, Norway and Finland. Together with Sweden they have gone further than almost all other nations in the elimination of poverty, the creation of full employment and the raising of health standards. With a population of 22 million—less than half that of England, one ninth that of America—Scandinavia leads the world in healthy babies, long life, literacy, newspaper readership, book publishing, outdoor sports and innumerable other measurements which say something about the quality of national life.

They are old societies with young ideas. Their cities look freshly minted. Their technology is advanced, and industrialization has made them rich, but their countryside is unspoiled. They have a high degree of social and economic organization. From the model farms of Denmark to the glaciers of Lapland, it is a place of wild strawberries and peaceful public affairs. It is seen from the outside world through familiar images and names: Garbo, Sibelius, Nobel Prizes, the welfare state, *smörgåsbord*, cooperatives, Swedish sex, Danish bacon, the Midnight Sun, Scandinavian Design.

It was relative isolation from the main currents of world affairs that enabled the Scandinavians to develop their unique civilization, and it is their emergence today from isolation that represents a new but considerably more peaceful eruption of the Vikings. Even during the days of Canute the Great, when Europe trembled at the approach of the Viking hordes, there was no counterinvasion of the North. Like the Japanese who stood apart from the Asian mainland, the northern peoples were able to develop slowly as homogeneous, closely knit societies little infused with foreign blood and only superficially infected by alien ideas. The Baltic served the Norwegians, Swedes and Finns as a moat which screened them from the influences of Central Europe. The Danes, occupying a scattering of territory at the entrance to the

Baltic and linked to what is now Germany by a narrow land corridor, somehow preserved their Nordic identity as well.

The privileged classes of Scandinavia eventually took on the trappings of Continental culture, and Christianity came to stay, but it was a selective adoption of foreign ways, much as the Japanese took what they wanted of Chinese culture and then no more. The Swedes and the Danes had their fling at great-power status from the Middle Ages through the Napoleonic era. Their armies took part in the Continental wars and fought each other for dominance in the North, but, on the whole, the Scandinavians remained a people apart—uninvolved, unconquered and un-diluted. Even Finland, as a grand duchy of Tsarist Russia from 1809 to 1917, functioned as an almost autonomous state, and with a greater measure of self-government than it had known in its six and a half centuries under Swedish rule.

Apart from the impact of a handful of cultural figures like Ibsen, Andersen and Strindberg, and some celebrated explorers, the Scandinavians of a century ago met the world as sailors and traders—and as a poverty-stricken mass. During the second half of the nineteenth century, more than a million Swedes and an-other million Norwegians, Finns and Danes migrated to America. Scandinavia's rise from rags to riches makes one of the most dramatic stories in European economic history.

Today's Scandinavian outburst is something more than con-quering hordes, merchant traders and refugees from poverty. The new breed are The Experts. They build telephone factories in Latin America, teach birth control in Ceylon, keep the peace in the Congo, and advise Arabian oil millionaires on how to spend their money. It was a Norwegian and a Swede, Trygve Lie and Dag Hammarskjöld, who ran the United Nations during the first fifteen years of its life, and a Finn, Sakari Tuomioja, who was the United Nations' political representative on Cyprus. Danish engineers have erected harbors in the Persian Gulf and cement factories in Korea. Norwegian experts are teaching the Indians how to develop a modern fishing industry. Sweden's Volvo company built the first European automobile factory in North America (at Dartmouth, Canada) and powerful Swedish bankers arranged the financing of the LAMCO iron-ore project in Liberia. Swedish economist Gunnar Myrdal, author of a classic study of the American racial dilemma, has completed a major work on the economic problems of underdeveloped nations. Ingmar Bergman has burst forth in the past decade as one of the most original and disturbing forces of the international cinema. Finland's Alvar Aalto, one of the handful of the world's great architects, and Denmark's Arne Jacobsen, who designed St. Catherine's College at Oxford, are just two of several hundred architects and artists who have made Scandinavian design a worldwide synonym for elegant functionalism.

The Scandinavian expertise which most commands world attention is expressed in the democratic welfare state. In the construction of a middle-way 'ultimate society,' they have built the kind of better mousetrap which the world envies, denounces, studies and often seeks to imitate. Hundreds of foreign economists, politicians, psychologists, journalists, labor leaders, city planners and social workers flock to Scandinavia every year to see if the thing really works. While American and British trade-union officials go to Stockholm to learn how the famous 'labor peace' has been achieved, the friendly chiefs of the great labor and management federations travel together to New York and London to explain why there was a fury of strikes several decades ago and few strikes today.

War and Cold War

World War II was a traumatic experience for the Scandinavians. The policy of neutrality had worked in the first world war, but with Sweden excepted, it fell apart in the second. Stalin attacked Finland, and Hitler marched into Denmark and Norway. Today's Cold War conditions have brought all four nations out into the world in a manner sharply contrasting with their prewar position. Denmark and Norway have abandoned neutrality and joined the Western alliance. Sweden bolsters its armed neutrality by trying to strengthen international peace-keeping operations. Neutral Finland, forced by circumstances to be more than friendly to

Russia, plays as large a role as it can in nonmilitary international organizations.

Denmark and Norway, as members of the North Atlantic Treaty Organization, are the first to admit that they rely on American nuclear strength for their ultimate safety. Sweden has refused to abandon its nonalignment policy, but at the heavy cost of maintaining armed forces of big-power proportions and elaborate underground shelters. Sweden's new role in international affairs is expressed mainly through its United Nations work and increasingly large foreign-aid commitments. It has been a major contributor of troops to United Nations forces in Suez, the Gaza Strip, the Congo and Cyprus. All this has meant an about-face in national attitudes. 'They used to turn instinctively inward,' said Prime Minister Tage Erlander of the Swedish younger generation. 'I sense a great change.'

Finland, which fought Russia during World War II as a reluctant ally of Germany, and then had to drive out the Germans at the end, has such a precarious proximity to the Soviet Union that it must be the most docile kind of neutral, doing nothing to arouse Russian ire. Yet it is a patently pro-Western nation which does four fifths of its trade with the non-Communist world. Finland is a partner in the Nordic Council, which promotes Scandinavian collaboration, and an associate member of the European Free Trade Association. Denmark, Norway and Sweden are EFTA members, and they would probably join the Common Market once their traditional best customer, Great Britain, is admitted. Sweden has said it would take such an important step only if it were assured that the Common Market would not be turned into a military bloc.

Aggressive Economies

It is the sheer dynamism of the Swedish economy, however, that is doing more than anything else to give this nation of just 7·7 million people—less than the population of New York or London—a new and disproportionate world influence. Because they are quietly competent experts in somber executive suits, the Swedish businessmen flying about the world in SAS jet planes are apt to be overlooked in the international scheme of things. And then it is reported that yet another automobile, telephone or ball-bearing factory has opened in a far-off country, or another complicated financial operation has been engineered by bankers in Stockholm. Sweden, in its own quiet way, has recently overtaken Britain as the world's biggest shipbuilder after Japan. The other Nordic countries are also far from being innocents on the world economic scene. Norway's merchant marine is one of the three largest. Denmark and Finland, although best known for their farms or forests, are rapidly expanding their industries and exporting everything from toys to icebreakers.

The Scandinavians must export to live, and they do so with agility and imagination. The combination of aggressive capitalists, an intelligent working force and 'socialist' governments far more pragmatic than doctrinaire has brought about an unprecedented standard of living. This in turn has played its part in the new Scandinavian emergence. Not only is the typical Scandinavian living better, in appliance-filled homes and apartments, but he has a television set to bring in the outside world, an automobile to give him a new mobility, and the extra income to permit him to travel. The Nordic peoples are becoming the most active tourists in Europe. Sweden's tourist revenues are now more than offset by the $185 million which 750,000 Swedes (one tenth of the nation) spend abroad each year. In all the Nordic countries, a huge business is being done by travel organizations which arrange chartered flights to the Mediterranean each year for hundreds of thousands of Scandinavians.

The importance of this tidal wave of travelers is that it has helped to strip away the provincialism which had been so marked in the northern countries. Today it is almost commonplace to find young Scandinavians who speak two or three languages, or who received part of their education abroad and vacation regularly in distant countries.

The outward movement of Scandinavians is reciprocated by the millions who now visit the four countries each year—a tourist intake many times greater than in prewar days. The influx of foreigners not only has vastly increased the worldly contact, but also, in Sweden, has caused so many traffic accidents that the Swedes are finally planning to join the rest of the Continent in driving on the right. Early one morning in the fall of 1967, in the critical phase of an eighty-million-dollar operation, police and a host of military and civic organizations will be out in full force directing traffic and switching signs and signals as all vehicles slow to a crawl and make a massive switch to the other side of the road.

A Feeling for Tradition

What travelers to Scandinavia find is a collection of countries which has made the leap from the rural past to the industrial, urban present without having strewn the land with ugliness. The industrial revolution came late to Scandinavia, well after other nations had experienced the blight of factory towns and the early battles of trade-unionism. The swing to a mainly urban society also came late, so that many mistakes were avoided, and change took place without unduly violating the look of the land or the essential pattern of Scandinavian life. There is a pervading sense of continuity in the North, with past and present living naturally side by side. Superhighways glide by eighth-century castles. Small factories are set unobtrusively in the forests. Lapps still follow their herds of reindeer across the northern wilderness but these days they often travel by weasel and helicopter. Nothing is more symbolic than the almost identical silhouettes of the great stone watchtowers surrounding the ancient city of Visby on Gotland and the five skyscrapers standing in a row like upended glass dominoes in the ultramodern heart of Stockholm.

In all the Scandinavian capitals and many other cities, a large portion of park space is set aside for a re-creation of the old pastoral life. Ancient farmhouses, barns, workshops and timbered townhouses from all over the country are lovingly reassembled to show how life used to be in simpler days. Viking ships are reverently displayed in Oslo, and the great warship *Vasa*, raised from the muck of Stockholm harbor after 333 years, is on view in a building where a continuous fine spray preserves it from disintegration. In thousands of small workshops all over the Nordic world, ceramists, glassworkers, silversmiths and furniture makers keep up the old traditions of craftsmanship which account for the high quality of Scandinavian domestic products. All of this traditionalism meshes easily with the modernism of hydroelectric projects, the European Space Research establishment in northern Sweden, and the shipyards turning out giant merchant vessels. The man who spends his day at the potter's wheel may well go skimming home at night in a hydrofoil water bus or drive his Saab to an atomic-energy-heated suburb.

Change in Scandinavia has been evolutionary, rarely revolutionary. The zeal for modern solutions has meant no rejection of the past. For all their democratic procedures, the Danes, Swedes and Norwegians still prefer to keep their monarchies. Similarly, in these overwhelmingly Lutheran countries, the vast majority of people hardly ever go to church, and they profess little interest in religion, yet almost all Scandinavians continue to be enrolled as members of the state church and pay a church tax. It is in their essentially conservative nature to do so. They accept change so long as it is nonviolent change. They have had their days of violence and have decided that it is better to talk things out and try to reach rational solutions. The harmony of today's labor relations is the result of management's willingness to move with the times and labor's willingness to restrain its militancy. The habit of peaceful solution gives the Scandinavian countries their special gloss of high civilization. It is rightly said that they are fortunate in having small populations and no racial or religious conflicts, but they have made the most of their good fortune.

Scandinavia?

There is no precise definition of Scandinavia as it is known today. It is often taken to mean only Denmark, Norway and Sweden, because of their similar racial origins and languages. The Finns racially and linguistically have more in common with the Estonians and Hungarians. They migrated in the dim past from some point deep in Russia. But Finland's more-than-600-year history as a part of Sweden stamped it indelibly as a Scandinavian nation with institutions and an over-all approach to life almost identical with those of its Nordic neighbors. ('Nordic,' according to Webster, is 'of or pertaining to the Germanic peoples of northern Europe, especially the Scandinavians,' but I am including the Finns for the sake of convenience.)

Swedish is one of the two official languages of Finland. The Lutheran Church, the parliamentary system, the rule of law, the pioneering work in social welfare, and even the character of the homes and schools—these are all common denominators of Scandinavia which apply as much to the Finns as to the Danes, Swedes and Norwegians. With its great northern reach of forests and icy lakes, and its stake in the Lapland wilderness, Finland has even more in common geographically with Norway and Sweden than does little Denmark.

Scandinavia is often defined as including Iceland. (In order to keep the focus on northern Europe I do not do so in this book.) This remote North Atlantic island, first settled by Irish monks and the Norwegian Vikings, was distantly ruled by Denmark for more than five hundred years, until it became fully independent during World War II. Iceland may actually be the most Scandinavian of all the northern countries. It has the purest Nordic language of them all—a language so little changed from the Viking days that the Icelander can read the old Norse sagas of the twelfth and thirteenth centuries as easily as he can read his daily newspaper. In contrast, the Norwegians and Danes find Icelandic incomprehensible.

The modern Icelanders have rightly been described as the ultimate Vikings. They have built up, especially during the last twenty-five years, such a vital and prosperous society that it is tempting to write about it at length on these pages. The trouble is that Iceland is so small that it only barely qualifies as a sovereign nation. Its population of 190,000 is no more than that of Salt Lake City, and until the Maldive Islands were admitted to membership in 1965 Iceland was easily the smallest nation in the United Nations. Furthermore, in its lonely ocean wilderness 645 miles to the west of Norway, Iceland is far removed from the intimate grouping of the four larger Scandinavian countries.

Some of the distinctions of the 'land of fire and ice,' including the fact that it has the oldest parliament in the world, are fascinating, to say the least, but they have such a small compass that everything seems more peculiarly Icelandic than Scandinavian. Iceland may belong to the Nordic Council, and its national institutions may look like Scandinavia in microcosm, but it is a unique society which has clung to a unique place for more than a thousand years. To add the particulars of Iceland to the generalities about the other Scandinavian nations would be to distort the whole. To ignore the Icelanders, on the other hand, would be to overlook a resourceful people who inhabit a land of awesome natural wonders. Iceland is therefore described in Chapter 33 as a postscript to this book.

Hard Land, Harsh Climate

Denmark is a small country of scattered bits and pieces, while Norway, Sweden and Finland together account for nearly a third of the territory of Western Europe. They are linked like sausages at the top of the continent. Sweden and Finland are the larger countries, but Norway, which is oddly shaped like a caveman's club, stretches north for more than a thousand miles. Its great length means that a citizen in southern Norway is closer to the Riviera than he is to the towns on the Arctic coast. Norway is creased by so many fjords or narrow inlets that if its land and sea frontier were ever straightened out it would reach halfway around the world.

The most important fact of Scandinavia is water. It has made the Nordic people natural seafarers, fishermen and merchant traders. Hydroelectric power has helped turn them into industrialists. The fact that most Norwegians live within a few miles of the ocean has made Norway one of the greatest of shipping, fishing and whaling nations. Sweden and Finland, which each have long sea frontiers, have between them more lakes than the rest of Europe combined. Almost all of Denmark is surrounded by water.

Norway is nature gone berserk.* Mountains erupt wildly along its whole length; fjords reach as many as 114 miles inland; and some 150,000 islands stand offshore like sentinels guarding the mainland from the fury of the Atlantic storms. Sweden, which shares some of Norway's mountains, is dimpled with 96,000 lakes and bristles with billions of trees. Finland is also heavily blanketed by forest, and its 60,000 lakes consume one tenth of the total area, or more than all of Finland's farm land. Southern Sweden with its bustling towns and lush farms looks more and more like Denmark as it stretches toward Copenhagen. It was once, in fact, a part of Denmark. The people in Skåne, the south-ernmost section of Sweden, complain like Danes about 'those stuffed shirts in Stockholm.' Copenhagen, with more than a million people, is Scandinavia's biggest and liveliest city. It holds fully a fourth of the Danish population. The rest of Denmark is a low-lying pastoral kingdom of prosperous farm land and gentle towns.

One quarter of Norway, Sweden and Finland lies above the Arctic Circle in the most thinly populated territory of all Europe. It is eye-opening to see just how far north these countries are. Even Copenhagen has approximately the same latitude as Moscow. If it were moved five thousand miles directly west it would sink into Hudson Bay, Canada. Norway, Sweden and Finland share a top layer of the globe with Alaska, Siberia and the North-west Territories of Canada.

The presence of the Gulf Stream means that Scandinavia's Atlantic coast is kept ice-free, and its warmth seeps far inland. The northern climate is classified as Polar Tundra, yet apple trees grow in coastal areas north of the Arctic Circle. Scandinavia is covered by snow for at least half of the year. The capital cities are placed well to the south in Norway, Sweden and Finland. Their winters are milder and their summers warmer than many people suspect. The mean temperatures for the four capitals in the coldest and warmest months of January–February and July are:

* A word stemming from Norse mythology which told of the *berserkr* warriors who fought with such frenzy that they were believed to be invulner-able.

Copenhagen, 33 and 62 degrees Fahrenheit; Oslo, 25 and 62·5 degrees; Stockholm, 26·5 and 64·5 degrees; and Helsinki, 21 and 64·5 degrees.

Even though the wintertime cold can be bone-chilling, the Scandinavians have, by long experience, learned to cope with it. Their well-built homes and apartment buildings, double windows and central heating enable them to live more warmly indoors through the winter than the British. *The Economist* has written: 'Nobody, they say, has been cold in Stockholm since Descartes died there, reputedly from working in Queen Christina's unheated royal library.' It is not temperature that counts with the Scandinavians so much as the northern extremes of prolonged winter darkness and summer light. This is most spectacularly expressed by the midnight sun, which is the primary tourist attraction in Lapland. In early summer the sun rises and forgets to go down, so that life must be lived in perpetual daylight. People walk their dogs or meet friends at two in the morning. To sleep they must cover their windows with black curtains.

The few bright months of summer are greeted almost deliriously by the Scandinavians. On the first fine days of May the heliotropic northerners lean back on park benches and drink in the sun's rays like prisoners let out of solitary confinement. There is probably no more beautiful sight in Scandinavia than the girls of Stockholm and Helsinki, sprawling like human sacrifices on the concert hall or cathedral steps, their skirts drawn up to their thighs, shoulders bared, eyes closed, and golden heads turned rapturously to the sun. Like so many butterflies released from their cocoons, the Scandinavians flock to the countryside, sleep little, swim, hike, burrow into sweet nature, and infect each other with a kind of midsummer madness. It has become almost impossible to find a doctor or a plumber at home in July.

There is a bittersweet quality to the Scandinavian summer, however. What is so alive so quickly dies. Too soon the long days fade into long nights. In the far north, in midwinter, the darkness lasts around the clock. The sun refuses to appear. In the south the pale sun rises reluctantly, clings to the horizon for a few hours and escapes. Midday looks like dawn in other countries.

The sky is leaden. Street lights shine in the morning and after-noon. The Swedes feel the grip of 'the winter sickness.' Life moves indoors, and people switch all too abruptly from a general melancholy to the ritualistic joys of a dinner party, which may end with boisterous singing on table tops. For the most part, it is a time for work and for dreams of summer. Nevertheless, Scandinavia can be magnetically attractive in the winter. It is then most like itself. People light fires to drive away the icicled gloom. Dinner tables and window sills glow with candles, and on St. Lucia's Day in Sweden the girls, wearing crowns of lighted candles, awaken their parents at dawn. The luxurious Opera Restaurant in Stockholm is ringed with flaring torches like Viking beacons. In the Nordic cities, there is a dry crackle in the air, but the snow muffles the footsteps and skaters glide silently on icy ponds. If there is an excess of darkness, there is also an abundance of light in the homes and shops of the most electrified part of Europe.

Quality and Teamwork

The Nordic countries provide less than one per cent of the total population of the world, yet they account for 10 per cent of the world's shipping, 5 per cent of international trade, and they make an outsized contribution in everything from science and sport to diplomacy and the arts. The emphasis is on quality, not quantity. Population densities, with the exception of Denmark, are the lowest in Europe. And even little Denmark has three times more elbow room than Britain and the Low Countries. There are 7·7 million Swedes, 4·7 million Danes, 4·6 million Finns and 3·7 million Norwegians. Sweden and Denmark have only recently turned into predominantly urban countries, with slightly more than half of the population now living in cities and towns. Finland and Norway are being so rapidly urbanized that they will turn the halfway mark in a decade or so.

Even with such a degree of city life in Scandinavia, there is still a persistence of thought patterns stemming from Scandinavia's rural past. Even the most sophisticated national leaders, most notably President Kekkonen of Finland, are only a step removed from the forests, farms and villages. The Swedish banker, Norwegian educator and Finnish engineer, for all their urban ways, like nothing better than to rough it in the most primitive kind of country shack. There are few really big Scandinavian cities, even in Sweden, and the largest industrial plants are usually only a few miles or a few steps from woods rich in wildlife or lakes sprinkled with sailboats.

Swedish historian Ingvar Andersson wrote that the central figure in Swedish history has always been the peasant. In medieval Sweden he 'retained his social and political freedom to a greater degree, played a greater part in the politics of the country, and was altogether a more considerable person, than in any other West European country.' The same was more or less true of farmers elsewhere in the North. Except for the Danes, they escaped the feudalism which so affected life in countries to the south.

Scandinavians have a long tradition of personal and political freedom, even allowing for the fact that Norway was for so long dominated by Denmark and Sweden, and Finland by Sweden and Russia. The average man felt himself to be a free man, not a creature at the disposal of an aristocracy. He was not ridden with a sense of inferiority. If anything, he was proud of his abilities, his independence and his self-sufficiency. Like the American frontiersman, his was often a solitary struggle to subdue his environment. In his immediate community he learned how cooperative effort could ensure survival, and this is the key to the extraordinary Scandinavian ability to work together as equals for a common goal. The most graphic demonstration of such teamwork in modern times was the way the Danish farmers in the nineteenth century organized themselves into cooperatives when economic forces compelled them to change from a grain to a dairy agriculture. Since then the producer and consumer cooperatives have played a more important role in the Nordic lands than anywhere else in the world. About a third of all Scandinavian families are members of at least one cooperative.

The five-nation Nordic Council is a kind of supercooperative which has had the effect of bestowing a common citizenship on the Danes, Finns, Swedes, Norwegians and Icelanders. They can move across the various borders and settle down where they please, with as much ease as Americans moving about the fifty states of the U.S.A. The Nordic Council was formed in 1953 to seek out areas of agreement and promote Scandinavian cooperation. It is by no means a Nordic parliament, and there is no sign that any member nation wants to federate. The last time that happened was in 1397, when Queen Margrethe of Denmark organized the all-Scandinavian Union of Kalmar which lasted fitfully until 1523. Although the Council has no real power except in its influence on public opinion, it studies and debates proposals for unified action on practical problems and helps put them into practice when all five nations agree. There are annual Nordic Council meetings of the five prime ministers and their associates, but the parliaments have the last word on major actions. The result is that Scandinavians do not need passports as they go from country to country, and workers can take on jobs anywhere and qualify for local social welfare. Some 100,000 Scandinavians are now at work in northern countries other than the lands of their birth. Some 70,000 of them are in Sweden. The Scandinavian states constitute a single postal, telegraph and telephone union. They collaborate on health measures, sponsor all-Scandinavian schools, and work on common economic problems. There is virtually a single legal system in being for the whole area. The fact of language similarity, which means that well-educated Scandinavians, excepting the Finns, can understand each other fairly well, has provided the basis for a growing amount of cultural cross-fertilization. Books and publications in Danish, Swedish or Norwegian can be read without translation in most of Scandinavia. Students and educators study and work in different countries under exchange programs; theater groups exchange visits; and a new institution called Nordvision is furthering cooperation in radio and television.

National Differences

Common history, common institutions and a common outlook on life would seem to make the Scandinavians, who have a higher proportion of blue-eyed blondes than any other people, so many peas in a pod, hardly distinguishable from one another. It is something of a shock, then, to discover how dissimilar they are, and how much they cherish their differences. There are striking variations in national character and some strong feelings of envy, antagonism and condescension. A lot of it is just amusing family feuding, but some of it is serious, sad and silly.

There are a good many stories dealing with national characteristics, and it is the Scandinavians who tell them most avidly. For example, two Danes, two Norwegians, two Finns and two Swedes are shipwrecked and cast up on a desert island. By the time they are rescued, the Danes have formed a cooperative, the Norwegians have built a fishing vessel, the Finns have chopped down all the trees and the Swedes are waiting to be introduced. A variation of this tale says that the Danes are making jokes, the Norwegians are fighting, the Finns are drinking, and the Swedes are still waiting to be introduced.

Another story tells of the four Scandinavians who get together to manufacture a new product which will make them a lot of money. The Finn designs it, the Swede makes it, the Dane sells it, and the Norwegian complains about it.

These caricatures are about as valid as the notion of the snobbish Englishman, amorous Italian or loud American; but, of course, there is something to them. Among the Scandinavians themselves, judging by many conversations, it is popularly held that the Danes are fun-loving, easygoing, shallow, shrewd, not altogether sincere and not inclined to too much exertion; the Norwegians are sturdy, brave, but a little too simple and unsophisticated; the Finns are dour, argumentative, courageous, a bit primitive and apt to be violent after too many drinks; and the Swedes are clever, capable, reliable, but much too formal, success-ridden and neurotic.

It is only after getting to know the Scandinavians close up that one can see how true these descriptions are—and how untrue. The Swedes are particularly fascinating to foreigners who find them 'cold.' They are said to be the Swiss of the North. Unquestionably, the Swedes are the most formal and reserved of the

Scandinavians but they are not so glacial as they seem. Closer acquaintance reveals hidden reserves of warmth and heartiness. I have known too many charming and quietly cheerful Swedes to be able to wholly endorse the view that they are gloomy Strindbergian characters. Nor can I agree with the French writer who declared that there is 'not a single, intelligent Swede who, on closer acquaintance, will not throw off his mask of a happy man, to reveal the face of a man in torment.' The Danes, on the other hand, are too easily thought of as happy-go-lucky charmers, when they are actually given to bouts of melancholy and discontent with their too blissful life. The Norwegians may be less sophisticated than the Swedes, but they are more clever and complicated than they appear. As for the Finns, they have a spontaneous as well as a reticent nature, and in their political life as a beleaguered nation squeezed into an uncomfortable corner of Europe they have developed a sophistication which ensures survival.

On the whole, the Scandinavians like each other and work well together, but there is a persistent unhappy note in their close relationship. In all the joking about national characteristics, it is always the Swedes who come out worst. In the popularity ratings, it is always the Swedes at the bottom.

'All this bitterness of the Danes and Norwegians toward the Swedes is ridiculous,' said a Danish Jew who had been sheltered in Sweden during the war. 'We are becoming more friendly all the time with people like the Italians, but we are not friendly with each other.'

The war, of course, hurt the Swedes in the eyes of their neighbors, even though they were generous in caring for refugees and providing economic help after the war. The Danes, blacked out and bearing the weight of the German occupation, could hardly help but resent the sight of the lights twinkling in Sweden just across the sound. And yet Sweden's only real crime was not to have been attacked; the Danes would gladly have sat out the war if Hitler had left them alone. Norway, however, had more substantial reasons for resentment. Sweden could not have helped Denmark, but it could have come to Norway's aid and did not.

Even if this was too much to expect, given Sweden's slight power in the face of the greatest military machine in Europe, the Norwegians say that at the least their next-door neighbor should not have permitted German troop trains to travel across Sweden to Norway during the occupation.

Finnish feelings about Sweden are mainly conditioned by the fact that Sweden was for so long the ruling power, and today still has a big-brother influence. The Swedish-speaking portion of the Finnish population is now down to 7 per cent but it still has great economic power and an important cultural impact.

The Standard of Living

The main reason for the peevish relations between Sweden and its neighbors, however, is simply the greater size, strength and wealth of Sweden. It is the largest, most populated and most fortunate of the four countries. Not only has it been able to progress for a century and a half without the interruption of war, but it has a better balance of natural resources to begin with. It is as if the farms of Denmark, the forests of Finland and the hydroelectric resources of Norway had been lumped into one thousand-mile-long country. Add to this one of the greatest treasures of all Europe: the storehouse of iron ore in northern Sweden.

Swedish industry dominates Scandinavia. Of the one hundred biggest manufacturing companies, sixty-nine of them, including the top eight, are Swedish. The Swedes work harder and more successfully than their neighbors and generally set the pace in Scandinavia. The result is a mixture of envy and awe. A Swedish diplomat in Oslo said: 'It is embarrassing how impressed the Norwegians are with Sweden. We just aren't that good.' He added: 'Norwegians are less interested in work than we are. A lot of people in Sweden work overtime or weekends. In Norway more than any other country I know, people devote themselves to freedom, to their time off. I'm not saying it's bad. It's just that the Norwegians take it easier, but they still want the same standard of living we have.'

By the end of 1964, there were 1·6 million automobiles in

Sweden, or about one for every four and a half persons. In the United States there is one car for every three persons; in Great Britain one for every six. More than a quarter million new cars are bought every year in Sweden, a rate of purchase equal to that of the United States. In television sets, appliances and other hard goods, the Swedes lead the rest of the Scandinavians—the order of affluence usually putting Denmark close behind Sweden, and Norway and Finland further behind. The Swedes, for example, have twice as many telephones per capita as the Finns. But more important is the fact that poverty has been outlawed in all four countries, and in most respects their living standards are much the same.

The trouble with high living, however, is that it means a high cost of living. In October 1965 the *Financial Times* of London produced a 'rough guide' to the cost of living in twenty-three of the major cities in the world. Using a 'food basket' of selected items as its principal yardstick, the paper concluded that the four most expensive cities were, in order: Stockholm, Tokyo, Oslo and Helsinki. New York was in seventh place and London in eighteenth. Copenhagen was not included in the survey, but undoubtedly would have been placed close to its Scandinavian sister cities.

In at least one important respect not usually counted in living-standard statistics the uncrowded Scandinavians have an enormous advantage over almost all other people in the world. They have a surplus of space and they live in comfort close to nature. Except for Iceland, which has just five persons per square mile, Norway is the least-populated nation in Europe, and Finland and Sweden are almost as empty.

(Using 1963 population figures, here is a sampling of population densities in persons per square mile: Norway 28, Finland 34, Sweden 44, U.S.A. 52, Denmark 282, Italy 435, West Germany 578, Japan 670, Belgium 790, England and Wales 824, and the Netherlands 922.)

With the world's runaway population increase making life ever more uncivilized, room for solitude may someday be mankind's most precious possession. Scandinavians have it in quantity. If

America is the country of two-car families, then Scandinavia is the land of two-house families. The first dwelling may be only a small city apartment, and the second a modest country cottage without running water, but together they make it easy for people to get away from it all. There are now some 350,000 country retreats in Sweden, and it is rare to meet a Dane, a Norwegian or a Finn who does not have his own place by the sea or in the mountains, or at least the use of a family or friend's cottage. They are so zealous about the outdoor life that it is probable that the Scandinavians (excepting the Danes) are the most physically fit people in Europe. Each country has sports organizations which enroll millions of people. The national ski competitions attract hundreds of thousands of participants. The idols of teen-agers are more often sports heroes than show-business personalities.

'These are a handsome people,' wrote Marya Mannes. 'They look clean, as their cities are, as their countryside is; and you feel that sea or mountain air has blown through them for so many centuries that their lungs too are washed. The Scandinavian love of nature has made them natural. To see men without the greenish pallor or larded white of our own city workers, to see girls with unfussed hair and uncaked skin, the blood near the surface of unlipsticked mouths, is to rediscover a lost beauty.'

Mass Culture

Gunnar Myrdal, who inhabits a modernistic office high up in a Stockholm skyscraper, pointed out that 'we Swedes are good at things which have to do with the body, not the soul. We go in for bodily culture, architecture, plumbing, furniture, textiles, glassware, but our cultural life leaves a lot to be desired.'

It is true that the Scandinavian arts concentrate on those functional, well-designed things which make for easier, handsomer living. There is less really good art for art's sake. Norway's Edvard Munch is the single Scandinavian painter of undoubted international stature in the past century. Cultural traditions are strong, however. Scandinavian literature, music and theater are excellent, people are exceedingly well read, and there is a gallery

of great names : Ibsen, Strindberg, Grieg, Sibelius, Nielsen, Kierkegaard, Saarinen, Thorvaldsen, Milles and others.

What is more impressive, even awesome, is the dedication of the
Scandinavians to cultural self-improvement. They attend 'continuation schools,' night schools and study circles by the millions.
They support the arts through public grants, allocate good percentages of building funds to works of sculpture and murals, erect
special studios for artists, and listen solemnly to the critics and
highbrows. The best newspapers are distinguished by their
cultural pages. Companies and banks form clubs to help employees
purchase works of art. Manufacturers of domestic products set
aside special studios, or 'little playpens,' where their more
imaginative designers are given free rein to express themselves.
It is all magnificently earnest.

No Paradise

There is no denying the modernity of Nordic life, yet there is a
pervading middle-class morality with goodly traces of the Philis-
tine and the Puritan. Despite the legends of Scandinavian sex,
many people still are shocked by 'immoral' behavior. The
atmosphere of freedom enables dissenters to have their say, but
avant-garde ideas must fight an uphill battle against the conservative establishment. The moralists who cry out against all
manner of sins and the teetotalers who would tighten the already
strict drinking laws have considerable political strength, particularly in the parliaments. Artists complain about the bourgeois
public. Women complain that they are not fully emancipated
despite Scandinavia's early lead in women's rights legislation.
Young people complain about the old guard in politics hanging
on to office decade after decade. And the older generation complains about youth.

Such ferment by itself suggests that all is not perfectly placid or
placidly perfect in Scandinavia. Proud as they are of their accomplishments, the Nordic peoples are annoyed at any suggestion
that they have built some kind of paradise on earth. Worst of all
is the notion that the welfare-state benefits they enjoy are 'free,'

as if the left-wing governments had brought them down from heaven. The truest thing to say about Scandinavia is that people work for what they have, and work hard. And they are the first to say that what they have is far from ideal. They have social security, health benefits and good pensions, but they also have some of the highest taxes in the world.

In the bigger cities there is an unbelievable shortage of housing despite a large building program. (One third of all Scandinavian homes have been built since World War II.) At the worst, people must wait eight or ten years for a new apartment in Stockholm, and the black market in housing is a black mark on Sweden. The problem is one of too-rapid urbanization, lingering rent control, high building costs and various inhibitions on private construction. From country to country, there are other kinds of shortages—schools, hospitals, old-age homes and child-care facilities. There are not nearly enough doctors and nurses. Norwegians complain about the inefficient telephone service, primitive roads and bureaucratic bungling. Finns cry out against the farm subsidies, the rising cost of living and some questionable spending on development programs. The Swedes have a catalog of standard complaints, and the ruling politicians found much to be embarrassed about in the Stig Wennerström spy case of 1963–64. The Danes worry about teen-age sex, inflation, shifting trade patterns and other things which disturb their snug little kingdom.

Political life is said to be dull in Scandinavia, but it has more controversies than outsiders believe. Because party differences are not extreme and there is general agreement on the welfare state, it is not always easy to say what all the shouting is about. In Finland, where politics is customarily tumultuous, the president is accused of acting like a de Gaulle and bowing too low in his relations with the Russians. Too many parties—none of which is able to gain a parliamentary majority—means repeated resort to coalition government.

In the other three countries, the Social Democratic or Labor parties have dominated the political scene most of the time since the mid-1930s. The opposition parties, however, have rarely been able to form united fronts against them. The pattern was dramatically upset in the September 1965 elections in Norway, when the 'nonsocialist' parties decisively took control of the government after three decades of Labor Party rule. Even though the system of proportional representation at work through Scandinavia has meant a multiplicity of parties, Denmark, Norway and Sweden have enjoyed remarkably stable political conditions. Tage Erlander of Sweden has been prime minister for almost two decades.

Perhaps the most notable feature of Scandinavian political life, particularly in Sweden, is the habit of consulting all parties and all manner of experts before legislation is introduced. Analysis of a problem by committees of competent authorities, consultation of interested parties, informal discussions by government and opposition leaders—all may precede the actual parliamentary debate of a proposed bill. Agreement, in other words, is already achieved, and there is nothing left but the shouting of a few extremists. The smoothness of such operations removes much of the blood and thunder of political life. It makes some people worry about the state of Scandinavian democracy. 'We are too inclined to leave things to the experts,' they say. During the political campaign before the 1964 election in Sweden, an American correspondent in Stockholm asked a Swede, 'What do you think about the election?' He was asked in return, 'Which one, the American or British?'

The Humanitarians

While the tendency to consult everybody in advance may make boring politics, it is part of a common Scandinavian concern for minority rights. Everybody is entitled to have his say, even if he is wrongheaded, and everyone should have a fair chance in life. The idea of equal opportunity lies at the root of the educational systems. Even if there is no general desire for a complete leveling-out of incomes, the over-all idea is that no one should be prosperous at the expense of others. The Swedish Social Democrats of the late 1920s even had a slogan, now happily out of date, which said: 'Poverty is to be tolerated only if it is shared by all.'

The great attention given to the safeguarding of everyone's rights has led to the creation of the Ombudsman, a Scandinavian institution which other nations are considering adopting. The Ombudsman, who stands apart from the normal processes of government and the courts, is a kind of one-man court of appeal for the citizen who has suffered an injustice, especially if it be at the hands of an unfeeling bureaucracy. The Scandinavian concern for simple human feelings, and an individual's right to privacy, is shown in the code of conduct which Scandinavian newspapers impose on themselves. They almost never report divorce actions, suicides and other family embarrassments. Children and rape victims are, of course, saved from harmful publicity. The gossip column is frowned upon; and yet, in contradiction, annual listings of taxable income are published privately from public records so that people can find out how much money other people make.

The humanitarian character of Nordic life is the most praiseworthy element of Scandinavia. It is at the root of the welfare state, which seeks to eliminate suffering and provide security for every citizen. There is plenty to be said against welfarism—as many a Scandinavian will testify—but it is hard to argue against a way of life which insures that *every* person is decently treated. It is no surprise that the enlightened prison systems treat inmates as human beings who have family responsibilities, or that great efforts are made to enable elderly people to live out their years in dignity. The help given unmarried mothers, the holiday facilities provided children of the poor, the retraining programs for workers displaced by machines, are all part of a singularly humane philosophy. Franklin D. Roosevelt once spoke of 'the forgotten man at the bottom of the economic pyramid.' There are no forgotten men in Scandinavia. It is perhaps best defined as a society without victims.

Such a society, almost by definition, is not bursting with color and drama. There is more excitement in a crowded slum than in an orderly suburb. In egalitarian nations there is no throbbing conflict between the offensively rich and the downtrodden poor. When life is so well ordered and everyone so sensibly behaved there are no outstanding vices, no thrilling crimes, no great causes to stir the blood and fill the streets with angry young men. The Scandinavians are forced to import issues like apartheid in South Africa or the war in Vietnam, in order to work up a demonstration. The Good Life has been so uniformly spread that professors and factory hands live in adjoining apartments and can scarcely be told apart by their clothes, their country cottages or the schools their children go to. Everything is so neat, so modern, so sanitary, so thoughtfully planned that it is a world far removed from the squalor and frenzy of other lands.

Does that, therefore, make it a dull place inhabited by bored people? It depends on the kind of excitement one is looking for. In my own experience, I have been constantly surprised at how much more there is to each Scandinavian country than meets the eye. For all their achievements, they are still unfinished societies still in pursuit of excellence. I have found them to have great powers of refreshment and rejuvenation. No amount of security or welfarism has dampened their essential dynamism. If anything, it has whetted the appetite for still more changes and improvements. Urbanization and industrialization plunge forward. New towns, new city centers, new universities spring up all over the North. Sweeping educational reforms and ambitious development programs for Lapland are part of the process of change which is so marked in Scandinavia. There is no slackening in the effort to raise living standards and welfare benefits to heights far beyond those envisioned by the social planners of the 1930s. There is a quiet excitement to the unfolding of this unique society. It is still on the far side of paradise, but so far so good.

Chapter 2

LOVE IN A COLD CLIMATE

I suppose you might call us well-protected sinners, but so what?
—SWEDISH EDITOR

More than 92 per cent of all brides under twenty married in Copenhagen are pregnant.
—DANISH ASSOCIATION OF
GENERAL PRACTITIONERS

Sex. Suicide. Socialism. I turn to these prickly subjects in this and the next two chapters in full knowledge that they are red capes waved in front of the Scandinavians. How weary they are of the clichés about sin and desperation in the too-perfect welfare state! Their countries are open books. Their statistics are the most ample and honest in the world. Freedom of inquiry is so complete that journalists are given the specific right to inspect government files and correspondence about almost everything short of state secrets. Several million foreign visitors each year move freely through four of the most open societies in the world. And yet some of the most vital things about Scandinavia remain a mystery to the outside world. It is seen through a glass darkly.

Everyone knows that these are immaculate, prosperous and law-abiding nations, and yet, in the popular imagination, something seems to have gone terribly wrong. There is sexual abandon and rampant alcoholism. Abortions are a dime a dozen, and every other baby is illegitimate. Sex-hungry Scandinavian girls go in droves to the Mediterranean to seek out Latin lovers. Scandinavian men hurl themselves out of windows at a fearful rate. Socialism has reduced a sturdy, self-reliant race to a pampered mass without ambition or joy.

This is putting it strongly but it is not too strong to say that such notions about sex, suicide and socialism have warped the image of Scandinavia to an almost unbelievable degree. It is not that the popular impressions are without some element of truth or that these are unimportant subjects. On the contrary, they are rightfully in the front rank of the special fascinations of the Nordic world. It is just that they have become distorted and overheated. During the past year it was a rare American or Englishman who, upon learning that I was preparing a book on Scandinavia, did not remark about the immorality, melancholy or welfare-unhappiness of Scandinavia—and of Sweden and Denmark in particular.

In Scandinavia itself I could feel the backlash. When I introduced myself to an amiable Gothenburg psychiatrist, Dr. Kjell Eriksson, he said wearily, 'Are you going to write about sin, suicide, juvenile delinquency and all our other so-called troubles?' In Denmark, another noted psychiatrist, Dr. Kirsten Auken (who dislikes being known as 'the Danish Dr. Kinsey') said, 'I'm so *tired* of talking about sex. There are so many other things going on.'

Why is so much attention given to Scandinavia's seamy side? Why is 'socialist' Sweden's high suicide rate more renowned then conservative Switzerland's equally high rate? During a panel discussion in Stockholm about youth problems, a psychologist named Richard Blomberg put it this way: 'We all know that Sweden has a reputation abroad for being unusually advanced, or progressive, or enlightened, or permissive—whatever word you care to use—in the area of sexual morals. Foreigners apparently *like* to think of Sweden as a den of iniquity, citing as evidence our high illegitimacy and divorce rates, the statistics for venereal disease, our attitude toward birth control, abortion and sexual education in the schools.'

It is undoubtedly true that a good many non-Scandinavians take perverse pleasure in detecting the blemishes on the Nordic

beauty queen. People from countries with glaring social disorders seem to find satisfaction in discovering that Scandinavia
still falls well short of perfection. Conservatives delight in discovering the cracks in the Social Democratic structure. The
Scandinavians, after basking in the reputation they acquired in the
1930s as builders of a middle-way 'model for the world,' now find
that they are in the uneasy position of the brightest child in a
classroom. They are admired, envied and resented. They stand
exposed. Their achievements are taken for granted and their
imperfections become embarrassingly prominent. Swedish ambassadors have told me of their dismay when they conclude a lecture
about national health insurance or democratic economic planning
and then have to listen to a succession of questions about suicides
and unwed mothers. One consequence is that the Scandinavians
have become unduly sensitive about foreign opinion and sharp
with the fellow citizens who provide fuel for the foreign imagination. Sweden, for instance, is proud of Ingmar Bergman's towering reputation as a film director, but I have heard Swedes bitterly
criticize him for portraying their country to the world as a morbid
land of illicit sex. In Denmark, a leading journalist who wrote a
humorous but nonetheless critical article in *Life International* called
'The Pursuit of Happiness in the Welfare State' was savagely
denounced on his home ground. A Copenhagen headline said:
'DANE DIRTIES THE DANES.'

Scandinavians complain that the foreign press ignores their
good news and sensationalizes their bad. They are only half right.
The routine news of progress in the Nordic world receives only
scant attention in the world press while there always seems to be
room for a story about (to quote a British headline) 'MY TEN
DAYS IN A LAND OF PASSIONATE PURITANS.' It is difficult,
however, to persuade editors that an election in Denmark or an
expansion of the pension system in Norway is more compelling
news than riots in Asia and revolutions in the Caribbean. Scandinavia is fated by its own orderliness and excellence to be a
virtual non-news area except when there is a royal wedding, the
discovery of a Soviet spy ring, or a sex scandal. The image con-
veyed by such stories is bound to be a distortion just as the heavy

emphasis in Scandinavian newspapers about American racial troubles and other social problems does not present a balanced portrait of the United States.

Two foreign criticisms have remained longest and most painfully in the Scandinavian memory. The first was a full-page *Time* magazine article in 1955 entitled 'Sin & Sweden.' The second was a statement by President Dwight Eisenhower in July 1960 which spoke of an unnamed Scandinavian country as an example of how the welfare state can destroy moral fiber and lead good folk to drink and suicide.

American Professor Philip Boardman at the University of Oslo has written about the reaction:

The President's remarks, uttered at a summer political gathering and not founded on impeccable research, apparently had no mission except to strengthen home faith in the Republican way of life. But the resulting uproar all over Scandinavia was an astonishing revelation of how proud these peoples are of their achievements and how trigger-happy toward critics. Swedes, from the prime minister on down, lashed at both Eisenhower and America with even more acrimony than was apparent in the 'Sin & Sweden' incident of 1955. Even Danish politicians and editors forgot their usual good humor to hurl denials and counteraccusations back across the Atlantic. In Norway the reaction was not only instantaneous but far more indignant in press and parliament than when the U.S.S.R. had threatened to wipe out alleged Norwegian bases for U-2 planes a month before!

President Eisenhower later admitted that he had gotten his facts wrong. As for *Time*, it has been a long uphill climb in its Scandinavian reputation. In the summer of 1964 it produced a cover story on the delights and accomplishments in Scandinavia, which the Swedish magazine *Industria* said 'represented as extreme a change of course as can be found in the publication's history. . . . Barely paying its respects to that old standby—Sin in Scandinavia —the magazine rather sensibly suggested that the "statistics on sexual and suicidal patterns are murky and conflicting."'

The Permissive Attitude

The desire to find something wrong with Scandinavia and the prurient character of press accounts about life in the North are two reasons for the twisted image, but not the most important ones. In the first place, to concentrate on the foremost subject, there *is* something special about Scandinavian sex. Or, more specifically, the Scandinavian *attitude* toward sex. Secondly, sex is one of the great, ceaselessly debated topics within the Nordic countries. It is a primary fact of life, widely reported in Scandinavia's own newspapers. Inevitably it draws the attention of the outside world. Finally, the notion of Scandinavia, and Sweden in particular, as a kind of neurotic free-love society has largely been brought on by a succession of films, mainly Swedish, which have caused raised eyebrows around the world. It may be no fault of Scandinavian moviemakers that foreign audiences are easily shocked, but the fact remains that they are offering the world a view of their own society which is bound to raise questions.

The something special about Scandinavian sex is its frankness, its absence of hypocrisy, and its calm acceptance—even approval —of premarital sexual activity. There is little inclination to equate sex with sin, even though a strong puritanical streak still runs through much of the Nordic world. While the Scandinavian outlook may be called enlightened or sophisticated, the actual sexual conduct differs little from the norm in other Western nations. It is simply less plagued by a sense of guilt. 'Scandinavian sex,' said a Swedish housewife, 'is what the Americans do but don't admit they do.' Scandinavians take their sex straight; other people take it furtively. The Swedes and Danes admit that permissiveness has perhaps gone too far, but they cannot agree that they are more immoral than other nations. If anything, they have reason to feel that they lead a considerably more wholesome sex life than other people who are steeped in moral ambiguity.

To the Nordic mind, Americans and Englishmen are sexual hypocrites: their pretenses are Puritan and Victorian, while their performance is entirely the opposite. It took the Kinsey Report to explode the myth of American innocence. Half the American females and 85 per cent of the males, it seemed, had premarital experience. The figures for homosexual and other variations of sexual activity made sensational reading. The American divorce rate was already known as the highest in the world. In the last decade a sexual revolution has swept the United States, bringing a fresh breeze of frankness but bombarding the newsstands, bookstores and movie houses with sex as the be-all and cure-all. The current American obsession with sex may well be a necessary convulsion before a time when the whole subject is taken in stride, as it is in Scandinavia. For the present, however, the scene is marked by confusion. Three quarters of the fifty states still have such strict sex laws in force that most Americans are technically lawbreakers. An estimated one million abortions are performed annually in the United States, well over 90 per cent of them illegal.

If anything, Great Britain is even more contradictory to a Scandinavian. While young Britons seem to be working out a code of conduct of their own, sex education is still backward and one out of every sixteen births (one out of nine in London) is illegitimate. Call girls and strip-tease clubs, almost unknown in Scandinavia, are institutions in England. Pornography is a multi-million-dollar business. Homosexuality is a national embarrassment. One headline asked: 'ARE WE GOING SEX CRAZY?'

The atmosphere in Scandinavia is relatively more natural and mature. A traveler in the North has the impression that there simply is less of a need for prostitution, pornography and constant erotic stimulation. Nonetheless, they exist, and in the biggest cities in particular. Oslo has its soliciting teenagers, Stockholm amateur and professional prostitutes in roomy cars, and Copenhagen its thriving pornographic industry. In many places, magazines offering uncompromising male and female nudity sell openly on the newsstands, and contraceptives can be purchased from coin machines as easily as cigarettes. Sex information is provided to schoolchildren, and the schools are wholly coeducational. The problems with deviates, masochists, child molesters and rapists are minor compared with those of other countries.

Homosexuals

The attitude toward homosexuality is indicative. It is not something that people approve of, but they deal with it as a fact of life. The effort is not to suppress it, but to keep it in its place. It is seen as a misfortune, but not a crime. Other nations, notably America and Britain, harass and prosecute their homosexuals. The Scandinavians view this as an invasion of human rights—an intolerable limitation of one's right to a private life. It is felt that homosexuals comprise a minority and must not be victimized by the majority so long as their activity is confined to 'consenting adults.' The abuse or recruitment of minors is another matter entirely. The adult homosexual's need for, and right to, the companionship of his choice is acknowledged. As in Holland and a few other countries, there are homosexual social clubs and publications in Scandinavia which operate openly, without persecution. In Sweden, clubs like Diana for women and The Circle and Albatross for men are joined in the Swedish Union for Sex Equality. A typical advertisement in the Union's publication, *The Companion*: 'I am a 20-year-old boy, dark, five-feet-seven-inches tall, and seeking a companion of about the same age. Intellectual interests. Apartment in center of town. Please answer with photo which will be returned.'

The homosexual publications which can be found on Copenhagen newsstands have a candid pictorial approach to the subject which has horrified many a tourist, but then the Danes think it even more astonishing that Washington policemen should be assigned to spy duty in men's rooms. It is my impression that the Danes are even more tolerant of homosexuality than the Swedes, and that in both countries it is more of a social phenomenon than in Norway and Finland. The people of these two nations pride themselves on being more athletic and less effete than the Danes and Swedes, who now live in cities and are said to be growing soft. The influence of hard-core Lutheranism is also more pronounced in Norway and Finland. Both countries take a sterner view of sex in books and films; they are inclined to censor some extreme material which passes easily in Denmark and Sweden.

Sex for All

Scandinavia's live-and-let-live attitude about sexual matters approximates the view of the English lady who said she did not mind what people do so long as they do not do it in the streets and scare the horses. It is an attitude firmly rooted in the Scandinavian's sense of justice. The sexual debate in Sweden in particular has more to do with human rights in a democratic society than with vague concepts of morality.

The concern for everybody's rights leads to such extreme views as those expressed in a recent Swedish book, *The Erotic Minorities*, by a young psychiatrist, Dr. Lars Ullerstam. The majority of people, he says, can get all the sex they require for their physical and mental needs, but what about such minorities as invalids, prisoners and mental patients? He argues that they too have a right to physical love but society does little to assist them. What about sexually vital older women who have lost their husbands? 'They would love to meet young men and for them a brothel would be the natural meeting place.' That is, a state-supervised brothel catering to all types and even sending out 'sexual Samaritans' to serve the needy. The author hopes that 'talented and cultivated people who understand the joy of giving' would embrace the calling.

On a more practical level, the merits of pornography can be heard argued in Sweden by eminent authorities. It is reasoned that the suppression of pornography deprives those people who want or need it of their right to have something which is not as harmful to public morality as people suppose. It is characteristic of the practical Swedish approach that the public debate on the subject in Stockholm did not deal in vague generalities but specifically discussed pornographic films which were screened as part of the program. In Sweden and Denmark, television programs deal more frankly with sexual matters than anything known in Britain or America. What the Scandinavians *do* censor rigorously is violence of the kind which is commonplace in American cowboy or crime programs. Cruelty, or anything which smacks of sadism, is scissored out. If a documentary program showing brutality in the Congo or Vietnam, for example, is to be broadcast, parents are warned ahead of time that it will be unsuitable for children.

Nudity

Brutality may be bad in Scandinavia, but there is nothing shameful about nudity. 'A lot of us may be Godless,' said a Swedish politician, 'but we seem to have more respect than some people for the human form that God gave us.' For the greater part of the year the Scandinavians are as thoroughly covered up as any people in the world. When the long gray winter is over and summer comes for only a few months of intense sunlight, the inclination to abandon clothing is strong indeed. They are instinctive nature lovers who quite naturally think of clothing as an encumbrance. Nothing is more purely and beautifully Scandinavian than the summer sight of a Swedish blonde toasting her backside on a private little island in the Stockholm archipelago or the winter sight of naked Finns running out of the severe heat of a sauna and rolling in the snow. The Nordic yearning for nudity is suggested by the fondness that even the most straight-laced middle-class families have for adorning their walls with little prints or paintings of nudes, and by the number of statues of maidens and athletes which can be seen in Scandinavian parks, their heads and shoulders adorned with snow or pine needles.

In the simpler days of northern Europe there was a greater easiness about the nude bathing which is part of the foreigner's image of Scandinavia. Today, when tourists swarm in hoping to see the naked North, the nature-loving Scandinavian usually limits his total exposure to the sun to strictly private surroundings. Writers of guide books to Scandinavia feel obliged to warn their readers that there is more bare skin to be seen on the Mediterranean than on a Baltic beach.

The idea of naked Scandinavia has been fostered by films like *One Summer of Happiness* which suggest that the Swedes and their Nordic neighbors leap out of their clothes with blinding speed. Such movies, rather than the more standard productions of Scandinavian studios, are almost the only ones which distributors of foreign films select for release in other countries. In recent years, Swedish films shown abroad have gone far to convey an image of a sex-ridden Scandinavia. 'It's time they stopped this muck from appearing on the screen,' said a middle-aged Stockholm lady. 'Sex is private and belongs behind doors.'

Morality

It is clear that the Scandinavians take a more tolerant view of sexual matters than most other people, but it would be wrong to suggest that they have reached agreement on sex or that they have found the final answers to these most human of human problems. Their worries about sexual behavior are not, after all, so very different from the concerns of people elsewhere. Parents still worry about their children going too far, and young people still grope for a practical code of conduct. During my visits to the northern countries during the past few years there always seemed to be some sort of argument going on about sex, usually on the theme that modern Scandinavian youth lacks morals. Those persons who moralized about sex were savagely denounced as archaic thinkers by self-styled progressives, and yet it seemed to me that the worriers were complaining not so much that young people had a sex life before marriage, as that they were going about it too carelessly and at too tender an age. A proclamation in Norway warning about sexual laxity was signed by 129,000 women. In Sweden, 140 prominent doctors and professors issued a protest which declared that 'chaotic relations between the sexes menace the vitality and health of the nation.' At the same time the Danes were heatedly arguing about a young woman writer's insistence, expressed on television, that teen-age girls as young as fourteen be fitted with diaphragms by school doctors because it was obvious that they would soon need them.

The Swedish girl who said, 'I still don't see what sex has to do with morals,' was expressing a common opinion that morality has to do with more important things than sex. It embraces the whole scale of individual conduct, but most especially the responsibility of each member of society for the dignity and well-being of every other member. Young Scandinavians have told me that rich men who ignore the hungry or racialists who abuse minorities are far more immoral than people who make love. Viewed in this light, the Scandinavian countries, where everyone is decently treated, are among the most moral and virtuous in the world. 'Christian sexual morality,' wrote Swedish author Lars Gustafsson, 'is unacceptable to a considerable number of modern Swedes simply because they do not accept the beliefs about sin, punishment and the will of God behind it.'

In Scandinavia's rural past there was, as Sweden's Alva Myrdal has expressed it, a 'habit of fairly lax authoritarian inhibitions of the sex life of youth.' Young couples were allowed considerable freedom, and trial marriages served to establish whether a girl was capable of providing the children needed for the family farm. Eldest sons in particular needed to be sure that they would have heirs. The pregnancy of an unmarried girl was not so much a shock as a signal to set the date for the wedding. The practices of a century ago were little different from the 'ring engagements' of some present-day Swedish couples. This is a kind of premarriage marriage, which includes the exchange of rings but stops short of the final official ceremony. 'Ring-engaged' couples will usually not set up a household, but their parents expect them to sleep together from time to time while they determine whether they are compatible enough for a legal, lifetime connection.

Long engagements, with sex taken for granted, are often considered by both the couples and their parents as the best solution when marriage seems impractical for the time being. Young people beginning work at a university or starting a career may prefer not to rush into all the problems of setting up a household. The housing shortage in the major cities has done much to delay marriages and encourage informal living arrangements.

In Denmark, the chief psychiatrist of the Mother's Aid organization told Look magazine: 'Most Danish parents expect their daughters to have sexual intercourse with boy friends, provided it takes place in the home and is with a boy they know.' Many Danish parents would deny that they are so liberal-minded, but I recall a conversation with a decorous and well-educated Copenhagen secretary who said she had spent the past summer touring Europe in a Volkswagen with 'a friend.' Only reluctantly did she admit that it had been a boy friend, and she hastened to say: 'We thought we were going to get married but we've broken off now. My parents knew about it. It was perfectly all right.'

I said: 'I'm sure it was, but in that case why didn't you say it was a boy friend in the first place?'

'I didn't think you would understand,' she said. 'I mean, most Americans can't.'

The Independent Girls

As this conversation suggests, Scandinavian girls have an independent air which makes them freer spirits than—to take the extreme—their more sheltered and chaperoned counterparts in the Mediterranean countries. They do not think of themselves as the fragile weaker sex. They are hearty personalities with minds of their own. The commingling of the sexes in the schools and in the lively outdoor life of Scandinavia helps to instill a sense of equality and self assurance. They hold many more positions in the professions and public life than women in most other countries. They have a strong sense of their own worth. They are expected to be self-reliant—to open their own doors and pay their own way on a date. They consequently expect to have as much social freedom as boys. Far from sitting by a telephone hoping to be asked out, they go out on their own, or more often with a girl friend, and they expect to dance with strangers at a restaurant or club.

Although to a lesser degree than in most countries, the double standard still persists in Scandinavia. The promiscuous male will be excused, but not the promiscuous female. A young lady is not expected to be a virgin, but she must not distribute her favors too widely either. It is illustrative of Scandinavian attitudes that some people, and especially certain leading women authors in Sweden, argue vehemently that such 'old-fashioned' viewpoints restrict women's rights. Scandinavian girls are usually more genuinely career-minded than, say, American and British girls, partly because the opportunities are greater for important jobs. They seem to be less anxious about getting married early, preferring to enjoy at least a few years of independence. They particularly want to travel and make a start at a career. The average age at marriage in Scandinavia is about twenty-three for females and twenty-six for males.

A Swedish girl at Uppsala University, a graduate student who had studied in the United States, told me with some disgust that 'American girls are terrified if they haven't found a husband before they finish college. They seem to go to a university simply to find a man, and if they don't they think their life is ruined.' Other students were caustic about the American dating system. They see something almost sinister about the way 'American mothers insist that their daughters be "popular" and do everything possible to win a husband, but to never, never surrender their virtue.' Professor Franklin D. Scott in *The American Experiences of Scandinavian Students* wrote that such students found much to admire about United States universities but they 'almost unanimously dislike the American customs governing relations between the sexes and cite them as prime examples of American immorality and hypocrisy.'

Compared with what is officially sanctioned on the average American campus, Scandinavian student life seems outrageously free. The essential difference is that students in Denmark, Norway, Sweden and Finland are treated as adults and act as adults. University officials and professors feel content to function as educators rather than nursemaids. They expect students to have a sex life. One educator put it this way: 'Is it fair for society to insist that young people spend more and more years at their studies, often into their middle twenties, and to remain "pure" at the very time of their greatest sexual drive?' A prominent clergyman in Stockholm said he would not personally say it was sinful if 'young people who feel deeply toward each other' have sexual relations before marriage. The official Swedish publication *Our Church* said the same thing about couples planning to marry.

Students of both sexes are often quartered in the same dormitory buildings but usually on separate floors. One of the most charming sights of my first visit to Uppsala was the view from a sociologist's apartment balcony of a student dormitory across the street. It was early evening and almost every room was lighted up, with the curtains parted, revealing a honeycomb of student life: girls studying in some rooms, boys studying in others, and some joint book work and light romancing in the remainder. It would be incorrect to suggest that every student in Scandinavia becomes a lover under such convenient circumstances. Foreign students who arrive at a Nordic university for a year's study often prove to be troublesome because they assume too much. As one girl expressed it, 'If you invite them to your room for a cup of coffee they refuse to believe that all you had in mind was a cup of coffee.' By expert testimony, a significant minority of girls, for all the conventional reasons, choose to remain untouched, so to speak, until marriage. What all insist on is their freedom to make such a choice—as adults. I remember a comment by an administrator at the Swedish University of Turku, Finland, when he was showing me the plans for new student quarters. 'There were proposals for putting the men in one wing and women in the other,' he said, 'but the students wouldn't stand for it.'

Sex Education

For many Scandinavians, instruction in sex begins in grade school. I was not surprised to learn that the subject was taught in school; rather, I was surprised that sex education is not so thoroughly imbedded in school curricula as I had expected. Perhaps 60 per cent of Danish schools have sex courses. Norway and Finland are still far from providing every student with the fundamental facts of life. There is still a strong opinion in these countries that that is a job best left to parents, though it appears that even in enlightened Scandinavia parents get tongue-tied on the subject. An official Swedish *Handbook on Sex Instruction* says flatly that 'the happiest solution would undoubtedly be for children to be taught in their own homes,' but since this often fails to happen 'the necessary guidance responsibility passes to the school.'

Norway's controversial sex-education pioneer, Dr. Karl Evang, said that Sweden is still the pacesetter in this field. Its program is the most comprehensive of any in Scandinavia. Simple instruction begins at age seven, when the Swedish child enters school, and is continued in more detailed doses through the nine compulsory school years. A cartoon in a Swedish magazine showed a little girl arriving home from school and being asked by her mother, 'Was your class in sexual instruction interesting, dear?' The child throws her books on the sofa in disgust and says, 'Ahh, it was all theory today.'

Sex education began in a modest way in Swedish schools as long as half a century ago but the subject was not made compulsory until 1956. One object is to 'create the necessary conditions for a harmonious sexual life' but another is to 'counteract less desirable sexual behavior, among other things too early sexual intercourse.' Family relationships are emphasized during the first years of schooling. The eleven-to-thirteen-year-olds get simple anatomy and reproduction lessons. Pupils from fourteen to sixteen are given more detailed material on the 'anatomic, physical, psychological, ethical and social aspects of the subject.'

In the light of all this, it is all the more astonishing that, to quote one authority, there is still so much 'ignorance, carelessness and simple irresponsibility.' It has been estimated that well over half the brides in Denmark and Sweden are pregnant at the time of marriage. Norway and Finland may not be too far behind Denmark and Sweden in this sphere. At a variety show in Oslo a comedian who was doing skits about 'those things which are typically Norwegian' received his most gleeful audience response when he spoke of the babies which appear four months after the wedding day.

Illegitimacy and Abortions

Where the Scandinavian countries show some interesting variations is in the rates of illegitimate births, or 'counterfeit children,' as the Danes say. Whereas the English and American rates are about 6 per cent of all live births, the Scandinavian rates are Norway and Finland 4, Denmark 8 and Sweden 12. As for busy little Iceland, the percentage is 25, by far the highest of all the world's developed nations. What is misleading about these figures is that they have to do with percentages of *all* live births. Thus a country like Finland, which still has fairly large families, certainly in contrast to Sweden, will show a lesser illegitimacy rate. If only 'first-born' babies are considered, then the rates are much higher and the differences among the four countries are not so great. Once again, Iceland is in a class by itself. There is such a casual attitude toward the whole business of love and marriage on that throbbing island that six out of every ten first-born babies are produced out of wedlock.

What needs stressing is that illegitimacy is no new phenomenon in the Nordic countries and is hardly to be blamed on the welfare state. The percentages (for illegitimates out of all live births) are lower today than they were in the early postwar years and about even with the figures of a few decades ago. To go far back in history, Stockholm in 1840 had 40 per cent illegitimate births. Today, perhaps because of contraceptive techniques, the figure is 15 per cent.

A pregnant but unwed girl in Scandinavia marries quickly to legitimize the child, or she remains unmarried and has her baby with the help of the state, or she tries to arrange for an abortion. If the baby is to emerge illegitimate, the welfare institutions go to great lengths to shield the mother and spare the child from being penalized for the manner of his coming into the world. Organizations like Denmark's Mother's Aid program, which gets some two thousand applications a year from pregnant girls under eighteen, stand ready to give free and kindly assistance. The fact that the prenatal care, delivery, medical treatment and other assistance is virtually free in each country has led some people to call it the 'subsidization of sin.' Scandinavians I have talked to simply describe it as a humanitarian approach which at minimum assures that innocent babies are protected.

The Scandinavian countries have a reputation, not entirely warranted, for easy abortions. A few years ago, at the time of the international thalidomide-baby tragedy, an American housewife, Mrs. Sherrie Finkbein, flew to Sweden to seek an abortion when she found it impossible to get one legally in the United States. The abortion was performed, and it was established that her child would have been tragically deformed. That incident led to a surge of applications for abortions from foreign women, but Sweden and its Nordic neighbors discouraged them and made plain that abortions are not automatically granted. It is easier to get a legal abortion in Japan, the Soviet Union and most East European Communist countries than it is in Scandinavia. Nonetheless, annual legal abortions run into the thousands, while a great many more illegal abortions are performed. There are more than four thousand legal abortions a year in Denmark, about half of all applications, and an estimated fifteen thousand illegal ones.

There obviously would be more legal and fewer illegal abortions if the authorities gave their approval in every case where no serious danger was involved. In this respect, the Finnish abortion authorities have become more liberal in their decisions during the past decade, while the Swedes have swung in the opposite direction. The peak year for Swedish legal abortions was 1951 when there were 6,328. In 1963, there were 2,703 in Sweden, while Finland, with a much smaller population, had 6,015. Illegal abortions were many times these figures.

There is a danger of reading too much 'immorality' into abortion figures. More married women, by far, seek abortions than unmarried. Only a quarter of Denmark's 8,000 abortion applications each year are from unmarried girls. What Scandinavians find more worrisome are the recent statistics which show that Sweden and Denmark, although not unique among well-to-do nations, have two of the highest venereal-disease rates in Europe.

The Erotic Young

The spotlight was thrown on the V.D. situation in 1964 when 140 medical men, to whom I have already referred, petitioned the Swedish government for action to restrain the promiscuity of the young. They said there was an 'alarming erotic situation' in Sweden and warned that the widespread premarital sexual activity was 'debasing to the personality and harmful from the point of view of the nation and society.' Sweden was 'in a state of progressive moral and spiritual decline.'

On the other hand, most Scandinavian sociologists, psychiatrists, youth workers and others to whom I spoke agreed with Norway's Dr. Evang that 'there has been no lowering of morals in youth.' There is, however, on the part of a number of young Scandinavians, a restlessness that has received much attention. It is part of an over-all phenomenon of Western Europe in its postwar prosperity. Again, the lead which the Nordic countries have taken in social legislation and welfarism makes such problems as juvenile delinquency and drug addiction look all the more extraordinary. It was my impression that Sweden has the only serious wayward-youth problem in Scandinavia (although as a professor in Finland said, 'Sweden is still ahead of us in this as in other matters, but we will catch up').

In Stockholm there is a kind of teen-age demimonde. When parents are out of town and an apartment is free, the word is passed that the site has been found for another orgy. The well-publicized *raggare* are the most visible of all. They cruise in packs of unmuffled cars, usually flashy secondhand American models, and pick up girls in a modern mating ritual worthy of serious anthropological attention. Minor-league versions of the same exercise can be seen in other Swedish cities. In Luleå in the far north the nightly traffic jam of cars by cruising Romeos finally forced the police to ban all vehicles from the main street after eight o'clock at night. When I looked into it, I found that the effect was simply to transfer the parade to another street one block away.

The combination of sex, automobile and youthful affluence gives Sweden something of the look of a well-scrubbed American suburb, with all its attendant problems of sophisticated delinquency. The most characteristic teen-age crime is car stealing. When asked whether the welfare state had anything to do with the situation, one Swedish boy said, somewhat facetiously, 'Well, with life so well arranged for all of us, there is a longing for adventure and excitement. But it is nice, anyhow, that there are so few horses stolen nowadays.'

Love on Ice

I have tried to suggest that Scandinavian sex, despite the over-all permissiveness and the refusal to equate sex with sin, is not in practice so extraordinary. Much of it may be more healthy than the furtive activity of other places. If young people seem unusually active, it is hard to prove that they are more or less so than the youth of the rest of Europe or North America. Reliable statistics on comparative sexual behavior are deplorably meager. Little work on the subject has been done within Scandinavia. It is a socially advanced territory, but its work in sociology is still at the teething stage. A Kinsey Report on Scandinavia has yet to be produced.

If there is anything distinctive about Scandinavian sex—and here I can speak only of personal impressions, not statistics—it is that it operates at a lower temperature. A great many emotions in the North are packed in ice. Inevitably, for reasons of geography and climate, it is not the ardent, spontaneous, hot-blooded world of southern Europe, and it becomes necessary to affirm at least some of the stereotypes about love in a cold climate. The Scandinavians have their own kind of love-making just as they make their own kind of happiness. If it lacks fire, at least it escapes disaster. There is neither great passion nor great shame. During a trip to Scandinavia, American writer Marya Mannes was told that love 'is more of an exercise than an emotion.' A young American in Stockholm, after thinking hard about the Swedish approach to sex, finally said, 'I know what's wrong. There's no mystery to it.'

Ingmar Bergman's *Summer Interlude* contained one of the most moving episodes of young love ever filmed, but it was a tragically short-lived affair. So it seems with many a Scandinavian romance. 'There is a brief time of love,' said one housewife, 'then you marry, and the romance is over. It all becomes so routine.' Despite the wealth of beauty in the Nordic world, the men tend to take their women for granted. 'They are so cold and mechanical,' complained a Swedish girl, thereby suggesting why Scandinavian women have acquired something of a reputation on the Mediterranean.

Nordic husbands seem embarrassed about displaying too much affection toward their wives. I have been in Scandinavian homes where mutual affection had long since given way to the common cause of maintaining the façade of respectability. A French writer on Norway felt constrained to say of 'Norwegian women and their suffering' that 'over there marriage entails a more or less peaceful form of coexistence, stripped, all too often, of any passionate elements.' Twin beds are popular in Scandinavia, and I was told in Sweden that 'the latest status symbol, for those who can afford it, is twin bedrooms.'

Much has been made of the divorce rate in Scandinavia. It is said to be shockingly high and to give further evidence of a breakdown in morality. Sweden's divorce rate, it is true, has tripled in the last three decades. There is now one Swedish divorce for every six marriages. But it seems to be a worldwide phenomenon that the more a nation prospers and becomes a fully modern state, the more its marriages will break up. The American divorce rate has doubled since 1918. The United States easily leads the world in divorces, while Denmark and Sweden are grouped with a number of East European Communist countries and the Soviet Union as the next highest divorce nations. Finland and Norway are further down the international divorce table, keeping company with France and West Germany.

Of all the ingredients of Scandinavia's social *smörgåsbord*, sex is the least likely to lend itself to the solutions of the reformers who restlessly seek to organize the Good Life of the model democracies. Certainly no magic answers have yet been found to all the familiar problems of love and marriage. What we are left with, after surveying the Scandinavian scene, is an extremely mixed picture. While it is not at all so scandalous as painted, neither is it particularly reassuring. If some Scandinavians seem almost recklessly advanced in their views on sex or indifferent to the consequences of overly permissive behavior, an even greater number are both circumspect and concerned.

Scandinavia's open approach to the subject has removed much of its mystery, but it has also brought about a healthy confrontation of sexual problems. The continuing debate on sexual morality is honest and vigorous. Above all, the subject is taken seriously. A typical young Swede taking part in a Stockholm forum on morals said: 'I don't think it's at all true that romance is dead, but there is a conflict for many people, particularly very young people, between romantic love and sheer physical desire. . . . One thing that really frightens me is this freedom in certain circles. They are trifling themselves away; they have no sense of romance or responsibility toward other human beings. I think that later in life they will find it difficult to live harmoniously: there will be big problems, and unfaithfulness will play an important part in their lives.'

Chapter 3

SUICIDE IN THE WELFARE STATE

Suicide is our national form of aggression.
                                    —DANISH DOCTOR

*A low suicide rate may conceal more human misery than is
revealed by a high rate.*
                                    —ENGLISH PSYCHIATRIST

One of the most intriguing of all Scandinavian puzzles is this:
Why do so many people commit suicide in such well-to-do welfare societies as Denmark, Sweden and Finland? Why should the
suicide rate for the gay Danes and the prosperous Swedes be higher
than that of the struggling Israelis or the poor Portuguese?
President Eisenhower was not the first to conclude that the 'almost
complete paternalism' of the welfare state drove people to self-
destruction. It appeared that with nothing more to struggle for,
people had nothing more to live for.

Three things can be said with confidence: 1. The over-all
Scandinavian suicide rate is high, but not nearly as high or as
significant as a great many people seem to believe. 2. The 'paternalism' and 'boredom' of the welfare state have little to do with
suicides. The fact that Norway, a thoroughgoing welfare state,
has a suicide rate far below that of its Nordic neighbors, and one
of the lowest in Europe, is the most obvious argument against
the easy welfare-suicide hypothesis. 3. Neither the Scandinavians
nor their critics are yet fully clear why they, or any people for
that matter, commit suicide, but that has not prevented the subject
from being used to prove that something has gone seriously wrong
in the Nordic social laboratory.

49

The Scandinavians are acutely embarrassed by the whole business. They can deal with the misconceptions about socialism by producing figures proving that capitalism is the real dynamo behind their prosperity. They can dismiss the sex stories about Scandinavia in the sure knowledge that other societies are in no position to criticize. But suicides present a more difficult problem of explanation. Unlike sex or socialism, it is hard to make a case for suicide as a good thing. The act of suicide looks too much like an act of rejection of the secure, happy life which the Scandinavians have so earnestly sought to create. Yet a reasonably high suicide rate, unfortunate as it may seem, is not necessarily something to be ashamed of. It may well be one of the signs of a modern, advanced society.

Customarily, the Scandinavians answer questions about their suicides with a brisk counterattack challenging the statistics. And well they might. 'Our statistics are honest,' they say. 'When somebody here commits suicide we mark it down. When you have a suicide you try to hide it. Anyway, we may kill ourselves more than we should, but you Americans kill *each other* at ten times our rate.'

In Denmark in 1962—the year offering the best international statistics at the time of writing—there were 883 suicides, most of them by people over fifty years of age, and only 23 homicides. (The year before there were just 781 suicides and 18 homicides.) In the United States that year there were 20,207 reported suicides and 9,038 homicides.

Thus it turns out that the American suicide rate of 10·8 per 100,000 of population was a bit more than half the Danish rate of 19·0, but the United States homicide rate was 4·8 as against just 0·5 for Denmark. (For England and Wales, suicides numbered 5,589 for a rate of 12·0, and there were 309 homicides for a rate of 0·7.) To put it another way, the United States had one killing for every two suicides, while Denmark had one killing for every 38 suicides. There was one homicide for every 20,800 Americans and one for every 202,000 Danes.

The Nordic countries are not at the top of the international list of suicide rates. As in abortion and divorce ratings, that distinction goes to the East European Communist countries, where people have undergone exceptional stresses and strains. Furthermore, if the statistics of other nations were as impeccable as the Scandinavian figures, then Denmark, Finland and Sweden would not look much more suicide-prone than other nations. In Scandinavia suicide may not be considered an honorable action (as it often is in Japan), but it does not receive the mark of shame as in the Catholic countries. Suicide is seen as a private matter and is treated as such by the press. Just as divorces are not publicized, so suicides are not mentioned in the newspapers, even if they involve prominent persons. At the most, a newspaper will say that a person died 'suddenly.'

Some Scandinavians will even argue that one of the rights of man is the right to end his own life. 'We didn't ask to come into this world,' one Dane said. 'Why should we need anybody's permission to leave it?' There is a good bit of support for euthanasia, particularly if a person suffering from an incurable disease pleads with his doctor to be allowed to die. It may be of parenthetic interest that one of the most famous of all Swedes, Alfred Nobel, the lonely dynamite king whose fortune was left to be distributed as Nobel Prizes, had such a life-weary outlook that he once sought to lend a helping hand to suicide. Sten Söderberg, a chronicler of Nobel's life, described a donation he wanted to make to the city of Paris:

> With the aid of an architect and a doctor of his acquaintance, he drew up a plan which he thought would be very attractive and which he considered ought to become a model for the whole world. Along a boulevard, which he proposed to buy, he would build a number of small, beautiful houses, in which anyone at all could, free of charge, commit suicide in a respectable and painless manner, in the full certainty that his dead body would be taken care of and his last will respected. Both doctors and lawyers would be available. Alfred Nobel considered Paris as the world's most civilized city, but unfortunately, he thought, suicide often occurred under abhorrent conditions. What most irritated him was that these human remains polluted the Seine. If the Paris police and the city's

other authorities had not refused this magnificent gift, what would probably have become the world's most original and most macabre street would have been founded.

The matter-of-fact Scandinavian attitude toward suicide is matched in few other countries. A leading statistician on suicides, Louis I. Dublin, has written that the number of American suicides is probably higher by one fourth to one third than recorded. The leading suicide authority in England, Austrian-born Professor Erwin Stengel, wrote in *Suicide and Attempted Suicide*:

> The suicide figures for Great Britain are probably no more reliable than those for the United States. But there are other factors which tend to falsify the suicide rates. In Roman Catholic and Moslem countries a verdict of suicide is such a disgrace for the deceased and his family that it is avoided wherever possible. This is why the very low suicide rates of the Republic of Ireland and Egypt are suspect. In many countries the methods of registration leave much to be desired. . . . However, it is obvious that highly industrialized and prosperous countries tend to have comparatively high suicide rates.

Catholic countries like Italy, Spain and Portugal are well down in the list of suicide rates. Catholics presumably are more inhibited about committing suicide than the Lutherans of Scandinavia, and if they do take their own lives, the truth may be covered up. And yet Austria and Hungary, both Catholic countries, have two of the highest suicide rates in the world—in some years higher than Japan or any Nordic country—and the rate for France is not far behind those for Denmark and Sweden. It is possible that the true rate for France is higher than that of any Scandinavian country. Religion obviously is only part of the picture. Some Protestant countries like Holland and Norway have low suicide rates while others are high. The least well-to-do of Americans, the Negroes, commit suicide at only a third of the rate of whites. In South Africa, black Africans kill themselves at only a fourth of the rate of prosperous 'Europeans.' The Scots are less suicide-prone than the wealthier English.

Even with all their statistical faults, the United Nations statistics for suicides per 100,000 inhabitants are worth recording. The rates for the leading suicide nations are given, as well as those for several other nations for the sake of comparison:

	1963	1961	1951
East Germany	28·4**	28·4**	29·0
Hungary	26·8	25·4	20·6***
Austria	21·7	21·9	22·7
Czechoslovakia	20·6*	20·6	—
West Germany	19·3	18·7	18·2
Finland	19·2	20·6	15·7
Denmark	19·1	16·9	23·6
Sweden	18·5	16·9	16·2
Switzerland	18·5*	18·2	21·1
Japan	15·9	19·6	18·3
Australia	15·7	11·9	9·5
France	15·5	15·9	15·5
Belgium	13·6*	14·7	13·8
England and Wales	12·2	11·3	10·2
(Scotland)	(8·6)	(7·9)	(5·4)
(N. Ireland)	(6·0)	(5·0)	(4·1)
U.S.A.	11·0	10·5	10·4
Portugal	9·6	8·7	10·2
New Zealand	9·6	8·4	9·9
Norway	8·0	6·6	6·5
Canada	7·6	7·6	—
Iceland	7·6	10·6	—
Netherlands	6·2	6·6	6·0
Italy	5·5*	5·6	6·8
Ireland	2·5	3·2	2·6

*   1962
**   1958
***   1955

The suicide rate is almost always higher in cities than in the countryside. For the past twenty-five years, Copenhagen's rate has usually been 35 to 40, and the average for 1946–50 was 42·6, or almost double the national rate of 24·8.

The Boredom Thesis

Interesting as these statistics are, it is more important for the purposes of this inquiry to see whether the Scandinavians are committing suicide more or less than ever. If it were clear that the Nordic people in their pre-welfare-state past took their own lives far less frequently than they do now, then it would seem to confirm the Eisenhower thesis. But this is not the case at all. To speak only of Sweden, its rate at the turn of the century was about 15 per 100,000 persons—only slightly less than the average of recent years. The number rose to 18·1 in 1910 before falling to a modern low of 10·0 in 1918. By 1932, when the Social Democrats came to power, it was up to 17·7. In that Depression year the suicide rate in the U.S.A. reached an all-time high of 17·4. The Danish rate in the postwar period has usually been higher than the Swedish—often exceeding 20 and once reaching 25. Finland for a number of years has had a rate hovering about 20.

Of course, even a rate of 20 means that only one person in every 5,000 commits suicide in a year. It might be supposed that even more would end their life in well-ordered societies which enable people to live longer than almost anywhere else in the world. Except for Finland, which lags behind by a few years, the mean expectation of life in Scandinavia is about 71 years for men and 75 for women. The Nordic statistics leave no doubt that older people account for most of the suicides. The disproportionate number of middle-aged and elderly people in West Berlin is given as one important reason for the high rate (about 40 per 100,000 persons) in that tense city.

One of the wisest statements yet made about suicides is this by Professor Stengel:

Contrary to popular belief, which associates suicide with frustrated love and 'poor moral fiber,' the majority of the people who kill themselves are elderly and many of them are physically sick. Their average age is in the late fifties. One of the reasons why highly developed and prosperous countries have higher suicide rates than underdeveloped and poor countries is that the expectation of life is far longer in the former than in the latter. The great medical discoveries of our time have benefited mainly the younger age groups. The diseases of middle and old age still remain to be conquered. Thus, more people are enabled to become old and sick today than were in the past. This is why scientific medicine, improved medical care, and material prosperity tend to increase the suicide rates. A low expectation of life of the general population makes for a low incidence of suicide. A low suicide rate may conceal more human misery than is revealed by a high rate.

The suggestion here is that the welfare state *does* serve to add to the suicide rate, but only in this strange way—by enabling people to live longer so that they can reach the age when suicide is more attractive. But this is not what the welfare-suicide critics have in mind. It seems to them that the welfare state leads to boredom, frustration and the crippling of individual incentive. A Swedish government official, Ernst Michanek, asked: 'Seriously, does any person really think it's probable that old-age security, adequate medical services, satisfactory housing and so forth cause people to feel unhappier?'

A study of the connection, if any, between suicides and the welfare state was made by Professor Maurice L. Farber, of the University of Connecticut, who reported his findings to the American Psychological Association in 1963. Among other things, he noted that Denmark had a high suicide rate of 20 to 30 for over a hundred years before it became a welfare state. If anything, the Danish rate showed a moderate decline after the advent of the welfare state, and 'there was a drop in the suicide rate for old people following the establishment of these extensive social-security practices.' Similarly, 'the suicide rate in the United States declined after the introduction of the social legislation of the New Deal.'

Professor Farber found that studies reveal that 'the Swedes are characterized by a *high* degree of incentive, throwing themselves into their jobs with perhaps a greater intensity than do Americans. In my own intensive interviews with suicide attempters in Norway and Denmark, I never encountered a case in which lack of incentive or boredom played a significant role . . . if anything,

Norwegians are more bored with life than are Danes (yet) the Danish suicide rate is much higher than the Norwegian. . . .' It seemed to him that 'welfare-statism need not be associated with low incentive.' He added: 'Are people in the welfare states, their moral fiber weakened by coddling, or, their adaptation level lower, less able to tolerate life's difficulties, as the hypothesis maintains? I could uncover no evidence to support this assertion.' On balance, it seemed to him that there was more of a case for saying that welfarism somewhat reduces the suicide rate: 'A man can look forward to an economically carefree retirement. His outlook is not marred by anxieties concerning the economics of illness or disablement. Such a favorable future–time perspective is an antidote to suicide.'

If the welfare state does not, per se, cause unhappiness, then it is also true that it does not necessarily bring happiness. The elementary things which trouble people in Scandinavia and many other places seem to remain, no matter how big the social-security checks become. There are innumerable psychological motivations. A frustrated person may become hostile, but he turns on himself instead of another person. As one authority says, there may be 'loss of love, feeling of rejection, feelings of guilt and desire for vengeance; and desire to escape from a physically painful situation.' Men almost always kill themselves at a greater rate than women. In 1961 in Sweden, 960 males and 313 females took their lives. Significantly, because Denmark has been called more of a matriarchal society, there were 514 male and 267 female suicides in the same year. It appears, furthermore, that women are becoming ever more suicide-prone as they achieve emancipation and play a less traditional housewife-mother role in the cramped cities of secular, industrialized countries. In more rural and rugged Norway, women commit suicide at only one fifth the female rate in Denmark.

Country living, strong religious views, a sound marriage, numerous children, membership in a lower-income group—all these are factors which work against suicide. On the other hand, such factors as these (as listed by Stengel) help to increase the likelihood of suicide: 'male sex, increasing age, widowhood, single and divorced state, childlessness, high density of population, residence in big towns, a high standard of living, economic crisis, alcohol consumption, history of a broken home in childhood, mental disorder and physical illness.'

In his classic study of suicide patterns in Europe at the end of the nineteenth century, the French sociologist, Emile Durkheim, illuminated the way persons who are strongly integrated in a social group are unlikely to take their own lives, while persons cut off from such groups become relatively more suicide-prone. The 'march of civilization,' he found, was weakening the strength of the family, the church, the village and other forces for social integration, and thus suicide rates were rising in Europe. But Durkheim also made it clear that too much integration—too much submission of the individual personality to the demands of the group—can, as sometimes happens in Japan, produce its own kind of suicide.

August Strindberg once wrote:

A suicide is committed. Business troubles, says the man of affairs. Unrequited love, say the women. Sickness, says the invalid. Despair, says the down-and-out. But it is possible that the motive lay in all or none of these directions, or that the dead man concealed his actual motive by revealing quite another, likely to reflect more to his glory.

The long, dark, depressing northern winters are often blamed for the high frequency of Scandinavian suicides. There has been a fascination with suicide in Nordic literature, and writers from abroad are fond of portraying the moodiness, neurosis and schizophrenia of the Scandinavians. They seem to be ready-made for suicide. And yet we are again left with Norway, a country which stretches farther than any other European nation into the dark and wintry north, and which has a lower suicide rate than Portugal. A friend in Finland, when asked about the suicide problem, simply recited an old saying that 'Finland is a wonderful, beautiful country, but hell's bells, just try living there.' Physical conditions seem almost beside the point, however; Denmark is the most comfortable of the four countries, while Norwegian life is the toughest, but their suicide rates work in reverse.

National Character

It has been my impression that much of the answer to the dilemma of the Nordic suicide pattern lies in the national character of the people concerned. It has not surprised me that the Norwegians commit fewer suicides. Not only do they seem to face the world aggressively from their long Atlantic coastline, but they argue, complain and boast with such extroverted heartiness that they work off most of their problems. In many ways it is a more 'natural' country today than either Sweden or Denmark, both of which have acquired a lot more polish.

The Finns in the harshness of their physical conditions and their emphasis on the tough, natural man are much like the Norwegians. Offhand, they might be expected to have the same low suicide rate. But in many ways they are the most extraordinary and mixed-up people in Scandinavia. They can be as charming and feckless as the Irish, as gloomy and close-mouthed as the Swedes, as hardheaded as the Russians, as spontaneous as the Italians—and sometimes all at once. The Finns, furthermore, live an almost West Berlin existence as a frontier of the Western world pushed up against the Soviet Union. For half a century their national survival was in question and they lived under such extraordinary trials and tensions that it is a wonder that their suicides have not been more frequent.

The high Danish rate has been no surprise, however, because I soon learned that the Dane is a much more complicated person than he appears. He presents himself as a gay, carefree fellow living in a story-book kingdom, but in business he is shrewd, in conversation his wit can be malicious, and in private he can become Shakespeare's melancholy Dane. Dr. Thorkild Vanggaard in Copenhagen said that 'there is plenty of bottled-up aggression. There are few outlets for exerting force or dominance in a situation where all are supposed to be equal. You don't order people around and you feel you must not be submissive.' He offered, as a 'strictly private philosophy based on observation but not scientific conclusions,' the thought that 'there is some loss of character when everything is so secure and comfortable that there is no need for assertion. The welfare state has achieved material benefits but not expression of the soul.'

As for the Swedes, it seemed to me that they had so many characteristics similar to the Japanese—introversion, great reserve, difficulties of communicating emotion, dedication to work, desperation to succeed—that it was only fitting that Sweden's suicide rate should be as high as Japan's. They are an extremely bottled-up, homogeneous people, who live according to a good many rigid rules of a highly organized society. As the newspaper *Expressen*, of Stockholm, said, Sweden's high suicide rate 'does not stem from our "dull" well-being. It's quite the opposite: Swedes commit suicide because Sweden is a hard country, one of the most competition-marked countries in the world.'

Expressen's sister newspaper, *Dagens Nyheter*, said:

A figure of between 1,200 and 1,300 suicides a year in Sweden is frighteningly high, higher than the death rate on the highways. As frightening is the knowledge of the despair, confusion and desperation existing right in the middle of the welfare state, which lies behind those thousands of attempts to voluntarily seek death or half-serious attempts at suicide as a protest, a cry for help when there was no help to be given. Every suicide could not have been prevented. But every attempted suicide is a warning, among many others, that psychological welfare does not automatically follow with physical welfare and cannot be bought with tax money.

The most ambitious attempt to analyze Scandinavian suicides in terms of national character or psychology has been that of Dr. Herbert Hendin, a psychiatrist of Columbia University. His book *Suicide in Scandinavia,* which appeared in 1964, gave the results of a four-year study of conditions in Denmark, Norway and Sweden. It was not well received in Scandinavia. The book was widely denounced; his conclusions about national foibles, after leaning heavily on interviews with persons who had tried and failed to commit suicide, led critics to call his work 'superficial,' 'unscientific' and 'funny.' Nonetheless, Dr. Hendin managed to throw some more light on a murky subject.

He decided that Denmark specialized in a 'dependency loss' kind of suicide, Sweden in a 'performance' type and Norway in a 'moral' type. He found the Danes to be exceptionally unaggressive and well-behaved. The homicide rate is low and in a recent year half the victims were children slain by their parents in connection with their own suicides. As a child, the Dane's aggressive tendencies are curbed. He grows up as a highly dependent mother's boy. She disciplines him by letting him know how much his behavior has hurt her. Hendin found that Danes of both sexes showed 'an extraordinary ability to arouse guilt in others through one's own suffering or misfortune.' Families in Denmark reveal a pattern of the passive father and forceful mother: 'The position of the Danish husband often resembles that of a privileged oldest child.' He concluded that the Danes are more likely than other people to plunge into depression if there is a breakdown of love or a deterioration of a personal relationship—in short, a dependency loss. And then the habit of suppressing aggression turns aggression inward, and 'the use of guilt-arousing techniques expedites the use of suicide as a method of dealing with the frustration and anger generated by a dependency loss.'

Hendin found a different story in Sweden, where youngsters are left to their own devices at an early age and are urged to be successful. Swedes 'push their children into an extremely early independence. "Key children" is the Swedish term for young school children who return to their homes before their parents come back from work. Since the child is too young to be trusted with a loose key, it is tied around his neck.' A Swedish child is caught up in fierce competition in school. He is likely to hate himself if he fails to live up to his own and his parents' high expectations. The ambitious Swede's 'intensive pursuit of money and material goods seemed as strong as anything seen in the United States.' The Swedish 'performance type' suicide is also seen in Germany and Switzerland, and, with important modifications, in Japan. Hendin wrote that 'it is the older men who are the core of the suicide problem in any country. In Sweden, men over 35 years of age seldom commit suicide simply over loss of dependency; it is rather their failure to reach ambitious goals or rigidly defined standards that motivates their suicide.'

As for the Norwegians, he found that they too had earlier freedom of movement, or less mother-dependency than the Danes, but that more than the Swedes they are permitted to express their aggression, making it 'less necessary for them to internalize anger.' In general, 'Norwegian faces were strikingly more expressive than those of Swedes and rarely showed the Swedish masklike quality.' He found Norwegians to be more outgoing and less caught up in a competitive struggle than the Swedes. All these safety-valve factors help explain why Norwegians commit fewer suicides than their neighbors, and more might have been said about Norway's more rural or traditional character, but what of those suicides they do commit? A 'moral' form of suicide was noticeable: 'It stems from aggressive antisocial behavior and strong guilt feelings aroused by such behavior, with the entire constellation cast in a puritanical setting.'

Obviously there is no simple answer to the suicide question. National character is important but so is a nation's economic condition and the level of its advancement on many fronts. It often seems in the high-pressure, technological age that the more progress, the more suicides, and yet some of the most advanced countries are low on the international suicide scoreboard. My conclusion is an undramatic one which parallels the viewpoint about Scandinavian sex: there is nothing really so extraordinary about Scandinavian suicides but there is a notably frank and open-minded approach to the subject.

'Of course,' said a Swedish social worker, 'we should do everything we can to see that people do not have to commit suicide. There may be some failing in our social conditions. But if they do take their own lives, that's their right.'

Chapter 4

THE NANNY STATE

There are no socialists in the Socialist Party.
—SWEDISH JOURNALIST

Why should I go to church? There's nothing more to pray for.
—DANISH CITIZEN

As long ago as 1906, Winston Churchill said in a political speech in Glasgow:

I should like to see the State embark on various novel and adventurous experiments. I am of the opinion that the State should assume the position of the reserve employer of labor. I am very sorry we have not got the railways in our hands. We are all agreed that the State must increasingly and earnestly concern itself with the care of the sick and the aged, and, above all, of the children. I look forward to the universal establishment of minimum standards of life and labor. . . . I do not want to see impaired the vigor of competition, but we can do much to mitigate the consequences of failure. . . . We want to have free competition upwards; we decline to allow free competition downwards. We do not want to pull down the structures of science and civilization, but to spread a net over the abyss . . . and I would recommend you not to be scared in discussing any of these proposals, just because some old woman comes along and tells you they are Socialistic.

What the young Churchill advocated came to pass in Scandinavia as well as in Great Britain. Are the Scandinavian countries, therefore, socialistic? One answer is that they are no more socialistic than America is capitalistic or Russia is communistic. The

United States, with its elaborate apparatus for government regulation of business, its public authorities, and its social-security and welfare programs, is now far from being the simple free-enterprise, self-reliant capitalistic society of the conservative dream. The Soviet Union, which controls the means of industrial production, describes itself as a socialist state (the Union of Soviet Socialist Republics) being guided to the communist utopia by the Communist Party.

Socialism, strictly speaking, has to do with government ownership and management of the essential means of production and distribution of goods. It opposes private 'exploitation.' In these terms, Denmark, Norway, Sweden and Finland are not, have never been, and probably never will be socialist. They are even *less* socialist than countries like Austria, France and Italy, which have a higher percentage of state-owned enterprises. Their basic economic system is capitalistic and it is free enterprise that has done the most to make all four countries among the most prosperous in the world.

Even though this is strikingly obvious to any visitor to Scandinavia, the four countries are still popularly thought of as socialist states where paternalistic big government has all but suffocated individualism and private enterprise. Right-wing speakers in American businessmen's clubs are sometimes hard put to explain why Scandinavia also has a reputation for high living standards but it is still widely asserted that the socialist Nordic nations are but one step from the communist grave. A great deal of the energy of the Scandinavian press-relations offices is spent counteracting this myth. Their descriptions of the economic system invariably start off by demonstrating how much private business there is and how little the state owns.

The misconceptions spring largely from a confusion of terms. If socialism is taken to mean a high degree of state regulation of industry and comprehensive social-welfare programs, then the Scandinavian countries are indeed socialist—and the United States is half socialist. Welfarism has gone far in Scandinavia, so far that many people are beginning to grumble that a kind of 'nanny state', has evolved which arranges and secures their lives as if they were inhabitants of a great Nordic nursery. But this is modern welfarism, not socialism.

The main reason for the image of a socialist Scandinavia rests on the Labor and Social Democratic parties, which have had the most powerful influence in Denmark, Norway and Sweden for more than thirty years. In their early days they called themselves socialist parties, their ambitions were socialist, and they saw themselves as part of a great European socialist movement. All that has changed, but the aura of socialism lingers on and the parties are reluctant to give it up entirely. They were once radical parties, which embraced doctrinaire socialism, but now they are pragmatic left-wing moderates. For a brief spell, the Norwegian Labor Party was a member of the Communist International. Even today, the Labor Party leaders in Norway manage to sound more left-wing than the Swedes or Danes. At May Day rallies they bring out, as if from mothballs, the old socialist slogans.

A Swedish diplomat in Oslo said: 'Norwegians talk more about socialism than we do. At our Labor Party conferences I haven't heard the word for years.' An American diplomat in Stockholm said that 'the Swedes just aren't impressed by packaged dogma.' The Finns still give about half their votes to left-wing parties but are ruled primarily by the Center or Agrarian Party. As for the Danes, a leading government economist, Eric Schmidt, said: 'No country in Europe has a smaller amount of nationalized and socialized industry than Denmark, and no similar stage of liberalism. There is less control of private undertakings here than in the United States. There is a lesser degree of intervention by big government, either by the use of state money or price control.'

Schmidt was only one of a number of Scandinavians who saw in America a greater degree of business regulation, much more protectionism for business and less devotion to free trade, and far more government intervention in management-labor relations. Scandinavian countries do not even have minimum-wage legislation. The opinion is that the trade union and employers' federations should be able to settle their differences themselves. Scandinavians view the British economy with wonder: management and labor in Britain look old-fashioned in their antagonism, while both the Conservatives and the Labor Party seem mired in outdated philosophies.

What the Scandinavians have is a practical mixture which has been called the Middle Way. It may ultimately become the Only Way as capitalist countries move left in their economic thinking and the Communist states move right. One Swede defined it as 'free-enterprise capitalism moderated by social aims and standards.' Another said more graphically that 'the socialist government likes to keep the capitalist cow fat in order to milk it.' Inevitably, there is disapproval. A Norwegian businessman said: 'We think we are free, but we are really working for the state.' And a Swedish student: 'There is no need for the state to socialize any more, because it decides everything as it is.'

Two things need description: the degree of nationalization of industry and the scope of the welfare state.

Nationalization

The Scandinavian countries have made state enterprises out of such public services as the postal, telegraph and telephone systems, power stations, railroads and airlines. Governments also own many of the forests, operate major mining, metal and wood processing companies, and control the manufacture and sale of alcohol. It is hazardous to generalize about nationalization, however, because of the many exceptions. State-owned railroads account for most of the mileage in the North, but each country has some private railway operations. The state dominates the electric power industry, but there are innumerable privately operated power plants. In Denmark and Norway the state owns most of the forest land but only 25 per cent in Sweden and just 35 per cent in Finland, where forestry is the backbone of the economy. In Denmark the state owns 51 per cent of the telephone service, which operates as if it were a private company.

Denmark and Sweden have the least direct government ownership or control of business enterprises, while Norway and Finland have the most. In Norway the state is the sole or principal owner of twenty-five firms and has investments in some fifty private companies. The government operates the huge and controversial Norwegian Iron Works at Mo-i-Rana in the north and the Syd-Varanger iron-ore mines near the Russian border. It has financed state-owned aluminum works in competition with private companies. In Finland the state has the major holding in a number of important pulp and chemical firms, and the lion's share in the country's biggest company, Enso-Gutzeit.

Such firms are expected to perform as if they were private companies. Even when they are wholly state-controlled they are led by experienced businessmen, including some who are stanch believers in free enterprise. They explain that the state has to function in some fields where the risks involved or the capital required are beyond the capacity of private companies. Norway, Sweden and Finland have all constructed steel mills close to the Arctic Circle as a means of spurring northern development. From a strictly business viewpoint they should have been placed elsewhere, but the state has chosen to take an economic gamble for the social good. The businessmen managers of state industry point out that the Social Democrats have almost completely abandoned their old ideas about nationalizing existing private enterprises. They shake their heads at the British Labour Party's efforts to nationalize the steel industry; Scandinavian 'socialists' wouldn't bother.

The most visible example of the state and private mixture is the Scandinavian Airlines System. SAS is a cooperative effort of Denmark, Norway and Sweden, with each nation sharing in the ownership (40 per cent Swedish, 30 per cent Danish, 30 per cent Norwegian) and with government and private business in each country going half and half on the shares. Significantly, one of the major forces in the success of SAS has been the Wallenberg financial dynasty in Sweden.

Capitalist Sweden

Although it is Denmark that has most studiously kept the state separate from the business world (the government, of course, manipulates economic controls), it is the Swedish story that is most revealing about Scandinavian economics. Sweden dominates the Nordic business scene. It is an economic wonder, having transformed itself in less than a century from a poor, underdeveloped country to a rich nation which has, after three decades of Social Democrat government, one of the most effective capitalistic systems on earth.

Less than 6 per cent of Swedish industry is nationalized; and most of the nationalizing was done decades ago, when the Conservative and Liberal parties ruled the country. The Social Democrats in thirty-three years in power have nationalized little more than one per cent of industry. They make it plain, however, that they stand ready to step in if private enterprise fails to do the job. As the *Daily Telegraph* of London reported: 'Sweden has proportionately more private enterprise than almost any other country in West Europe. The Swedish Social Democrats work through, rather than against, private enterprise.' A Swedish banker said: 'Actually, we are more radical than they are. All they want to do is keep the economy on an even keel.' And a trade-union leader said: 'Only if industry remains progressive and prosperous can we maintain and improve our standard of living.'

Going by employment figures, private enterprise in Sweden owns more than 90 per cent of mining and manufacturing, wholesale trade, insurance and commercial banking. Private firms are predominant in almost all other fields. The state still controls less than half of the nation's electric power stations. It is the sole owner of the tobacco-processing plants, and has put the liquor business under a monopoly company in which the government dominates. Broadcasting is a semiofficial monopoly, not a state-owned operation, and has the press, radio industry and several national organizations as shareholders.

The most controversial recent state enterprise is the huge steel mill erected at Luleå in northeastern Sweden to provide a magnet for the industrial development of the relatively backward north. The iron ore for the Luleå plant comes from the great mines at Kiruna and Malmberget. These national treasures have now passed into state hands. It was a conservative government which first maneuvered for a state share in the private mining enterprise and laid down the conditions which gave the government the right to buy up control of the mines. The Social Democrats began to exercise the option in the 1950s.

Despite such postwar activities, the Swedish business community is confident that the state has no interest in nationalizing industry. Marcus Wallenberg, the country's leading financier, said: 'First and foremost, it should be remembered that free enterprise and a free market economy have always characterized Swedish economic life.' The Social Democrats, although they have imposed heavy progressive income taxes on the rich, have been generous with companies. The over-all corporation tax is about 50 per cent, but companies are permitted a wide latitude in leveling out annual results, building up tax-free reserves, and writing off capital equipment.

Similarly the Social Democratic government has been generous in its dealings with cooperatives, which form a kind of third economic force in Scandinavia between private and public enterprise. The Swedish cooperatives grew up in close sympathy with the Social Democratic Party, but they operate independently. They have an unusual importance in retailing and agriculture, but they play a lesser role in manufacturing than their early enthusiasts expected. Everyone agrees that the cooperatives are valuable, but private companies still dominate the Swedish scene—under the watchful eye of the state.

Welfarism

Sweden's veteran prime minister, Tage Erlander, has said that his government's economic policy has a twofold purpose: 'To stimulate industrial development and to meet the actual and urgent demands of our citizens.' It is in the meeting of these demands that the governments of the Scandinavian countries act more like the socialists they are assumed to be. The welfare state is a reality in all four countries and something which virtually every Scandinavian of every political persuasion wants to preserve. It isn't perfect, but it works; and the trend is for more of it, not less, even though a certain saturation point has been reached.

Scandinavian welfarism is no longer so extraordinary. All the more prosperous West European countries are now welfare states in about as thoroughgoing a fashion as Sweden or Denmark. Each has a galaxy of accident, health, old-age, unemployment and other insurance available to all citizens. West Germany spends a higher proportion of its government revenues on social welfare than even the Scandinavian countries. Great Britain's 'socialized medicine' is more 'free' than anything known in the Nordic world. Britain is an old hand at welfare measures; its 'Beveridge Plan' had a major influence on Scandinavian social planning. It is hard to find an industrially advanced nation today which does *not* have a welfare-state apparatus. The United States, while clinging to its old notions of every-man-for-himself, spends more money on welfare than any nation in history. It is more social-security-minded than most Americans are prepared to admit. Legislation to protect the workingman and regulate business was first introduced decades before the New Deal. What Theodore Roosevelt helped to begin, Franklin Roosevelt expanded to fit the growing American social conscience. It was under a Republican President, Dwight Eisenhower, that the Department of Health, Education and Welfare was created. John F. Kennedy proposed the Medicare program, finally enacted in 1965, which takes a long stride toward the Scandinavian-style medical-care programs. Lyndon Johnson proclaimed the goal of a 'Great Society' and launched such ambitious social programs that he was soon 'outdealing' the New Deal.

The actual welfare-state differences from country to country are therefore not so great as they seem. What makes Scandinavia special is the way these welfare solutions have been carefully and democratically built up, brick by brick, over almost a century, but with particular impetus in the last three decades. In many respects the Nordic countries have set the welfare pace for the world and served mankind as social laboratories. It has not been ruthless experimentation, but a carefully programmed effort for the improvement of society which the guinea pigs, so to speak, voted for themselves. There has been an awareness throughout the whole construction of the welfare state of the danger that too much security might lead to too little personal liberty. The constant object has been to bring everybody into the welfare tent without taking away any citizen's individual freedom. What was wanted was a safety belt, not a strait jacket. My own conclusion is that the Scandinavians, even though they have their own misgivings, have succeeded. An English educator in Trondheim told me that 'the Norwegians still show a fierce independence and capability.' Swedish Prime Minister Tage Erlander, who sees the state 'as an instrument of cooperation between individual human beings,' said: 'I am fully aware that some people fear that the increase in government influence implies a serious threat to personal freedom and may risk impairing private initiative and responsibility. But I wonder whether these fears are not exaggerated. We believe that increased security is in fact a way to enlarge the freedom of choice. To open new possibilities for everybody to build his future according to his own wishes. It is our concept of an open society.'

Imperfect and incomplete as they may be, the Scandinavian welfare-state systems are well conceived and well administered. They have a smaller bureaucracy and a greater degree of decentralization than is generally realized. In a recent year in Sweden, the state accounted for 44 per cent of the total expenditures on welfare programs, the communities 28, employers 6, and individuals made up the remaining 22 per cent by paying welfare charges. People deal with a community-administered health-insurance and pension office, and they go to the doctors of their choice—doctors in private practice who earn some of the highest incomes in Scandinavia. There is little talk about corruption or abuse of the welfare system. All of this seems natural for the efficient Scandinavians. They have had a social conscience for a long, long time and have fashioned a way of life which seems eminently suitable for their own conditions.

The Swedish public-health system began as far back as 1681. There has been a Scandinavian pattern of public hospitals and medical services for several hundred years. Systems of free elementary schools began well over a century ago. Locally administered programs to help the poor formed the nucleus of later social-welfare developments. The industrial revolution came late to Scandinavia, but when it arrived over a century ago it was soon followed by legislation protecting workers. Trade unions and the Social Democratic Party began to be influential late in the nineteenth century. Conservative and Liberal governments, which nationalized a number of public services, began several insurance programs in a modest way before and after the turn of the century. But it was in the 1930s that the 'Home for the People,' as the Swedish Social Democrats called it, began to take its modern shape. The existing programs of relief, worker protection and social security were greatly enlarged. Sweeping legislation to improve health and housing standards was pushed through parliament. 'Baby bonuses' were devised to stimulate the birth rate. Family allowances were created to enrich home life. Full employment was the major goal of the reformers, and its eventual achievement is greatly to their credit.

For better or worse, womb-to-tomb protection was provided on a scale greater than in any other part of the world. Emphasis was put on the prevention of distress rather than on simple relief. Today, Sweden and Denmark have the most elaborate welfare arrangements in Scandinavia, while Norway is close behind and Finland is hurrying to catch up. Roughly 13 to 15 per cent of the net national incomes are spent on welfare; slightly more than in Britain, twice as much as in America. For the average Swede, for instance, the welfare state means that he gets medical care at little cost, free hospital treatment and operations, a furniture loan when he is setting up a household, assistance in building a house or paying for an apartment, a cash allowance if he is unable to work, free care and a 180-dollar cash grant for his wife when she has a baby, 120-dollar annual cash allowances for each child under age sixteen, free books, meals and transportation for his school children, free tuition and a loan for expenses for his children who go on to a university, a generous pension and housing allowance in his old age, and more.

Health insurance is now compulsory in all four Nordic countries, a fact which some conservatives heartily resent, but in Denmark, for example, it is possible to be just a 'passive' or 'C' member of the national 'Sick Chest' insurance system. All that is required is a contribution of about $3.50 a year for insurance against invalidism.

The most revealing summation of the welfare apparatus in Scandinavia is the listing in the Swedish publication *Social Welfare Statistics of the Northern Countries*. Under the heading 'Scope of Welfare Measures' are these items:

Health Insurance and Corresponding Benefits
Doctors, Midwives and Nurses
Hospitals, etc.
Care of the Mentally Defective
Dental care
Occupational Injuries Insurance
Unemployment Insurance
National Old Age Pensions
Disability Pensions
Widows' Pensions
Occupational Therapy and Rehabilitation Centers for Partially
    Disabled
Homes for the Aged and Pensioners' Flats
Welfare Measures for Mothers and Infants
Day Nurseries, Nursery Schools, Leisure Centers, etc.
Children's Allowances
Maintenance Advances
Children and Young Persons under Public Supervision and
    Care
Children's Homes, Homes and Special Boarding Schools for
    Young Persons, etc.
School Meals
Health Services for School Children
Social Home Help Services
Marriage (Home-furnishing) Loans
Rent Subsidies to Families with Children
Holidays for Children
Holidays for Housewives
Social Assistance

'Holidays for Housewives' is an example of welfarism carried to extremes or welfarism showing great compassion, depending on one's viewpoint. The idea is that housewives from poor families who are badly in need of a rest because of 'many children, illness, poor health' and other reasons should be assisted by the state. In Sweden the housewife gets free holiday transportation once a year to and from any place in the country. The holiday must last at least ten days and may be spent at a holiday home. Well over 20,000 work-worn Swedish housewives receive such help each year and presumably return to the bosoms of their families in improved condition. Norway and Finland follow Sweden's method of state assistance, but the Danish solution provides an example of how public and private welfare sometimes interlock in the North:

> There is no special legislation in Denmark concerning house-wives' holidays. A number of private benevolent societies, however, provide holidays for housewives of small means, and these activities are subsidized by the Ministry of Social Affairs out of football pool profits.

The High Cost of Welfare

Welfare costs may amount to one third of total public expenditures in a Nordic country. The benefits and protection are not 'free.' Scandinavians have become increasingly conscious that they are paying for everything they get. Some pay more and get less; some pay less and get more. It amounts to a considerable redistribution of income. But in these countries, where few are really poor or rich, the average man in the long run pretty much gets back in welfare-state benefits what he parts with in taxes, minus the cost of administration. The real value for his money is peace of mind: he will never be crippled by medical bills; he will be comfortable in his old age. He would not, therefore, choose to give up the welfare state even though he resents paying so heavily for it.

Listen to John Johannessen, an angry Norwegian who wrote to *Life International* after it published a critique on the welfare state:

The article might leave the impression that the welfare state itself is an independent and inexhaustible gold mine, the gifts of which are relieving people of all their financial worries. I therefore think it should be stressed that our so-called welfare state is actually based on the most extensive and rigid taxation system by means of which the state simply confiscates one's money and then redistributes parts of it in forms of social welfare as the state itself considers appropriate.

In Norway, the average income of the industrial workers is about $2,500 yearly of which direct taxes take $620 if single and $200 if a five-member family. On incomes of $7,000, approximate taxes are $2,600 and $2,100 respectively. Besides a purchase tax of 10% of all goods sold, special dues and taxes are innumerable. A Chevy II costs $4,930, a bottle of ordinary Scotch $8. A license, annual fee, $23, is required for radio-TV. The system is so intricate that when serving martinis restaurants are known to split the price on the bill in three, viz., the price of liquor (gin), of wine (vermouth) and of food (olive).

No wonder some people get tired.

The Scandinavians pay some of the highest taxes in the world. Taking all direct and indirect taxes into account, approximately 50 per cent of the average man's earnings go to taxes. The size of the direct tax bite has gotten so big that Sweden and Denmark are planning to make a wholesale switch to an elaborate system of indirect taxation. Businessmen insist that the severe progressive taxation will be the downfall of free enterprise. I have never heard such incessant and angry cries against high taxes as I did in Norway. The Swedes are not such ready complainers as the Norwegians, but their resentment of high taxes was almost equally ill-concealed.

Although the mayor in Stavanger, Norway, told me that 'high taxes are the admission ticket to civilization,' an important turning point has been reached for the welfare state. A great many people are beginning to think that still higher taxes are too high a price for still more benefits. There is uneasiness about the fact that cheating on taxes has become fashionable. It is clear that many people are not working as hard as they might, because additional earnings are lost to the tax collector. Doctors and other professional people are taking longer vacations. In labor-short Sweden a good many housewives who could go to work have decided that the only effect would be to raise the family income into a still higher tax bracket. In Denmark the tax laws requiring the incomes of working husband and working wife to be added together means that it is cheaper to 'live in sin.'

A good many Scandinavian welfare officials are convinced that the state must use the ordinary citizen's money for social purposes because he is too foolish. They speak of all the money that people waste on liquor and lipstick; they say that all too many people do not have the good sense to save their money for a new home and that the state, therefore, has been obliged to take tax money from them in order to hand it back as housing loans.

There is obviously a good case for such a viewpoint, even if it is almost insultingly paternalistic. But now that a great many basic needs have been met by the welfare state, the feeling is growing that enough has been done. People want to use the money they have left after taxes the way they choose.

The trouble is that this current of thought collides with a torrent of demands for (1) improvements in the existing welfare services, (2) additional measures to take care of the unfinished business of the welfare state, and (3) still more spending on other kinds of public services. Let us take them in turn:

1. The existing services still leave much to be desired. There are shortages of hospital space, medical and nursing personnel, child-care and old-age institutions, and other welfare facilities. The state has come to be responsible for sponsoring new housing but has failed to meet the demand. One oddity of the welfare state is the way the solving of human problems creates new and allied problems. I remember talking to the administrator of the new central hospital in Tampere, Finland. I asked, naïvely, why huge medical facilities were necessary if people were becoming healthier than ever. The answer was that with inexpensive and even free medical treatment available, people were making use of it in a way which would never have occurred to them before the rise of the welfare state. In the old days they just suffered in silence.

Now they had become aware of the wisdom of seeking medical treatment and were turning up with all manner of ailments. One physician said that the increase in the number of mentally ill in Scandinavia is due mainly to the new availability of treatment and the detection of cases which would have remained hidden in former times. The mentally ill and their relatives, no longer so ashamed as they used to be, are coming forward for help. Similarly, the over-all improvement in health conditions means that people are living longer and that hospitals must devote more of their time to old-age ailments. There is an ever greater need for facilities to care for the aged. There is a constant cry for such new welfare wrinkles as free trips to Mediterranean health resorts for patients who need sunshine. 'Everybody demands more welfare of the government,' wrote Ernst Michanek. 'No one demands less.'

2. The unfinished business of the welfare state is anything that any group still feels entitled to and clamors for loudly enough. For Norway and Finland, it can also be defined as anything that Sweden and Denmark have and they still lack. The major welfare effort at the moment in Scandinavia is the universal pension plan which gives everyone in his retirement years an income of about two thirds of his peak earnings during his working days.

3. The demand for spending on other public services has to do with such things as the improvement of roads to meet the growing flood of automobiles, the reshaping and expansion of cities as the urban movement continues, the construction of more schools and the creation of new universities. All of these 'Great Society' demands are common to any prospering industrial society. They cost money, and the money comes from taxes.

Laziness?

Does the welfare state make people too comfortable, too lazy? Does it destroy their ambition and initiative?

A quick answer is 'no.' A safer answer is, 'not noticeably.' As already mentioned, some people are cutting down on their effort or ambition, but this is due to taxes, not to oversecurity. In

Scandinavia, as anywhere else, more work means a higher scale of living, less work means a lower scale. Most people want more and are willing to work for it.

Scandinavia has historically been a hard-working part of the world. It took prodigious efforts to build a civilization in countries where nature presents a daily challenge. People have built-in work habits. In Sweden, industriousness is so chronic that a lazy man is likely to be considered sick and in need of treatment. Certainly there is a movement in the North toward the shorter working week (it is still about forty-five hours as against the American forty) and the longer vacation. After the long winter months of hard labor most people feel they have a right to take it easy in the few sunshine months. An American diplomat in Stockholm said: 'During the summer it's difficult to raise a warm body in the Foreign Office. If you telephone you get a recorded message.'

Even so, in my visits to factories and offices in Scandinavia I have always been struck by the pace of work and the dedication to the job. The piece-rate system is widely used in industry even though trade-unionists in other countries see it as an exploitation of labor. Scandinavian workers like the idea of being able to earn more if they produce more. They are working hard to get the luxuries they are sure they need. Today's laborer is thinking about a new Volvo, a country cottage, a holiday in the Canaries. Some people worry about this outlook; it may be the good life, but it seems to lack the idealism and cultural uplift which the early Social Democrats envisioned when they prepared the blueprints for utopia. 'We are getting too materialistic,' said an editor in Copenhagen. 'People are talking about money more than they ever did before.'

Does the welfare state limit freedom? Does the individual smother under the nanny state's warm blanket? If the answer is yes, then it has to be added that the Scandinavians have asked for it. The welfare apparatus has not been imposed on them. They have voted it in and they could vote it out. These are still parliamentary democracies, with all the traditional political freedoms. Few people are conscious of a loss of liberty except for those who complain that taxes have cut deeply into their freedom to spend the money they earn. Many will point out all the deficiencies of the welfare system and then say that it has enhanced their freedom. Assured that their living standard will not be seriously affected if they become ill or lose their jobs, they feel freer to spend their money on luxuries and travel. 'Perhaps I have lost my freedom to worry about losing my job or paying for the doctor,' said one Swede, 'but I am willing to make the sacrifice.'

The Pursuit of Happiness

Does the welfare state bring happiness? Critics of Scandinavian life are sure it doesn't. Much has been written about gloominess and frustration in the Nordic welfare states. But another question should be asked: Is the welfare state supposed to bring happiness? Some of the Social Democratic pioneers thought so, but the contemporary view was expressed by Viggo Kampmann, a self-styled socialist and a former prime minister of Denmark, when he said it was not the job of government to make people happy but to create conditions which would enable people to find happiness for themselves. 'It is up to the individual, not the state, to make himself happy.'

The Scandinavians have had so many people accuse them of being unhappy that they now ask, as does Sweden's Lars Gustafsson: 'Why should we be happier than other people and not be able to feel bored? That is, of course, what the whole matter is about. Thorough social legislation and a high standard of living are not sufficient conditions for happiness. They cannot possibly be, but it is not their fault that they aren't. They are sufficient conditions for a humane life, and that is enough. The mechanisms of boredom and happiness are controlled by subtler laws than that.'

Knud Meister, a Danish journalist, goes further:

It is indeed a good question whether Scandinavians ever have been happy. Certainly the roaring laughter of the Dublin pub and the songs of Naples have no counterpart in the Gothic twilight of Ibsen's wild duck, Strindberg's Miss Julie and

Andersen's nightingale; amid the mists of the fjords and the rains of the northern valleys happiness is a far different thing from happiness in the lands where Caesar's and Charlemagne's legions roamed. Denmark's substitute for happiness is *hygge*, an untranslatable word that undramatically indicates content, and embraces good food, good company and a blaze in the fireplace.

The Nordic welfare state has settled into a comfortable middle age. Even though fully half the Scandinavians consider themselves more conservative than the Social Democratic architects of welfarism, it is hard to find anyone in the whole of the North who would now tear down the welfare-state structure. Even the right-wing political parties vote for welfare measures and pledge to carry on the social system if they should come to power. The essence of the welfare state is now almost above criticism in Scandinavia. The argument constantly under way in the Scandinavian press and parliaments centers almost entirely on whether it is economically prudent to take the further welfare steps which the Social Democrats propose from time to time. The left-wingers say 'now,' the right-wingers say 'later.' There is a growing body of opinion, however, which is saying 'enough.'

The Scandinavians are happy to have the welfare state, but they are not wholly content with it. It is their creation, but it seems to have a momentum of its own, so that it threatens to get out of hand. The more it does, the more it is called upon to do. And the more it *likes* to do. A Danish social worker commented sourly that 'the welfare state does not love the poor and the lost. The welfare state as we know it loves the ideal of the complete state; in other words, it loves itself.'

Scandinavians I have spoken to betray a sense of unease about so much welfarism. They vaguely feel that their everyday lives are too much caught up in the impersonal machinery of the welfare state. They wonder whether they might be better off if everything were not so tidy and secure. 'Everything is too well arranged,' they say. 'We don't even have the opportunity to feel miserable.' There is worry about the fact that young people do not express great ambitions. They echo the concern of foreign critics that too much security deprives a society of its excitement and challenge. And yet people want the welfare state even if they don't love it. Väinö Linna, the Finnish author of *The Unknown Soldier*, said: 'I would rather have a welfare state where people are not fully satisfied than the old world where people had no choice but to suffer.'

Part Two

Denmark

Chapter 5

THE COZY COUNTRY

Have fun in Denmark, sleep in the next country.
— DANISH TOURIST OFFICIAL

*The Danes are superb salesmen of themselves. They play their
Little Mermaid, Hans Christian Andersen image to the hilt.*
— A SWEDE

A cartoon by Danish humorist Bo Bojesen tells the story of
Denmark. A typical, well-fed, contented Dane with straw hat
and picnic box goes down on all fours to look at his reflection in
a pool of water. What he sees is not his usual plump, smiling self
but his vision of the Dane he once was: a fierce, bearded Viking
with horns projecting from his helmet and a knife at his hip.

There was a time, a thousand years ago, when the Danes were
part of the horde of Nordic warriors who terrorized Europe. For
long centuries afterward the Danes were constantly at war with
the Swedes, Germans, British and many other peoples of greater
power and numbers. In Iceland, Greenland, the Faroe Islands and
territory in the Caribbean they had the start of a colonial empire.
Their guns at Kronborg, 'Hamlet's Castle' at Helsingør (Elsinore),
exacted payment from merchant ships passing through the gate-
way to the Baltic.

Today's Dane, however, is no ruthless Viking or combat hero
but a fine fellow who likes to be liked and who enjoys life more
than his earnest Scandinavian brothers. On the whole, he is quite
pleased with himself. A story is told about the time a poll was
taken to see which of the Scandinavian peoples was most popular
within Scandinavia. To no one's surprise, it turned out that the

83

Norwegians liked the Danes the best, the Swedes liked the Danes the best, the Finns liked the Danes the best, and the Danes liked the Danes the best.

The day before Nikita Khrushchev's arrival in Copenhagen in June 1964 for an official visit, Danish Foreign Minister Per Haekkerup told foreign correspondents that 'Russia is one of the few countries that Denmark has never attacked.' Despite this piece of unfinished business, Denmark has sworn off aggression. It has the appearance of being the most peaceful country in all Europe. It takes a visit by the Beatles or a football game to work up anything resembling a riot. Denmark's handful of juvenile delinquents are choir boys compared to the Swedish breed. Hardly anybody resorts to violence in the Finnish fashion. The sharpest-edged weapon is the cutting Danish humor. In World War II the German occupation was an accomplished fact for several years before the Danes got around to putting up any hard resistance. Today Denmark is a NATO power, if power is the word, but this tough stance is offset by a pacifist, neutralist strain in Danish political life.

The Danes like to say: 'But we are only a little country.' And yet the little place has done some big things. It is the world's oldest kingdom and probably the most efficient agricultural country on earth. Its milk, cheese, butter, bacon, beer and cigars are unsurpassed. It is the world's biggest manufacturer of diesel engines for merchant ships. Danish engineers are world famous. The Royal Ballet is one of Europe's finest. The late Niels Bohr was only the best-known of a number of Danish scientists who have won the Nobel Prize. Except for the Bible, the stories of Hans Christian Andersen have been more widely translated and read than any other works of literature. Søren Kierkegaard was one of the great European philosophers, and Arne Jacobsen is today one of the foremost European architects. Copenhagen is the only truly cosmopolitan city in Scandinavia, and its Tivoli Gardens is the finest pleasure park in the world. The Folk High School and the cooperative movement have planted their roots more deeply in Denmark than in any other country, and nowhere have they produced such visibly beneficial results. The healthiness of

Danish life, the strength of Denmark's democracy and the scope of its educational and social-welfare institutions all justify the envy of larger, stronger nations.

It is a serene and pleasant country. The temptation is great to call it Europe's land of milk and honey, or Shangri-La without mountains. To drive across Fyn, 'the orchard of Denmark,' and to see the smiling fields, cozy homes and radiant people, is to be reminded of a description by one of the Spanish conquerors of Peru in the age of the Incas:

> We found these countries in such a condition that there were no thieves, no vicious men, no idlers, no adulterous or evil-living women. . . . Cultivated land, mountains, mines, pastures, hunting, woods and everything else were organized and shared in such a way that each one knew and owned his heritage; no one else could occupy or seize it, and there was no need to go to law. . . . Everything, from the most important to the smallest detail, was planned and coordinated with great wisdom.

Reality intrudes, of course, on any suggestion that Denmark is so idyllic. Not everyone is happy. The divorce rate is one of the world's highest. Drug addiction is high; pornography has become a big business. Copenhagen has slums and a quarter million Danish families live in sub-standard housing. Class feelings still persist. Political extremists appeal to the 'working population' against the 'bourgeois exploiters.' Personal attitudes are such that the foreign minister has said that 'The U.S. is much more genuinely democratic than Denmark.'

A Knack for Fun

A century ago, Denmark's great poet, bishop and educator, N. F. S. Grundtvig, foresaw a land 'where few have too much, and still fewer have too little.' Denmark today is still seeking such a happy state, but, as Danish writer Mogens Lind explained, 'nobody looks down on a man who is a millionaire. We know that the taxation system will not allow him to go on being one for very long and anyway he is not happier than the rest of us.'

Or, as another Dane put it, 'You mustn't judge a man by an accident of birth. After all, it was not his fault that he was born a count.'

Although there is still a marked fondness for titles, every Dane knows that he is as good as anybody else. Most people live at about the same level, look alike, dress alike, and indulge in similar pleasures. The royal family mingles in the market place with an ease unknown in monarchies outside Scandinavia. It is predominantly a middle-class life without too restrictive a bourgeois discipline. Ninety-seven per cent of the population belong to the official Lutheran Church, but only a fraction are actively religious. A Greek who spent some time in Denmark said that the Danes 'show tolerance, understanding and love for their fellow countrymen, contrary to some other northern countries. But I was surprised to find that their spiritual life was to my opinion lower and/or different from ours. They consider wealth and higher living standards the sole purpose of man on earth, and now, somehow having achieved this, they seem to be lost in an ocean of euphoria.'

Most Danes are surely moral and upright, by anybody's standards, but pleasure is not frowned on and the over-all attitude toward private conduct is permissive. It is almost, but not quite, hedonism. To suggest hedonism as the Danish ethic is to unfairly discount the plain hard work and social responsibility which have made Denmark a thriving and enlightened country. Nonetheless, the Danes have a knack for enjoying themselves. They are not suited to austerity. They are an indulgent people, who prolong the joys of childhood into middle age. The knowledge that they are inhabitants of an ancient kingdom seems to inspire them to play the part of happy subjects who throng merrily to Tivoli and raise their children on their shoulders to see the King's sentries marching through the streets to the palace.

'The Danish national drink is beer,' wrote Mogens Lind, 'and the Danish national weakness is another beer.' A friend in Copenhagen explained that 'Denmark is a kingdom where the parliament has the legislative power and the breweries have the executive power.' The Danes of a century ago were the hardest-drinking people in Europe, with an annual consumption of two and a half gallons of pure alcohol per head of population. Today the Danes take their hard liquor far more moderately, but they are among the greatest beer drinkers and cigar smokers in the world. Depending on the season, three to four million bottles of beer are consumed every day, yet the total population is less than five million. A six-week brewery strike in 1965 was considered a national calamity. It forced people to buy expensive imported beer and cost the government more than 12 million dollars in taxes. The end of what the Associated Press called 'one of the most unpopular strikes in Danish history' was announced in special news broadcasts on the state radio.

The Danes do not hurl themselves into drinking bouts so compulsively as the Finns, Norwegians and Swedes. They space out their drinking and produce fewer drunks. Although Danish authorities are as severe as other Scandinavians on people who drive after drinking (including bicyclists), the restrictions on the sale of alcohol are minor compared with those of the neighboring countries. It is possible to sit drinking in one Copenhagen night spot until it closes at five o'clock in the morning and then find another place which is opening at exactly that hour. For its young people, Denmark—or, more specifically, the dairy industry—has created a wholesome hangout called the 'milk pop.' In Copenhagen and a number of towns around the country, teen-agers drop into stylish milk bars where they can talk, flirt, do their homework, and listen to pop, jazz and classical music while gulping down milk shakes.

The Danes eat more food—and good, rich food at that—than their Scandinavian neighbors. Their consumption is the highest for potatoes, sugar, meat, fats and coffee. Thick cream is poured into coffee and lavished on almost everything else. The average man's day is a succession of little meals. He may have breakfast at eight o'clock, nip out for a bite at ten or eleven, lunch at twelve, and eat again at three, six and nine o'clock. The famous national snack is *smørrebrød*, literally 'buttered bread.' The bread may be white, or light or dark rye. The butter is laid on as if with a trowel. Artistically placed on the butter are pieces of cheese, herring, smoked salmon, beef, pork and anything else edible. Oskar Davidsen's restaurant in Copenhagen offers 178 different kinds of *smørrebrød* on a menu almost four feet long. Number 56 is 'raw, scraped meat, export caviar and two Limfjord oysters flanked by two rows of shrimp.' Number 128 is 'Bombay toast: macaroni, chicken giblets in curry, mayonnaise with egg and smoked salmon.'

I remember entering a small hotel restaurant in Sønderborg on the island of Als late one evening. The waiter said it was past supper time. He could not serve me a meal but wondered whether I could make do with a *smørrebrød*. 'Anything,' I said. He brought me a hot roast beef dinner. Lurking under the slabs of fine red meat was a thin slice of buttered bread. That made it a *smørrebrød*.

One of the pleasures of Denmark for a visitor is watching the Danes at their leisure. There is something graceful and effortless about it, nothing frantic or competitive. It is a country ideally suited for bicycles. There are some three million of them and in many communities there are special bicycle paths between the streets and sidewalks. The fact that automobiles have come to Denmark in profusion has meant a speeding up of the easy pace of Danish life, but it is still a land where families go bicycling, sailing or walking the beaches. The Danes are not the kind of determined Nordic athletes who run off with Olympic medals for track or other sports which require great exertion. They do better at archery, yachting and kayak rowing. Even so, some two million Danes are card-carrying members of sports clubs of one kind or another, and that's almost half the population.

Heavenly Bliss

To a remarkable extent, the Danes have succeeded in reducing all the usual conflicts of life to insignificant size. Denmark is a place of doting parents and easygoing children, and of natural relationships between boys and girls. The remaining feelings of antagonism between bosses and workers are usually smoothed over. There is an over-all politeness and law-abidingness. Taxi drivers leap out to open the door for their passengers. People wait obediently for traffic lights to change, even on a deserted street at midnight. Visually in Denmark there is little to give offense. The roads are devoid of billboards or junkyards. There is a sense of design in most shops and homes. Meals are arranged and served with an Oriental feeling for appearance as well as taste. It is an altogether comfortable country.

If there is anything wrong with Denmark, it is probably just that: it is comfortable, too comfortable. Russia's young poet, Evgeny Yevtushenko, wrote:

> We were sitting about taking coffee
> In the aerodrome café at Copenhagen
> Where everything was brilliance and comfort
> And stylist to the point of tedium.

As many Danes will admit, the country lacks excitement and challenge. The Norwegians in their rugged kingdom have natural forces to contend with. The Finns live perilously at the edge of Russia. The Swedes have an inner drive to succeed and excel. The Danes not only present a picture of national contentment but seem to be past masters at 'how to succeed in business without really trying.' In their own tourist propaganda they promote themselves as a carefree folk living in a fairy-tale kingdom. A guide book to Denmark states: 'Even in the soberest moments, these stalwart people are almost completely free from repressions, and, in such matters of tourist interest as eating, drinking and night life, they set the pace for the rest of Scandinavia.' The most overworked of Danish words is *hygge*, pronounced *hug-ga*, that state of bliss which is peculiarly Danish. *Hygge* and the adjective *hyggelig* keep popping up in Danish advertisements and in conversations, especially when people say they are planning a *hyggelig* evening with friends. The Danish Psalms speak of *himmelsk hygge*, or 'heavenly bliss.' A disenchanted Danish-American journalist, Jack Lind, wrote that 'an old farmhouse can be *hyggelig*, the sidewalks are filled with *hyggelig* people, one has a *hyggelig* time just sitting curled up in a chair with a good book—preferably surrounded by pictures on the walls and flowers in pots. Implicit in the word *hygge* is the sharing of it with somebody nice and pleasant, and freedom from worry and the trouble of thinking of annoying things.'

Evelyn Waugh once spoke of the Danes as 'the most exhilarating people in Europe' but a foreign resident in Copenhagen said that 'if you need stimulation, then this isn't the place to get it. The Danes have a tendency to pull their feather quilts over their heads.' The noted Danish cartoonist, Robert Storm Petersen, said that if you ask a Dane what he thinks of the world situation he is likely to say, 'Nothing; I've got something in my eye.' The Dane likes to play the fool. He is Scandinavia's court jester. The only Scandinavian humorist of international stature is a Dane, Victor Borge. When I watched an all-Scandinavian television quiz program in Copenhagen, it was amusing to note that the Finnish contestant was well in the lead, the Swede and the Norwegian were anxiously trying to win, and the Dane was cracking jokes.

Dr. Herbert Hendin, in his analysis of Danish suicides, wrote that if there is 'a socially acceptable outlet for aggression among the Danes, it is their sense of humor. They are very fond of teasing and are proud of their wit. Their humor will often cloak aggressive barbs in such a manner as to get the point across without actually provoking open friction.' A Norwegian sociologist told me that 'satire is a deadly weapon in Denmark. It is sometimes used as a kind of blackmail. If someone doesn't do what a Dane wants, then he is sure to make fun of him. If a Dane disapproves of something, then he will try to destroy it by making fun of it. He uses jokes to pull people down. In contrast, the Norwegian is directly outspoken and the Swede just withdraws.'

If I were to go only by my own experiences I would have to say that the Danes are among the most agreeable, charming and hospitable people in the world. And so I believe they are. But elsewhere in Scandinavia there is a widespread opinion that the Danes, while a delightful people, are insincere and not always to be trusted. Businessmen in London and in Scandinavia described the Danes as shrewd salesmen, 'who are not above pulling their little tricks.' A Norwegian who was telling me everything that was wrong with the Swedes suddenly said, 'The Danes are more fun, but you can't trust them. You can trust a Swede any time. He is a man of his word.'

It was also frequently said that the supposedly gay Danes are vaguely discontented in the manner of people who finally move into their dream house and then wonder what to do next. They inhabit a country which has come to be symbolized by the Little Mermaid statue in Copenhagen, a circumstance which many a Dane finds tiresome. There were muffled cheers recently when vandals put a saw to the Mermaid's neck and removed her head. 'It was about time,' said one Dane. But, as might be predicted in the tidy little kingdom, a new head was soon grafted to the statue and all was *hyggelig* in Denmark once again.

Chapter 6

DANISH PASTRY

I love these big, sunny meadows in the middle of the wood, these green stretches where deer and roebuck skip away so airily . . . I can wander about for hours in silent wonderment.

—HANS CHRISTIAN ANDERSEN

The highest mountain in Denmark is shorter (by 416 feet) than the Eiffel Tower. The mightiest waterfall is four feet high, a fact which explains why Denmark is the only Scandinavian country without an abundant supply of hydroelectric power. The whole country is smaller than forty-one of the fifty American states and is only one sixteenth the size of Texas. The entire population is outnumbered by ten of the world's big cities. Denmark may have once ruled a fair-sized empire, but today it is just a set of stepping stones across the mouth of the Baltic.

The loyal Dane, naturally convinced that good things come in small packages, will protest that there is more to Denmark than meets the eye. It is larger in area, for example, than Albania, Belgium, Holland or Switzerland. It has in Jutland one of Europe's greatest peninsulas. Denmark, moreover, owns the world's largest island, Greenland, which spreads icily over 840,000 square miles, four times the size of France.

Denmark lies halfway between Great Britain and Russia. Norway and Sweden loom above it. On the map they have the shape of a barracuda with its jaws wide open to snap up the bits of Danish pastry. Although Denmark is as far north as Scotland and Moscow, it is geographically only barely in the Nordic world. It has a softer climate than the other Scandinavian countries. The

92

winter winds sweeping across Jutland can pierce like daggers, but on the whole it is a flat, comfortable country with scarcely any of the noble fjords, mountains, lakes and wildernesses of the rest of Scandinavia. It is not the setting for the haunting loneliness of a symphony by Sibelius or the bitter introspection of a Strindberg.

A visitor has the feeling in Denmark, as he does not in the rest of the North, that nature has been subdued. Man seems more assuredly in control of his environment, and because of Denmark's compact size there are more people about. Some 1,300,000 of them crowd into Copenhagen and suburbs. At least half the Danes now live in cities. The pace of industrialization is blurring Denmark's familiar image as a simple land of lush farms, fat cows and blonde milkmaids. Farm families now comprise only a fifth of the population, even though 75 per cent of the land area is devoted to agriculture—one of the highest percentages in the world. The mechanization of Danish agriculture has gone so far that most cows are now milked by machines, pigs are electrically stunned before being slaughtered and sliced into Danish bacon, and the number of tractors has increased more than thirtyfold since World War II.

The whole recent thrust of the country has been to make up for its notable lack of raw materials by developing engineering skills and turning out specialized industrial products. Today there are more than six thousand manufacturing companies, big and small, and Copenhagen is the biggest industrial complex in Scandinavia. Most of the Danish firms are so modest in size and so widely scattered that they are unobtrusive in their bucolic surroundings. Their clean-lined architecture puts them in good company with the dashingly modern Danish schools and apartment blocks, and the invitingly designed shops and shopping centers.

Denmark is crisscrossed by some of the best roads in Europe, but it can take an exasperating amount of time getting from one part of the country to the other. One hundred of the 482 islands are inhabited, and for many Danes life is just one ferryboat after another. Jutland, however, is connected to the large central island of Fyn (or Fünen) by bridge, and the big step from Fyn to the largest island of Zealand (or Sjælland) can now be made by what is described as the biggest ferry in the world. Even when Copenhagen on the eastern coast of Zealand is reached, it still takes another long boat ride to reach Bornholm, a little paradise of an island ninety miles farther out in the Baltic below the southern coast of Sweden. The Faroe Islands and Greenland, of course, are far off in the Atlantic.

As it turns out, Denmark *does* have more than meets the eye. It is a geographic *smörgåsbord*. Here is a sampling of the main dishes:

Jutland

Jutland is not the cute Denmark of the fairy tales and travel posters. It is almost a country by itself, accounting for two-thirds of the total Danish territory. To stretch a point, it is the Wild West to the soft Dane sipping his coffee in a Copenhagen café. Jutland is bigger than Belgium and in its extreme reaches it can be as rough as Scotland and as sand-swept as the Sahara. Storms sweeping in from the North Sea (West Sea to the Danes) batter the jagged coastline, but in the summer the sun and the salt-laden breezes make it one of the finest (as well as least crowded) places in Europe for getting away from it all.

Jutland is supposed to be more provincial than other parts of Denmark. I have heard farm people on Jutland speak about going to Copenhagen with the apprehensive tone of cowboys talking about New York or Siberians planning a trip to Moscow. A few older inhabitants of Jutland, in fact, have never seen the capital. The idea of a rural backwash, however, is a little hard to sustain when good paved roads lead up to farmhouses which have a car in the driveway, a television antenna on the roof, books, musical instruments and the latest appliances indoors, and machinery working the fields outdoors. The Jutland highways lead south to Germany and the Jutland ships and ferries make frequent daily connections with England, Norway and Sweden. There is an over-all atmosphere of a prosperous and well-organized community which makes intelligent use of its physical and human resources. Significantly, the cooperatives and Folk High Schools which have had such an impact on Danish life originated in Jutland.

Although the thousands of farms seem to cover the whole peninsula, one tenth of the land is made up of dunes, lagoons, salt marshes and moors rich with heather. For some 250 miles of western coast there is an almost uninterrupted stretch of sand and frothy surf. Broad beaches reach far inland, some as many as two or three miles. The offshore islands like Fanø and the little resort towns along the beaches are lively and lovely in the summer but forlorn in winter. In northern Jutland, where Skagen and Frederikshavn are the chief fishing ports, there are rugged people still speaking a dialect spiced with ancient words. They are still struggling to make a living in a part of Denmark which is roughly comparable to the underdeveloped northern regions of the other Scandinavian countries. For centuries the people of Jutland have been draining the peat bogs and bringing the heath under control, but nature has not yet completely surrendered.

Along the eastern coast there is a more settled and less primitive atmosphere. Overnight ships bring people home from Copenhagen and cars stream steadily over the bridge to Fyn. Charming little towns and harbors line the coast. Some of the ancient communities, especially Ebeltoft with its miniature buildings and streets, are so authentically quaint that they seem too good to be true. It is in the delightful open-air museums or parks-of-the-past in Denmark (and the rest of Scandinavia) where the old days of craftsmen, cobblestone streets, log-cabin farmhouses and timbered townhouses can be seen most vividly. Everything from churches and windmills to barns and distilleries has been saved from destruction and painstakingly re-erected. One of the best re-creations of an old Danish market town is Den Gamle By, or The Old Town, in a dale in the center of Århus, a thousand-year-old port in eastern Jutland. Århus is Denmark's second-largest city, but with only 190,000 people it is a far distant second. It has a twelfth-century red-brick cathedral, which is the longest in Scandinavia, a town hall of controversial modern design, and the second of Denmark's two universities. (The first is in

Copenhagen.) The city of Viborg in Jutland has a cathedral, originally built in 1130, which is called the largest granite church in the world. Ribe, the oldest town in Denmark and possibly in Scandinavia, has a cathedral just about as ancient. Both Ribe and Randers are known for their storks and large roof-top nests. The stork population is gradually thinning out, but the hundreds which remain live a millionaire's life as they spend the summer in Denmark and fly to South Africa for the rest of the year.

Rebild in northern Jutland makes the news once every year. In 1909, a group of Danish-Americans led by Dr. Max Henius, a Chicago scientist, bought a 300-acre tract of land at Rebild and later turned it over to Denmark as a national park where the historic connections between Denmark and America could be celebrated annually. Statesmen, celebrities and some twenty to fifty thousand other persons gather in a hillside amphitheater every Fourth of July to stage the biggest Independence Day celebration held outside America. It has been going on now for over fifty years. (In 1963, Norwegians and Norwegian-Americans began a comparable annual Independence Day celebration, complete with hot dogs, ball games and fireworks, at Sandefjord, the whaling city south of Oslo.)

There is another kind of international story in south Jutland. Close to the German border the Danish towns take on a special character. A fifth to a quarter of their inhabitants speak German. On the other side of the frontier, the same situation is in reverse: German towns with a sizable minority of people speaking Danish. At Rudbøl, the frontier runs right through the center of the town, leaving it in a state of permanent schizophrenia.

This, of course, is Schleswig, the upper half of the old disputed territory of Schleswig-Holstein. Lord Palmerston of England said that only three men ever understood the Schleswig-Holstein problem: 'The first was Prince Albert, who is now dead. The second is a German professor, who has since gone mad. The third is myself, and I have forgotten the details.' Schleswig, historically Danish, is today divided between Denmark and Germany. For almost four centuries it was a duchy under Danish rule, as was

German-speaking Holstein. Eventually much of Schleswig became German-speaking as well. In 1848–50, Prussia tried to seize
Schleswig-Holstein in order to bring the two territories within a
united Germany but the Danes fought off the assault. Then in
1864, Prussia, now allied with Austria and commanded by Otto
von Bismarck, tried again. The Prussian forces crashed easily
through the Danish defenses and won both duchies. It was a
disaster for Denmark and the biggest blow yet to its dying empire.
Two fifths of its land and a million persons were lost to the enemy.
The peace treaty promised that a plebiscite would be held 'later,'
but Bismarck struck out the clause. The plebiscite was finally
forced on Germany by the Allies at the end of World War I. The
North Schleswig citizens voted decisively for Danish rule, and the
present border was fixed.

During the rise of Hitler life became difficult for the Danish-
speaking Germans in southern Schleswig while a good many of
the German-speaking Danes in North Schleswig became active
Nazis. The German armies invaded Denmark through Schleswig,
and during the occupation years the Germans found some of their
best collaborators among the German-Danes in southern Jutland.
At the end of the war, a strong pro-Danish movement began in
southern Schleswig. Its supporters included Germans who felt
that Germany was finished and that life would be better under
the Danes. Although there were strong patriotic arguments
in the Danish parliament, mainly by the right-wing parties, in
favor of recovering the lost territory of 1864 from the World
War II wreckage, the government wisely decided to let the
frontier stand. It had no taste for swelling its German-speaking
minority and giving future German leaders a cause for territorial
claims.

Today the border is quieter than at any time in over a century.
There is no serious movement under way to shift the frontier
again. The two countries are cooperating in keeping their minorities content. There are Danish-language schools in German
Schleswig and German-language instruction in Danish Schleswig.
One of the most significant recent developments is the establishment of a number of Danish manufacturing subsidiaries in

Flensburg, the biggest city in German Schleswig, as a means of getting a foothold in the Common Market.

Fyn (Fünen)

By its location midway between Jutland and Zealand, Fyn is at the heart of Danish life. It is Denmark at its most idyllic, and it serves the nation as a lovingly cultivated front garden. Fyn's soil and climate are kind enough to permit the growth of everything from tobacco and sugar to plums and cherries. The island is an artist's palette of colors—colors in the freshly painted cottages, the flowers planted in the most unexpected places, the flags flying as if every day were a holiday, and the bright clothing of the school children. Fyn is studded with pretty little villages, manor houses and castles. Svendborg in the south is the yachting center of Denmark, the Danish version of Cowes in England. At Ladby in the north, in an air-conditioned underground chamber, the Danes display the remains of a thousand-year-old Viking ship. To make sure that a Viking chieftain reached Valhalla in a manner befitting his station, the 72-foot ship was put into a grave and filled with his corpse, his best weapons, his favourite hunting dogs and twelve horses.

Odense is the biggest city on Fyn and the third largest in Denmark. Before a visitor can say Hans Christian Andersen the local patriot will start talking about the great cathedral, the open-air historical park, and Odense's busy commercial life. But, inevitably, the conversation turns to the miserable little boy who was born in Odense in 1805. Hans Christian Andersen lived seventy years and became the most famous of all Danes, and Odense hasn't been the same since. Andersen made the world laugh and cry. He was the most influential creator of the Little Mermaid image of Denmark. Today, long after his death, he is a one-man tourist industry worth millions of dollars in foreign exchange for Denmark every year. After having ignored Andersen's success during most of his lifetime, Odense has since gone all out to proclaim itself as Andersen's home town. The old neighborhood of charming wooden houses where he once lived has been preserved, and a large Andersen museum, remarkably uncharming, has been erected to house his books and personal effects. The structure looks like a tired, gray mausoleum, but there are Danish delights within. Andersen was a vain as well as self-doubting man, and he seems to have saved every letter, photograph and piece of string which came into his life. He wrote, sketched, cut out silhouettes and traveled with furious energy, and everything has been saved, including his umbrella, hat, love letters and leaves from Charles Dickens's garden.

The popular image of Andersen today is that of a cheerful Danny Kaye, dancing and story-telling his way through life. His real life, however, was full of sadness and frustration as well as spectacular success. His father was an unskilled shoemaker whose earnings were not enough to get the family out of the Odense slums; his mother was a shrew; his grandfather was insane; his grandmother was a pathological liar; his friends laughed at him; his country paid tribute to his genius only after he had become celebrated abroad; his native town paid little attention to him until just before his death. He suffered through impossible love affairs and never married. He amused other people's children. In 1847, he wrote from London to a friend:

> I suppose I have reached the pinnacle of glory and recognition . . . it is a fact that I am a famous man. Members of the aristocracy, so disparaging towards their own poets, have received me as one of themselves. I am overwhelmed with invitations—it is all like a dream . . . but Denmark—Copenhagen—I am less than nothing to them, not a scrap of interest, no participation . . . they spit on me, and Europe has honored me.

Andersen was an ugly duckling who began daydreaming as a boy and never really stopped seeking a fairy-tale world as a refuge from his despair and his sense of being an outcast. It was just such sensitivity and suffering that gave him an insight into the human soul and graced the plays, poems, books and fairy tales which were acclaimed around the world. He wrote 168 fairy tales altogether, and they have been translated into more than eighty languages. Many of them, like 'The Emperor's New Clothes,' were satirical comments on the follies of the world he knew. Some of them contained passages which lampooned Danish society, but these gems are often lost in translation. He had enormous powers of description.

Andersen's fame as a writer for children has obscured his social significance. Although he did much of his writing in some of Denmark's finest manor houses, after he became successful, he remained a poet of the poor. He seemed to be crying out for the welfare state or compassionate society which Denmark has become today. One critic, Edvard Lehmann, wrote:

> Social literature, that which moralizes on community spirit to the point of deafening our ears and often makes us long for the ancient realms of literature once more, began with Andersen without anyone realizing it. No crowds of begrimed laborers, with their strikes and threats and agitators, but the hardship which really exists, and which then, as now, ought always to move our hearts: the washwoman, standing every day in the cold water, with only her drop of gin to give her a bit of warmth, until at last she drinks herself to death; and her boy, with the battered peak cap, who had to stand meekly in front of the town bailiff's window, and hear his mother being scoffed at; the little half-starved, shivering creature, striking all her matches to give the last gleam of life; the poor lonely boy, sitting, poverty-stricken and forlorn, with the faded rose he would keep forever.

Zealand

If Fyn is Denmark's front garden, then Zealand is its office, workshop and throne room. It has been the seat of power in Denmark for nearly a thousand years. The ancient Danish capital of Roskilde is on Zealand. Today, as it has been for the last five centuries, Roskilde is best known as the burial place of Denmark's kings and queens. Copenhagen became the capital in the middle of the fifteenth century, when it was still a small town. The city is now a ravenous urban monster, swallowing up the countryside so fast that Zealand's whole northwest corner is in danger of turning into a single great suburb.

Even with this domination of the capital city, Zealand remains beautiful and bucolic. It is a flat, easy country of tidy little farms, elegant manor houses and a dazzling sprinkling of castles. In the south, one of the world's longest bridges, a two-mile-long structure, connects Zealand to the island of Falster. A shorter bridge leads to the smaller island of Möen with its glorious beech-woods and white cliffs which rise as high as 400 feet above the blue Baltic. I remember a Sunday at a friend's place near Frederikssund in north Zealand. A blue-beamed, thatched-roof cottage lay nestled in wild grass, a horse grazed in a nearby pasture, and across the sound we could see the coves where the Vikings once kept their vessels. In such a setting it was easy to think of Denmark as a spot on earth singularly blessed.

For many people one of the main attractions of Zealand is Helsingør, not so much for its castle, shipyards or close proximity to Sweden but because it is famous for a legendary Danish prince, the creation of an English poet who probably never set foot on Denmark. The visitor finds Hamlet's castle, Hamlet shops, the Hamlet hotel, Hamlet beer, Hamlet souvenirs, and it is vaguely suggested to him that he is in the presence of Hamlet's bedroom and Hamlet's grave. In short, much ado about nothing, but good for tourist income.

The trouble with Hamlet's ghostly presence is that he takes the real glory away from Kronborg Castle, one of the finest structures in Europe. Kronborg was built in such a strategic position that for 428 years until 1857 Denmark was able to exact a toll from foreign ships passing through the sound between Denmark and Sweden. Ships were obliged to stop at Helsingør in order to have their cargoes inspected. The town became the most international in Denmark and a wealthy one besides, since the ships took on provisions as they waited for the Danish officials to let them pro-ceed. The captain of a ship was obliged to state the value of his cargo, to provide a basis for the toll. To make sure that an honest evaluation was given, the king of Denmark gave himself the right, exercised through his customs officers, to buy any part of the cargo at the price stated. If a customs officer thought that the value of a cargo was understated, he would simply buy all or any part of that cargo on behalf of the king, and then the government would sell, for a profit, what it had bought.

Copenhagen

Copenhagen is as wicked as a picnic. It is a seductive city, but its excitements are strangely innocent. It has never learned how to be coarse. Its beauty has not yet faded, even though it is called 'the Paris of the North.' (The Danes describe Paris as 'the Copenhagen of the South.') Greater Copenhagen is more weathered and not so sleekly modern as Stockholm, but that only makes it less an 'American' city and more a Continental capital, which still savors of Old Europe. While this may please a visitor looking for charm, it inspires many a Copenhagener to complain that one eighth of the city has substandard housing, and that the new apartment buildings are as cramped as rabbit warrens. There are certainly places in Copenhagen which are slums by exacting Scandinavian standards, and the housing shortage is one of the government's major headaches; but I have seen worse, much worse. At any rate, it is a clean city, and the sight of the surrounding sea is always welcome. Foreign residents are inclined to feel that the people of Copenhagen have become less polite and more grasping as the years go by. The famous Danish hospitality, they say, is marred by a new offhandedness about the foreign visitors, who now come in such numbers that they account for tourist revenues of 150 million dollars a year.

Even if this is true, Copenhagen is still one of the most agreeable cities in the world. It is a study in graceful urban civilization. It glitters with good-looking people and smart shops offering beautifully designed goods. The bicycle bells, ship bells and church bells seem to be playing a love song to a red-brick city bright with green copper roofs, red-coated mailmen, and blue trolley cars. Free beer flows for visitors at the two great breweries. Flowers cascade from the balconies of apartment buildings. There are breathtaking views from roof-top restaurants of the spires, statues, gabled townhouses, palaces, parks and cathedrals, and of the narrow little streets, the maze of waterways, and the bridges opening and closing like jackknives.

There is much about Copenhagen that is stunningly contemporary—even the mayor's name, Urban Hansen, sounds up to date—but the city's old age shows in its circus, its stock exchange, and its leading newspaper, *Berlingske Tidende*, all of which are said to be the oldest in the world. Copenhagen has been inhabited off and on for at least six thousand years, according to archaeologists, but it dates its life as a city from 1167, when the warrior-priest, Bishop Absalon of Roskilde, built a castle to protect the people from enemy fleets. The city has since been gutted by fire several times, attacked by the Swedes, shelled by the British and occupied by the Germans. It has also grown prodigiously, swallowing a quarter of the Danish population and getting ever more corpulent with suburbs. The city has a fondness for playful buildings. The Stock Exchange has a spire of entwining dragon tails. The Round Tower built by Frederik IV is the shape of a gigantic salt shaker and has a wide spiral ramp inside; Peter the Great, of Russia, and/or his Tsarina is supposed to have driven to the top in a horse-drawn carriage. Grundtvig's Church, honoring the clergyman-educator and built only a few decades ago, looks like a mammoth pipe organ made of five million blond bricks.

It is a fanciful city. In December, Copenhagen looks like an old-fashioned Christmas card. The days are short and the street lights are switched on early. Children throng to the shop windows to see imaginative dramatizations of Christmas legends. The crowds stop to watch the palace guards in towering bearskin hats march by behind a brass band. Candles burn brightly and brass bells tinkle in this toytown world. As a visitor leaves a little bookshop after browsing, the owner reaches into a child's pail and gives him a few pieces of Christmas candy. The winter-chilled city glows with good cheer.

In the late spring and summer the days grow longer, and people stepping out of a bar at 3 A.M. complain about the light and the chirping birds. The beaches, sand dunes, summer cottages, deer parks and yacht clubs are all within bicycling distance. Despite the crush of private cars, which Danes seem able to buy despite a staggering tax, the city still has some 300,000 bicycles and the girls provide a leg show worthy of a Ziegfeld. In June the city explodes with students wearing their new white caps. They have just passed their matriculation examinations which will permit them entrance to the universities. They celebrate night after night with parties and noisy rides through town in the rear of gaudy trucks or horse-drawn vans.

The signs which say 'God Mad' are not what they seem; they mean 'Good Food.' It is served from hot-dog stands, outdoor cafés, heated terraces during the winter, and a score of superior restaurants like Nimb's, Krog's, Frascati's, Coq d'Or and Lang-eliniepavillonen, which is a mouthful by itself. *Smørrebrød* is sold everywhere, the Copenhagen favorite being *leverpostej* (liver paste and pickled cucumber with a dab of jelly). There is a restaurant chain known as the 'K.A.R.'s' or 'Women's Alcoholfree Restaurants.' This nonprofit organization dispenses twenty-five 'food scholarships' each year to deserving students in Copenhagen. The awards entitle them to free meals at any K.A.R., but they have to do their drinking elsewhere.

At Nyhavn ('New Harbor'), a stubby canal lined with gaudily painted eighteenth-century merchant houses, there is a honky-tonk atmosphere for sailors and adventurers. The dives have names like Shanghai, Safari and Hong Kong. According to a Swedish literary editor, Åke Runnquist, 'the fun consists of entering—or descending into, as the case may be—any or all of the various cafés that take your fancy, ordering a beer and, if you like, a glass of *snaps*, and peering through the haze at the more or less sober gentlemen dancing with the often very stalwart girls with blue bruises on their legs.' The sounds from these establishments are of crashing bottles, bellowing seamen, blaring strumpets, and the occasional splash of a tipsy Swede falling into a canal. (It is a Danish saying that 'even a Swede can have fun in Denmark.') During the war so many German servicemen were mysteriously dropping into the canal and not coming up for air that the Nazis had to declare Nyhavn out of bounds.

Nyhavn tries hard to keep alive its rowdy, bawdy reputation, but it is too Danish to be really dangerous. It is, after all, just around the corner from the Academy of Arts, the Royal Theater, and the aristocratic D'Angleterre Hotel, all grouped around the late-seventeenth-century Kongens Nytorv ('King's New Square'). Similarly, the beatniks and their long-haired girl friends listening to deafening jazz at nearby spots like the Montmartre try hard at being bohemians, but they can't quite pull it off. They are just nice Danes with their shirttails out. Even the few leather-jacket types padding about the neighborhood look more sheepish than sinister.

Stretching between Kongens Nytorv and that other main square of Copenhagen, Rådhuspladsen, is Copenhagen's 'walking street,' called Strøget. It means 'sweep' or 'stretch' and is really five different streets strung together to make a crooked mile. This is Fifth Avenue, Bond Street and Via Veneto, all squeezed into a narrow package, labeled 'for pedestrians only,' and lined with some of the best shops in Europe: Georg Jensen, Dansk Designs, Illums Bolighus, Ny Form, Magasin du Nord, A. C. Bang, Royal Copenhagen Porcelain, Bing & Grøndhal. It is a Danish cornucopia of silver, mink, toys, porcelain, jewels, books, art, antiques and teak furniture. The pedestrian street ends (or begins) close to the city hall. From there it is only a few steps to Tivoli, the most captivating pleasure park in the world. There is something singularly Danish about the fact that the Danes maintain a twenty-acre playpen, which is closed seven months of the year, in the very center of their capital on some of the most expensive real estate in the country.

It is easy to say that Tivoli is just one more manifestation of the childlike disposition of the Danes, but, as usual, there is shrewdness behind it. Today it is a colossal tourist attraction for Denmark, as well as a sound business enterprise. The idea was originally sold to King Christian VIII on the grounds that it would help take the people's minds off politics. A wandering Dane named George Cartensen—writer, architect, diplomat and troubadour—argued that Copenhagen needed a pleasure park along the lines of London's celebrated Vauxhall Gardens, but laid out with the Renaissance grandeur of Italy's Tivoli Gardens. In August

1843 the park opened as Tivoli and Vauxhall and attracted 3,615 people. The name Vauxhall was later dropped.

Tivoli now draws well over 50,000 people on a good day, or some four million a year during the May–September season. For only 14 cents admission, they can enjoy the nearest thing in this world to fairyland (the Danes say that Tivoli spelled backward is practically 'I love it'). It is a corner of paradise, complete with flowers, fountains, fireworks, glass dragonflies, Japanese lanterns, games, puppet shows, miniature cars, bandstands, dance halls, roller coaster, Ferris wheel, Chinese pagoda, Moorish palace trimmed with lights, and twenty-three different eating places. It is a magical creation of 85,000 lights, cheerful gardens, sparkling water and rollicking Danes. Its enchantment is absolute in an ingenious underground chamber where little boats, as if in a tunnel of love, glide silently through a whimsical world of luminous butterflies and pixielike winged creatures. Tivoli has all the fun, and more, of a first-class amusement park, but without the usual vulgarity.

The only thing wrong with Tivoli and all the other delights of Copenhagen is that for the casual visitor they obscure the fact that it is a big working city and the premier port of Scandinavia. It is the unchallenged governmental, educational, cultural, scientific, financial, industrial and commercial center of Denmark. It dominates Danish life even more than London rules England and Paris reigns over France.

Swift hydrofoils as well as fat ferryboats beat a steady trail for eleven miles or so across the sound, between Copenhagen and Malmö, Sweden's third-largest city. One of the most visionary projects in Scandinavia is to connect Copenhagen with Malmö by having each city build a bridge over the sound to the island of Saltholm, where the greatest international airport in Scandinavia would be built. This effort, combined with a shorter bridge or tunnel farther to the north, linking Helsingør to Hälsingborg, would ultimately create a conurbation, or urban merger, of some two million people of Denmark and Sweden.

Chapter 7

WAR AND PEACE

We used to be quarrelsome people, you know—quite recently, too
—time of Napoleon. Fight anybody. Fight about anything.
Wars all the time. Now all that energy is still boiling around,
but there's no use for it. Too well organized.

—DANISH POET

'Once upon a time, a thousand years ago, there was a king of
Denmark named Gorm the Old. All through the years his family
has ruled the oldest kingdom of the world, and the present King
Frederik the Ninth is a descendant of the Old King Gorm.'

This fetching capsule history of Denmark is found on a Danish
poster which depicts the fifty-one consecutive rulers of Denmark,
beginning as far back as the year 900. The early monarchs had
such extraordinary names as Harald Bluetooth, Sweyn Forkbeard, Magnus the Good, Eric the Very Good and Eric Plough-
penny. Denmark's only ruling queen, Margrethe, took the throne
in 1387. Less than a century later Christian I appeared, and then
King Hans, followed by Christian II and Frederik I. From then
on, it has been nothing but Christians and Frederiks right down
to Christian X, who reigned throughout World War II, and his
son, Frederik IX, the present king of Denmark. Looking at the
list of Danish monarchs for the last five hundred years is a little
like watching a long volley in tennis. An interruption in the
Christian-Frederik pattern is impending, however. There is no
Danish crown prince, no son to be Christian XI. The next ruler
will be a new Queen Margrethe, now the eldest of three Danish
princesses.

Although the present royal line can be traced back to Old King Gorm in 900, there was a King Godfred in 804 who constructed the 'Danewerk' in the south of Jutland as a defense against Charlemagne's armies. Denmark gradually came into being as a union of tribes. Godfred's successor, King Hemming, made a treaty with the Frankish armies in 811, which established the Eider river, now in German Schleswig, as Denmark's southern frontier. Amazingly, it remained just that for more than a thousand years, until the Danish-Prussian war of 1864. During the Viking Age the independent kingdom of 'Danelagh' was established in England. Alfred the Great rallied the beleaguered Englishmen for a time, thus setting the stage for the emergence of the English crown, national consciousness and sea power. But those mighty Danes, Sweyn Forkbeard and Canute the Great, conquered England and Norway in the eleventh century to form an Anglo-Scandinavian empire which included parts of Sweden.

It is a long, long history after that, with Danish power repeatedly expanding and contracting. A Baltic empire which incorporated Estonia was forged by Valdemar II. More than a century later, in 1397, Queen Margrethe masterminded the Union of Kalmar, which united Scandinavia for the first and only time. It lasted more than a century and came to a bloody end. Denmark's Christian II crushed the Swedish aristocracy and executed eighty-two leaders in what has become known as the Stockholm Bloodbath. One of Sweden's foremost heroes, Gustavus Vasa, then drove out the Danes in 1521. From then on, Swedish power was on the ascent as Denmark weakened. These were also the days of the Reformation, some five hundred years after the introduction of Christianity in northern Europe. It was a mild and relatively bloodless shift of the religious scenery. Scandinavia has been predominantly Lutheran ever since.

Over the next three hundred years Denmark and Sweden fought repeatedly for supremacy in the Baltic. There were particular days of glory in 1588–1648 during the rule of the best-loved of Danish kings, Christian IV. He was a jovial, supremely talented administrator, who put his stamp on Copenhagen as surely as Napoleon reshaped Paris. He ate and drank, and he fathered a flock of illegitimate children with all the gusto of Henry VIII. He poked into everything and was the prime mover in the building of the Naval Arsenal, the Round Tower, the Stock Exchange and numerous other structures which now adorn the capital. Christian IV built two royal palaces, founded new towns and began a chain of fortresses on Denmark's frontiers. He strolled through Copenhagen with a ruler in his pocket to see how well the masons and carpenters were working. He dropped into the shops to check whether merchants were cheating on their weights and measures. He sought out the common man and woman, to have a chat with one and a bit of fun with the other. He pushed reforms in Danish education, agriculture and the administration of Norway. He sent off explorers to find the Northwest Passage and began trading companies to do business in the Far East.

Christian IV was a romantic, impulsive, self-indulgent ruler who went too far in trying to restore Danish greatness. He over-reached himself by entering the Thirty Years' War and as a result suffered crushing defeats, first at the hands of the Germans and then the Swedes. Like Admiral Nelson, he lost an eye in a naval engagement and in the end spent a bleak old age living with his chambermaid. He is remembered by Danes as they sing the national anthem, 'King Christian Stood by the Lofty Mast.'

Both Denmark and its major possession, Norway, were impoverished when he died, but the Danes have a talent for recuperation and for sheer survival. An old motto says, 'What is outwardly lost is inwardly won.' The English bombarded Copenhagen in 1801 and 1807 and smashed the Danish fleet when Denmark became involved in the Napoleonic Wars. Denmark lost Norway to Sweden in 1814 and was defeated by Prussia and Austria fifty years later. Denmark was neutral in World War I, but felt it expedient to sell the Danish West Indies (the Virgin Islands) to the United States for 25 million dollars. The Danes hoped to stay out of World War II as well, but they were conquered by their old rival, Germany, and Denmark was occupied for more than five years. In the process they lost yet another piece of property when Iceland declared its independence.

World War II

Denmark's wartime experience was unique. What began ignominiously ended gloriously. The Danes ran the gamut from reluctant collaboration with the German occupiers to bitter resistance. Denmark was overpowered by the Germans in just two hours, one of the swiftest conquests—and capitulations—in history. Only thirteen Danes were killed. 'They took us by telephone,' said a Foreign Ministry official. Officially, both the occupier and the occupied pretended that it had not been a conquest after all, but just the German way of throwing a protective arm around a small neighbor. Hitler sought to conquer the Danes with kindness. In the early years it was the most benign and indulgent of all Nazi occupations. Eventually, 'this ridiculous little country,' as Hitler's plenipotentiary in Denmark called it, found the German presence too much to stomach. The Danes added courage to cunning and proceeded to make the German overlords look ridiculous. Thousands of them came out of the war as full-fledged heroes.

When the Germans first struck, Denmark's response was realistic. It was hopelessly outgunned and outnumbered. Denmark was so geographically close to Germany, without any natural obstacles, that the Nazis could have come in on roller skates if they had chosen to. The Danes could expect help from no one. Winston Churchill had said that 'Sweden and Norway have a ditch across which they can feed the tiger, but Denmark is so terribly close to Germany that it would be impossible (for us) to bring aid.' The Danes gave in, and lived to fight another day.

Neutrality had been Denmark's foreign-policy line for half a century. It had not been at war for seventy-six years. Norway and Sweden, similarly neutral, had remained apart from Europe's family quarrels for 126 years. When Hitler in 1939 sought non-aggression pacts with all four Scandinavian countries, Denmark was the only one to sign up. Like British parliamentarians during the days of Baldwin and Chamberlain, Danish politicians of almost all the parties deluded themselves into believing that the Nazis could be appeased by a massive display of nonpreparedness.

Denmark actually reduced the strength of its army after the start of the European war in 1939. Ostrichlike, the government ignored the persistent warnings of its diplomats in Berlin that the Germans were planning to take Denmark and use it as a springboard into Norway. When the naval attaché in Berlin arrived in Copenhagen on April 4, 1940, to warn that the invasion would start in a matter of days, the government still refused to mobilize, despite the pleas of the commander in chief. The navy was put on the alert, but after the action started it never got around to firing a single shot, even though the Danish waters, including Copenhagen's naval harbor, were thick with German ships.

At 4 A.M. on April 9, German troops began pouring across the Jutland border. Soldiers stepped ashore in Copenhagen from their hiding places on an innocent-looking German merchant ship. As parachute troops were dropped at key points around the country, surprise air attacks wiped out most of the small Danish air force on the ground. The Danish army of merely 14,000 men never really got out of its barracks. A few detachments fought briefly in Jutland. The Royal Life Guards at Amalienborg Palace in Copenhagen, however, were issued live ammunition and managed to hold off the German detachment which had been assigned to capture the King. Christian X conferred with the heads of government, who urged capitulation. He heard the commander in chief argue for resistance, but at 6 A.M. he gave the order to surrender. The Danish population awoke that warm spring day to learn that Denmark, as a free democracy, had died during the night.

There was little for the Danes to do but go on about their business. They streamed as usual to their fields and factories and offices. Life was strangely normal in the wake of the national humiliation. The Germans insisted that they had only stepped in to save Denmark from being attacked by the British. They promised to respect Denmark's integrity and political independence. Denmark was to be a 'model protectorate.' The Danish Jews were left alone, and the Danish armed forces were not even disarmed until 1943. Seeking to make the best of the bad situation, the major political parties formed a coalition government under Social Democratic

Prime Minister Thorvald Stauning, a forceful, bearded ex-trade-union organizer, who had been premier since 1929. He had been a key figure behind Denmark's appeasement policy.

The government's object was to outwit the Germans and ward off any attempt to foist a Quisling-type government on Denmark. It also believed that Germany would win the war and that Denmark had better secure itself a place in the New Order. The most prominent spokesman of this 'realistic' viewpoint was Erik Scavenius, Denmark's foreign minister during World War I. He was known for his pro-German sympathies, although he was not a Nazi. He was once again installed as foreign minister and immediately issued a declaration promising cooperation with the Germans. Cooperation under Stauning and Scavenius often looked more like collaboration. The Danish economy was put at the service of the Germans. The German debt at the end of the occupation totaled $1,700,000,000. So many supplies were required, and Denmark's normal trade situation was so upset, that shortages developed and strict rationing was imposed. Even so, the Danes were far better off during the war than most Europeans and had enough extra food to send generous shipments to hungry friends in Norway. Stauning and Scavenius echoed the German claim that the invasion was merely a move to head off a British attack. They aligned Denmark with the Axis powers by signing the Anti-Comintern Pact, thus touching off the first important anti-German demonstrations in Copenhagen. And they agreed to the formation of a Danish Free Corps to fight with the Germans on the eastern front. Danish torpedo boats and destroyers were turned over to the Germans. The Communist Party was outlawed, and some of its leaders were arrested.

Beginning of Resistance

An increasing number of Danes began to feel that this was too high a price to pay for their being allowed to run their internal affairs. The passive-resistance movement, which had begun as soon as the first German troops arrived, now turned into The Resistance, complete with sabotage, strikes and underground newspapers. When a German entered a restaurant the Danes would get up and leave. When a German band arrived to give a free concert in a park the Danes would walk away. The crowds for Danish open-air concerts were huge, however, until the Germans caught on to the fact that these were nationwide gatherings to sing patriotic songs. Danish children took to wearing red-white-and-blue caps, the British colors, until the Germans cracked down.

King Christian X, a bony, mustached man of immense dignity, helped to establish the mood in the early occupation years by coming out of his palace on horseback every day, as he was accustomed to doing, and riding unescorted through the streets of the capital. 'Who guards him?' the Germans asked. 'We all do,' the Danes replied. The King would return greetings from his Danish subjects, but he studiously ignored the salutes of German officers and soldiers. The 'telegram crisis' of November 1942 was touched off by King Christian's curt reply to Hitler's effusive message of birthday greetings. The enraged Nazis retaliated by forcing the Danes to install a still more compliant government.

By the fall of 1943 the war had begun to turn against Germany. The Danish Resistance, now being supplied by the Allies and stimulated by Free Danish broadcasters in London, began to gather momentum. Railways and factories were sabotaged, and strikes broke out around the country. The Germans employed Danish hoodlums—ex-convicts who had originally been recruited to fight on the eastern front—to help crush the saboteurs, and this in turn led to more revolts. A German officer was trampled to death when he fired on demonstrators at an Odense shipyard.

The Nazis handed the government an ultimatum to declare martial law, ban all strikes, and impose the death penalty on saboteurs. Even though Erik Scavenius was now the prime minister, the government dug in its heels and refused. The German army then took over the administration and applied martial law. Now the Danes moved into their finest hours. The navy scuttled its ships before the Germans could get to them. A Freedom Council of Resistance leaders was formed to act as an underground Danish government. The King was now virtually a prisoner in his palace, and leading citizens were arrested and shipped off to concentration camps. The Germans began arresting the Danish Jews but thanks to the courage of their fellow Danes and helpful Swedes, some 7,000 Jews were hidden from the Nazis and smuggled to Sweden. Only 500 fell into German hands and were shipped to concentration camps in Czechoslovakia. Of these, 485 survived and returned home after the war. In contrast, most Norwegian Jews were killed. Altogether, during the war, about 18,000 persons were successfully shipped across the sound to Sweden by a well-organized refugee system.

Recovery of Freedom

In 1944, sabotage became more commonplace, and strikes and demonstrations broke out all over the country. The biggest was the Copenhagen uprising in June. For five days the city was a battleground, with the Danes erecting barricades in the streets, while the Nazis cut off gas, electricity, water and food supplies. Amazingly, it was the Germans who finally weakened and made a number of concessions which the Freedom Council demanded. But the action cost the lives of eighty-eight Danes. The Germans consistently misjudged the Danes and often seemed bewildered by their stubborn refusal to see things the German way. For their part, the Danes began to feel superior to their conquerors. Even today, Danes remembering the war years will say, 'The Germans were *so* stupid!'

By the spring of 1945 it was clear that deliverance from oppression would soon be coming. The nation listened with desperate anticipation to every broadcast from London. Then, at 8:35 P.M. on May 4, an excited voice on the BBC said: 'It has been announced, in this very moment, that the German troops in northern Germany, Holland and Denmark have surrendered unconditionally . . . I repeat . . .'

Those few words began a time of ecstasy—of singing, dancing and bonfires of blackout curtains—which no Dane who was there will ever forget. Spontaneously, Danes from one end of the country to the other put lighted candles in their windows. The five-year agony was over, but there was a strange anticlimax. Even before the liberating British forces and the Danes began the work of disarming the 200,000 German soldiers who were still in the country, a new invading German force swept into Jutland: tens of thousands of ragged and fearful men, women and children fleeing the holocaust of their homeland. For a year after the fighting was over, Denmark had to care for 200,000 refugees from the country which had stolen its freedom.

Foreign Policy

The German invasion and occupation were a traumatic experience for Denmark. Although the Danes wanted nothing more than to be able to cultivate their little garden and stay out of trouble, they had found that neutrality was no guarantee of survival for a small state. Soon after the war they promoted the creation of a Nordic defense union which would make Denmark, Norway and Sweden armed allies in a Scandinavian bloc standing apart from the big powers. Sweden was after the same thing, but Norway, which had been a wartime ally of America and Britain even though it was occupied, decided that a Scandinavian military group could not be strong enough to defend itself. It would have to be associated with the West. Since Sweden, which had enjoyed a successful policy of neutrality for over 130 years, would not accept that solution, the Nordic talks broke down.

Prime Minister Jens Otto Krag told me that 'at the end of the war we were the weakest of the Scandinavian countries. Germany was still on our border, and Russia had moved closer. We were ready for almost any solution. We even thought of a Danish-Swedish defense union, but nothing came of it. The Swedes very reasonably declined. Now I wonder whether any kind of Scandinavian military bloc would have worked on its own. It could have been cripplingly expensive.'

Badly shaken by events in postwar Europe, especially the Communist take-over of Czechoslovakia, both Denmark and Norway decided to join the North Atlantic Treaty Organization. It was a

100 per cent switch from the old doctrine of pacifism and neutralism, but Social Democratic Prime Minister Hans Hedtoft insisted: 'Never again an April 9!' The pro-NATO vote in the Danish parliament was a solid 119 to 23. Years later, when the Russian threat to Western Europe seemed to diminish, a number of Danes began to wish that they were not involved in the military machinations of NATO after all. The extreme left-wing parties, with highly vocal support from some student groups, campaign ceaselessly for Denmark to pull out of NATO. Early in 1965, young demonstrators tried to halt the arrival of 160 West German soldiers for NATO maneuvers on Jutland with British and Danish troops. Much of the anti-NATO sentiment is inevitably anti-American, but so far most Danes find the whole attitude distasteful. In both Denmark and Norway there is general, if unenthusiastic, support for remaining within the Atlantic alliance.

Both countries, however, have a special position in NATO insofar as nuclear weapons are concerned. For a number of reasons —Norway's border with Russia, Finland's delicate relationship with Russia, Sweden's neutral stance—Denmark and Norway feel that it is more prudent not to station missiles with nuclear warheads on their soil. To this extent they have heeded Russia's warnings of nuclear devastation if they become too provocative, but they have stubbornly resisted Soviet pressure to promise not to accept nuclear arms in any circumstance. They have retained their freedom of action. Per Haekkerup, who was Denmark's foreign minister until late in 1966, explained:

> Today Scandinavia is *de facto* a nuclear-free area. But this does not mean that there is any treaty obligation to prevent the Scandinavian countries from equipping their forces with nuclear warheads. Neither Denmark and Norway as members of NATO nor neutral Sweden have wished to commit themselves to such a step. That is why they have been unable to agree to the proposal by President Kekkonen of Finland to establish an atom-free zone in Scandinavia by treaty.

Haekkerup said that Denmark is 'content with the present arrangement whereby the nuclear defense of the alliance rests in reality with the United States.' For the long-run business of keeping the peace, however, the Danes as well as all other Scandinavians prefer to look beyond the immediate defense problem. The Danes speak of NATO membership as just one of the four planks of their foreign policy; they also seek to strengthen the United Nations, create greater European political and economic unity, and bring the Scandinavian countries together in closer association. In short, Denmark has a small nation's interest in international movements, and its contribution to the work of United Nations agencies is impressive even if the per capita amount of its aid to underdeveloped countries is low. Although their Western sentiments are obvious, the Scandinavian peoples tend to think of themselves as a mediating force in world affairs. If their numbers and armed forces are relatively slight (although Sweden has unusual strength for its size), they feel at least that they possess unusual moral authority. Conversations about foreign affairs in the Nordic countries are therefore inclined to have an idealistic tone. Scandinavians speak with fervor and righteous indignation about the treatment of natives in South Africa or the troubles in Southeast Asia, and their frustration about not being able to do much about it is all too obvious.

Day-to-day foreign policy, however, is another story. It is almost wholly concerned with economic matters. For Denmark, free trade is a national gospel and its trade relations with such major customers as Great Britain and the Common Market countries are crucially important. It has been estimated, for example, that Denmark's agricultural production is enough to feed as many as fifteen million people a normal European diet, or three times Denmark's own population. With two thirds of farm production and a quarter of all manufactured goods earmarked for export, Danish foreign policy concentrates on keeping the markets open.

Greenland

Although Denmark has come down in the world as a colonial power, it still controls a collection of territory in the North Atlantic which is vastly greater than its own size. It was the

Norwegians who first settled Iceland, Greenland and the Faroe Islands, but they came under Danish rule after Norway, beginning in the 1380s, became a partner and then a subject of Denmark. Iceland developed more swiftly than the other possessions, and after 1918 it became a self-governing country under the Danish crown. World War II threw it so completely on its own that the Icelanders decided to declare their independence in 1944. Denmark, then under occupation, could do little about it but send a cable of congratulations. 'Rather like kicking a man when he is down,' commented a Danish historian.

Greenland and the Faroes remain under Denmark's wing but, as they say, the natives are restless. Greenland is little more than an enormous sheet of ice as much as 11,190 feet thick on top of the largest island in the world. It was discovered by a Norwegian in the early tenth century. Erik the Red went to see for himself in 982, stayed three years, and then organized the first colony. In order to persuade enough Icelanders to sail east to the bleak land, Erik called it Greenland. He may have been the world's first advertising man. Nearly ten centuries later, one of his successors in the trade, a director of tourism for Denmark, wrote that 'in spite of the ice the summer temperature in southern Greenland is like that of spring in Western Europe. Bees buzz above the grass while cows low, sheep bleat, and horses whinny.'

The settlement of Europeans died out by the fifteenth century, but recolonization began in 1721 under the Danes. A Norwegian missionary who hoped to seek out the descendants of the original Norsemen found only a few thousand Eskimos, but he stayed and managed to get others to join him. Denmark's colonial policy sought to preserve the native culture and keep the place in Danish hands. Greenland was all but closed off to outside contacts for about two hundred years. Denmark was like a mouse trying to keep a firm grip on a great cake of ice, since Greenland is almost twice as large as the whole of Scandinavia. Most of the world came to recognize Denmark's sovereignty over Greenland, perhaps figuring that owning it would be more trouble and expense than it is worth. Shortly after the American Civil War, during the Andrew Johnson administration, Secretary of State William H.

Seward proposed that the United States purchase Greenland from the Danes just as it had bought Alaska from the Russians. An angry Congress told him that one 'Seward's Folly' was enough. Seward saw Greenland as a worthy strategic base in case of conflict with the Russians—which is precisely why America today, almost a century later, has poured millions of dollars into military installations on Greenland.

Greenland figured in one of World War II's more fascinating footnotes. When Hitler moved into Denmark the Danish minister to the United States was the experienced and courageous diplomat, Henrik Kauffmann. Perceiving that the instructions he was getting from Copenhagen were being dictated by the Nazis, Kauffmann disobeyed them. He said he felt like a loyal son whose father had been kidnaped by gangsters; he decided to waive his oath to the King and use his own judgment. Among other things, he told Danish ships to stay in American ports or head for pro-British countries instead of making for such pro-German 'neutrals' as Italy and Spain, as his government had ordered. In April 1941, a year to the day after the German invasion of Denmark, Kauffmann, 'acting on behalf of the King of Denmark,' signed an agreement turning over Greenland to the United States for the duration of the war. King Christian and his government, clearly under German pressure but still feeling in authority to some degree despite the occupation, protested to the Americans and denounced 'the Kauffmann usurper government.' The United States was in the odd position of maintaining diplomatic relations with the Danish government while recognizing as its minister a man whom that government had renounced. The happy ending after the war, of course, was that Kauffmann was hailed as a hero, thanked by the King for his outstanding services, reinstated as minister in Washington, and given the prestige assignment of leading the Danish delegation to the United Nations meeting in San Francisco.

The Greenland agreement with the United States, which the Danish parliament unanimously ratified in May 1945 immediately after the liberation, paved the way for the 1951 pact which puts the defense of Greenland jointly in Danish-American hands.

Construction then began of the giant American air and radar base at Thule. Greenland's colonial status ended in 1953, when it became a 'special, integrated territory' of Denmark, with full political rights and two permanent seats in the Danish Parliament. The island's administration comes under the Ministry of Greenland in Copenhagen and a governor sits in the capital, Godthaab, which has a population of slightly over 3,000.

Greenland's total population is only 35,000, almost all of them weather-beaten Eskimos. Strictly speaking, they are 'Greenlanders' and prefer to be known as such, now that they have mingled with the Danes for nearly six centuries. Many Greenlanders still live in igloos and turf huts, and they hunt and fish in the wilderness much as Eskimos have done for centuries. Most of them, however, have had enough of a taste of modern civilization to want more. They are clustering in the several towns along the southern coast, living in wooden or brick homes, eating meat and canned foods, going to schools, using electricity instead of blubber lamps, and reaching for a more modern economy.

Prosperity and improved medical conditions have raised both the living standard and the population. The population is growing four times faster than Denmark's and it may reach 100,000 in the next quarter century. Denmark invested more than 110 million dollars in Greenland between 1950 and 1964. It announced early in 1965 that it planned to invest five times that amount, or well over 500 million dollars, for a ten-year development program which would go far to modernize the fishing industry and give Greenland a surface coating of industrialization. It is likely to be a long time before Greenland will emerge as a fully independent nation, but the training for self-government is under way.

The Faroe Islands

There are few serious cries in Greenland for independence now. The story is different in the Faroes, a sprinkling of nineteen rain-drenched, storm-lashed little islands anchored just north of Scotland and southeast of Iceland. They are, altogether, only about 1/1555th the size of Greenland, yet they have almost exactly the same population: 35,000. The economy is almost entirely dependent on fishing and whaling.

Originally Norwegian but tied to the Danish crown for centuries, the Faroese speak an antique language which is more Icelandic than Danish. The proud and roughhewn fishermen and lonely shepherds are fiercely nationalistic. They have their own flag and their own currency (actually a version of the Danish krone). They run many of their own affairs through an island assembly and send two representatives to the parliament in Copenhagen. During World War II they were taken over by the British and did some notable work in supplying the Allies with fish. But that experience only fired their zeal to be independent, and they are not wholly sovereign now only because they doubt whether their isolated economy could survive on its own without the regular Danish subsidies.

This conflict of nationalistic passion and realistic restraint has left the Faroese more than a little frustrated. There are occasional reports of clashes between the islanders and visiting Danes. 'You'd think we were suppressing some colony of savages,' said a Danish naval officer after a few of his seamen had gotten the Danes-go-home treatment. The local view of the relationship with Denmark was expressed by a Faroese newspaper, which described the Danish government as 'a schoolmaster wagging an admonishing finger.' The Danes are dismayed by the friction with the rugged islanders, but the Copenhagen newspapers *Politiken* told them: 'One understands nothing of what is happening in the Faroes if one assumes that the islanders are Danish. They are not. They constitute the sixth Nordic nation.'

Chapter 8

ROYAL DEMOCRACY

The King reigns, but the people rule.
—SCANDINAVIAN SAYING

The state must be careful not to become too big and oppressive.
—JENS OTTO KRAG

It is said that when Princess Margrethe was thirteen and learned for the first time that a proposed change in the Constitution meant that she would someday become Queen of Denmark, she exclaimed: 'I wish I were an ordinary girl who could grow up like everybody else and marry a man named Olsen.'

The Danes would not approve of her marrying a man named Olsen. That would be carrying democracy too far. It would dilute the whole idea of royalty. But in all other respects the Danes, like the Swedes and Norwegians, treat the royal family with an appealing folksiness, and the royal family is able to live more like Olsens than it would be permitted to in other monarchies. Probably nothing better illustrates the common-sense approach of the Scandinavians than the way the Danes, Swedes and Norwegians have managed to mix monarchy and meritocracy into a satisfying kind of royal democracy. Although the royal families are surrounded by all the trappings of monarchy, and are expected to earn their keep by plenty of pomp and ceremony at appropriate times, they are able to be informal and unregal much of the time.

It is now one of the clichés about Scandinavia, but a generally accurate one, that patrons in a shop in Copenhagen, Stockholm or Oslo are not too surprised to find that they are standing next to the King or Queen or one of the royal children. People understand that it is not proper to stare at them. The King of Sweden, an accomplished archaeologist, is a veteran browser in Stockholm bookstores. The King and Queen of Denmark have often been seen eating in the Tivoli restaurants while the princesses were standing on line for the Ferris wheel. Royal children in Scandinavia are used to going to schools where they receive no special treatment. Their comings and goings are reported by a generally protective press, and there is obvious affection for the royal families, but I have not found that the Scandinavians hold their majesties in any great awe. They are seen not as superior beings, but simply as people with a particular history and a particular role to play. Since the royal personalities are so much in the public eye, they are much gossiped about. I have heard much unrestrained chatter in the several countries about one royal person's sex life or another's slow-wittedness. There is speculation about the effects of inbreeding. But it has been casual rather than vicious talk. While there are few passionate royalists about, there are still fewer antiroyalists.

Several decades ago, when socialism had an appeal, a good many people demanded that the three crowns be swept away with the rest of the baggage of the old days. Today most Scandinavians prefer to keep their kings. The monarchies are held to be useful institutions, if only to give tourists something to look at. They provide a necessary touch of color and glamour to societies endangered by too much uniformity and conformity. They make a focal point for the preservation of worthwhile national traditions. 'We have had a king for so long that I would feel naked without one,' said an outspoken Swedish lady. In their roles as chiefs of state, even though they have been shorn of political power, the monarchs carry out an important governmental function.

Finland is the only Scandinavian state without a king—although it almost had one back in 1918—but it has found it necessary to have a president as well as a prime minister. In contrast to the political impotence of the royal chiefs of state, the Finnish president is the most powerful politician in Scandinavia. The usefulness of the kings was well demonstrated in World War II. Indeed, the wartime experience was enough to guarantee royalty a long life in the North. In Norway and Denmark especially, the behavior of the rulers, though it took very different forms, was exactly what was needed to give expression to the national will. Denmark's Christian X, as we have seen, chose to take responsibility for the capitulation. He stayed with his people in Denmark and was the first among his countrymen to cold-shoulder the German occupiers. Norway's King Haakon refused the German demand to appoint a Quisling government. He gave backbone to the Norwegian resolve to fight the Germans rather than surrender, and he directed Free Norwegian forces during the war from his place of exile in Britain.

Who's Who

It might be wise to pause for royal identification. This can be treacherous, as well as confusing. The Scandinavian monarchies are so interlocking and so entangled that they defy simple description. For example, the Danish and Norwegian kings are cousins, and each married a Swedish princess. The youngest daughter of the Danish King and his Swedish-born Queen is now the Queen of Greece, whose husband, King Constantine, is the great grandson of a Danish king.

The royal house of Denmark is the oldest dynasty in Europe. It dates back to 1448, when the House of Oldenborg succeeded to a throne which had already been occupied by Danish kings for well over six hundred years. Christian I was the first of the Oldenborgs. His successors and their children have married so many other members of European thrones that everyone of royal blood in Europe is probably part Danish. Christian IX, who ruled from 1863 to 1906, was called the 'father-in-law of Europe' and 'the grandfather of Europe,' because four of his children ascended thrones:

1. Frederik succeeded to the Danish throne as Frederik VIII.
2. Alexandra married Britain's King Edward VII in 1863.

3. Vilhelm was recruited by the Greeks in 1863 to become their monarch, George I. He was assassinated at Salonica after ruling for half a century.
4. Dagmar married Tsar Alexander III of Russia.

Frederik VIII's eldest son, King Christian X, led his country through two world wars and died in 1947. His second son, Prince Carl, was asked to become King of Norway soon after the turn of the century. After insisting that the Norwegian people vote whether they wanted him as monarch, he was installed as King Haakon VII and ruled Norway until his death in 1957. Christian X was succeeded by Denmark's present monarch, Frederik IX. He and Queen Ingrid, daughter of the King of Sweden, have three children, all girls: Margrethe, Benedikte and Anne-Marie, now the Queen of Greece.

Danish Royalty Today

King Frederik's full title is: His Majesty King Frederik IX of Denmark, of the Wends and the Goths, Duke of Schleswig, Holstein, Stormarn, Ditmarsken, Lauenborg and Oldenborg. His full name is Christian Frederik Franz Michael Carl Valdemar Georg. In common with other Scandinavian kings and the President of Finland, Frederik is a big, rugged, sports-minded man. He is extra tall: six feet four inches. His ears are of noble proportions, his chest has a splendid set of tattoos, and he has the kind of squinting face common to seamen who have spent years staring into the wind. He was, in fact, trained in the navy and has been an enthusiast for the open seas all his life. Although he has slowed down a bit in his sixties, the King has long been an avid swimmer, rower, hunter, tennis player and indoor exerciser. He is also a music lover, pianist and amateur orchestra conductor.

'The King has dignity,' a Danish authority said. 'He knows how to be a king, but it's the Queen who has the real brains in that family.' Queen Ingrid, once a Swedish princess, has succeeded in the difficult job of becoming a Dane in Danish eyes. The royal family lives in relatively modest apartments in one of the four adjacent Amalienborg palaces in the heart of Copenhagen. They also have the use of at least half a dozen other palaces and residences in Denmark. Once a year on the King's birthday, March 11, thousands of school children assemble below the monarch's windows and shout in chorus: '*Konge, Konge, Konge, Kom nu frem, ellers Gaar vi aldrig hjem*' ('King, King, King, come out or we shall never go home').

A casual reading of the Constitution would suggest that the Danish king has great authority: 'The form of government shall be that of a constitutional monarchy. . . . The legislative power shall be vested in the King and the Folketing (parliament) conjointly. The executive power shall be vested in the King. . . . The King shall not be answerable for his actions; his person shall be sacrosanct.' In practice, however, the king acts as the government decides, and he must live under considerable restriction. He must be a member of the Evangelical Lutheran Church and 'shall not enter into marriage' without the consent of parliament. The heir to the throne must also have permission to marry or else forfeit his right to succession to the throne.

For a century until 1953 the right to succession was restricted to male heirs, but then Denmark faced up to the fact that it had no crown prince, only three little princesses. That meant that Prince Knud, younger brother (by only one year) of King Frederik, would ascend the throne if he outlived the King. In 1953 the parliamentarians, taking up the delicate matter of whether the amiable Prince Knud would make a suitable king, and his son after him, decided to amend the Constitution so that the crown could pass to Princess Margrethe, who was then only thirteen years old.

By all signs so far, Margrethe will make a splendid queen. She was born just a week after the Germans occupied Denmark. Although her father once said that she was a girl with 'certain bad habits, like all other children,' she has grown up into a good-looking, strong-minded, serious young lady with a fondness for archaeology. She has artistic talent and a nice sense of humor. After a trip to the Far East she gave a television report which showed that she had the ability to present her country at its best advantage. Late in 1966 she became engaged to a young French count whom she had met during her student days at the Sorbonne. It was little Anne-Marie, however, who was the first of the three princesses to become a bride. The spotlight shone least of all on middle sister Benedikte, and yet one Dane who has reason to know said that 'she is the smartest of the princesses, by far.'

Anne-Marie's storybook romance with Constantine, the dashing Greek prince, held the Danes enthralled for several years. He was a naval cadet on a Greek training ship, and she was not quite eleven when they first met in 1957. The rumors began four years later. It was noted that they were distant cousins; both had had the same great-great-grandfather, King Christian IX. Anne-Marie was growing up as the prettiest and liveliest of the Danish princesses. She was a leggy girl of five feet eight inches, with blue eyes and dark-blonde hair. An admiring Greek newspaper called her 'a little wildcat.' Her girl friends in Copenhagen described her as a sort of fun-loving 'girl next door.' Suddenly the fun stopped. The death of King Paul made young Constantine the ruler of the Hellenes, and the little princess was to become his queen as soon as she reached her eighteenth birthday. 'It's terribly difficult becoming a queen when you're only eighteen,' she told a friend. 'I hope people will be understanding because we're so young.'

The royal wedding in 1964 was, of course, magnificent, but what was most intriguing about the whole affair was the relief of so many Danes that the princess had married royalty instead of a commoner. Democratic and egalitarian as the Scandinavians may be, they take the view, as one Dane expressed it, that 'royalty plays a useful role in our society. We set them apart and give them a job to do. If they get too democratic themselves by marrying commoners, then there's no sense in giving them special privileges. They should marry among themselves.' It was felt to be particularly important that Princess Margrethe, the future ruling queen, should not marry a commoner. Similarly, the Norwegians had made it plain that their Crown Prince Harald should stick to royalty when he chooses a wife.

'Lose this little bit of mystery,' said a Copenhagen editor, 'and then the whole illusion's gone. The welfare state loses very early every kind of distinction. You get mass production, common housing, common dress. There's a great asset in having a king who can appear in a uniform and look like no one else in the country.'

Professor Christian Elling, a member of the Danish Academy, also made clear his feeling that royal informality and democratic gestures were all very nice, but only up to a point:

The concept of monarchy is undoubtedly an anachronism in our day and age. It can sustain itself and exist only by virtue of its exclusivity, which is its very being. One cannot make a stylized art work by robbing it of its style. If you do, you kill it. The more a royal family assimilates with the ordinary citizens of a country, shares their tastes and way of living, the more one can see a president and his family emerging instead. You cannot have your cake and eat it too. If you want to maintain royalty with all its majestic apparatus and its total symbolic nature, then it must dutifully remain within its archaic framework and be willing to make sacrifices in order to maintain its extra-ordinary being.

The essence of the attitude, however, is this: It would be regrettable if royalty were watered down; it would be abominable if certain ordinary people were, so to speak, watered up. The Scandinavian is at his most intolerant when he suspects that anyone in the society of equals is trying to set himself above everyone else. Politicians, by virtue of their office, have an elevated position, but it is a rare Scandinavian who holds them in awe or who will tolerate any seeking of privilege. They are expected to live in small apartments and ride the streetcars like everyone else. The politicians who last longest are those who live most humbly.

Danish Politics

It would be comforting to think that a society which has solved most of the important problems of the human condition would be characterized by a daily life of lofty thoughts and ennobling action.

This may yet be possible, but the tone of Danish public affairs is all too often one of churlish petty-mindedness. It is as if a poor family, after the most prodigious efforts, had succeeded in raising itself from the slums and had moved into an elegant country mansion—only to spend its energies complaining about the faults of the central heating system and the servant problem. Phoebe-Lou Adams of *The Atlantic* magazine noticed this too:

> Nebulous, difficult to pin down, largely unjustifiable on any practical grounds, there ran through the talk of these young Danes a steady current of exasperation with efficiency, comfort, and good order. They complained not that it is difficult to grow rich, but that it is almost impossible to stay poor; not of the quality of housing, but of the red tape involved in finding a place to live, or, much worse, in getting permission to build one; not of deficiencies in social or medical services, but of their enervating, pervasive, constantly improving embrace.

I recall arriving in Copenhagen late in 1964 to make some further inquiries into the political situation. There had just been an election, and the Social Democrats were once again in power, but only by their fingertips. 'That's usual,' said a Danish friend. 'There's nothing exciting about that. It's the mudflap scandal that people are talking about. That's what you ought to look into.' He was right. People were much more worked up about mudflaps than about the possibility that the government might fall or the argument whether Denmark ought to try to go into the Common Market on its own.

The story was that the Social Democratic government, in the latest squeeze of its 'constantly improving embrace,' had decreed that Denmark's 650,000 car owners should install rubber mud-flaps behind the rear wheels of their automobiles in the interests of road safety and public neatness. Sweden, after all, had made mud-flaps mandatory for years. They prevented mud and stones from being hurled on following cars. There were some cries of protest. Sweden is a far larger country, with many thousands of miles of unpaved roads, while little Denmark's modern road network is almost all hard-surfaced. Were mudflaps really necessary? Had the government thoroughly researched the problem before laying down the law? Apparently not, but the government was sure it knew what was good for the people. The Danes, for all their complaining, are exceptionally well-disciplined and law-abiding, and so the automobile owners went to garages and paid five to ten dollars each to have mudflaps installed. Some people paid even more, and the total outlay was said to be more than five million dollars.

To add insult to injury, it then developed that the flaps were doing more harm than good. On rainy days they deflected mud sideways onto the windshields of other cars at the very time they were trying to pass. Pedestrians and bicyclists all over Denmark were being drenched with mud. Surveys by auto associations showed that the mudflaps were making things worse. The government was acutely embarrassed. The man who had originally ordained the mudflaps, Justice Minister Hans Haekkerup, brother of the foreign minister, was removed from the office he had held for a decade and made minister of the interior. The new minister of justice told the Danes that they could take the mudflaps off their cars if they wanted to.

The mudflap fiasco at least had the virtue of enlivening a political scene which is not marked, except superficially, with deep divisions in political thinking. There is not the same gulf between Labor and Tories, as in Britain, nor must Danish politicians grapple with such a multitude of social and economic issues as in the United States. The emphasis is on moderation and compromise. The political scene changes only slightly from year to year, and the relative strengths of the competing parties shift only slightly. For all the squabbling they do, the Danish politicians work well together and the cabinets of the coalition governments have a high degree of stability.

In a way, it has always been so. In its thousand-year history Denmark has had its share of turmoil and bloodshed, but as one parliamentarian, Per Federspiel, said, there has been 'a remarkable absence of violent revolutions.' Political changes have come through 'a gradual process of evolution.'

Paule Lauring wrote:

Revolutions in Denmark have a habit of taking place in their own special way. In 1660, when absolute monarchy was introduced, the King merely had a talk with some of the leading men in the country and then announced that from then on there would be absolute monarchy—and that was all. In 1848 there was unrest all over Europe. Shots were ringing out in the streets of Berlin and Paris. In Denmark, feelings mounted to such extraordinary heights that a number of honest citizens donned their top hats and frock coats, went to see the King and told him that from now on they wanted a free constitution. They got it.

The easy winning of the Constitution of June 1849 was all the more amazing for the fact that the Danish king for 189 years had ruled under a Regal Law so absolute that there was no kind of parliamentary curb on the monarch, as in other European countries, and it was treasonable to even propose a reduction in the king's authority. But Frederik VII had permitted the development of a system of consultative provincial assemblies after 1834 and then had the wit to read the handwriting on the wall in 1848. The final constitutional breakthrough came in 1901 with the adoption of the modern idea of a democratic parliamentary government based on the majority in the second, or popularly elected, chamber. Such a breakthrough occurred in Norway in 1884, in Finland in 1906, and in Sweden in 1917.

The Parties

Denmark's Social Democratic Party has been the largest for more than thirty years, but it has never had a majority of the seats in the Folketing or a majority of the popular vote. After the 1966 elections it had 69 of the 179 seats. It normally rules by forming coalition governments—usually teaming with the Radical Liberals, a group representing small landowners, intellectuals and professionals. Labor-oriented but seeking to appeal to rural and middle-class voters, the Social Democrats have been the prime movers of the welfare state. Their emphasis is on full employment and social security, with little interest in the nationalization of industry. They led Denmark into NATO and have championed Scandinavian cooperation.

The formal opposition is composed of the Moderate Liberals, Conservatives and Independents, who are all essentially conservative in their outlook and oppose encroachments of big government or excessive welfarism. The Independent Party is so far to the right that it opposes social welfare expenditures in general. At the other end of the political spectrum is the Socialist People's Party with its strong Communist flavoring and its vociferous opposition to NATO and military preparedness in general. The party is a fascinating mixture of warmed-over Communists, far-left neutralists, pacifists, ban-the-bombers, anti-Americans and assorted malcontents. What puzzles many Danes, not to mention foreign observers, is why the Socialist People's Party has as much support as it has in a land seemingly so serene. In the November 1966 elections the party doubled its representation in the Folketing from ten to 20 seats.

One explanation is that the Socialist People's Party provides the kind of political fireworks which a good many Danes seem to want. When things are too cozy and settled some people have a terrible urge to break things. The People's Party boss, Aksel Larsen, is a veteran at breaking things in Danish political life, first as a Communist agitator between the wars and then as chairman of the Communist Party of Denmark. After an internal power struggle he was thrown out of the party in 1958 and formed the Socialist People's Party. It is like the outer skin shed by the Communist Party when it shriveled in the 1950s. The Communists, outlawed by the Nazis during the occupation, performed notably in the Danish Resistance. Largely for this reason the Communists won as many as 255,236 votes and eighteen seats in the Folketing in 1945. But two years later they were down to nine seats, and they have been out of parliament since 1960.

Jens Otto Krag

Denmark's Prime Minister Jens Otto Krag is every inch the modern, pragmatic Danish politician. His relative youth, energy, good looks and fast rise to power give him the appearance of a Scandinavian Jack Kennedy or Willy Brandt. Two unfortunate events as well as his own abilities account for his swift ascendency. Social Democratic Prime Minister H. C. Hansen died in 1955 and then his successor, Viggo Kampmann, suffered two heart attacks and was forced to retire from active politics. Krag, who had been foreign minister under both prime ministers, took over the top job in August 1962, a month before his forty-eighth birthday, as Denmark's youngest premier ever.

Krag is a new-style Social Democratic leader in the sense that he did not come up from the factory floor or the trade-union ranks. His father ran a tobacco shop and was a political radical. Young Krag saw the breadlines in the Depression days of the 1930s and was struck by 'how badly our society was functioning.' He joined the Young Social Democrats when he was sixteen. He had early ambitions to be a journalist but worked his way through Copenhagen University and emerged as an economist. He entered the parliament in 1947 and was immediately installed in the cabinet.

Krag has twice married an actress. He met his second wife, Helle Virkner, one of Denmark's best-known stage and screen performers, at a diplomatic reception for President Sukarno of Indonesia. He married her in 1959. When he became prime minister three years later, Denmark—like America in those days of the Kennedy administration—could boast a vigorous young leader and a glamorous leading lady. Helle Virkner was such a stunner that she once snapped that 'I'm getting damn tired of hearing people tell me how beautiful I am.' There were some grumblings from straight-laced citizens about the prime minister's wife continuing to appear in movies—for example, playing the part of a circus trapeze artist in a mediocre film. The prime minister's response was: 'What about it?' He didn't object, nor did he attempt to deglamorize her, as the wife of the head of the workingman's party, when they went politicking around the country. She continued to dress elegantly, while he wore neat, executive-style charcoal-gray and blue suits which, according to a Copenhagen journalist, 'gave the appearance of upper-class correctness.'

Krag is an effective and respected political leader but not a wildly popular one. It is doubtful whether any Danish politician could inspire the politically sophisticated population to give him passionate, unquestioning support. When things have reached the stage where some people complain that there isn't enough to complain about, then the leading politician is bound to attract all the pent-up criticism. Krag is said to be 'too slick and smart-alecky,' but then he is also described as 'too serious and humorless.' The Left says he isn't enough of a man of the people while the Right sees him as yet another socialist big spender.

Jens Otto Krag is a relaxed, solidly built man with a broad, almost boyish face, a strong jaw and a thick crop of dark hair. He has the first-class, calculating mind of a thoroughgoing economic pragmatist. He is strikingly less 'socialist' in his approach to public affairs than the Social Democratic leaders of Norway and Sweden, who are themselves far removed now from doctrinaire socialism.

It is Krag's opinion that Denmark, far from being a placid society, is undergoing the greatest change of all the Scandinavian countries. He explained that before World War I, Denmark was the best off of the four nations. 'Sweden was poor then.' But after that war Denmark was hard hit by the Depression and suffered a severe agricultural crisis. There was high unemployment. Sweden was less badly hurt and began to draw even with Denmark in living standards. It pulled ahead during World War II while Denmark and Norway were occupied, and was in a favorable postwar position for more rapid industrialization. Denmark was still wrestling with serious economic problems and high unemployment of about 10 per cent well into the 1950s.

'The real change,' Krag said, 'began here in 1957. Industrialization started to take hold. Unemployment went down. Our annual growth in industrial investment and national product had been behind Sweden's, but since 1957 it has gotten much stronger. Our industrial exports have picked up by 10 to 18 per cent every year. There has been a take-off. This is no longer a simple agricultural society. Gone is the feeling of living in a never-changing world. I don't find it so sad, because it has solved a lot of problems.

Where I grew up near Herning in Jutland I could ride a bicycle down a long street lined with small one-story houses, and that would be the whole village. Today it is a big industrial town. We have achieved a lot to make a better life for people. When I was a boy, there were many people who were poor, *really* poor. Children lived in very unsatisfactory conditions. Their education was bad. The chances for a poor boy were rather limited. Unemployment was a natural thing. All this has been changed.'

The Ombudsman

It is probably in the nature of government, however well meaning, that at any point in time it will abuse or oppress some members of the citizenry. The problem of protecting the individual from a heavy-handed bureaucracy is one which the Scandinavians have worried about for a long time. One answer is the Ombudsman, which *The Times* of London has called 'Scandinavia's most distinctive contribution to the art of government.' The Ombudsman is a public watchdog, 'the people's attorney,' a parliamentary commissioner and a 'grievance man.' A Danish journalist, however, called it 'an overrated institution.'

All four Scandinavian countries have Ombudsmen, beginning as long ago as 1809 for Sweden and as recently as 1963 for Norway. 'Ombudsman' is an ancient Nordic word which originally referred to the official in charge of the king's castles and possessions. A few countries like New Zealand and West Germany have followed the Scandinavian lead with Ombudsmen, or parliamentary commissioners, suited to their own needs, and Great Britain is taking steps to provide itself with an Ombudsman who would work closely with members of parliament. It remains an open question whether an institution which works in a small Scandinavian society would do as well in a larger context.

Sweden has three Ombudsmen; the first keeps his eye on the military establishment, the second is the king's legal adviser, and the third is the civil Ombudsman. The latter hears complaints from the public and reports to the parliament but the king's man also listens to the public's problems. Finland has two Ombudsmen;

one is the chancellor of justice, who reports to the president, and the other reports to the parliament. In Denmark and Norway the Ombudsmen are answerable to parliament. In all cases, the Ombudsmen have far-reaching authority to listen to public complaints and undertake investigations. They are important and highly respected figures who are well paid and operate with a great air of independence. Much trivia comes their way, but in many cases they can perform as modern knights slaying the dragons of a heavy-handed government. The Norwegian Ombudsman, for example, is Andreas Olai Schei, a vigorous legal authority who left the Supreme Court in Oslo to take the job, which pays 71,800 kroner ($10,260) as compared to just 64,000 for the prime minister. Well over a thousand complaints reached him in his first year in office, most of them having to do with social-security problems. Invalids claimed they were getting the wrong amount of pension, and others said their insurance cases were being delayed by doctors or lazy civil servants. As in the other countries, Norwegian prisoners are permitted to communicate directly with the Ombudsman. When it seemed to the Ombudsman that conditions at one prison were not what they should be, he conducted his own on-the-spot investigation and saw to it that the administration was improved.

In Sweden, the Ombudsman often pursues cases which his office spots in the newspapers. One press report said that a drunk resisting arrest was subdued when the policeman hit him with a bottle which he had pulled out of the drunk's pocket. The Ombudsman ordered the police superintendent to investigate. In the end the policeman was charged with an offense for using an unsuitable and dangerous weapon. In Finland, a soldier complained to the Ombudsman that he had been unfairly put under arrest for malingering. He had insisted that his knee was out of joint, but the army doctor had found nothing wrong. Armed with a certificate from a noted specialist, the soldier was able to convince the Ombudsman that he was suffering from a rare disease and required treatment, not time in jail.

The Ombudsman in Denmark is one of the most powerful and influential figures in the country, but he occupies an unpretentious

suite of offices in the attic of a building close to the parliament.
He is Dr. Stephan Hurwitz, a quiet and courtly former professor
of criminal law at the University of Copenhagen. A handsome,
silver-haired man, now in his sixties, Hurwitz had to flee to
Sweden during the occupation when the Nazis began to round
up the Danish Jews. He was put in charge of the refugee office at
the Danish legation in Stockholm and later joined the Danish
military mission in London. He was an observer for Denmark
at the Nuremberg war-criminal trials. In 1953, when Denmark
was revising its constitution, it was decided to create the office of
Parliamentary Commissioner for Civil and Military Administration. Hurwitz wrote an article saying that the man who got the
job would certainly be in an exposed position. A few days later
he was asked to take the post himself. He has been at it ever since.
The Ombudsman is hired by the parliament after each election
and, as a servant of the parliament, can be discharged if he loses
the confidence of the parliamentarians. He is the highest-paid
civil servant in the kingdom. Hurwitz has just six lawyers and
four stenotypists helping him. Any member of the public can
drop in to see him, although the caller may have to talk to an
assistant first. 'Many people who come to see me are mentally
disturbed,' he said, 'and the best advice I can give them is to see a
doctor. Some of them get angry with me, but astonishingly many
say that I am right and follow my advice.'

The number of cases the Ombudsman handles increases as the
office becomes more widely known. Well over a thousand cases
come before him annually. Some hundred and fifty to two hundred
call for closer investigation, and perhaps forty or fifty result in the
Ombudsman finding fault with the administration and pressing
for reforms. While most complaints come from individuals, a
good many industries, associations and trade societies protest
about all manner of government regulations and how they are
applied. Hurwitz is not a policeman, and he has no authority to do
more than look into cases and make his criticisms and proposals,
but he has the power to turn on the spotlight of publicity when
he chooses. 'Some high-standing personalities have been re-
proached,' Hurwitz said. In one well-publicized case, the Foreign

Ministry was so lax and inept in the handling of a spy in its midst that the Ombudsman's report was highly critical of the minister of foreign affairs, a man who later became prime minister. 'This turned out to be one of the foundations of our authority,' said Hurwitz. 'We were able to criticize the highest offices in the land.'

Chapter 9

LAND OF MILK AND MONEY

Whoever could make two ears of corn, or two blades of grass, to grow upon a spot of ground where only one grew before, would deserve better of mankind, and do more essential service to his country, than the whole race of politicians put together.
— GULLIVER IN BROBDINGNAG

The Danish farmer, tilling an indifferent soil, has been a miracle worker for the past century. Over-all agricultural production has doubled since the last war. With his yields among the highest in the world, he has been justly rewarded with a standard of living which is also one of the very highest in the world.

The farmer is still the most essential figure in Danish life but times have changed and he no longer carries the nation alone. His own efficiency has helped deplete the rural population, and Denmark's industrial upsurge has meant that only one ninth of the national product comes from the land, even though farm products account for 35 per cent of Denmark's exports. It was 90 per cent at the turn of the century.

Although the tremendous outflow of bacon, beef, butter, cheese and the rest accounts for exports of some 750 million dollars every year, the Danes are worried because business has not expanded. It seems that more and more of Denmark's old customers are putting up barriers to protect their own farmers. As one Danish economist put it, 'there are scarcely any free foreign markets open to Danish farm products. The British market has been the only important one to which there has been free entry. For that very reason, this market has been glutted with agricultural products from many countries, including goods produced with substantial government subsidies, with the result that the prices obtainable by exporting to Britain have generally been unsatisfactory to Danish producers. Consequently, the export prices obtained today are not much higher than twelve years ago. In the same period the level of costs has risen 50 per cent.'

No wonder, then, that Denmark has been the Scandinavian country most anxious to get into the Common Market (E.E.C.). Its dilemma, however, is that its two biggest customers are Great Britain and West Germany—the first having unsuccessfully tried to get into the Common Market and the second already firmly inside. Going into the Market on its own would mean a break with Britain and EFTA (European Free Trade Association), which Denmark cannot afford. But remaining outside E.E.C. is making its trading life more difficult. General de Gaulle's guillotining of Britain's bid for Common Market membership was an even more bitter blow to the Danes than to the British.

Despite such matters, which cause gray hair in the Copenhagen ministries, there is reason for confidence, because of Denmark's historic ability to overcome its problems. Denmark's agriculture was backward a hundred years ago, but a quiet revolution has been under way ever since with a series of land reforms strengthening the small farmer. Today there are 196,000 farms in Denmark, 95 per cent of them owned by their operators. Numerous large holdings, including 1,900 'estates,' bring the average farm size to about 38 acres, which is larger than the average for any other West European country with the exception of Britain. The unusually high yields per acre of wheat, barley and oats result from good management, heavy use of fertilizers and a high degree of mechanization.

Until a century ago the Danish farm economy was based on the export of grain. When cheaper grain began to flow into Europe from North America, the reaction of most countries was to raise their tariffs. The Danes, on the other hand, turned to a new line: processed livestock products. Danish dairying got a boost when a Dane invented the cream separator. When dairies and bacon factories were needed, the Danes found the capital, production techniques, and then the means to market their products by forming cooperative associations. The country's first cooperative enterprise was a dairy, set up at Hjedding on Jutland in 1882. Within a few decades, operating entirely outside the government, the cooperative movement grew into a great national force.

The Cooperative Life

Denmark today is one of the most cooperative-minded countries in the world, but it has all come about so naturally that the co-ops are just part of the scenery. A farmer does not *have* to belong. Ninety-five per cent of the farmers are joined together in the dairy cooperatives, but that still leaves 5 per cent on their own. But it does not take long in the Danish countryside to see how advantageous it is to be a part of the cooperative movement. Ask a farmer whether he belongs to a co-op and it takes him half an hour to name all his memberships. He might belong to the local dairy and bacon cooperatives, the fertilizer society, feeding-stuffs society, poultry-dressing station, cooperative seed association, cattle-export and egg-export associations and the cattle-breeding or artificial-insemination society. He probably is a member of a co-op bank, a co-op laundry, and co-ops which help him buy machinery, fuel and cement. He borrows money from one of the co-op credit societies. He and his wife undoubtedly shop at the local consumers' cooperative, which could be a little corner grocery or an ultramodern supermarket. They thus belong to one of Denmark's 1,865 consumers' cooperative societies. The societies now have 647,000 members throughout the nation, but if all persons in a family are counted, the co-op customers number over two million, or 40 per cent of the population. (One sign of the times is that the urban membership is now far greater than the rural.) There are even cultural co-ops like the Cooperative Theater.

There is no need to go on, except to say that all of the co-operatives for production, marketing and supplies are linked together in the great Federation of Danish Cooperative Societies. This is just one of three main groups of farm organizations, however. The others are the Farmers' Unions and the Smallholders'

Unions, both nonpolitical. Add to them the political and social groups and the picture is complete: the real 'organization man' in this world is the Danish farmer.

The American farmer, for all the freedom he enjoys, is more dependent on the government than his counterpart in Denmark. He and his fellows look to the federal government for billions of dollars in subsidies every year. The Danish farmer is neither controlled nor subsidized by the state, although he depends on the government to fight for Denmark's agricultural trade rights in the world markets. He is protected, insofar as a farmer can be protected from the shifting economic winds, very largely by his own voluntary organizations. He has his complaints, but he can also be heard to sing at country meeting places a song which celebrates the 'simple, cheerful and active life on the land, which I would not change with kings.'

Industry—Little Things Mean a Lot

The Danish factory worker is also a thoroughly organized individual, who enjoys some of the best wages, fringe benefits and working conditions in Europe. Denmark's trade-union movement began as long ago as the 1870s and now encompasses virtually all the workingmen in the country. Not only are the unions closely tied to the Social Democratic Party, but the chairman of the giant, 158,000-member Central Organization of Metalworkers, Hans Rasmussen, has been called 'the most powerful man in Denmark.' Management–labor cooperation is so well oiled that strikes are few and productivity is high. There is now full employment, and even the constitution insists that everyone must have work.

Even though Denmark has no iron, coal, oil or water power, industry has now become so solidly rooted in the Danish soil that twice as many Danes work in manufacturing today than in farming. In a recent ten-year period, industrial production rose 80 per cent and exports by 250 per cent. One third of the country's over-all production is exported. Denmark's advantage as a manufacturer and seller is a geographic location which gives its factories easy access to the sea and puts the whole country in the center of a circle which reaches from the top of Scandinavia to the toe of the Italian boot, and from Iceland to Moscow.

It is possible to make too much of the handful of superlatives which any country can produce. I have seen one listing for Denmark which goes like this: 'The biggest diesel-engine producer in the world is in Denmark (Burmeister & Wain); two of the biggest breweries in Europe (Carlsberg and Tuborg); the biggest food canner in northern Europe (Plumrose); the biggest tobacco manufacturer in Scandinavia (Scandinavian Tobacco) . . .'

More to the point is the adaptability of the Danes and their concentration on the few things they do extremely well. Denmark has a large cementmaking–machinery industry. Its host of engineering firms are so talented that they give the Germans, Swedes and British hard competition for international projects from Korea to Latin America. In the postwar period Denmark has developed the largest production of mink in Europe; anyone looking for the finest furs now makes a beeline for Copenhagen. There are hardly any trout streams in the country, yet the Danes have so neatly made a little industry out of artificial ponds full of trout that they have won an important share of the American frozen-fish market. There is a steady outpouring of goods which are celebrated for 'Danish Design,' and in their audacious way the Danes export pipes to Britain, whisky to Scotland, snails to France and chewing gum to America.

Even by Scandinavian standards, Danish manufacturing firms, with only a handful of exceptions, are embarrassingly small. Sweden, Finland and Norway have many more big industrial firms than Denmark. The story is different among the trading companies. The biggest trading firm in Scandinavia, far larger than any other in the North, is the East Asiatic Company of Copenhagen. It was founded in 1897 by a Dane, H. N. Andersen, who went to the Far East and was elated by the prospects for trade and plantation development. Today it is a worldwide enterprise with annual sales of over 600 million dollars.

It was East Asiatic, in 1912, which went to sea with the world's first ocean-going motor (as opposed to steam) vessel. Denmark lost half its merchant marine in World War II, but the tonnage today is more than double the prewar figure, and Denmark ranks among the leading dozen shipping nations. For many decades until his death in 1965 at age eighty-eight, the greatest name in Danish shipping—and Danish business—was that of Arnold Peter Møller. Owner of the Maersk Line and many other international enterprises, he was known as the wealthiest man in Scandinavia. He preferred, however, to be known as 'the world's only multimillionaire who sails a boat to and from work every day, fair weather or foul.' While other Copenhagen executives engaged in a daily battle with traffic in order to get to work, Møller was driven in a chauffeured car from his suburban home to his 60-foot sloop, which then sailed across Copenhagen harbor to a mooring near the Little Mermaid statue, where a second limousine waited to take him to his nearby office.

Carlsberg

One of the great Danish business institutions is Carlsberg, a 120-year-old brewing company, which produces 785 million bottles of beer every year (plus 134 million bottles of mineral water). A quarter of the beer goes all around the world to further Denmark's reputation as a country devoted to good beer. The Carlsberg Breweries, a landmark in Copenhagen, is perhaps the only large company in the world controlled by five professors. It is owned by the Carlsberg Foundation, which the professors manage; they are chosen by and from the members of the Royal Danish Academy of Science and Letters. Every time a Dane, or anyone else, buys a bottle of Carlsberg beer, he is furthering the good work of Denmark's most notable foundation. Remarkably enough, the rival Tuborg Brewery also turns over much of its profits to good works.

The Carlsberg profits have had an impact on Danish cultural and scientific life in a way comparable to Rockefeller or Ford money in America. The name Carlsberg stands for Carl, the son of Jacob Christian Jacobsen, a doctor of philosophy who founded the company in 1847. Carl, who was also a Ph.D., ran his own beer company, New Carlsberg Brewery, for a number of years in competition with his father before succeeding as head of the family firm. Both father and son established foundations which remain separate (but jointly administered), even though the two beer companies were combined in 1906 as the Carlsberg Breweries. They receive two million dollars a year from the beer profits and the interest on capital, and use the money for scientific research and work in the arts. The Little Mermaid is the most noticeable of many statues which beer profits have paid for, but the most outstanding Carlsberg creation is the great Copenhagen art museum, the New Carlsberg Glyptotek.

Free Enterprisers

It is likely that the Danish firm best known around the world is the Lego company, whose Lego System is one of the most original creations and outstanding successes in the history of toymaking. The company began in the most modest possible way in the Depression year of 1932 in the little town of Billund in central Jutland, when a carpenter named Ole Kirk Christiansen started to make wooden toys. He sometimes bartered them for groceries. The business grew slowly and was given the name Lego, a contraction of *leg godt*, which is roughly 'happy games.' The firm had only forty employees in 1952 when one of the founder's four sons, Godtfred Kirk Christiansen, made the decision to use new techniques in plastics to produce interlocking toy bricks the size of sugar cubes to make toy houses, trucks, trains and anything else a child fancies. Germany, traditionally a leading toymaking country, was the first big market which Lego conquered. Since then it has been an unending success story. Today there are thirty-five persons in Lego product development alone and two thousand in the whole organization, including factories in America and other countries. Annual sales now exceed 30 million dollars.

Lego has been pointed out to me as one of many striking examples of uninhibited free enterprise in welfare-state Denmark. There are others. In Viborg, a workman who had been crippled in an accident has used his insurance money to start a ladies' underwear firm which is now doing a flourishing export business. In Herning, an eccentric businessman named Aage Damgaard has become not only an important shirtmaker but also a high-powered collector and patron of abstract art. In Copenhagen, a virtuoso businessman, Oscar Petersen, has made a success out of restaurants, catering, hotels and his Nordair airline. High taxes make it unlikely that anyone will ever become as wealthy as A. P. Møller, but it is true in Denmark as well as the rest of Scandinavia that there is still room for the ambitious, and it is still possible to become wealthy. One name has come up most often when Danes discuss their most successful self-made businessmen. It is that of the late Mads Clausen, founder and owner of Danfoss, the biggest manufacturing firm and the second-largest industrial employer in Denmark.

The Danfoss works on the sleepy island of Als is an impressive complex of factories, warehouses and office buildings—Europe's largest plant for making refrigeration and heating-control equipment. The firm has factories in half a dozen countries, including the United States and Germany.

Danfoss is Denmark's foremost demonstration of the kind of industrial role the country expects to play in Europe from now on. Recognizing that Germany, France, Britain and other large nations with huge industrial organizations and immense home markets are bound to have an advantage in manufacturing the complete automobile, appliance or other piece of major equipment, the Danes will concentrate on making specialized components for such products. Danfoss, for example, studiously refuses to make a whole refrigerator and try to sell it in Germany, but it knows it can make certain components better and more cheaply than the German refrigerator companies themselves.

The company began in a farm boy's bedroom and has grown up, literally, in the front yard of the farmhouse. As a young engineer, Mads Clausen worked briefly for firms in the new field of refrigeration and decided that it had a bright future. Most Europeans and Americans were still using iceboxes in the 1920s and '30s. Clausen became his own boss and made his first piece of apparatus, an automatic expansion valve, in the family farmhouse on Als in 1933. Danfoss grew gradually in the Depression years and managed to survive World War II. Its great advance came after the war, as refrigerators and other appliances became common in the European home. The number of employees rose from just 179 in 1943 to 7,300 today. The workers, enjoying superior working conditions in a company which has been attentive to housing and welfare problems, have gone on strike only once in more than thirty years, and that was a reluctant sitdown as part of a nationwide general strike.

Mads Clausen died in 1966. Despite the trappings of wealth, including a large private plane, and his fondness for big-game expeditions to distant continents, he remained a rather shy, self-effacing man who worried that his new executive suite might be considered too showy for a mere country boy. During my visit to the company I found it enchanting to be able to look down from Clausen's luxurious office to the old family farm where his elder brother in overalls was happily at work.

When I drove away from the Danfoss works I was immediately engulfed again in idyllic Denmark—contented cows, soft fields of sugar beets, gentle villages and slumbering country churches. It was hours before I saw another factory. It was as if the Danes, determined not to let the new industrialism intrude too much on their *hyggelig* land, had done an artful job of camouflage.

Chapter 10

THE HUMANIZED SOCIETY

The care of human life and happiness . . . is the first and only
legitimate object of good government.
                                                —THOMAS JEFFERSON

How can you Americans afford to destroy so many people?
                                        —DANISH PRISON OFFICIAL

'The attitude here is that nothing should go wrong. But that's
just a dream. There should be some risk in life. They want to stop
everything from happening. You can't even drive your car if
you've had a drink. They try to avoid all mishaps. Now that we
have only a one-chamber parliament, the new legislation is
coming out too quickly. There's always something to stop you
from doing something you like. But does anybody complain
about it? I think we must have the lowest rate of letters-to-the-
editor in the world. The papers themselves are weak-kneed.
They're so reverent about officials. There are a lot of people who
would like to get the Social Democrats out of there and have a
change, but they shrug their shoulders and say, "What can you do
about it? They'll be in there forever."'

The speaker was a prominent Danish broadcaster. The viewpoint may not be representative of majority opinion in Denmark,
but it is part of the picture. There is widespread support for
individual pieces of social legislation and for the continuing efforts
to improve the welfare state. Many Danes feel uneasy, nonetheless, about the totality of it all. They worry about the high cost
and the way so much of an individual's life becomes involved

with the state. There is concern that individuals are surrendering traditional responsibilities to the government. One woman said, 'People use their extra income for television and cars instead of helping to support their old folks. They figure that's up to the state.'

Denmark spends 13 per cent of its net national income on welfare. It makes a heavy tax load but it cannot be denied that the Danes get a lot for their money. The social services began in the last century, but were pulled together and extended after the passing of the Social Reform Acts of 1933. The refinements in the system over the last three decades have left virtually nothing undone short of social workers tucking the people into bed at night. Even that is already being done on a small scale by the Home Help Service, which provides domestic assistance to sick housewives.

A full description of the soup-to-nuts comprehensiveness of Danish welfarism could take up the rest of this book. Children get free dental care. Young couples get financial help when they start married life and substantial assistance as their babies start coming. Everybody, rich or poor, gets an old-age pension. For the really down-and-out, there could not be better, cheaper care anywhere. The whole nation is enrolled in the comprehensive medical-insurance system called *Sygekasse* (literally, Sick Chest). Everybody, including the 'passive' members in the 'C' group, pays some insurance fee. The 'active' members in the 'A' and 'B' groups usually pay about $2.50 a month for an adult. For higher-income members of the 'B' group, *Sygekasse* pays two thirds of their doctor bills. The 85 per cent of the nation in the lower-income 'A' group have the whole of their medical costs taken care of; the physicians bill *Sygekasse* directly. Even though there are certain limitations on his freedom to charge what the traffic will bear, the Danish doctor does not see himself as a victim of 'socialized medicine.' The Danish Medical Association negotiates with *Sygekasse* on basic money matters, and doctors have enough opportunities to bolster their earnings to place them with company executives, businessmen, big landowners and lawyers in the top 2 per cent bracket of Danish incomes. On the average a

Copenhagen physician earns three times the wages of an ordinary factory worker, or more than $10,000 a year.

Sixty per cent of the total Danish social-welfare expenditure of well over a billion dollars a year comes from the state; community spending accounts for most of the rest. The Ministry of Social Affairs itself spends about 400 million dollars a year—more than Defense, Education, or any other ministry. Yet the central government's welfare bureaucracy is not unduly large. To a great extent the welfare programs have been localized. The Dane deals with a community-administered health-insurance office, not with a distant national office. A senior Social Welfare Ministry official said that 'Denmark probably has a more decentralized, localized welfare operation than you have in the United States. Our welfare programs are undergoing constant revision, and there is still much to be done. Our system of family allowances is not as developed here as in West Germany, Sweden, Norway and France. But perhaps we Danes don't need it as much. Our old-age, accident, sickness and other insurance programs are well developed. We oversee all this, but we don't operate the insurance. The staff of this ministry is not so large.'

The official added that 'public assistance is not simply charity. It is a humane thing, not degrading. People who are in need go to their commune and get liberal treatment. We give more or less the same old-age assistance regardless of what a person had been earning. In France, for example, if people enjoyed a well-to-do life in their younger days, then they have a good old-age assistance. But you can see pitiful old ladies selling things on the streets in Paris because their husbands had not earned much money.'

In Denmark, concern about the welfare of old people led to the building of Den Gamles By, the now famous Old People's Town, where hundreds of the aged live in comfortable dignity. Their surroundings are cheerful and colorful, nature is close at hand, and they receive tender care. Yet even this is not enough for the Danes who now think that it is a mistake to segregate the oldsters from the community at large. The newer solutions mix the old with the young. The same attitude influenced the design of the big 'collective house' for the physically handicapped, which was opened in Copenhagen in 1960. It is ingeniously equipped with devices to aid the handicapped in operating their own apartments, yet the handicapped comprise only a third of the tenants. 'The other tenants are sound persons,' says an official description, 'since it is desired to avoid the sense of isolation which tends to affect the sick when they are restricted to one another's company.'

Neurotics

The prisons, mental hospitals, juvenile homes and correctional institutions in Denmark are impressive for the humane character of their operations and the high caliber of their directors. A prison or mental asylum in Denmark does not have the customary look of defeatism and the smell of degradation. They are often surprisingly cheerful places. They suggest that their inmates have a better life to look forward to.

What marks the Scandinavian institutions is the pervading confidence that people can be improved and restored to a useful role in society if enough care is taken with them. Whether the person is a juvenile delinquent or a dangerous criminal, he or she is treated as an individual with private feelings and personal dignity. Except in extreme cases, a mentally disturbed person is able to enjoy some normal home life; a prisoner is permitted close contacts with his family, perhaps even sexual intimacy with his wife; a prostitute undergoing reform in an institution is not altogether cut off from the normal world of men.

I first met Dr. Kirsten Auken (now at University Clinic of Copenhagen) at the Montebello 'Day and Night' Hospital close to the capital. It is a handsome institution—a cluster of low, whitewashed buildings placed around a central courtyard and backed by trees and gardens. It could be an elegant new motel, complete with restaurant and game rooms. There is a library which doubles as a music room, a quiet place where patients can prepare their own coffee, a lot of pleasant modern art, and other effects which reduce the institutional atmosphere to the minimum. Staff members, patients and visitors mingle in the dining room.

The patients are neurotics and psychotics. One hundred of them come to the hospital to spend the day, while another twenty-seven or so stay on around the clock. The whole effort, Dr. Auken explained, was to keep the patients in touch with the real world and restore them to normal society as early as possible. Patients are confined only when it is really necessary, and are treated with compassion. It is as far from being a 'Snake Pit' as any mental institution can be, but it requires a large staff and a high expenditure per patient, much more than most countries are willing to spend. Dr. Auken's caustic view of the American mental health scene is that '90 per cent of the psychiatrists treat 10 per cent of the population, while 10 per cent of the psychiatrists treat 90 per cent of the population.' She asked: 'Isn't there something wrong when a mental patient pays forty dollars a day for treatment at a private institution, while half a mile away the state institution gets only five dollars a day for each patient?'

Crime and Punishment

The Scandinavian treatment of lawbreakers is far removed from traditional methods of imprisonment and punishment. It is enlightened—and successful. 'We have detention institutions,' said one prison official, 'and you have destruction institutions.' As in the whole field of health, there is a heavy emphasis on preventive measures so that potential criminals are put right before they verge into crime. Denmark has a notably low rate of juvenile delinquency, partly because of an extensive youth-club program and other means of coping with youthful restlessness. When young people break the law, they get special treatment outside the prison system.

Scandinavian penal authorities look upon the term of imprisonment for adults not simply as punishment but as an opportunity for rehabilitation. Where necessary, the security measures are strong, but they are unobtrusive. Where possible, the prisoner is kept in an open prison or under such conditions that escape would be easy, but his growing sense of responsibility keeps him inside until he is released. The prisoner at both minimum- and maximum-security institutions is not made to live in the bleakest possible cell conditions (although he may still get solitary confinement if he rejects all discipline) but in rooms with a good measure of privacy and homelike conditions. In some of the newer Swedish institutions each prisoner carries a key to his room. The approximation of normal living conditions helps preserve a man's humanity and enables him to make an easier transition back to the civilian world. Capital and corporal punishment in Denmark were abolished in 1933. There are extensive probation programs, and a prisoner can earn the right to leave prison from time to time for family visits.

It is true enough that the Scandinavian countries are smaller, well-behaved, homogeneous societies, with nothing like the criminal problems of America or Britain; the Danes at any one time have little more than three thousand prisoners on their hands, including six hundred or so awaiting trial. But what problems they have are dealt with intelligently. They make heavy use of the growing armory of modern social-science weapons to increase the likelihood of a prisoner going straight after his release. Apart from the humanity of it all, the statistics on results make it clear that it is the more efficient approach. Society gets its money's worth when prisons need not be run like fortresses, when sentences can be reduced, and when crime is effectively contained.

But what can be done about the incorrigibles, psychopaths, 'sex fiends' and dedicated criminals? The modern answer is the preventive detention institution with indeterminate sentences. There are two in Denmark. One is at Horsens in Jutland. The other is the Herstedvester Detention Institution for Abnormal Criminals in Glostrup, a distant suburb of Copenhagen. I drove out one day to call on Dr. Georg K. Stürup, its medical superintendent and an internationally known psychiatrist and penal authority.

Herstedvester, as Dr. Stürup explained it, is a place which gets 'mostly chronic criminals whom no one wants in the prisons, or in the mental hospitals, or in the institutions for mental defectives in Denmark.' It could be expected to be bristling with armed guards and surrounded by a wall which only a helicopter could scale. Instead, in the farmland outside the capital, I found a none-too-formidable wall and a set of ordinary-looking buildings for the wards, workshops and offices. The guards were not armed, but weapons were in reserve, and a rigorous security system was in force. There was an air of quiet discipline.

Herstedvester has its own prison farm without walls only a few miles from the main buildings for those prisoners well advanced in treatment. The farm usually has thirty prisoners and eight staff members. The institution as a whole has room for two hundred prisoners and a staff of 150 plus four psychiatrists, four psychologists and seven social workers. This is an extraordinarily large staff, but then Herstedvester has been given an unusually demanding job to do. It was opened in 1935 to take in criminals, most of whom are psychopaths, who are in 'a more or less permanent state of mental disturbance or debility, including sexual abnormality . . . persons who, on account of their insufficiency of character, were not able to get on in life without resorting to fairly serious crimes or to recurring criminality.'

When I walked about the place with Dr. Stürup we were surrounded by thieves, rapists, arsonists and thugs of all kinds, but they greeted the director with fond respect (or so it seemed to me) instead of fear or antagonism. Dr. Stürup is a scholarly-looking man with rimless glasses and white hair. He was wearing a beret. Similarly, the prisoners were permitted a certain latitude to dress with individuality. One man we spoke to had a beard. In the residence for trustees there were two men each in rooms which had a number of paintings, books and flowers. There was a group television set, a small library and a room where prisoners could make coffee. In wards with tighter security, prisoners had private cells, which were given a homey touch by various personal effects, including books, pin-ups, paint sets and perhaps a small rug on the floor. Inmates could earn cigarette and candy money, and money for the bank, by their activity in the workshops. Dr. Stürup was not worried if it seemed to some visitors that the prisoners were being coddled. 'Loss of freedom is punishment enough.' He said it was well established by now that it is not the harshness of prison life which stops men from being criminals. On the other hand, 'there is no doubt that this is a prison. When the new men come in I make it clear that it is exactly that. I tell them that the state is very generous—you can stay here as long as you want; but if you want to get out you have to convince me first that you should be released, and then we will try to convince the court.'

Most of the men sent to Herstedvester are depressed, suicidal, or otherwise disturbed types who react badly to normal prison treatment and seem to be compulsively criminal. They are committed to Herstedvester for an unlimited time, but they have social care 'guardians' who make sure that a man is not forgotten. Furthermore, every prisoner has a chance at least once a year to appeal to a court for release. The inmate is told from the beginning of his open-end sentence that he is not going to be forced to undergo therapy to change his attitudes. Rather, it is up to him to want to be cured. Dr. Stürup has written:

> 'Cure' here means, of course, not subsequently committing a crime. His self-respect will be greatly developed by his own realization that, in spite of his many handicaps, he has managed with assistance to develop himself sufficiently to live out a respectable pattern of behavior in the community. This recidivating [repeatedly imprisoned] minority group of serious criminals—the prototype criminals—do not trust us and do not want our help; their whole past experience has been antipathetic to such an expectation. In Herstedvester we make no promises to them. They have been sent to us by order of a court for the protection of society and our main duty is to fulfill the court's order. The whole burden of the future, legally and in fact, rests on their shoulders; the decision genuinely is theirs; we are here to help them to avoid the force of the segregating order if they want us to, and only if they want us to.

Despite the prisoner's suspicions, he begins to perceive that if he wants to get out he had better make himself available for treatment. This means 'integrating, individualized growth therapy,' a collection of words which Dr. Stürup uses apologetically to mean the specialized kind of 'total approach' therapy which the institution has developed. The inmate undergoes the kind of analysis which sticks to the single great objective of turning him away from crime. 'We consider it a success if the man stops being criminal, even if he isn't happy.' Most of the prisoners, he said, are unrealistic; 'they want to be big businessmen.' Under therapy they begin to see that they must live more realistically, and that in fact they are capable of doing so. 'The staff must demonstrate in their daily behavior that life in the world can go on without too many difficulties, without disturbing other people too greatly, and that this is the more comfortable way to live.'

The prisoner's relations with his therapists and the staff, the way of life of the prison, group activity and theatrical production —all are intended to show him that there is a reasonable way of life. When he makes it clear that he can fit into such a life on the outside, the security on him relaxes. He may be able to work at the prison farm or be allowed to have monthly six-hour leaves with his family or go about the town escorted by a warder in plain clothes. Eventually he becomes capable of demonstrating to a court that it is safe to parole him. Even after release he gets after-care attention from the Herstedvester specialists.

Dr. Stürup took charge at Herstedvester in 1942. At that time the prisoners were fighting in the wards several times a week. 'Now the fights are only several times a year,' he said. 'The atmosphere here just doesn't give support for that kind of activity.' In the institution's early years the average inmate undergoing treatment for the first time stayed four or more years before parole. Now the usual stay for the first-time prisoner is two-and-a-half years. Experience over the last thirty years has shown that 50 per cent of the first-timers who are released are able to fit into general society. The other 50 per cent who slide back into criminal activity and are returned to Herstedvester usually stay a briefer time before being released, and about half of them give up the criminal life. Some men return a number of times, but the end result is that something like 90 per cent of all those who have passed through the institution are restored to normal society. Since these are 'severe criminals,' the hardest types in the whole prison system, Dr. Stürup seems justified in finding the results 'clearly satisfactory.' He said proudly that 'the whole prison system in Denmark has been humanized. The cold awful institution is out.'

'Mothers in Unfortunate Circumstances'

Every year there are about 80,000 babies born in Denmark. Some 7,000 of them are illegitimate. What happens to the 7,000 or so girls each year who are in the embarrassing position of having a baby without having a husband? Sixty years ago when the percentage of illegitimate births was higher than it is today, the unwed mother was likely to be thrown out of her home, scorned by society and perhaps driven to infanticide or suicide. An organization formed in 1905 to help unmarried mothers was obliged to use a euphemism: 'The Association for Help to Mothers in Unfortunate Circumstances.' A few years later another group was more specific: 'The Committee for Help to Destitute Single Women with Children.'

The two organizations combined in 1924 under the simple name, 'The Mothers' Aid,' one of Denmark's most celebrated contributions to the panorama of Scandinavian social welfare. It is a living, breathing demonstration of the Danish attitude that a mother is a mother whether married or not, and a baby is a baby whether legitimate or not. Even if some people view the unwed mother as immoral, as a few Danes still do, virtually everyone agrees that the baby should not have to suffer through life as a bastard.

One Dane who knew what it was like to be illegitimate in the old days was Egmont H. Petersen. In 1878, when he was seventeen, he started a tiny printing business in his mother's kitchen and grew up to be a wealthy man. Just before World War I he built Gutenberghus in Copenhagen, then the most modern printing plant in Scandinavia, and died at fifty-four, before he could set foot in the building. His will led to the founding of the Egmont H. Petersen Foundation, one of the largest in Denmark. It owns the biggest printing and publishing establishment in the country. Part of its work, as Petersen stipulated, was 'to assist needy solitarily placed mothers with children under their care.'

The most visible sign of this assistance is a seven-story, yellow-brick building of contemporary architecture in Copenhagen known as the Collective House. It houses 113 unwed mothers and their babies in small but very personal apartments during that difficult time in their lives when they first face the world together.

The head office of the Mothers' Aid centers is attached to the Collective House. It was there that I spoke to the director, Mrs. Vera Skalts. She is a relaxed and cheerful woman whose office on top of the building has the warm natural-wood look of a Scandinavian country home. She admitted that it helped to put the pregnant girls who came to see her at ease. (She put me at ease by offering me a cigar.)

Mothers' Aid began as a privately-financed operation to help pregnant girls without husbands. It has evolved into a nationwide organization with some private support but primarily financed by the state. It operates under the Ministry of Social Affairs. The eleven Mothers' Aid centers now deal with more married women than unmarried, on a 60–40 ratio. Forty thousand women a year ask for assistance and they get it entirely free. Every fifth married woman in Denmark comes into contact with Mothers' Aid before, during and after childbirth. The centers are available to give birth-control information in the first place to any woman who wants it (with parental permission if she is under eighteen). When a baby is on its way a mother can get advice, medical attention and even economic help.

There is family counseling as well, and courses in infant care for both fathers and mothers. Mothers' Aid is also the institution to turn to for the woman who wants an abortion. A group of three experts—usually a psychiatrist, gynecologist and social worker or lawyer—must give unanimous approval before permission is given, and their decision comes after an intensive investigation of the circumstances. A woman can get a legal abortion if a birth will endanger her health, if the pregnancy resulted from a proven crime such as rape or incest, or if the child 'might suffer from a serious hereditary taint.' A woman who is suicidal or clearly worn out with childbearing or coping with an alcoholic husband will usually be able to get a legal abortion.

Each year half of the eight thousand women, most of them married, who ask for an abortion are given the permission. Of those refused, 80 per cent go ahead and have the baby. The rest presumably arrange for an illegal abortion.

The Danish way of running the Mothers' Aid centers is more psychological and sociological than is the practice at the comparable institutions in Sweden and Norway. 'They have a more medical approach,' said Mrs. Skalts. Mothers' Aid costs the state about two and a half million dollars a year. The four hundred persons who work at the eleven centers include social workers, legal experts, gynecologists, psychologists and psychiatrists. All of these experts are brought to the aid of the girl who walks in and announces that she is pregnant but has no husband. Almost all the unwed mothers in Denmark are brought into contact with Mothers' Aid. Doctors and midwives are legally bound to report an illegitimate birth to Mothers' Aid, and the institution is legally bound to help the mother in making sure that the child's father helps support him.

For the sake of the child, the unmarried mother must identify the father whether she wants to or not. Legal machinery then goes into action to try to make sure that the person named is the father and that he assumes his responsibilities. The principle is that a child born out of wedlock has the same rights in relation to his parents as a legitimate child. He has the right to his father's name and the right of inheritance. The father is duty-bound to help support the child up to eighteen years of age, and possibly to age twenty-four if an extended education is involved. The support usually amounts to about three fifths of the cost of maintaining the child. Mothers' Aid provides money to the unwed mother while the paternity case is being established. The girl is helped before and after her pregnancy. She may be placed in a private home, if her parents cannot help her, during her last month of pregnancy. After the birth the centers may help place the baby in an infants' home while the mother looks for a job and makes preparations for a new life.

The unmarried girls often say they want to give the baby away for adoption, but after the birth 96·5 per cent of them want to keep the child. Even so, Mothers' Aid arranges about 350 adoptions a year. There are ten times as many parents who want to adopt a child as there are legitimate and illegitimate children for adoption.

A guiding principle of the whole Mothers' Aid operation is that 'if you want to help the child you must help the mother.' The practical approach is maintained throughout. 'We don't preach morals to the girls before or after,' said Mrs. Skalts. 'We stress their responsibility and help them to make a home for the child. There has been a steady change in the attitude of the community over the last twenty years. It used to be that many parents wouldn't take a girl or her child back into their homes because of what their neighbors would say. Now they are more willing to.' The Collective House in Copenhagen accepts a girl and her baby for a year or two while she is getting established as a new mother without husband. Each apartment has a combination bedroom-living room, a small child's room, tiny kitchen and bath. With their teddy bears and other personal possessions, the young mothers live much like girls in a college dormitory. They may have male visitors, but only up to eleven o'clock at night. They run the risk of expulsion if they let their boy friends stay overnight, but even then something is done to make sure the babies don't suffer. While the mothers are at work during the day, or learning an occupation, the children are cared for in the building's big nursery. The whole atmosphere is one of loving kindness.

The happy ending for at least half the unmarried mothers is that they get married within a few years, and often to the same man who got them in trouble in the first place.

Chapter 11

CULTURE IN DEPTH

We were fighting for dear life against the culture of larger nations like Germany. They could have swallowed us. What Grundtvig did was to teach us that we had a culture of our own.
—FOLK HIGH SCHOOL PRINCIPAL

Lines must be pleasing. There must be life, blood and heart in the things we make. They must be human, warm and alive.
—DANISH DESIGNER

It takes three ministries of the Danish government just to give a guiding hand and financial help to the whole teaching, preaching and creating process which occupies so much of the energy of the Danes. The Ministry of Education grapples with the problems of an exploding demand for more and more learning. The Ministry of Cultural Affairs spends nearly 20 million dollars a year looking after the interests of everything from museums, theaters and foundations to the aesthetics of the Danish countryside itself. The Ministry of Ecclesiastical Affairs busies itself with the Lutheran State Church, whose bishops and ministers are essentially civil servants in clerical garb. (Oddly enough, the head of the State Church, insofar as it has a head, is the politician who runs the Ecclesiastical Affairs Ministry, and he need not be a Church member. He could even be an atheist. A professor of theology has called the Church 'a fairly well-organized anarchy that has proved its ability to function.')

Religion in a nation of disinterested churchgoers no longer has the force it once had. 'People are embarrassed to talk about God,' said a Danish psychiatrist. 'It is almost a taboo word.' But religion still has a cultural influence, and culture in Denmark is a serious business as well as a subject of endless controversy. One of the most recent arguments was over the parliament's decision to award a 3,000 dollar annual income for three years to fifteen young writers, artists and composers in order to allow them to devote their full time to creative work. Inevitably, there was a storm about the particular creators selected—the committee seemed inclined to put its money on sure-fire talent who needed the help less than others. Some taxpayers asked why they had to support writers and painters in the first place. Wasn't it enough that they lived in the welfare state? Or was this the welfare state taking another expensive leap forward?

There has been, in fact, a history of official assistance to artists of all kinds: stipends to needy authors, life pensions to painters and composers, annual support of the Royal Theater, and much more. Writers in particular have been deemed worthy of some assistance because the few million who use the Danish language are not enough of a market to support the average author. Nonetheless, about eight million books in all languages are sold in Denmark every year. Another thirty-one million are borrowed from libraries. To keep Danish authors in business, the library system, working through the Authors' Union, gives a writer 50 øre (roughly six cents) per annum for every copy of his book available in libraries. It is a state royalty which acknowledges that the sales of a book are reduced when it is made freely available in the public libraries.

Quite clearly, the Danes, like other Scandinavians, are voracious readers. They are addicted to newspapers and they publish more books per capita than any other people except the Icelanders, according to the U.N. *Statistical Yearbook*. They publish one book each year for every 1,000 people, while Americans publish one for every 7,000 people. Their rate even exceeds that of the Russians, who are easily the world leaders in the number of books published annually. (The U.S.S.R., because of its multitude of nationalities, publishes books in about 125 languages; the annual total of 80,000 titles, half of them first editions, far exceeds that of any other nation.)

To speak only of Scandinavia, America and Britain, the ranking in terms of book production per 100,000 inhabitants in 1963 is as follows:

	Total Titles	First Editions	Titles per 100,000 Inhabitants
Iceland	230	127	121
Denmark	4,753	2,308	100
Norway	3,148	2,690	90
Sweden	5,703	4,250	75
Finland	2,680	1,169	60
United Kingdom	26,023	20,367	50
United States	25,784	19,057	14

The Danes are fifth in the world in per capita newsprint consumption and tenth in per capita newspaper circulation. All the Nordic countries are high in the lists. The twelve leading per capita newsprint consumers are: (1) United States, (2) Australia, (3) *Sweden*, (4) United Kingdom, (5) *Denmark*, (6) New Zealand, (7) Switzerland, (8) *Finland*, (9) Canada, (10) The Netherlands, (11) *Norway*, (12) *Iceland*.

The twelve leading nations in terms of daily newspaper circulation per 1,000 population in 1963 were:

	Number	Circulation	Per 1,000 Pop.
1 *Sweden*	121	3,791,000	499
2 United Kingdom	112	26,200,000	490
3 Luxembourg (1960)	5	140,000	445
4 *Iceland*	5	82,000	443
5 Japan (1962)	160	39,877,000	420
6 New Zealand	41	1,018,000	401
7 *Norway*	82	1,424,000	388
8 Australia (1962)	58	4,011,000	375
9 *Finland* (1960)	64	1,597,000	359
10 *Denmark*	71	1,598,000	341
11 West Germany	428	18,175,000	315
12 United States	1,754	59,905,000	311

The national newspaper circulation in Denmark (1,600,000 for a population of 4,700,000) is high, and the number of individual daily newspapers is unusually high, particularly in view of Denmark's compact size. The press has long had a key political role to play, and the result has been a multiplicity of newspapers espousing many viewpoints to small audiences. In 1913, when Denmark had 143 separate daily papers, there were thirty towns with three or four newspapers each. There are still a number of such towns; and Copenhagen, with ten daily newspapers, has more than many other major cities in the world. Even so, it was patently uneconomic for so many dailies to exist in little Denmark, and a process of contraction has been under way. Between 1938 and 1963 the number of daily newspapers decreased from 125 to 71. The surviving papers, with stronger circulations, are vigorous competitors.

The Nordic passion for newspapers and books is often said to be due to the long winters and the remoteness of the northern countries; but this clearly applies less to the Danes than, say, to the Finns. The phenomenon is better credited to the lengthy history and high quality of public education in Scandinavia.

Education

Early compulsory education, beginning a century and a half ago, led to early universal literacy. Today Denmark is carrying on a major expansion and streamlining of its educational system as good times enable ever more young people to spend more time in the schools. The clamor for more education, particularly in the last few years, has resulted in a shortage of space and a dearth of teachers. The country needs more teachers' colleges, more universities. 'But this isn't a sign of poverty,' said an Education Ministry official. 'It shows the kind of sudden pressure you get when living conditions improve and people take up new opportunities.'

Just five years ago, 50 per cent of Danish youngsters left school at age fourteen, after the seven-year compulsory period. Now only 20 per cent do. 'It was a change we hadn't foreseen,' said the official. With 80 per cent of its pupils now staying in school beyond the compulsory seven years, Denmark is having to build new schools in a hurry. Its investment in education in comparison to national income is 5 per cent, one of the highest in Europe. A shortage of university space has developed now that there are 11,500 students crammed into Copenhagen University and 5,000 at Århus. A new university at Odense will open shortly, and there are long-range plans for more. University education is free, once a student has passed the examination to get in; scholarships and loans pay for his board and lodging. There are now some 25,000 students in the higher-education institutions of all kinds. At the same time, there are thousands more in the whole range of 'after schools,' or continuation schools, for those early drop-outs who have decided to return to studying.

Folk Schools

The most interesting institution in the Danish educational spectrum, and one which stands apart from the regular school system, is the Folk High School, or People's College. It helps explain why so many quite ordinary Danes—most noticeably in the farming areas—show a remarkable familiarity with books, read two newspapers a day, and easily hold their own with their sons and daughters who are going to a university. The Folk High Schools are traditionally rural institutions which serve as finishing schools for farmers. They are intended mainly for those who have been through the compulsory school and desire to expand their knowledge in their late teens and their twenties. The founding father was a many-splendored Dane who lived for ninety busy years (1783-1872) as a poet, preacher, historian, politician and popular educator. He was Nikolai Frederik Severin Grundtvig, a bishop who wrote a third of the Danish hymns and transformed the cold, austere religion of Luther into a more joyful Christianity. He believed in learning for learning's sake, not just in order to acquire a trade. He first propounded the Folk High School idea in a book on Scandinavian mythology as long ago as 1832. The first school was opened in Jutland in 1844 by a group of clergymen and leading citizens inspired by Grundtvig. But it was a brilliant educator named Kristen Kold, a rebel against learning by rote, who, in Grundtvig's words, 'first grasped the High School idea and practiced it.' It was idealism in action, and the motto was 'For the love of God and the happiness of Denmark.'

The Folk High School was to operate privately, but in a low-fee, Spartanlike manner, and stand clear of the regular schools so that teaching could be done more freely and informally. There were to be no examinations and the teacher-student relationship was to be far more intimate than was the practice in regular schools. The intention was not simply to provide knowledge, but to awaken the spirit and instill a love of learning. The High Schools took on the ambitious job of giving farm hands culture, or at least a feeling for culture. Sixty per cent of the Danish population was then rural. The nineteenth-century conservative politicians and the conservative press, according to a history of the movement, 'took delight in caricaturing the mythology of the High Schools as well as their modern but just as despised liberalism.'

Nonetheless, the movement grew and workers' organizations in the towns founded similar schools. Like the cooperatives, the schools developed outside the government although eventually the state helped provide some financial support. The High Schools turned out to be 'the only specially Danish form of education' (later imitated in the other Scandinavian countries) and one which helped give Denmark's agricultural community its singular character. Most of the country's cooperative leaders, for example, have attended the Folk High Schools.

In the little more than a century of their existence the schools have been attended by some 400,000 students. The typical school —small, rural and residential—has a winter course of five months' duration. It is attended mainly by young men between eighteen and twenty-five years old who are fully occupied with farm work in the summertime. There may be a three-month summer school for young girls and perhaps a two-week 'family course.' Some seven thousand students attend the regular courses annually, and thousands more attend the summer events. Several decades ago there were eighty Folk High Schools. There are now sixty-seven.

In an interesting way the schools have created their own competition. They set the pattern for the continuation schools and
agricultural schools, and sparked the whole, vast adult-education
program which is a striking part of the Danish scene.

The beauty of the Folk High Schools is that in an age of specialization they are still teaching general subjects for the whole man.
The typical syllabus is strong on the humanities, as N.F.S.
Grundtvig and Kristen Kold would have wished. The purpose is
still personal enrichment, not the acquisition of a degree. There
continues to be an emphasis on 'the living word' of lectures and
free discussion as opposed to heavy use of books. The fervent
singing of songs and all the talk of brotherly love and social
responsibility make it clear why the early Folk High Schools, in
more Christian-minded days, had the character of a religious
revival. It is hard not to admire a country where a farm boy or
factory hand decides to spend half a year studying arithmetic,
economics and Scandinavian history and literature, and attending
lectures on 'Greek civilization, natural philosophy, or involved
social problems.'

The teaching of such subjects is conducted much more informally—more as seminars or teacher-student discussions—than is the
custom in Denmark's formal school system, and the teachers
themselves are often more experienced in life than in teaching.
Robert Petersen, the head of a new Folk High School I visited at
Herning in central Jutland, told me that 'it is impossible to use
university-trained people in these schools. They have no experience working with people. This is a place where the teacher
doesn't have to be regarded as a prophet.' Petersen was himself a
typographer and economist before going into Folk School work
with his wife. One of his instructors is a former sailor who took
up folk-school teaching in Ghana. The Herning school is a splendidly modern establishment which the local Damgaard family,
particularly the shirt manufacturer, Aage Damgaard, began by
raising the first one million of the six million kroner ($870,000)
needed to build it. If a Danish community can raise one sixth of
the cost of a Folk High School, the state will provide half the
total and the remainder can be borrowed.

The 108 pupils of both sexes at the Herning school when I saw it came from both city and countryside and were to stay together for an unusually long fall-to-spring program, which would include an eight-day, midwinter train excursion to Austria's Tyrol mountains. It seemed to me that the school glowed with a sense of idealism among both teachers and students which would have pleased Bishop Grundtvig. 'These are young people,' said one teacher, 'who do not have soaring or selfish ambitions, but rather an acute sense of social responsibility.' They were, needless to say, strong defenders of the welfare-state philosophy. I was told by a student: 'Those who complain about the welfare state are those who are themselves rich enough to have provided for their own welfare.' That might be, I replied, but did they ever seriously question whether welfarism in the long run was good or bad for people? 'Oh, yes,' a teacher said. 'We had a lively welfare-state discussion a while ago. One of the students who attended was a spastic. He sat quietly just listening for a long time, and then he simply said, "I like the welfare state." That stopped the argument cold.'

Great Danes

High cultural ambitions and standards were bound to produce important creators in the arts and sciences, and Denmark, for a small country, has had more than its share. The most popular figure, Hans Christian Andersen, was not just a clever nineteenth-century spinner of fairy tales; as has already been noted, he was Denmark's first important proletarian writer and a sensitive man who had a deep perception of human nature. His contemporary, Søren Kierkegaard, was an author and philosopher, whose arguments for religious individualism came to have a large impact in Europe. In many respects he was the original existentialist. No Danish composer managed to achieve anything like the international standing of Grieg or Sibelius, but Carl Nielsen, who died in 1931 and was not really 'discovered' outside Denmark until more recent years, has been growing in stature. In the new art of the cinema, Carl Dreyer, born in 1899 and still turning out controversial films, is the most celebrated of Danish directors. Two of his masterpieces out of a lifetime of moviemaking are *Jeanne d'Arc* (1928) and *Day of Wrath* (1943). In the silent-film days Denmark was one of the world leaders in film production, turning out 1,628 movies between 1907 and 1931. Since there was no need to know Danish to appreciate a Danish film, they won an international audience. The introduction of sound reduced the Danish cinema to a lean, small-country operation, which produced only 421 sound films between 1930 and 1963, or about a dozen a year.

When the Danes talk about their foremost writers of this century they mention Johannes V. Jensen, who won the Nobel Prize in 1944, Kaj Munk, Martin Hansen, H. C. Branner and a few others, but none of these achieved anything like the international following of a gifted, almost magical, Danish baroness named Karen Christentze Blixen-Finecke, who wrote under the pseudonym 'Isak Dinesen.' Her father, Wilhelm Dinesen, was a professional soldier who lived for some years among the American Indians. He published an outstanding collection of letters about his hunting expeditions under the Indian pseudonym, Boganis. Her brother fought with the Royal Canadian Highlanders in World War I, won the Victoria Cross, and wrote the war book *No Man's Land* in 1929. Young Karen, who had published a few short stories when she was twenty, also craved a live of adventure. She got it when she married her cousin, Baron Bror Blixen-Finecke. They became entranced by Africa and bought a coffee plantation near Nairobi shortly before World War I. The baron became a white hunter and turned up as a character in Hemingway's *The Short Happy Life of Francis Macomber*. The marriage broke up after seven years. The Baroness stayed on alone in Africa and managed the plantation until the bottom fell out of the coffee market in 1934. She returned to Denmark and within a few years had established herself as one of the great poetic writers of her time. Nonetheless, it remained a puzzle for years whether Isak Dinesen was a man or a woman. Her *Seven Gothic Tales* became a classic, and *Out of Africa* was acclaimed as one of the most moving books ever written about that continent. For those who still hadn't grasped the identity of Isak Dinesen, even after the secret was out, Baroness Blixen-Finecke confused matters still further by using another pseudonym, Pierre Andrézel, for a wartime romantic novel, *The Angelic Avengers*. An old friend, Eugene Walter, called her 'a creature as mysterious as Andersen's Snow Queen . . . [an] eternal human mystery crystallized in a ninety-pound Danish lady of any age you might care to guess.' It is reported that 'she subsisted on fruit, oysters and champagne and the resources of her own indomitable spirit' before dying in 1962.

Another great Dane died soon afterwards: Professor Niels Bohr, nuclear physicist and Nobel Prize winner of 1923, the most famous of many distinguished Danish scientists. He was the head of Copenhagen's Institute of Theoretical Physics, a position now held by his son, Aage Bohr. Professor Bohr was a cofounder with Max Planck and Albert Einstein of the quantum theory, the foundation of all nuclear research, and a developer of the basic theory of the structure of the atom. 'One of the greatest scientists of this century,' said *The New York Times*, 'but also one of the intellectual giants of all time.' He was also a Dane of gentle, pipe-smoking informality. He was still bicycling to work in his seventies. During the war he was spirited away to America, where he helped work on the atomic bomb. His name for security purposes was 'Dr. Nicholas Baker.' He was ordered to stick to this name and to admit his true identity only to authorized persons. But one day in New York an old friend from Denmark spotted him in an elevator and said she had no idea that he had come to America. Bohr said, 'I'm sorry, madame, but Baker is my name, Dr. Nicholas Baker.' The astonished lady insisted, 'But you are Niels Bohr. I knew you in Copenhagen.' He said again, 'My name is Nicholas Baker,' tipped his hat and walked away. But then he turned, and called out to her, 'And how have you been, Mrs. Olsen?'

Louisiana

Of all the Scandinavian painters of this century, only Norway's Edvard Munch has achieved undoubted world stature. Denmark has produced a galaxy of important modernists, especially Asger

Jorn and Carl Henning Pedersen, and a number of first-rate sculptors, but the country's greatest strength is in the excellence of its architecture and the genius of its domestic design. The most dramatic place to see all of these arts in action is at the Louisiana Museum on the 'Danish Riviera' eighteen miles north of Copenhagen.

First there is a park thick with exotic trees and a Japanese setting of seaside landscaping. Then an elegant white villa, almost like an antebellum mansion of the American South, built more than a century ago by a Danish nobleman who married three wives, all conveniently named Louise (hence, Louisiana). The big house, itself a treasury of art, is the starting point for a walk through glass passageways to contemporary rooms where paintings and other works of art are seen in soothing chambers of natural wood and raw brick. Nature is always close at hand, as the window walls reach toward a woodland pond and a sculpture park.

Louisiana is a jewel box set in shimmering greenery and swept by sea breezes. The abstract art Louisiana displays is playful with its forms and colors. Where there is madness, it is funny-mad, not angry-mad. There are giant old millstones scattered in the park to serve as benches and stepping stones. Children are lured into an artist's studio of their own where they can splash in paint. The whole estate pulses in the evening with concerts, chamber music, experimental jazz, and ballet and dramatic performances.

The founder of the Louisiana Museum and the impresario of this intermingling of the arts is Knud W. Jensen, a public-spirited businessman who heads one of the country's major publishing houses. The special Danish touch to the story of his imaginative patronage of the arts is that he owned one of Denmark's major cheese companies until he sold out a few years ago, and his wealth comes from cheese. The Danish cow, we are once again reminded, brings all things.

Arne Jacobsen

There are two outstanding names in Scandinavian architecture today: Finland's Alvar Aalto and Denmark's Arne Jacobsen.

Aalto's distinctive creations brought him to world attention long before World War II. Jacobsen is a late bloomer whose reputation has soared in the postwar period. They are both in their sixties now and both are busier than ever. Aalto, four years older than Jacobsen, stuck doggedly to his warmly personal idiom while the world gorged itself on 'international style' metal and glass boxes. Jacobsen has been more of an internationalist in this sense, but all of his work, however functional, has shown a traditional Danish appreciation for the landscape. Danish buildings are made to keep company with nature, not to fight it, and Jacobsen is as talented a landscape artist as he is an architect. Like Aalto, he is a meticulous craftsman, who makes sure that every building is impeccably finished. Not content with that, both of these versatile artists prefer to design the interior fittings as well, particularly the furniture and lamps.

Jacobsen, whose father was a wholesale merchant, was born in 1902. His more-than-forty-year career has been a steady, quiet rise to the top rank of world architects. He has ignited controversies inside Denmark, but he is not a flamboyant performer in the manner of a Le Corbusier or a Frank Lloyd Wright. 'Danish architecture,' according to one expert, 'is devoid of great and dramatic traits.'

One architect who is the exception which proves the rule is Jørn Utzon, whose Sydney (Australia) Opera House, now being built at the cost of 45 million dollars, has been called 'the most exciting new building in the world,' as well as the most difficult to engineer. It has forty-six enormous precast concrete shells thrusting as high as 185 feet above the ground. In its finished form it will look like a cluster of magnificent yachts with their white sails billowing in a high wind. Utzon has also designed an unusual art museum for the Jutland town of Silkeborg. The building has large underground galleries with spiral ramps and snouts which reach just above the ground to catch the sun. Now in his forties, Utzon may well emerge as the most illustrious of modern Danish architects, but so far the almost utopian quality of much of his work has severely limited the number of actual buildings which have been completed.

Jacobsen's buildings, on the other hand, can be found all over Denmark, and increasingly abroad. He began winning competitions early in his architectural life, including a 1929 prize for a circular 'House of the Future' with a prophetic helicopter pad on the roof, and (with Eric Møller) the important commission to design the town hall at Århus. Jacobsen was strongly influenced by the Stockholm Exhibition of 1930, which was a breakthrough for functionalism in Scandinavia. The architect of the Stockholm Exhibition was Sweden's foremost modernist, Gunnar Asplund, a man twenty years Jacobsen's senior. They were close friends until Asplund's death in 1940. Jacobsen was forced to flee from occupied Denmark to Sweden in 1943; but, with the help of his talented wife, he struck out in new directions with successful textile and wallpaper designs.

Returning to Denmark after the war, he created private villas, housing estates, schools, factories, town halls and office buildings in dazzling succession. He was responsible for the most formidable modern building in Copenhagen: the stark glass slab of the twenty-story SAS Royal Hotel which looms above Tivoli in the heart of the capital. Jacobsen designed everything in the building from the lamps to the crockery. The spacious, softly lighted lobby makes a stage setting for his swiveling, black-leather 'egg' chairs which wrap around the sitter like a man-eating plant. Unoccupied, they seem to be talking to each other. They are luxurious and expensive, but Jacobsen has also designed a simple stacking chair which looks like a large black ant. It has three metal legs attached to a single piece of molded wood. Both chairs, egg and ant, are now familiar around the world and bring in a large extra income.

Jacobsen's imaginative design for Copenhagen's Munkegårds School—a feat of giving a huge institution a feeling of intimacy— led to his being chosen as the architect for St. Catherine's College at Oxford. He upset many traditionalists by putting down a boldly modern structure in the Gothic setting of the old university, but there was high praise for its elegance and dignity. 'It is as you work or linger in these buildings,' said the *Guardian* of England, 'that you become aware of the formidable order that pervades the entire undertaking, from the huge precast beams to the small spoon with which you stir your coffee. This phenomenal capacity for ordered simplicity is the root of Arne Jacobsen's art.'

Arne Jacobsen looks like a man any child would choose for an uncle. He has white hair, a large and jolly face, and an ample figure which relaxes easily into one of his own egg chairs. He is unmistakably a Dane: a nice sense of fun keeps bubbling up into serious conversation. He is one of the few architects I have met who did not seize the opportunity to denounce the work of other architects. He would only say that within Scandinavia the Danes were doing better than the Swedes ('they study with engineers instead of artists'), while the Finnish architects were the most inspired of all. Of his own work, he said that 'I have no style. I am interested in quality. It is important to do all the small things and to have a unity in the work.'

Danish Design

The beauty of everyday objects in Denmark is a distinguishing mark of the country, but it was not always so. Although there were strong roots in rural handicrafts, the machine age produced offensive household goods until the good design breakthrough in the 1920s. Poul Henningsen, an architect, designer, creator of ingenious lampshades, and propagandist for the arts, called for a democratic revolution:

> Dear craftsmen friends! How can you expect us to go on respecting you, while this swindle continues in the name of art, and while you ignore all your obligations to the modern world? We have no proper tumblers, plates, water sets, spoons, knives, or forks, while richer homes are flooded with trash and rubbish at fantastic prices! Think a little, and consider your obligations to make things for the delight of your fellowmen in their daily life! Throw away your artists' berets and bow ties and get into overalls. Down with artistic pretentiousness! Simply make things which are fit for use: that is enough to keep you busy, and you will sell vast quantities and make lots of money!

That is precisely what happened. Even before Henningsen and other rebels began their agitation, Kaare Klint, an architect, designer and educator, was studying how people lived and working out proportions for furniture and household objects. His aim was to create a system which would have efficient everyday thing, sufficiently standardized to make the most economical use of space. He and his pupils went about sizing up people and furniture to see how they would best fit together, and measuring Danish and foreign cups, saucers, plates and silverware in order to plan the most sensible kind of storage space. Suitability of purpose and economical beauty were the practical aims of a new wave of designers who made a modern art out of the old traditions of craftsmanship. The craftsmen themselves, particularly the Cabinetmakers' Guild of Copenhagen, organized exhibitions and took other steps to make sure they survived in the industrial age, and thus reinforced the new movement.

The result is Danish Design: warm, colorful, graceful, imaginative, strong in texture, rich in natural materials, rich in artist-artisans. The names are familiar to anyone with an interest in the applied arts: Nathalie Krebs in ceramics, Marie Gudme Leth in textiles, Børge Mogensen, Hans Wegner and Finn Juhl in furniture, Søren Georg Jensen in silver, glass and sculpture, and dozens more, particularly those who have been attached as resident artists to the two celebrated porcelain firms, Royal Copenhagen and Bing & Grøndahl. Both companies, like the great glassmaking firms of Sweden and the Arabia ceramics plant in Finland, subsidize artists under conditions of almost unlimited freedom. The results are soaring flights of the imagination which end up in museums or private collections and provide the inspiration for beautiful but inexpensive production-line objects.

'Denmark is a little country,' said Poul Kjaerholm, one of the brightest of the new furniture designers. 'We have no wood, no metals, nothing in the ground. We have to import everything. We have people who feel they must use these things in a fine way. We have fantastically good craftsmen.'

Part Three

Norway

Chapter 12

RUGGED INDIVIDUALISTS

What is there to write about Norway? Nothing ever happens here.
—NORWEGIAN POET

Sweden is a monolithic country: the same people in the same towns all over. There is much tighter communication and administration north to south. But Norway is a conglomeration of mountains, valleys and fjords, and people can live quite separately from one another.
—COOPERATIVE LEADER

Norway is still a virginal land. Despite its ancient Viking history, its millennium of struggle for national identity, and its hard-won breakthrough as a modern state, Norway has the clear-eyed appearance of the freshest, cleanest and most natural nation in Europe. It is almost as if the weary and sophisticated Continent had set Norway apart as a national park or royal preserve and had appointed the Norwegians as custodians to keep the waters clear, the mountain snows untouched by industrial soot, and the wonders of nature unspoiled by thoughtless trespassers. It has less than half the population of New York or London. It occupies a territory larger than Britain and Ireland combined, and it is longer than any other European nation except Russia. In some miraculous way the Norwegians have harnessed the angry sea and mined the 'white coal' of the roaring mountain waters to give themselves one of the world's highest living standards. It is a society as modern as hydrofoils and hydrogen plants, but the most typical Norwegian

179

scene is still a lonely but cheerfully painted wooden house perched on the mossy shore of an infinitely blue and silent fjord.

There is such a crystalline quality to the countryside that it can be intoxicating. Visitors return from Norway with the feeling of having been nourished at a fountain of youth. They have taken deep draughts of northern air and concluded that the rest of the world is ugly, frenzied and hard on the lungs. Because the great outdoors is virtually in everybody's backyard, the Norwegians have something which money cannot buy. Far from being blasé about their wealth of space and nature, they have gone to great lengths to save their natural beauties for the common good, and to use them with uncommon enthusiasm. In no other nation that I know of do people in the cities make a point of working through the normal lunch hour, pausing only for a sandwich and cup of coffee at the desk, in order to be free by mid-afternoon to go hiking, sailing or skiing. In some mysteriously sophisticated way, the Norwegians have managed to achieve the affluence of an industrial society without sacrificing the simple art of living. They have their cake and are eating it too.

Uneasy Self-Confidence

That much being said, is there anything more to say? 'We never seem to hear anything about the Norwegians,' said a guest at a London cocktail party. 'They're so much quieter than the Swedes or Danes. Doesn't anything happen in Norway?' Occasionally a Swede will needle his Nordic neighbor by saying, 'Norway . . . Norway . . . Isn't that a town in Sweden?' To which the inflamed Norwegian will reply, 'No, by God, it's the other way around.'

It is more than a little galling to the proud Norwegian to know that the Swedes, who once dominated Norway, are richer and a few steps ahead in building a prosperous welfare state. This has not stopped the Norwegians from following Sweden's lead in economic and social measures, or learning from its mistakes, but it is in spite of their intensely nationalistic feelings. Even now, more than two decades after the event, some Norwegians are unable to forgive or forget the early war years when Sweden permitted German troop trains to cross its neutral territory to replenish the army of occupation in Norway. But at least the Nordic differences are usually spoken of with a smile these days. A government official in Oslo said, 'People like to say that the Norwegians get good ideas, the Swedes systematize them, and the Danes turn a good profit on them.'

It is a commonplace that the Norwegian has neither the polish of the Swede nor the cosmopolitanism of the Dane. The stereotyped Norwegian is not a particularly quick or clever person. He is a little shy and sluggish, like an awkward country boy still trying to fit in with big-city ways. He may cover his shyness with a boast or a bout of drinking; it is true enough that on a Saturday night in Oslo or Bergen the rafters ring with the shouts of the inebriated. According to Agnar Mykle, one of Norway's more controversial modern novelists,

> Melancholic desperation rages in the body of every Norwegian who has to show the world how gallant and daring he is. . . . You wouldn't think that there was any man in the world as brave and carefree as the Norwegian when he stands smiling or laughing, hands in his trousers' pockets and jacket nonchalantly unbuttoned, at the street corner, on the amateur stage, in the witness box; but women and critics and examiners and judges and executioners will tell you that in his heart of hearts the Norwegian is full of uncertainty and terror. . . .

This is one man's opinion, of course, and it is hard to prove that the Norwegian is *not* seething with doubt and worry under that robust and self-confident exterior. Nonetheless, I find more satisfying some remarks by Denmark's Willy Breinholst. He said that if you ask a Norwegian to analyze himself to see what he is like as a human being, he will 'set about the task with natural suspicion, and with an undertone of indignation he will say: "I suppose you are out to uncover all my faults, so that you will have something to counterbalance the virtues of the Danes and the Swedes." Whereupon he will warm up to the task, until he stands before you as an impressively steep and inaccessible granite mountain from which you couldn't wring as much as a single drop of self-criticism, even if you kept wringing till the end of time. "What I'm like as a human being? Why, *for fanken* [mild Norwegian oath], I'm a hundred-per cent success, of course!"'

Many would agree that he is indeed a success as a civilized human being. Most of the assessments of the Norwegians are favorable ones. Norwegians are usually described as self-reliant individualists or as rugged and resourceful modern Vikings who sail the seven seas. They have none of the sexual or suicidal notoriety of the Danes and the Swedes. Judging by the international homicide statistics, they share with the Danes the distinction of being the least violent, certainly the least murderous, people in the world. The cheerful Norwegians are not so complicated as their neighbors. They do not analyze life down to the bone or brood endlessly about their disappointments. Their emotions are not so bottled up, and they speak their minds more readily than the Swedes. Less pressured to succeed, they grow up as useful citizens without soaring ambitions—which may be just as well for a small society with few high places for the ambitious to reach. Most Norwegians seem content with a life without frills, although, of course, they want all the modern conveniences. If Sweden is seen as a high-powered Cadillac gleaming with chrome, then Norway gets along just fine as an economy-size Rambler with skis lashed to the roof.

Norwegians are said to have an inferiority complex vis-à-vis the Swedes. Certainly they often sound envious of their more elegant neighbors. One Norwegian girl told me that she feels like a hick when she goes to Stockholm and sees the exquisitely dressed women. And yet I have heard Swedes speak enviously of the Norwegian's capacity for enjoying life and for not treating everything with ultraseriousness. 'The Norwegian is not lazy,' I was told in Bergen. 'He works hard—when he works.' Because eight or nine months of the year are spent in harsh weather under leaden skies, there is little to do in Norway but work. The first suggestion of friendlier weather, however, will drive even the most dedicated doctor or profit-minded tycoon into the hills to fix up his summer hut. In Trondheim I was told of the bulldozer operator working on an important development project who left his machine one day to go off on a brief holiday during an unexpected succession of sunny days. It turned out to be the nicest summer in years and the man did not reappear until three months later.

Set against this carefree image is the undoubted fact of Norwegian indomitability. No other people in Europe are in such a constant struggle with the elements. Their personalities are shaped by the forces of nature. Farmers wrestle with a stony soil in a land of granite mountains which is only 3 per cent arable. Fishermen go out day after day to work an icy, wind-swept sea. Almost half the country lies above the Arctic Circle in a bleak world which is shrouded in darkness for long winter months. For centuries Norway has gone to sea, and today, with only one-fiftieth the population of the United States and one-fifteenth the population of Britain, it operates the world's third-largest merchant marine. A host of Norwegians, from the Viking adventurers to Nansen, Amundsen and Heyerdahl, have performed incredible feats of exploration. During my recent travels in Scandinavia a Norwegian youth was attempting to ski across the North Pole. Oslo University Professor Ragnar Christophersen has said that the Norwegians 'are perhaps the counterpart—in Scandinavia—of the Irish in the British Isles, with some of the Irishman's love of the crazy. Who but a Norwegian would have thought of drifting on a raft for four thousand miles across the Pacific?'

In these exploits, Norwegian individualism shines, and yet they have an equally strong ability to cooperate and as much of a taste for the security of the welfare state as the rest of the Scandinavians. It is also true that they complain about taxes more than any other people I have ever encountered, but then they pay some of the highest taxes in Europe. Norwegians also complain about each other and about themselves. 'I have never seen people who are so fond of disparaging themselves as the Norwegians,' wrote George Mikes. 'This healthy dislike of each other is symptomatic of a deep inner harmony. Every human being and every nation is in need of discharging a certain amount of dislike, just as a motor has to discharge a certain amount of fumes, and those who discharge these psychological fumes on the home market can adjust themselves to communal life at large.'

Superdemocrats

The Norwegians are as belligerently democratic and egalitarian as any people on earth. True, they have a king, but they *voted* for their monarchy, and they are quick to say that they will vote it out 'if it ever gets too above itself.' As long ago as 1821, they abolished the nobility and all the fancy titles which used to set apart the elite from the common herd. Everybody is as good as everybody else. Social equality is nearly complete, and taxes and welfare measures are bringing about a greater economic equality than can be seen almost anywhere else. This ascendancy of the common man is the logical result of the Norwegian habit of reverse snobbery, which looks down on whatever is up. Henrik Ibsen said that 'Norwegians can only agree on one sole point, to drag down what is most lofty.'

A Bergen businessman told me that a Norwegian worker given the choice of a 10 per cent pay rise for himself or a 10 per cent reduction in his boss's salary, would cut down his boss every time. While I suspect that this as an exaggeration, I felt more keenly in Norway than in the other Scandinavian countries that there was a greater zeal for leveling out the differences between the average man (since there are few genuinely poor people left) and the well-to-do. The favorite Norwegian whipping boy is the millionaire shipowner: there are several dozen of them who are notably rich and powerful. And yet every Norwegian knows that they make an extraordinary and absolutely vital contribution to Norwegian well-being. 'We are a one-crop economy,' said an Oslo banker, 'and that crop is shipping.'

In this atmosphere, Norway's wealthy men avoid ostentation. They live sumptuously, but they do not make a show of it. '"Thou shalt not display" is our eleventh commandment,' said Norwegian sociologist Johan Galtung. In his excellent book, *Norwegian Democracy*, American Professor James A. Storing wrote:

The Norwegians themselves admit to being insecure, perhaps more in their relationships with each other than with people in other lands. This insecurity manifests itself in many ways, but perhaps most importantly in critical attitudes heard expressed on the street and found written in the daily press. Events that in many countries would be dismissed after a single report in the press remain in Norwegian newspapers for days the subject of public scrutiny and debate. If a police officer has made an 'improper' arrest, or if a public official has made an error, these infractions are labored long and hard. Perhaps by doing this the critic may be genuinely concerned with correcting a wrong, but he may also be building up his own ego. Another manifestation of insecurity can be found in the manner in which innovation is accepted. Generally, new products and new ways of doing things are viewed with suspicion. There are many Norwegian housewives who still refuse to accept milk in paper cartons, and many would not buy frozen foods, even if they were more readily available. This conservative attitude extends into the social life of the people; Norwegian dinner parties, though delightful in the extreme, present no surprises to the initiated guests.

It is trite to describe any nation as a 'land of paradox,' and I have so far avoided the temptation in this book, but there is something compelling about the fact that Norway is at once the most puritanical of the Scandinavian states and the most socialist. It is a fairly lukewarm kind of socialism by now, despite the ardent May Day speeches, but during World War I and in the following decade the Norwegian Labor Party was one of the most radical in Europe. All the while, a deep-rooted conservatism characterized the Norwegian people, and it is still possible to feel the hold of old ways and old attitudes.

Norway is still a largely rural civilization in the sense that those who have moved into the towns in such numbers in recent decades are still close to the soil. 'I sometimes think,' said one observer in Oslo, 'that every other person in this city has just come off the farm.' The Norwegians are so widely scattered over their long and craggy land, with their villages isolated in valleys or on islands, that there are strong regional differences. 'The separation of the communities has given people a fierce independence and capability,' said an English scholar in Trondheim. Norway's 'Bible coast' in the south still offers hard religious views and the rural precepts of duty, work, austerity and abstinence from corrupting pleasures. In an effective combination of clerical and Labor Party views on the Sabbath, no Sunday newspapers are sold in Norway and it is impossible to buy a drink. Even the fishing fleet stays home on Sunday in the height of the season.

All this may suggest that a great many Norwegians go to church, but very few do so with any regularity. They find their religion in the great outdoors, like most other Scandinavians. The clergy, like the rest of the civil servants, are paid their wages and pensions by the state. The church plays almost a bystander role in Norwegian life except in the most pious areas. In everyday Norwegian life a more vital institution is the conciliation council. There are about 460 of these in the country, and they serve the unique and highly useful purpose of settling disputes between argumentative Norwegians without anyone having to go to any great legal bother. Each community has a conciliation council of three average citizens elected for four-year terms by the town council. With certain exceptions, every civil case which might go to the regular law courts must first go to the conciliation council to see if simple mediation will settle the matter. The two parties in a dispute are not allowed to be represented by lawyers; they argue their side of the matter as best they can. If they accept the settlement proposed by the council (more than a third of the 25,000 annual cases are quickly resolved) then they have been spared the expense of a court fight and the courts are left free to get on with more important business.

'Having no real problems,' said George Mikes, 'the Norwegians are desperately anxious to create some.' One that they make the most of is the language issue, which comes down to a heated struggle between the advocates of Riksmål, a Danish-influenced tongue, which is favored by the townspeople, and Landsmål, an invented 'Norwegian' based on rural speech, which the more ardent nationalists champion. There is even a kind of middle-way language between the two. No wonder it is said in Norway that 'if a man knows eight languages, seven of them are Norwegian.' The eighth language, of course, will be English. As elsewhere in the Nordic world, it is the one foreign language which every Norwegian must learn in school, and they learn it and use it remarkably well. It is partly a result of Norway's open face to the world and its long history of seafaring. Finland, in contrast, is backed into a far corner of northern Europe and its 'ocean' to the east is the great and forbidding expanse of Russia.

The Big Change

I think of Scandinavia as an oyster which is tightly hinged at the Finnish–Soviet border but which opens up most widely where Norway meets the Atlantic. Four fifths of all Norwegians live within twelve miles of the sea, and it is said that 'a Norwegian is never happy if he is too far away from the smell of fish.' Because Norway is one of the most mountainous countries in Europe, it was not until 1909 that a railroad link was made between the two biggest cities—Bergen on the west coast and Oslo (then Christiania) in the east. Before that connection it took a citizen of Bergen five or six days to sail to the capital of his country and about half that time to reach Scotland or England. Bergen's historic importance, in fact, stems from the days when it was one of the key Hanseatic ports. The lingering German influence still makes Bergen seem a little foreign to Norwegians in other parts of the country.

The nationalism of the Norwegians, which inspires them to run a flag up a pole at the slightest excuse, is understandable when it is realized that the country only became fully independent in this century. True enough, it has had a constitution and a large measure of autonomy for about 150 years, but it was a Danish colony for centuries and then it was obliged to be loyal to the Swedish Crown until 1905. In the sixty years since then it has achieved the prosperity which finally put a stop to the emigration that brought three quarters of a million Norwegians to America. A broad program of social benefits begun under Conservative and Liberal governments has been carried forward and embellished by the Labor Party, which ruled almost without a break for three decades, to 1965. A country which had only 17 per cent of its population living in towns a century ago is now 57 per cent urbanized. Norway's economy, like Denmark's, is no longer something which can be summed up by simply mentioning the obvious. Shipping, fishing and forestry are still crucially important, but the hydroelectric installations which have made Norway the most electrified country in the world have spawned scores of new industries, from chemicals and aluminum to cash registers and tape recorders. The creation of a giant trade union organization and its sensible dealings with management's own great union have given Norway an enviable postwar record in labor relations.

Of all the Scandinavian states, Norway came out of the war with the brightest record of resistance to aggression at home and on the high seas. Not given the opportunity to be neutral like the Swedes, and enabled by geography to defend itself in a way denied to the Danes, the Norwegians fought off the Germans for several savage weeks and then established a government in exile in London rather than surrender. The Norwegian merchant marine was an invaluable weapon for the Allies. But it was a costly war. More than half of Norway's ships were sunk, the retreating Germans burned and destroyed almost everything in the Norwegian north, and the development of the national economy was slowed to a crawl. The early postwar years meant self-discipline and belt-tightening but a miracle of reconstruction took place. The Labor government pushed the economy as hard as it would go, and it indulged in more economic planning than any of its Nordic counterparts. Norway has had one of the highest rates of investment in the past decade.

Norwegian conditions, according to the inhabitants, are still unsatisfactory. They grumble about the housing shortage and bad roads, the queues for telephones, and the high taxes and high cost of new state enterprises. The over-all postwar achievement, however, is something that even the most critical Norwegian can be proud of. Theirs is not a life of ease and luxury, yet the

Norwegians are living better than ever. Half a million of them, or one out of seven of the entire population, now go abroad during their holidays. Most Norwegians actually have more living space in their homes than the Swedes. One thinks of the Swede in a modern utility apartment and of the Norwegian in a sturdy bungalow painted red and facing a postcard view of a lake or mountain. Nearly half a million homes have been built since the war, which means that about a third of the nation is now under a new roof. There is said to be a shortage of as many as 100,000 dwellings, but that is not a measure of the Norwegian homeless. It is a sign that ever more people want a home of their own, or a better home. Furthermore, most Norwegian families either own a cabin in the countryside or have the use of one. 'When I go back to Oslo,' said a Norwegian diplomat in London, 'I seem to be the only one who doesn't have a hut in the mountains.'

The Norwegians do not have as many automobiles per capita as the Swedes, and they are not likely to, so long as the duty comes to about 100 per cent on the retail price of a car. But the nation's car population has climbed dramatically nonetheless. So too with television. In 1957 the planners predicted that there might be as many as 70,000 television-set owners in Norway in 1964. As things turned out, the actual number was over 400,000. Television facilities have now been extended to communities far above the Arctic Circle. One of the greatest obstacles in the development of Norway is the high cost of public facilities. The distances and the ruggedness of the terrain mean that every mile of road and every foot of cable is more expensive to install and maintain than almost anywhere else in Europe. In addition, the small population means that the per capita use of any facility is almost prohibitively low. These obstacles are matched, however, by Norway's high ambitions, and so the development work is pressed ahead anyway even though conservatives complain that 'we are living beyond our resources.' It is popularly felt that every Norwegian from Kristiansand to Kirkenes should enjoy the same Good Life.

To an astonishing extent this has come to pass. In Tromsø, Hammerfest and Kirkenes on the very roof of Europe I found supermarkets and modern hotels. In Spitsbergen, a Norwegian outpost even farther north in the Arctic Ocean, the coal miners are rewarded with free spring holidays in Greece and autumn holidays in Italy. And in a land where skiing is about as common as walking, even the blind have been put on skis and sent racing down the slopes, guided by sound-emitting signals along the track.

Chapter 13

SURVIVAL OF THE FITTEST

I've lived in good climate, and it bores the hell out of me. I like weather rather than climate.
— JOHN STEINBECK

The sea is the true Norwegian highway.
— WILLIAM SANSOM

In 1944–45, in the savage Götterdämmerung of Hitler's European empire, the German forces in Finnmark in northern Norway destroyed virtually every town, port, factory, farmhouse, cottage, vessel, tractor, machine and telegraph pole in their path as they retreated to the south. Determined to leave nothing and no one to assist the Russian forces whom they expected to pursue them, the Germans burned and exploded facilities which the Norwegians had laboriously constructed over the years on the bleak northern rim of Europe. They drove more than 50,000 settlers to the cities in the south, a gunpoint expulsion of the population which could have become a death march if there had not been good weather, clear roads and calm seas. When the war ended, Finnmark, a Norwegian county as large as Austria, was a wasteland practically denuded of people.

It was an event which passed almost unnoticed on the larger canvas of World War II. In Norway itself, it was counted as one of the major wounds of the war, and the government began to plan for a slow and orderly redevelopment of an area which would be too costly to revive at any great speed. The northerners were offered jobs and a new life in the south. But then the planners

191

were confronted with the fact that the Norwegians who had been forced out of their Arctic homeland were leaving the relative ease of the south to return to their shattered towns. They had practically no resources to carry out the reconstruction on their own, but they went anyway, to live like pioneers on the frontier of glacial soil and twenty-four-hour nights. Their return compelled the government to act sooner than it had intended and brought about measures to aid the settlers in their task of making Finnmark a working community again.

I had not known this story until I saw Norway as it should be seen: by driving a small sports car from the southernmost tip of this curiously stretched-out land to Hammerfest, Europe's most northern city, and on to the Russian border. It was a twisting, turning, exhilarating, 2,500-mile obstacle course; the straight-line distance is slightly more than a thousand miles. It was on that journey, and especially in the brutally beautiful northern reaches of Norway, that I came to understand just how much a creature of his environment the Norwegian is. The Norwegians and the Finns are the true and final Spartans of Europe. Those settlers who returned to the cold emptiness of Finnmark did so because their natural appetite is not for the easy life. Their instincts take them to the sea, the forests and the mountain valleys, where a man can still survive by using his primitive talents. There is food in the water, fire in the timber, and clothing on the animals.

To describe Norway's natural man, then, one must describe his natural surroundings. Norway is a peculiarly shaped country: 'a giant long-armed lute,' a caveman's club, a lamb chop, a limp dumbbell. Whereas Sweden has almost a rectangular shape, Norway is bulbous at top and bottom and so thin in the middle that it amounts to a ragged narrow corridor roughly twenty to forty miles wide between the sea and Sweden. At one point (at the head of the Tysfjord) Norway is merely four miles wide. Although the land border with Sweden, Finland and the Soviet Union is 1,587 miles long, the coast line is longer still—1,650 miles. But it is a coast shaped like the edge of an old saw, with fjords cutting in so deeply that the longest of them, the Sognefjord, is 114 miles long. If the actual coast line is measured by including the fjords and the shores of the larger islands, then the total is 12,000 miles.

This exercise in stretching out Norway is one of the favorite games of amateur geographers. Another is pivoting the country on its bottom. Because it is 1,089 miles long, Norway would bump into Italy and Ireland if it were ever swung in a circle. This is a meaningless indoor sport except to make the point that the Norwegians in the more populated south—in Oslo, Bergen and thereabouts—are physically closer to the English, Irish, French, Germans, Russians and practically everyone else in Europe than they are to their countrymen in Finnmark. Most Norwegians in the south have never been north of Trondheim, which is only a third of the way up the coast. Built under fantastically difficult conditions, a railroad now reaches as far north as Bodø, just above the Arctic Circle, and there are roads now which can take a summertime traveler by car or bus all the way to the North Cape and Kirkenes. But after the onrush of winter in October the passes are blocked for seven months or so. Although airplanes now service the far north, the most common means of travel throughout the year is still that old reliable, the coastal steamer.

The Sea Road

The steamer is a seagoing stagecoach which travels a regular 1,200-mile route from Bergen to Kirkenes, day and night, summer and winter. It stops at every town of any importance to drop off and take on mail, cargo and passengers. There are thirteen vessels in all, owned by five separate shipping companies, and all together, they travel nearly a million miles a year. The twelve-day round-trip journey to Kirkenes on an attractive and amiable steamer is one of the most unusual as well as relaxing tourist excursions in Europe, and a superb way to mix with the Norwegians who circulate along the northern coast. My own long drive up the spine of Norway was twice relieved by these coastal steamers, which picked up the car in a rope sling and took me along on a seagoing short cut. The leisurely, folksy journey recalled the days of Mark Twain, when the steamboats sailed majestically up the Mississippi. For the lonely towns scattered along the riverfront, the arrival of the steamboat was the great event of the day. So it is in Norway when the local Tom Sawyers, Huckleberry Finns and their girls ride down to the wharf on their bicycles to stare at the passengers and inspect the strange crates and packages arriving from the outside world.

From the sea, Norway seems uninhabited except where life is sustained at the water's edge with handkerchief-size farms and small fishing boats. Of the 119,000 square miles of Norwegian land, only about 6,000 can possibly be cultivated and little more than 3,000 actually are farmed. Yet, almost miraculously, Norway has become self-sufficient in meat, vegetables, dairy products and a number of fruits. The green-and-gray-granite kingdom is so thick with hills and mountains, so creased by rivers and fjords, and so high above sea level that it defies men to tame it. Just consider the fjord. It is a word and a natural phenomenon which is almost always identified with Norway. Indeed, my dictionary says it is 'a narrow inlet of the sea, between high banks or rocks, as on the coasts of Norway and Alaska.' But 'inlet' is a weak little word for these thrusting ocean fingers which stab so violently into the body of Norway. The fjords are also immensely varied, so that some look like rivers which have drilled their way through the mountains, while Oslofjord and a few others are more like expansive lakes which have reached out to the sea.

A quarter of Norway is forest and most of the rest is mountain-ous land above the tree line, where little can grow. Although the north is an awesome, threatening wilderness, the greatest natural spectacles are in the south, where the longest river runs close to Oslo and the longest fjord lies just above Bergen. This is where travelers find a glacier nearly large enough to cover New York City, a waterfall six times as high as Niagara Falls (though only a fraction of its width), and the tallest of Norway's mountains.

Only 2,000 of Norway's 150,000 islands and skerries are in-habited, and the over-all sparseness of population—the gaping absence of mankind—is as much a part of the Norwegian scenery and atmosphere as are the crowds of people shouldering by in other countries. A visitor can have mixed feelings: a clinging loneliness but also a wild sense of discovery and possession, as if he were the first man to see and to claim these stark mountains and heavenly valleys.

While there is no doubting that Norway is the least crowded land on the continent, it is also a fact that the Norwegian population has had a substantial increase over the years. Two centuries ago there were only 700,000 persons in Norway; today there are 3·7 million. As in the rest of Scandinavia, the birth rate has fallen sharply in this century, from 28 births a year per thousand inhabitants sixty years ago to just 17 today, but the infant mortality rate is one of the world's lowest, and people are living healthier, longer lives.

America Fever

Norway would have many more people than it has if 861,000 Norwegians had not left during the hundred years between 1836 and 1935. This was a staggering number of people for a nation of Norway's modest size to lose, and it is the most eloquent testimony of all to the fact that Norwegian prosperity and well-being is a phenomenon of only very recent times. The overwhelming majority of the emigrants went to America, which offered not only escape from poverty but also boundless opportunities for ambitious men. As Ibsen repeatedly said in his plays, the Norwegian society in the nineteenth century was far too parochial and straight-laced for people of spirit and enterprise. The nation was not even wholly free of foreign rule; the king lived in Stockholm. The United States, on the other hand, was the great new and revolutionary democracy—a vast open society.

In a commentary on this upsetting period in Norwegian life, the *Norway Yearbook* calls it a period of social change in a nation groping for new ways and modern institutions.

Social and political discontent flared up among the farmers and workers, and into this restless and changing society poured an endless stream of letters from abroad, describing in glowing colors the economic opportunities, the democratic institutions and the social equality in the U.S.A. These letters, together with prepaid tickets and the activity of steamship agents, undoubtedly stimulated emigration.

The Norwegian–American love affair began in 1825 when about fifty persons sailed off in a small vessel to the United States. Another group left a decade later, and then the sailings became more frequent. The end of the Civil War in the United States coincided with 'America Fever' in Norway. In the fifty years from 1865 to 1914, 674,000 Norwegians left the country, 90 per cent of them bound for America. The flow was not really stopped, or greatly slowed down, until the American Immigration Act of 1924 which restricted the flow of immigrants. Most of the Norwegians settled in the six states which had a particular attraction for all the hardy Scandinavians: Wisconsin, Illinois, Iowz, Minnesota, and North and South Dakota. From there, many moved on to the Pacific Northwest and to Canada.

One pleasant consequence of this flood of Norwegians to the New World is that an American traveling in Norway today feels immediately that he is among his own kind of people. Every Norwegian seems to have a relative in the United States, and no wonder—there are more than two million Norwegian-Americans, or more than half the population of Norway. The Norwegians not only have an emotional attachment to America, but it sometimes seems as if every other Norwegian has *been* to America. Thousands of young men—and women—join the merchant marine each year and are soon as familiar with Brooklyn as they are with Bergen. They speak English in foreign ports. The thousands who eventually leave the merchant marine for a more settled life give the country an interesting transfusion of worldliness. It mixes oddly with the pervading provincialism.

For the full flavor of Norway it is essential to see something of the home life. The Italian or Frenchman may spend much of his time with his friends on the streets or in cafés, and some Englishmen may make the pub the center of their social life, but for the greater part of the year the Norwegian is necessarily a dedicated homebody. When it is black and below zero outside, the home must be a glowing, spotless and cheerful retreat. Great importance is attached to books, candles, plants, flower patterns, bright colors, paintings from nature, deep-pile rugs, solidly comfortable furniture and ceremonial food and drink. It is wrong to imagine that the Norwegians, or any Scandinavians for that matter, surround themselves with furnishings so starkly functional that all the warmth is gone. They are devoted to good design, of course, but the emphasis is on bourgeois comforts, not on an avant-garde style of living. A Midwestern American would feel more at home than a New Yorker. Happily for foreigners, almost all Norwegians have an outgoing nature which makes for relaxed and informal hospitality. More readily than the Swedes, for example, they will invite a new acquaintance home for an impromptu meal of coffee, sandwiches and pastry. When I learned that only 10 per cent of the married women in Norway go out to work, instead of the 25 per cent in Denmark, Sweden and Finland, my first thought was that it could only be because they are kept so busy preparing snacks for visitors.

Although their winters are rigorous, the year-round life of the Norwegians is more pleasant than might be supposed for a country at the latitude of Greenland and Siberia. The Gulf Stream makes the difference. This tropical ocean-river touches the Norwegian coast all the way up to the Russian border and beyond, so that the northern coastal towns are ice-free through the winter, despite the unrelenting Arctic night and the blanket of snow which descends on them. The ice-laden fishing craft continue to operate, and the coastal steamers, sometimes bucking howling Arctic blizzards, carry on the only reliable midwinter transportation. Winter can close in on Lapland in October like the switching on of a refrigerator, freezing the roads and blocking the passes. My own September–October drive to the summit of Norway turned out to be a close and chilling race with the elements.

Rough Riding

In 1948, entering Scandinavia for the first time, I had taken a Norwegian ship from Newcastle, England, to Bergen on Norway's western coast. This time the starting route was Newcastle to Kristiansand on the southern coast. From there it was a long journey, broken frequently by ferry trips, to Stavanger, Bergen, Ålesund, Molde, Kristiansund, Trondheim, Mo-i-Rana, Bodø, Svolvaer, Narvik, Tromsø, Alta, Hammerfest, Karasjok and Kirkenes. Later, after zigzagging through Finland and Sweden, I returned to Norway through its eastern door for a further swing through the Oslo region and the southern counties.

It is tempting to describe the journey in personal detail—the wildly pitching ferry ride from the Lofoten Islands to the mainland when the car and all its contents were almost hurled into the angry sea, the frightening drive across mountain passes suddenly encrusted with ice, the snowstorm near the North Cape when a truckload of Lapps arrived in time to pull me out of a drift. But this is not an adventure story. What might be said is that no country has so much to offer a traveler who has tired of the crush and commercialism of the more familiar tourist nations.

The Norwegians deplore the fact that so many of their roads are primitive compared with the smooth highways of Denmark and Sweden, and yet, to look on the bright side, no one else's roads are so full of surprises. It is an attraction of Norway in the age of traffic jams that it is able to offer adventure to travelers who may have forgotten that a road can have a personality. Norwegian roads are individualists which reject such encumbrances as traffic lights, billboards, garages, junkyards and drive-in restaurants. They ramble through a countryside which can be deliriously beautiful when the sun glistens on the frosty mountaintops and the mist settles in green valleys speckled with brightly painted cottages. It is a poor traveler who does not stop occasionally at the edge of a cliff to fill a cup from his Thermos of coffee and take in the grandstand view of the spectacular country.

Kristiansand and Stavanger

The first thing the Norwegians said to me as I arrived in each new town was: 'You should have come during the good weather. Now you will find it not so nice.' I had to explain that I had seen plenty of Norway in its time of sun and flowers and berries; the time had come to see the country in the raw. As expected, it rained a great deal and the September–October nights were cold as I moved farther north, but the gathering gloom was frequently punctuated by outbursts of sunshine. The sun was blazing when my ship sailed into Kristiansand. The port was created by royal command in 1641, and it is still marked off from most other Norwegian cities by its precisely rectangular street pattern. A journalist who doubles as a social worker, Theodore Torjussen, took me almost immediately to the handsome new school gymnasium where a good percentage of the town's 27,000 citizens were sitting under the acrobat rings listening to the local orchestra playing a rousing rendition of 'Oklahoma!'

The road from Kristiansand to Stavanger twists like a cow path through a regiment of dark-green hills. It slides around the curves of river basins and fjords and passes across a strange terrain, resembling the surface of the moon and suggesting a geologist's paradise. And then Stavanger looms up out of all the primitiveness as one of the brightest and most up-to-date cities in Norway. It is the fourth-largest city, after Oslo, Bergen and Trondheim, and was about to increase its population from 85,000 by incorporating a number of the surrounding communities. The move was part of a 'streamlining of municipalities' which was taking place in many parts of Norway. In Stavanger's case, a lot of streamlining has already been accomplished in the city center, which surrounds the 860-year-old cathedral. There is a pleasing assortment of new glass-faced buildings, an inviting modern library, and other structures which add up to a large-scale urban renewal. Stavanger was not damaged during the war, yet it looks as if it had been created fresh out of bomb sites. The city planners have wisely left intact the narrow streets and old wooden buildings which crowd around the harbor. They make a capsule version of a Norwegian port in the old days when the country literally lived on fish.

Today Stavanger is turning into a service center for its southwestern corner of Norway, but as an important shipbuilding town and the center of the canning industry it is still dependent on the sea. I had my first clear impression of the size of the Norwegian fishing business when I called at the Bjelland

Canneries, one of 170 canning firms in Norway and the largest in Scandinavia, and saw some of the billion fish which pass in and out of the plant each year. The canning companies buy the fish from the fishermen's sales cooperative at a price fixed *before* each season, a system which contrasts with the auctions of most other fishing nations. In addition to processing herring, salmon and other fish, the Bjelland Canneries, in 'the sardine capital of the world,' produce about fifty million tins of sardines a year. Since there are fifteen silvery fish to a can, that makes 750 million sardines—and three quarters of them go to America.

Soon after the sardines are caught at sea they are transferred to a freezer ship, which eventually delivers them imbedded in slabs of ice resembling thin gravestones. These are stored in a great freezing room until they are needed, a circumstance which has turned canning into a year-round, instead of seasonal, industry. The sardine slabs are sent through a shower bath to release the fish from the ice. After that a series of ingenious automatic machines sort out, cook, guillotine and otherwise convey the sardines to their ultimate end in a flat little can.

Bergen

Norway's fabulous 'Discovery Route' lies between Stavanger and Bergen. It is a natural wonderland, where every turning of the road produces another view of a deep-blue fjord or a village nestling at the foot of a mountain whose diamond tip of ice etches the sky. When I arrived in Bergen it was, of course, raining. It is said that a horse in Bergen will bolt at the sight of a man who does *not* have an umbrella. The much exaggerated rain, however, only makes Bergen sparkle more when the sun bursts through the clouds and reveals the nine-hundred-year-old port in its full glory. First there is the harbor churning with ships, then the mixture of ancient and modern buildings at the base of the backdrop of mountains, and finally the rising tiers of wooden houses clinging to the green slopes. It is a small-scale San Francisco with crying seagulls, cobblestone streets, a boisterous fish market and a row of fine old Hanseatic buildings facing the ocean.

Bergen is a city bottled in brine. It has the kind of atmosphere which comes with great age and which no travel agent can manufacture. The seasoned old town is a metropolitan version of the Viking-age stave churches which stand like Nordic pagodas in scattered places in Norway. Bergen was Norway's capital in the twelfth and thirteenth centuries and a powerful commercial center during the Hanseatic period in the fourteenth to sixteenth centuries. Like the rainy, self-reliant city of Gothenburg in Sweden, it has always seen itself as more international and sophisticated than the nation's capital. In its history it has often been closer to Hamburg and London than to Oslo. It is the country's second city (population 150,000), but it is first in civic pride. Norwegians tell of the boy whose family moved to a new town. When he entered his new school he refused to reveal where he was from. Only later did he say, 'I didn't want to boast on my first day, but I'm from Bergen.'

The fishing industry is still important, but manufacturing, banking and trading now provide most of the work. Bergen University (founded after World War II) and the Norwegian School of Economics and Business Administration are two of a number of rapidly expanding educational establishments. As a cultural center the city blossoms for a fortnight every June when an international festival of music is staged in memory of its most famous citizen, composer Edvard Grieg.

Trondheim

North of Bergen the landscape changes so abruptly and so often that it is like sitting in a theater and watching the stagehands constantly changing the scenery. The mountains, fjords and valley towns are so picturesque that they seem to have been invented for postcards and color slides. The larger towns are placed like signal lanterns along the coast. They are crisp and modern ports, which are all undergoing great change. Ålesund, for example, is a town of about 20,000 persons living on a Venice-like necklace of islands. It has been known as the country's 'largest fishing village' or 'leading herring town,' but the herring have not been so plentiful in recent years and the city fathers have had to step up the movement to textiles, furniture and other manufactured products. In Molde, some two hundred downtown buildings were destroyed in German air raids in 1940, but today it is a small polished gem of a city with a waterfall rushing through the middle of town and new buildings lining an elegant little main street. One of the most attractively designed new churches in Scandinavia towers above the city center. Here as elsewhere in Norway it was hard to find anyone who did not look in ruddy good health, who was not well and comfortably clothed. The glassy new library was full, and every child seemed to be attached to a bicycle. Kristiansund too was severely damaged in 1940, losing 724 houses and most of its old buildings, but it has since been transformed into one of the handsomest small cities in Scandinavia.

Trondheim, in contrast, was not particularly damaged by the war. It still has, amid the outcropping of modern office buildings and hotels, enough weathered old wooden structures to preserve its look of a pioneering town. Splendid old wooden warehouses lean against each other along the canal banks, and the great stone bulk of the Nidaros Cathedral is the largest medieval building in Scandinavia. The city has a few sizable factories, but it is mainly a service and educational center for the area which connects the main body of Norway to the long arm reaching northward. The population is now 115,000, after the incorporation of suburbs. Since Trondheim is less than a hundred miles from the Swedish border, it is the biggest city around for many persons in the northwestern regions of Sweden. One of the town's more peculiar problems, according to the police chief, is the regular invasion of prosperous young Swedes who come roaring over the mountains in their big cars and then cruise around Trondheim looking for girls and a good time.

Whether or not it is entirely due to Swedish influences, a number of young Norwegians in Trondheim, Bergen and other cities have picked up the habit of somehow acquiring an automobile and driving it about in loud, aimless circles. The fashionable youthful crime in Norway (a distinctly uncriminal land, where the police do not carry guns) is car stealing. It is perhaps to be wondered why there isn't more trouble with teen-agers and restless youth in Norway. In the typical Norwegian town, by any standard of the indulged youth of the world, there is 'nothing to do' except for an occasional dance and an amazing amount of walking and bicycling around. In time, sex and drink add a little excitement; the first is often easier to get than the second. The fact is that Norwegian youngsters simply do not take naturally to being delinquents. 'Swedish youth is more rebellious,' said a city official in Trondheim, 'but then they have more to rebel against.' Young Norwegians, as a whole, seem content with their relatively simple life, and there are plenty of ways for them to work off their energies. Residents of Trondheim are surrounded by mountains and sea; they can be on the ski slopes fifteen to thirty minutes after leaving their front doors.

Narvik and Tromsø

It was on the drive north of Trondheim, moving on to the Arctic Circle, that I saw the man in earmuffs eating an ice-cream cone. He was a harbinger of the colder weather and sudden swirls of snow which were to become commonplace. It became more necessary at night to cling to that strange pillow-blanket (a kind of pregnant quilt) which serves as an all-purpose covering for the sleeper in Norway. Its disadvantage is that it slithers away from anyone who turns too vigorously in his sleep but it has all the warmth of several layers of regular blankets.

Just short of the Arctic Circle the old mining town of Mo-i-Rana, which had only 1,500 people before the war and was virtually owned by a single family, has been wholly transformed in the postwar years by the erection of the great state-owned steelworks which overshadows the life of the entire area. Mo-i-Rana now has 15,000 residents, who occupy the new homes and apartment blocks of the expanded town. Although Norwegians have been debating for years about the wisdom of placing a steel mill so far north, it came into being (and is now producing 400,000 tons of steel a year) at just the time when the fishing towns along the coast and in the Lofoten Islands were facing a serious unemployment problem as the sea harvest dwindled. The steel plant employs some 2,400 persons and indirectly provides several thousand more jobs. Aluminum, chemical and hydroelectric establishments in the same area add up to an important industrial complex, which is one of the northernmost in the world.

Above the Arctic Circle stretches a misshapen territory which accounts for a third of Norway's land area and less than 10 per cent of the population. There are about 450,000 people in the three northern counties of Nordland, Troms and Finnmark. A few thousand people leave every year because work is more plentiful and life is more comfortable in the south, while a number of adventurous souls come up from the south each year to take part in the national effort to develop the north into a more prosperous region. The birth rate is higher in the north. 'Our winter nights are twenty-four hours long,' said one resident. 'What else do you expect us to do?' The Oslo winter is figured to be four months long, while in the topmost parts of the north it is nearly six months. It is inland, away from the warmth of the Gulf Stream, where Norway becomes coldest. Karasjok, the old Lapp town on the Finnmark plateau, has seven months of winter, two of summer and one and a half each for spring and autumn. It was at Karasjok where the weather experts recorded Norway's lowest temperature ever: –59·8 degrees Fahrenheit.

Bodø is the first of the several key towns above the Arctic Circle. Most of it was leveled in the German bombing of 1940, but it is now an important military town, transportation center and stepping stone to the Lofoten Islands. Narvik is a better-known city because of its importance as an outlet for Swedish iron ore and the British–German naval battles which took place in the waters around Narvik early in World War II. The Germans captured the city, but they were thrown out by Norwegian, British, French and Polish forces after some spectacular British naval victories. But then the Allies had to let the Germans retake the city when the Allied forces were needed for urgent duty in the south. The fighting largely destroyed Narvik, but the recovery has been impressive. The life of the city is centered on what is said to be the world's largest ore-loading installation. It is owned by Sweden's giant LKAB iron-ore company, now a Swedish government enterprise. The amount of business it does makes it the biggest taxpayer in Norway and makes Narvik an unusually wealthy little city.

Farther to the north, Tromsø is a famous old whaling and sealing town, which escaped serious damage during the war. It was the scene, however, of a celebrated action in November 1944, when British planes destroyed the German battleship *Tirpitz* in the nearby waters. The old section of the port still has the rough look of the old frontier town which sent off the first Arctic sealing ships and a succession of Arctic expeditions led by Roald Amundsen and other Norwegian and foreign explorers. In the last few years Tromsø has had such a surging growth that land prices have doubled, and the city planners have the problem of a serious housing shortage. The city has a graceful new suspension bridge (the largest in northern Scandinavia), a new airport, a new hospital, and a new cable lift to a mountain perch which offers one of the greatest scenic views in Europe.

Spitsbergen

Some four hundred miles north of Tromsø, on a direct line to the North Pole, lies Spitsbergen, an island group which has red snow, white coal and the lowest income taxes in Norway. (The coal mines have a white frosting of ice crystals, while the snow above ground often has a reddish hue because of a coating of algae.) Strictly speaking, Spitsbergen is not so much Norwegian as it is a territory over which Norway has sovereignty under international agreement. Svalbard, 'the land of the cold coasts,' is the over-all name for Spitsbergen and several other islands north of Norway. The international treaty of 1920 which recognized Norwegian sovereignty gives the citizens of all the nations which signed the treaty (the United States, Britain, Russia, France, etc.) the same rights in Svalbard as the Norwegians. A number of nations tried their hand at mining the coal in Spitsbergen, but only the Norwegians and Russians have made it a permanent enterprise. In fact, of the 3,500 inhabitants of the territory, which is approximately the same size as Ireland, about 70 per cent are Russian, 30 per cent Norwegian.

Spitsbergen is only seven hundred miles from the North Pole. Tourist boats make a few trips to the islands in the summer when the Gulf Stream melts a passageway through the ice. Since 1965 visitors have been able to stay at the 'world's northernmost tourist hotel' at New Ålesund. They experience the odd sensation of living in a place where there is nothing but daylight for four months. At the same time, the coal miners go skiing and marvel at the strange flowers which seem to spring out of cold storage. Then in August the sun begins its somber retreat. By November Spitsbergen is once again locked in ice and entombed by darkness.

The Lapps

On the northern Norwegian mainland, the only people who seem thoroughly accustomed to the odd pattern of the midnight sun and the noontime moon are the Lapps, but they have been roaming the glacial wilderness ever since the end of the Ice Age. Today, like the American Indians and the Canadian Eskimos, they are outnumbered in their own land, but they continue to wander freely over a thousand-mile-long wilderness at the top of Europe. Most of them, about 22,000, live in northern Norway, but there are about 10,000 in Sweden, 2,500 in Finland, and 2,000 in Russia. In other words, there are only about 36,500 Lapps left in the world—hardly enough to fill the seats at a big-college football-game—but they have nonetheless managed to preserve their separate racial and linguistic identity.

No one is certain where the Lapps originally came from. Very likely they once lived below the sheet of ice covering Scandinavia, perhaps in Russia or central Europe. They were first mentioned in historical accounts in 98 A.D., when the Roman historian Tacitus wrote of the rumors that north of the wild Germanic tribes there were an even wilder people, the 'Fenni.' The language of the Lapps (or the Same people, as they prefer to call themselves) belongs to the Finno-Ugric linguistic family, which puts them in company with the Finns, Estonians, Hungarians and a few others who once came out of the heart of Russia. But because the Lapps and the Finns are so different in appearance it is believed there was an earlier Lapp language which was blotted out by too close association with the Finns. Most of the Lapps (or Sames) are short, slender, dark-haired, brown-eyed, and sometimes almost gnomish in appearance. About a third of them, however, because of mixing with the Scandinavians, are tall, blond and blue-eyed. The most stunning blonde I have ever seen was a Lapp girl in northern Finland. She was resplendent in a colorful costume of blue and red, and she was surrounded by bowlegged little Lapp men who barely came up to her chin.

The life of many of the Lapps still revolves around the reindeer, an animal of wondrous ability to provide food, clothing and shelter. An eighteenth-century author wrote that the reindeer are 'the fields and meadows of the Lapp, his horses and his cows. They give him all that we have from land and sea, from India and the Levant.' Ask a Lapp how many reindeer he has and he will be insulted. It is the same as asking how much money he has. To their credit, the Norwegians, Swedes and Finns respect and protect the Lapps. Steps are taken to see that their old customs and nomadic rights are preserved. Lapp children go to special Lapp schools and are taught in Lappish as well as in a Scandinavian tongue. All the thoughtful attention, however, cannot alter the fact that the Lapps are having to give way to 'progress,' and that their ancient way of life is all but finished. In the old days, as Swedish writer Elly Jannes has observed, the Lapps were encroached upon by everyone from the Vikings to county governors who compelled them to transport iron ore with their reindeer. Yet, in spite of it all, Lapp culture survived in the roadless wilds.

The Lapps merely retreated higher and higher in the mountain areas. Now there is nowhere they can flee. Railways and roads spread across their nomad routes. Mining towns, stations with built-up communities and power stations spring up where once the reindeer herds grazed in peace. The new age has arrived, so solidly and so abruptly that the individual easily becomes swept aside.

The Lapps now have modern conveniences, but reindeer herding is not enough to pay for them. The men take jobs in the mines or on construction gangs. Families settle in towns. If they wear the same clothing as the Scandinavians they become lost in the crowd. If they wear their traditional costumes with oddly peaked hats they give encouragement to travel agents promoting tours of Lapland. Inevitably, the Lapps have become characters in a living museum. One of the saddest of all stories in modern Europe is that a resourceful people who challenged the worst that nature could offer above the Arctic Circle must now be fated to live as tourist attractions.

Hammerfest and Kirkenes

I drove into Hammerfest in a howling blizzard, grateful for its warmth and bright lights after a day of fearful driving in icy mountain passes. Hammerfest lies just below the North Cape, the top knob of Europe. Its ice-free harbor has kept it busy trading with both northern Russia and Western Europe ever since the Viking Age. It has officially been a township since 1789 and its citizens are quick to say that around 1889 it became the first town in the world with street lighting. Some clever citizen had returned from the Paris Exposition with an Edison generator and set it to work. No town anywhere has a greater need of day-and-night lighting. The sun disappears completely from mid-November to mid-January and there is little natural light for several more months.

Hammerfest has always led a perilous life. It lies at the foot of a mountain which sends down an avalanche every so often. In 1809, during the Napoleonic Wars, it was shelled by the British, a distinction which put it in the same league as Copenhagen. It endured repeated fires and then was utterly destroyed—except for the mortuary chapel—by the Germans in 1944. One leading citizen mentioned offhandedly that his home had been bombed by the Russians in 1943, burned by the Germans in 1944, and smashed to bits by an avalanche in 1950. The repeated business of building anew has made Hammerfest a thoroughly modern-looking town with a lively main street of new shops and office buildings. The old seal-catching port has a population of 7,000 now, double the prewar size, and it lives mainly by processing fish by the most up-to-date techniques. Its fleet of trawlers operates throughout the year. In many respects it is a one-industry town, since half the work force is employed by the Findus fish plant, which prepares frozen fillets for supermarkets all over Europe. Interestingly enough, Findus is 80 per cent owned by the Nestlé's chocolate company of Switzerland.

Thanks mainly to the regular service of the coastal steamers, Hammerfest residents can get almost everything they need from the south of Norway. The end of the line for the steamers, and for everything else that moves in Norway, is at Kirkenes, the remote mining town which nuzzles against the Russian border. At first glance, Kirkenes might seem to be yet another well-built community where life centers on a single big industry—this time the Syd-Varanger iron-ore company, 62 per cent government-owned. The mines and the ore-concentrating plant rule the life of the town as surely as do the Swedish ore-loading works in Narvik, but Kirkenes leads another, more shadowy life. I first became aware of it when I read the 'Proclamation' which was posted in the hotels and other public places. It was addressed to 'all who travel or sojourn in the districts bordering on the Norwegian-Soviet frontier.' The message, 'by Royal decree,' was to the effect that no one should cross the frontier without permission, or fire a gun at Russia, or photograph Soviet territory, or talk to anyone on the other side of the border, or 'show offensive behavior on the border directed against the Soviet Union or its authorities.'

The residents of Kirkenes and a number of imported slave-laborers were forced to work the iron mines for Germany during the occupation. Kirkenes was also the supply center for Germany's defense of its northern acquisitions. There were only 7,000 Norwegians in the area and 70,000 German troops. As a consequence, Kirkenes became one of the most bombed cities in Europe. There were 1,012 air alarms and 328 air attacks by the Russians and other Allies. During the Battle of Kirkenes before the German retreat some 3,500 people hid and starved for three weeks in the railway tunnels. The Germans had destroyed what was left of the town before retreating. The Russians swept into northern Norway as liberators, behaved well and left, but the cordial relationship did not result in a friendly, open border which citizens of both countries could easily cross. The Russians strengthened their frontier posts and only rarely would permit anyone to enter the U.S.S.R. Until the recent installation of a telephone link the border commanders could only signal each other by raising flags. Suddenly in 1965 the Russians announced that the nearby area was open to visits from Scandinavians only. It was soon apparent, however, that the Russians were mainly interested in selling vodka to the Norwegians who swarmed over from Kirkenes and the other towns of a vast 'dry' area where no liquor stores exist. Norway was then obliged to impose its own restrictions on border crossings.

Oslo

Few foreigners get as far north as Kirkenes, but the visitors to Oslo each year outnumber the natives. The city likes to call itself the oldest capital in Scandinavia. It was founded by a Viking king and celebrated its nine-hundredth birthday in 1950. Nonetheless, Oslo has the look and feel of the youngest and rawest of the major cities of the North, a circumstance which gives it a more purely Nordic character than Continental Copenhagen, 'Americanized' Stockholm or Eastern-influenced Helsinki. For all its long history, it is like a gangling youth who has grown up overnight and feels more at ease on mountain trails than on traffic-clogged city streets. The way its citizens pour out of town en masse on weekends to rough it in the countryside suggests that they are still unconverted to urban life.

Oslo was a fair-sized city in its ancient days, but it fell on hard times when the Black Death wiped out a great part of its population and the worst of its many fires almost completely destroyed it. Rebuilt by Christian IV of Denmark and renamed Christiania (which remained until Norwegian nationalists succeeded in bringing back the old name in 1925), the city had a population of only 7,500 at the time of the first census in 1796. Its population is now close to 500,000. The city also expanded its boundaries so ravenously that Oslo today, with 175 square miles of territory, is geographically the world's fifth-largest city. Four fifths of its area is taken up with hills, forests, farms, lakes and rivers. Oslo is the nation's governmental, commercial, cultural and educational center, and its factories and shipyards make it Norway's greatest industrial concentration. Even so, it takes an effort to locate the industry while it needs only a glance to see the panorama of pine-clad hills which envelop the city on three sides and the blue expanse of the Oslofjord which washes the capital's front steps and reaches out sixty miles to the sea.

In Oslo's full summertime bloom the fjord is delightfully alive with tourist boats, private sailboats gliding by the freighters and tankers, and hydrofoil water buses which run a commuting service to hamlets down the coast. During one August visit to Oslo I stood with my family on the deck of the American nuclear ship *Savannah*, 'the vessel of the future,' and watched a vessel from the past sailing across the fjord. It was an exact replica of the thousand-year-old Viking ships, three of which can be seen in one of the ship museums on Oslo's Bygdøy peninsula.

There is little else in Oslo that is particularly old. The only medieval building of consequence is the Akershus Fortress, which sits broodingly at the city's front door. Almost all the wooden buildings of old Oslo were destroyed in the repeated fires. There has been a burst of new construction in the last decade. The city is full of clean-cut new buildings with bright glass faces, but none of the architecture is as distinguished as the best of the new structures in Helsinki, Stockholm and Copenhagen. One of Oslo's more original buildings was designed by the late Finnish-American architect, Eero Saarinen. It is the American Embassy, a triangular structure made to fit a triangular site, with triangular corner offices and odd shapes everywhere. Even the elevators are not quite square.

When the Norwegians build, or make statues or murals, they are inclined to do it on a grand scale—insofar as their limited resources will permit. One of their newest tall buildings houses the largest Design Center in Scandinavia, even though Norwegian design ranks well behind that of the other Nordic countries. The most noticeable building in the city is the Town Hall, which stands resolutely at the rim of the harbor with its back to the downtown business district. Whereas the Stockholm Town Hall is a work of Renaissance splendor, the Oslo version is a far more functional creation in dark-red brick on reinforced concrete, with a massive central block and two severely squared-off towers. Although some people dismiss it as a warehouse trimmed with sculpture, at least it has a strong silhouette and it is filled with paintings and frescoes, including what a Norwegian guidebook insists is 'the world's largest monumental painting, 85 by 43 feet.'

Gustav Vigeland

One of the most amazing civic sponsorships of an artist in all history was Oslo's support of the sculptor Adolf Gustav Vigeland (1869–1943), a man who apparently had formidable powers of persuasion and doggedness of purpose. The city supported Vigeland and his assistants at high cost during the several decades that he labored on a grandiose sculpture park, which covers over a hundred acres of city property at Frogner Park. It is a disturbing place. There are fifty sculptural groups of 1,600 'erotic-primitive' figures. Norway's 'Neanderthal Rodin' froze mankind into grotesque postures of birth, love, life, strife and incipient death. The whole of existence is shown from embryo to old age in columns of figures, collections of bodies, explosions of forms, and a 50-foot monolith of 121 naked creatures struggling to reach the light. The babies are built like little barrels, the men are as bull-necked as Prussian wrestlers, and the thick-limbed women are formidable maternal figures.

Some visitors find the world of Vigeland inspiring, others leave in disgust, but no one is able to remain indifferent to the collection, if only because it is such a prodigious feat by one single-minded sculptor. Norwegians themselves are sharply divided about its merits. The descriptions in their tourist guides sound almost apologetic as they warn visitors that the sculptures are not to everyone's taste. Vigeland didn't believe in fig leaves. It is said that the late Dr. Alfred Kinsey made a special trip to Oslo, not to see the nude statues but to see the people who had paid for them with their taxes. Evelyn Waugh wondered what hope there was for the people who made it. He saw it as a 'multitudinous sub-human zoo . . . the most depressing spectacle it is possible to encounter; something far more awful than the ruins of Hiro-shima.' Such reactions are understandable, but it needs to be said as well that to the Norwegians the place is not all that forbidding. A typical Sunday afternoon scene has swarms of radiant children and their neatly dressed parents happily strolling and playing in the midst of the muscular granite.

Edvard Munch

The reactions to Frogner Park may be mixed, to say the least, but it is hard to do anything but lavish praise on the trim white jewel of a museum which opened in 1963 to display the works of Edvard Munch (1863-1944), Norway's—and Scandinavia's—greatest painter. It is easily one of the world's greatest museums devoted solely to the lifetime output of a single artist. Munch was to painting what his friend and fellow Scandinavian August Strindberg was to writing: an anguished man feverishly searching for some meaning to life. Though pursued by demons, he was capable of setting down his obsessions for the world to see. He wrote that 'the black angels of disease and insanity were on guard at my cradle . . . I always felt that I was treated unjustly, without a mother, sick and threatened with punishment in hell.' He named some of his best-known creations 'The Shriek,' 'Anxiety,' 'Jeal-ousy,' 'Melancholy,' 'The Sick Child' and 'Death at the Helm.' They have unnerving undulating lines and are full of hollow-eyed children and the living dead. But at times in his life he found joy and could produce, as one critic said, 'a grand tribute to healthy, vigorous humanity.' Such lively works can be found in paintings and murals all over Oslo.

Munch's mother and elder sister died of tuberculosis. His father 'was a severe disciplinarian obsessed by the anxieties of a Protestant religion,' according to one biographer. Munch spent his formative years abroad, mostly in Berlin and Paris, where he added mastery of lithography and wood carving to his abilities as a painter. After a breakdown in 1908 and successful treatment at a sanatorium, he returned to Norway and spent the remaining thirty years of his life at home as a prolific artist who hated to part with his creations. This was fortunate for Oslo, because he bequeathed them to the city, and they number over 1,000 paintings, 15,000 prints, 4,500 drawings and watercolors, and six sculptures—in short, a remarkably complete and varied collection.

Simple Pleasures

Oslo's critics say that 'if you have nothing to do, Oslo is a wonderful place to do it in.' It is not a flashy city, and the entertainment is quietly respectable. There are no real night clubs except for a few summer spots to attract tourists. It is a major port and very much a sailor's town, but there is only the vaguest kind of honky-tonk atmosphere. Visitors are warned by the International Press Club's guide not to 'fraternize with the young stuff' drifting around behind the City Hall and on a stretch of Karl Johansgate. In common with the other Scandinavian capitals, Oslo has begun to fret about the sex life of its youngsters. 'They are starting too soon, and they are damned careless about it,' said one journalist. The press has reported the activities of restless kids looking for kicks, and a racy novel by Axel Jensen chronicles the *dolce vita* of Oslo youth in the wealthier residential districts.

The main impression is of a city which is more a hometown than a metropolis. The main street, Karl Johansgate, is surrounded by the palace, the parliament building, the National Theater, the old buildings of Oslo University, and the main hotels, shops and restaurants. It is more of a park than a street, and in good weather it teems with Norwegians buying hot dogs, eating ice-cream, basking in the sun, and listening to band music. A few of the restaurants are first class by any standards, but Norwegians like to complain about the service. It is said that a customer entered a leading restaurant one day in late December and greeted a waitress with a cheerful, 'Merry Christmas!' She snapped back, 'That isn't my table.'

Oslo is known for its pioneering work in municipal social welfare. An official account says that 'the wide-awake eyes of the Municipality follow the citizens from the cradle to the grave.' This sounds almost as if the city's welfarism is being carried to Big Brother lengths but there is no denying that its citizens, like almost all Norwegians, have a particular glow of ruddy good health. It was in Oslo where I was told the story of the two Danes at Copenhagen airport who were amusing themselves by trying to guess the nationalities of the airline passengers. Puzzled about one man, they stopped him and asked, 'Are you a Swede?' He smiled and answered, 'No, I'm a Norwegian, but I've been sick.'

Chapter 14

THE LONG AWAKENING

From the wrath of the Northmen, O Lord, deliver us.
— ANCIENT FRENCH PRAYER

In the beginning there was the ice. For tens of thousands of years it covered Norway and the rest of northern Europe like the icing on a cake. When it finally retreated, in the last of three glacial periods, it was at a speed of 400 yards a year. After six thousand years Scandinavia was free of ice and inhabited by man.

The experts say that Norway has been populated for about fourteen thousand years and governed for one thousand. What is so fetching about the country today, for all its modern ways, is that it has not been civilized out of all recognition. Most of it looks as it must have looked many millenniums ago, and it is possible to find in the reindeer-oriented life of Norway's Lapps some suggestion of the Norwegian scene in the days of scattered tribes of hunters and fishermen. The original Norwegians seem to have come from central and western Europe by way of Denmark, Sweden and Russia. The earliest runic inscriptions, from the third century A.D., are in an archaic Germanic language which was the root of the Scandinavian dialects. At some point in the eighth century the Norsemen began the small pirate raids on the Europeans to the south, which gradually became large-scale plundering assaults on monasteries and towns, and finally elaborately organized expeditions of conquerors who became colonizers. There were the Vikings—Norwegians plus Danes and Swedes— and their thrust for more than two centuries, from about 800 to

216

1030 A.D., took them as far afield as Arabia and America. While the Swedes were swarming through western Russia the Danes and Norwegians were commanding great portions of France, England and Ireland. The Spaniards used the Arabic term *Madjus* to describe the Vikings as 'heathen wizards.'

Considering that Scandinavia today is the least-populated part of Europe, it is noteworthy that authorities on the Vikings have often given Nordic overpopulation as one of the main reasons for the eruption of the Vikings. The custom of polygamy and the pride of northern men in fathering as many sons as they could from their various wives and concubines undoubtedly produced a splendid birth rate. European reports of a thousand years ago, according to Danish historian Johannes Brøndsted, speak of the 'enormous size of the Viking armies; like storm clouds, swarms of grasshoppers, waves of the ocean, and so on.' In his view, however, the major cause of the Viking raids was the expansion of European commerce and the development of new trade routes, which made piracy attractive, rewarding and inevitable for a people who lacked the luxuries of wealthier and more fortunate lands. Adam of Bremen, a European historian of the eleventh century, wrote of the Norwegians: 'Forced by the poverty of their homeland, they venture far into the world to bring back from their raids the goods which other countries so plentifully produce.' There was something else not to be overlooked, wrote Brøndsted in *The Vikings*: the Viking way of life.

I am thinking here of their disposition as we know it to have been: proud, adventurous, with a yearning for glory, a desire to excel in battle, and a scorn for death. These qualities of heroism and virility, combined with their mercantile skills, made them a powerful and dangerous race. Early monastic historians, in their records of the Vikings, emphasized the cunning, cruelty, and treachery of this warlike people. The sagas, on the other hand, show them in a different light; telling of the boldness, generosity, frankness, and self-discipline of these famous warriors. No doubt in the aggregate they possessed all the qualities, complimentary and otherwise, which were ascribed to them: the Vikings were not all alike. But one thing they did have in common: a daring resoluteness that made their period the greatest in the history of the North.

The Discovery of America

Although plunder was the original purpose of the Viking expeditions, the Norsemen turned to the more ennobling task of striking out to remote territories across the Atlantic to establish new settlements. Iceland was the most important one. Its ancient sagas not only describe the early history of the island but tell of the Norsemen who sailed to 'Vinland the Good,' a bountiful grassland on the North American coast. According to the sagas, it was Bjarni Herjolfsson and his companions who were the first Vikings—and the first Europeans—to sight the American continent. They had sailed from Iceland for Greenland in 986 but lost their way and three times sighted land well to the west of Greenland. It was left to Leif Eriksson, however, to make the actual landing and exploration.

Described as 'big and strong, of striking appearance, shrewd, and in every respect a temperate, fair-dealing man,' Leif bought Bjarni's ship and, about the year 1000, led a thirty-five-man expedition west from Greenland to seek out the territory which Bjarni had sighted. He arrived first at a glacial island and then moved southward along the North American coast. After looking over wooded flatlands which he called *Markland* ('Forestland'), he landed at an idyllic place which offered salmon, timber and fine grazing grounds. The sagas say that Leif and his fellow Vikings built large houses and stayed a year before returning to Greenland. Leif Eriksson's brother Thorvald, later slain in a battle with Indians, was one of several other Vikings who led subsequent expeditions to Vinland. One group of 160 men and women arrived in three ships and stayed for three years until they withdrew because of constant clashes with the Indians.

The authors of the sagas were obviously in no doubt about who had discovered America; but, while dealing with real people and real events, they were inclined to romanticize and embroider. The hard evidence of Viking settlements in America was finally unearthed in 1963 and 1964 by a Norwegian couple, Dr. Helge Ingstad and his wife, Anne Stine Ingstad, at L'Anse aux Meadows, at the tip of the island of Newfoundland, a place which may well have been Leif Eriksson's Vinland. The gentler climate on the Canadian coast in Viking days might have permitted grapes to grow there. The Ingstads had spent a decade searching for Viking remains and at last found them: the layered turf foundations of nine ancient structures, one of them a house 70 by 55 feet, and a Viking Age soapstone spindle whorl which the *National Geographic* has described as 'the earliest-known household artifact yet found in North America.' Radiocarbon dating of the ruins established their age at a thousand years.

The discovery inspired the United States Congress in 1964 to pass a joint resolution honoring the Viking explorers and naming October 9 as Leif Eriksson Day. In the words of Hubert Humphrey, it was a 'long-overdue recognition of this courageous Norseman who first explored the North American continent.'

And then, just one year later, came the announcement from scholars at Yale University that they had established the authenticity of a map, probably drawn by a monk in Basel in 1440, half a century before Columbus sailed to the New World, which identified the Vikings as the discoverers of America. A British Museum authority described the simple line map in faded brownish ink as 'a document of crucial importance on one of the greatest events in world history.' The map and its inscriptions indicate that as early as the twelfth century the rest of Europe knew about the Viking discoveries. It depicts the North American coast as a huge island (complete with Hudson Bay and the Gulf of St. Lawrence) to the southwest of Greenland and its Latin caption states:

By God's will, after a long voyage from the island of Greenland to the south, toward the most distant remaining parts of the Western Ocean Sea, sailing southward amid the ice, the companions Bjarni and Leif Eriksson discovered a new land, extremely fertile, and even having vines, the which island they named Vinland. Erik, legate of the Apostolic See and Bishop of

Greenland and the neighboring regions, arrived in this truly vast and very rich land, in the name of Almighty God, in the last year [1117–1118] of our most blessed father Pascal [Pope Paschal II], remained a long time in both summer and winter, and later returned north eastward toward Greenland, and then proceeded in most humble obedience to the will of his superiors.

The Yale announcement and the publication of a book setting down the history of the map and the eight years of scholarly detective work needed to authenticate it, dramatically revived the old controversy about who should be credited with the discovery of America. The Italians insist on Columbus; the Irish say that they were there first; and claims are made, of course, for the forebears of the American Indian, the Asians who reached North America via the Bering Strait more than 15,000 years before the Europeans. What is inescapable, however, is that the Vikings in their remarkable ships conquered the ocean a thousand years ago and were sailing repeatedly between and around Iceland and Greenland. It needs only a glance at the map to show how easily they could have sailed on to the coasts of North America.

The Dark Centuries

In Norway, it was Harald the Fair-haired who was the first to establish himself, beginning in 872, as the ruler of the entire country. He began a royal succession which included such vivid names as Erik I Bloody Axe, Harald II Gray Fur and Magnus IV the Blind. The Norwegian empire grew in the Viking centuries with the acquisition of the Faroe Islands, the Shetlands, the Orkneys, the Hebrides, and, of course, Iceland and Greenland. Christianity became a powerful influence in Norwegian life, especially after the death of King Olav Haraldsson in 1030, a monarch who came to be a national saint and was enshrined in a new church in Trondheim. This church preceded the erection of the great thirteenth-century cathedral which now dominates the weathered old port. Medieval Norway developed as a more mature European state under Haakon IV (1217–63) and his son

Magnus the Lawmender; but the beginning of the end for independent Norway came when the country became dependent for its grain imports on the Hanseatic merchants who gradually took over control of Norwegian trade. And then in the middle of the fourteenth century the great plague known as the Black Death struck Norway and killed off half its population of 350,000. Norway was already the weakest and most vulnerable of the northern nations but now the plague wiped out 240 of its 300 noble families.

Almost by default, Norway gradually passed under Danish control, first as a member of the Union of Kalmar under Queen Margrete of Denmark in the 1380s. The Hanseatic merchants became a state within a state in Norway, and Norwegian national feeling was almost extinguished after 1536 with the introduction of the Reformation. Norway was no longer a separate realm, but merely a part of Denmark; and so it remained for almost three centuries until 1814. Danish became the official, ecclesiastical and school language, and Danes swarmed into Norway to exploit its resources. The national economy grew on fishing, shipbuilding, sawmills and the mining industry. Although most Danish monarchs were bored by the affairs of their Norwegian colony, the imaginative Christian IV took a special interest. He revitalized Norway's public life and ordered a new city, Christiania, to be built after a fire in 1624 almost completely destroyed Oslo.

Later in the seventeenth century, Norway began to develop the merchant marine which became one of the largest in the world. National pride began to grow at the same time, but only a few faint signs of revolutionary ambitions could be seen when Norway, as an appendage of Denmark, found itself involved on France's side in the Napoleonic Wars. Denmark and Norway were subjected to a ruinous blockade by British ships. Sweden, on the other hand, was allied to Britain; but it suffered a humiliating defeat when it lost Finland to the Russians. By way of compensation, Sweden demanded Norway as its reward for taking part in the coalition to crush Napoleon. In the Peace of Kiel of January 1814 the Danish king was forced to cede Norway to Sweden, but he was able to keep Iceland, Greenland and the Faroes.

Struggle for Independence

The infuriated Norwegians refused to submit supinely to Swedish domination. Christian Frederik, the heir to the Danish–Norwegian throne, was serving as viceroy in Norway at the time of the decision to give Norway to Sweden. He still aspired to be King of Norway despite the Kiel agreement, and his ambitions coincided with the plans of Norwegian patriots to declare Norway independent of foreign rule. They persuaded him to recognize the sovereignty of the Norwegian people and to summon a constituent assembly, which was held at Eidsvoll, forty miles north of Oslo, in April 1814. The delegates had been elected by citizens who gathered in their churches to vote and to swear to defend the country. The historic meeting in a wealthy factory owner's mansion lasted five weeks and produced a constitution on May 17th, the date which Norwegians now celebrate as their national day even though complete freedom was not achieved until 1905. On that day, which also saw the unanimous election of Christian Frederik as king, Norway was, by its own will, free and independent. It now had a constitution, a parliament (the *Storting*) and a king.

The Swedes objected to these revolutionary moves and fought the Norwegians in an eighteen-day war, which ended with a peace treaty that was a compromise for both sides. The Eidsvoll Constitution remained in force, but Christian Frederik had to abdicate and the Swedish king was recognized as the ruler of the union of Sweden and Norway.

The Norwegians felt free and acted free, even if their king sat in Stockholm; but they became increasingly resentful of the fact that the conduct of foreign affairs was kept in the hands of the Swedes. There were other aggravations, particularly the efforts of the Swedish kings to amend what was then the most democratic constitution in Europe and to extend the royal authority. Over decades the Norwegians became more nationalistic, and more insistent on more power for the parliament in Oslo. The friction and bad feeling came to a climax at the turn of the century, when the Norwegians demanded the right to maintain their own consular service in foreign countries. It was an understandable desire, since Norwegian shipping interests were considerably greater than Sweden's. Finally the Storting in May 1905 passed an act establishing such a service. When King Oscar II vetoed the bill, the Norwegian cabinet under Christian Michelsen resigned. The King was unable to find another party leader willing to put together a cabinet. The Storting then took the decisive step of declaring the Swedish–Norwegian union dissolved.

It was a declaration of independence which could have inspired the militarily stronger and numerically superior Swedes to go to war to restore the union. Tempers were high in Sweden and a minority called for war, but by now the Scandinavians had become too accustomed to peaceful ways to want to return to the internecine slaughters of the old days. (In fact, it was only four years earlier when the Norwegian parliament first took up the work of selecting the recipients of the Nobel Peace Prize, a task assigned to it by Swedish industrialist Alfred Nobel in his will.) The Swedish parliament said it would agree to dissolution of the union if a plebiscite in Norway showed that the people favored it. They did, by a lopsided count of 368,208 to 184.

The New Norway

After a conference to work out the problems of separation, Oscar II abdicated as King of Norway. It is hardly surprising that at this point there were strong currents favoring the establishment of a republic in Norway along American or French lines. Norway had already abolished its titles of nobility, installed universal suffrage for men, and given women a limited right to vote (full suffrage came in 1913). The Norwegian Labor Party had been founded in 1887 and was beginning to challenge the Liberal and Conservative parties, which were themselves more democratically inclined than their Swedish counterparts. Even so, most sentiment still favored having a king for Norway. When the Swedes coldly refused the overtures suggesting a Bernadotte prince for the Norwegian throne, Prince Carl of Denmark was offered the job. He would agree to take it only if a plebiscite decisively proved that the Norwegian people wanted him. When he received three quarters of the vote, Prince Carl took the throne as Haakon VII and began the first Norwegian royal house in six hundred years.

The Norwegians chose well. The Danish prince was only thirty-three when he became king. He was eighty-five when he died in 1957 as the world's oldest and longest reigning monarch. No Norwegian king had ever been on the throne so long. He lived two decades longer than his wife, Queen Maud, who died in 1938. After World War I, during which Norway remained neutral but lost half its merchant fleet to German U-boats, agitation for abolishing the monarchy rose with the increase in power of the Labor Party, despite Haakon's cautious exercise of what few real powers he had under the constitution.

Haakon was not then a notably popular king; he was much too reserved, and his language and cultural interests were too patently Danish to transform him easily into a Norwegian. But he knew how to overcome the deep-seated socialist antagonism to the monarchy. 'As late as the 1930s,' wrote *The Times* of London, 'it was the party line that Labor members of the Storting should refuse invitations to dine at the royal palace at the opening of the parliamentary sessions. King Haakon refused to be offended. When the Labor burgomaster of Oslo did not invite him as king to the laying of the foundation stone of the new Town Hall, he asked if he might attend as a subscriber to the building fund.' In 1928 the King had surprised the socialists (and almost everyone else) by asking them to form a government for the first time instead of attempting to return the Conservatives to power after they had lost a vote of confidence. The Labor government lasted only two weeks, however, because the alarmed right-wing forces, after having been told by the governor of the Bank of Norway that capital was starting to leave the country, organized to unseat the socialists. Labor did not win the government again until 1935. The King's action muted the demands for a republic, and his courageous role in World War II made him such a national hero that the subject was seldom heard again during his lifetime.

Largely because of the intensity of the antagonism between the owners and workers of Norwegian industry, Norway developed a much more revolutionary Labor Party than Denmark or Sweden. Beginning in 1927, Labor became the strongest single party in the Storting. When it finally came to power it pursued a pacifist foreign policy. Although the defense budget was increased, the government refused to keep the Norwegian armed forces at anything like the strength demanded by those who feared that Norway would be brought into the approaching war against its will.

World War II

Norway, along with its Scandinavian neighbors, declared its neutrality in 1939 when the war began, but Norway was too important to both the Allies and the Germans to be able to sit it out. Britain and France were the first to put pressure on Norway. They requested, but were refused, permission to cross Norwegian territory in order to help the Finns when they were fighting off the Russians in the Winter War. (One unspoken Anglo–French objective, however, was to gain access to Swedish territory to prevent the treasury of iron ore from falling into Hitler's hands.) Early in 1940 the British Navy entered Norwegian territorial waters to rescue Allied prisoners from the German vessel *Altmark*, which was hiding in a fjord. And then the Allies announced their intention to mine those same waters to try to stop the transit of merchant vessels which were bringing Swedish iron ore down from Narvik to feed the German war machine. To make sure that he continued to get the ore, and to make use of Norwegian territory, Hitler invaded Norway on April 9, 1940.

Although Denmark, attacked the same day, succumbed almost immediately, Norway proved to be a tougher nut to crack, despite its appalling unpreparedness. As in Denmark, the high authorities had refused to take seriously urgent warnings from sources in Germany only days before the invasion. The army was still unmobilized and the waters at the approaches to the principal cities still unmined when the attack came. In a series of lightning moves the Germans seized almost all the Norwegian airports and every important city in the south and west, from Kristiansand to

Narvik. They would have reached Oslo on schedule if a small force at the old fortress of Oskarsborg at a narrow passageway in the Oslofjord had not opened fire on the 10,000-ton German cruiser *Blücher* and sunk it. The Germans lost nearly two thousand men n that quick, magnificent action, including a key Gestapo force and the administrators who had been assigned to organize occupied Norway. The several hours' delay before the German fleet could reach Oslo enabled King Haakon, Crown Prince Olav, the government and almost all members of the Storting (plus twenty-three truckloads of gold and secret papers) to make their getaway.

The parliament assembled in the countryside and authorized the government to act for the nation until it could meet again. Thus was set the legal basis for a government-in-exile, if things should come to that. It was in a village near the town of Elverum, close to the Swedish border, where the Norwegian government made its decision to refuse the German demands to surrender and to call on Norwegians to resist even though the Germans now controlled the key cities and facilities of the nation. King Haakon, a tall, spare, flinty man, gave inspiration to his ministers at that meeting of the Council of State with an eloquent statement which said that he would understand why the government in the perilous circumstances might feel it prudent to accept the German demands for capitulation, but that if it did so he would be obliged to abdicate. He could not, in good conscience, appoint the Norwegian fascist, Vidkun Quisling, prime minister as the Germans demanded. The Germans tried to bomb King Haakon and the government when they continued to reject all demands for capitulation. They were pursued as they fled through the valleys and up the Romsdalsfjord to the port of Molde. The Luftwaffe bombed the town, but the Norwegian leaders were spared and boarded a British cruiser the same night to sail north to Tromsø, to set up a provisional capital on May first.

The fighting in Norway and along its ragged coast during the next month broke the quiet of the 'Phony War' and stopped Hitler's advance for the first time since he began his lightning conquests of European territory. The Norwegians still held the northern third of Norway. After several classic naval engagements between British and German ships, a combination of British, French, Polish and Norwegian units recaptured Narvik, the crucially important iron-ore port, which a Norwegian commander, under threat of naval bombardment, had surrendered to the Germans during the first days of the invasion. Not only were the Norwegians fighting back like Vikings, but in the occupied portions of Norway people were refusing to cooperate with their new leaders. Quisling, who had proclaimed himself as the new prime minister on the very afternoon of the invasion, had proved to be so unpopular that the Germans told him to resign just a week later. It was not until some months later that the occupiers set him up again as the head of a one-party 'National Unity' state.

Occupation and Resistance

The Germans finally conquered the whole of Norway, despite the heavy resistance which they were encountering, as a direct consequence of their invasion of France. The crucial situation in France and the Low Countries forced the Allies to withdraw the forces which they had sent to help the Norwegians. There was little choice for the King and the Norwegian ministers but to give up the struggle in Norway and retire to England, where they could establish a government-in-exile and prepare a Free Norwegian fighting force. They left on June 7, 1940, two months after the invasion. When King Haakon returned to Norway exactly five years later, on June 7, 1945, the delirious Norwegians greeted him as a fighting monarch who had saved the nation's honor. In the intervening years, Norway had mounted an astonishing war effort for a small-population country under occupation. The merchant marine of 25,000 men and more than a thousand ships, half of them sunk by the time the war ended, was worth a million soldiers to the Allies, according to an American admiral. Not only were the Free Norwegian army, navy and air force involved in direct combat with the Axis powers, but an underground army in Norway, supplied and directed from London, and numbering more than 40,000 men at the end of the war, served to tie up heavy German forces in Scandinavia and to sabotage vital industrial and military installations. Some of the classic actions of World War II involved Norwegians and other Allied special forces, who parachuted into Norway or paddled ashore from naval vessels and sabotaged such vital installations as the Glomfjord hydroelectric station and the plant at Rjukan which was producing heavy water for potential atomic-bomb use.

Altogether, Norway lost about 10,000 lives in the war, including some 4,000 merchant seamen and 2,000 Resistance fighters. These numbers, as Norwegians are the first to say, are small compared to the millions of Russians, Germans, Poles and others who were in the main path of the war, but they are significant for a nation of Norway's size which could excusably have taken the easy way out. Nearly 40,000 Norwegians were arrested and imprisoned, while 336 were executed by the Gestapo. Many of the most prominent men in Norway today, including Labor's postwar prime minister, Einar Gerhardsen, and ex-foreign minister Halvard Lange, were among the influential younger leaders who were hustled off to German concentration camps, where 1,400 Norwegians lost their lives. The entire Jewish population of Norway was forced to leave the country. Half of the Jews escaped to Sweden, while 760 were seized and deported to Germany, where almost all were killed; only twenty-two returned to Norway after the war. Thousands of Norwegian civil servants, teachers, judges, clergymen and others who refused to serve the occupiers were imprisoned or made to work in the mines in Kirkenes and elsewhere. Teacher and student resistance forced the closing of Oslo University, and thousands of Norwegian boys hid in the mountains and forests rather than be enrolled in the national labor service which the Germans tried to mobilize.

As in Denmark, the ordinary people of Norway conducted psychological warfare against their occupiers, using all means of making their distaste clear without necessarily giving cause for arrest. The Germans were treated like lepers. The Norwegians would refuse to sit next to them, and when they were obliged by regulations to do so on streetcars and buses they preferred to get off and walk. When the Germans ordered Norwegian men to stop wearing flowers in their lapels on patriotic occasions, particularly the birthday of their exiled King, the men started wearing paper clips instead. Professor James A. Storing wrote that this was 'certainly an interesting period for the student of national psychology, since most of the so-called Norwegian traits were dramatically exposed during the occupation years. Subtle obstructionism, dogged individualistic enterprise, stubborn resistance to the invasion of privacy, disregard for personal safety (sometimes manifested even today by motorcyclists in Norway), and a passionate love of country, both as a geographic and a spiritual entity, all came out in sharp relief. . . .'

Norwegian newspapers, when compelled to print German propaganda material, would use as many German words as possible to alert their readers. Underground newspapers began to appear, but indiscriminate sabotage activity or guerrilla warfare was discouraged in favor of a longer-range plan of building up a home force under the nose of the Germans. The 'Home Front Command,' which was headed (unbeknown to the Germans) by the president of the prewar Supreme Court, numbered about 47,000 men and would have gone into direct action against the Germans at the end of the war if the surrender had not come abruptly in Germany, leaving an undefeated army of some 350,000 in Norway to give itself up to the Norwegians and the Allied forces. Of the thirty Norwegian Nazis condemned to death for treason, Quisling and twenty-four others were executed. There were some five hundred persons sentenced to long prison sentences for collaboration, and many more for shorter terms, but by 1957 all had been released, including those sentenced for life.

The war years were hard for the Norwegians, and the nation's over-all conduct was glorious; but it is remarkable how little people have to say about their experiences unless they are directly asked. What remains sharply etched in memory is the occasion in the salon of a coastal steamer when Norwegian faces froze with rage when a hearty and prosperous German tourist said in all friendliness: 'Ah, what a wonderful country this is. I have such fine recollections of my first visit here. It was in 1940 . . .'

Norway's wartime experience obviously shattered the nation's old foreign policy, which put its faith in good will and neutrality instead of strong defenses and alliance with stronger powers. The nation had relied heavily on the League of Nations, an understandable position in view of the extraordinary role that Norwegians had played in the formation and functioning of the League. The work of Christian Lange, Fridtjof Nansen and C. J. Hambro set the pattern for Scandinavia's special contribution to international organizations. Christian Lange, father of Halvard Lange, was an outstanding Norwegian diplomat, Secretary of the Interparliamentary Union from 1909 to 1933, and a winner of the Nobel Peace Prize. While World War I was still under way he prepared a blueprint of a world organization which was influential in the planning of the League of Nations. Similarly, Fridtjof Nansen, before and after the formation of the League, was a tireless advocate of international machinery for the settlement of disputes between nations, and as High Commissioner of the League he was its outstanding humanitarian figure. C. J. Hambro, an important Norwegian author, editor, Conservative Party leader and Speaker of the Storting, was an influential voice at Geneva and served as president of the Assembly in the League's final years.

Fridtjof Nansen

It was Fridtjof Nansen in particular who played a heroic role as a practical idealist in the bitter decade after World War I. If this superlative man with his white walrus mustache, broad-brimmed hat and Viking bearing had come from America, Britain or any of the larger nations, he would be even more celebrated than he is as one of the greatest men of the past century. Like Winston Churchill, he had an appetite for life, enough talent and energy to supply a dozen men, and a stunning record of accomplishments. Both men were famous in their youth for great feats of daring, but while Churchill had his finest hours in time of war, Nansen shone as a peacemaker and humanitarian. In his lifetime (1861–1930) he was, among other things, a zoologist, polar explorer, oceanographer, author, artist, sportsman, diplomat, ambassador, international civil servant, and winner of the 1922 Nobel Prize for Peace for his incredible achievements in refugee and hunger-relief work. (In a sense, he won the Nobel award a second time, eight years after his death, when the peace prize for 1938 went to the Nansen International Office for Refugees, which the League had set up to carry on Nansen's work.)

In 1888, as a young scientist of twenty-seven, Nansen amazed the world by crossing Greenland on skis. Five years later he began an even more imaginative and hazardous adventure by leading the expedition of the *Fram* ('Forward'). The ship is now on permanent display in Oslo. By tracing the movement of Russian timber and the wreckage of ships across the top of the world, Nansen had become convinced that the ice of the Polar sea drifted from Siberia to Spitsbergen. He wondered whether this offered a different way to the North Pole since the efforts of explorers to reach the Pole over the ice had so far failed. 'If a solidly built boat is steered as far north as possible,' he wrote, 'and is allowed to be caught in the ice, and if it is left to the current, then it will follow exactly the same course as the drifting timber and will easily arrive at the other side of the earth by way of the North Pole or thereabouts.' Although other polar explorers criticized the plan, the Norwegian parliament voted to pay two thirds of the expenses of the proposed expedition, and King Oscar II led private subscribers in raising the rest of the money. The *Fram*, which was designed to be lifted up, instead of crushed, when it was trapped in the ice, sailed away from Christiania (Oslo) in June 1893 with Nansen and twelve associates. By September it was frozen in the ice north of Siberia. Just as Nansen had predicted, it drifted across the top of the world and emerged three years later above Spitsbergen. While eleven men stayed on the ship during this odd, slow-motion voyage, Nansen and a companion set off in March 1895 to spend an exhausting and often terrifying year traveling by skis, kayak and dog sledges on a mission which brought them closer to the North Pole than any explorers before them. (The Pole was finally reached in 1909 by Robert E. Peary.)

Nansen's years of scientific work were followed by a quarter

century of diplomatic activity, beginning with his efforts to build
world support behind Norway's secession in 1905 from its union
with Sweden. He served as Norway's ambassador to London, was
involved in the formation of the League of Nations, and for two
decades led the Norwegian delegations to the League meetings.
He organized the repatriation of some 450,000 former prisoners
of war of twenty-six nations after World War I. He arranged for
the settlement of a million and a half Russian political refugees
and hundreds of thousands of others. He devised an international
proof of identity for stateless persons which became known as the
'Nansen Passport.' He led the immense famine-relief operation
in Russia in 1921–23 which saved the lives of more than seven
million persons, six million of whom were children. And, at the
same time, he directed the greatest mass exchange of peoples in
history, when one and a quarter million Greeks were moved from
Turkish to Greek territory and half a million Turks were transported in the other direction in the aftermath of the Greco–
Turkish war.

Fridtjof Nansen set the style, so to speak, for daring feats of
exploration which have engaged such other Norwegians as Roald
Amundsen and Thor Heyerdahl, and for Scandinavian service in
international organizations, which saw Trygve Lie of Norway
and Dag Hammarskjöld of Sweden appointed as the first two
Secretary Generals of the United Nations.

Foreign Policy

The high idealism of Nansen and his Norwegian colleagues was
admirable but ultimately ineffective as the League of Nation's
impotence became only too apparent and Mussolini and Hitler
began to feed on their neighbors. When it became clear that major
countries like Britain and France were not seriously going to apply
sanctions against an aggressor like Fascist Italy, Norway felt
justified in backing away from sanctions itself, and took a neutralist posture. It continued to be such a fervent advocate of disarmament, however, that it reduced its own arms even when others
did not. Some Norwegian voices warned that Norway would

someday have to protect itself from a Nazi Germany so clearly bent on aggression, but the overwhelming sentiment of the ruling Labor Party was for a weakly armed neutrality to prove that it meant to be an innocent bystander if war should break out in Europe.

The lesson Norway learned when war did come was that big powers were not likely to respect a small nation's neutrality if it occupied a strategic geographic position and was involved in economic activities (shipping iron ore, for example) which affected the vital interests of the belligerents. As one of the victorious Allied powers of World War II, Norway was a founding member of the United Nations at San Francisco and for a short while was hopeful that this would turn out to be an international organization that kept the peace. Soviet engulfment of Eastern Europe, however, most particularly the Communist take-over of democratic Czechoslovakia in 1948, made all the Scandinavians uneasy, and the Danes, Swedes and Norwegians began to discuss the practicality of a Nordic defense union. Sweden insisted on a Scandinavian military block which would be neutral and have no connection with America and its Western allies, even though it was clear that Scandinavian sentiment in the Cold War was with the West. In the opinion of Denmark and Norway, it would not only be staggeringly expensive to undertake the arming of a Nordic union, but even the greatest efforts could not stop the Russians if they ever chose to take Scandinavia. As the discussions continued, the United States, which made it plain that it would not be willing to provide financial and military help to a neutral bloc, sought to persuade the Nordic countries to join the prospective North Atlantic Treaty Organization.

In the end, as already noted in Chapter 7, Sweden clung to its neutrality while Norway and Denmark joined NATO. The Norwegian Parliament's vote in March 1949 was a resounding 130 for NATO and 13 against (11 Communist votes, two Labor). Nonetheless, the deed was not done without misgivings which have persisted to this day. Initially, there was worry about how the Soviet Union would react. Moscow had aimed strong warnings at Norway not to take the provocative step of joining

NATO, and Norwegians were well aware that they shared a northern border with the Russians. They stuck to their determination to seek security within the Western alliance but partially placated Russia by stating that they would not station foreign troops on Norwegian soil or otherwise let Norway serve as a base for foreign powers.

Chapter 15

THE GOLDEN MEAN

Norwegians are not sure whether they're happy, but they do feel safe.

—BERGEN BUSINESSMAN

They tell the story in Scandinavia about the Dane who moved to Norway, went into business and after a time became well known as the country's biggest hotel owner. Then one day he was introduced to King Haakon, who said, 'I am proud to meet a Dane who has made out so well in Norway.' The hotel owner responded, 'And the same to you, your Majesty.'

It was King Haakon VII who started, in Norway, Europe's youngest royal house, but it has ancient antecedents as a branch of the House of Oldenborg (originally a North German princely family) which has occupied the Danish throne since 1448. Although Haakon was a Danish prince elected King of Norway, his son, who was Crown Prince for fifty-two years before succeeding his long-lived father, is regarded as a thoroughgoing Norwegian by his respectful subjects. King Olav V looks Norwegian, speaks Norwegian (something his father never quite mastered), and he has the vigorous outdoor interests that every Norwegian admires. He was born in England as the only son of the then Prince Carl of Denmark and Princess Maud of Great Britain. He was only two years old when he was taken to Norway, where his father became king. In keeping with the democratization of the Nordic monarchies, he was sent to an ordinary secondary school before attending Norway's Military College and going on to Balliol College, Oxford, to study international law and economics. As a Balliol man, he is one of a distinguished company of personalities, including former British Prime Minister Harold Macmillan, Arnold Toynbee, Julian and Aldous Huxley and Graham Greene. The husky, dashing Crown Prince excited the nation as a first-class yachtsman who won a gold medal in the 1928 Olympics in Amsterdam. He married Princess Märtha, of Sweden, and they had two daughters and a son. She died after the war, just three years before he succeeded to the throne.

In World War II, Olav helped direct Norway's last-ditch stand against the invading Germans. Later, as part of the exiled Norwegian leadership in London, he served as commander in chief of the Free Norwegian armed forces. As monarch since 1957, he has traveled to every corner of Norway and satisfied his watchful subjects as an earnest, working king who manages to be regal without being stuffy. He is a large, almost portly man with seafarer's eyes, strong facial lines and a swiftly receding hairline. The state provides him with $230,000 a year for royal salary and expenses. Although he occupies the big but not particularly impressive palace in the heart of Oslo, he has managed to spurn the ostentatious living which Norwegians would heartily resent. In my travels through Norway I have heard the King spoken of with respect, but not with particular reverence; in fact, a good many comments were highly irreverent, but then it is a rare Norwegian who wants to appear too enamored with royalty. They prefer to be thought of as republicans who choose to have a monarchy—tolerating it, so to speak—because it is useful, sentimental and colorful in a society where equality has been bought at the cost of diversity. 'Almost as much as the Swedes,' wrote *The Times* of London, 'the Norwegians view the monarchy soberly. A good king justifies the system, and the people are content to leave it at that.'

As a monarchy without a court, the royal family is an extremely small and exposed little island in Norwegian life. There is only the widower King, the two princesses who married commoners and Crown Prince Harald, born 1937, the sole person in the line of succession (it is only possible through the male line). If Harald should not have a son on his own, it would finish the dynasty, and Norwegians (judging by present attitudes) would probably choose to elect a president rather than search about for a prince from another royal house.

The Norwegian constitution concentrates the executive power of the nation on the King and the Council of State, or Cabinet. The Cabinet, which consists of the prime minister and seven or more other members who head the various government ministries, supposedly exists simply to advise the King about his decisions, but it works quite differently, of course. The Cabinet decides and the King agrees. Formal meetings are held on Friday mornings in the palace, with the monarch and Cabinet seated about a long table and taking up fifty or more matters which require decision. The Crown Prince is permitted to sit in on the session, but just to observe, and the King prudently confines himself to asking a few searching questions instead of trying to argue with the decisions. A modern monarch must be a master at demonstrating his great interest in the nation's affairs without letting his true feelings about controversial matters become public.

Labor Party

For thirty years, until 1965, the real power in Norway was held by the Labor Party. It was organized as long ago as 1887, but did not achieve important strength until the time of World War I; the Liberal Party had won many of the working-class votes by championing expanded suffrage. At the close of that war, Labor swung toward revolutionary policies of the kind which brought the Bolsheviks to power in Russia. In 1919 the party quit the old Socialist International at Amsterdam in favor of the Communist International which was being formed in Moscow. The more moderate members of the Labor Party, protesting its drift to the far left, walked out to set up a Social Democratic Party. And then, when the Labor Party began to balk at the obligations imposed by Comintern membership, its extremist elements went off to establish a Communist Party. These developments persuaded the Social Democrats to return to the Labor fold. The reunited party was able to capture the allegiance of the workers so thoroughly that by 1930 the Communist representation in the Storting was eliminated. The Communists enjoyed a brief revival immediately after World War II, but soon faded out again.

Labor, which has sought 'the Golden Mean' for Norway, ruled with the support of the Agrarian Party (now the Center Party) during its first decade of power but after that it enjoyed an absolute majority in the Storting—the only Scandinavian Labor or Social Democratic party to have that advantage. It was able to override the objections of the 'bourgeois' or 'nonsocialist' parties and push through a full-scale program of welfarism and economic planning. In the climate of change, however, the Liberals (or 'Radical Left') could be as avid as Labor for social reforms, and the Conservatives, Agrarians and members of the Christian People's Party were not so much obstructionist as they were more cautious and selective in their reforms. Although it was discouraging for the opposition parties to see Labor cleaning up in election after election, some signs of hope began to appear in the 1950s.

Labor had reached a peak of eighty-five seats in the 150-man Storting in 1949, but by 1961 the party was down to seventy-four, with two of its lost seats going to a newly formed Socialist People's Party, which was opposed to Norway's NATO membership and to a strong defense force. The new party argued the Communist viewpoint in the Cold War. It was able to claim the attention of those numerous Norwegians, notably students and intellectuals, who are strongly attracted to pacifism, despite Norway's World War II experiences. Their outlook on international affairs, judging by conversations I have had with a number of them, is both charmingly innocent and dangerously ignorant. There is nothing innocent, however, about the men who control the Socialist People's Party.

The slump of the Labor Party and the creation of the socialist splinter group led to a fascinating political situation. Labor had lost its majority and was evenly matched with the seventy-four-seat Center-Right opposition. The balance of power was therefore held by the two-seat People's Socialists. They voted with Labor and thus served to keep the Norwegian Left in power. The

Socialist People's Party leader, Finn Gustavsen, became a man of undeserved importance, because he could bring down the government almost at will. The stage was set for Norway's political melodrama of 1963. In the previous November the nation was shocked when twenty-one miners lost their lives in a gas explosion at the King's Bay coal mines in far-off Spitsbergen. It was the latest of a series of accidents in the state-owned mines since 1949, and there were scathing charges of negligence directed at the Labor government. When the government White Paper on the mine disasters was debated by parliament in August 1963, the whole country followed the arguments closely on radio and television. The climax came when the two People's Socialists lined up with the regular opposition parties in a vote of no-confidence in the Labor government.

Out went Prime Minister Einar Gerhardsen, who had ruled the Labor Party since the end of the war. Out went Halvard Lange, the fixture as foreign minister for seventeen years. Out went all the familiar faces who had been so long in power. A great many Norwegians found it difficult to realize that Labor was no longer running the country. The four center-right parties, themselves surprised at their sudden chance to take over the affairs of state, somehow managed to bury their differences long enough to agree on the Conservative leader, John Lyng, as prime minister, and to parcel out the various ministries among them.

It suddenly seemed that an era had ended for Norway; it was almost a revolutionary step to have a Conservative prime minister, even if the modern Conservatives could hardly be called hard-shelled reactionaries. Everyone realized, however, that the new government, even more than the old, would lead a precarious existence at the mercy of the two Marxist members of parliament. John Lyng simply said: 'After twenty-eight years, it's about time somebody else had a chance. Not that I count on hanging on for anything like that long.' As it turned out, it was only twenty-eight days. The hastily devised program presented by the coalition was an inoffensive plan to carry on the welfare state. Its economic plans, as Einar Gerhardsen complained, seemed to have been 'lifted from the Labor Party.' Labor, however, promised far more radical steps to an improved Good Life, including a compulsory four-weeks holiday and a fattened pension system which would be about as sweeping as Sweden's. The much-wooed People's Socialists naturally voted against the center-right coalition, and the new government fell.

At first glance it seemed that the only effect of the political drama was to force the Labor Party to push for even more drastic welfare-state measures than it would have presented normally, but my own inquiries in Norway revealed a more significant consequence. I was told by people of all political colors that the events of the fall of 1963 had stirred the nation into a fresh and more questioning interest in national politics. People suddenly discovered that the 'bourgeois' parties would not necessarily turn back the clock on the welfare state as the Laborites had insisted. A leading banker and Conservative leader, Sjur Lindebraekke, said that the brief period of non-Labor government 'made people aware for the first time since the 1930s that there *could* be another kind of government—that an alternative was possible.' There was a widespread eagerness to get on to the next scheduled election in the fall of 1965.

In that election, Labor was hobbled by its tired-old-men image and the opposition's emphasis on the government's mismanagement of several state enterprises. The veteran Labor leaders found it hard to counter the arguments against high taxes and the smothering role of the state in everyday affairs. Many Norwegians clearly felt that it was time for a change. Although there was no change in the *percentage* of the vote for the two left-wing parties, the center-right coalition swept into power with eighty seats as against Labor's sixty-eight and two for the splinter socialists. The mere fact that Labor was decisively out made it seem like a revolutionary change, but appearances deceive. It was more a shift of emphasis than of national purpose. The promise of the new coalition government was not to dismantle the welfare state but simply to run it more efficiently.

Although the Conservative Party is by far the largest member of the four-party coalition, the premiership went to Per Borten, the leader of the Center, or Agrarian Party, which—like the

Liberal Party—dramatically increased its share of the seats. A tall, athletic and soft-spoken man in his early fifties, Borten is a farmer turned politician who has divided his time since 1950 between the Storting and his large acreage in central Norway. 'He looks like a farmer,' commented an Oslo newspaperman, 'but he behaves like an intellectual. Even his opponents say that it is impossible to make him angry.' He is the kind of solid, quiet citizen who suddenly bobs up in Scandinavia as the leader of his nation— unknown to the world outside.

For the Labor Party, defeat in 1965 signaled the emergence of a new generation of leadership. The most visible figure is Trygve Bratteli, who has succeeded Einar Gerhardsen as party chairman. After entering the Storting in 1950 he served in several cabinet posts and became Labor's parliamentary leader. Now in his mid-fifties, Bratteli began his political career in the socialist youth organization and was secretary of Labor's youth movement until it was banned during the German occupation. He was shipped off to a Nazi concentration camp, but was saved shortly before the end of the war when a Swedish mission led by Count Folke Bernadotte succeeded in transferring thousands of Scandinavian inmates in Germany to neutral Sweden.

Einar Gerhardsen

It will be many years before another political leader achieves anything like the stature enjoyed by former Prime Minister Gerhardsen during the critical postwar period. The shape and style of the Norwegian social-security state stem greatly from his driving ambition to create an easier and more secure life for the average man. Appropriately enough, he rose to power as an authentic average man, a plain Norwegian worker.

Humbly born in 1897 and only modestly educated, Gerhardsen was a roadworker during the First World War, before he became deeply involved in Labor Party affairs. In 1925 he was jailed as a pacifist demonstrator, but as prime minister a quarter century later he unswervingly insisted on strong defense forces for Norway and membership in the Atlantic alliance. Even those Norwegians

who oppose Gerhardsen's political views have invariably described him to me as a completely trustworthy, down-to-earth
man who represents some of the finest qualities of the Norwegian
character.

He is a spare figure with bony features and a nearly bald head
fringed with white hair. His eyes are bright blue and there is a
hint of gold in his smile. He told me once that during his early
days in politics 'we actually had people in this country who went
hungry and a great many people who were unable to find work.
In the beginning of the 1930s during the economic crisis there
were strong class contrasts and we had difficult labor relations.
We could see the rise of Nazism in Germany, and there was some
fear here that the small fascist movement in Norway would
grow and appeal to the farmers and workers.' Gerhardsen believed
that Labor's policies held off that threat. 'We gained influence
through a realistic plan for society, not just promises.'

When I asked him whether a government, however well-
intentioned, might go wrong in doing too much for people,
Gerhardsen said, 'there is always the danger that a person will not
feel responsible for his own life, but that has not been a problem
in Norway. It might be in countries where nature is kinder, but
here people have had to work hard to survive. It is ingrained in
our character.'

Work and Welfare

Another Norwegian, a businessman whose political outlook is
worlds apart from Gerhardsen's, said that 'the effect of the welfare
state is to subsidize the least deserving while holding down the
most enterprising. There is no room any more for real initiative.'
I protested that most Norwegians seemed to be living a good life
these days. Would he tear down the welfare state if he got the
chance? 'No,' he said, 'it's too late for that. It has given most
people a decent life, but it's all been financed by private business.
The socialists have never made a dollar on their own. Anyway,
Norwegians look well-off because they have some blessings given
by God, not by Gerhardsen. We have so much room that almost

anyone can buy himself a little holiday island and go there in solitude in his own boat, all very cheaply. In New York you would have to be a millionaire to do the same.'

Despite hearing a lot of grumbling of this sort, I was impressed by how often Norwegian welfarism is identified with work. 'The feeling here still is that work is a blessing,' said Dr. Karl Evang, the Director of Health Services, 'and all efforts to make a man able to work are worthwhile.' Olav Gjaerevoll, then the Minister of Social Affairs, stated: 'There was a time in Norway when things were so bad that men simply broke down, just as machines can break down. You can't get good quality out of a man who is unable to get out of economic difficulties. In their desperation some people will even become antisocial. I don't see how we are damaging moral character or willingness to work by providing minimum benefits as a human right. People work hard here, as they do in your country.'

A section of the Norwegian constitution says that 'it is incumbent on the authorities of the state to create conditions which make it possible for every person who is able to work to earn his living by his work.' That is a plain enough reason for a government to make full employment one of its primary objectives and to equip as many people as possible for employment. Just as the classic idea of welfare as charity has been replaced by the concept that everyone has certain basic rights in a humane society, so the simple idea of help to an unemployed or injured worker has been transformed into training and rehabilitation programs to promote self-help. An official explanation even speaks of it in terms of a 'moral impact: the stimulation of the individual's own responsibility for his destiny, which will induce him to realize that assistance from the community may ultimately depend on his own efforts.' There is much in this that even the most crustaceous conservative would have to applaud—which may explain why so many of the major social-welfare programs in Norway receive unanimous approval in a parliament which is described as 'half-socialist, half-bourgeois.'

It is now the responsibility of a non-Labor government to administer one of the most thoroughgoing welfare structures of any society in the world today. Although Norway's comprehensive health-insurance program began as early as 1909, it was not until 1936, a year after Labor took power, that a modest nationwide old-age pension system was started. 'In the beginning,' said Gjaerevoll, who was once the mayor of Trondheim, 'we gave the unemployed and sick the minimum they needed to survive. In the 1930s we gave old people a minimum standard, to be compared with those earning low wages. We said that they had taken part in building the present community and were entitled to be unafraid of tomorrow. It was, if you will, the spirit of Franklin Roosevelt. We now take the next step to give all citizens the possibility of keeping, when they become old, the standards they enjoyed while they were working—their house, their car, their holiday cottage.'

The 'next step' is the sweeping 'People's Pension,' which an official bulletin describes as one of the most important social reforms in Norway's history. Promoted by the Labor Party and enacted with the support of all parties in 1966, it is a comprehensive pension system which resembles the Swedish pension apparatus recently adopted after a major political battle. It calls for a total pension for all Norwegians corresponding, for most people, to two thirds of their average income during their twenty best working years. The financing of the pensions comes from individuals, employers and government. The fascination of the compulsory system is that high-income earners will draw a lesser percentage of their peak earnings, while persons in the lowest income levels will get such a large pension, relative to their earnings, that it will amount to an old-age raise. Thus all Norwegians who start drawing their pension at the normal retirement age of seventy will have incomes which are not too far apart from one another. It will be Norway's closest approach yet to the 'leveling-out of incomes' which some social planners have zealously sought.

Womb to Tomb

Although I had the feeling in Norway, as I did elsewhere in Scandinavia, that the well-meaning but ever-tightening embrace

THE GOLDEN MEAN 245

of the welfare state would be more than my American temperament could bear were I to take up Norwegian citizenship, I also felt strongly that the social and economic system which the Norwegians had freely chosen was suited to the peculiar conditions of the country. Professor James A. Storing has written:

> The private practice of medicine, reliance on charity, savings, and private security plans to care for the aging would be as impossible in Norway as would private ownership of the railroad system. The topography, the climate, the limitation of resources, the dependence on relatively few types of economic activities, and the consequent austerity that this has brought to certain classes in society, as well as the uneven spread of population, all have contributed to make a modest system of state ownership of transportation lines and certain industrial facilities and a fairly elaborate system of social security inescapable in Norway.

One of Norway's most important welfare administrators, and possibly the country's most vivid personality, is Dr. Karl Evang. He has had a stormy career as a pioneer in sex education, a battler for the scientific outlook in a land where provincial superstitions have been deeply implanted, and as a leading architect of Norway's health services. Internationally, he is known as one of Europe's foremost authorities on health-insurance programs. He helped the American military government devise a new public-health service and medical plan in postwar Germany.

Dr. Evang is a compact, energetic man with brown eyes and bristling gray hair. His outward manner is brusque and combative, but there is great warmth inside. He takes a puckish delight in being outrageously outspoken. As Norway's Director General of Public Health, he occupies a somewhat frantic office in a new glass-box building in Oslo. His struggles with Norwegian 'puritanism' are now mostly past history, but he can still speak vividly of his troubles with the 'anti-fluoridation types and religious zealots.' He said that 'there is a remarkable unanimity on welfare in Norway, except, of course, for a little group of crackpots who have managed to get in the way.' Such matters as legalized abortion and sex education in the schools had taken longer to be put into practice in Norway than in Sweden, Dr. Evang pointed out, but Norwegian attitudes on social matters are becoming ever more open-minded. He said he was not worried about the so-called immorality of the young: 'The percentage of children born out of wedlock used to be more than twice what it is today.' More important, 'we have one of the lowest rates of infant mortality in the world. We provide great care for children.'

There is no denying the virtues of Norwegian medicine. Few countries in the world have made such a thoroughgoing effort to surround everyone with the highest possible health standards and the best of medical attention. The Norwegians even claim to have more dentists per inhabitant than any other country. In this passion for good medicine, the Norwegians, of course, are in good company, with the Danes, the Swedes and the Finns. In 1965 the four nations signed an agreement providing for a joint labor market for doctors. It means that a doctor educated in any one of the countries may practice in the three others. The Norwegian system allows doctors a greater scope for private practice than might be imagined, and the coverage—deliberately—is not so total or 'free' as it is, for example, in Great Britain. I have heard it called 'a Nordic Blue Cross, except it is compulsory.' The cost of the health program is paid by the premiums of all persons covered, plus contributions from employers, municipalities and the state. While most doctors are independent operators, it is the public-service doctors who make the difference between medicine and no-medicine in the more remote valley and island communities which are scattered along the great length of Norway.

Patients choose their own physicians. A doctor's fees are fixed by his professional medical association (though he can charge more if patients are willing to pay from their own pockets), and the patient gets 60 to 100 per cent of the money back from the local health-insurance office. Thus the typical out-of-pocket cost of a visit to the doctor is about one dollar. Patients also buy most of their medicines, except special ones for severe or chronic ailments. Hospital costs are covered, including essential drugs and medicines. Eighty-five per cent of all the hospital beds in Norway are in public institutions. 'We regard them as workshops for specialists,' said Dr. Evang. 'Private doctors cannot follow their patients into our hospitals. We doubt that we could sustain full confidence otherwise.' Those who do not like the system can go to a private hospital, but even there the costs are at least partly defrayed by the national medical plan. The compassionate society embraces one and all, like it or not.

Chapter 16

MUSCLES TO BRAINS

The trouble is, we don't have any means of making the trees grow faster or persuading the herring to come back.
— NORWEGIAN ECONOMIST

Shipping is our sacred cow.
— OSLO STUDENT

It is the woods and the sea with their abundance of timber and fish which provided the foundation for Norway's evolution into a modern economy, and it is now the mountains with their tumbling waters converted into hydroelectric power which give a solid foundation to Norway's new importance as an industrial nation.

Even more than Denmark, Norway has managed to disguise its instruments of economic strength so that a visitor is mystified as to how the Norwegians have managed to achieve such a high living standard with the few factories, shipyards and small fishing vessels which come into view on an excursion through the country. It is possible to drive a thousand miles through Norway and be only dimly aware of industry. Could the Norwegian prosperity rest only on gaily colored sweaters and the three million tourists who drift in every year?

The real economic strength of Norway is either off the beaten path or far beyond Norway's borders. The great merchant marine, for example, is mostly out of sight. Nine tenths of the ships almost never touch Norwegian shores as they make the rounds of foreign ports. The important Norwegian fishing vessels are no longer the small craft operating close to home, but large trawlers which operate far from Norwegian waters for weeks or months at a time. The hydroelectric stations which have made Norway, per capita, the most electrified nation in the world, are not only well removed from the main centers of population but, for security and other good reasons, are often buried deep in the mountainsides. The big new metal and chemical plants are in the north or tucked away in valleys or on islands which few tourists visit. As for mining, Norway's principal iron deposits are in Kirkenes, the most distant cubbyhole of the country, and the coal comes from Spitsbergen.

Obviously, appearances deceive. There *are* factories, despite all the scenic mountain greenery, and Norway is fast becoming an industrial nation. Manufacturing and mining account for the lion's share of the work force and for 25 per cent of the gross national product, while agriculture, forestry and fishing total just 10 per cent. The typical Norwegian is not a farmer, a seafarer or a lumber-jack (he has often been all three at once), but a factory hand or a white-collar worker.

The Public-Private Mixture

To argue politics in Norway is to argue economics: the whys and hows of making the fragile economy work and of forcing the growth of national wealth. It is an oddly exciting story. There is even a cliffhanger problem which goes like this: Can Norway, with little room for farming and few raw materials for industry, survive in an increasingly competitive world, when its traditional activities in whaling, fishing and forestry have come on hard times? Can it keep pace with larger nations, when its merchant fleet has been put under enormous pressure by the swift trend to expensive supersize vessels, and when the industrial world is putting ever more premium on huge integrated plants, heavy research and costly technological changes?

As one government authority put it, 'the dominant problem of the Norwegian economy of the future is that we cannot expand production in the traditional fields of exports, because of limitations in the availability of natural resources.' To state it more graphically, the whales are disappearing from the sea, the fish sometimes flee the Norwegian coastal waters, and the trees which cover a quarter of Norway do not grow fast enough to provide the paper and pulp industry with all the timber it requires. Even before the war, Norway had to import wood from Finland.

The Norwegian economy had been extremely one-sided, with only a few products accounting for most of the exports. This is true even today, as metallurgical and electrochemical products have been brought along to make up for the limitations of the traditional lines. Perhaps inevitably, the state has indulged in a greater degree of economic planning and industrial ownership than in Denmark and Sweden. A Scandinavian magazine said that economic planning in Norway 'is probably together with the French the most well established in Western Europe.'

The state controls most of Norway's transportation, communications and power production. There is a state grain monopoly and monopolies for imports of animal fodder and fishing equipment. The government has a major stake in mining and in some of the biggest metal and chemical operations. It holds all the shares in the biggest aluminum company and nearly half the shares of the giant chemical concern, Norsk Hydro. In both cases the government stepped into the picture at the end of the war, when it took over the German ownership of the shares as enemy property.

Government activities as a whole ('the public sector') now account for one third of the gross national product as against less than 20 per cent before the war, but Norway is still an essentially free-enterprise society with the individual companies overwhelmingly in private hands. Even the most hidebound capitalist admits that the vulnerability of the economy—its unusual sensitivity to fluctuations in world markets—obliges any government, left or right, to keep a close grip on the economic machinery. If world shipping or the timber business slumps, for example, Norway feels the shock immediately. It must have the export revenues to pay for the multitude of things which it cannot supply in full itself.

The struggle with the Germans and the long occupation had a devastating effect on the Norwegian economy. Many towns were completely leveled, the coal industry in Spitsbergen was ruined, and half the merchant fleet and 70 per cent of the whaling fleet were destroyed. Practically no new houses were built during the war, and by 1945 the nation's industrial machinery was all but worn out. The total cost of the war for Norway has been calculated at five billion dollars.

It is no wonder then that Norway, despite having lived through five years of rationing and controls, decided it could recover its economic strength only by undergoing a peacetime period of austerity. Rationing and a full armory of economic controls continued for a number of years after the war as the Norwegians worked feverishly to get the country back on its feet. For at least three years there were only the most elementary things to buy in the shops. Consumption was well below that of most other West European countries. It can be said of the Norwegians, as of the Finns, that they were admirable in this period of enforced denial. Somehow they managed to sublimate their usual squabbling to the primary task of reconstruction.

The Marshall Plan was a godsend, especially since Norway was badly hurt by the international economic crisis of 1947. The 480 million dollars in Marshall aid enabled Norway to carry out the planned reconstruction without taking on a staggering burden of foreign indebtedness. And, of course, the aid to other nations encouraged the whole trade situation in Europe, to Norway's benefit.

The unexpected need to spend large sums on defense after the Soviet threat became apparent was a setback but Norway's prodigious effort brought about a national recovery within a few years. By 1950, the merchant marine tonnage was higher than it was at the beginning of World War II, and even that was doubled by 1960. Consumer rationing was almost entirely lifted by 1952. Full employment was reached, except in certain northern areas, and the welfare program, including family allowances and higher pensions, was stepped up even as early as 1946. Today Norway's gross national product (at current prices) is *eight* times greater than the prewar figure, while personal consumption is about double that of 1938.

It has been a heady journey to new economic heights after the crippling wartime years. Norway is well-off, and wealthier than ever before, even though it lacks the cozy look of Denmark or the sleek appearance of Sweden. And yet it cannot afford to breathe easily. It is under constant pressure from economic forces. It is plagued by a balance-of-payments problem as imports continue to outpace exports. (About half the imports are ships and other requirements for the merchant fleet.) Norway has had to borrow heavily from foreign sources, and it is fashionable for Norwegian conservatives to point out that the high prosperity is illusory because the nation is deeply in debt.

The small size of the home market has made it difficult for Norway to develop the production of manufactures as much as other nations. Even the more basic metal and chemical industries which Norway has been developing may not be large-enough units to keep up with the rapid technological development taking place in the world. Norway is reluctant to allow foreign investment in Norwegian industry, but several arrangements have been made in order to gain access to the technical know-how and marketing abilities of larger industrial countries. For example, Alcoa, the American aluminum giant, is a partner in a Norwegian aluminum enterprise.

Two of Norway's main hopes for the future are more hydroelectric power and greater use of its brain power. It proposes to double its electrical capacity and make the maximum industrial use of this abundance of cheap energy. The stage will be reached, however, in about twenty years, when the exploitation of water-power sources will have gone about as far as it can go. According to its planners, Norway will then 'have to live more by "wits and skills" than by exploitation of natural resources.' It is believed that 'talent industries' manned by Norwegians of finely tuned technological abilities will come to play a dominant role. In the coming years the nation will have to greatly expand its educational research facilities. The new breed of Norseman is likely to be a highly trained laboratory specialist or expert on automation instead of the familiar roughhewn outdoorsman. In the meantime, let us look at the traditional pursuits which still give Norway its special flavor.

The Blue Meadow

Like farmers standing in the shade of front porches and gazing across shimmering fields of grain, the Norwegians put their backs to the mountains and look out across the great ocean which they call 'the blue meadow.' They have farmed it for a thousand years and more, and their kinship with the sea is written in the lines of their faces. They are still the world's foremost seamen and fishermen. Their harvest from the sea and their constant journeying across it have fed and enriched a nation which could not live on the land alone.

For centuries Norwegians dwelling in the small ports which cling like barnacles to the ragged coast went to sea in small boats to bring in fish for drying, salting and exporting to the world. It was a seasonal business, and the fisherman during his time on land would work a small farm or cut the forest trees to supply Norway's lumber, paper and pulp industries. At the turn of the century, fish and forestry products accounted for three quarters of Norway's exports. Even today they provide a third of the exports. One of the most familiar sights along the Norwegian coast has been the cod and other 'stockfish' hanging like socks on a clothesline (after being decapitated, gutted and washed) as they dry out in the crackling cold air for six to twelve weeks before being shipped abroad, or the klipfish carefully spread out on rocks to dry for a month or so in the sun and wind.

Norwegian fishermen for centuries led a hard life, but they were their own bosses. They owned and sailed their own small boats. Fishermen of other nations had to go far from their coastal waters to find fish, but the Norwegian fisheries were close to home in the warm waters sheltered by thousands of islands. The fish instinctively came to spawn just offshore. 'A century and a half ago,' states a Norwegian business publication, 'the fisheries were a pillar of the economy. Not that the fisheries then, any more than now, were a sure or safe living. The men who ventured with net and line to haul the fish from the sea were pawns in the fickle hand of nature. Unorganized, they were not in a position to bargain strongly with the merchant either. Since then, the fishermen have gained in technical efficiency and organizational strength, so their economic condition has improved out of all recognition compared with 1814.'

Half a century ago the annual landings of fish were about 600,000 tons. In 1965 they reached a record 2,400,000 tons. Business would appear to be booming, even though the number of fishermen has decreased, yet there have been alarming fluctuations in the size of the catch during the past decade. For reasons that still baffle the experts, great multitudes of fish began to spurn the coastal waters. The annual landings were reduced by nearly a million tons between 1958 and 1963. An almost catastrophic reduction in the herring catch took place: from a record 1·1 million tons in 1956 to a pitiful 70,000 tons in 1961. The disappearance of the fish took the life out of the great annual winter spectacle at the Lofoten Islands, when some twenty thousand fishermen would go out into the cold choppy water in small boats and exhaust themselves as they landed 39 or 40 million cod in a good year. Sometimes (as I was solemnly assured on a visit to the islands) the nets were so heavy with fish that whole boats were pulled under the sea, never to be seen again. When the cod moved to more distant waters the islanders themselves began to drift away. Fishing villages along the whole length of the coast were affected, and the process of converting a life of rugged individualism to a rationalized industry of modern techniques was drastically speeded up.

Even before the current wave of modernization, the small-craft fishermen began to equip themselves with radios, echo sounders and other gadgets, and they cooperatively conducted their operations like a military campaign. The fleets were directed by headquarters on shore to the shoals where the fish were reported to be most thickly concentrated. Vessels were sent out to relieve the catcher boats of their loads so that the campaign at sea could continue. The fish were then sold by the big fishermen's cooperatives, while the fishermen, all but frozen from their long hours on the icy seas, warmed up with some heavy drinking ashore. Legislation strictly limited the number of trawlers, as the independent fishermen demanded, even though other nations from Britain to Japan were converting swiftly to trawlers. (The world's leading fishing countries in terms of the tonnage of the annual catch are, in order: Peru, Japan, China, U.S.S.R., U.S.A., Norway, Canada.) The individualistic Norwegians feared the trend to a fishing industry of larger vessels run by a few owners and manned by employee-fishermen. The decline in coastal fishing, however, has forced them to change.

Today, Norway is expanding its fleet of trawlers. They sail off across the North Atlantic—to Iceland, Greenland and beyond— for days and weeks at a time, and the operation is run as a modern industry. The traditional fish-drying procedures have given way to freezing techniques which begin aboard the trawlers themselves as the fish are packed in ice.

The Disappearing Whales

Although Norwegian fishing can survive through new techniques, Norwegian whaling has come on rough seas. They are so rough, in fact, that Erik Brofoss has said that 'the prospect is only one of continual decline, and the final end of a once prosperous industry can be foreseen within a few years.' Norway was the world's foremost whaling nation during most of the past century, first in the Arctic waters and then in the Antarctic. Original methods were primitive, and as dangerous as anything depicted in *Moby Dick*. Then in 1868 a Norwegian seal hunter named Svend Foyn invented the grenade-tipped harpoon which explodes after penetrating the whale. Used on steam-driven whaleboats, the new weapon enabled the hunters to go after the swifter and stronger blue whale (the largest animal in existence, up to 100 feet long) as well as the finback whale and humpback whale. The slaughter then began on a grand scale, with about one million whales plucked from the sea by all the whaling nations by the time World War II gave the great creatures a much-deserved rest.

It was also the Norwegians, soon after the turn of the century, who began to operate in the Antarctic and to use the 'floating factories' which processed the whales on the high seas instead of hauling them to shore. The next great step, in 1925, was the Norwegian-invented slipway in the stern of the factory ship, which enabled the whalers to draw the whales inside the vessel for flensing (stripping the blubber from a whale like peeling a banana). This meant that the job did not have to be held up until calm water permitted it to be done alongside the ship; now the processing could be done on board, in rough weather as well as fair. After that step the whaling industry boomed and other nations scrambled to get in on the kill. The number of factory ships of all nations in the Antarctic rose from fifteen in the 1925-26 season to forty-one in 1930-31. The forty-one accounted for a record kill of 40,200 whales and the production of 3,608,000 barrels of oil. Norway was responsible for roughly half of the world's whale catch and oil production in those days; Britain and Argentina, and then Germany and Japan, accounted for the rest. About 7,000 Norwegians were involved in the arduous whale hunt each winter.

World War II was a heavy blow to the industry, but like Norwegian industry in general, the reconstruction was astonishingly swift. By the end of 1948, Norway had ten factory ships (and some one hundred catcher boats) operating in the Antarctic, as against seven for the five other whaling nations all together.

Within a few years, however, it found itself facing cutthroat competition from Japan and the Soviet Union. It was an unequal struggle, in view of the immensely greater manpower and resources of the other two countries. They built giant new factory ships and went after the whales with a vengeance. The owners of Norway's whaling armada, in the meantime, were unable to expand. Not only were they operating without government subsidy and paying high duties in Norway, but the international prices for whale products were much reduced after the boom years. A number of companies decided to switch from whaling to the far more profitable tanker and dry-cargo trade. According to the Federation of Norwegian Whaling Companies, the Japanese were able to expand rapidly because of 'cheap labor and the fact that they have a domestic market for frozen and salted whale meat for human consumption at good prices. There is no corresponding market for whale meat in Western Europe. The Soviet Russian whaling industry is hardly conducted on usual economic principles, and its expansion must be said to be based more on political than on economic considerations.'

The number of Norwegian whaling expeditions to the Antarctic each year has been cut from ten to two while Japan and Russia take precedence. A few figures on the whale catch tell the story:

	1948–49	1964–65
Norway	16,570	7,887
Japan	3,331	18,257
U.S.S.R.	3,122	10,864

More important, there are no longer enough whales to go around. The destruction has been alarming. Just as the Norwegian harpoon gun depleted the Arctic whale stocks, so the Norwegian-designed factory ships started the overkill which now threatens to destroy the industry. In 1938–39, for example, 13,849 of the great blue whales were caught, but only 1,191 in 1958–59. Norway and Britain, the traditional whaling nations, took the lead in the 1930s for international restrictions on the slaughter, and for overall conservation measures. The whaling countries have attempted to reach international agreements on the size of the catch and the number of expeditions each one would send out each year, but for many reasons, including Russia's refusal to accept an inspection system and the anxiety of the Japanese to get the most out of their investment in whaling, the international understandings have been nets full of gaping holes. Some experts say that the number of whales killed each year must be reduced by one half or more if whales are not to become extinct.

The Big Ships

The decline in Norwegian whaling is more than overcome, however, by the tremendous expansion of that far more important part of the Norwegian economy: shipping. This is Norway's pride, joy, and, at the moment, headache. I have heard it called 'the goose that lays our golden eggs' and 'our only big industry.' It is hard to turn round in Norway without running into conversation about ships, shipping or shipowners. It has reminded me of Texas and the obsession with oil. The shipowners are talked about like oil millionaires: they are seen as heroic figures who breathe life into the economy; yet, in the eyes of many Norwegians, from leading government officials to plain workingmen, they are tainted by the mere fact that they are rich men who have the knack of making money. It is almost a love-hate relationship. In any event, the shipowners are absolutely vital figures in Norway's growth, and even the most rabid socialists hesitate before suggesting that a nationalized shipping industry could perform a better service for the nation than the big capitalists.

Although Norwegians have always been famous sailors, it was not until the middle of the nineteenth century that the conditions were ripe for Norway to emerge as a shipping nation out of all proportion to its population. The English Navigation Act of 1651, requiring that only English ships carry the trade between England and its colonies, had been the main obstacle to Norwegian shipping expansion until the last vestiges of that law were repealed in 1849. The villages along the Norwegian coasts turned into gold-rush towns as people hurried to build and sail in bigger ships to have a part in the new bonanza on the high seas.

It was a fiercely competitive time, a period of frenzied free-enterprise activity which, coinciding as it did with the waves of emigrants sailing to America, gave the impression that all of Norway was going out to sea. According to an official account, 'Norwegians entered the timber trade from Canada and the White Sea to England. They sailed the Great Lakes. Their ships carried more and more British coal and American grain. Norwegian tonnage was multiplied by five in the thirty years to 1880. Crews increased from 19,000 to 60,000 men, and capital accumulated.' Norway was slow to switch to steamships—two thirds of the tonnage in 1900 was still made up of sailing ships—but the nation once again demonstrated that amazing Scandinavian capacity to make almost overnight changes when the need becomes obvious. By 1914, four fifths of Norway's huge fleet of 2·5 million tons, the world's third-largest, was made up of steamships. Then came two crushing blows and two miraculous recoveries.

Although a neutral in the First World War, Norway lost half its fleet and 2,100 seamen. The reconstruction was so thorough that by 1940 Norway had a fleet of nearly five million tons— 40 per cent in tankers, which were the new Norwegian specialty. Once again Norway was caught in a world war. As already related, half the fleet and nearly 4,000 men were lost but great service was performed. Norwegian tankers carried nearly half of the oil that reached Britain during the war. This time the recovery was still more astonishing. The merchant marine was down to two and a half million tons in 1945, and many of the ships were in battered condition. Within a few years the industry was back to its prewar size and by 1966 the tonnage was over 16 million, representing more than 2,750 ships of over 100 gross tons each. This amounted to a tenth of the world's shipping tonnage for a nation with less than 0·2 per cent of world population. Britain and America have larger fleets, but Norway actually has more tonnage in active service than the United States. The net income to Norway from shipping is over 450 million dollars annually. It is the single greatest saving factor for an economy which often runs a yearly balance-of-trade deficit of 200 million dollars.

Norwegians are proud of their great ships, but they seldom see them. Despite the large expansion of the Norwegian shipbuilding industry, most of Norway's ships are produced in Swedish and other foreign yards, and then, as already noted, nine in every ten spend all their time moving between foreign ports and seldom return home. The average Norwegian's contact with them is through the 51,000 merchant seamen of Norway. (The fleet's over-all crew numbers 64,000. Nearly a third of the 13,000 foreigners are Asians and a quarter are Spaniards.) From seamen's school to retirement, the well-paid Norwegian sailor is protected by an ocean-going welfare state which gives him all the benefits of the Norwegian worker at home—and then some. Among other things, the merchant mariner is entitled to a periodic free

trip home (half paid by his employer, half by the state) and free
return to Norway if he is ill or injured. Scandinavian welfarism
does not falter even in extreme situations. An official description
of the rights of sailors states that 'a seaman suffering from venereal
disease has no claim to a free passage home, but may be sent home
for treatment in Norway at the expense of the Treasury.'

Another particularly Norwegian touch is the fact that the ranks
of the merchant mariners include 4,000 women, 200 of whom are
officers. The officers are mostly radio operators, while almost all
the ordinary seawomen serve as galley and mess workers or as
stewardesses. A boy can go to sea, with parental permission, as
early as sixteen, but a girl must be at least twenty. I have spoken to
a number of seamen and they insist that having women in the
crew does not create important tensions; on the contrary, they
are said to have a humanizing influence. There are shipboard
romances, of course, and many a marriage. There is a further
humanizing factor: seamen are sometimes permitted to take their
wives along on a voyage.

The credit for the dramatic postwar rebuilding of the merchant
fleet goes almost entirely to the much-maligned shipowners. They
do not, as in some countries, receive subsidies. In fact, because of
Norway's capital shortage, the government compelled the shipowners to seek their shipbuilding funds abroad by refusing them
credit at home. When the shipowners protested that this was a
serious interference with private business, the government candidly said that they were better able to raise money abroad than
any public authority or any sector of private business—'In the
national interest of a fast development of our national resources
the shipowners have to submit to this inconvenience.'

Even as they grumbled, the shipowners energetically and
ingeniously got credit on a grand scale. Fortunately, shipyards
from West Germany to Japan were so hungry for work that they
joined the financial institutions in offering financing of up to 80
per cent of the cost of a ship. One common technique is to win a
contract from an oil firm to ship its oil in a new tanker for, say, a
ten-year period, and then use the signed charter as a gilt-edged
security for the financing which gets the actual ship built. Nor-

wegians have been particularly successful in obtaining financing from leading American banks.

But even more to the point is the way the shipowners set out, soon after the war, to anticipate trends in international trade and to order the specialized ships which traders would require. These include freighters for hauling small European cars to America a thousand at a time; they have special decks which can be swung away to permit the same ships to take on coal, grain or other bulk cargoes for the return voyage. Special tankers have been created with special insulation to carry cold liquefied gas or hot asphalt.

One of the most prominent shipowners is Niels Onstad but mainly because he is married to Sonja Henie, the best-known of all Norwegians in the days when she was an ice-skating champion and show-business personality. (There is a story that an inebriated patron in a night club once handed Sonja Henie an ice-cube and mumbled, 'Here. Do something.') When I went along on a tourist cruise on the Oslofjord the sight-seeing director, acting for a moment like a guide in Beverly Hills, pointed out the white mansion 'where Sonja Henie lives.' The Nazis took over the house during the war and, according to Miss Henie, 'they stole everything, everything.' She avoids the 'terrible God-awful' winters in Oslo, preferring to visit her house in Beverly Hills or the Onstad apartment in Lausanne, Switzerland, but she and her husband spend their summers in Oslo. All three residences are full of modern art, perhaps Norway's greatest private collection. The art will be turned over to the public for its enjoyment around 1967, when a museum which the Onstads are having built near Oslo will open.

Although such companies as Bergesen, Wilhelmsen and Høegh are giants on the high seas, the shipping firm which bears the name Anders Jahre is the biggest of them all. Jahre owns the largest fleet of tankers in Norway, and his dozens of ferries, freighters and other ships make him the nation's wealthiest shipowner. He has long been the dominant figure in the whaling industry as well. A hard-driving, outspoken man in his seventies, Jahre is both a vehement free enterpriser and a generous philanthropist. Most of his ships and those of other owners are built abroad (Norwegian orders have made Sweden one of the Big Three of the world's shipbuilding nations), but enough are constructed on home grounds to make Norway one of the half dozen largest shipbuilders.

Although the shipowners are almost exotic figures in egalitarian Norway, most of them are too busy keeping pace with the revolutionary changes in the industry to have time to enjoy their wealth. Not only do they have to worry about Russia's rapidly expanding merchant marine, American shipping policy which rewards shippers who use United States vessels, and the competition of the various 'flags of convenience' (countries like Liberia provide tax-free havens for many rival shipowners), but they must cope with the international swing to monster ships. It is a bigness movement of awesome proportions. Compared to today's new oil tankers the prewar vessels were veritably rowboats. The latest Norwegian tankers delivered from foreign shipyards are even larger than the *Queen Elizabeth*.

Big ships are more economical, once they are in service, but the impact on Norway is that its exceptionally modern fleet is becoming 'obsolete' much sooner than anyone had imagined. Perfectly sound ships only seven or eight years old may have to be scrapped or sold and replaced. Inevitably, there has been a leveling-off of the shipping industry's net income, even though the fleet has been expanding at a rate of more than a million tons a year. It amounts to a major 'capital intensification' problem which can be seen elsewhere in Norwegian industry as ever bigger and more expensive units are required to keep pace with world competition.

White Coal

Shipping may be the backbone of Norway's economy, but the new muscle power and the nation's hope for its future prosperity is being delivered by the 'white coal' of hydroelectricity.

Once again, as in fishing, whaling and shipping, it all starts with water. Norway is spiked with mountains, dappled with lakes, drenched with rain, coated with snow and bejeweled with ice.

The result is a roaring surge of water—the greatest wealth of hydro power in Europe. It is expensive to harness. Few things in the world look more impressive and expensive than a hydroelectric installation in its full glory, but once harnessed, it needs relatively little manpower or maintenance, and it pours forth cheap energy without end. 'It is perhaps the nearest approach in practice to the ancient dream of perpetual motion,' says a gleeful Norwegian government publication.

Even before the last war Norway had become, per capita, the most electrified of all nations, with an annual output of 8,000 million kilowatt hours. Today the output is six times greater, or nearly 50,000 million kilowatt hours. On the human level, it means that 99 per cent of the population is supplied with electricity. Not only is Norway now beginning to export electricity, first of all to Sweden, but its engineers go abroad to build hydroelectric works in other countries, including the Soviet Union. Norway is pushing its hydroelectric expansion rapidly in order to get a jump on atomic or thermoelectric power development which other nations may use in competition in the future.

The Norwegians, like the Swedes, have made a point of building all their major stations deep within mountains, where they are safe 'even from hydrogen bombs.' Enormous generators hum inside white-walled cathedrals of power hewn out of solid rock. They are watched over by technicians who handle the machinery like high priests attending the national gods. The state and the municipalities own the plants which produce about three quarters of the hydroelectric power, but private industry still accounts for a quarter. A special touch of state socialism is revealed by a government report which says that 'Norway's water power is jealously guarded, and its exploitation even by Norwegians is governed by strict regulations.' One important stipulation is that power plants built by others than the local authorities become the property of the state after a certain term of years, usually fifty or sixty, and without compensation.

It is hydropower, of course, which accounts for the spectacular expansion of Norway's metal and chemicals industries. 'Spectacular' is the right word, I think. Because low-priced power is the decisive factor in the production of metals, particularly aluminum, Norway has been able to build up an outsized industry even though it is obliged to import most of the raw material it needs. Norway is now the biggest exporter of magnesium in the world and Europe's leading exporter of aluminum. American, Canadian, Swiss and other aluminum makers have been financing plants in Norway, often on the basis that they will revert to Norwegian ownership as the foreign companies are paid in the aluminum produced.

The old seafaring country's new industrial look depends as much, however, on the smaller firms which are leading the way toward a more diversified economy. In Bergen, for instance, a self-made man named Jørgen S. Lien is the owner and business genius behind a company bearing his name which is exporting cash registers and adding machines all over the world. Another leading entrepreneur, Vebjørn Tandberg, started the Tandberg radio and tape-recorder works in 1933. When it eventually turned into one of Norway's biggest little businesses he continued as chairman, but turned the whole operation over to his employees. They plow all the profits back into the business, enjoy top wages and a 39-hour week, and studiously avoid any blue-collar-versus-white-collar distinctions. This odd enterprise is a sort of halfway house between the typical company and the co-op.

Cooperatives

As in the other Scandinavian countries, the cooperative movement in Norway is important, but not so important as some foreign observers once thought. Eager Asians and Africans arrive in Oslo to study the Norwegian co-ops in order to learn non-capitalistic economic methods and then find that it is still capitalism that makes the national engine turn over so efficiently. In fact, the trend in the cooperatives themselves is toward attitudes and operations which are identical with normal business practices, except for the fact that the surplus profits go to the multitude of member-owners, not a fewer number of shareholders.

The cooperative idea has found its most useful expression in the fishing, farming and housing co-ops, but it is the great National Consumers' Cooperative, or N.K.L., that enlists nearly a third of the nation through its membership of 330,000 families. Although membership in N.K.L. is growing by about five thousand families a year, much of the membership has become indifferent to the original purposes of the co-ops. The old idealism can still be found, but the consumers no longer feel exploited by private manufacturers and retailers, perhaps partly because co-op competition improved the tone of the private firms. There is even a certain snob appeal in *not* joining a co-op.

'Before the war,' said Harald Korsell, the N.K.L. secretary, 'this was a bread-and-butter movement having to do with the most simple, basic things. The dividend just before Christmas meant a lot when wages were small. Since the war there has been an economic revolution. People want more things, better and fancier things. Our distribution system was set up for basic items. We had to have a new look and get away from being too conservative.' Thus a chain of large self-service stores has been in the making. 'Old members were attracted to us by the ideal; now people first come to buy, then they may become members. Many members let their dividends accumulate with us; we call it "friendly capital."' He added that 'the pattern for the future is less on "cooperative principles" and more on the practical application of nonprofit service.'

Trade Unions

Almost all of Norway's industrial workers belong to a union, and the five thousand local branches are joined in the massive Trade Union Federation known as L.O. It is the most powerful organization in Norway. The membership of 575,000 encompasses a third of all the families in the nation. (There are another 80,000 or so members of independent trade unions covering white-collar employees.)

Such a formidable machine needs its management counterpart. The Norwegian Employers' Confederation, or N.A.F., embraces 8,900 different companies, which employ more than 300,000 persons. It works closely with a number of other employer groups, notably the shipowners' association, whose member firms employ over 50,000 persons. Necessarily, because of the strength of L.O., individual companies turn over most of their authority in labor negotiations to N.A.F.

The result of having such great, tightly controlled management and worker organizations is a degree of labor peace which stands in utter contrast to the bitter disputes, prolonged strikes, angry lockouts, and frequent breakdowns of the economy's forward movement of a few decades ago. During several recent years there were virtually no strikes whatsoever, although in the postwar period Norway has not been quite so tranquil as Sweden and Denmark. The last major labor conflict was in 1931, when 100,000 workers struck in protest against wage cuts made by hard-pressed companies in that Depression year.

Chapter 17

INDOORS AND OUTDOORS

The prevailing image is of Norwegians as adolescent geniuses, bursting with ideas, which they broadcast about without following through.

—OSLO SOCIOLOGIST

The Norwegian is presented with too much external beauty to feel the need of producing his own.

—MARYA MANNES

During a long weekend I spent at Svolvaer in the Lofoten Islands soaking up the atmosphere of fish and ships I met a young Norwegian schoolteacher at dinner in the Lofoten Hotel. He was over from the mainland for a brief holiday. He wore horn-rimmed glasses, spoke flawless English, and had all the appearance of being a studious, serious-minded scholar. He was also a little drunk. He was still drunk when we met again at breakfast, and he was inebriated to the point of incoherence at all the other meals during the rest of what I took to be a Lost Weekend. At the Saturday night dance in the hotel he staggered about asking girls to dance, and he would drink still more wine every time he was refused. His room was awash in beer and wine bottles. He was one of the most dedicated drinkers I had ever met, but his friends assured me that it was simply a rare and deliberate binge: 'He probably won't touch another drop for the next six months.' By the time I left Svolvaer he was due to return to the mainland himself. Now he was sober, ashen-faced, and embarrassed by the spectacle he had made. The next day he would be back in the classroom, the very picture of a proper schoolmaster.

'Norwegians are not heavy drinkers,' I was told, 'but when they do drink, they go all out.' The same thing was said in Finland, even more emphatically, about the Finns. Both countries, and Sweden as well, are in an isolated part of the world, where physical conditions are often harsh. For the fisherman just in from the stormy sea or a lumberjack coming out of an icy forest, a good stiff drink means a lot. Alcohol has always meant a lot to the northern peoples, and alcoholism has been a persistent social problem. The Norwegians, nonetheless, consume less alcohol than the French, Italians, Germans, Americans, British and many other people, and even less than the Swedes.

Statistics compiled by the Swedish alcohol monopoly gave the following as the annual per capita consumption in liters of pure alcohol, from spirits, wines and beer, for eleven countries: France 17·9, Italy 13·2, Switzerland 8·7, West Germany 8, United States 5·6, United Kingdom 5, Denmark 4·3, Sweden 4, *Norway* 2·7, Netherlands 2·5, Finland 2. These statistics are misleading unless it is observed that in nations like France and Italy many people drink regularly and moderately, while in Norway and Finland fewer people drink, and those who do are apt to do it irregularly and immoderately. After a visit to Norway, an American journalist cabled his editors: 'Whatever the figures show, the most conspicuous social problem in Norway is alcoholism. Drunks are a more common sight on the streets of central Oslo than in any major city I can remember.'

I have even heard alcoholism described as 'Norway's number-one vice,' but if true, it is only because there is a shortage of vices. Dr. Herbert Hendin found more shame and disgrace attached to alcoholism in Norway than to suicide:

> The Norwegian attitude toward alcoholism is partly a reaction to a genuine problem and partly a carryover from the puritanical tradition of the country. Excessive drinking is considered an important social problem in all three Scandinavian countries [and in Finland as well], as it is in the United States. However, the Norwegians' attitude is more moralistic than that of Swedes or Danes. 'Alcoholic' has a pejorative implication in Norway that cannot be compared with any-

thing in the United States or the rest of Scandinavia. Consequently Norwegian patients are ashamed of their drinking and will minimize it, cover it up, or lie about it to an unusual extent.

Norway, like Finland, introduced total prohibition after World War I, but 'its manifest fiasco led to final repeal.' Today Norway has a kind of near-prohibition. The state says: We will permit you to drink but we will make it difficult for you to do so. The cost of alcoholic beverages, in the first place, is among the highest in the world. Sales of spirits and wines are in the sole hands of a government monopoly which, significantly, operates under the Ministry of Social Affairs. What is most important, it is up to local communities to decide by plebiscite whether a liquor store should be established. Many communities have voted against local liquor sales, thus giving Norway the kind of patchwork of wet and dry areas which I hadn't seen since India. Special arrangements are made at tourist hotels to see that foreigners can get a drink during certain hours, but local people in some areas are left high and dry. It is little wonder that some folk turn to moonshining.

Zest for Culture

In looking into other aspects of Norwegian life, I found education booming, the written word avidly read, the arts more ambitious than accomplished, religion marked by apathy except for the fervent few, and the sporting life as bracing as it is supposed to be. That is too simple a summing up, of course, but I am speaking only of broad impressions. I doubt whether many Norwegians would disagree that religion has, for most people become just a part of the national furniture, comfortable to have at hand, but only for ceremonial occasions. There is the Lutheran State Church, of course, with the King as Supreme Bishop and 96 out of every 100 citizens enrolled as members. Well over 80 per cent of all Norwegians are baptized, confirmed, married and buried by the Church, but few people regularly attend services.

They leave that to the 'religious types.' Hard-core Lutherans in fundamentalist areas denounce sex, dancing, movies, theaters and even beer as sinful, and they even more vigorously let fly at Church leaders who seek to move the Church into some kind of harmony with this secular, scientific age. The arguments within the Church about whether, for example, the story of Adam and Eve should be taken literally have hardly won much enthusiasm from Norway's younger generation which tends to think of the official Church as an anachronism. The Pentecostals and Roman Catholics, although drawing on only a fraction of the population, have more vitality.

In contrast to the emptiness of the churches, there is the pressure of youth for more education, and especially for more places at the university level. Norwegians start school at seven, and for a long time there has been a compulsory seven-year elementary course, but the nine-year course has now become standard over much of the country. Not only are youngsters staying in school longer, but a rapidly increasing number every year are banging on the doors of Norway's too few universities and institutes. In 1935, only 4 per cent of their age group took the university entrance examination. In the spring of 1965 the percentage was 18. It is expected that by 1975 a quarter of all Norwegian youngsters will go to a university.

Until the end of World War II, Oslo University was the only such institution in the nation. Now there is also Bergen University, and the excellent Institute of Technology in Trondheim is being expanded into a university. A fourth institution is being planned for Tromsø. Oslo University has more than doubled its enrollment in the past decade to over 10,000 (about half of all higher-education students in Norway) and is now operating out of a fast-expanding campus of vigorously contemporary buildings. The shortage of higher-education places, not to mention the dearth of teachers and professors, compels some 3,500 young Norwegians to go to foreign countries for their studies. There are even some who go to Iceland for their medical training.

Some Norwegians admit that it is a great advantage to have been educated abroad. Despite Oslo University's high qualities, it still seems a little provincial when compared with such elderly Swedish universities as Uppsala and Lund. A visitor senses that there is more contentment than intellectual thrust at a Norwegian university, but much the same can be said for Norwegian education in general. It is good and solid, well suited to the Norwegian temperament, which is less concerned with 'success' or outstanding performance than the Swedish. Once the horrendous problem of finding a place in a higher-education institution is solved, the Norwegian students are less driven to excel than their Swedish counterparts.

The Uneasy Arts

Norway is a difficult country for scholars, truly creative artists and intellectuals ambitious enough to want to leave their mark on the world. It is simply too small, self-contained and isolated from the main stream of international cultural affairs. And yet, for an artist or writer of more modest attainments or ambition, Norway has many elements of the ideal cultural state. Although its population is small and scattered, it has a fully literate and educated citizenry, which devours books at a rate equaled by few societies. (The Norwegian's love of the printed word is a story by itself. There are about 1,700 daily and periodical publications of all kinds in Norway, possibly the greatest number per capita in the world. Despite the trend to fewer newspapers throughout Scandinavia, there are still about 160 in Norway including 84 daily papers. Oslo, a pint-sized capital in relation to others in the world, has eleven daily papers.)

It is a public, moreover, which holds artists and intellectuals in high esteem. It is so fond of the theater that the state since 1949 has financed a traveling Riksteater which moves constantly about the country to perform in communities too small and remote to have a stage of their own. In addition, all the state-supported theaters tour the nation. The state and municipalities support seven theaters and subsidize a number of artists, writers and stage managers—even to the point of providing some with lifetime salaries and special housing. They give financial backing to the designers and craftsmen in the applied arts. Gustav Vigeland's astonishing sculpture park in Oslo is the most striking example, of course, but parks, city halls and other public buildings from one end of Norway to the other are full of paintings, murals and works of sculpture by local artists engaged by the government. Private business too is culture-conscious. Such thing as murals in factory cafeterias and the amply stocked libraries on the ships of Norway's merchant marine are part of the climate of encouragement.

And yet, the effect is not wholly satisfying to many Norwegians, and some speak earnestly of Norway's 'cultural stagnation.' Few people really argue against all the official encouragement; without it, many writers and artists would be unable to survive in a small society with a population no larger than Chicago's. What is disturbing is the dearth of truly first-class work and of creations which have an impact outside Norway. There is, at the time of writing, not a single living Norwegian writer, poet, artist, architect, dramatist, composer, or film maker who has a truly important international reputation. When Norwegians boast about their great names—as well they should—they must look back to the giants like Henrik Ibsen, Bjørnstjerne Bjørnson, Edvard Grieg and Edvard Munch. Even then, it is a short list. Knut Hamsun and Sigrid Undset, both Nobel Prize winners, were probably the two best known Norwegian writers of this century, yet even they had only a limited following outside Scandinavia. Such contemporary writers as Johan Borgen, Tarjei Vesaas, Axel Jensen, Johan Falkberger and Cora Sandel are well read in Norway but only barely known abroad. Vesaas won the Nordic Council prize in literature in 1964 for his excellent novel *The Ice Palace*.

To the disgust of those who find his novels second-rate, Agnar Mykle may be the best-known of the current authors because his *The Song of the Red Ruby* was the focal point in a classic censorship case only a few years ago. A bible-belt critic charged that it was pornographic; the publisher was prosecuted, found guilty and ordered to destroy the type; the Supreme Court reversed the decision; the book went on sale again, and the steamy passages of a student's love-making and personal anguish guaranteed substantial sales both in Norway and in translation abroad. *Red Ruby's* notoriety also spurred the foreign sales of Mykle's other sex-packed books. In the meantime, 'mykle' became a five-letter Norwegian verb which need not be translated.

The great difficulty for writers in Norway is that few persons outside the country read Norwegian, and even in Denmark and Sweden, where the languages are similar to Norwegian (or the varieties of Norwegian), probably only a fraction of the population turns to Norwegian authors. Writers are inhibited by the fact of their own small market and the difficulty of getting translated into English, German, French or other international languages. They are also inclined to be intimidated by both the huge reputation of their few great writers in history and the quality and quantity of literature which comes into Norway from other countries. The Norwegian trying to make an impact on the larger, more powerful and confident world of the arts in the rest of Europe is like a Canadian at the edge of the American colossus. 'At one time,' said Henrik Groth, a leading Oslo publisher and an angry champion of Norwegian culture, 'we talked about a Scandinavian cultural bloc of at least fifteen million people who spoke more or less the same language. We have a great deal of economic integration and almost a common citizenship, yet most Norwegians don't read the Swedish writers and vice-versa. We missed the bus, and now it's too late. We had hoped to go from a national culture to a Nordic culture to an international one, but we were too slow and the world came in too fast.'

The bookshops in Oslo and elsewhere in Norway are full of works in English and other foreign languages. The big theatrical hit in Oslo is likely to be an American musical. Concerts lean mostly on foreign works, and those Norwegians interested in painting must look to London and New York for new works and new movements to talk about. In fact, one gets the impression of a great deal of knowing and critical talk about cultural matters without a matching brightness of performance. There is also a significant inferiority complex—the 'little brother' mentality, which Norwegians themselves comment about. It is the feeling that culturally Norwegians do not quite measure up to other Europeans, and in particular to their nearest neighbor. 'The Swedes,' said Henrik Groth, 'have double the population, four times the wealth, and they are eight times as gifted. Their music, theater, literature are all ahead of ours, although thirty or forty years ago, when Knut Hamsun and Sigrid Undset were alive and writing, no one would mention Swedish literature with the Norwegian. The trouble may have been that such a fantastic amount of our talent went into politics. In 1920 we very nearly had a revolution.' Now he finds that with Labor having been so long in power, there is a dullness and a sense of conformity in Norwegian society which hardly makes fertile soil for the arts.

My main impression after sitting in on some gatherings of poets and authors was one of great dissatisfaction and frustration. Even though these intense individualists were inclined to be 'more socialist than the Socialists,' they were sharply critical of the Labor Party not only for its foreign policy but for neglecting the arts. The talk would go like this: 'They finally, after all these years, got around to holding a cultural conference.' 'There isn't even a decent concert hall or conservatory of music in Oslo.' 'Our orchestra has to live like a bunch of nomads.' 'A writer can hardly live in this country, the pay's so poor.' 'The Minister of Culture? He's nothing but a dentist.' Anyway, they insisted, there was nothing going on in Norway that was worth writing about. When I observed that they might be unduly critical of their own country, two writers picked up the cue:

'Nobody in the world speaks against themselves so much as the Norwegians.'

'But we don't want anyone else to agree.'

'That's right. Only Norwegians are allowed to criticize Norwegians.'

What they were really complaining about was that Oslo is not Paris, and Norway is not a sufficiently inhuman society to allow them full scope for artistic outrage. They were stuck with the fact that Norway is a pleasant land of wholesome people.

The Sporting Life

It may be that Norway's cultural energies have been dissipated by good times, but at least the country is in championship form in sports and in its traditional zest for the outdoor life. A 'National Society for the Promotion of Physical Culture' began as long ago as 1861, and today's nationwide sports confederation has a third of a million members. Organized sports are important, especially football and athletics, but it is the universality of the sporting life in Norway that makes it a country rare in its dedication to vigorous activity. Whole families troop off to the seashore, forest trails and ski slopes to pit themselves against nature. Children learn to ski almost as soon as they can walk, and it is skiing which is the national passion.

Scandinavians were probably the world's first skiers. Ancient skis found in the North are believed to be 5,000 or more years old. A Norwegian rock carving dating from about 2000 B.C. is the oldest known depiction of skiing. The Norwegians claim that it was in the little valley of Morgedal in Telemark, more than a century ago, that skiing was elevated from mere transportation to sport and pleasure. 'When the snow comes to this Scandinavian country,' wrote John Lovesey, a British sports authority, 'it is almost unheard of not to ski, and equally unheard of if you are a boy, a real Norwegian boy, not to jump. They say only half-jokingly that if King Olav had not jumped he could have hardly mounted the throne, and his real popularity is reckoned to date from the time he competed in the great competition of Holmenkollen Day.'

Holmenkollen is one of the mightiest of about ten thousand ski jumps of all sizes in Norway, a country with a long record of winning Olympic gold medals for ski jumping. Holmenkollen is a landmark on the outskirts of Oslo—a beautifully sculptured hill topped by a great scaffold which supports the run-in to the jump. It has a forlorn look in the summer when it sits neglected amid the pines, but in the winter it wears a long, glistening robe of ice and snow. During the annual February or March jumping contest some 100,000 spectators squeeze together in the cold to watch the international champions perform. The jumbo-sized Holmenkollen jump measured just 20 meters in 1892 but it has since grown to 90 meters, or nearly 300 feet. At the very top of the jump the skier stands poised like a potential suicide on a wind-swept wooden bridge. Crouching between his knees, he hurtles down the 42-degree slope and then shoots into space at sixty miles an hour like a deadly missile flung from a catapult. Using the new aerodynamic style, the skier leans so far forward that his nose comes within inches of his ski tips. For a breathtaking moment, in a picture of pure grace, he is a flying man, alone and unsupported in the sky. If he only had more time he could look down into the eyes of the pretty girls buried in their fur coats or admire the panorama of Oslo and its beautiful fjord. But the flight lasts only about three seconds, and the skier, taking the shock of contact in his knees, hits the sloping deck like a jet fighter whooshing onto the deck of an aircraft carrier.

Understandably, Norway's foremost ski jumpers are national idols who outshine movie stars or pop singers in the eyes of teen-agers. Toralf Engan, one of the two or three greatest ski jumpers in the world in recent years, recovered for Norway the supremacy in ski jumping which it had temporarily lost when Finnish, Russian and Central European jumpers seized on the new aerodynamic technique. He is the trim, fair-haired and blue-eyed son of a road inspector from a village near Trondheim. Now in his late twenties, Engan was rated as too nervous a jumper ever to be a national champion even though he had won a county championship for boys when he was thirteen. He was not even able to make the Norwegian team to the Winter Olympics in Squaw Valley in 1960. His response was typically Norwegian— and then some. He ruthlessly trained himself by diving from springboards, running hundreds of miles through the woods, sweating through squatting and jumping exercises, and agonizing his way up and down the steps of a sports stadium with a 30-pound bag of sand lashed to his back. He swept up almost all the competitions he entered and became a gold medalist in the 1964 Winter Olympics.

For Norwegians as a whole, over their thousand years of

national identity, life has always been an uphill struggle, but it has been a challenge cheerfully met. Perhaps it is symbolized on the big jumping days at Holmenkollen when tens of thousands of ordinary Oslo men, women and children, knowing that there will be room for only a few on the little railway to the ski jump, arise in the early morning darkness, put on their boots and sweaters, and trudge for hours up the mountain in the capital's snowy backyard.

Part Four

Sweden

Chapter 18

THE PERFECTIONISTS

Why is the pretty girl smiling? She lives in a country where everybody has a job and enough to eat, where crime is practically nonexistent, where there are no slums or ghettos, and there hasn't been a war in 150 years.
—SAS ADVERTISEMENT

If the Swede starts analyzing himself it quickly develops into a highly complex affair, for the Swede doesn't like himself at all!
—WILLY BREINHOLST

The most untypically Swedish event in history occurred on August 10, 1628, when the King of Sweden's newest, most expensive and most elaborately outfitted warship, the *Vasa*, set out across Stockholm harbor with five hundred persons aboard for her maiden voyage. It was the evening of a balmy Sunday. Thousands of Swedes watched proudly as the tall, 64-gun man-of-war moved slowly away from the Palace of the Three Crowns. And then a strong but quite ordinary breeze billowed the topsails. The great ship keeled over and sank ignominiously to the bottom. The *Vasa* remained there until she was raised in 1961, three and a third centuries later, and put on display in a special museum.

It was not only a catastrophe for the hard-pressed Swedish armed forces during the Thirty Years' War, but the kind of engineering blunder which would horrify any proper Swede. The Swedes are a practical, pragmatic, thorough, industrious people, who make careful calculations and do things well if they do them at all. They prefer to leave little to chance. The persistent question in Sweden is: Does it work? Neutrality, for example, works—at least it has, ever since 1814—but to make sure it does, the Swedes have built the sixth-most-powerful air force in the world, and they maintain a state of military and civil-defense readiness that is matched in few other countries. Even more to the point, they have gone to considerable effort to reduce the possibility of war by sending out some of their most talented citizens as peacemakers and international civil servants.

The same kind of thoroughness and devotion to thoughtful solutions characterizes the Swedish scene from the bountiful farms of the Baltic south to the bleak mountains of the Lapland north. It is doubtful whether any other country in the world has been so totally organized, socialized, mechanized and modernized as Sweden. It is hard to imagine a more efficient nation in terms of exploiting to the full the available natural and human resources, and the aids of science and technology. The United States is known to be the world's technological giant and the most advanced of all societies, but its distribution of the 'blessings' of prosperity to every citizen in every corner of the land is less impressive than Sweden's. The Soviet Union, after nearly half a century of Communist leadership, would appear to be the most socialized of all nations, but the quality, the actuality, of Swedish social security is well in advance of the Russian brand. (Dictionary definition of social security: 'Public provision of the means necessary to enable individual citizens of a country to lead a personally satisfying and socially useful life, including adequate housing, education, recreation, health safeguards, and full employment, as well as adequate income.')

The Swedish blend of capitalism and socialism has produced not simply the well-known welfare state but a far different creature— the wealth-and-welfare state. In Swedish eyes, the United States has wealth and freedom, but has yet to secure full employment and full social security for the whole population, while the Soviet Union, despite its social and technological advances, still provides its citizens with insufficient wealth and far too little freedom. Several favorable circumstances (homogeneous population, natural resources, escape from war), plus native genius and sheer industriousness, have enabled the Swedes to construct a way of life which in *material* terms is the most successful in Europe and one of the three most successful in the world.

Precisely how well-off the Swedes are today, and how they have surged in the postwar period to a level of prosperity which ranks just behind that of the Americans and the Canadians, will be told in the following pages. Liberal use will be made of statistics—not from any fondness for figures on my part, but because this is the way the Swedes themselves like to tell the story of their achievement in affluence. They are the most statistical-minded people I have ever encountered. A veritable army of economists and statisticians is at work in the government and in private banks, companies and associations, assembling the figures on 'per capita gross consumption of electric energy' (Sweden is fourth in the world, after Norway, Canada and the U.S.A.) or the number of people who play tennis outdoors (140,000) and indoors (60,000). I have sometimes suspected that the plethora of statistics is a kind of smoke screen which the Swedes lay down to ward off further inquiry into their private lives, much as a clever public relations man will so overwhelm an inquiring reporter with press kits and publicity handouts that his more penetrating questions are smothered before they are asked. It is probably more correct, however, just to say that the Swedes are what they are—not Irishmen, not Italians, but a cool, precise, purposeful people who use the slide rule almost as a magic wand.

Unfortunately, an atmosphere of hard facts and cold statistics does little to warm up the standard image of the cool Swede. Ambition and efficiency are not the most charming and endearing characteristics of a people, admirable as they may be. They do not suggest emotional, sensitive or impassioned human beings who have the usual quota of foibles. But do appearances deceive? Is there fire under the ice? What *are* the Swedes like, anyway?

'Oh, yes,' said a Swedish lady to a visiting American writer, 'the Swedes are hardheaded and down-to-earth, practical materialists. Who can deny it? And also they are a bit heavy and unimaginative, as a general rule—who can deny that either? But it is not so simple. For in this same hardheaded, practical, down-to-earth Swede, one will generally find a deep, persistent brooding that likes to lose itself in abstract considerations and is obsessed with the idea of perfection.'

The Lonely Crowd

The Swedes are possibly the most complex people in Europe. They are tremendously accomplished yet seemingly unable to fully enjoy the superior standard of living they have achieved. As word of their well-being and their social problems has spread, the individual Swede has come to feel that he is some kind of bug on a pin undergoing an intense scrutiny by the outside world. There is a widespread fascination about the Swedes, if only because they seem to be living proof of the adage that money does not bring happiness.

The Swedes *ought* to be happy, content, satisfied, delighted with life. Seemingly, they have everything, but it isn't enough. Amid such great material prosperity something is missing. A picture book on the delights of Sweden published in Stockholm says quite candidly that 'spiritual unease—the plague of an anxious heart and a mind dissatisfied with plenty—has grown.' Foreigners arrive in Sweden and wonder why everybody is taking life so seriously.

It is doubtful whether welfare, prosperity and the commonplace tensions of the complex modern life have much to do with the Swedish unease. The Swede is not by nature a jovial, happy-go-lucky character; he never has been and never will be. It is in the Swedish nature, as one writer put it, 'to analyze life down to the bare bones, penetrate the soul, talk, talk.' From August Strindberg to Ingmar Bergman, the message seems to be that life brings disappointment and despair. A great quest leads not to fulfillment but to emptiness. There is this passage in Strindberg's *The Road to Damascus*:

LADY. Did you ever see visions?
STRANGER. Never. But I've often thought that two beings were guiding my destiny. One offers me all I desire; but the other's ever at hand to bespatter the gifts with filth, so that they're useless to me and I can't touch them. It's true that life has

given me all I asked of it—but everything's turned out to be worthless to me.

LADY. You've had everything and yet are not content?

STRANGER. That is the curse . . .

LADY. Don't say that! But why haven't you desired things that transcend this life, that can never be sullied?

STRANGER. Because I doubt if there is a beyond.

So many of Bergman's films have dealt with tormented, soul-searching Swedes that he has been accused by some of his country-men of giving the world a distorted image of Swedish life. His controversial *The Silence* is an unnerving study of people virtually unable to feel or communicate. The professor emeritus in *Wild Strawberries* says that 'our intercourse with other people consists chiefly in discussing and evaluating the character and behavior of our neighbors. This has caused me to refrain—of my own free will—from practically every form of so-called social life.' Later on, during a harrowing hallucination, he asks an inquisitor, 'What is my crime?' He is told, 'Indifference, egoism, lack of consideration.' The penalty? 'The customary thing: loneliness.'

The Swedes are known as a reserved, formal, withdrawn people whose submerged personalities may not be exposed unless there is sufficient alcoholic lubrication. It is said that 'Swedes don't tell jokes. If they have enough drinks they stand on tables and sing.' Visitors return from Scandinavia glowing about their encounters with the Danes and Norwegians, but less enthusiastic about the 'standoffish' Swedes. An American diplomat said that after three years in a Stockholm suburb he had yet to see the inside of his neighbors' homes. Nor had he, in fact, been able to make much contact with them. One day, after he had rushed a neighborhood child to a hospital for emergency medical treatment, he was sure that her parents would call on him at last. 'They sent me flowers,' he said, 'and a note of thanks.'

Yet it is the Swedes themselves who are among the first to deplore the Swedish personality. I have actually met Swedes living abroad who described themselves as 'anti-Swede Swedes.' They couldn't stand the life back in their home country. A leading Swedish diplomat said that things back home were too cut-and-dried. 'There should be prizes given to those people who create controversy and amusement in Sweden.' A Danish writer said that a Swede 'will tell you with great conviction that he is *urtråkig*—not only dull, but dull in the most extreme sense of the word—deadly dull. To prove it he will tell you that he's too formal, too reserved and ceremonious at parties, too bashful, too proud, and too unapproachable in daily life.'

The Need for Ritual

In these and other ways, the Swedes seem much like the Japanese. Their personal defenses are up. They wear a mask, and it seldom slips. They are anxious to be seen at their best, hence the reluctance to have callers unless preparations have been made. They have, over the centuries, spun out a web society which is almost Japanese in the interlocking of its human components. 'Things are too well arranged,' one student complained. 'Life is organized to the smallest detail.'

The Swedes surround themselves with ritual and an elaborate code of conduct. They have a strong sense of duty and obligation, with the result that they hesitate to become involved with others. New relationships only mean new duties and obligations. The high degree of social organization seems to be a way in which the individual can be assured that things are being handled properly without his having to be personally involved. His inclination is to leave it to the proper or responsible authorities, while he remains uncommitted.

If there is a traffic accident the Swede is less likely to spring to a person's aid than he is to look on, without expression, without involvement, until the police or doctors arrive. Behind the wheel of a car, again like the Japanese, he may show surprising antisocial traits. Sealed inside the automobile, racing toward pedestrians he does not know personally, he is apt to drive with the kind of ill-manneredness unthinkable in his face-to-face contacts. The gentle Swedish cities screech with the sound of strained tires as cars take the corners fast and dangerously. In 1964, Sweden had 63,800 traffic accidents, in which 1,189 persons were killed, despite some of the most vigilant traffic police and stiffest drunken-driving penalties in the world.

Once personally involved with a stranger, however, the Swedes could not be more solicitous. One day I telephoned a city government department in Gothenburg for some information but the call went to someone in the wrong agency—a fact not discovered until I had stated my problem. The official insisted on getting the information for me anyway. At the end, when I thanked him for his help and apologized for bothering him, he protested, 'Oh no, it is my duty to be bothered.'

Willy Breinholst, viewing the Swedes through Danish glasses, has noted that they are 'especially keen on carrying the titular formality to its utmost consequence.' He wrote: 'There is a classic example of two Swedes who would have liked to start a conversation during a long and tiresome train journey, but who were prevented from doing this because they didn't know each other's title or profession. At long last one of them solved the problem by addressing the other as "Mr. Express-train Passenger." The other man was highly ingratiated, seeing that he was in fact traveling on a slow, local line, and so a lively conversation was embarked upon.'

The fondness for honorifics is of Germanic proportions. Letters are addressed to 'Herr formerly Chief Inspector of Schools, the author Carl Gustaf Jönsson, B.A.' In conversation it is advisable not to use the second person, as in 'What do you think of the play?' but to say, 'What does the professor think of the play?' The ritual at a dinner party is likely to be bewildering. A guest raises his glass, catches another's eye, says *Skål*, drinks, and gives a polite little nod—still keeping his eyes locked with his drinking partner—all in one fluid motion. A guest is supposed to raise his glass with a number of people, not forgetting his own wife, and respond agreeably when someone catches his eye. The hostess, however, who must keep the refreshments coming and see that things are in good order, is spared from being drawn too much into the drinking routine. At the start of the ceremonies the host will give a 'welcome-to-the-table' speech. A sufficient quantity of akvavit and wine may inspire other speechmakers. Swedish dinner parties with their ritualistic toasting, speechmaking and creeping gaiety, as well as the beautifully arranged bits of food presented on handsome trays and dishes, have always reminded me of the ceremonious-then-uproarious evenings I have known in the inns and geisha houses of Japan. In both cultures, personalities are unlocked with the passkey of alcohol.

It must be added, however, that the Swedes only carry to more formal lengths the food and drink customs which are common all over Scandinavia. Because so much of the social life is carried on in the home, people in the Nordic countries have developed much the same ritual for a convivial evening. Above all, guests must be plied with more food and drink than they can possibly consume. Even when the visitor arrives unexpectedly at a Scandinavian home, the lady of the house manages to produce an elaborate serving of coffee, sandwiches, cakes and assorted delicacies. When invited to a dinner party the guest is well advised to take a gift of flowers to the hostess. At the end of the meal he lines up with the others to shake her hand and express his thanks. And when he meets her later on the street he must make a point of thanking her once again.

Elaborate politeness and an involved code of conduct are crutches for any people whose emotions are suppressed and whose tongues are tied. 'Swedish silence' has now become a cliché, and like most clichés it is an unfair exaggeration of the truth. In my own experience, Swedes are voluble enough. It would be ridiculous to suggest that it is a land of stark silence. Nonetheless, Swedes have difficulty about fully expressing their feelings, and difficulty in communicating satisfactorily with each other. Girls complain about their boy friends who seem incapable of saying tender words of love. Wives complain about their silent husbands.

The recent Swedish film, *A Sunday in September*, was a disturbing study of two young Swedes trying, unsuccessfully, to make a go of their marriage. A poignant love affair was followed by the dreariness of each other's company. The girl's mother was convinced that 'most marriages are unhappy.' The young husband's father 'died of disappointment.' There were these bits of dialogue: 'You wrap yourself in silence.' 'What keeps us together is our habits.' 'He's dead to me.' 'You know how it is with parents. At first you hate them. Then you begin to understand them. And finally you love them, but then it's too late.'

Young people I have spoken to in Sweden say that their parents make little effort to understand them or to say anything to them beyond tedious instructions to work, succeed and conform. The older generation complains that it cannot understand the younger generation. A number of Swedes suggested that the outbreaks of juvenile delinquency could be traced to the cold war between the generations in some Swedish homes. A visitor certainly gets the impression that there are dark impulses toward violence underneath the Swedish skin. Not much gets out, to judge by the statistics on crime and violence, but Swedish youth as a whole seems much more rebellious than youngsters elsewhere in the North. To take only a minor instance, the male teen-age fad of the mid-1960s for long hair, cosmetics and modish clothing found its most extreme expression on the streets of Stockholm, where the boys out-Beatled the Beatles.

Cracking the Shell

The Swedes are most Swedish when they are brooding, something they do more than most people. They become lost in thought and seem to be sitting wrapped in a shroud of their own making. Their mask is riveted on. When asked to explain what it is all about, the Swedes fall back on the word *grubbel*. It has to do with melancholy and longing. *Grubbel* is an atmosphere peculiarly Swedish even though I have been reminded of it in Norway and Finland when I have heard people say wistfully, 'Will we ever see summer again? How I hate winter!' It seems to stem, at least in part, from the brevity of life's most exhilarating moments. The joys of summer are over much too soon. They have to be enjoyed with almost too much intensity, like a feast eaten ravenously. Afterward there is too much time to reflect and find fault. All too often in Sweden, marriage is like that—a brief, glorious romance in the golden hours of youth, and then stolid conventionality. I have often had the impression that Sweden's

precisely organized, middle-class, right-conduct society closes in
on people much too early in life. Husbands and wives become
melancholic about the carefree time of youth. They wonder
where it all went. They brood about it, in separate beds.

Mixed in with brooding is introspection. For a seemingly
nihilistic people who are said to prefer cleanliness to godliness,
the Swedes do a powerful amount of soul searching. It was only
after his death that it was revealed how much Dag Hammarskjöld, the quietly competent, serenely self-confident diplomat, was
really a mystic who had worked out a personal philosophy about
the idea of life as a sacrifice. His posthumously published diary,
Markings, which became an international best seller, was, by his
own account, 'a sort of "white book" on my deliberations with
myself—and God.'

A good many Swedes, as well as other people, were amazed to
learn how religious a man Hammarskjöld was, and how he seemed
to equate his sacrificial role on earth with Christ. A leading
Swedish editor, Olof Lagercrantz, said it was perhaps fortunate
that Hammarskjöld died before becoming too carried away by the
parallel, otherwise he might have moved too far from reality. He
saw Hammarskjöld as one of those top-society Swedes, one who
'fights in the clouds at the same time that he plays a role on earth.'

Hammarskjöld wrote: 'I ask the impossible that life shall have
a meaning. I fight the impossible that my life shall have a meaning.' Only months before his death he put these words in his
diary:

I have reached a time and a place where I know that my road
leads to a triumph that is perdition and to a perdition that is
triumph, that the price of a life's deeds is vilification and that
the depths of abasement offer the heights to which man can
aspire. The word courage has lost its meaning, since I have
nothing to lose.

All of this fits in with the stereotype of the despairing, joyless
Swede; but it is too simple, not to say unfair, to write off a whole
people as soul-tortured. 'Come on now,' a friend said one day.
'Look at me. Do I look gloomy?' I had to confess that he did not,

nor did most of the Swedes I knew. Not only did they lead full and satisfying lives, but they appeared to be happily married and they often displayed a warm sense of humor. They were not stiff, or cold. At one Stockholm dinner party with a mixture of film, stage, business and government people, I conscientiously tried to carry out the usual eyeball-to-eyeball *skål* ritual but was told not to bother. 'It's too much trouble,' they said. 'If you feel like drinking, then drink.' Even Ingmar Bergman is far from being a 'typical' Swede. 'He looks French more than Swedish,' wrote a British critic, 'and he is extraordinarily gay. A young actress who has worked with him says of him that he has the largest laugh in the whole of Sweden.'

I have also come to feel that the number of Swedes who deplore the darker side of the Swedish character may someday outnumber those who fit the standardized image. 'We are technicians, not artists,' said a psychologist. 'We are a stressed people,' said a restaurant manager. 'We are so damned stiff,' said a banker; 'we are afraid of putting a foot wrong.' But the psychologist had a bubbling personality and was about to write a book on Israel. The restaurant manager, showing no signs of stress, had only recently flown a private plane all the way to India. And the banker, who has friends all over the world, was so unstiff that he could as well have been a Dane or a Norwegian. I have met some extraordinary people in Sweden—sophisticated, accomplished, open-hearted individuals—and can recall almost no instances of stand-offishness. They simply take a little longer to get to know than other Scandinavians. You enter into a lasting relationship with a Swede one step at a time, not by plunging in.

Down deep, the Swede is anxious to be liked, and his sometimes awkward efforts to be hearty and informal with a foreigner can be winning. In any event, Sweden's over-all release from its protective shell, its more active role in world affairs, has helped to make the Swedes easier-going and easier to know. They are not so austere and formal as they used to be, and they care less about what the neighbors will say. Young people in particular assert themselves in a way they would not have ten or twenty years ago. I remember asking a Danish student who had just returned from a visit to a Swedish university what he thought of the Swedish students. 'I was really surprised,' he said. 'They laugh just like we do.'

The slow emergence of the extroverted Swede is coupled with running debate in Swedish intellectual circles on the need to fashion a more spiritually rewarding society now that the physical side of life has been satisfied. Jörn Donner, a Finnish-born author and one of Sweden's new wave of film directors, has spoken of 'the spiritual unrest which has troubled Swedish society for the last thirty years.' He wrote:

> In Swedish society today, the motive of economic security as a factor in human conduct has been partly pushed into the background. This is not true for all citizens, but it is valid for large segments of society. . . . The social question which remains to be solved, when outward security has been achieved, is the question of balance on the personal level, in the inner life. This aspiration can never lead to a definitive result, since perfection and happiness are remote mirages which man sets up for himself.

It is this search for an inner satisfaction to match the outward security that makes Sweden a particularly fascinating and even exciting society. An effort seems to be under way to take in hand the deep-rooted Swedish personality and see whether it might be reshaped to suit the new Swedish age of affluence and outgoingness. But at the same time the Swedes are earnestly tackling the problems—familiar to all technologically advanced societies—of how to make the most rewarding use of leisure time and how to find cultural and spiritual satisfaction in a land of plenty. 'We have nothing to look forward to,' grumble some of Sweden's indulged youth. The challenge is to give them a challenge, and something to look forward to.

Land of Plenty

When they are not worrying about themselves the Swedes are working, and working with a will which is becoming out of date even in such industrious countries as Germany. It is still a part of the national ethic to stick to the job, and to do the job well. Having pulled themselves up by their own bootstraps, the Swedes have achieved an astonishing momentum in their drive toward the Good Life. It is true enough, as the Swedes are the first to say, that not everyone is living in luxury, but it is also true to say that Sweden is likely to achieve mass luxury sooner than any other nation in Europe. Even now, Sweden shares the heights with the United States and Canada in innumerable economic measurements.

For example, using 1963 figures on ownership of goods per 1,000 people, the top three *automobile*-owning nations are the U.S.A. (366), Canada (267) and Sweden (204). For the sake of comparison, the figure for the United Kingdom is 152, for Italy 77.

The top three nations in *telephones* per 1,000 people are the U.S.A. (443), Sweden (423) and Canada (349). The U.K. figure is 174, the Italian 100.

The top three in *television sets* per 1,000 people are the U.S.A. (280 homes with TV), Sweden (239 TV licenses) and the U.K. (237 licenses). Canada has 222 homes with TV, Italy 85 TV licenses. Amazingly enough, regular television broadcasting did not start in Sweden until October 1956.

The 1963 figures for *per capita gross national product* show only four nations above $2,000 (£714): the U.S.A., $3,090 (£1103); Canada, $2,263 (£808); Sweden, $2,045 (£730); and Switzerland, $2,010 (£718). The U.K. figure is $1,564 (£558), the Italian $899 (£321).

The Swedes may be, man for man, the best-dressed people in the world. They have a psychological need to appear at their best, and they have the means to purchase the highest-quality clothing. Personal consumption of food and goods has nearly doubled since 1939, and the Swedish people as a whole have become accustomed, like the mass of Americans and Canadians, to luxuries which are still beyond the reach of most people in the world. Sweden is not only nearing the American ratio of one car per family but the most popular automobile in Sweden is a costly Volvo model, not the cheaper Volkswagen, Saab or the least-expensive Volvo. In addition to 350,000 weekend cottages for a nation of just 7·7 million people, there are some 250,000 motorboats and 30,000 sailboats in Sweden, and the average man's expenditure on travel may be the highest in Europe. To a greater degree than anywhere else in Europe, the Swedes have filled their homes with appliances and most modern kinds of furnishings.

It is also worth noting that the Swedes have given an exceptional amount of attention to devising the most functional and well-designed yet inexpensive components for the modern household. As it was expressed in the 1940s, the approach takes in everything 'from cutlery to town planning.' The whole design for living starts with the simplest utensils. The size and shape of knives and forks is a factor in determining the design of a drawer, and, in turn, of its cabinet, the other kitchen units, the kitchen itself, the whole apartment, the multistory building it is in, and the place of the building in the whole scheme of urban life. Massive research into space requirements, practical furnishings and the standardization of units was put together in the 1958 report, *Living Habits and Standards*. Domestic guidelines were set down for designers, artisans and architects. Among the results was the integrated, cleverly equipped 'Swedish kitchen,' as it is well known in Europe.

The Housing Dilemma

With 40 per cent of the population now occupying homes built since the end of World War II, Sweden has as modern and well-designed a housing structure as any nation in the world. Yet it is housing—the shortage of housing and the cramped size of the average home—that is one of Sweden's most nagging social problems. It is a state of affairs, moreover, which raises the question whether Swedish living standards are as lofty as they seem. There is no question but that Sweden is more prosperous and socially secure than almost any other country, but it is also true that most other people in the Western world have more living space in their homes and a greater choice of housing. Virtually every European country is having to cope with an insistent demand for more and better housing, but people whose incomes have substantially increased can usually find a better home to move into when they want to. Not so in Sweden. Only the exceedingly well-to-do Swede or the exceedingly fortunate can move into a new home when and where he chooses.

The Swedish housing problem is not so much a shortage of dwellings as it is a shortage of dwellings in the right place. The essence of the problem is that Sweden has undergone one of the most rapid social and economic changes of any nation in history. The once poor peasant country—which lost a fifth of its entire population to America because of widespread poverty—has been transformed almost overnight into a rich nation of city dwellers. Barely one lifetime ago, three quarters of all working Swedes were farmers, foresters and fishermen. Today the percentage is less than 15. The portion of the total labor force engaged in agriculture has dropped from about 30 per cent just before the war to 10 per cent today. (At the same time a stunning increase in farm productivity has made Sweden agriculturally self-sufficient.) 'In a few generations,' said a Swedish official, 'we have advanced from an old-oaken-bucket economy to automated industry and broad social benefits.'

Three quarters of the Swedes now live in towns and cities. The national movement from the country has been so rapid that the building of new dwellings has never caught up with the demand. Meantime, a lot of rural housing has been abandoned, torn down or converted into summer homes for city dwellers. Prosperity for all has meant an unrelenting pressure from families seeking better and roomier housing, and from single persons anxious to acquire their own dwellings. These include young people and pensioners who in former times would have stayed with their families or relations.

It was estimated in 1964 that more than 400,000 new living units were needed in Sweden in order to alleviate the existing housing shortage, and yet postwar Sweden has had the highest postwar home-building rate in Western Europe with the sole exception of war-devastated Germany. More than one million new dwellings have been erected in the two decades since the war, a high figure for a country of only 2·7 million households, and Swedish officials quite naturally cite it to prove that the housing problem is being tackled with vigor. But it must be added that a third of a million dwellings have been demolished or converted into offices in the same period, so that the net gain is about 700,000 homes. Furthermore, 70 per cent of the new units are apartments, not private homes, and they are small apartments, certainly by American standards.

The housing problem is clearly not a case of neglect by Sweden's Social Democratic government, but rather a result of some built-in Swedish problems of resources and manpower, and of an almost too-conscientious effort by the government to provide all Swedes with decent housing. The Swedish state has been involved in housing construction and regulation ever since World War I. The present housing policy was devised in the 1940s. It aimed at making available, for a rent of 20 per cent or less of the average income, a modern family dwelling of two rooms and a kitchen. In one respect, the policy has been successful, since the typical family man in Sweden pays less than 25 per cent of his income for an apartment with three rooms and kitchen. But the trouble is that there are not enough apartments, and a great many people suspect that there would be a sufficient supply if the government had kept its hands off and permitted a free market in housing.

Sweden has had rent control since 1942. Although it is no longer so universally applied, it still remains in force in most cities and covers more than half the population. Rent control has undoubtedly been a boon to many persons who would have suffered in an open-market situation, but it has discouraged private building companies and led to many abuses.

The government and local authorities erect a third of all new dwellings, and almost all housing projects are backed by government loans. It is the government that decides on the number of housing starts each year, enforces building standards, and subsidizes pensioners and low-income families to about 25 per cent of their rent. The government insists that it has had to exercise housing controls because the high cost of land, materials and labor would mean sky-high rents in a free market, and because the manpower shortage forces it to try to allocate labor on some priority basis. What it boils down to, however, is a surplus of state regulation and a shortage of housing. Critics of the Social Democrats say that housing is one of their greatest failures, and government leaders themselves sound defensive about their policies. They are now moving toward the abolition of rent control, but with agonizing deliberation. Said one Swede: 'We've kept a bad system going so long that it is hard to change it today.'

Rent control has brought about a black market in housing in Stockholm and other cities, where owners let their apartments through private agencies which have been charging tenants 'key money' ranging from $1,000 to $15,000, depending on the quality of the dwelling. The luckiest people are those who acquired flats before the days of rent control. Some elderly single persons occupy older midtown apartments with many big rooms, while large families are packed into small modern apartments. At one point in 1964 there were 170,000 people in the Stockholm area registered for new housing, and undoubtedly there were many who, out of sheer hopelessness, did not register. Only a small percentage of these were 'without roof.' The rest were looking for a place of their own, or something better than what they had. The people on the housing queue might have to wait five to ten years before they are offered a new apartment by the authorities. Not only is there a queue for housing, but there is also a one-to-two-day queue just to telephone Stockholm's housing department. Swedes have had to resort to ingenious methods to find a place to live. One woman explained that she and her husband had succeeded in obtaining a flat in the popular Stockholm suburb of Vällingby by arranging a three-way deal. They were living in Uppsala at the time and learned that a Vällingby family was seeking an apartment in Gothenburg. They then discovered a Gothenburg family which was searching for an apartment in Uppsala. The obvious negotiations took place. One day all three families moved at once, and all were amazed at their good fortune.

Cliff Dwellers

What might be wondered about is why the Swedes, a nature-loving people who live in a country with more than enough space for everyone, choose to dwell in crowded apartment buildings. Sweden seems made to order for the private homes and sprawling suburbs which characterize the American scene.

In the first place, the average Swede does not have much choice in the matter. He is pretty much obliged to take what housing is available. Faced with the need to provide a lot of housing in a hurry, the government went along with the over-all European answer of the high-rise apartment project. But three other points are more indigenous to Sweden: 1. The long Nordic winter has convinced the Swedes that it is more sensible living in a centrally heated apartment than struggling along in a private home. 'There is no snow to shovel,' said one Swede. 'No worries about heating or something going wrong with the house.' 2. The Swedes, like the Norwegians and Finns, have evolved a two-house way of life. They are willing to put up with the crowding in a small city apartment most of the year in order to enjoy their private and often quite primitive country cottages during the good-weather weekends and the brief but glorious summer. 3. The Swedes are more gregarious than their reputation for diffidence and reserve suggests. They like to have company and to hibernate en masse through the dark months. 'We like to be alone,' a Swedish journalist said, 'but alone together.'

The result is a country of forests, lakes, empty spaces and millions of people stacked up like cliff dwellers in apartment buildings, which are getting taller all the time. For a long time the standard height was three stories; but as the cities began to fill up, the apartment blocks became more vertical than horizontal. The elevator is now the principal means of transportation in Sweden. When a twenty-seven-story residential skyscraper was opened in Malmö, Sweden's third-largest city, in 1964, it was hailed as the tallest apartment building in Europe. A few months earlier, in downtown Malmö, the city's newest and largest department store had sprouted a little community of twenty-one adjoining roof houses. Stockholm, Gothenburg and every other city in Sweden bristles with new apartment towers, most of them equipped with little balconies to bring some semblance of the outdoors to the average man's filing-cabinet life.

Homogenized Prosperity

The abundance of new apartment towers and cleanly designed housing projects help give Sweden its look of supermodernity. They also give it a look of monotony. The buildings seem the same from one end of the country to the other. The new Swedish schools are marvels of functional design, but they too look the same from north to south. It is a standardized society, with all the homes, shops, cars and people seemingly produced from the same limited number of cookie cutters. Thousands of 'Tempo' and 'Konsum' retail chain stores appear on main streets, with a wearisome inevitability. Everything from furniture to street lighting fixtures has a nationwide sameness, which is all the more noticeable because, although incomes have not been leveled out as much as might be imagined in a high-tax welfare state, there is little difference to be seen in the look and dress of a laborer and a professional man. They may not share the same cultural interests and probably have little to do with each other socially (class differences being given greater weight in Sweden than elsewhere in the North), but they may well have adjoining flats in the same housing project. Their children will attend the same school and have equal possibilities of a university education if they merit one. They each get four weeks' vacation every year, and both will display a feverish joy in their summer pleasure to match the fervor of their working life.

The uniformity of it all takes something away from the drama of Swedish everyday life; but, for anyone who is interested in the way societies develop, there is a special excitement in the rapidity with which Sweden is changing. Far from having achieved a comfortable, settled existence and being content to leave it at that, the Swedes are altering and modernizing their way of life at a faster pace all the time. For an essentially conservative people who have a great pride in their past, they have an amazing passion for progress. Their social problems have not been as easily engineered, but in material terms the Swedes have virtually forged a wholly new society during the past few decades.

The whole country has been pulled together by hydroelectric lines, by a highway and rail network which is one of the most advanced in the world, and by communications facilities which are the best in Europe. Sweden is one of the world's great producers of telephones and the efficiency of its telephone system is rivaled only in the United States. Sweden shares with Britain the distinction of having the highest per capita newspaper readership, and the several major newspapers in Stockholm which recently erected new skyscrapers for their offices and printing plants probably have the most modern equipment of any newspapers anywhere. Automation and computers have swept the Swedish industrial scene during the past few years. Nikita Khrushchev was so astonished by the way the Swedes made giant ships in a new assembly-line shipyard that he told a Russian television audience that they were being turned out 'like stuffed sausages.'

The Swedes are rushing into automation and other labor-saving methods with a greater zeal than other nations because they have one of the most serious labor shortages in Europe. It is a shortage which would be worse if it were not for the postwar importation of 300,000 foreign workers, nearly half of whom have become citizens. These newcomers in turn have altered Sweden, made it less uniform and ingrown. The whole society has been on a labor-saving binge during the last few years. As just one indication of the change in home life, partly brought about because so many married women have a job as well as keep house, the Swedes have become Europe's greatest consumers of frozen foods.

It would be nice to believe that the Swedes are still devoted to such traditional dishes as 'Grandmother's Eye' (raw egg yolk, chopped pickled beets, onions, anchovies, capers) and 'Jansson's Temptation' (sliced potatoes, onions, anchovy fillets), but times have changed. 'The awful truth,' wrote Willy Breinholst, 'is that the highly civilized, super-Americanized Swede of today mainly lives on semimanufactured, mass-produced, cellophane-wrapped, vitaminized industrial foods that are quickly bought, quickly eaten and quickly forgotten.'

Swedish shopping habits have done a complete about face. The number of self-service stores in Sweden grew from only 200 in 1950 to 8,500 in 1965. The number of retail shops of all kinds is decreasing at the rate of a thousand a year, as many little ones give way to fewer larger ones. The housewife who once walked to the corner grocery now drives to a shopping-center supermarket. Sweden has become a nation on wheels. In 1950 there were only 250,000 automobiles in the whole country. Today Swedes buy more than 250,000 new cars every year.

It all adds up to a dynamic new society grafted onto an ancient land which still exudes an atmosphere of trolls and Vikings and elderly gentlemen wearing monocles. Whether Sweden has become a truly better and happier society is something for the Swedes to say. They are obviously not wholly satisfied with the results, and they are searching on. They can say, however, as did one Swede, that 'if there is apathy and boredom, it is at least a more sophisticated social problem than slums and poverty.'

Chapter 19

EVERGREEN KINGDOM

The leafless trees and every icy crag
Tinkled like iron; while far-distant hills
Into the tumult sent an alien sound
Of melancholy.
                                    —WILLIAM WORDSWORTH

Space and unspoiled nature are Sweden's solace for its troubled soul. The surrounding sea and snow-covered mountains make it almost an island civilization. The lakes give it serenity. The forests, which cover well over half the total area, give it depth. The vastness of the land in relation to the fewer than eight million population gives it extraordinary privacy. A Danish psychiatrist muttered that 'the Swedes have all that space and practically the lowest birth rate in the world. They could easily have twice the number of people and live comfortably.'

It is a long haul from the gentle, rolling, lake-dimpled south through the great forests to the glacial mountains of the north. Sweden has the shape of a sausage—a highly punctured sausage, since the lakes number 96,000 and take up 9 per cent of the total area. The California-size country is 990 miles long and generally 200 to 250 miles wide. One seventh of it lies above the Arctic Circle. The southernmost province of Skåne almost touches Denmark and is only sixty miles from the Baltic coast of East Germany. Most of Sweden's west coast lies abreast of Norway. As already noted, Sweden is only a few miles from the Atlantic in that region where Norway squeezes into a narrow corridor. Gothenburg and the other cities on the southwestern coast, however, have ready access to the North Sea and the ocean. Sweden has a coastline of 4,737 miles, beginning at the Norwegian border just below Oslo, sweeping around the south and running up to the Finnish border at the top of the Bay of Bothnia. There are few fjords, but Sweden has a natural wonderland in the fringe of tens of thousands of little islands which shelter the mainland. During the winter most of the Bothnia coast freezes up from November to April or May. In exceptional winters almost the whole of Sweden is locked in ice.

Sweden's northern frontier is wedged between Norway and Finland in that Lapland world which lures hikers, skiers, mountaineers, hunters and fishermen. To travel north is to go deeper and deeper into the forests—vast, silent, broodingly beautiful evergreen forests. There are said to be 51 billion trees in Sweden, a figure which boggles the imagination and makes one grateful that the Swedes haven't tried to count the pine needles. Some 300 million trees are cut down each year. A great logging network of streams and rivers carries the trees to the sawmills and pulp mills. The forests are carpeted with moss, and the lichen-covered rocks are said to be trolls turned to stone. The wanderer through the Nordic jungle marvels at the play of light and shadow, and at the infinite shadings of green in this great green world. Sweden has a subtle, dewy beauty far different from the lush colors of southern lands.

Despite the rush of traffic and the roar of industry, Sweden has a calm and settled air over most of its parts. The thousands of industrial plants are woven quietly into the landscape, almost hiding the fact that peasant Sweden has become one of the most potent manufacturing nations in the world. Because the country has almost no coal and depends on hydroelectric energy and oil imports for its energy, there is little industrial grime. Scrubbed cities rise cleanly from the landscape. Towns take care to keep their natural surroundings unspoiled. It is rare to see either a townhouse or farmhouse that is not spruced up and well painted. Like berries on a Christmas wreath, the dark-red houses with their white-rimmed windows stand solidly in the country greenery. It is a perfect equestrian country and horses are still to be seen; but they have lost the race to the tractor, whose numbers have multiplied tenfold in twenty years.

Only 9 per cent of Sweden is suitable for cultivation, and agriculture now accounts for only 5 per cent of Sweden's gross national product; yet the traveler in southern Sweden feels that he has found a farming paradise. Skane accounts for only 2·5 per cent of Sweden's total area, but it has 12 per cent of the population. As the 'breadbasket of Sweden,' it was the original settlement of the nation. The prosperous farmland is sprinkled with ancient runic stones, medieval castles and splendid manor houses.

North of Skåne the pastoral scene shifts to the rocky ground and beech forests of Småland where there lives a tough, resilient people with the stuff of pioneers. There is a story that while God was busy making Skåne into a natural garden, the devil sneaked past Him and made Småland. By the time God caught on, it was too late to change the hard face of the land, 'so He made the people.' In their wondrous way the Smålanders have prospered by grouping in little workshop communities—the Swedish *bruk*—and making specialized high-quality articles for sale in Sweden and abroad.

Anchored just offshore from Småland is the long and narrow island of Öland, a poetic place of cornfields, wild flowers and harsh winds which sweep over a great treeless steppe. Öland, like Småland, was disastrously hit during Sweden's nineteenth-century days of poverty. At least a quarter of its population sailed to America. The challenge to a visitor to Öland is to find a single native who does *not* have a relative in the United States. A number of Öland farmers over the decades have turned into dollar millionaires overnight when news came from the American Midwest that 'Uncle Sven' had died and left them a fortune.

Northeast of Öland is the larger and historically more important island of Gotland. Few places in Europe can so quickly transport a modern traveler into the world of the Middle Ages than the Gotland capital of Visby. Now known as 'the city of ruins and roses,' Visby in the twelfth century was one of the wealthiest trading centers in the world. It grew up under the sponsorship of the Hanseatic merchants of Lübeck and eventually dominated the trade of northern and most of western Europe. The rich merchants of Gotland put up no fewer than seventeen churches within the relatively small confines of the town. The old, encircling, tower-studded wall, nearly two miles long and as tall as six medieval soldiers, still stands. The farm land still comes up to the very gates. It is as if the old City of London had stopped growing in the fourteenth century and now stood forlornly in a quiet corner of England.

The rest of Gotland is simply a nature lover's paradise. The island hibernates in the winter and then takes on an onslaught of visitors during the summer. Many more Swedes, however, head for the great lakes which lie between Gothenburg on the west coast and Stockholm on the east. The largest of them, Lake Vänern, 90 miles long and 50 wide, happens to be the greatest lake in Europe, excepting Russia. It is one of the links in the delightful 350-mile waterway which meanders nonchalantly across southern Sweden from Gothenburg to Stockholm. The Göta Canal, which opened in 1832 and has 65 locks, accounts for 115 miles of the waterway. I was amazed to discover that it is the longest ship canal in the world, longer than the Suez and twice the length of the Panama Canal. It does not, however, have much width, depth or traffic. Its days of commercial glory are past, and its occupation now is nostalgia. The ships it accommodates are tubby white boats which carry vacationers on a leisurely cruise through the lakes and farmland. The full Gothenburg–Stockholm journey takes three days and two nights. One of the more astonishing sights in Sweden, if a visitor stands well back from the canal, is to see the ships sailing across the landscape as if on a sea of grain.

Gothenburg (Göteborg)

Ships of a different kind are seen in Gothenburg, Sweden's biggest port and second-largest city. It is the home for 40 per cent of the country's merchant fleet of about 950 vessels. It takes in a third of Sweden's imports and sends off a fourth of its exports.

Gothenburg became Great Britain's principal depot for trade with northern and western Europe during the days of Napoleon's continental blockade. The city has been called 'Little London' and takes pride in its many associations with England and Scotland. It is a place where the proper Swede with his black derby and rolled umbrella looks more like a proper Englishman. It is said that 'when it rains in London the umbrellas go up in Gothenburg.' Gothenburgers are at pains to emphasize that the city is not just a half-size Stockholm but a quite different, more vigorous and much friendlier metropolis. 'The best thing in Stockholm,' said a banker, 'is the train back to Gothenburg.'

King Gustavus Adolphus founded the city in 1621, and its name is an appropriate one for that part of Sweden known as the Land of the Goths. Dutch builders were called in and they gave the central part of the town the canals and narrow townhouses which suggest Amsterdam. The city has some handsome parks, an outstanding art museum and considerable elegance, but it is primarily a business city, where commerce has always taken precedence over culture. It is the best place in Sweden to feel the full impact of the nation's industrial strength. SKF ball bearings, Volvo cars, Eriksberg and Götaverken tankers, Mölnlycke textiles and innumerable other products all come pouring out of fast-expanding factories, which would grow even more rapidly if there were workers enough and housing enough. Greater Gothenburg has now burgeoned to 520,000 people, and despite a prodigious building program it still can take five years or more to get an apartment.

Going North

What makes Gothenburg particularly blessed as a big industrial city is its nearness to some of the finest seaside resorts and getting-away-from-it-all islands in northern Europe. North of Gothenburg and running up the coast to the Norwegian border is Bohuslän province, an escapist's wonderland of rocky peninsulas, craggy islets and jagged inlets, and a scattering of fishing villages, castles, rustic old hotels and weathered holiday cottages. One entranced foreign visitor decided that the Bohuslän islands look something like 'a school of gigantic whales caught and turned to stone in some unrecorded cataclysm in the youth of the world.' In the full glory of summertime Sweden they make a haven for yachtsmen and a heaven for girl watchers.

Central Sweden begins above the great lakes in the romanticized province of Värmland. It is an idyllic region, which became legendary when Sweden's most celebrated authoress, Selma Lagerlöf, a winner of the Nobel Prize in Literature, wrote *The Saga of Gösta Berling.* This remarkable novel, so very Swedish, told the story of a parson who drank to relieve his aching loneliness and was finally condemned by man and God to tramp the country roads as a hungry embittered outcast. Värmland today is a gentle place which glows with good times. It is proud of its reputation as Sweden's 'literary province.' Certainly poets and novelists can find a fertile soil in its rolling farm land, birch forests, sinuous rivers and stately manor houses. In a grave close to a lake at Filipstad lies John Ericsson, the nineteenth-century engineer who is best known to the Swedes as a prolific inventor and to the Americans as the builder of the ironclad, revolving-turret *Monitor,* which defeated the South's *Merrimac* in the Civil War. Although its factories are well camouflaged, Värmland is the home of several of Sweden's premier industries, including the Bofors armaments company and the huge Uddeholms company, which owns enough property to cover Rhode Island. Once a little seventeenth-century ironworks, Uddeholms has become an industrial empire embracing everything from sawmills and steel mills to chemical plants and hydroelectric stations.

In Dalarna province, just to the north of Värmland, another great business empire, Stora Kopparberg, not only is a still larger company but its more than 700-year history makes it the oldest industrial firm in the world. Dalarna (Dalecarlia in English) is probably Sweden's most purely peasant region—at least it is more conscious of its rural traditions, more inclined to dress up in the old costumes and make the most of its folklore. On Midsummer Eve when maypoles are raised on every village green, the whole of Dalarna becomes a little mad, as normally prim and proper

SWEDEN

people whirl about in their gay costumes and dance to fiddles and accordions until sunrise. Dalarna is the source of the orange, hand-carved, toy Dala Horse, a popular souvenir which has come to symbolize Sweden's rustic past.

Now, in moving north from this upper layer of the more populated portion of Sweden, the forests begin to deepen and the soil becomes more resistant to the farmer's plow. Yet the traveler from the south still has not come halfway up the length of Sweden. The great north stretches for another five hundred and more miles. Because the Norwegian frontier to the west is a rough and nearly empty mountain country, the customary way north is along the Bothnia coast. In Västerbotten province it is called the Gold Coast because of the mining of gold and other valuable metals which has kept the Swedes busy for more than a century. The Gold Coast's less celebrated industry is the production of arsenic.

The prosperous cellulose city of Sundsvall is a famous old lumber town which was an early battleground for trade-union rights. Umeå is the site of the fifth and latest Swedish university, which is now being built in order to speed the development of the northern half of the country. As in Norway and Finland, there has been a steady drift of people in the north to the south, where jobs are more plentiful and life is easier (providing, of course, that the newcomer can find a place to live). There is an undoubted feeling of remoteness in the north, and yet cities like Umeå, Luleå, Boden and Haparanda are surprisingly well appointed with new buildings and all the required modern facilities. Luleå is not only the major Swedish outlet for the iron ore from the northern mines but also the site of a huge and controversial state-owned steel mill—controversial because it is a state- instead of private-enterprise venture and because it was placed far north in a city where the shipping lanes are blocked by ice for a third or more of the year. After a slow beginning during the war, the steel plant began to pay for itself in the late 1950s. As an investment in northern development, however, it had already paid off in jobs and stimulation to business activity.

Luleå is in the bottom right-hand corner of Norrbotten (North

Bothnia), the largest province in Sweden. Most of it lies above the Arctic Circle and it covers the northern fourth of the country. Its population of fewer than 300,000 inhabits an area as large as Britain, Holland and Switzerland combined. Despite the giant iron-ore industry which is the heart and soul of the area, Norbotten is still the most backward region in Sweden. After all the evidence of good times in the Swedish south, it was a change to hear about an unemployment problem, make-work projects, significant support for the Communist Party, and incentive programs to attract industry. As the capital of Norrbotten, Luleå has grown suddenly from a prewar town of wooden buildings and 12,000 people to modern steel-and-concrete buildings and 33,000 people. It is a bright little city which not only has roulette tables in its leading hotels but also has some interesting problems with its affluent younger generation. The fact that a good number of restless Luleå youths go driving aimlessly about in their own cars, just like their Stockholm cousins, is as sure a sign as any that the Swedish north is beginning to get its share of prosperity.

Iron Kingdom

Inland from the coast but still within Norrbotten province is Swedish Lapland, a wilderness of tough farmers, 10,000 Lapps—a third of them reindeer herders—and 270,000 animals. As in some other regions a traveler finds signs cautioning motorists about moose crossing the road. The best-known Lapp town in Sweden is Jokkmokk but only a fraction of its 3,000 population are Lapps. It has been the site of a great winter market for more than three and a half centuries, and now has a Lapp college. Two of the leading Jokkmokk citizens are Mr. and Mrs. Nils Hövenmark. Their way of life puts to rout all glib generalizations about Swedes living in cramped urban apartments. The Hövenmarks live in a rambling three-story wooden house which is solidly built against the rigors of winter north of the Arctic Circle. The ground floor has an *apotek*, or pharmacy, which they own and operate, as well as an office and a workshop. The upper floors have spacious rooms and hallways with bearskin rugs set before the fireplaces and the skins of wolves, wolverines and wildcats hanging on the walls. Part of the top floor is devoted to an assortment of tape-recording equipment and a broadcasting studio. The Hövenmarks work for Swedish Radio as a sideline and do a half-hour weekly broadcast to the Lapps all over northern Sweden. In this direct way they play their part in the official Swedish effort to save the Lapps from being swallowed up completely by industrial Sweden, and to allow them special grazing, hunting and fishing rights. Only a Lapp, for example, is permitted to herd reindeer. But, as in Norway, the hydroelectric lines and the highways march forward and the Lapps are, foot by foot, pressed back. Resentfully, they appear in town only occasionally to buy a few things before retreating to their huts and reindeer; resentfully, they huddle around the fringes of Jokkmokk, work fitfully, make souvenirs for tourists, and get drunk. Everyone agrees that it is a shame, but no one knows quite what to do about it.

'Our friends think we're crazy to live up here,' Nils Hövenmark said, but he and his family enjoy the pioneering spirit of the north, and they delight in having a surplus of living room in their home. In Kiruna, still farther north, I asked a junior executive of the LKAB mining company why he had decided on a life far from his native south. 'I was working in Stockholm for a company and had just been married,' he said, 'but I simply couldn't find a place for us to live. I was offered a job up here, and an apartment to go with it. I know it's a long way to go to find a place to live, but that's how it is in our socialist paradise.'

Kiruna is a city of superlatives. It has mushroomed at just that point on the Swedish landscape where the tundra begins to replace the forest. It is Sweden's most important northern town, and its 26,000 population makes it the world's largest community north of the Arctic Circle. Its far-flung boundaries and 8,700 square miles—more than five million acres—make it the world's biggest city, geographically speaking. The city limits include Sweden's highest mountain.

Kiruna's reason for being is a great iron mountain called Kiirunavaara, which produces some of the highest-grade iron ore to be found anywhere. Surface mining is giving way almost completely now to below-surface activity of such proportions that Kiruna claims to have the biggest underground mine in the world. It is certainly the greatest iron-ore concentration in all Europe. Sweden has nine tenths of Europe's high-grade ore (50 per cent iron or better). Since the ore still to be dug out is reckoned at about two to three billion tons, all of it eagerly sought by the international steelmakers, a case could be made that Kiruna is the wealthiest of the world's cities. Few others, anyway, have such a practically bottomless pit of riches in their back yard.

Kiruna and its sister city of Gällivare sixty miles to the southeast tear out of the ground twenty million tons of iron ore each year, enough to fill more than 400,000 of the ore cars which trundle toward Narvik on the Atlantic Coast and Luleå on the Bay of Bothnia. Both mining centers are dominated by the Luossavaara-Kiirunavaara company—L.K.A.B. for short (the 'A.B.' means 'Inc.'). One of the dozen biggest Swedish industrial companies, LKAB is a unique organization because it operated for fifty years as a half-private, half-state enterprise, until the Swedish government exercised its option in 1957 to take over virtually all the private shares in the company.

The miners are some of the best-paid and most pampered workers in all Scandinavia, a far cry from 1898, when the first of the miners arrived in the nothingness which was Kiruna. Today an excellent highway as well as the railroad connect the city with the south, and an airport makes it possible to fly to Stockholm sooner than anyone can walk to the city limits. 'Kiruna,' wrote Eric Linklater, 'is a modern town that applied science and modern technology have endowed with all the comforts necessary to defeat the malignity of Arctic darkness and the eternal enmity of Arctic weather. A spacious town, a well-paid town, a masterpiece of human enterprise and ingenuity, set down in the midst of desolation . . .' It is also a schizophrenic city. It lives both above ground and below ground, and it lives part of the year in total sunlight and part of the year in total darkness.

Kiruna below ground is undoubtedly one of the most efficient mining operations in the world, starting with the fact that the miners are driven to the mine faces in buses, which rumble along the miles of subterranean roads. (Visitors are driven luxuriously through the dark galleries in a Mercedes sedan.)

Kiruna above ground is no slapdash Klondike town but a smart city of supermarkets, cinemas, department stores, a stunning indoor swimming pool and a thirteen-story glass-faced headquarters building for LKAB. It is a remarkably complete and modern town for its wilderness setting, but in an odd way it is disappointing. The central-heating comforts and the forest of television antennas have robbed the Lapland outpost of its rugged glamour. It might as well be a suburb of Stockholm. Even in the world's biggest city, with a ridiculous amount of room to spare, apartment-house living has taken over from the oldtime barn-red private houses with big fireplaces. During the winter, when it is about as dark above ground as it is in the mines, the city keeps its artificial lights on around the clock. 'We sit waiting for the spring,' said one native of Kiruna, 'but it never really comes. Winter turns into summer just like that. We have been dying for the sun, and now we get too much of it.'

Stockholm

It is as hard to imagine a Swedish gondolier as it is to conceive of an Italian Garbo. Nonetheless, it is inevitable that the capital of Sweden should be called 'the Venice of the North'—or 'the city that floats on water.' The rippling waterways of Stockholm free it from the suffocation of most big cities. Its twelve islands and forty-two bridges save it from being ironed out into the typical monotonous metropolis of the twentieth century. Stockholm was founded in 1255, when a powerful noble named Birger Jarl fortified several islands. The Old Town with its labyrinth of streets is one of the best preserved in all Europe and a complete contrast to the modern city, which has exploded all around it on other, larger islands. The palace guard in the Old Town still struts as it did in the days when the monarchy was all-powerful. In the Riddarholm Church the floor is paved with the tomb slabs of every Swedish monarch since 1632, except for Queen Christina, who gave up her throne to become a Catholic and was buried in Rome.

Stockholm was made the capital of Sweden by Gustavus Vasa in 1523, just three years after the single time in its history when a foreign power (Denmark) briefly occupied it. Since then it has been spared all the usual assaults of war-prone Europe, including artillery barrages and bombings. The city is now vulnerable from the air, of course, but it is protected by rockets and supersonic aircraft. Elaborate civil-defense measures probably make it the safest big city in Europe.

A foreign navy would find it difficult to get near Stockholm. Not only are there destroyers ready to spring out of caves along the Bothnia coast but the city is set thirty miles deep inside an archipelago and can be reached only by threading through some twenty-thousand islands and skerries. This is a summer sailor's dream world. It means that the average man in Stockholm can cast off from a pleasure-boat pier near his apartment house and be sailing into unspoiled nature within minutes.

When I first visited Stockholm soon after World War II the stately beauty of the city was overwhelming—the constant play of sunlight and blue water . . . fishermen lowering their umbrella-like nets into the canal by the royal palace . . . the tawny yellow of elegant old buildings . . . the seagulls crying as they swooped beside the new apartment towers which were barnacled with balconies . . . the Renaissance splendor of the Town Hall, where Nobel Prize dinners are held in the Golden Room . . . the silent, sun-worshipping Swedes and their glowing children. It was almost too pleasant, too serene, when so much of Europe was still picking its way through the rubble of war.

Years later, when I returned to Stockholm to find the pace of life much quickened, a banker friend drove me at three o'clock of a summer's morning to a hill which overlooks the city. I wasn't sure whether the sun had just gone down or was about to come up, but the whole of Stockholm was bathed in an eerie blue light which made it as enchanting as any place on earth. I have returned to Stockholm many times since and have not changed my view that it is one of the handful of the world's truly beautiful cities. But it has not been beauty which has lured me so much as the peculiar challenge of the city to find its mystery beneath the scrubbed and composed exterior. There is a constant suggestion in the Stockholm air that some kind of smoldering passion may be found just below the crust, if only the crust could be broken.

Stockholm has a great sense of decorum. The orderliness of its life makes it comfortable, but also a little smug. It offers little to the bohemian, the nonconformist or the disreputable. There is no Soho, Greenwich Village or Montmartre to draw the wild ones and the weird ones. 'If your idea of a night club,' says a government tourist booklet, 'is a big, brawling place with a row of amateurish chorus girls kicking up their heels while you are forced to drink champagne at double or more the normal price, Stockholm's night clubs are going to be a pleasant surprise for you.' The 'pleasant surprise' is that there aren't any real night clubs in Stockholm. There are a few passable imitations catering to visitors during the summer and several costly restaurants with music for dancing and occasional performances by cabaret artists. They do their best despite the drinking law, which bans hard liquor after one o'clock in the morning.

It is the tourist, perhaps spoiled by Copenhagen, who complains the most about the night-club situation. Stockholmers seem to care less; most of their entertaining is done at home. A night out is more a question of ordering a sumptuous meal, getting in enough drinks before the deadline, and working up to a gregarious good time. Since the 'foreign food invasion' began, in the 1950s, Stockholm restaurants have advanced from parochial menus to an international cuisine satisfying enough for even the most temperamental palate. It is said that the revolution started when Tore Wretman discovered garlic. As the city's leading restaurateur, he has built up (with the backing of the Wallenbergs), the Operakällaren, the Riche and the Stallmästaregården into luxurious dining places which can compete with the best in Europe.

Stockholm's younger generation flocks to dance halls like the Nalen which a Swedish Olympic broad jumper, Topsy Lindblom, founded in the 1940s as a place where the city's energetic youth could let off steam. The music is deafening and the dancing frantic, but behavior is closely supervised and the well-dressed youngsters hardly fit the image of a wayward generation. In contrast, there is the late-evening mating ritual already referred to in Chapter 2. Big, gaudy, secondhand Fords, Chevrolets and Chryslers—'bedrooms on wheels'—move slowly in parade down Kungsgatan, the Broadway of Stockholm, at about the time the cinemas, restaurants and dance halls empty out. The sallow-looking young drivers and their friends, never smiling, never eager, look over the girls drifting along on the sidewalk. A toe touches an accelerator and an unmuffled exhaust pipe emits a deep burbling sound. A girl, or two or three girls, respond to the call by opening the rear door of the car and tumbling into the back seat. The car cuts out of the procession and careens into the night.

The hard-looking youngsters aggressively wheeling their pack of automobiles are known as the *raggare*, the Swedish teddy boys who have their restless counterparts all over the world, from the *Stilyaga* of Russia to the Wild Ones of California. The word *raggare* is a new addition to the Swedish language, apparently a concoction of English and Swedish arising from the way the Swedish car cowboys hang a rag or piece of fur from their aerials as a sign that they are on the prowl for girls. In any event, the *raggare* succeed in shocking their elders, as do the long-haired girl beatniks and the homosexuals who have made one side of a Stockholm park their favorite meeting ground. The efficient Stockholm police deal briskly with the drunks who are a predictable part of the nighttime scenery in every Scandinavian capital.

Despite these activities, there are few disturbances of the Stockholm peace. It is one of the few cities in the world which finds public behavior good enough to permit it to set out in one of the busiest downtown parks—Kungsträdgården, 'The King's Park'—a series of glass showcases which display fine articles of Swedish craftsmanship like jewels glittering in a shop. They would not last long in Central Park or Hyde Park, nor would the glass globes, as big as basketballs, which light the footpaths. Kungsträdgården in summertime is filled with people on benches turning their faces to the sun, and in the wintertime with heavily clothed Stockholmers enjoying the sight of skaters twirling on the outdoor rink. The great granite headquarters of major Swedish banks watch over the scene. The financiers can look across the park to the iron gates and black fortress walls of the 'Match Palace,' where Ivar Kreuger once commanded his industrial empire. At one end of the park the shoppers hurry into N.K.—Nordiska Kompaniet—the colossus of Swedish department stores. At the other end of Kungsträdgården there is the massive opera building with its flaring restaurant torches. At the water's edge, sleek tourist cruisers sail off for a tour of the city.

Stockholm is an ideal city for strolling, even if there is little outside the Old Town which is authentically quaint, and even though it sometimes seems that every other building is a bank or a bookstore. A visitor stepping out of the Grand Hotel, one of the best, and best-positioned, hotels in Europe, needs only a few minutes to walk to an old white schooner with towering masts which serves now as a youth hostel or to the quays where the big white liners leave for Finland. It is not far to the Royal Dramatic Theater which has spawned a score of internationally known performers. Farther down the water's edge are the delights of Djurgården ('The Deer Park'). This is a massive playground, which has been left in its natural state except for an amusement park (Stockholm's Tivoli) and the re-creation of Old Sweden in the transplanted dwellings and workshops of Skansen. To step from this nostalgic garden to the new business center of Stockholm is to make a dizzying leap through time.

For the past decade Stockholm has been so busy creating a new world in the city center that the people in the country have said that there's no sense going to the capital 'because it's closed for repairs.' Greater Stockholm has grown ten times in the past century. The population is now 1,200,000, and it is gaining by about 20,000 a year. The growing pains have meant a constant struggle by civic authorities to provide living room and office and factory space without turning the capital into yet another urban eyesore. Although the housing shortage which still persists is a mark against them, they have been successful in keeping the civic explosion under control. More than most cities in the world, Stockholm has grown pretty much according to plan, and has benefited from the action of the foresighted city fathers of half a century ago who bought up all the available land within the city's boundaries. It was one of the first cities to erect garden communities and housing projects in the modern style. The Stockholm planners not only studied the ideas of urban experts like Le Corbusier, Lewis Mumford, Sir Patrick Abercrombie and Clarence S. Stein, but put a good many of them into action. In 1961 Stockholm won the International Union of Architects prize for its 'organic growth and international reconstruction.' It was 'an example to all other cities, because they show foresight in land policy and intelligent coordination of the many problems confronting the modern city.'

One crucial Stockholm decision was not to succumb, like Los Angeles and many other cities, to the onrush of the automobile, but to attempt to make civic transportation so effective and attractive that it would carry most of the traffic load. In the postwar years, while lacing the city with new motorways, Stockholm has installed the most modern and handsome subway system in the world. The 'Tunnelbana' has now grown to fifty-eight stations—some of them breathtakingly deep—with more to come.

The new subway lines reach out to the satellite cities of Farsta and Vällingby. Each was planned to create a suburban community for some 30,000 people. The focal point in both towns is a pedestrians-only shopping center with branches of Stockholm stores and restaurants. The rest is nature, preserved by the builders as much as possible, and an assortment of apartment towers in various shapes, sizes and materials. As in comparable projects in other countries, residents appreciate the fresh air and the spaciousness of it all, but seem to miss the advantages of living in the crowded but more stimulating inner city. Nonetheless, the waiting list for an apartment is so long that it can take ten years to get one. In Farsta, the supermodern touch is the atomic-energy heating system for the project's 9,500 apartments. Two-and-a-half miles from Farsta a nuclear reactor and heat-exchangers are packed into a 165-foot-long cavern in a granite cliff. Hot water produced after a complicated nuclear process is piped to Farsta's underground and between-walls network of pipes. The atomic heating installation is being operated at a loss by the government as a pilot plant to see whether Sweden, which has almost no coal, oil or other fossil fuel, can effectively harness the atom for everyday life.

The feeling of living in the future is duplicated in downtown Stockholm by the Hötorget project, one of the biggest surgical operations ever performed on a city. Several acres of old buildings have been swept away to make room for five eighteen-story towers and the surrounding complex of shops, banks, cinemas, garages, fountains and a long, traffic-free piazza. It is a city planner's exercise in traffic separation, so that the pedestrian's world is isolated from the flood of cars on the surrounding streets. The towers have all the latest in equipment, but their Lever House look is less distinctive than that of the twenty-five-story Wenner-Gren skyscraper, one of the most striking modern structures in Europe, which stands at the edge of the city center.

Stockholm blooms in the summer, as does all of Sweden. It lifts its face to the sun, and its glacial beauty melts into soft contentment. But the soul of the city is best felt in the dead of winter, when the ice heaves underneath the bridges and icicles hang from roof ledges. There is a crackle in the air and the snow crunches under the boots of citizens who huddle like Russians in their greatcoats. Life moves indoors and candles burn to keep spirits bright. The muffled city waits for spring.

Chapter 20

GOVERNMENT BY CONSENSUS

*Seventy-five years ago Sweden was one of the most conservative
countries in the world. And despite all that has happened since,
the advent of what is called the welfare state and such, a great deal
of that conservatism remains.*
—STOCKHOLM PROFESSOR

*The King is Sweden's watchman; he opens the country in the
morning and locks it up at night.*
—SWEDISH SAYING

Sweden appears to be a wholly contemporary society, but beneath
its democratic superstructure, its welfare establishment and its
automated industry are firmly imbedded old institutions and old
habits which have survived the onslaught of modernism. It is still
far from being a completely classless nation. There is still a widespread use of titles, just as there are millionaires who ride in
limousines and Herr Professors who run their classrooms like
Junker generals. Aristocracy still exists. It has been subdued since
its special privileges were withdrawn a century ago, but there are
still 25,000 nobles in Sweden and a House of Nobility in Stockholm. There are some 150 manorial estates still in private hands.
Sweden is the one remaining Scandinavian country with a two-
chamber parliament because its local governments, which elect
the Upper House, remain strong despite centralization. The
Riksdag dates from the fifteenth century and is one of the world's
oldest legislatures, but a fully democratic system did not emerge in
Sweden until World War I.

Most strikingly of all, there is the monarchy, still an important fact of Swedish life, still occupying the largest lived-in palace in the world, though in fact only a few of its five hundred rooms are regularly used by the royal family. In the palace courtyards the rituals of the changing of the guard, set down by King Karl XI, has continued with hardly a change for nearly three hundred years. There are some Swedes, particularly doctrinaire Social Democrats, who insist that the time has come to sweep out the monarchy and bring in a republic, but most people find it hard to imagine Sweden without a king. It is an open question, however, how they would react if the present dynasty should die out and the nation had to decide whether to search about for a new royal family or establish a presidency. Young Swedes are fond of saying that they have no interest in royalty.

The original kings of Sweden reigned more than a thousand years ago, well before the Viking Age. Because he appears in the Icelandic sagas, Olof Skötkonung, who ruled about 1000 A.D., is the first Swedish king whose life is known in some detail. Christianity was established in Sweden during his time. Erik IX (1150–60), by undertaking a crusade against the heathen Finns, began the Swedish dominion over Finland. From 1248 to 1266 a great statesman, Birger Jarl, was the virtual ruler of Sweden; he made history not only by founding Stockholm but also by preparing the way for the abolition of serfdom. During the period of the Kalmar Union, beginning in 1397, Sweden and Norway were ruled by Denmark. Swedish resistance to Copenhagen's efforts to make Sweden a mere vassal country was so strong, however, that for most of the time the country was virtually independent. A noble with the compelling name of Engelbrekt Engelbrektsson (in other words, Engelbrekt, the son of Engelbrekt) led a peasant revolt in 1434, which turned into a national fight for freedom. The end of Danish domination was touched off by the Stockholm Bloodbath in 1520, when Christian II tried to bring Sweden completely under Danish rule.

Two of the eighty-two massacred nobles were the father and brother-in-law of a young nobleman named Gustavus Vasa. Having just escaped from a Danish prison, Vasa learned of the slaughter after arriving in Sweden. He quickly set about raising a peasant army to drive out the Swedish overlords who supported the union with Denmark. Vasa swept to power as the people's hero. He became the new king and put an end to the Kalmar Union. He turned Sweden into a national state along the lines of those states which had developed in Europe during the Middle Ages. Vasa was to become the most celebrated of all the kings of Sweden—'the organizer of the Swedish nation.' While fighting off his enemies inside and outside Sweden, Vasa stabilized the country's finances and initiated the measures which led to confiscation of the Roman Catholic Church's properties, which covered one fifth of Swedish soil, and the establishment of a Lutheran State Church. A description of Vasa by the historian Ingvar Andersson makes him sound a very Swedish king indeed: 'His astounding memory and prodigious capacity for work, his practical talents, his energy, which, however, was not proof against occasional fits of black depression, . . . combine to produce one of the most vivid personalities in Swedish history.'

Gustavus Vasa's eldest son succeeded him in 1560 as Erik XIV. He was a cultivated but temperamental and unbalanced Nordic hothead. He moved to the brink of insanity when his marriage offers to Queen Elizabeth of England and Mary Queen of Scots were rejected. He eventually married his low-born but devoted mistress, Karin Månsdotter. Erik was overthrown and imprisoned after he took to assassinating his noble enemies. Erik's nine years in prison ended one day when a guard served him a bowl of poisoned pea soup.

The long line of Swedish kings included a few who were nearly as mad as Erik, several who were wholly incompetent to rule, and a few truly great kings, particularly Gustav II Adolf (Gustavus Adolphus). He was Gustavus Vasa's grandson and a political and military genius who turned Sweden into a major European power by leading it through a great national expansion. Under Gustav II, Sweden took part in the Thirty Years' War against the House of Habsburg and the Catholic League, which were bent on crushing Protestantism. By raising huge peasant and mercenary armies and spurring the development of Swedish mining and the armaments industry, he was able to make a spectacular drive into

Poland and Prussia. He spread Swedish rule to both sides of the
Baltic and then was killed in 1632 leading a cavalry charge. Most
of Sweden's Baltic possessions were lost during the next century.
The precocious Charles XII became king at age fifteen in 1697 and
was not yet out of his teens when he led the Swedish armies in a
historic rout of Russian forces many times their size. The number
of prisoners taken was so much greater than the number of
Swedes that they had to be released. Other brilliant victories
followed, including a bold expedition which went so deeply
into Russia that when it collapsed Charles was able to flee
south to Turkey. There he was held captive for a time. He was
killed a few years later while leading an attack on a Norwegian
fortress.

In 1719, a year after Charles's death, a new constitution was
established and a parliamentary system launched but it was submerged later in the century when Gustav III restored the authority
of the king. 'At the very time when the Revolution bursts upon
France,' commented one writer, 'the king of Sweden rises against
the Swedish parliament!' The 'Era of Liberty' had lasted only
fifty-three years, before giving way to 'Gustavian Absolutism';
but the idea of representative government had taken hold and
would see daylight again. For all his despotic ways, Gustav III
turned out to be 'one of the most captivating and colorful figures
in the whole succession of Swedish rulers.' He was an avid patron
of literature and the arts, who founded the court theater at
Drottningholm, the eighteenth-century Nordic Versailles on the
outskirts of Stockholm. The 62-foot-deep stage still has the original
curtains and equipment for producing thunder and waves. It is
Europe's oldest court theater in use, now that it has been rescued
from the dust and indifference of the nineteenth century. Gustav
III wrote a number of plays himself and made his reign one of
great cultural ferment. He founded the Swedish Academy which,
among other things, has the task today of selecting the Nobel
Prize laureates in literature. Sweden under Gustav III in 1783
was the first country after France to recognize a new and promising country called the United States of America.

One night in 1792, while enjoying himself at a masquerade at the opera house, Gustav III was assassinated by a political conspirator. He died speaking of his vision of 'Sweden's happiness.' Then and now a controversial king, he is remembered as the monarch who drove the Swedes to drink. He made the manufacture of spirits a royal monopoly and ran a campaign to persuade people to drink more and thus provide the government with more tax revenue. Sweden's dark age of alcoholism, however, got going in earnest under Gustav IV (1792–1809), when the potato became popular, especially after it was discovered that it could produce alcohol. Gustav IV was a luckless, hot-tempered monarch. Only thirteen years old when he became king, and seventeen when he took the government into his own hands, he lost Finland to the Russians, ruined Sweden's finances, and was finally judged to be so unbalanced that he was dethroned by a *coup d'état* and exiled. Sweden became a constitutional monarchy.

Gustav's elected successor was his uncle Karl XIII, but since he was childless the Swedes had the problem of naming a successor. When the first crown prince they selected died, they called on one of Napoleon's most talented marshals, Jean Baptiste Bernadotte, to come to Stockholm and prepare to start a new royal line. He arrived in Sweden in 1810 and, as a more forceful figure than the aging and not overly bright king, virtually took over the direction of the nation. He lined up Sweden in the last coalition against his old chief, Napoleon, thus winning possession of Norway when Denmark, Napoleon's ally, was forced to relinquish it. That helped make up for Gustav IV's loss of Finland—at least until the Norwegians severed the union with Sweden ninety-one years later. The French marshal became King Charles XIV John in 1818. He was a strong-minded ruler who led Sweden well, but never did learn to speak Swedish with any great fluency.

The Bernadottes

The Bernadotte dynasty has occupied the royal palace in Stockholm through the past century and a half of peace, social upheaval, emigration, industrialization, and vigorous development of democratic institutions and social-welfare concepts. The present king is Gustav VI Adolf, the sixth ruling Bernadotte. He did not reach the throne until 1950, when he was in his sixty-eighth year. His father, Gustav V, had ruled for nearly forty-three years, the longest reign in Swedish history, and died at the grand old age of ninety-two.

Although Sweden has the oldest written constitution in Europe (since 1809), Gustav V was still able to exercise considerable authority when he came to the throne in 1907. Despite all that had been accomplished in the name of democracy, only 9·5 per cent of the population was then able to vote. It was necessary for a voter to own property. But in that year there was a franchise reform which doubled the electorate, and universal suffrage was achieved in 1918. True parliamentary rule began only in 1905 and was not conclusively established until 1917. Although Gustav V was obliged to turn over the job of national chief executive to the prime minister at the beginning of his reign, he did not step aside entirely from policy making. He was a formidable, aristocratic figure, who helped keep Sweden out of both world wars while leaving no doubt about his pro-German sympathies. He had married the daughter of the Grand Duke of Baden. Sweden's aristocracy and its military, professional and business classes were strongly influenced by Germany, with which they had innumerable connections. German was then the principal foreign language taught in Sweden; today it is English. There was agitation within Sweden for intervention in World War I on Germany's side, but the government decided not to become involved.

Pro-German sympathies were considerably reduced in Sweden when World War II began. Nonetheless, Gustav V took it upon himself to write a personal letter to Hitler after the attack on Denmark and Norway saying that he hoped Sweden would not be attacked next and assuring the dictator that Sweden would remain neutral in the war. This and other assertions of an executive power he was not supposed to have, earned him much bitter criticism.

What is more important, however, is the fact that the monarchy under Gustav V survived despite the republican sentiments which grew up with the rise to power of the Social Democrats. In its early years the party had committed itself to the establishment of a republic, but later decided it was more trouble than it was worth, especially after the king gave up the royal prerogative to rule the country himself in the last resort. The present king has probably done everything a modern monarch can do to keep from throwing his weight around; he has impressed the Swedish public as a truly regal figure who has the nation's interest uppermost in his mind.

Unlike some of Sweden's teen-age rulers of the old days, Gustav VI served a long apprenticeship for the throne. He became King several years after the usual age of retirement. Apart from his duties as Crown Prince for forty-three years, he devoted himself to archaeology and led a number of scientific expeditions to Egypt, Greece, China and elsewhere. He was known as 'Sweden's number-one professional man,' a specialist in Etruscan art, and an accomplished gardener who grew superlative rhododendrons. He lived the quiet life of a country squire and had little interest in the race horses, vintage cars, yachts and other playthings of princes. His first wife was English, Princess Margaret of Connaught, the mother of his five children. In 1923, three years after her death, he again turned to England for a bride. She was Lady Louise Alexandra Mountbatten, the German-born second daughter of the first Marquis of Milford Haven. (Her father had been Prince Louis of Battenberg, but he became a British subject in 1917 and took the name of Louis Mountbatten, Marquis of Milford Haven.) Queen Louise was the great-granddaughter of Queen Victoria, the sister of Princess Alice of Greece and Earl Mountbatten, and an aunt of the Duke of Edinburgh. As Queen of Sweden from 1950 until her death in 1965, she devoted herself to good works, wore everyday clothes much of the time and accompanied the King on unescorted strolls about Stockholm. She gave her occupation as 'housewife' when she was enlisted in the National Health Insurance Program.

The king of Sweden has influence but no real power. He does, however, preside at the weekly meetings of the State Council, or Cabinet, at the Royal Palace. The Swedish cabinet is composed of the prime minister and fifteen other ministers, with and without portfolio. The object of the exercise, which ordinarily lasts only fifteen to thirty minutes, is to make the final, formal decisions on perhaps 800 different items. Since most of them have to do with appointments and minor matters, the business is quickly dispatched as both the king and the minister most concerned sign and countersign the decisions. The results are announced as the work of 'the king-in-council' but in fact the king is simply told what has already been decided. 'He is the perfect constitutional monarch,' said one government official, because 'he doesn't interfere, although he may ask a few questions if something strikes his interest.'

There is a story that the King was driving through a Swedish town in an open car and was being greeted by friendly crowds, when a voice called out, 'I, Alf Eriksson, am as good as anyone else. I'm a republican and I don't give a damn for the King!' As a policeman grabbed him for disturbing the peace and the angry crowd closed in on him, the King restored the good mood by calling out: 'And the King doesn't give a damn for Mr. Eriksson!'

Gustav VI's eldest son and heir apparent, Prince Gustav Adolf, was killed in the same Copenhagen airport plane crash in 1947 which took the life of American opera singer Grace Moore. His son, Carl Gustav, the King's grandson, is now the Crown Prince. When he was eighteen, in January 1965, he stood before the parliament to take the oath of allegiance to the 'King of Sweden, the Goths and the Wends.' In the event of the early death of the King the young prince would not be able to mount the throne until age twenty-five, because of a recent parliamentary action which raised the age of succession from twenty-one. The second in line of succession is Prince Bertil, now in his fifties and unmarried. The King's two other living sons married commoners; by doing so they renounced their rights to the throne. Sigvard is a noted Scandinavian industrial designer who lives in Copenhagen and is a founder of the design firm, Bernadotte & Björn. Karl Johan is a Stockholm businessman.

The King's daughter, as we have seen, is the Queen of Denmark. His four granddaughters—the daughters of his deceased eldest son—

have greatly enlivened the Swedish scene. Princesses Margretha, Birgitta and Désirée were married, respectively, to a British businessman, a German prince and a Swedish baron. The youngest, Christina, made headlines when, as one Stockholm newspaper put it, she flew off to Radcliffe College in Massachusetts 'for a fun-packed year of good-fellowship and collegiate love affairs.'

The Durable Prime Minister

Gustav VI Adolf is Sweden's grandfather figure. Tage Erlander, the world's longest-lasting prime minister, is its father figure. He has been in office four years longer than the King has been on the throne. He became the Social Democratic chief executive of Sweden when Stalin ruled Russia, the British controlled India, and the Communists were waiting to seize power in China. Hitler had been dead only a year, Harry Truman was still new to the White House, and Winston Churchill was warning that an Iron Curtain had come down on Europe. 'I'm just an average person,' said Erlander when he became prime minister in 1946. 'There is nothing exciting to write about me.'

One of the wonders of Sweden, and one of the explanations of its present-day prosperity, is its political stability. The Social Democrats have ruled with little interruption for more than thirty-three years and under only two prime ministers. Even though a good many Swedes find the whole business tiresome and say that it is time for a change, they clearly like and respect the tall, cunning, hard-driving, infinitely effective prime minister, who is a master at sugar-coating the bitter pills of politics. Too much of a moderate for the taste of the radical Left, too left-wing for the conservative Right, he has nonetheless held the center and managed a ship of state which lists toward socialism while driving ahead under capitalist power.

The Social Democratic Labor Party was founded in 1889, at a time when socialist ideas were just beginning to sprout. Today it is Sweden's oldest, as well as its largest, party. Hjalmar Branting, who was to become the first Social Democratic prime minister, was the first member of the party elected to the parliament, in

1896. A landslide in 1914 made the Social Democrats the largest party in the Lower House, and they have held the lead ever since. The formation of a minority government by the party in 1920 marked the first time in the world that a socialist or workers' government achieved power by democratic, nonrevolutionary means. Branting was prime minister three different times in the 1920s but it was his successor, Per Albin Hansson, who started the almost unbroken dominance of the Social Democrats when he took office in 1932. They have ruled ever since except for one hundred days in the summer of 1936. During World War II, when Hansson shared with the King the responsibility for keeping Sweden out of the war, the Social Democrats led a government of all parties except the Communist.

Under Branting and Hansson the party abandoned doctrinaire socialism. It put aside its notions about nationalizing industry and settled for social reforms, full employment, a general leveling of incomes and greater control of the economy. The Social Democrats championed the welfare state and the strengthening of the trade unions which provided their main support. It was clearly a workers' party, but one which was willing to work with big business. The Social Democrats guided the country through the Depression years, the war years, and the postwar drive to full employment and greater social security.

It was symbolic of the new look in Swedish politics under the 'socialists' that the gentle and simple-living 'Per Albin,' as Hansson was popularly known, should die on a streetcar while going home at night after a hard day's work. As Hansson's successor, Tage Erlander was yet another politician known to live an average-man's life. The son of a schoolteacher and organist, Erlander entered the parliament in 1933 and soon established himself as one of the most forceful figures in the Social Democratic Party. As prime minister, he has carried on the extension of the welfare state, while giving businessmen enough incentives to build the wealth state. He is big and shambling, and is so packed with energy that he characteristically leans forward—as a sailor might lean into the wind—when he walks at high speed through the corridors of power. His television appearances have revealed a man of considerable good humor. Even his political enemies find it hard to say much against him except that he has been around too long. Mrs. Erlander, whom he met when they were both students at Lund University, is a teacher of mathematics and chemistry, an author of several books, and a housewife who runs their modest home in one of Stockholm's new apartment projects.

Erlander leads such a typically Swedish home life that it seems almost a political technique, but his associates insist that he simply has no taste for luxury or ostentation. In any case, he and his family have the use of Harpsund Manor, the prime minister's official residence outside Stockholm, which has thirty rooms and two guesthouses. The Erlanders use it for their formal entertaining and as a weekend retreat. The prime minister's habit of holding consultations in the big house with businessmen, politicians and leading figures of the professions has given birth to cynical comments in Sweden about the 'Harpsund democracy,' something similar to the 'kitchen cabinet' of President Franklin Roosevelt's New Deal days.

The Problems of Progress

Erlander had been described to me as a man of 'tremendous intellectual curiosity'—a scholar-politician to complement the scholar-king. When I called on him in Stockholm and found him full of youthful vigor, it was hard to believe that he had held office for nearly two decades, starting with the dreary first postwar year when even lucky Sweden was still rationing its food. So much had to be done, and so much was done to give Sweden prosperity and security, that it was astonishing to see how much enthusiasm still welled up in a man who was in his mid-sixties. He was even able to say, cheerfully, that 'there is much, much more that we have to do. New problems arise out of the solving of old problems. And in many ways the new problems are more fascinating.'

The prime minister's office is in a triangular government building close to the parliament, with a grand view of the Stockholm waterways, the floodlighted Town Hall and the heavy flow of traffic over the bridges of the old inner city. The office is decorated in contemporary Swedish style, which is warmed by the tasteful use of deeply grained woods, comfortable furniture, a thick blue rug, a wall of books, and a painting of a Swedish country scene which almost covers another wall. Erlander explained that the painting portrays several Swedish loggers staring incredulously at a pair of scientists who are examining an ancient rock carving. 'They think it's a frivolous way to spend your time,' he said. 'It would seem that despite all our social changes and higher living standard, Swedes are still working very, very hard, with a good bit of tension and little relaxation.'

Erlander is himself a man of much nervous energy, but during our talk he was able to relax like a great rag doll. He sprawled engagingly in an armchair with an almost un-Swedish informality. He has a large square head, with thinning hair, and an animated face which pursed, scowled and twinkled as he thought over the questions and spun out his answers like a professor at a seminar. He is full of self-assurance, but there is little sign of arrogance. 'You don't have to agree with his ideas,' one Swede said, 'but you can't help but trust him. He is dedicated to improving the country. That's all there is to it.'

The Social Democrats had steered the ship of state to Welfareland. Now what? Erlander stared out the window for a moment, then said: 'It is better to begin at the beginning. The early Social Democrats were Marxists, of course. The original principles stemmed from the German socialists, but we developed our own Swedish program. It was very Marxist at first; nationalization of industry was considered essential. But Hjalmar Branting did not accept this theory. He saw that the need was to create a social-security society. It is now fascinating to see just how much that he envisioned actually came about in the first decades we were in office. It was our own creation, this social-security society.

'And then we turned to make our society responsible also for employment. At that time, in the 1930s, Lord Keynes and other authors were having a great influence. And now we have very nearly solved the problem of employment, but our work is never really completed. It is always a question of standard. If the standard of living is going higher and higher, for most of the population, then we must be sure to raise it as well for the old and the sick. You can say, however, that we have in principle solved what the first generation of Social Democrats considered the most important things. And yet we are just discovering that we are really in the beginning of the work. If people are given security and full employment, they rightly come to expect that wages and salaries are going to increase every year, and this gives people the feeling that by 1975 living standards will be 50 per cent better than they are now.

'Then the question is, What shall we do with this prosperity? We obviously must have more planning. In the past, when people didn't have so much, it was much more difficult to make plans for the future. You weren't sure you had a future. But if you know you will have more and more, then you are more interested in the future. You begin to think not so much of food or clothing but of your children's education and your home. And this is very largely a job for the state. The individual cannot build a university or make well-planned cities for homes. He wants to know what society is planning. And there you have a new task for the party, one which it could not play in the past. It is a job which is demanded by a society with very huge resources.'

Erlander was sure that it made no sense to say that the economy could be let free to take a natural course now that prosperity had been achieved. 'Conceivably in America, with such great variety and space, it would be easier to let things go, but for us planning is absolutely necessary. There is not such a great party difference about it, except that I don't think the other parties are taking it as seriously as we are. The controversy has more to do with taxation, but we feel we must have the money to do the job.' He added that there is not too much centralization of power in the government's hands, although big businessmen say there is too much. 'We are *really* trying to realize a society with a mixed economy. Nothing has happened to shake our belief that it is much easier to realize results if we cooperate with big business. If there is some conflict of interest, well, we who represent the people will act on their behalf, but we haven't had this situation.'

Erlander talked about many other things, but none so fervently as his feeling that the sense of solidarity which Swedes have with each other is now being extended to a sense of responsibility for what is happening to people elsewhere in the world. 'Swedes are now asking, What are we doing for the rest of the world? What about the millions who are dying while we live well? There is a feeling of moral responsibility. It was absolutely impossible fifty years ago to have discussed such things among students. There is now an entirely new spirit.'

Luncheon Government

It was interesting to observe in Sweden that there was no such thing as a cult of personality attached to the man who had led the nation for so long. Swedes by nature are not inclined to build up one man above the rest. If anything, the inclination is in the other direction. 'Royal Swedish envy' is a well-known term. Even the government press-relations officers make no effort to 'sell' Erlander to visiting writers; it took me a while simply to obtain some copies of his speeches. 'After all,' said one official, 'he is just one of our ministers. There are many others.'

At the moment there are fifteen others, and Erlander as the prime minister is 'the first among equals.' Sweden is said to have a 'luncheon government,' because it is the practice of the ministers to gather at lunch every day in a private dining room to talk over issues and reach informal decisions. The government ministries are small; they usually have no more than fifty to a hundred persons, including clerical staff. They are involved in the decision-making process, while the task of carrying out the decisions is in the hands of the central administrative boards—for example, the Social Insurance Board and the National Board of Education. The boards operate under the relevant ministries, but are headed by government-appointed directors general. This is the Swedish Civil Service, said to be stuffily bureaucratic, but obviously a highly professional and competent corps. Civil servants are appointed for life under almost absolute security of tenure, and even appointed officials are seldom removed. One notable feature is that civil servants, as well as military and police personnel, are free to take part in politics and to hold political office. They express their political views quite openly.

Since Scandinavians seem more honest than most people in an imperfect world, it is not surprising to be told that Swedish politicians and bureaucrats are seldom marked by corruption. 'Seldom' is obviously a safer word to use than 'never.' After all, the Liberal Party was badly shattered in 1932 when it was revealed that its leader and prime minister, Carl Gustav Ekman, had accepted secret funds from Ivar Kreuger. There have also been cases from time to time of just plain maladministration—most recently in Sweden's foreign-aid program which has been overhauled and given fresh leadership. One thing that keeps the government clean and on its toes is the right of the press or any private citizen to examine the official files of any administrative office. The only things held back from such scrutiny are 'secret' matters having to do with national security, foreign relations or certain medical, criminal and other records about individuals. In practice, Swedes do not go poking through the government's file cabinets, but if the press should get the whiff of a scandal it can ask for and see the relevant documents and correspondence. In the United States, which is more of an open society than most, embarrassing material may not come to light except through a Congressional investigation, or a leak to the press by a disgruntled civil servant.

'The principle of publicity' is the term given to the open-files policy. And, as related in Chapter 8, the power of the Ombudsman rests largely on his ability to put the spotlight of publicity on Sweden's dark corners. It might also be noted that for almost a decade Sweden has been televising its parliament, one of the few countries in the world to do so. The original full-scale transmission of proceedings has given way to the more practical custom of presenting recorded condensations of the day's events each evening, plus excerpts on news programs, with full coverage reserved for major debates. In many ways, the politicians, officials and civil servants of Sweden are exposed men, and yet, as the press code of ethics shows, Swedes are also passionate about the individual's right to privacy.

Advice and Consent

Concern for the individual is matched by a concern for the viewpoint of the group. To a remarkable extent, Sweden has government by consensus. Consultations and still more consultations oil the smoothly running machinery of the Swedish state. In my own experience I have never seen a country where such a total effort is made to make sure that every interested party has its say. Commissions of experts are established by the parliament to investigate and deliberate a problem in order to lay a factual foundation for legislation. ('Sweden is an almost maddeningly rational society,' an American diplomat said. 'The Swedes deal in facts like no other aggregate of human beings I know.') The commissions may include members of interest groups and representatives of the relevant professions. Not content with this, the authorities then submit the commission reports to a variety of organizations outside the government for criticism. In short, an issue can be thoroughly thrashed out by the experts and run through a mill of criticism before a bill is even presented to the parliament. It can make parliamentary debate superfluous.

The various organizations (of trade unions, salaried employees, businessmen, farmers, cooperatives, women, teachers, tenants, landlords, etc.) also have their say when they sit on administrative boards or are invited to comment on government proposals. It is said that just about every Swede belongs to some kind of organization, even if it is only a sports federation or scientific body, and the government and the parliament make the most of this fact. The opposition parties are in the thick of this recording-of-opinion process, so that in an interesting way they are involved in the actual running of the government. Their views are not simply the cries of a frustrated opposition, but opinions which help shape legislation.

It sounds, and is, very Swedish, but simple political facts also make it advisable for the Social Democrats to rule with a gentle touch. Except for a special situation during the war, when the electorate gave, in effect, a 54 per cent vote of confidence in the government's neutralist policy, the Social Democrats have never been able to win half or more of the seats in the popularly elected second chamber of the parliament, where members sit for four-year terms. In 1965, they held 113 of the 233 seats. (For some time, however, they have had a majority of seats in the first chamber, which is elected by provincial assemblies for eight-year terms.) The Social Democrats could be defeated if all the other parties combined against them, but the 'non socialist' parties are seldom able to see eye to eye. The 1966 municipal elections, however, were a nightmare for the Social Democrats and greatly increased the chances of a major political turnover in Sweden.

Although communism seems irrelevant in Sweden, the true 'workers' paradise,' the Reds in the 1964 elections increased their second-chamber representation from three to eight seats, thanks largely to the attractive personality of the new Communist Party leader, C. H. Hermansson. Even so, there is no likelihood of their achieving any important strength in Sweden. It is not only a well-to-do society but, as a foreigner in Stockholm said, 'the Swedes just aren't interested in packaged dogma.' Nor does there seem much prospect that the Social Democrats will soon lose favor, even though many people speak of the desirability of a change of government. Even when the opposition parties manage to pull together, their view of the Swedish welfare state differs only in detail from that of the Social Democrats. Harry Hjorne, the owner-editor of the *Göteborgs-Posten*, when asked what will happen to the Swedish government in the future, said grumpily, 'Nothing! Even if we have a change of parties it wouldn't make much difference. Things would be just the same.'

Next Generation

What seemed to discourage those Swedes who insisted that 'our politics are boring' is that the political parties are led by 'a lot of tired old men' who refuse to make room at the top for fresh blood. 'It is difficult for a Jack Kennedy to rise up suddenly in Swedish politics,' a journalist commented. 'The bright young men are squeezed out.' This is not entirely true, but it seems clear that in many parts of Swedish life a fairly rigid hierarchical structure dampens the hope of younger men to soar past their elders to commanding positions. The noted economist and veteran leader of the Conservative Party, Gunnar Heckscher, once wrote that 'American society is characterized by a mobility—geographic, occupational, even social—which is almost entirely absent in Sweden. Swedish society is probably even more static in this respect than other European countries.' And yet it is not all that rigid: Heckscher himself, after heading his party for many years, stepped aside in 1965 for a fellow Conservative member of parliament, Yngve Holmberg, who at age forty became the country's youngest party leader.

Within the Social Democratic Party, which will soon have to look for a new generation of leaders, one of the brightest young men in the ranks is Olof Palme. He is a dark-haired, quick-witted minister of communications in the government, and he serves as an aide and adviser to the prime minister. Born in 1927, he spent a year at Kenyon College, in Ohio, before attending Stockholm University, where he took a law degree. As chairman of the National Swedish Union of Students, Palme was in the thick of the effort in Europe to wrest control of the international student movement from the Communists. He was elected to parliament in 1958. As a member of the prime minister's office, part of his job is to deal with problems of Swedish youth—and, while he is at it, to persuade them to vote the Social Democratic way.

A self-confident, pragmatic visionary, like Erlander, Palme is the other side of the coin from those disgruntled young Swedes who complain that they have nothing to look forward to because all the challenges are gone. Like some other new-generation Swedes I have met, he is positively ebullient about the work that still needs to be done in Sweden. 'It is necessary to have an ideology,' he said. 'I am against wet-finger politics—testing public opinion before you do anything. All the pioneers had the simple, classic solution. Now things are much more complex, but we still have some values as our driving force. Our job is to translate them into practical things. What drives us is the ideology of equality; the desire to give everyone an equal chance. There is so much that we want to do. We are not content to lean back and take it easy. That would be our death anyway. The economic problems are tough. We are always living in a type of crisis and pushing our resources to the limit. But that is the pain of progress. We are deliberately putting pressure on the system, and by presenting the vision of what society should be, we are putting the spotlight on our shortages.'

The shortages in Sweden of housing, schools, hospitals and various social and civic amenities have arisen, Palme said, because of the over-all sweeping changes in Swedish life and because 'in an affluent society people demand more and more services.' John Kenneth Galbraith has written that 'in recent times no problem has been more puzzling to thoughtful people than why, in a troubled world, we make such poor use of our affluence.' It is Olof Palme's view that Sweden is one of the very few nations which is coming to grips with the problem of finding a proper balance between private wants and public needs—the problem of making the most intelligent use of society's resources.

Chapter 21

NEUTRAL PORCUPINE

*Every attack against the freedom and independence of the realm
will be met with force. Every report that resistance will cease is
false. Sweden can and will defend itself.*
— CIVIL DEFENSE PAMPHLET

Sweden has had the most successful foreign policy in the world.
— FINNISH DIPLOMAT

The story of Swedish foreign policy is summed up in the career
of Alfred Nobel. He began by inventing dynamite and ended by
establishing a peace prize. The image of Sweden today as the
peaceful neutral which has not shot a bullet in anger for 150 years
makes it hard to recall that the old Viking country used to be one
of the most aggressive powers in Europe. Only a few centuries
ago it was involved in constant warfare. 'Significantly enough,'
says a Swedish historian, 'the armament industry was the first
large-scale industry to be developed in Sweden.'

Even today, many Swedes seem to have a special fascination for
the military arts. The *New Statesman* has commented on 'the
Viking delight in military things that persists in a belligerently
neutral country.' Apart from atomic weapons, Sweden has, in
relation to the size of its population, the most formidable military
establishment in Europe. The Swedes, moreover, make most of
their own military equipment, including the most vicious breed
of supersonic aircraft, an astonishing feat for a nation with a
population less than that of Ohio. And, of course, the love of
peace has not stopped Sweden from doing a profitable business
in armaments.

338

In the old days when Swedes went to war almost by habit, it was striking how often they managed to do their fighting on other people's territory. Except for brawling with the Danes in the southern portion of the country, Sweden itself was rarely at the mercy of foreign armies. It was almost always the other way around. It was said by the Swedish strategists in the seventeenth century that 'it is better that we tether our horses to our enemy's fence, than he to ours.' By avoiding war for a century and a half—since the days of Napoleon and nearly fifty years before the American Civil War—Sweden has accomplished the first purpose of foreign policy, which is to assure the survival of the nation and save it from harm. Sweden has resolutely stayed neutral and non-aligned through all the struggles and the two world wars which have engulfed Europe since the beginning of the nineteenth century. This fixed policy, plus plain good luck, has left Sweden unscarred, but not untroubled.

Neutrality has brought the Swedes peace, but not peace of mind. A policy which seems so obviously correct and is so thoroughly supported in the nation still leaves the Swedes feeling uneasy. Safety has been bought at the cost of noncommitment and a nagging conscience. With considerable asperity, a Swedish architect, seconded by a young banker at a dinner party, said that 'Sweden shouldn't just go on always being in the middle, never deciding or choosing, always staying out of things. It just seems too selfish and cautious.' A British writer, Kathleen Nott, commented that many Swedes 'are tiresomely guilty about being the only Scandinavians who are not battle-scarred.' This odd sense of guilt is less noticeable today than it was just after the last war, but the business of being peaceful—a virtue of necessity for a small nation—still makes quite a burden. 'The virtue,' wrote Miss Nott, 'lies in losing the habit of war to the extent that you won't be fooled into fighting even for a good cause.'

The new habit of peace restrained the Swedes from moving against their weaker neighbor, Norway, when it dissolved the Swedish–Norwegian Union in 1905 and refused to recognize King Oscar as its sovereign. It was Dag Hammarskjöld's father, Hjalmar, who was the prime minister in 1914-17, when Sweden managed to avoid becoming embroiled in World War I. The country suffered, however, from being cut off from its normal supplies of food, raw materials and manufactured goods. The prime minister was called 'Hungerskjöld' by political opponents who blamed him for the food scarcities. After World War I, Sweden accepted with surprising calm the League of Nations' decision which gave the Swedish-speaking Åland Islands to Finland.

World War II

There were twenty European states which declared their neutrality in September 1939, when Hitler set off World War II. By the end of the war only five remained: Ireland, Portugal, Spain, Sweden and Switzerland. (Of course, some were more neutral than others.) In the late 1930s there had been a general Scandinavian expectation that the Nordic countries would be able to stay out of the impending war, just as they had kept out of World War I. The Hitler–Stalin pact and the Russian attack on Finland altered the picture.

'Finland's cause is ours' was the logical and popular slogan in Sweden in 1939, and Sweden responded to Finnish pleas for help by sending a generous amount of economic and military aid and permitting 9,000 volunteers to go to the Finnish front. But that was all that was done, despite the centuries of intimate Swedish–Finnish relations and despite the fact that Sweden dreaded the likely possibility that the boundaries of Soviet Russia would be extended to the Swedish border itself. With Russia allied, as it then was, with Nazi Germany, the Swedes felt that they could not risk sending regular troops to Finland. They also refused to permit British and French forces to cross Swedish soil to go to Finland's aid. As the Swedes correctly suspected, the Allies were primarily interested in getting a foothold in Sweden in order to seal off the northern iron mines and cut the flow of ore to Germany. If that had been done, Hitler would have felt impelled to strike into Sweden himself; Swedish ore provided almost half of Germany's imports of some twenty million tons of iron ore each year and could not be given up. Later, when Germany attacked Denmark and Norway, the Swedes felt themselves to be in a helpless position. Sweden was suddenly isolated from the West. Hitler ruled the Continent. There was no doubt of Germany's ability to smash the Swedish defenses at will, and it may have been only Sweden's threat to blow up its iron-mine power stations if invaded that stopped Hitler from swallowing Sweden along with the rest of the Continent.

Even those Danes and Norwegians who complain about Sweden's wartime stance will acknowledge that it was too much to expect the Swedes to hurl themselves into certain slaughter. What they do say is that Sweden need not have continued to supply iron ore to Germany or allowed the passage of German troops and war materials across Swedish soil (though it must be noted that the transit facilities were not granted until *after* the Nazi conquest of Denmark and Norway had been completed). In the summer of 1941, for example, a whole German division and its equipment was permitted to move across Sweden from Norway in order to reach Finland for the campaign against Russia, which was then one of the Allied powers.

These were hardly the acts of a neutral, and Swedes will admit as much. But neutrality really only works when there is some balance between the opposing big powers, as there was in World War I and as there is now between the Soviet bloc and the NATO countries. From 1940 until the middle war years, Germany was the master of Europe. Sweden either had to make concessions or be conquered. Winston Churchill told Swedish Ambassador Gunnar Hägglöf after the war that in the dark days of the struggle for Europe he had often looked at the map of Scandinavia and thought of isolated Sweden. 'My advice to Sweden,' said Churchill, 'was always: to keep quiet and rearm.' Sweden was, in fact, rearming as swiftly as it could—helped, paradoxically enough, by imports obtained from Germany in exchange for supplying the iron ore.

By the end of 1942, when Germany was beginning to falter, Sweden felt more capable of resisting German demands. The troop and war-material arrangement was canceled in 1943.

During the following year the shipments of iron ore and ball bearings were stopped, and Sweden found itself able to get along without the German imports which had been vital to its economic survival. Stockholm announced that it would not give asylum to war criminals; it would be no sanctuary for fleeing Nazis. Even before these moves, Sweden was serving as a vital listening post for the Allies and as a haven for refugees, especially when the Germans began to root out the Danish and Norwegian Jews. Sweden was also a middleman for the exchange of prisoners and a training ground for Danish and Norwegian forces. Officially, these men were training to be policemen, not soldiers, but part of the exercise was instruction in the use of field artillery.

As the war drew to a close, the Swedish Red Cross, led by Count Folke Bernadotte, a nephew of the King, managed to secure the release of some 30,000 prisoners of twenty-seven nationalities from German concentration camps. Two thirds of them were Danes and Norwegians. And Raoul Wallenberg, a member of the most important banking family in Sweden, was able to liberate a number of Jews in Budapest while serving there as the first secretary of the Swedish Legation. As a footnote to the war, Raoul Wallenberg later disappeared after greeting the Russian forces when they arrived to drive out the Germans from Hungary. After great diplomatic pressure the Russians eventually stated that he has died in Lubianka Prison in Moscow, but no fully satisfactory explanation of his seizure, imprisonment and fate had been given. The case has continued to be a sore spot in Soviet–Swedish relations.

Some 300,000 refugees, a quarter of them children, were sheltered in Sweden during and immediately after the war, and another 100,000 Finnish children were cared for in private homes. As soon as the fighting was over, Sweden shipped 400,000 tons of food and millions of dollars' worth of clothing, shoes and other materials to its Scandinavian neighbors and to other countries. Total postwar relief, primarily in the form of credits to Denmark and Norway, came to over 600 million dollars. I have seen several low-cost housing developments which were erected by the Swedes in neighboring countries to meet the immediate postwar shortage. Despite all the help, some Danes and Norwegians have not felt that it made up for 'Sweden's pro-German actions early in the war.' Said one man in Oslo: 'Yes, the Swedes finally did a lot to help Norway, but it was very slow in coming, very grudging, and not always pleasant.' On the other hand, Norwegians who escaped to Sweden and were helped by the Swedes could not be more grateful. Norway's wartime prime minister said soon after the liberation: 'We are sufficiently honest now to acknowledge that Sweden's neutrality was a blessing for Norway.'

It was also clear in wartime Sweden that most people were anti-Hitler and anxious for an Allied victory. Some Swedish newspapers had been as anti-Nazi as any in the world before the war, and they continued their attacks both on the Germans and on Swedish policy even when Sweden's position was the most imperiled. The government finally imposed a limited censorship on the most virulent anti-Nazi expressions, but the newspapers continued to be critical. (The present constitution expressly prohibits any repetition of the censorship.) Probably the most outspoken editor was Torgny Segerstedt of the respected *Göteborgs Handels-och Sjöfarts-Tidning*. Among other things, he called the profits earned by Swedish Railways in transporting German men and material 'blood money,' and suggested that they be turned over to the Norwegians after the war. Those wartime days are now two decades in the past, but many Swedes still say they remember the shame and sense of helplessness they felt at the time of the German troop movements through the country. They know that Sweden's actions made the country's postwar relationships within Scandinavia difficult, despite the 'little Marshall Plan' which Sweden began after the war. 'They don't love us very much,' Prime Minister Erlander said. 'There isn't much we can do about that. It goes up and down.'

Postwar Policy

At the end of the war, as the United States and other victorious powers began to dismantle their military establishments, Sweden was one of the few nations to keep its armed forces in a high state of preparedness. It was only too aware that the Soviet Union was now a far greater force in European affairs than ever before. Moscow was exerting great pressure on Finland, and its forces occupied Eastern Europe just across the Baltic from Sweden. The beginning of the Cold War and the proposed formation of NATO presented Sweden with the dilemma of going it alone as usual or seeking allies. Sweden had already joined the United Nations in 1946, but this did not offer security in the face of the Soviet threat in Europe. Thus, the Swedes in 1948 proposed to the Danes and the Norwegians that the three countries form a Nordic defense union. As already related, the talks came to nothing, largely because the United States declared its unwillingness to supply arms to a neutral defense grouping. In the end, Sweden stood alone, while Denmark and Norway joined the Atlantic alliance.

It seems hardly believable today, when practically every Swede supports the neutralist policy, but in the late 1940s and 1950s there were some powerful voices in Sweden demanding that the country join the West in the great effort to contain communist expansion. A number of noted editors, most prominently Professor Herbert Tingsten of *Dagens Nyheter*, argued that for moral as well as strategic reasons Sweden belonged in the Western alliance. But others doubted that NATO aid could reach front-line Sweden in time, and they said Finland's independence would be compromised if Sweden permitted the NATO defense line to reach the Finnish border; Russia might feel obliged to put still greater pressure on the Finns, or take them over entirely.

Prime Minister Erlander told me that he still felt that a Nordic defense union would have been the best answer for Scandinavia, but 'today it is very dangerous to alter the status quo.' Despite its high cost, most Swedes feel that armed neutrality is the nation's most satisfactory course. Interestingly enough, Sweden's go-it-alone policy has not made it cringe before Soviet power. The Swedes have made clear their distaste for both communism and for many of Moscow's Cold War policies. The Raoul Wallenberg case, several spy scandals, and a number of incidents of Soviet interference with Swedish ships and planes have kept relations at a frosty temperature. Nikita Khrushchev's 1964 good-will visit to Sweden was accurately summed up by British journalist Patrick O'Donovan in these words:

> The visit was not a failure, it was a nothing. It was a coin dropped into a bottomless box. The icy civility, the Northern correctitude, the self-disciplined demonstration of non-interest —these were part of the most eloquent answer that the West has ever made to the East. And it was made by an authentic neutral.

Global Policy

As an armed neutral, Sweden is a porcupine—unwilling to attack but capable of inflicting punishment if abused. But far from staying curled up in their Nordic shelter, the Swedes have gone all out to build up the international peace-keeping machinery. Sweden has made an outstanding contribution to the United Nations and to aid programs for underdeveloped areas. The two most notable UN martyrs were Swedes: Count Folke Bernadotte, who was assassinated by terrorists as the chief UN representative in Palestine in 1948, and Dag Hammarskjöld, who died in the Congo after serving eight years as Secretary General. Some 25,000 Swedish troops have taken part in UN peace-keeping operations —at the Gaza Strip, the Congo and Cyprus—while other Swedes have been sent on missions to places like Kashmir, Korea and Lebanon. My own first knowledge of Swedish technical aid came in Ceylon, where I found Swedish advisers working in a family-planning program, and in South Korea, where Swedes and other Scandinavians had equipped and staffed a hospital for training Korean doctors and nurses. Even so, Swedish foreign-aid activity moved slowly until the last few years, when it became a large-scale operation costing about 45 million dollars a year.

Some cynics call this 'conscience money,' like the assistance Sweden gave its neighbors after the war. In this case, it is said to be the uneasy conscience of a rich man dining well while the hungry world presses its nose to the window. If so, the response is more to be commended than scorned. Swedes have sometimes been labeled 'honorary Afro-Asians,' because of their almost too automatic United Nations support of those countries which claim to be struggling against 'neocolonialism.' Sweden's greatest contribution to the underdeveloped world, however, is probably made by its more disinterested businessmen. The LAMCO iron-ore project in Liberia is only one of hundreds of examples of profit-seeking Swedish investment money serving to advance the economies of backward regions.

As an important trading nation, Sweden has been one of the foremost advocates of free trade. 'It embraced the British gospel of free trade with enthusiasm in the nineteenth century,' wrote *The Economist*, 'and, with its Scandinavian fellows, stuck to it tighter than the original sponsors did.' In the early postwar years Sweden was an active supporter of the O.E.E.C.—the Organization for European Economic Cooperation—which was an outgrowth of American Marshall Plan aid to Europe, and it has encouraged the development of a European free-trade area. Sweden was instrumental in the formation of EFTA, 'the Outer Seven,' seeing it as a bridge to the Common Market and working to bring the two associations closer together. The British bid for membership in the Common Market touched off a national debate in Sweden on whether it too should join the E.E.C. once Britain became a member. It was feared that Sweden's neutrality would be compromised, so the decision itself was a compromise: to seek associate membership instead of full membership. The Common Market's rejection of the British bid was, on one hand, a step away from the dream of a European free-trade area, but it also saved the Swedes from having to do anything immediately about becoming a part of the E.E.C.

Self-Defense

For a nation which has not been at war since 1814, and which is so obviously 'peace loving,' Sweden's preparations for defense and survival in case of war are extraordinary. At first glance they not only seem excessive, but obsessive. It is as if a prim lady making her way at night through a disreputable neighborhood were armed not with a long hat pin or even a little pistol but a submachine gun and a dozen hand grenades. More than any other nation in the world, Sweden has committed itself in advance of hostilities to a total defense effort. It involves every man, woman and child from the first order to evacuate the cities to the operations of guerrilla units fighting to the last in the depths of Lapland. 'Our whole effort is to make Sweden the hardest possible nut to crack,' said one defense authority.

No other nation has gone underground to such an extent as Sweden. No other nation has made such thorough plans to save itself from nuclear annihilation. And no country this side of the major powers has mounted such a powerful and self-contained defense capability as Sweden. It produces aircraft, tanks and heavy guns which are equal to the best of the big powers. The Swedish air force, with about nine hundred combat planes, is larger than those of nations with ten and more times its population. The only thing lacking is nuclear weapons, and only because the Swedes have decided—for the moment, at least—to do nothing to upset the international efforts to limit the spread of nuclear arms. Sweden is pressing ahead with its development of peaceful uses of atomic power.

Sweden's annual defense spending, including civil defense, comes to 865 million dollars, or about 17 per cent of the national budget. Except for the Communist Party, there is unanimous political backing in Sweden for this scale of effort, with the result that the Swedish military is able to work on a four-year budget and engage in long-term planning to a greater extent than in almost all other countries.

Two keynotes of Sweden's defense measures are specialization and versatility. The nation concentrates on the particular problem it would have to face in case of aggression; and the equipment it has given itself—from tanks and planes to underground shelters and power stations—can be used in multiple ways. Like the NATO forces, Sweden's defenses face mainly toward Russia. The Swedes assume that they would have to fight off an enemy alone and not count on help from abroad, at least not in the early stages. But it is obvious that they think it unlikely that America and its NATO allies would sit idly by if Russia were to threaten, invade or obliterate Sweden. Swedes feel that the Soviet threat is less today than it was a decade ago, but they are far from ready to let down their guard. They feel geographically exposed and are confident that a strong military posture by itself reduces the chances of an enemy even attempting political coercion.

Sweden would be not only difficult to attack and invade, but also difficult to occupy. 'The planning of Swedish defense,' said one official, 'does not reckon with capitulation.' Nearly total mobilization would come into being from the first warning, and it has been stated to the nation that no orders to surrender are to be believed. Every household in Sweden has been given a copy of a defense manual entitled, 'If War Comes.' Everyone is expected to know what to do and where to go when the orders are given. Elaborate evacuation plans covering some three million people have been readied so that the cities can be emptied within a matter of hours. If a nuclear attack seems imminent, then every urban dweller knows to which shelter he should go. Since 1945, every new apartment building in towns of more than 5,000 persons, and every new school, hospital, factory and office building, has had to include a civil-defense shelter in its construction plans. The exceptions are the central districts of the fourteen biggest Swedish cities, where giant community shelters have been built to take thousands of persons at once. All the shelters, standard and special, can accommodate more than two million persons, which means practically everyone in the likely target areas. More than a billion dollars has been spent since World War II on shelter construction. The Swedes have also been prudent enough to strengthen and widen selected portions of the national highway network in order to provide alternative landing strips for their military planes.

Sweden has national conscription for both the military services and civil defense organizations. Every male from eighteen to forty-seven is subject to compulsory military service and some 50,000 are called up each year. Conscripts get basic training for ten to fifteen months and then are called back three more times every six years for thirty to forty days of refresher training each time. Sweden's permanent military establishment numbers about

60,000 men, but the force can be rapidly expanded to some 600,000 in an emergency. Every man in the stand-by force would report to a local depot to join a preassigned military unit. The basic military organization is supplemented by the Home Guard (a voluntary branch of the army recruited mainly from men above and below military age) and by a score of national voluntary organizations numbering about a million Swedes of both sexes.

'We have a special situation as regards equipment,' a military spokesman said. 'A great power must have everything from the most sophisticated to the most minuscule. It needs to have personnel and material to fight war everywhere. But a small country like Sweden is not going to send out an expeditionary force. We do not need aircraft carriers, nuclear submarines, intercontinental missiles, strategic bombers or reconnaissance planes like the U-2. We need certain special kinds of equipment—unified equipment.'

Sweden spends 85 per cent of its defense money within its own borders. Private firms like Bofors, SAAB, Volvo, Ericsson and Kockums make weapons and equipment to precise Swedish specifications. (These companies do half, usually well over half, of their business in civilian goods.) Defense imports consist mainly of certain types of electronic equipment and American and British ground-to-air and air-to-air missiles.

The Bofors company, whose antiaircraft guns were famous during World War II, is one of the largest private producers of big guns and powder in the world. The company has now developed an amphibious 'S' tank, which has a low profile, a powerful gun and a top speed of thirty miles per hour. In 1964, about 100 million dollars' worth of the 'S' tanks were ordered from Bofors, the largest contract ever placed by the Swedish army.

The SAAB company (Svenska Aeroplan Aktiebolaget) is best known for its snarling little cars, but its major role in Sweden is as the manufacturer of specialized jet planes as well as trainers, light attack aircraft and missiles for the Swedish Air Force. The planes are produced on an underground assembly line. The SAAB *Draken* (Dragon), a supersonic, delta-wing, all-weather jet interceptor, is currently the backbone of the Air Force. But it is the

SAAB *Viggen* (Lightning Bolt) which is to become the single most important piece of Swedish military equipment. The Swedish Air Force is planning to buy eight hundred of the new planes during the next decade as part of a 'System 37' program which will cost more than one and a half billion dollars. It has been called 'the greatest national project ever undertaken in Sweden.'

The *Viggen* is a multipurpose STOL (short takeoff and landing) combat plane. It has a SAAB-made digital computer for weapons control and guidance. It is said to be a 'very advanced aerodynamic configuration' with a small delta wing at the nose to control the flow of air over the main delta wing. What delights the cost-conscious Swedes is that the plane, they say, was developed at less than half the cost of comparable American and other foreign aircraft. It will replace all the existing combat planes, because the same body can be turned out in three different versions—for attack, interception and reconnaissance.

Subterranean Sweden

Of all the Swedish defense measures, none is so striking as the way the nation has gone underground to help insure its survival. This does not mean that the Swedes, who are almost fanatic about the great outdoors, have turned into moles, but four things have combined to persuade them that a great many of their most vital installations and defense equipment should be placed below ground. First, the fact that much of the country, especially the northern two thirds, is covered with solid bedrock which can be blasted into perfect subterranean caverns. Second, the severe climate, especially in the north, where the temperature can drop to 40 degrees below zero, makes it difficult to build and maintain above-ground plants. Underground plants can operate throughout the year and often at a lower cost. Third, Sweden's long experience and expertise with blasting and drilling techniques makes the whole exercise relatively simple. It is enough to say that Alfred Nobel invented explosives and that Sweden's Atlas-Copco company is a world leader in compressed-air drilling equipment.

Fourth, Sweden's neutrality and its exposed geographical position compel it to take special protective measures.

Most of the Swedish navy now operates out of caves and tunnels blasted out of the rock of the Swedish coast. A number of air bases have their vital parts hidden underground, and hundreds of missile and gun emplacements have been carved out of rock. More than half of Sweden's hydroelectric power is produced underground; the installations include some of the world's biggest power plants. A number of vital defense plants of Bofors, SAAB, AGA and other companies are underground. Millions of gallons of oil and gasoline, as well as enough emergency food and other material to keep Sweden going for several months, have been stored in old mines or new excavations. Most of the civil-defense control centers are underground, as well as many municipal water and power installations.

There are fourteen large nuclear shelters in the nine largest cities. The four in Stockholm serve in peacetime as garages. The largest one, carved out of the Katarina hill close to the center of town, has three stories inside a 1,700-foot-long tunnel. During an air raid, 17,000 people can find safety under seventy feet of solid rock. In normal use it accommodates six hundred cars. (It also has a drive-in bank.) In Västerås, home of the giant ASEA company, the community shelter for 5,500 persons serves during peacetime as a civic social center complete with theater, club rooms, gymnasium, restaurant and garage. As one foreign observer said, 'the whole military and civil defense effort is the best example you can find of Swedish thoroughness.'

Chapter 22

CAPITALIST SWEDEN

A bold exposure to the battering of world markets has helped to transform one of Europe's poorer rural societies into easily the most prosperous country in Europe today.
— *The Economist*

So often the adventure of an individual, either in the realm of ideas or capital investment, is the sole reason for the appearance of an industry and its later prosperity.
— ROY MILLWARD

In a single lifetime, 'poor Sweden' has become 'rich Sweden.' Economically, it was still a medieval state as late as the beginning of the nineteenth century. At that time, wrote Gunnar Heckscher, 'the overwhelming majority of the Swedish people lived under conditions which in many respects closely resembled those prevailing as early as the thirteenth century.' There was a time lag in the nation's economic development which was not corrected until the last few decades. In the mid-nineteenth century only 10 per cent of the Swedish population lived in cities and towns. It was a peasant nation, and a notoriously poor one. An essay published in those days was entitled, 'The Significance of Swedish Poverty.'

When crop failures came on the heels of a soaring birth rate, Sweden took on the look of a Nordic Ireland. As many as one and a quarter million Swedes flooded to America between 1860 and 1930. The great exodus amounted to 20 per cent of the Swedish population. According to Vilhelm Moberg, author of *The Emigrants*, 'the Swedes in America, Swedish-born down to the third generation, today total about two and a half million persons.

Approximately a fourth of all Swedes in the world now live in the United States.'

The contrast between today's good times and yesterday's hard times could not be more striking. Sweden is setting the pace for other European economies instead of lagging behind. Its modern history points up John Kenneth Galbraith's observation that 'the experience of nations with well-being is exceedingly brief.' Sweden was late in joining the industrial revolution, but when its time came the Swedes were ready with a native talent for manufacturing, a strong sense of organization, an instinct for co-operative effort, and a certain background of business experience. The Riksbank had begun as early as 1668; it is now the oldest central bank in the world. The Stora Kopparberg company was so old that its records included a document in Medieval Latin dated June 16, 1288. Sweden was a pioneer ironworking country and for a long time was actually the foremost iron-producing country, accounting for a third of the world's total output. And Sweden had long since begun to exploit its timber and water-power resources. But in most respects Sweden was an unlikely-looking industrial country, with neither the natural endowments nor a large-enough population to compete with its betters in the rest of Europe.

Even today with only about 10 per cent of the work force engaged in agriculture, most of Sweden still looks as if it is waiting for the industrial revolution. The most characteristic manufacturing situation is the *bruk*, the factory community deep in the countryside, where life centers around a single company. In a *bruk*, workers of several generations feel a special family loyalty to the company and the company has a sense of obligation to its workers that is paternalistic but not oppressively so. The managers and workers, despite differences in status and income, get along together in an easy democracy of proud and skilled men. More than half of the 25,000 factories and workshops in Sweden have no more than ten workers each. In Anderstorp, a small town of 3,700 in the once poverty-stricken southern province of Småland, there are no fewer than 134 industries. Most of the several thousand Småland factories have fewer than fifty workers, and they make everything from furniture and plastic goods to hinges and coat hangers. The owners of the little companies, many of them former workers who decided to strike out on their own, are fiercely competitive free-enterprisers who are quick to detect a demand for a new product, and to make the most of it.

It is, however, the array of big companies, big banks and big financiers that gives bantamweight Sweden the economic punch of a heavyweight. Virtually all of the nation's industrial units are in private hands. The LKAB iron-ore mines and the government steel plant in Lulea are the most notable exceptions. Of the total number of people in industry, private enterprise employs 90 per cent, the cooperatives 4 per cent, and national and local government enterprises just 6 per cent. Private enterprise accounts for 99 per cent of shipping, shipbuilding and textiles, 98 per cent of engineering, 95 per cent of the forest industries, 94 per cent of steel and metalworking, 93 per cent of banking, and so forth. In the retail trade, it is 83 per cent private firms, 16 per cent co-operatives, one per cent government.

In short, socialism has only lightly brushed the economic machinery of welfare Sweden. It has a predominantly capitalistic system, and it is capitalism at its most dynamic and responsible. For a small-population country, Sweden has an extraordinary number of corporations with worldwide reputations—corporations which look far beyond the narrow Swedish market for their sales. Their 1,200 factories in more than 60 countries outside Sweden provide jobs for 175,000 persons. This, plus the foreign workers laboring within Sweden itself, means that the Swedes are providing a livelihood for more than 300,000 foreign workers and their families—to speak only of direct employment.

The easiest way to appreciate Sweden's dominance of the Scandinavian business scene is to look at the ranking of Nordic countries published annually by the Swedish business magazine *Ekonomen*. In 1965, its listing of *manufacturing* companies according to their 1964 sales figures revealed that Sweden had 101 of the 141 Scandinavian firms which had sales of 100 million Swedish kroner (21 million dollars) or more. Finland had 28 companies on the list, Norway 14 and Denmark 9.

The total national sales figures for the listed companies were Sweden $9,400 million, Finland $1,778 million, Norway $784 million, Denmark $435 million.

Although not always counted in the listing of the major Nordic industrial concerns, the largest manufacturing and trading organization in Scandinavia is actually KF, the Swedish Cooperative Union. This collection of factories and food plants under the cooperative banner has annual sales to the KF retail cooperatives of about 700 million dollars, in comparison to SKF's worldwide ball-bearing sales of some 500 million dollars.

Apart from KF, which is really in a category of its own, the dozen largest Swedish industrial corporations according to sales are:

No. Company	Main Products
1 SKF	Ball bearings
2 Volvo	Automobiles
3 ASEA	Electrical machinery
4 L.M. Ericsson	Telephones
5 Skånska Cement	Building materials
6 SAAB	Airplanes, automobiles
7 Scania-Vabis	Trucks
8 Alfa-Laval	Separators
9 Stora Kopparberg	Steel, pulp, paper
10 LKAB	Iron ore
11 Swedish Match	Matches, machinery
12 Electrolux	Electrical appliances

The Wallenberg Dynasty

It is one of the arresting facts of Swedish life that nine of the top dozen firms, as well as many other important companies (Atlas-Copco, Astra, etc.) are powerfully influenced by a single banking family: the Wallenbergs. Only Volvo, Skånska Cement and LKAB of the top twelve are outside the Wallenberg reach.

The Wallenbergs play a role in Swedish economic life even greater than that of Vanderbilt, Morgan or Rockefeller in American life when they were at the peak of their economic power. It

is doubtful whether any important nation anywhere is so influenced, and beneficially influenced, by the financial genius of
one family. This can be said even though Sweden is tremendously
rich in talented business figures. For example, Thore Browaldh of
the Svenska Handelsbank and Lars-Erik Thunholm of the
Skandinaviska Bank not only command the country's two largest
banks, but also serve as spark plugs in the growth of Swedish
industry. Browaldh played a distinguished role in the postwar
recovery of Europe. Industrialists like Erland Waldenström of
the adventurous Grängesberg company—he is a musician and
philosopher as well as a shrewd executive—are constantly pushing
into new business ventures. And yet, despite such personalities
there remains something special about the Wallenbergs: a certain
aura, a golden touch.

The family's most dynamic figure is Marcus Wallenberg. He
is the second son and the namesake of one of the two sons of the
founder of the dynasty. When asked how the Wallenbergs had
reached their unique position in Swedish life, he said, 'We're in a
blind alley up here. If this Stockholm office were in America we
would be up in Hudson Bay. A century ago we were just a small,
underdeveloped country. But Sweden began to have a breakthrough in forestry in the middle of the nineteenth century. We
started to make use of pulp and to develop water power and
electricity. Ours was a very active family, and my father, Marcus,
was probably the most active of them all. One of our greatest
activities was finding capital abroad for Swedish enterprises. We
had to find partners to develop iron ore in the north. Our pattern
has been to develop things which should be developed and which
seem interesting. If there is jealousy directed toward the Wallenbergs it is only because those companies in which we have been
interested have grown so much. We have always taken our
responsibilities to heart.'

It is not surprising that the Wallenbergs should have the
authority they do in Swedish life. The country has been uniquely
served by its outstanding inventors, industrialists and financiers,
and the Wallenbergs have been in the thick of things for more than
a hundred years. It has been estimated that something like 10 per

cent of Sweden's manufacturers are based on Swedish inventions. John Ericsson, for example, not only built the *Monitor*, but also was the coinventor (with Francis Pettit Smith of England) of the marine propeller. G. F. Göransson's improvement of the Bessemer method of steelmaking a century ago brought it to the practicable stage and began the production of steel in large quantities. This and later innovations turned Sweden into an important steel-producing country despite its lack of coal. The recently developed Swedish Kaldo oxygen process is yet another milestone in international steelmaking.

Gustaf de Laval, who designed a new kind of steam turbine, revolutionized the dairy industry by inventing the centrifugal cream separator. The blind inventor, Gustav Dalen, won the Nobel Prize in physics in 1912 for his automatic beacons and light buoys—developments which dramatically increased the safety of ships at sea. After Sven Wingquist created the self-aligning ball bearing in 1907, the world's output of ball and roller bearings increased from 10,000 to several millions a day, and SKF became the premier firm in this vital industry.

Lars Magnus Ericsson, a contemporary of Alexander Graham Bell, was one of the pioneers in the development of the telephone. By the time he died at age eighty, in 1926, the L. M. Ericsson company had installed telephone systems everywhere from Moscow to Mexico City, and was ranked as one of Europe's foremost corporations. Alfred Nobel, of course, became an important industrialist after his numerous discoveries in explosives. The Bofors company was largely his creation. Although it still turns out big guns and powder, a strong diversification program has converted Bofors into a major producer of civilian products. More than half of its sales now come from such varied non-explosive items as steel, turbines, bassinets and heart pills.

Ivar Kreuger, for all his skulduggery in high finance, developed a number of important Swedish companies and built Swedish Match into a worldwide giant—as it still is today, despite the Kreuger crash. Another legendary name in Swedish finance is Axel Wenner-Gren. He made his fortune with the Electrolux company, which manufactures and sells home electrical appliances all over the globe. Wenner-Gren was a secretive, scientific-minded salesman, industrialist and philanthropist who died in 1961 convinced that one of his creations, the monorail, was destined to become a standard means of transportation on every continent. Still another powerful figure was Axel Axelsson Johnson, who took over a steel mill and other works begun by his father and turned them into an industrial empire comprising everything from stainless steel, oil and chemicals to heavy machinery, a fleet of passenger-cargo vessels and an international bus line. He died only a few years ago, but the third generation carries on 'the Johnson group of Sweden.' It is a family company which employs 27,000 people and operates in sixteen countries besides Sweden. Its annual sales come to about 450 million dollars. It is the second-largest company, after SKF and Volvo, but because it is a family enterprise and not a corporation it does not publish an annual report. Thus it is usually not included in the lists of the biggest Swedish companies.

Some Swedish authorities say that the Johnsons are the wealthiest people in Sweden. Others insist that the greatest fortune is in the hands of the most powerful shipowner, Dan-Axel Broström, who commands the Tirfing Steamship Company and the Swedish-American Line. Still others speak of the Wehtje family, whose most prominent personality is Ernst Wehtje. Now in his seventies, he is the son of a noted businessman and the eldest of four brothers who all became important figures in Swedish industry. Ernst Wehtje turned a small cement factory into the mighty Skånska Cement company, one of the top half dozen Swedish firms. His brother Walter Wehtje has been closely associated with the Wallenbergs and at the time of writing is the president of Investor, one of the Wallenberg investment trusts. His daughter is married to Marc Wallenberg, son of Marcus and the president of the old family bank, the Stockholms Enskilda Bank.

And so it seems, in Sweden, that any trek through the national economy eventually leads to the Wallenbergs. Whether they are wealthier than the Johnsons, the Broströms or the Wehtjes is a debatable question, but there is no doubt that they control one of the largest pools of investment capital in Sweden. Their real importance, however, has less to do with their money than with the unique kind of influence they wield in the executive suites of Sweden.

Not everyone, of course, is happy about such a concentration of wealth and power, and the Wallenbergs for decades have made an irresistible target for left-wing sharpshooters. There was a time after World War I, when 'the mass of the people,' as Marquis Childs reported, looked upon the influence of the Wallenbergs as 'sinister and all-pervasive, dominating the financial and industrial life of the country, opposed to all progress and reform.' If this was the popular conception at that time, then things have drastically changed. My own impression after having studied the family in some detail is that it has a profound sense of public obligation. As Marcus Wallenberg expressed it, 'Many people think we have inherited a fortune, but what we have inherited is a debt.'

The debt or the obligation is to advance the well-being of Sweden and enhance its influence abroad. An associate of Marcus Wallenberg said 'he loves to see new enterprises, new buildings, new activity.' The Wallenbergs were instrumental in the creation of the Scandinavian Airlines System, and Marcus has served periodically as its chairman.

Similarly, the Wallenbergs were the central figures in the organization of Swedish, American and German steel, mining and banking interests into the great 230-million-dollar LAMCO (Liberian American–Swedish Minerals Company) project. LAMCO has a seventy-year contract with the government of Liberia to exploit the more than 300 million tons of high-grade iron ore in the Nimba mountains. Bethlehem Steel is the major American partner in the project. Grängesberg, the Swedish shipping and steelmaking complex, supervised construction and is now managing the mining operations. *The New York Times* said in 1961 that 'the deal marks the emergence of Swedish industrial management skill to a position of prominence in areas of the world often associated with so-called "colonial powers."' Another commentator said more jocularly that it was 'Sweden's largest overseas investment since the Thirty Years' War.' For Marcus

Wallenberg the LAMCO exercise is just one of many foreign operations. He plays an incredibly busy role as an international financier. To mention just three activities at the time of writing: he is a member of a team of top-level counselors advising the government of Kuwait on how to spend its oil riches; he is president of the International Chamber of Commerce; and he is chairman of ADELA, the first multinational private investment company for Latin America, a private counterpart to the United States government's Alliance for Progress.

Creative Capitalism

The heart of the House of Wallenberg is the black granite building which sits like a brooding citadel at the side of Kungsträdgården in central Stockholm. It is the headquarters of Stockholms Enskilda Bank (Private Bank of Stockholm), Sweden's third-largest bank in assets and deposits, and the country's principal pipeline for more than a century for the flow of foreign capital into Sweden. It is now a public-stock company, only partly owned by the Wallenbergs, but controlled by them as the main instrument of their financial power. It was founded by Oscar Wallenberg, vastly expanded by his sons Knut and Marcus, as well as their three brothers, and brought to its present eminence by Marcus's sons Jacob and Marcus. They have run the bank as a brother act for almost forty years.

The Wallenberg emphasis is on creative capitalism, not the simple accumulation of wealth. Their power in Swedish affairs comes not so much from ownership as it does from the authority of their expertise. The dozens of 'Wallenberg companies' are firms which have benefited from the golden touch of a family steeped in experience and information, and ingenious in the arts of management. Wallenberg money is committed on a grand scale, but it is widely spread and usually does not amount to a controlling interest although the stake is heavy (5 to 10 per cent) in major concerns like SKF, ASEA and Stora Kopparberg. The family does not even hold the majority of shares in the two investment trusts, Investor and Providentia, which they control.

The combined assets of the two trusts, whose portfolios are heavily laden with major holdings in the 'Wallenberg companies,' were 215 million dollars in early 1965. 'It is a matter of principle with us,' said Marcus Wallenberg, 'not to own or seek majority control in any company. It is our experience, and the accumulated experience of our family, that has landed us on many of these boards.'

In 1965 Jacob Wallenberg was the chairman of the board of fourteen different companies, while Marcus and Marc were board chairmen of another eleven. These included all but a handful of the largest corporations. In addition the three men held directorships in about fifty other companies and in one way or another influenced still more companies. The Wallenberg hand is felt over the whole range of the Swedish economy, from steel and airplanes to Stockholm's largest department store and three of its most luxurious restaurants.

That subtle thing called 'Wallenberg management' does not mean the day-to-day running of companies. It is more a matter of finding the right man to manage the firms and being useful at times of vital decisions. It is not any blatant, obvious use of great power, but quiet deliberation and decision-making behind the scenes: nothing flamboyant, nothing (preferably) that makes headlines.

Even though the family has spoken out more openly about its affairs in recent years, it still operates with the traditional reticence of private bankers. A *Fortune* article in 1962 was the first detailed foreign dissection of 'The Wallenberg Dynasty.' It said that 'as individuals the Wallenbergs are misty figures to their own countrymen. Strictly abiding by their motto—*Esse non videri* (To be, not to be seen)—they live in the style of a great bourgeois family of a century ago, shunning ostentation and publicity.' This description made me feel apprehensive when I went to see the Wallenbergs in Stockholm, but they proved to be far more engaging and outgoing than I had expected. They were more approachable, certainly, than the Rothschilds of London, whose reluctance to be interviewed was painful to behold. Perhaps there is something symbolic in the fact that the massive front doors of the Enskilda Bank now open automatically as a visitor passes through the beam of an electric eye.

The Wallenbergs are cosmopolitan financiers who each speak at least four languages. They served apprenticeships in foreign banks and spent a great deal of their time traveling outside Sweden. Young Marc is a graduate of the Harvard School of Business Administration. In 1965, he was forty years old, father Marcus was sixty-five, and uncle Jacob seventy-two. The two older men are each six feet tall or more: sturdy, white-haired, still-athletic figures. Jacob is a noted yachtsman who has successfully competed in the Baltic race, a grueling 340-nautical-mile course from Stockholm to Helsinki. Marcus was the amateur singles tennis champion of Sweden in 1920 and 1926.

During World War I, their uncle, Knut Wallenberg, was Sweden's foreign minister; he did much to keep the country neutral. And their father, Marcus senior, was a key figure in the restoration of Europe's finances after the fighting. In World War II, as Sweden again sought to stay neutral and keep its economic head above water, Marcus was drafted to maintain Sweden's contacts with Great Britain while Jacob was assigned to deal with Germany, a job which eventually involved him with the German underground. In the postwar world, Marcus has been a corporate Mr. Fix-It in Sweden and an increasingly active figure on the international scene, while Jacob, as chairman of the Enskilda Bank as well as companies like SKF, Stora Kopparberg and Alfa-Laval, has minded the store and concentrated on affairs inside Sweden.

At the Enskilda Bank, or wherever he lights, Marcus Wallenberg's aim is 'uncluttered management.' He has an intense dislike of all the paper which is the curse of modern corporate life. 'Open lines of communication' are established at the bank by heavy use of the telephone, a lot of personal visiting back and forth, increasing use of computers to process information, and a minimum reliance on interoffice memos. Swedish businessmen resort to the telephone more than their counterparts in other countries. In many parts of Swedish life a letter is regarded almost as an imposition, and may not be promptly answered, if at all, but a telephone call will put you straight through to the man you want. Eric Boheman, the board chairman of SAAB, said that Swedish companies have few people in the top echelon. 'They work together without a lot of paper work.'

The tycoons of Sweden form a closely knit business establishment. 'The big companies are in constant contact with each other,' said a Danish journalist. 'The leading people are all close, close friends. They went to school together. They support the same politics, finance each other, and sit as members on each other's board.' It is a business hierarchy which resembles the British 'Old Boy Network,' but with the crucial difference that there is not a breath of amateurism among the Swedish old boys. The Swedes are not playing at business; they are deadly professionals. For all their competitive zeal they also have a remarkable capacity for teamwork. Like the tycoons of Japan (another nation always conscious that it must 'export or die'), they reserve their ultimate weapons of business combat for their foreign competitors, not for each other.

The gentleman's-agreement character of Swedish business life begins at the very roots. In Småland, for example, a worker who has trained in a *bruk* and decides to go off to start a little company of his own may well receive both aid and encouragement from his former boss, but the unwritten understanding is that he will not set up a directly competing firm which takes business away from the first company. In like spirit, the major firms of Sweden pretty much divide up the chores: one makes telephones, another makes generators. It is not absolute, of course; there are a number of specialty steel firms jostling for the same business, for example, but they jostle most gently. In their invasion of foreign markets the Swedes march forward as a united front. Even the scrappy little entrepreneurs of Småland have banded together (120 of them at the time of writing) in an exporting outfit called Swed Expo, which has erected a permanent exhibition hall at Värnamo. It all seems natural to a country which, as Gunnar Heckscher wrote, 'is far from being torn by dissension and conflict. Compromise and cooperation rather than competition have been the vehicles of social change.'

Swedish Match

In the days when Ivar Kreuger was riding high, Swedish Match controlled three quarters of the world's production of matches. The crash of his financial empire had global repercussions. The most celebrated financial genius of his day was unmasked as a swindler of historic proportions. Millionaires lost their fortunes and small investors were ruined. A number of companies went bankrupt and many more were crippled. The Match King's maze of match companies in scores of nations seemed to have been dealt a fatal blow, and the heart of the match empire, Svenska Tänd-sticks (Swedish Match), looked as if it might never recover. But recover it did, in one of the greatest reconstruction jobs in business history. Today Swedish Match controls a quarter of the world's match industry through majority or partial interests in some forty foreign match companies operating sixty factories. This accounts for slightly less than half of the company's business as it expands into precision machinery and an array of other products.

Ivar Kreuger was a Napoleonic business figure who was said by British economist John Maynard Keynes (before Kreuger's crash) to possess 'maybe the greatest financial intelligence of his time.' In his greatness he did not feel encumbered by ordinary ideas of right and wrong. The Kreuger & Toll Building Company, which put up buildings and bridges all over Sweden, and its off-shoot, Kreuger & Toll, Inc., were his original instruments for financial aggression. He created Swedish Match by merging important match interests within Sweden. Eventually his 'little wooden soldiers' gave him control of some 250 match factories all over the world which turned out about 30 billion boxes of matches a year. He invested deeply in the L. M. Ericsson Tele-phone Company, SKF and other key Swedish firms, and he borrowed millions of dollars from the Skandinaviska Bank. By adroitly juggling his holdings, inventing fictitious companies, forging bonds, and inflating values, he gave the appearance of having twice as much wealth as he actually had. According to his latest biographer, Robert Shaplen, the net assets of his companies were 200 million dollars instead of the 400 million he claimed, and his personal liabilities at the time he committed suicide in Paris in 1932 amounted to 265 million dollars.

For Swedish Match, the debt was a staggering 28 million pounds, but the hardheaded financiers like the Wallenbergs who formed the rescue squad decided that it could be salvaged. It was an essentially sound business and it was still producing billions of matches with the best machinery in the world. As Shaplen wrote, Kreuger had always regarded it as 'the most legitimate part of his business, and he had kept its affairs pretty well apart from the inflations and fictions with which he had riddled his other concerns.' By World War II its debt had been reduced by half, and by 1948 the company was out of the woods at last and able to pay dividends on its shares. Its vigorous young president, Bo Ehrner, told me that 'in 1954 we had almost as much money in the bank as we had debts in 1935.' The company's annual sales are now about 185 million dollars, and half of this is accounted for by highly specialized equipment and other non-match products, which stem from its pioneering development of match-making machinery.

Volvo

In the past decade Volvo has become the most widely known of the great Swedish companies, because of the worldwide success of its conservatively designed, painstakingly manufactured automobile. Volvo is now second only to SKF as the biggest Swedish manufacturer. It is a producer of cars in Canada, a leading foreign-car competitor in the United States, and it makes the best-selling automobile in Sweden, a title once possessed by the cheaper Volkswagen.

A country of Sweden's size and small home market should not be expected to make its own vehicles, but Sweden has not one but three important companies producing automobiles and/or trucks. SAAB is still principally an aviation firm (and expanding rapidly into computers), but its rugged, front-wheel-drive cars account for about half its sales. Scania-Vabis, which is Scandinavia's largest producer of diesel trucks, makes buses and engines as well, and serves as the sales agent for Volkswagen, Volvo's biggest competitor within Sweden. Like SAAB, it is a 'Wallenberg company,' and it has been a staggeringly profitable one in recent years.

Volvo makes trucks as well as marine jet engines, agricultural machinery, printing presses and other products. It is one of four companies which have the lion's share of Sweden's armaments exports. But the car is still the heart of the matter. With the help of capital from its Gothenburg neighbor, SKF, Volvo in 1927 began producing an automobile tough enough to stand the rugged conditions in Sweden, where most roads were yet to be paved. By 1940, sales were still less than 6,000 a year. Volvo's big push to become an important manufacturer began in the 1950s, when Gunnar Engellau became the managing director. He is one of the most accomplished of the new, breezier breed of Swedish tycoons, and his arrival on the scene coincided with the sudden outburst of spending power which has made the Swedes the greatest car owners outside North America. Volvo now makes 120,000 cars a year, including an elegant sports model, and they are internationally acclaimed for quality and safety. Volvo was the first auto manufacturer anywhere to install seat belts in every car as standard equipment.

While Volvo's sales inside Sweden have risen dramatically, the company's chief importance lies in its superlative export performance. 'If we want to survive—and I don't just mean Volvo— we must export,' said Engellau. 'If we don't, we die.' In the quarter century before he took charge, the company had exported only 1,000 cars, mostly to Norway, where the roads were even worse than in Sweden. Today some 60,000 Volvos are exported every year as the nation's number one export item, accounting for 4 per cent of Swedish exports. The total annual value of Volvo's exports is approaching 200 million dollars. Although there are now several overseas assembly plants, most of the cars are coming out of a new, half-mile-long factory outside Gothenburg, the biggest industrial building in Scandinavia. It is packed with computers, television cameras, electronic eyes, all manner of automated equipment, and novel systems for handling the inflow of parts from Swedish and foreign suppliers. The heavy reliance on subcontractors means that perhaps 100,000 Swedes and foreigners work for Volvo, in addition to its own 20,000 employees. Every tenth Volvo worker, conspicuous in his yellow boiler suit, is an inspector checking on the quality of the work of the other nine workers.

The company is trying not to be unrealistically optimistic about the future, but just in case business continues to boom, it has designed its new factory in a way which would permit an exact duplicate ('a mirror-image plant') to be erected beside it. If the double factory were to work two shifts Volvo could conceivably make 400,000 cars a year. It could, that is, if it were able to solve its two knottiest problems: where to find more workers, and where to house them. Sweden is now so dangerously short of workers for the best-paid jobs in Europe that Volvo may have to build more overseas plants like the new one in Belgium instead of expanding home production. And even for its present labor force Volvo has had agonizing housing problems. It had to invest in a ship and moor it in Gothenburg harbor, just to provide temporary accommodation.

ASEA

ASEA can be translated as Swedish General Electric. The name in Swedish is formidable: Allmänna Svenska Elektriska Aktiebolaget. It is one of the world's dozen leading makers of electrical equipment and the third-largest Swedish manufacturer. The company began in an attic in 1883 and for the past half century it has been the overshadowing presence in the life of Västerås, a city in a rural setting sixty miles to the west of Stockholm. The soaring brick tower of the ASEA headquarters (there are quaint chimes every half hour) is often mistaken for the city hall.

The Wallenbergs rescued the company from bankruptcy soon after the turn of the century and have been quietly masterminding its affairs ever since. It is ASEA which has supplied most of the equipment for Sweden's outsized hydroelectric establishment and for the electrification of Sweden's railroads. Its annual sales are more than 415 million dollars a year. The ASEA group controls over two dozen different companies and has 49 per cent of the voting rights in Electrolux. Its products range from generators and atomic heating equipment to fiberglass and industrial diamonds. The diamonds are only the most exotic of a parade of new processes and products which have been presented to the world by the brilliant teams of ASEA research scientists.

Some years ago ASEA began to grow much too big for little Sweden. Like a household cat turned into an overfed tiger, it was too fenced in and too unwieldy for its own good. The answer was a bold thrust into world markets. ASEA, for example, is supplying all of the twenty-two generators for the immense Snowy Mountains hydroelectric project in Australia, but its most powerful effort has to do with advanced systems for the long-distance transmission of electricity.

The problem of unwieldy administration was attended to when the Wallenbergs plucked a young executive out of the ASEA ranks in 1961 and set him loose as the company's new president. Curt Nicolin was just forty years old at the time. He had made his mark as the aviation engineer at the head of the team which developed Sweden's first jet engine. Another team he directed produced the country's first commercial gas turbine. Nicolin served for six years as president of an ASEA subsidiary before being catapulted to the top position in the corporation. He had hardly begun to shake up the company when Marcus Wallenberg switched him to the presidency of SAS, when it needed emergency surgery. Since returning to ASEA in 1963 he has carried out a corporate streamlining operation of classic proportions. By concentrating the manufacture of products into one instead of two or three factories, Nicolin was able to close down four plants. Whole factories and many of their workers were moved from one town to another. The payroll was drastically reduced by lopping off jobs like floor cleaning and warehousing, which could be more efficiently handled by outside specialists. No worker lost his livelihood in the massive reshuffle; ASEA simply did not replace workers who left the firm under normal circumstances, and it set up a large-scale retraining program. In the process,

Nicolin's name entered the Swedish vernacular as a word for sweeping the cobwebs out of an organization.

What makes Curt Nicolin particularly noteworthy is that he symbolizes the oncoming space-age generation of 'American-style' Swedish executives. They are hard-driving, self-assured men, whose informal manners and brash methods upset some of their older or more stolid business associates. For all of their enterprise, Swedes still put an excessively high premium on conventional behavior, and Nicolin is audacious and unconventional. When I called on him at Västerås it was not for the standard interview I expected, but a nine-hour athletic day spent racing about the country in a private plane as he called on a succession of factories and delivered a speech in southern Sweden—a speech in which he managed, as usual, to step on a few toes.

'The man oozes confidence,' said a foreign diplomat in Stockholm. 'He is one of the three sharpest people I have met in Sweden.' Because Nicolin made his reputation overnight he has been in danger of being billed too often as a miracle worker. 'Royal Swedish envy' has made its appearance. 'Some people would dearly love to see me fail,' Nicolin said, 'but it only makes me more determined not to. It's an unfortunate part of our character that we are jealous about other people's achievements.'

Nicolin is a handsome and dark-haired six-footer who could play himself in a film about the corridors of corporate power. In the manner of men who enjoy the risks and responsibilities of leadership, he is relaxed and refreshingly candid about life at the top. 'You have to have an aggressive attitude about the future,' he said. 'I want to see the future of this company while I'm still alive. The only way is to quickly get an advantage over the competition.'

He said that Swedish industry 'has always lived under very keen competition from abroad.' It could go on making headway so long as it continued to produce ideas and was able to reward incentive. Typical of modern Swedish businessmen, he did not consider himself anti–welfare state. He felt that there had to be protection from distress, but thought it would be fatal not to have a climate where people could get something for achievement. 'Money isn't everything, but it can bring more freedom. If a man has some capital behind him he can argue with his boss, try out new ideas, pursue his whims. I don't just mean rewards for businessmen, but for anyone doing something outstanding: artists, scientists, members of parliament and so on. They may only amount to a tiny percentage of the population, but it is the creative percentage.'

Nicolin said he was worried about the extent of progressive taxation in Sweden, how it might deprive people of their willingness to show initiative; yet his outlook for Sweden was exceedingly rosy. In his enthusiasm, speaking as a dedicated free-enterpriser, he sounded remarkably like another young Swedish leader and dedicated Social Democrat already quoted, Olof Palme. Where the politician was thinking of what great works in welfare and public services the government might accomplish, the businessman spoke in terms of the business system as a cornucopia of wealth. Said Nicolin: 'In former times the only way to get wealth was to steal or make war or belong to a very small privileged class. Now, for the first time in history, we have the possibility of multiplying our wealth tremendously and providing enough for everybody.'

Chapter 23

A TALENT FOR TEAMWORK

The strike is no longer a weapon we use. It is too old-fashioned.
We lift the pistol, of course, but we never fire.

—TRADE-UNION LEADER

Our idea is that competition is good for society. You are forced to be
efficient.

—COOPERATIVE LEADER

The star performers of the Swedish economy are the private companies, but they work in a favorable climate of reasonable government and responsible trade-unionism. Sweden could be called the Common Sense Society. It is one of those rare and fortunate nations which have managed to harmonize their conflicting interests so that their people work with one another instead of against one another. The accent is on the positive. Businessmen are not opposed to the welfare state. The Social Democrats are not against the capitalists. State enterprise is not set against private enterprise. The cooperatives serve as a useful third force in the economy and help protect the consumer and the farmer. And the trade unions are not infected with that 'bloody-mindedness' which cripples production from Liverpool to Pittsburgh.

Great credit must be given to the capitalists of this hard Nordic land; their socially responsible business performance has made Sweden the most eloquent example of free-enterprise vitality in all Europe. But as much credit must be given to those political figures of the moderate Left who, in a way, had an even harder

371

task to perform: to rid themselves of a doctrinaire Marxist approach to society and to find a pragmatic formula to suit the genius of Sweden. Before they went too far in the socialization of Sweden, they stopped short, took stock, and chose moderation. In essence, they left business to the businessmen and concentrated on social problems. It could be said that they had no choice in that they never were able to receive a majority-vote mandate from the citizenry to build a Red Sweden. But the Social Democratic rejection of Marxism had already begun at the very time between the two world wars when they came to power with ever-increasing popular support.

Prewar writings about Sweden, most notably that memorable book *The Middle Way*, by Marquis Childs, gave only hurried (and often critical) attention to the activities of private business in Sweden and concentrated on the cooperatives and the widening range of the government's social and economic activities. A partnership of private and public enterprise was correctly envisioned, but it was not foreseen that the Swedish capitalists thirty years later would play the role they do today, or that the 'socialists' in the Stockholm ministries would function as guardians of free enterprise as well as champions of social security.

The cooperatives deserved the publicity they received in the 1920s and 1930s, because they have indeed been a vital element in the development of modern Sweden. Among other things, they helped break the octopus hold of the cartels and they induced Swedish companies to become more conscious of their social duties. They were, and are, major factors in the modernization of Swedish agriculture and in the development of an efficient retailing industry. The cooperatives, however, never achieved anything like the revolutionary role in the economy which their well-wishers envisioned, or which many outsiders imagined. Albin Johansson, the brilliant Swede who led the consumers' union, KF, during its most vigorous decades, was a great persuader. As a Swedish publication said some years ago, 'it is not unusual for visitors from abroad, particularly journalists, to come away from an interview with him with the impression that the co-operatives control the commerce and industry of the nation—

this in spite of the fact that nine tenths of business in Sweden is in private hands.'

According to a leading industrialist (and former ambassador to the United States), Eric Boheman, 'The Social Democrats can say that "they" have achieved our prosperous society because they have spread the income of the nation to an astonishing degree, but they never thought it could be achieved without another kind of society. Reorganizing society into a socialist state was the original idea, but it has turned out that private enterprise is the absolutely dominant economic factor in Sweden.'

Just how true this is was brought home to me when I read a Stockholm news release which said that 'the government has complete control over only one sector of the economy—the production of peat briquettes.' Of course, the government has enormous ultimate power to control the use of money in Sweden, and it undoubtedly does regulate business to a greater degree than capitalists prefer, but, as Marcus Wallenberg said, 'the necessity to maintain industry's international competitiveness has ruled out centrally directed planning of industry, trade and shipping. As the government authorities either have not wanted or have not dared to shoulder the responsibility for an attempt at such central management, they have had—particularly in view of our goal to maintain full employment in our free economy—to rely on the propensity and ability of private business to invest. Consequently, they have had to see to it that the investment climate has not been too unfriendly to private enterprise.'

In Sweden, a lot of responsible people are busy discussing how the economy and society should develop. Weighty reports are produced to suggest what might be done to make a better future. There is even a 'Long-term Planning Commission,' embracing everyone from bureaucrats and bankers to labor leaders and cooperative chiefs. Its main purpose is to give policy makers in the many branches of the economy some idea of what their counterparts have in mind for the future. There is, however, virtually no real long-term planning for the whole economy, certainly nothing on the scale being attempted by the Norwegians, despite the notions about Sweden being a planned society. It was my impression that businessmen feel that too-rigid blueprinting of the future for the whole economy would cramp their style. They are also conscious of how swiftly conditions change in a dynamic economy. The Swedish dynamism stems largely from the over-all urge for new products and production methods to keep Sweden ahead of the competitive game. About 300 million dollars are spent by Swedish industry each year on research and development. An authoritative study says that since this corresponds to just under 2 per cent of the gross national product, Sweden ranks tenth in the world in *total* research and development spending.

The momentum of Swedish industry is also due to the incentives for investment and modernization which Swedish private business has been provided during the years of Social Democratic rule. There are exceptionally liberal rules for inventory valuation and for the depreciation of machinery. A remarkable 'investment-fund plan,' aimed partially at leveling out business fluctuations, permits companies to set aside for future investment purposes a *tax-free* amount corresponding to 40 per cent of a year's profits. Later on, if government permission is granted, a company can use the funds for the immediate write-off of investments.

State Enterprises

It is noteworthy that the state enterprises do not receive any particularly favored treatment from the government in their operations. Talented businessmen are put at their helm and they are expected to perform as if they were directing private firms. Arne Lundberg, the widely respected president of the iron-mining giant, L.K.A.B., said, 'There is no human being in Sweden who is more against government subsidies than I am.' The fact is, however, that state enterprises play a lesser role in Sweden than they do in Austria, France, Italy and most other European countries. Manufacturing is almost wholly in private hands, while most of the state enterprises are in such predictable areas as transportation, power and communications. There is no sense underrating government business, however, since it accounts for a tenth of all workers. The nation's biggest employer (58,000 employees) is the State Railways, which also happens to be Sweden's greatest gardener; every station prides itself on its flowers. The state's alcohol monopoly is the largest purchaser of wines and spirits in the world. The state mines provide a fifth of the world's iron-ore exports.

The surprisingly small amount of expansion of the public sector by the Social Democrats since 1932 can be readily seen in the following tables adapted from those produced by the Stockholms Enskilda Bank.

AUTONOMOUS CENTRAL GOVERNMENT TRADING AGENCIES

Name	Government activity in this area since
State Railways	1853
Post Office	1636
Telegraph-Telephone Board	1853
State Forest Service	16th century
State Power Administration	1909
Ordnance Factory Board	17th century

JOINT-STOCK CORPORATIONS IN WHICH THE GOVERNMENT HOLDS 50 PER CENT OR MORE OF THE PAID-UP CAPITAL

Name	Government holds part of paid-up capital since	Government holds entire paid-up capital since
LKAB Mining	1907	1957
Swedish Restaurant Chain	1915	—
State Forests	1927	1941
Norrbottens Steelworks	—	1940
Alcohol Monopoly	1917	1955
Tobacco Monopoly	—	1915
Central Bank	1923	1951

In short, only one of the thirteen principal government enterprises—the Norrbottens steel mill—was initiated by the Social Democrats. The single important act of nationalization in their three decades of power was the take-over of the LKAB mining works, and this was a completion of a process begun half a century earlier by a conservative government. (The World War I intervention by the right-wing government in the restaurant, liquor and tobacco businesses was principally for reasons of health and sobriety.)

Cooperatives

The cooperatives play a neutralist or nonaligned role in the Swedish economy. They are in business like the private firms, without having a capitalist ownership, and they have the blessings of the Social Democratic government while operating independently of the state. They have carved out their special niche in Swedish life, as have the co-ops in the other Nordic countries. If they have not become as powerful a force in the Swedish economy as early enthusiasts expected, then at least they can say that where they are big, they are very, very big. And their mere presence on the economic landscape gives it a pleasant kind of wholesomeness.

The farm co-ops dominate Swedish agriculture. They are linked together as the Federation of Swedish Farmers' Associations, and their annual sales are more than a billion dollars. The consumers' cooperatives, operating separately from the farm co-ops, sell goods to a third of the nation's households through a network of retail stores. The consumers' union (KF), which embraces the retail outlets and other enterprises, has greater sales than any other business institution, industrial or trading, in Scandinavia. The central organization of KF sold nearly 700 million dollars' worth of goods to its member societies and other purchasers in 1964. The sales of the member societies, through local co-op shops and other outlets, exceeded 900 million dollars. The many housing cooperatives, particularly the nationally organized Tenants and Savings Bank and Building Society (H.S.B), have played a vital role in Swedish homebuilding. One quarter of the new homes in Sweden are financed by co-ops, and 10 per cent of all new homes are constructed by co-op building organizations.

Three things stick most in mind after an inquiry into the Swedish cooperatives: (1) the strong current of idealism which still courses through the movement; (2) the competitive spirit of the co-op leaders, who insist that they want to compete with private industry, not eliminate it; (3) the rapid-fire modernization of the whole cooperative structure to keep pace with the sweeping changes in Swedish living habits and standards.

The idealism was there from the beginning. The cooperative movement rose out of the social and economic discontent of the late nineteenth century. Like soldiers forming a ragged front line, the cooperators, trade-unionists, socialists, suffragists, temperance workers, adult education and 'free church' leaders, all advanced on the evils of society. They fought their battles with general success and moved on into a more tolerant middle age.

The co-op was originally a means for society's 'little man' to band together with his fellows as a force to combat the enemy. In the old days, the enemy was only too obvious: the laissez-faire economic system with its mysterious cycles of boom and bust, the big capitalists who didn't mind squeezing the consumer if it meant greater profits, and the cartels which sought to eliminate competition and inflate prices. The co-op movement marshaled an army of consumers made up primarily of working-class people, and thus it was called 'the third wing of the labor movement.'

The cooperatives, however, like the Social Democratic Party and the trade unions (the other two wings of the movement), became less and less radical as their primary goals were achieved. They also zealously remained independent of their political and labor allies. Their operations today are markedly pragmatic and businesslike, yet the old idealism is still there. It can be seen in the 'education and propaganda activity' of Kooperativa Förbundet, which has a magazine called *Vi* (We) with the amazing circulation of nearly 600,000. (A comparable circulation in the U.S.A. would be about 14 million.) KF also has such other periodicals as *The Cooperator, We Will* and *Our Paper.* They all preach the practical virtues of togetherness. KF operates a Cooperative College and some 4,500 study circles around the country. It produces films to teach families how to make the best use of their incomes. When I called at the KF headquarters in Stockholm, the latest project was a movie to inspire affluent Swedish youth to save their money for more serious things instead of throwing it away on cosmetics, cheap entertainment and other frivolities. It sounds like stern rectitude, but the emphasis was simply on creating a wholesome life in Sweden, an aim shared with a great many other volunteer organizations. From the trade unions to the mass sporting associations, the country is full of organizations which still pay much more than mere lip service to the ideals which inspired them.

The original Swedish cooperatives in the mid-nineteenth century were modeled after the famous movement in Rochdale, England—the Equitable Pioneers Cooperative Society. The co-op formed by the Rochdale weavers succeeded where others had failed, because they retailed their goods at market prices instead of trying to undersell the private shops. The Swedish co-ops began in the same way, but after they had gathered their strength they began a series of attacks on monopolies by providing consumers with lower-priced products purchased abroad or made in their own factories.

The first co-op retail stores were created by consumers who put up a certain amount of share capital and then conscientiously patronized the shop they partially owned. Then, as now, the co-ops made a point of voluntary membership, democratic management, political and religious neutrality, and the general idea that a member would receive a dividend from the surplus, or profits, according to the amount of his purchases. Nonmembers were welcomed as shoppers but received no annual dividend—that is, no rebate on their purchases over the year. The isolated and struggling societies finally joined forces as the Kooperativa Förbundet in 1899, but it was not until World War I that KF became a major economic force. Membership then was only 100,000. Today it is 1,300,000 persons. Since most members represent families, it seems that half the Swedish population is involved in the consumers' cooperatives.

The resistance of private businessmen (retailers threatened to boycott wholesalers who sold goods to the co-op societies) pushed KF into wholesaling and manufacturing. KF started to produce margarine, flour, soap, rubber shoes, light bulbs and other goods when it appeared that the monopolies were charging excessively high prices for these items. A series of classic battles took place. KF's little Luma light-bulb works, for example, took on the great international electric cartel and brought bulb prices down by 37 per cent. The cooperatives succeeded in giving consumers a wider choice of products at lower cost. Sometimes the mere threat by KF to enter a new field served to reduce prices. Competition from the co-ops had innumerable side effects, mostly good for society and often good for private business. Lower prices meant more customers, more business, more jobs. Private companies were compelled to rationalize their production costs to meet the co-op challenge and thus increased their own business efficiency.

The war between the co-ops and the cartels in the 1920s and 1930s received much international attention and was chronicled in *The Middle Way*. Since then, government regulations and the changing attitude of private firms have largely reduced the sound and fury. The co-ops and private firms now coexist amiably, and there are even some instances of joint ownership of factories. KF remains vigilant, nonetheless, and is ever ready to go into battle on the consumer's side. Its own account of 'KF's fight against monopoly' celebrates, for instance, the postwar 'competitive struggle between the consumer movement and the private washing-powder factories.' America's soap giant, Proctor & Gamble, moved into the Swedish scene in 1954 with an assortment of detergents and new soaps. KF dropped the prices of its own products, created some new soaps and detergents, and greatly stepped up production, thus thwarting some of the more ambitious plans of an international corporation which has three times the annual sales of KF.

'One might even say,' a KF history states, 'that the mere existence of a strong cooperative enterprise is sufficient to prevent private manufacturers and manufacturers' organizations from demanding unreasonable prices. They know that at any time the cooperative movement can take action. The measures which a powerful monopolistic enterprise can use against a troublesome private competitor have little effect on a cooperative enterprise.'

The cooperative movement is a prime example of strength

through numbers. KF's huge membership makes a powerful interest group. On the other hand, it is noteworthy how many Swedes do *not* belong to a cooperative. Some people say that they wouldn't dream of being seen in a co-op. 'Middle-class people,' said a KF spokesman, 'used to think of the co-ops as the back door to nationalization, but our retired chief said that if that's true, then nationalization will take seven hundred years.'

The great developer of the consumers' co-op movement, Albin Johansson, made a distinction between the 'working capitalists' he admired and the 'finance capitalists'—the monopoly creators— he abhorred. In his dedication to KF, Johansson would take a salary of only about $5,000, far less than the executive standard in the business world. It is a sign of the times that KF decided this was an old-fashioned approach when the present head of the organization, Harry Hjalmarson, took office in 1957. He earns about $24,000 a year. Hjalmarson is a friendly, down-to-earth administrator, now in his late fifties, who has spent about thirty-five years in the co-op movement, starting as a co-op shop assistant in Västerås.

He has one of the most demanding executive jobs in all Scandinavia, since KF is more an empire than a company. The KF umbrella takes in four hundred cooperative societies, a variety of food associations, a complex of factories making everything from china to vegetable oil, the Swedish Household Association, the Domus department-store chain, a group of funeral cooperatives, the Folksam cooperative insurance company, and more. KF in the postwar period took the initiative in creating the National Oil Consumers' Union in partnership with the motor owners' co-operative and other groups. The idea was to provide gasoline and heating oil to customers in the co-op manner. There are now some four hundred co-op filling stations on the roads of Sweden. (Many of them, like many privately operated stations, expect the customer himself to man the pump. Self-service Sweden has also been introducing coin-operated and banknote-operated gasoline pumps.) Significantly, KF moved into the oil distribution business soon after the war, in order to forestall a government plan to nationalize the petroleum industry. Experience has shown that the co-ops are no more anxious for state industry than is private business.

A great change is underway in KF's retail-store structure. The co-op societies handle about 17 per cent of Sweden's total national retail trade and 25 per cent of the food trade. They are getting increasingly stiff competition from the thousands of private-enterprise I.C.A. and Tempo chain stores, which monopolize the rest of the retail and food trade. And, as earlier mentioned, the small neighborhood shops are giving way to supermarkets and other large self-service outlets as customers become more mobile and congregate in cities. KF is responding to the challenge by rapidly reducing the number of its retail outlets so that there will be fewer but larger units served by a network of superwarehouses. At the same time, the number of societies is being reduced from the 700 of only a few years ago to today's 400 and tomorrow's 100.

In an even more drastic move, since it involves one of the fundamental principles of the cooperative movement, the KF leadership has suggested to the member societies that they consider abandoning the annual dividend which they pay members. The dividend is a rebate in proportion to their purchases. (If a society is able to afford, for example, a 5 per cent rebate in a good year, it means that a family which purchases $500 worth of goods at the co-op would get $25.) About a quarter of the one and a third million members are 'sleeping buyers,' who either shop infrequently at the co-op or just don't bother to send in their receipts to have them tabulated. They seemingly care more about the price of goods at the time of purchase than about a year-end bonus. The existence of the rebate plan means that goods at the co-op shop are actually often more costly than those at the private stores. There are signs that the co-ops are losing out to their price-cutting competitors. It is an ironic situation, which may have to be remedied by the cooperatives functioning less like cooperatives.

The Wonder of 'Labor Peace'

Saltsjöbaden means the Salt Sea Baths. It is a luxury resort east of Stockholm, less than an hour away by car and a pleasant hour and a half by boat. I once drove out there on a chill October Sunday and lunched on a mountain of succulent shrimp in one of the cathedral-sized dining rooms of the Grand Hotel Saltsjöbaden. The windows overlooked a slate-gray sea and a flotilla of misty islands. A statue of an ice skater set close to the water's edge spoke of the winter pleasures soon to come. But it is in midsummer, at the time of the international regatta, when the old hotel and the beaches, tennis courts and golf links of the fashionable resort evoke memories of an aristocratic, turn-of-the-century Sweden of the rich few and the many poor.

It was in this stylish setting in December 1938, just five days before Christmas, when representatives of Sweden's powerful trade union and management organizations signed one of the great documents in the international history of labor relations. It deserves that kind of description because it is still, many years later, a model working agreement between mature labor and employer institutions, and because of its stunning success in making Sweden the land of 'labor peace.' It would be misleading, however, to suggest that perfect harmony has been reached. In 1966 there were serious strikes of civil servants and school teachers, including the wife of the prime minister. It is likely that the country's fast-rising cost of living will touch off still more disputes.

Workers and bosses used to be at each other's throats all the time. In an average year in the 1930s there were 1,450,000 man-days lost through strikes and walkouts. In 1961 there were just 2,000 man-days lost, the equivalent of a one-day strike in a 2,000-worker factory. Sweden, as the Stockholm magazine *Industria* put it, 'reacts to disturbances on the labor front with the mingled horror and fascination of the ex-drug addict who tries an innocent reefer just to make sure that the cure has been taken.'

It is no coincidence that the last twenty-five years in Sweden have seen both a tripling of industrial output and a drastic reduction in labor disputes. There was a crippling metals-industry strike just after the war but in the entire period from 1946 through 1965, Sweden suffered only one major dispute: a six-week food-distribution strike in Stockholm in 1953.

The following table drawn up by Stockholms Enskilda Bank gives an indication of the state of labor-management relations in Sweden and eight other countries:

WORKING DAYS LOST DUE TO LABOR DISPUTES

Country	Days lost in 1962	Per 1,000 Inhabitants	Days lost in 1963	Per 1,000 Inhabitants
Sweden	5,000	0·7	25,000	3·3
The Netherlands	9,000	0·7	38,000	3·1
Denmark	15,000	3·1	24,000	5·0
West Germany	451,000	8·2	1,846,000	33·1
Norway	81,000	22·2	226,000	61·5
Belgium	271,000	29·3	247,000	26·6
France	1,900,000	40·5	5,991,000	124·4
U.S.A.	18,600,000	99·7	16,100,000	84·4
United Kingdom	5,798,000	108·7	1,755,000	32·5

How long and how rough was the road to Saltsjöbaden? Although much can be written about the exploitation of the un-organized workingman in Sweden, it needs to be said that Sweden was spared many of the worst labor conditions of the industrial revolution. A British trade-union leader, Jack Cooper, wrote that 'Sweden's relatively late transition to an industrial economy was comparatively peaceful and did not create deep "class" divisions. Sweden's trade-union movement, therefore, does not have its roots in the bitterness and strife of an Industrial Revolution such as was the seedbed of British industrial relations.'

The rural character of Swedish industry until recent decades and the traditions of the small, self-contained factory communities fostered agreeable relationships between owners and workers. Nonetheless, old Sweden was a starkly conservative society, and there was plenty of rough dealing by the political and business establishment. As *The Economist* reported in a special edition on Sweden:

Only one full lifetime ago, a Swedish worker who lost his job (as many then did) could be jailed for vagrancy. Long after the British trade unions had won legal status, a wholly orderly local strike provoked by severe wage cuts, at Sundsvall, a sawmill center, in 1879, was swiftly repressed by troops backed by gunboats, the strikers being jailed or herded back to work at gunpoint. In 1899 an act imposed penalties of up to two years' imprisonment for strike agitation. The 1907 depression set off a wave of strikes and lockouts that culminated in a grim four-month general strike in 1909, involving 300,000 workers and temporarily paralyzing the economy: its collapse set trade-union membership back by ten years. And in the early 1930s industrial warfare was widespread enough to evoke a chorus of demands for vigorous state action to protect the public.

The supreme Swedish labor organization, Landsorganisationen, or L.O., was founded in 1898. It had little to build on, because of the small number of big factories and trade unions. In the beginning, L.O. was mainly a central body for gathering statistics and raising money to help support unions involved in labor conflicts. Today, in relation to population, it is the biggest trade-union organization in the world, accounting for one out of every five men, women and children in Sweden.

Of the 2,800,000 wage earners in Sweden, more than two million of them are in the trade-union movement as a whole. 'Being a member of a union here,' one Swedish expert said, 'is taken as part of normal life, like voting. It's not a question of choosing sides. It's the natural thing to do. If you work you join a union.'

Sweden has four major trade-union organizations. L.O. is the powerhouse of the labor movement since it has a membership of 1,500,000 from thirty-eight national unions. L.O. unions range in size from the 1,000-member Chimney Sweeps to the 300,000-man Metal Workers. It spends over two million dollars a year just on the education of its members, and it operates two colleges. L.O. also publishes twenty-four magazines and owns one quarter of Sweden's daily newspapers. The other three organizations represent salaried employees (500,000 members), university graduates (75,000) and civil servants (18,000).

Inevitably, Sweden also has an employers' organization, which similarly operates as a highly centralized, tightly disciplined force. It makes the National Association of Manufacturers in the United

States look like a mere debating society. American employers sometimes complain that they have been compelled to sign away their rights to the unions; Swedish employers, in contrast, have voluntarily signed away many of their rights in dealing with their own workers to the employers' organization. Responding directly to the challenge of a central labor body, the owners of industry in 1902, just four years after L.O.'s founding, joined together in the Swedish Employers' Confederation (Svenska Arbetsgivare-föreningen, or S.A.F.). Today S.A.F. embraces more than 24,000 companies employing 1,200,000 persons. It works closely with the associations of agricultural employers and shipowners who employ another 63,000, and its decisions influence the employers of a million more Swedes.

Individual companies in S.A.F. are not permitted to reach agreements with workers or declare lockouts without S.A.F. approval, and they must comply if S.A.F. orders a lockout. It amounts to a hard, united front of well-heeled companies. But L.O. is rich too. The total capital of L.O. and its affiliate unions is about 150 million dollars (a worker pays one hour's wages a week to his local). Such resources are hardly needed at a time when serious strikes are rare and management is so willing to go along with improved wages and work conditions.

The employers' federation had the upper hand in the early days when the labor organization was slowly gathering its strength after being almost crushed by the failure of the 1909 general strike. L.O. managed to acquire the kind of centralized power needed to combat S.A.F. when it overcame the bitter opposition of the craft unions and formed itself on the principles of industrial unionism. This has been a blessing for the big shipyards and manufacturers of Sweden, because they can deal with a single strong union instead of a myriad of craft unions.

L.O. and S.A.F. battled savagely in their early days; but familiarity, instead of breeding contempt, created understanding. Whereas the employers once held most of the winning cards, the rise to power of the labor-oriented Social Democrats gave the trade unions the advantage. Interestingly enough, the strong possibility in the mid-1930s that the parliament would enact legislation to put the state in the thick of labor disputes served to bring the unions and employers together. They preferred to create their own machinery for industrial peace rather than have anything imposed on them. It took fully two years of talks at Saltsjöbaden to iron out their basic differences, but the result was the Basic Agreement of 1938.

The Basic Agreement, which has since been supplemented by other agreements, is both a peace treaty and a code of conduct. It is a declaration of mutual respect and willingness to talk instead of fight. It is a nonaggression pact in the sense that neither side will seek to destroy each other or take unfair advantage. 'Both trade-unionists and employers in Sweden recognize that power and responsibility are inseparable,' wrote Jack Cooper, who added that 'the Swedes seem to have a natural bias towards compromise rather than conflict; a disposition to discuss rather than to argue; an inclination to concentrate on expanding areas of agreement rather than on indulging in trials of strength.'

The Saltsjöbaden agreement, most importantly, made it obligatory to negotiate disputes. The procedure is set forth in detail and strong-arm methods or coercive actions by either side are outlawed. The agreement put limitations on secondary boycotts and set up a Labor Market Council to help settle questions about the use of coercive measures. The employer's basic right to hire and fire as he sees fit, originally accepted by labor in 1906, was reaffirmed, but employers recognized labor's need for protection against sudden, arbitrary and unfair dismissals. While the boss still has the ultimate word on dismissals, numerous safeguards now surround the worker. The Labor Market Council is also brought into the picture when a labor conflict might harm essential public services. The Basic Agreement came on top of the Law of Collective Bargaining passed by the parliament in 1928 which established a Labor Court to settle contract disputes and violations. The Labor Court was imposed by right-wing forces over the objections of the unions and the Social Democrats, but both have come to accept it as a valuable instrument.

Favorable economic conditions, rising prosperity and full employment have, of course, made it easier for the two sides to live up to their agreements. The big L.O. unions and the employers associations of the S.A.F. get together every two years to hammer out industry-wide contracts. They work from the general 'frame agreement' drawn up by top-level L.O. and S.A.F. negotiators in all-night 'mangling' sessions, which hold the attention of the nation. It is a kind of industrial world series played by the two strongest outfits in the country. The participants are friendly enemies; they go into the sessions grim-faced and they come out smiling. Arne Geijer, Sweden's topmost unionist, has said: 'We have a good system. Wages, conditions and social security are excellent. But you cannot take all this from heaven. Production is the only answer.'

Because they are in general agreement about the cold economic facts and statistics which underlie the negotiations (both L.O. and S.A.F. employ an army of economists and statisticians), the management and union representatives concentrate on practical possibilities. If the talks fail, government-appointed mediators are brought in. Strikes are seldom necessary, since the locals and individual companies usually have no trouble following the pattern set up by the industry-wide confederations. In the last resort, the Labor Court will step in to deal with wildcat strikers or bosses who break the contract. The court has seven members: two chosen by L.O., two by S.A.F., and three outsiders, two of whom must be judges. The unofficial strikes which plague labor relations in Great Britain are simply not tolerated in Sweden. Considering that L.O. has in its ranks more than 90 per cent of all manual workers in industry, the discipline which runs through the whole structure is remarkable. When there is an unofficial strike the L.O. leadership moves promptly to snuff it out. If workers become too obstreperous they will be compelled by the Labor Court to pay damages to their employers. In 1964 a number of Gothenburg dock workers had to pay damages of up to forty dollars each.

This kind of situation calls for a high level of sophistication on the part of both the trade-union leaders and the rank and file. The L.O. attitude was expressed by Arne Geijer when he said that 'we try to view society as a whole, because if society is successful it affects us.' A Swedish trade-union official recalled attending a union meeting while on a visit to England. He heard a shop steward reel off a long list of things which had to be done for 'the British worker.' The Swede's reaction: 'Why only for the British worker? Here in Sweden we talk about doing things for the Swedish people.'

What is intriguing about the union-management climate in Sweden today is that both parties not only have reached a great understanding but also have gone beyond it to a point where no one wants to make the kind of drastic move which would damage Sweden's reputation as an almost strike-free country. 'Labor peace' has become not only a thing of national pride but a kind of foreign-aid item offered to socially less-developed countries. The labor-relations experts of the trade unions and the employers' confederations are in constant demand abroad. The *New York Herald Tribune* said that 'no self-respecting conference on labor-management relations is complete these days without one.' Every so often those friendly warriors, Bertil Kugelberg and Arne Geijer, the presidents, respectively, of S.A.F. and L.O., travel as a team to America, Britain, Canada and elsewhere to testify to the rewards of labor-management togetherness.

The two leaders are powerful, respected figures in Swedish life. Kugelberg, now in his mid-sixties, is a learned man with a plump Pickwickian face. He began his career as a lawyer, served in the government, and has been involved with management-labor affairs since 1928. He became president of the employers' federation in 1942. Geijer, ten years younger, is a rugged, self-educated son of a laborer who has had the kind of from-the-bottom-up career one expects of a trade-union leader. He was, literally, a child of the L.O. His father was an ironworker. Young Arne went to work in the same plant as his father when he was fifteen. He joined the Metal Workers Union and the Social Democratic Youth Club. He became a machine-tool mechanic and studied at both the union-sponsored adult-education evening classes and at the L.O. 'graduate school' for party functionaries. By the time he was thirty-eight Geijer was president of the Metal Workers, the largest union in Sweden. He was elected to the parliament in 1949, and by 1956 he was the obvious choice for the presidency of L.O.

A year later he was also elected president of the 55-million-member International Confederation of Free Trade Unions.

The discipline within the labor movement which keeps the industrial peace is due largely to the centralization of authority in L.O. Its high command is so powerful, in fact, that a good many people worry about apathy at the local level. One device for keeping union members alert is to involve them in Works Councils, so that they can work with employer representatives in improving productivity, working conditions and vocational training. There is much collaboration on the incentive-work system which is a striking feature of the Swedish labor scene. Sixty per cent of wage earners work on piece rates, and elaborate time-and-motion studies are constantly under way by beady-eyed men with stop watches.

A drawback of the piecework system, however, is that it contributes to wage 'drift,' which is known in Sweden by the vivid word *glidning*. A worker who gets paid according to the number of items he turns out may well increase his earnings when the management installs a more efficient machine. In addition, some companies have been offering higher wages than the agreed levels because of the labor shortage. All of which, of course, contributes to the inflationary situation which has pushed the cost of living in Sweden to the American level. The sense of responsibility which marks the Swedish trade unions has been most strikingly expressed on those occasions when they went along with wage freezes which the government sought in order to reduce the inflationary pressures.

Wages in Sweden have more than doubled since World War II. A typical workingman's pay is now $3,500 a year, and in many households the income is $6,000 a year, since a quarter of all wives hold jobs. Inflation has reduced the value of the wage increases, but not enough to alter the fact that the average Swede is sharing in his nation's expanding wealth as never before. Between 1959 and 1964 consumer prices went up 18 per cent, but wages rose 44 per cent. The Swede's 45-hour work week is moving toward 40 hours, and a month's paid holiday is now standard. Sweden's annual rate of growth has been running at 4 to 6 per cent, and there is every reason to believe that the economy will keep on booming.

One of the most striking symbols of Swedish prosperity is the rising popularity of the 'salary check payment system.' Major companies like Volvo and Skånska Cement turn over their payrolls to a bank, and the bank in turn credits the latest wage and salary payments to the accounts of the employees. At first, workers drew out all their money, but they are now inclined to let much of it stay and gather interest. Wage banking has helped make Sweden such a checkbook society that customers on buses and trolleys have been known to pay their fares with checks when they found they had no cash in their pockets.

The farsightedness of both labor and management in Sweden has made the nation more prepared than any other for the revolutionary changes which are being wrought in every advanced nation by the computer and the rush of industry to automated equipment. While Sweden has had a successful full-employment policy, it is widely recognized that this does not mean that workers are guaranteed that they are safe in particular jobs in particular places. Technological change inevitably means that many workers must change their job habits, their jobs, or even their employers. Labor and management organizations have joined forces for the training of workers, and they collaborate with government representatives on the National Labor Market Board, which is concerned with the movement and retraining of workers. The laborer made redundant by a machine can look forward to considerable assistance in making the transition to new employment. If he must move his home, then he gets financial help. The result is a highly mobile society, unafraid of change.

Chapter 24

WELFARELAND

*All those things which come out of the American pioneering heart
are institutionalized in Sweden.*
                                                —U.S. DIPLOMAT

*Swedish girls are extremists. They can be the most dignified of
young ladies—or the beatest of the beat.*
                                                —RICHARD JOSEPH

The irony of Sweden is that, man for man, it is the greatest
producer in Europe, yet its output of babies is just about the
world's lowest. 'Swedish sex' has become well known, though
not well understood, yet the permissive love life of the Swedes
has not led to any bumper crop of babies. What is captivating
about Sweden's low birth rate is that it is hard to imagine any
other country outside of Scandinavia where the conditions for
children are so ideal or where so much encouragement is given
to people to have more children.

The health facilities in Sweden are among the very best in the
world, and the rates for maternal and infant deaths are about the
lowest. The child-care institutions are pioneers in their field. The
combination of the wealth state and the welfare state means that
every Swedish child is guaranteed an upbringing which lacks none
of the essentials. Sweden is a country with not nearly enough
people for its space or for its job openings, and young people are
literally being paid to get married early and produce large families.

Despite such attractions, Swedes don't breed, at least not enough
to give the country sufficient manpower to meet its needs. Only
Hungary and Rumania have lower birth rates. (The Swedes are

in questionable company: the three other countries among the four with the lowest birth rates are Communist.) Sweden's population increases at only half the speed of America's, and merely a sixth of Mexico's.

The adjoining table, adapted from the *Demographic Yearbook of the United Nations*, 1964, reveals that among the Scandinavian countries and a selection of other nations which have extensive social welfare programs, Sweden is extraordinary in its low birth rate and low rate of population increase. But it is also a country where babies have the best chance in the world of surviving at birth and living on to a ripe old age.

Where Have All the Babies Gone?

Thus, Sweden is one of those rare countries in the world with a population problem in reverse: an insufficient supply of new babies, rather than a surplus which calls for stern birth-control propaganda. Interestingly enough, it is not simply a postwar phenomenon, but a Swedish headache of long standing. It was in 1934 that the noted social scientists Gunnar and Alva Myrdal published their explosive volume called *Crisis in the Population Question*. They shook their countrymen by setting out the facts of Sweden's declining birth rate and warning that it could destroy the nation's social structure unless drastic measures were taken.

The Myrdals argued for a whole new attitude by the community toward individual families. They said ways must be found to permit people to have children without being penalized by a drop in their living standards. It has been a general Scandinavian phenomenon that birth rates went into a decline after a tremendous outpouring of babies in the nineteenth century. Other countries in Europe, notably France, showed a similar pattern and began vigorous countermeasures to encourage patriotic citizens to produce larger families. It was the Swedish birth rate that dropped most sickeningly of all, however. Until 1880, the birth rate was 30 to 35 per 1,000 of population as against today's 15. (Of course, infant mortality was much higher then, and the life span was shorter, thus reducing the effect of the high birth rate.) The

DEMOGRAPHIC SITUATION FOR SELECTED COUNTRIES IN 1964
(All figures except life expectancy are per 1,000 of population.)

Country	Marriages	Divorces	Births	Deaths	Infant Deaths	Rate of Population Increase	Expectation of Life at Birth[4] Male	Female
Sweden	7·5	1·2	16·0	10·0	13·6	6·0	71	75
Denmark	8·4	1·4	17·6	9·9	18·7	7·7	70	74
Norway	6·5	0·6	17·9	10·0	16·7	7·9	71	75
Finland	7·5	1·0	17·6	9·3	16·9	8·3	65	72
Iceland[1]	7·8	1·1	25·9	7·2	17·3	18·7	71	75
U.S.A.	9·0	2·3[3]	21·2	9·4	25·2	11·8	67	73
England and Wales	7·5	0·6[2]	18·4	11·3	20·0	7·1	68	74
West Germany	8·7	0·9[1]	18·2	11·0	27·0[1]	7·2	67	72
France	7·2	0·6[1]	18·1	10·6	23·4	7·4	67	74
U.S.S.R.	10·0	1·3[2]	21·2	7·2	30·9	14·0	65	73

[1] 1963 figures   [2] 1962 figures   [3] 1961 figures
[4] Life expectancy figures based on various dates: Sweden 1962, Denmark 1956–60, Finland 1956–60, Norway 1951–55, Iceland 1951–60, U.S.A. 1963, England and Wales 1961–63, West Germany 1961–63, France 1963, U.S.S.R. 1960–61.

In 1964, the twelve countries with the world's lowest birth rates were:

1 Hungary	13·0	7 Belgium	17·1[1]
2 Rumania	15·2	8 East Germany	17·5[2]
3 Sweden	16·0	9 Greece	17·5[1]
4 Bulgaria	16·1	10 Denmark	17·6
5 Luxembourg	16·5	11 Finland	17·6
6 Czechoslovakia	17·1	12 Japan	17·7

[1] 1963 figures   [2] 1952 figures

Swedish birth rate then slipped to 25–30 at the turn of the century, and by 1934 it had dropped to the dangerously low figure of 13·7.

To the population experts who think in terms of 'net reproduction rates' (the extent to which a society is replenishing its stock of people), this low birth rate meant that the Swedish race was in real danger of dying out, even though this might not be immediately apparent. The threat was obscured by the fact that people were living longer because of better social conditions, with the result that the population continued to show a small annual increase instead of a decline.

After the Myrdals sounded the alarm, Sweden introduced a full range of 'baby bonuses' and other family aids. These include maternity payments, annual grants for each child, and free school lunches. Since 1938, for example, Sweden has provided marriage loans to help young couples set up households and free confinement care for pregnant women. Logically, the welfare officials should have played down their family-planning programs, which provided married couples with birth-control information, but that would not have been in keeping with the spirit of the times. Large families were all right, it was felt, but not at the sacrifice of the new-found principles of planned parenthood. Today the Swedes, with sex education in the schools and contraceptives dispensed by vending machines, are probably more birth-control-conscious than any other people. (Not that knowledge equals wisdom, however. The newly pregnant but unmarried young heroine in the film *The Baby Carriage* explained to a friend that it happened because 'I left my pessary in my other coat pocket.')

Although the first official actions to stimulate the production of babies were taken in the 1930s, it was not until after the war that the most substantial family-welfare measures came into being. Ironically enough, that was just the time when, for reasons peculiar to the unsettled wartime and early postwar days, the birth rate had gone up to about 18 per thousand. In 1944 and 1945 it actually rose above 20—close to the current American figure. But just five years later it was down to 16, and in 1960 it hit a low of 13·7, the same mid-1930s rate that had alarmed the Myrdals. The rate has been gradually rising since then—but just gradually.

Why don't the Swedes have more children? Why, for that matter, don't all the Scandinavians, a virile people in a northern world of long winter nights? The Danes, Finns and Norwegians also have relatively low birth rates, despite almost identical programs of children's allowances and other family benefits.

No one pretends that there is any single or simple answer. It might be enough just to say that a low birth rate, like suicide, divorce and mental illness, seems to be part and parcel of an advanced society in the mid-twentieth century. There is a world of difference between family life in a simple farming society and family life in a complex, industrialized, apartment-dwelling civilization. A Gothenburg psychiatrist gave me an eloquent explanation of 'what is wrong with society today.' He said: 'There is a cold feeling among people in the city. A child screams on the street. Twenty mothers stick their heads out of apartment-house windows. They say, "that's not mine," close the windows and go on about their business. But the child is still crying.'

Such things as the apartment shortage and the fact that young people spend ever more time at higher education are birth-rate factors. A great many couples in the large cities, despairing of finding a home of their own, simply postpone their marriage for several years even though they carry on as if they were wed. But even after young people are married and settled down, the babies may be slow in coming, and then not more than one or two. I have visited dozens of Swedish homes and have seldom seen a young family with more than three children. When I mentioned that I had four of my own the usual response was a blend of astonishment, admiration and profound sympathy; it seemed to them that anyone with four children must be impossibly burdened and confined to the home.

One foreign resident in Stockholm put it bluntly: 'The Swedes are self-centered; they don't like a lot of children getting in the way of their private lives.' But how does one square this with the charming family scenes in Sweden when parents and children go off on skiing expeditions or enjoy to the fullest that wondrous lakeside month in the height of summer? A distillation of many conversations with Swedish parents would go like this:

'We are a modern people trying to live in the modern world. There is much more to life than just working and raising a family. We have been educated and it is only natural that we should feel a need for self-fulfillment. We prefer to have an independent life of our own before marriage. After marriage, we want to have children, of course. Swedes love children; you can see that. But two are enough, and many of our friends just have one. Large families simply present too many problems. A wife feels trapped at home, and despite the child allowances and such things, you cannot maintain the same living standard. With just one or two children a woman can return to work after they reach school age. You have greater possibilities for traveling and enjoying life. You aren't so tied down.'

Career Girls

The fact that urban Swedes live mostly in small apartments undoubtedly makes them feel more claustrophobic than the American housewife in her suburban split-level or the English-woman in her roomy semidetached-with-garden. It is also true that the modern Swedish woman, despite the national compulsion to make the home spotlessly well ordered, is not so sold on the romantic notion of the 'homemaker,' that paragon of domestic bliss celebrated by the American women's magazines. Her thoughts have more in common with the career-girl heroines of those same magazines thirty years ago. As already observed, a quarter of all married women in Sweden (and one third of all married women with small children) have jobs outside the home. A great many more would join them if there were enough child-care facilities or if there were such a thing as a maid in Scandinavia.

Women in Sweden play a much greater role in public life, and they have many more career opportunities immediately open to them, than do, for example, American or English women. One of the ministers in the Social Democratic government is a woman and 45 of the 233 members of parliament are female. Alva Myrdal not only is the wife of Sweden's most famous economist and the mother of a talented young author (Jan Myrdal), but also has had a distinguished career both in sociology and government, has served as ambassador to India, and has lately headed the Swedish delegation to the disarmament talks in Geneva. There is an impressive number of women doctors, scientists and other professionals.

It has been a full century since the pioneering Swedish champion of women's rights, Fredrika Bremer, went about the world saying that 'freedom and future, the bread and wine which gives lust to life, is something from which women are excluded.' Decades of struggle have brought about the laws on inheritance, property and divorce which release women from the bondage of men. Ellen Key in the 1890s attacked the ultrafeminine conception of women and shocked the staid nation with her notions of free love. Selma Lagerlöf in 1909 was the first woman to win the Nobel Prize. From Jenny Lind to Greta Garbo and Ingrid Bergman, a number of Swedish women have become world figures.

Surfeit of Honey

All of this fits in with the popular conception of the emancipated, sexually liberated Swedish woman, a blonde, of course, who has known coeducation all her school days and is now undoubtedly the equal of any man. Or is she?

The truth is that just as less than half of Swedish females (about 40 per cent) are blond, so their total equality and emancipation is more apparent than real. Their status, in fact, is still surprisingly ambiguous, given the extent of Sweden's social enlightenment. In many important ways they are free spirits with plenty of room for the expression of their desires and talents, but they exist in a society where the rules are still laid down by men. This might be tolerable were it not for the fact that a strange tension exists between male and female in Swedish life. Theirs is a nervous, not entirely happy, coexistence, and I have come to feel that it goes a long way in explaining why Swedish families are not larger and the birth rate is not higher.

After giving due attention to the amount of feminine participation in Swedish public life, it is necessary to say that it is somewhat illusory. It may amount to more than in the United States and

Britain, but there is less of it than one expects in 'progressive' Sweden. The women of Russia and Finland, for instance, are more thoroughly and naturally involved in public life than their Swedish counterparts. The female factory managers and judges in Russia, and the female doctors and dentists in Finland, seem more sure of their status and their acceptance by men than the Swedish professional women. (Like Sweden geographically, Swedish women stand midway between the more fully emancipated Finns and the more conventional, homespun Norwegians.)

It is true that Swedish women got the vote in 1918 (twelve years after the Finns), but it was not until 1947 that a woman became a minister in the government. And the fact that females have 19 per cent of the seats in the parliament is only one way of saying that men have 81 per cent in a nation where women outnumbered the men. Women have almost no importance in the executive ranks of industry, labor, publishing and many other fields. It was not until 1960 that the first three women were admitted to the clergy of the Evangelical Lutheran Church, which embraces 95 per cent of the population. It was an historic event to have women priests; but, as one Swedish church reporter wrote, 'far from enjoying unanimity of opinion, the decision to admit women to Holy Orders has caused the fiercest debate ever witnessed in Swedish church history.' Even more to the point, the fact that Swedish employment is still so often divided into male and female jobs has tended to lessen the effect of the long fight, now mostly won, for the same wages for the same work.

Of course, as some of the girls of Sweden will tell you, there is such a thing as too much equality. 'A characteristic common to all Scandinavians is their politeness,' wrote Willy Breinholst. 'They will always let the ladies get onto the trolley first—if they are young ladies with short skirts and pretty legs. They usually give up their seat on the train to some old woman—if they're tired of sitting down or have to get off at the next stop anyway.' There is no great fuss about gallantry, and a Swedish girl expects to pay her own way on a date and open her own doors. This may be charmingly democratic, and a tribute to the self-reliance of Swedish women, but it may just be that the Swedish male has a surfeit of honey. 'They don't *deserve* their women!' cried an indignant Italian in the Grand Hotel bar. It is as if Swedish men are unaware that among the women of Scandinavia—to quote Richard Joseph of *Esquire*—'the really one-in-a-thousand, knock-you-off-your-feet, breathtaking beauty is likely to be a Swede.'

I remember the editor in chief of a leading Stockholm newspaper telling me that some of the wives of his editors had complained to him that they knew almost nothing about their husbands' work; they said their husbands seldom discussed the events of the day with them. He therefore proposed to his editors that a few of the wives be invited to sit in on some of their occasional evening conferences about Swedish and world affairs. He even suggested that it might be beneficial to the paper to have the female slant on things. He was astonished at how vehemently the men were opposed to the whole idea, and nothing further was done. 'They kept telling me,' he said, 'that it would be too awkward—their wives wouldn't understand what was going on and "they would be too embarrassed."'

Dr. Herbert Hendin's comments in *Suicide and Scandinavia* are worth noting:

> In general, [Swedish] men were found to be far less able to utilize women as a source of comfort than are Danes or Americans. Since the woman is seen chiefly as someone for whom to perform well, she is likely to become something of a strain. In Sweden, far more than in Denmark or the United States, men like to relax in each other's company; in the absence of women they feel free to be themselves and enjoy themselves. . . .
>
> In her teens the girl's interest is expected to center around her popularity with boys, and her self-esteem depends on her success with them. Her self-confidence, if already impaired, is not helped by the boy's coolness. It is ironic that in a country known for the beauty of its women, these women are rather insecure about their attractiveness. Some girls accept successful work or a career as their goal, although too much achievement or success tends to be regarded as unfeminine. . . .
>
> The whole combination of circumstances leads to more disappointed women, more impotent rage and self-hatred, and

in a somewhat greater number of female suicides than are seen in the United States.

Many Swedes, male and female, would disagree violently with such conclusions, but I know from numerous conversations in Sweden that others would agree. Many women feel that they are not able to blossom and be fulfilled in a male-dominated society which has, as one writer put it, 'despotic, sultanic tendencies.' There is a saying that 'the Orient begins at Malmö.' It is a Nordic Orient, however, in a certain state of revolution. Such avant-garde women commentators as Eva Moberg and Kristina Ahlmark-Michanek have already set off a number of bombs. In her book, *Belief in Virginity and the Double Standard*, Mrs. Ahlmark-Michanek argued that there is no true equality for women so long as society is permissive about a man's sexual behavior but is shocked when a woman tries to enjoy the same freedom. She even went beyond the fashionable view that premarital sexual relations are all right if love is involved and said that friendship can be sufficient. As for Eva Moberg, she raised the temperature of the old debate about the role of women with her essay, 'The Conditional Release of the Woman.' In a memorable sentence, she said that 'mother love is history's most exploited emotion' and argued that just because a woman has the exclusive function of childbearing does not mean that she necessarily must bear the whole burden of child rearing. She would bring about such a change in the social patterns that after the first three years of the child's life mother and father would equally share the daily burden of raising the child and caring for the home. This might even mean that both parents would work at part-time jobs at different times, as they share the responsibilities at home. If this is too radical, then at the very least, she wrote, there must be more facilities for the daytime care of children outside the home so that women can be released to make use of their talents and brain-power. Eva Moberg's call is for nothing less than a wholesale re-examination of the sex roles of men and women.

Young author Lars Gustafsson noted in a critique on these proposals that 'it has perhaps been significant that more of Eva

Moberg's opponents have been women than men.' Nonetheless, she may be pointing the direction in which Sweden is moving—moving amid a seething struggle on the intellectual front between old prejudices and new ideas. 'That such a debate exists in Sweden,' said Gustafsson, 'is one of the reasons for finding it exciting to live here.'

Guaranteed Affluence

The Swedish (and Scandinavian) welfare state presents a remarkable paradox: the more wealth, the more welfare; the richer Swedes get, the more social security they want. Instead of withering away as the nation leaves poverty behind and enters the broad uplands of prosperity, the welfare apparatus finds itself bigger and busier than ever. Where once it provided soup to the starving and shelter for the homeless, now it guarantees affluence.

Although welfare is defined, in the first instance, as the 'state of faring, or doing, well,' it is often associated in one's mind with charity. And understandably so, because welfarism began as charity. In the beginning there were simply the local poor laws and the dole. Gradually the state began to play its part. In the late eighteenth century, for example, the Swedish Royal Board of Health appointed a number of 'provincial physicians' to care for indigents in their regions and supervise public-health activities. But the really decisive steps toward comprehensive social-security programs in Scandinavia were not taken until the very end of the nineteenth century—the inspiration coming, first of all, from Germany, where full-scale social-insurance reforms were launched in the 1880s. It was Denmark that took the social-insurance lead: it had programs covering old age, disablement, health, unemployment and employment injuries in being by 1922. Swedish programs did not cover all these contingencies until 1934, while Finland and Norway followed some years later. Today, however, it is Sweden which is setting the welfare pace.

Swedish Conservatives and Liberals began the welfare process; it was made the national gospel under the Social Democrats; and, as one Swede put it in admirable Americanese, 'now it's every-body's baby.' Despite the arguments in the parliament whenever new social-security legislation is proposed, all the parties line up in favor. Welfare has long since graduated from charity to univer-sality. The social stigma is gone. Now it is felt that everyone, whether chimneysweep or millionaire, is entitled to basic pro-tection and benefits.

About 90 per cent of all welfare spending goes to people not because their earnings are too low but for reasons of age, health, number of children or other family circumstances. Full employ-ment, good wages and the general leveling of income differences through tax and wage policies have, in fact, come close to elim-inating the poor from the Swedish scene. Offhand, it would seem that this would mean a reduction in welfare expenditure. As people become better off, however, they demand better medical care, greater job security, expanded opportunities for their children, and a guarantee of high living standards in their old age. The more people have, the more they have to lose, and the welfare state has been fashioned to make sure there are no losers.

It is not too difficult to appreciate the Swedish viewpoint, how-ever opposed an outsider might be to the whole welfare-state concept. Even in the most capitalistic and competitive society the person most concerned with security is the rich man. Before starting to enjoy his wealth, he makes sure his family is protected by an array of insurance policies; he sets up funds to guarantee that his children will be financed through college; and he spreads his capital through a variety of securities to spread the risk. He becomes venturesome only after he has spread out a safety net beneath him. The Swedes would say that that is exactly what they are doing, collectively, through their social-security legislation.

They also argue that they are not simply buying security with their taxes but helping to spur on prosperity. In other words, welfare helps produce wealth. The child allowances paid to families lead to greater purchases of food, clothing and children's goods. The pensions for elderly people enable them to continue

playing an economic role as consumers. The training of the handicapped, and the over-all provision of the best possible medical
care, puts more people on the production line. The numerous
state efforts to retrain and move workers who have lost their jobs
because of economic or technological change restores them to their
full capacities as producers and consumers.

The Cost of Welfare

Within Sweden, the conservative argument today is that the
welfare state, now that it has gone as far as it has, should think
twice before embarking on any further expensive responsibilities.
Somehow the economy has managed to carry the enormous
welfare load, but it has all come to pass in a time of rising prosperity. What would happen in bad times with greatly reduced
government revenues?

Total welfare expenditures by the state and local governments
are now coming close to two billion dollars a year. This is about
a third of total public spending and 12 per cent of gross national
product. Needless to say, income taxes are high in Sweden. They
start at low-income levels and allow for fewer and smaller exemp-
tions than in the United States. Middle-income people pay a
third of their earnings in taxes and the effective ceiling is 71 per
cent. There is a wealth tax, however, which takes an extra bite
out of the well-to-do. The sum of national and local income tax
and net-wealth tax must not exceed 80 per cent. Taxes now take
more than a third of the national income; it was 20 per cent before
the war. The Swedish worker now not only loses a quarter or
more of his income to taxes but pays exceptionally high taxes on
every purchase of gasoline, liquor, beer, chocolates, cigarettes
and other items. There is a general 10 per cent sales tax.

Lavish Pensions

The pension system is the backbone of Swedish social welfare.
First, there is the basic pension financed by national and local
governments. It goes to everyone at age sixty-seven—about $1,200

a year to a married couple, $670 to a single person. The payment may be more under special circumstances, and local increments can raise the sum still higher. The same benefits provide disability pensions and family pensions to widows and orphans. Every year some one million Swedes draw a pension; more than three quarters of them are old-age pensioners.

The basic pension program has put a solid flooring under the elderly and bereaved in Sweden, but to many Swedes it did not seem to be enough. And so in the late 1950s the nation was rocked by a controversy over the Social Democratic proposal for a 'supplementary pension' program. The question became a major issue and brought about the dissolution of the lower house of the parliament. New elections were held, and the reconstituted chamber passed the measure in 1959 by the hairbreadth majority of 115 to 114. Conservatives and Liberals said it should be left to individuals, or to the companies and unions, to develop their own plans for further protection on top of the basic pension. One of the fears of opponents was that the multimillion-dollar pool of pension money which would be created after a few years would be used by the left-wing government as an instrument of economic power. Since the extra layer of pensions came into being, however, hardly any politician would dare to suggest that it be scrapped.

The objective of the supplementary-pension plan is to sweeten the basic pension with a further sum so that a pensioner will receive two thirds of the average annual income he had during his best fifteen earning years. Thus a worker who had been earning $4,000 a year would get a pension of about $2,700, which means that old age need not compel him to suddenly shift his standard of living sharply downward.

The pensions in Sweden are tied to the cost-of-living index, rising automatically as prices go up. The supplementary fund is financed by employer contributions, according to the wages paid each employee. Self-employed persons pay their own premiums. Widows and children bereft of a breadwinner are already getting the full benefit of the new program, but for others the extra pension will come into effect gradually, as the fund grows. It will not be fully effective (that is, paying full pensions) until 1980.

Voluntary Security

One of the most eye-opening aspects of Sweden's splurge on pensions is that only about 10 per cent of the self-employed persons—farmers, shopkeepers, dentists, authors, etc.—have exercised their right to stay outside the supplementary pension plan if they wish. A powerful persuader is the fact that the self-employed person who stays out of the pension plan must remain outside the health-insurance plan too.

Even more startling is the fact that the increasingly elaborate pension and compulsory health-insurance programs have not hurt the private insurance business. On the contrary, private health- and life-insurance policies are being purchased at a higher rate than ever. This is all the more remarkable in view of the fact that in 1962 the employers' and trade-union confederations agreed on a group life-insurance plan (the employers paying the premiums), which overnight covered more than a million workers. Individual life-insurance spending by the Swedes is the highest in all Europe. The experts say that people originally bought life insurance to protect their loved ones against poverty, 'but today it is in order to protect their high standard of living.'

Since there continues to be a considerable spread of incomes in Sweden (there has been a leveling *up*, not *out*), some people obviously live better than others. Swedish welfarism makes sure that such people continue to enjoy their advantages in their illness or old age, since presumably they have earned them. For example, a middle-income person receives greater 'sickness benefits' while he is unable to work than an unskilled worker; both get about two thirds of their normal income. Similarly, the higher a man's earnings during his working days, the higher his old-age pension.

Socialized Medicine

'Socialized medicine' terrifies the American Medical Association, but even the A.M.A. is smart enough to use the British rather than the Swedish medical-insurance system as its primary target. A New York physician, Dr. Theodore M. Sanders, after a close on-the-scene look at what Swedish medicine is all about, wrote the following in the alumni quarterly of the Columbia University College of Physicians and Surgeons:

I wish that a great many American doctors, in addition to our Nobel Prize winners, would visit Sweden with open eyes and open minds. Such an eyeful would be a wholesome antidote for the cliché-ridden thinking that permeates so much official discussion of the socio-economic aspects of medicine, and might help to quiet the hysteria engendered by that little-understood phrase 'socialized medicine.'

Half a century of development of small local health-insurance programs into a more national approach led to the compulsory health-insurance system which was instituted in 1955. (Norway has had a compulsory system since 1956, Denmark since 1961, Finland since 1964.) This was not such a drastic step as it might appear, since practically everyone was covered already by some kind of medical-insurance plan. It was essentially a nationwide tidying-up operation which all the political parties supported. The medical profession accepted the plan, since it meant that patients still had a completely free choice of doctor, and there was no question of nationalizing private physicians. It just meant that three quarters of the doctors' bills would be paid by the insurance program.

Whatever a doctor charges above the government scale of fees must be paid by the patient. In practice, more and more doctors are charging more than the scale. The average Stockholm patient, for example, pays 40 per cent of the bills instead of 25 per cent. Many people pay half or more. This is a long way from the 'free medical treatment' which many foreigners believe Sweden to have. However, there is no charge for care of up to two years in the public wards of state or municipal hospitals, and the system pays half the cost of prescription drugs above sixty cents. Cash benefits go to persons unable to work because of illness or disability.

Individual fees ($30 to $60 for average wage earners) pay half the 810-million-dollar annual cost of the program, while employers and the state pay the rest. Swedes may quibble about details of the system, but everyone I have met prefers it to the kind of 'competitive medicine' which can wipe out the life savings of a family if one member becomes seriously ill. 'It is barbaric,' one Swede said, 'to force a person to resort to charity if he has no money to pay for his illness.' Swedish doctors will say the same thing. They complain about the paper work of the system, but their own earnings are excellent. House calls are sternly discouraged in Sweden, and doctors in larger towns take part in a night and weekend emergency-service system which puts a few on duty while the rest relax. Stockholm has six chauffeured radio cars which speed around the city on emergency calls.

A distinctive feature of the Swedish medical scene is the preference for a large, general, central hospital in each sizable town and county, instead of having many smaller ones as in America and Britain. The per capita expenditure on hospitals in Sweden is vastly greater than it is in Britain, where medicine still revolves around the general practitioner and where there are many more doctors per unit of population than in Sweden. As one Swedish authority put it, 'there is an increasing tendency to regard the hospitals as medical fortresses, which shall serve not only for the care of in-patients but which are in the position of supporting and integrating also a considerable portion of out-patients and field work.'

Dearth of Doctors

Sweden has an acute shortage of both doctors and nurses. The country has some 8,000 physicians, a figure which means that there is only one for every 1,000 inhabitants. Only Finland, with one doctor for every 1,300 persons, is worse off, among the leading West European countries. A Swede may have to wait a year or two before he can get booked into a hospital for non-emergency surgery. The problem was highlighted by a London headline, 'Hospital in Italy Sought by Swedes.' In order to get some of its chronically ill and aged patients off their hands, Swedish authorities were considering buying or renting a hospital near Rome to be staffed by Italian doctors and nurses at Sweden's expense. If it should come to pass, it will be a classic case of a poorer country helping to solve a wealthier country's problems of affluence.

Officials say that Sweden needs twice as many doctors (16,000) to handle the medical load in Sweden. The load is caused by at least three things: (1) the rising demand for medical services from a population which has come to expect the best of treatment; (2) the swelling number of elderly people; and (3) the disturbing increase in the number of mentally ill. It is an open question whether there are actually more persons with mental problems in Sweden or simply more detection and treatment of mental cases, but the information director of the Swedish Medical Association said that 'mental illness and disorders are a more pressing concern today than geriatric care.'

Unfortunately, Sweden (and Scandinavia in general) is astonishingly laggard in its psychiatric facilities and in the number of trained psychiatrists, therapists and analysts. The social planners have been so busy attending to the body that they have neglected the mind. On the other hand, a mentally ill person can receive virtually free treatment under the health-insurance plan, and the treatment is enlightened and compassionate. I spent an evening in Gothenburg with one of Sweden's best and busiest psychiatrists, Dr. Kjell Eriksson, the head of the Lillhagens Sjukhus. As one of several other chores, he looks after mentally disturbed students at Gothenburg University.

'I don't think there is any greater number of mentally ill today,' he said. 'It's just that many hidden or undetected cases are now being brought out in the new atmosphere. There is a new acceptance of psychiatric treatment and an understanding that mental illness is not something to be ashamed of. Since 1955, we have been able to take mental patients as you would in an ordinary hospital. They don't have to go through legal formalities and they can leave when they want. About 90 per cent of all psychiatric patients are under this free system now. Under 10 per cent have compulsory treatment.'

Inevitably, we are brought back to the old welfare-state-versus-happiness question. The chief neurosurgeon at the huge Södersjukhus in Stockholm, Dr. Ragnar Frykholm, wrote in Sweden's leading conservative newspaper that 'the existence of numerous neuroses is a typical welfare phenomenon.' Maybe so, but, as with suicides, I suspect that the neurotic Swedes who are crowding the hospitals get that way from a combination of deep-seated reasons of national psychology and the peculiar pressures of a highly advanced industrial society. Welfarism might possibly add to, or subtract from, the number of neurotics, but it seems to be the lesser factor.

Friendly Prisons

The dearth of psychiatric care is particularly noticeable in Swedish prisons. An admirable amount of care is taken in assessing a prisoner's mental condition before he is assigned to an institution, but once under detention he is highly unlikely to meet a psychiatrist or therapist. And yet Swedish prisons are among the most humane and enlightened in the world, and are run by decent people. At a prison near Gothenburg called Fångvårdsanstalten Skogome, I asked the superintendent, Per Lafqvist, what was done about escaping prisoners, since none of the guards had guns and the walls were not exactly formidable. 'It is better to let the man go than to put a hole in him,' he said. 'We can always catch him later.' It was his job to look after prisoners awaiting sentence before they went on to permanent prisons. 'Bad or unkind treatment,' he said, 'would make them resist the care they will get in prison, and the aftercare.'

The Swedish prison population at any one time is about 4,000, and most of the prisoners serve in open or semiopen institutions which have none of the traditional high walls and guard towers. In labor-short Sweden the inmates make a useful work force, and more than half of all prisoners are engaged in industrial production, often with first-class assembly-line equipment. The rest work on farms, in forests or at other jobs. The heads of the prison system are said to have a slogan, 'First we build a factory, then we add a prison.' Almost all the jobs are on an incentive or piecework basis, to encourage prisoners to work, and while the pay may be a quarter or less of what it would be on the outside, it adds up to important money in the bank for a newly released prisoner.

The logical next step the Swedes have taken is a prison-factory which pays full wages, but charges the inmates for room and board, and sees to it that they pay their debts and taxes, and provide support for their families. Well-behaved prisoners are given frequent weekend leaves to visit their homes. The aim is to keep family life intact and not destroy an offender's dignity or capabilities.

Superintendent Lafqvist said that 'loss of freedom and social shame are the main punishment. There is discipline, of course. Some people *want* discipline, but it is kindly done. It is still an open question just how much punishment is required, but the whole trend is toward shorter sentences and even shorter times in prison, and the prisons themselves are getting smaller all the time. They shouldn't have more than two hundred to four hundred men. We have never before built so many new prisons and abandoned the big old ones as we are now.'

Like many another Swede, this quietly competent professional (twenty-five years in prison work) revealed some hidden depths once the ice was broken. His enthusiasm for his work and his earnestness about doing the best for both his staff and his prisoners were infectious. As he showed off the new recreation quarters for his guards he mentioned that because he had felt it to be 'democratic' he joined the younger men in regular judo training. He is a bespectacled, slightly stoop-shouldered man of about fifty. We were standing at the doorway of the practice room. A green sheet of canvas covered the layer of rubber on the hardwood floor. Suddenly, without warning, he hurled himself into the room and did a series of violent somersaults punctuated by explosive slaps of his hands on the canvas. And just as quickly he was at my side again, puffing slightly, his hat still firmly on his head and his overcoat none the worse for wear. 'It looks even better when I've got a pipe in my mouth,' he said.

Chapter 25

NO BLIND ALLEYS

*The American dating customs would break up our school system.
We haven't time for such frivolities.*
— SWEDISH SCHOOLTEACHER

*The Swedes are the freest people in the world but they allow the
state to decide where they can buy their spirits. We don't give a
damn for Swedish freedom.*
— DANISH NEWSPAPER

One of the most winning characteristics of the essentially conservative Swedish society is its willingness to undertake radical
reforms, but only after a careful groundwork has been laid.
Sweden today is in the midst of a great educational revolution. It
is partly an effort to carry forward the ideal of universality—to
give the best possible education to everyone regardless of family
income or other factors. It is also an attempt to make sure that no
youngster, particularly the late bloomer, is victimized by any
rigid selection process as he moves up the educational ladder.
'There should be no blind alleys,' say the Swedes. Finally, it is a
response to a tremendous demand for more education from an
exceptionally literate—and now wealthy-literate—citizenry.

Sweden has had good schools for many centuries, a fact made
evident by the founding dates of the two oldest universities:
Uppsala 1477, Lund 1666. A common compulsory school did not
begin until 1842, however; and it was not until the end of the
century that the pupils from this *folkskola* were admitted into
academic secondary schools. While it came to be accepted that
everyone should have a basic education, only the wealthy and a

few bright members of the poor were expected to go on to higher education. In the words of Teddy Brunius, a scholar at Uppsala University, 'The traditional image of a student was not single but double: the upper-class student, who took things easily as regarded study and had a good time, whilst his parents met the bill, and the student from a peasant family, who scraped together the money by borrowing and starved and kept adversity at arm's length with severe Latin quotations.'

In the underdeveloped society that was Sweden until not too many decades ago, there was, in fact, no reason for having too large a well-educated class. There were only a few openings for scholars and scientists. Today the tables have turned. 'There is a tremendous demand from parents and youngsters for more education facilities,' said Hans Löwbeer, the head of the National Board of Education, 'and there is a huge demand from the labor market for better-educated personnel. We have come to see that education pays, that it is a necessary condition for the further growth of the economy. In the 1930s when we introduced the seven-year compulsory school there were a lot of protests. Now we have started the nine-year compulsory comprehensive school, and it is the other way around. The pressure is for still more expansion of facilities beyond the nine years, perhaps to eleven years. Furthermore, adult education is expanding at a terrific rate.'

Forty per cent of the young Swedes between sixteen and eighteen years are going on to further education, as compared with 20 per cent in the early 1950s. The percentage is expected to go over 50 in a few years. The number of pupils seeking admission to the gymnasiums, the three-year academic step toward the universities, is expected to double between 1963 and 1970. The number of university students rose from 33,000 in 1958 to 55,000 in 1964, and it is expected to be 80,000 in 1970. The new university at Umeå was established to take some of the load off Uppsala, Lund, Stockholm and Gothenburg, and there may have to be another. What came across most forcefully to me in talks with educators was the fact that it is not so much the state imposing ever more education on the country as the communities clamoring for more, and the state valiantly trying to keep the explosion under control. As it is, the national spending on education *doubled* in just the few years from 1958 to 1964, and there is an acute shortage of teachers. 'We started establishing the new school in 1950,' said Löwbeer, 'and we have been rushing it lately, but the problem is that the communities are queueing up for it. If we didn't restrict them, they would organize facilities for 150 per cent of our younger population.'

Comprehensive Schools

The new school is a nine-year comprehensive school, which has the same curriculum for all until the final years, when there are options for those of special abilities. And at the end it is the pupils and their parents, not society, who decide which 'streams' the pupils will enter as they move into more specialized training. If this sounds as if the bright pupils will be slowed down by the less bright, the Swedes say that their studies and experiments show that it is not necessarily so. And anyway, they ask, what about the rights of the slower students who have been shown to suffer by being deprived of the company of their brighter fellows? In any case, as Jonas Orring of the National Board of Education said, 'the greatest of current problems is the inability of people to live and work happily together—not the attainment of new and greater intellectual performances.'

This has a very Scandinavian welfare-state ring to it: a celebration of mass order and 'happiness' as against high individual performance. Are one's individual talents or special gifts to be crushed in an awful bear hug of togetherness? It remains to be seen just what kind of young people emerge from the comprehensive schools, but it is noteworthy that Swedish educators are convinced that social harmony and individual expression are twin goods which can be attained, and which need not cancel each other out.

If anything, it seems to me that the balance is moving toward the individual in Sweden. The ideal is that all are to be encouraged, and none are to be left behind. Jonas Orring said:

The school should place the pupil in the center of interest to a greater degree than formerly, and the work of the school must be based on respect for the personality and individuality of each pupil. This is in keeping with the fundamental democratic conception that all human beings are equal in value, regardless of their capabilities in one direction or another.

The Great Experiment

The British, who are themselves groping toward comprehensive schools out of an academic maze of many schools, early selection, early specialization and too many blind alleys, have been fascinated by the educational upheaval in Sweden. There is widespread recognition in Britain that school reforms are needed, and that greater opportunities must be provided, but it has been a shrill argument of many voices still divided about the kind of society Britain should be. The Swedes know the kind of environment they want, and they have gone after it with sure confidence. 'Educational reforms, even very radical ones, are not only necessary but natural,' said Jonas Orring.

Once a decision for change is reached in Sweden, the pace can be exhilarating, but the steps leading up to a decision are cautious. There was a ten-year experimental period before an act of parliament in 1962 approved the final shape of the comprehensive school and ordered its general introduction. A decade ago, Stockholm launched a five-year experiment which literally divided the city in two : the comprehensive system was introduced in the southern part of the capital, while in the north the old system was retained. Under the old system, brighter children were selected for a more challenging grammar school and ordinary types were streamed off to lesser secondary schools. The results of the test were compelling enough to convince the Stockholm school authorities to go all-comprehensive. Other areas tried out the new school, and by now nine out of ten Swedish pupils are in comprehensive schools. The process will be completed by the early 1970s.

In the first six of the comprehensive's nine years, there is a uniform general education. In the seventh and eighth years (ages fourteen to fifteen) pupils may select some optional subjects. In the ninth year they must choose one of nine different streams, depending on whether they want to undertake the mainly theoretical studies which lead to the gymnasium and perhaps on to a university, or other variations of theoretical or practical training. About a third go on after the final comprehensive year to a gymnasium, and 80 per cent then pass the qualifying examination which entitles them to enter a university. About a quarter of those emerging from the comprehensive schools go on to a two-year continuation school which gives them further general education, and another quarter enter a trade school for one or two years.

The fact that the new schools have small classes (in principle no more than twenty-five pupils in each) and superb equipment in modern buildings lessens the concern about bright children being slowed down by others. Language training, for example, makes use of tape recorders and other equipment to get the best out of a pupil. English is the compulsory foreign language for all, beginning in the fourth grade, and German and French are optional in the seventh grade. It is a rare Swedish youngster who is not competent in at least one foreign language, and many are fluent in several.

I have heard American educators complain that there is too much rigidity, formality and rote in Swedish classrooms, from the early grades into the universities. Many a visiting professor has been disturbed by the tendency of students to swallow the gospel from the teacher unquestioningly. 'They just sit there taking notes,' I was told. 'You can't get them to argue with you. They're too respectful. They don't use their imaginations.' Hans Löwbeer and others acknowledged that Swedish pupils are perhaps too burdened with work and under too much pressure as they study for their matriculation. 'They're too career-minded,' said one educator. 'They should have more time for social interests.' A Swedish teacher, commenting about Sweden's relatively late school-starting age of seven, said, 'When you start you play. We work.'

Special Education

Swedish schools are coeducational, needless to say. There is neither segregation of the sexes nor much mystery about sex. Education is free from the first grade to the top of the university. Books, lunches and certain other expenses are provided free to pupils, and grants and loans are available to university students to meet living and traveling costs. Even so, there are still about twenty-five private schools in Sweden. They have some 10,000 pupils as against the 1,200,000 in the public schools. Far from crushing the private schools as anachronisms in a democratic welfare state, the Swedish government regulates them through the National Board of Education, and gives them financial assistance. 'It is quite free for anyone in this country to start a school,' one official said.

Also allied to the public-education structure, yet operating with an independent air, are Sweden's one hundred Folk High Schools with about 12,000 adult students. Most intriguing, however, are the country's 95,000 'study circles.' They involve some one million Swedes every year, or one eighth of the entire population, an incredible number in a restless automotive society. It is also a rising number: the 1950 figure was 385,000 participants. The popularity of the study circles testifies to the Swedish zeal for self-improvement, but the explanation for the current vogue probably lies in the fact that they have moved away from their classic role. Whereas the study circle enthusiasts once concentrated on humanistic studies and solemn literary and philosophic explorations, today the swing is toward more practical knowledge, particularly foreign languages and economics.

University Life

Although university education for the masses is gradually becoming a reality, the student in Swedish higher education is still a special creature, whose mere presence at a university will give him a higher status in the larger society for the rest of his life. He makes a jarring transition from the disciplines of grade school and gymnasium to the absolute freedom of Swedish university life. Suddenly he is an adult, and on his own.

Assistant Professor Teddy Brunius wrote in the Uppsala publication, *The Intellectual Face of Sweden*:

> Everyone who has passed the *student-examen* has the right to study at a Swedish university. This examination is also called the 'maturity examination'—that is to say, the successful examinee is regarded as being mature or adult. And this is not all; as a student he has to look after his own interests. He is responsible to himself and to the group of students to which he will belong . . . the student has a private life and it is not supervised. The university exercises no moral control over the students. The nation (student organization) assists the student with advice and fellowship. But there is nothing that distinguishes a student from an ordinary wage earner. He takes his meals where he likes. He is at liberty to drink alcoholic liquors and have sexual relations, if he does so within the law. In short, the student is independent.

The 'nations' at Uppsala University are much like American college fraternities, except that each is a gathering of students from a particular province or major city. For Swedish universities in general it is the powerful student unions and their national superstructure that provide the focus for student life on campus. The unions not only take care of much of the student housing but also play an important role in the conduct of university affairs. 'It can still be said,' wrote Professor Brunius, 'that the university authorities are excluded from the actual organization of student life.' In the Swedish classroom Herr Professor is a kind of demigod, but on the campus the student is his own master. On Walpurgis Night, the last day of April, he takes over completely. In Uppsala, the ancient city shudders as thousands of white-capped students, still in their winter coats, race through the streets, hell-bent for a long night of eating, drinking, dancing, singing, speechmaking and uninhibited merriment, all in homage to spring.

Lukewarm Religion

The relentless statisticians of Sweden, not content with telling us that 1,500,000 Swedes are members of the National Alliance of Swedish Sports Federations, have even stated that 2,080,000 adults who live in cities take part in 'nature walks, bilberry or mushroom picking.'

These nature-loving Swedes have been described as 'blue domers.' Their church is the great outdoors; God's handiwork is in the green moss of the forests and the blue of the sky above. As a result, Sweden, despite its postwar 'new wave of church building,' may be said to have some of the most beautiful empty churches in the world. Only a quarter million Swedes, or just 3 per cent of the population, go to church every Sunday.

My personal interest in religion in Sweden began in 1964 when I attended the ceremonies on the occasion of the eight-hundredth anniversary of the founding of the diocese in Uppsala by Sweden's first archbishop. Christianity had been introduced into Sweden more than three centuries earlier, in 830. The jubilee celebration in the great 700-year-old, red-brick cathedral in Uppsala attracted hundreds of leading church figures from around the world. It was easy, in such surroundings, to feel that Sweden was an old and profoundly religious nation, but the fact is that there is a greater percentage of practicing Christians in the Soviet Union than in Sweden. And yet it is not a simple situation. The Swedes appear to be indifferent to religion, but below the surface many of them are yearning for religious concepts which could give them the same satisfying certainty that was enjoyed by their unquestioning ancestors.

The seemingly unreligious Swedes pay church taxes, approve of religious instruction in the schools, put up with a heavy Sunday schedule of religious radio broadcasts, buy newspapers which devote a surprising amount of space to religious topics, and look on approvingly as new churches in striking contemporary design are built in the new suburbs and housing projects. Many modern Swedes will insist that they never go to church and do not believe in God, yet they do not exercise their right to give up their membership in the official Lutheran Church, and they are happy enough to have the religious institutions continue as they are. The Church, however, must keep its place quietly in the background. It must stay out of public affairs. Sweden is not a country like the United States, where ministers join civil rights demonstrations, or like England, where the canons and bishops sound off on everything from teen-age morals to nuclear bombs.

The prevailing Swedish attitude was demonstrated in the public reaction to a project of the present Archbishop of Sweden, the Most Reverend Gunnar Hultgren, who in the course of a visit to France had been impressed by the accomplishments of French worker-priests. The Archbishop organized five worker-priests of his own and sent them out to the factories and down into the mines. It was a short-lived experiment; the Swedes disliked being the objects of missionary work, and they asked why the priests were not in their churches where they belonged. In another example, a priest with strong moral views refused to marry a couple because the girl was pregnant. There was a storm of criticism from the public. People said he had the right to his own views, but he should not force them on others.

The Church in Sweden seldom functions as a community social center as it does in America, where Sunday attendance is still strong. Swedes tend to think of the Church as a branch of government and of the priests as civil servants. And for good reason. There is still an intimate church-and-state relationship despite the long decades of 'socialist' rule. The King is the official head of the Church, and cannot be king unless he is of the faith. The prime minister, in fact, could not have been prime minister unless he had taken his first communion. A paragraph in the Swedish constitution says so. School children sing a hymn in the morning as they start the school day, and they attend classes on religion. Carl Boethius, a leading church editor, said: 'The teacher does not say that God exists or Christ is our Saviour. He says that Christians believe that this is so.' A recent government plan to reduce the number of hours of religious teaching sparked a heated debate in the Swedish press. Petitions objecting to the plan were signed by more than two million persons.

Civil-Service Church

The state-church system means that every Swede is considered a member of the official Church unless he applies for non-membership or was born to parents who were outside the Church. A 1951 religious-freedom law gave people the right to withdraw from Church membership, but only one per cent of the Swedes have done so. The percentage may rise a bit now that the deed can be done just by mailing a letter. Previously a member had to go in person and state his reasons for withdrawing. 'It was too embarrassing,' a Swedish woman said.

If he relinquishes his membership, a citizen will not have to pay the full church tax (not a large amount in any case), but even the dedicated atheist has to pay something. A good percentage of the tax revenue goes to meet the cost of the Church's civil-registration work—the recording of vital statistics—which the Church has carried out for centuries. Although the Church gets some income from its properties, it is the state-administered church funds which provide most of the money for the salaries of bishops and priests. As one writer has commented, 'the livelihood of ministers of religion is assured, no matter what the size and devotion of their flock.' A good many of the 3,800 clergymen feel that they should be doing more priestly work and less clerical work. Swedish radicals who call for the disestablishment of the Church would agree, but there is not much momentum behind disestablishmentarianism. In their more radical days the Social Democrats would advocate that the Church be separated and its property revert to the state and local authorities. In recent years, however, they have simply put on pressure to liberalize the Church—for example, by permitting remarriage in the Church of divorced persons, introducing women priests, and simplifying withdrawal from membership.

Of the quarter million regular church attenders, nearly half are members of the so-called 'Free Churches,' which have about 300,000 members as against the more than seven million of the Church of Sweden. The Free Churches are the heirs to the revival movements of the nineteenth century, and they are separated from both the state and the state church. The two biggest units are the Mission Covenant Church with some 95,000 members and the Pentecostal Movement with 90,000, and there are several thousand zealots of rigorous puritanical faiths. There are about 28,000 Roman Catholics in Sweden, 4,000 persons in the Eastern Orthodox Church, and fewer than 7,000 Jews.

Although weekly church attendance is almost as low as it can be, there are statistics to show that one fifth of the Swedes worship once a month, and that 87 per cent of all youths are baptized and confirmed in the church. Almost all Swedes marry in church and wish for a church funeral. They turn up in church in great numbers on Good Friday, Easter, Advent Sunday and Christmas. All Saints' Day is widely observed with much decorating of graves and lighting of candles. A great many Swedish customs, including the charming ritual of little girls wearing candle-studded crowns on St. Lucia's Day, spring from religious traditions. The Swedes would not dream of giving them up.

National Hangover

Sweden's troubled spirit is not unconnected with its trouble about spirits. A century ago a visiting Englishman called Sweden 'the drunkenness center of the world,' and the powerful temperance movement which resulted from those deplorable days had all the power of a religious revival. Even today, when the alcohol consumption by the Swedes is one of the lowest in the world (see page 268), the movement still carries on as a kind of a Church of Sobriety, with 6,000 local temperance societies and a teetotaling membership which has increased from 300,000 to 450,000 in the last fifteen years.

The national drinking problem which has brought about such a massing of antialcohol forces cannot be overlooked in any study of Sweden. It seeps through Swedish modern history like whisky aged in wood; it illuminates all manner of national traits; and it is brought immediately to a visitor's attention when he is warned not to drink if he is driving. The penalties are severe, and, as Fodor's *Scandinavia* advises foreign motorists, 'No exceptions are

made for anyone, so you'd better take a taxi if you've been out
on the town.' Swedes take a taxi to a party, or hire someone to
drive them home, or else a husband and wife will decide before-
hand who will drink and who will drive. For the past two
hundred years, alcohol and its consumption and regulation
have caused some incredible complications in the lives of the
Swedes.

The modern problem began with the introduction of the humble
potato. That exotic curiosity of the seventeenth century began to
be popularly accepted in the eighteenth century, when ordinary
Swedes learned that its juices could be converted into strong
drink. As one historian says, 'the increasing addiction to drink,
with its detrimental effects on health and behavior, was a serious
blot on eighteenth-century life.' Gustav III, the king who did so
much to advance Swedish culture, decided to ban private distillation in 1775 and turn the manufacture of spirits into a royal
monopoly. His intentions were more fiscal than noble, however.
He badly needed money, and the sale of spirits exclusively by the
Crown would obviously fatten his treasury. Drinking suddenly
became a patriotic duty, and civil servants were ordered to
encourage people to drink. Bars were placed outside the churches
in order to attract the citizen on his way home from the services.
The ban on private production naturally led to bootlegging, and
there were so many unpleasant political consequences of this that
the restrictions were lifted in 1800. By that time the drinking habit
had become so ingrained that the nation literally set off on an
alcoholic binge.

'A torrent of liquor burst forth,' says the author of a history of
Sweden. Whole crops went into the bottle instead of into food.
Many workers were paid in alcohol, and bottles of spirits became
a kind of currency, like cigarettes in Germany soon after the last
war. The annual consumption of alcohol for every man, woman
and child in Sweden actually reached ten gallons just a century
ago (the figure today is 1·5 gallons). Alcoholism led to a steep
increase in violent crimes as well as the early deaths of bread-
winners and misery for the families of drunks. Young executives
at the Stora Kopparberg company were warned: 'Never intoxi-

cate yourself with Strong Drink and do not associate too much with Womenfolk. The former is, however, the more dangerous, for it grows, but the latter declines with the years.'

Sweden's national hangover was so bad that the temperance movement began as a great crusade. It was encouraged and partly financed by the government, as it still is. For well over a century the temperance enthusiasts have wielded a strong influence in Swedish life and they still have significant power in the parliament and in other organs of the nation. For all the obvious good they have done, they loom as a restricting, puritanical force to many Swedes, who deplore the preaching and prying that have been the price of Sweden's semiprohibition. The temperance organizations took their cues from similar groups in Britain and the United States, and then added their own refinements.

Just a century ago, when Swedish drunkenness was at its height, the 'Gothenburg System' was adopted. The saloons were closed; the sale of spirits was shifted to restaurants where they had to be consumed on the spot; and manufacture was restricted. Other measures over the years brought the situation under control and dropped the annual per capita consumption to about two gallons after the turn of the century. Confirmed drinkers, of course, drank much more than this figure and the sight of wage earners reeling down the street on Saturday night after blowing their week's pay inspired the more extreme teetotalers to demand all-out prohibition. After all, Norway and Finland as well as the United States voted for it right after World War I. A national plebiscite was held in Sweden in 1922. It was a close vote—925,000 to 890,000—but the prohibitionists lost. Sweden then concentrated on the famous 'Bratt Liquor Control System,' devised by Dr. Ivan Bratt, which it had instituted during World War I. This was semiprohibition: manufacture and sale of alcohol were confined to the state's tightfisted hands, spirits were rationed, and they were denied altogether to 'alcohol abusers.'

The Swedes put up with the Bratt System for almost forty years, until they scrapped it in 1955. It unquestionably had some good results in a notoriously hard-drinking nation, but they were at the cost of numerous unedifying spectacles. Ordinary, sober, law-abiding citizens were made to feel like criminals, as details of their private lives were probed in order to determine whether it was safe to let them have a passbook for purchases in the dreary state liquor stores. Customers were limited to about three quarts of alcohol a month, and their purchases had to be entered in their passbooks. Wine was not rationed, but it too had to be noted in the book. Excessive purchases of wine could lead to warnings, reduction of the alcohol ration, or withdrawal of the passbook. No one under twenty-one was allowed to purchase spirits, and women were given only a small allocation. With few exceptions, married women were not given a passbook.

In the Bratt System days, people who went to a restaurant for a drink could get only a small amount, and it could be taken only with a meal. There were two inevitable consequences: A lot of food was wasted, because people ordered it just to drink; and, of course, restaurateurs took to serving the same boiled egg or the same plate of cold peas over and over to different customers. The 'rubber sandwich' was a popular device to make it seem as if the drinker was also a diner. But proprietors had to be on guard against the official snoopers who skulked about trying to catch waiters serving too many drinks, or drinks without food.

Predictably, Swedes took to moonshining, bootlegging and the black marketing of ration books. People in southern Sweden sailed regularly to Copenhagen, where they drank furiously to the amusement and disgust of the Danes. Protests against the Bratt System mounted, and Dr. Bratt himself came under such abuse that he took up residence in France. It appeared that the system, far from curbing drinking, was making it more desirable, especially to the young. An investigation showed that 75 per cent of all the alcohol offenses were committed by persons who had been denied the passbook. The worst of the situation was that a law-abiding nation was breaking the law right and left, and a democratic nation was putting up with a disturbing amount of state control of private behavior.

The Difficulty of Drinking

The reform in the control system a decade ago brought about a more realistic and sophisticated approach, but it still amounts to a degree of big-brother regulation which people in many other countries would find intolerable. The state decides who can drink, and where, when and how, and how much. Furthermore, the extremely high cost of a bottle of liquor in Sweden (the state sets the price and then nearly doubles it with taxes) is one of the official ways of controlling drinking, but it obviously affects the workingman more than the wealthy man. It is one of the least democratic sides of Swedish social democracy.

Under the present alcohol policy, the state continues as the exclusive manufacturer and distributor of alcoholic beverages, and the ordinary citizen over twenty-one who is not on a black list of 'alcohol abusers' can buy as many bottles of akvavit, whisky and wine as he wishes. But he may be asked to show an identity card if there is any suspicion that he is one of the alcohol abusers on the black list. A recent ruling says that the card must have a photograph and an attested signature. The larger liquor shops have installed automatic photo machines to assist the customers. To make sure that spot checks are made, a device with a red light flashes every so often, and the customer is obliged to produce his identification. The more than 13,000 persons forbidden to buy alcohol are those who have been twice convicted of drunken driving or were caught moonshining or have been branded as habitual drunks by local temperance boards. These boards, which are mainly financed by the state, have broad powers to persuade or coerce people to stay sober. And the confirmed drunkard is forced to submit to treatment.

The Wine Mountain

The state retail shops are organized as the Systembolaget. It buys all of its supplies from the Vin-och Spritcentralen, the state monopoly which produces, imports and wholesales alcoholic beverages. It is a big business operating in a businesslike way. It produces glossy annual reports which describe its annual sales of more than 60 million dollars' worth of alcoholic liquor, more than 26 million gallons of all kinds. There is a still higher figure of over 400 million dollars for the total annual expenditure by Swedes on spirits, wines and beers, including those lighter, domestic beers which are widely sold outside the monopoly shops. The liquor taxes and duties (90 per cent on retail cost of a bottle of akvavit) earn the state about 350 million dollars a year, or over 7 per cent of its total revenue.

Some Swedes complain that the profits of the wholesale and retail monopolies amount to a hidden tax, but a spokesman for the Vin-och Spritcentralen said, 'We are supposed to make a profit like any business, but a fair profit.' It amounts to four million dollars a year. The company is the world's largest single importer of alcoholic beverages. The fact that it buys seven million dollars' worth of wine from France each year, and ships the wine to Sweden in a 300,000-gallon special tanker with enamel-lined insides, means that the Swedish buyers get favored treatment and the best from the vineyards when they go to France. The strictest quality controls give the Swedes an unexcelled selection of the world's finest wines. The monopoly imports more than seven million gallons of wine a year, mostly from France, Spain and Italy. The business is so big that the wine is stored in immense cellars which have been blasted out of rock. The greatest of these is the famous 'wine mountain' in Stockholm, which is being enlarged to hold about twelve million gallons of wines and spirits by 1967.

When the restrictions on purchases were lifted in 1955 there was a sudden leap in sales, as everyone expected, and then a leveling off. Swedes are drinking more than they did a decade ago, as might be expected with their increasing prosperity, but not significantly more. The 'Drink More Wine' campaign by the alcohol monopoly and the temperance forces, combined with the higher prices put on stronger drinks, has led to a change of drinking habits. Swedes are swinging away from their traditional favorite, *brännvin*, the potato alcohol (akvavit), toward wines and beer. Furthermore, they are spacing their drinking in Continental fashion rather than saving their drinking for all-out Nordic binges. Sweden's 200-year hangover is finished.

Chapter 26

THROUGH A GLASS DARKLY

It was Sweden which first made the world realize that there really is an art of the motion picture and that it is worthy of respect.
— *The History of Motion Pictures*

After Strindberg, Lagerlöf and Garbo, Ingmar Bergman is today the only world celebrity created in and through Swedish art.
— JÖRN DONNER

The Swedes have a special culture in a cold climate, seldom noticed and little understood by the outside world, but deeply ingrained in the individual citizen. Long isolation from the main currents of world affairs has made them unusually conscious of their cultural heritage, while the universality and excellence of their educational system has given them an admirable familiarity with the best of foreign cultures.

The national zeal for self-improvement has already been noted, and the Swedish passion for the printed word is evident. Not only are they the most voracious newspaper readers in the world, but the production of books in Sweden is phenomenal. In 1964, for example, there were 7,304 titles published, an increase of more than a thousand over the previous year. The country is full of heavily patronized bookshops. Writers are encouraged to keep writing through a variety of inducements, including the fact that they benefit financially whenever people take their books out of the library. Sweden has a distinguished literary history, with August Strindberg, Selma Lagerlöf and Pär Lagerkvist probably the three best-known of the several score outstanding writers. Similarly, the Swedish theater has a rich background, and it was

427

because of its appreciation of his work that Eugene O'Neill turned over to the Royal Dramatic Theater the manuscripts of four plays which had their world premieres in Stockholm after his death.

The Swedes have produced great performers of the stage and screen, and world-famous singers like Jenny Lind and Birgit Nilsson, but not a single Swedish painter or composer ranks with the greatest international figures. Carl Milles is an exception as a world-famous sculptor. The Swedish genius seems to be expressed less in art and more in the art of living. It excels in functional, though not daringly imaginative, architecture, and in the design of glassware, silverware, furniture, ceramics, textiles and other things which enrich the domestic scene. The greatest care has been taken to preserve the handicraft traditions, and one of the brightest sides of Swedish life is the encouragement and status given to individual designers. In glass companies like Orrefors and Kosta, which do most of their business in assembly-line glassmaking, a visitor has the impression that the whole factory has been created to respond to the whim of superstars like Vicke Lindstrand, Mona Morales-Schildt, Ingeborg Lundin and Sven Palmqvist. An outstanding designer like Sigurd Persson, who produces some of the most inspired jewelry and silverware to be seen anywhere, has become a major figure in the life of his nation; his work ranges from candelabra for churches to knives and forks for Scandinavian Airlines.

Much of what is being accomplished in the arts in Sweden deserves greater notice, but it is a fact that only one living Swedish creator has become an undoubted international figure: film director Ingmar Bergman. He has been at the heart of a cultural drama in Sweden which saw the near eclipse of a once celebrated film industry and then its amazing resurgence through a characteristic combination of private and government action.

Past and Present

Swedes were making motion pictures as early as the 1890s. Their largest film company, Svensk Filmindustri, began as long ago as 1907, as the Swedish Biograph Theater. Charles Magnussen, one of the earliest newsreel photographers, was put in charge of production. The early Swedish films were strong on rhapsodic views of the great outdoors. Modern Swedish film makers, including Bergman, are still inclined to linger lovingly over the dark forests, rushing waters and moody lakes of the North. Magnussen's master stroke was to hire two theater actors, Mauritz Stiller and Victor Sjöstrom, and turn them into film directors. Their imaginative work made the world notice that Sweden had mastered the strange new medium. David Robinson wrote in the *Financial Times*:

> From the start, also, Swedish film makers showed a willingness then unique in the world to treat the cinema seriously, as an art, and to use it for the discussion of wholly adult themes. Oddly enough, this sophistication, at a time when the rest of the world's film industries were in a baby stage, was probably helped as much as anything by the inauguration in 1911 of a state system of censorship which clearly classified films by suitability for various audience categories.

One of Victor Sjöstrom's early films was a 1913 social documentary on the Swedish poor, which led to important welfare reforms. His superb picture, *The Phantom Carriage*, was a 1920 classic about the struggle between good and evil. It was a forerunner for Bergman's own classic in 1957, *The Seventh Seal*. Mauritz Stiller was an equally formidable director, who filmed a number of Selma Lagerlöf's writings and achieved an early breakthrough into such daring themes as adultery by treating them with a sophisticated comedy touch. He is most often identified, however, as the man who converted an up-and-coming actress named Greta Gustafsson into Greta Garbo. Garbo was a graduate of Stockholm's Royal Dramatic Theater, which has also been the fountainhead of such famous Swedish actresses as Ingrid Bergman, Signe Hasso, Viveca Lindfors, Ingrid Thulin, Eva Dahlbeck and Mai Zetterling. (Surprisingly few Swedish males of either stage or screen have achieved the same kind of recognition.) In Sweden there has been a close and significant connection between the theater and the cinema, one which has persisted right up to the present. Ingmar Bergman has been the director of the Royal Dramatic Theater and such outstanding performers as Harriet Andersson and Bibi Andersson are equally at home on stage or screen. American and British films, in contrast, grew out of a tradition of vaudeville, music halls and other forms of light entertainment.

The galvanic early days ended with the doom of the silent film. With the advent of the talkies a language barrier suddenly went up, and the industry in Stockholm switched to light-entertainment movies strictly for the Swedish market. Sjöstrom (known in America as Victor Seastrom), Stiller, Garbo and other top names were lured to Hollywood. The insularity of the Swedish film became almost total during World War II. It encouraged the kind of films which one critic described as 'lighthearted, easily middle-class and highly moral comedies.'

A little ray of light, a promise of a renaissance of the Swedish cinema, appeared even during the war. One of Sweden's greatest modern film directors, Alf Sjöberg, famous for his Shakespeare productions on the stage, produced a psychological drama about a sadistic high-school teacher. The title was *Hets* (*Frenzy* in Britain and *Torment* in the United States). Rune Waldekranz, a leading producer and film historian, wrote: 'The author of this, the best film manuscript in Swedish motion pictures since the period of Sjöstrom and Stiller, was the young student and dramatist, Ingmar Bergman. With *Hets*, Swedish films broke through their provincial isolation with explosive power and again could demand a favorite place in the international cinema.' Bergman reached the front rank of international film directors with a steady output of more than two dozen highly individualistic films. Now, with Bergman still in his prime, have come a number of ambitious young directors taking up bold themes.

These directors and a handful of enterprising producers came into the arena at a time of economic depression for the film industry which threatened to close up the studios altogether. The Swedish cinema was almost strangled by two of the most visible signs of the nation's new affluence: television and the automobile.

In 1952, before the age of TV, Swedish studios turned out forty feature films each year. Ten years later they made only twelve annually. In the same period the number of people who went to the movies was reduced by more than half. In the early 1960s, the movie companies were losing money on four out of every five films they made. A former head of Svensk Filmindustri, Dr. Carl Anders Dymling, said, 'The wonder is that the industry exists at all.' The studios, as a matter of fact, were existing not as film makers, but as owners of the nation's movie houses where over 90 per cent of the films shown were American or other foreign productions. But even this business suffered from the fact that the entertainment tax on films was one of the highest in the world. When television began spreading like wildfire in 1956, the Swedish film looked doomed.

Rescue

It was saved in part by the endeavors of movie enthusiasts and the government's willingness to give the industry a tax break. The most influential voice outside the professional ranks was that of Harry Schein, a young and wealthy Austrian-born businessman who has lived in Sweden since his boyhood. A wiry bundle of energy with a restless mind and high organizational talents, he made a fortune in water purification and sewage disposal equipment, and then decided to retire at thirty-five to make a vocation of his avocations. The greatest Schein avocation was the cinema, an interest further stimulated in 1956 by his marriage to Ingrid Thulin, best known for her roles in Bergman's *Wild Strawberries* and *The Silence*.

In 1962, Schein wrote a hot-tempered little book entitled *Can We Afford Culture?* 'It came along at just the right time,' said young director Vilgot Sjöman. 'The welfare state had achieved most of its goals, and people were ready to do something about improving our cultural life.' The book appealed for a national cultural policy and made some proposals on how to save and improve the Swedish film. Schein himself admits that after the book came out 'we began to get fantastically fast results.'

What was done was inspired and unprecedented, and was one of the most vivid demonstrations ever of the Swedish ability to come to grips with a problem of national concern and produce a common-sense solution. It has been called 'the Swedish film reform of 1963' and its success was so immediate that Denmark, whose own small film industry had been all but paralyzed, soon copied the Swedish reform.

The new approach was unanimously voted by the Swedish parliament. It wiped away the onerous 25 per cent entertainment tax on movie tickets (it had once been as high as 39 per cent) and put in its place a 10 per cent 'tax' to be used to finance a newly created Film Institute. The Institute's annual income of two and a half million dollars is used in a variety of ways to encourage production and appreciation of films in Sweden, most importantly through a system for rewarding movies of outstanding quality. A rotating panel of film critics decides which films deserve to get a bonus for unusual merit, without taking into consideration either production costs or box-office success. It is stated in an appendix to the government-industry agreement setting up the Film Institute that 'the conception of quality must be applied in its widest sense, to make possible the unfettered development of film art in Sweden.'

The award system offers a powerful incentive to a producer to make sure that his pictures have some merit. It means that a studio can take a risk with an experimental film or with a promising young director. The production chief at Sandrews studio said: 'This puts a net under the tightrope. We have been in constant fear that we would break our necks with any film outside the routine. Now we can perform more daring tricks.'

Harry Schein is the first director of the Institute, which operates under an eight-man board of directors, half of them government employees and half film industry representatives. A film school has been started in an effort to breed new directors. 'No one knows,' said Schein, 'whether creators flourish on plenty or on adversity. It may be that nothing will come out of this chance. But if we turn up one director in five years, I think we'll have done very well.'

With the tax load lifted and financial incentives offered through the Film Institute, Swedish moviemakers have dramatically pulled out of their slump. Production doubled, from twelve to twenty-five feature films between 1962 and 1964, and cinema attendance figures began going up—the only country in Europe to show an increase, according to the Institute. Attendance has been helped by another fact of modern Swedish life (and another example of the cooperative streak which runs through the whole society): the national television system does not show films on Saturday and Sunday nights, the most popular moviegoing nights.

The Times of London has said that 'Sweden thus becomes the first country officially to recognize cinema as an art in its own right, freed of the tyranny of numbers imposed by box office control, and with the status of, say, opera in Britain.' It is also true that young talent is now flourishing and that the Swedish cinema is no longer a one-man show. There is more to it than Ingmar Bergman.

Bergman's Poison Pills

The English film critic, Penelope Houston, wrote recently that Bergman, 'that rock on which so many critical toes have been stubbed . . . has the immeasurable advantage that behind him piles up a whole unshakeable tradition of film making.' His work is a logical extension of a cinema which had such giants as Sjöman and Stiller in the silent days and a master like Sjöberg, with whom Bergman worked as a youth, in modern times. A superb and imaginative craftsman, Bergman is less a film radical than a traditional, nationalistic, but fiercely creative writer–director. He has worked almost entirely in his own painstaking Swedish way with Swedish performers on themes which are so introspectively Swedish that a good many modern-minded Swedes find them embarrassing. They feel that God and the devil and the large, philosophical questions about life and death and suffering are more than a little old-fashioned for the contemporary cinema. Many Swedes dislike or fail to understand Bergman's work at the same time that they take pride in his international reputation.

That reputation is enormous. He shares the heights with only a handful of directors: Kurosawa of Japan, Satyajit Ray of India, Antonioni and Fellini of Italy, and a few others. When I called on Bergman one busy day at Stockholm's Royal Dramatic Theater, it was in order to talk mainly about the state of the international cinema. I found a trim, dark-haired, slightly bony man in his mid-forties, wearing a brown open-necked polo shirt with a brown suit. I have seen him at other times in the city hurrying about in a windbreaker and a wool beret.

In this first encounter, Bergman seemed, at the beginning, a little wary and hostile. He is not particularly fond of journalists. He claims that they have made too much of his rebellious boyhood and his love life (he has been married four times), and they keep on repeating those old stories about how he used to throw chairs through windows and tear telephones off walls during moments of rage in the studio. He has calmed down since then, but he still rules the set with the iron discipline of a Nordic Captain Bligh. 'He is an extremely possessive man,' said Harry Schein. 'It is better not to know him too well.' Although I have heard an associate call him a slave driver, it was said with affection. Bergman has been making films for two decades. He likes to work with the same performers and technicians, and he commands every aspect of his films from the first word he puts on paper to the decision whether to let them be released in countries which wield the censor's scissors.

Bergman was sitting behind a small desk in his sparsely furnished office in the ornate theater building. There wasn't much to it except the gray walls, green carpet, a few indifferent pieces of furniture and a full-length portrait of an old Swedish actor playing a role in *Pickwick Papers*. Two telephones and two bottles of mineral water stood on the desk. I sensed a shyness and a graciousness which wiped away the description of him as a cold, arrogant man. It seemed to me that he had too searching a mind and too great an understanding of human frailty to be truly arrogant. But he is unquestionably an intense and forceful personality. It was instructive to see that he still had a small-boy's enthusiasm for films.

'I think that the whole world of the cinema is going through an enormous revolution,' he said. 'I make a film as I write a book and as a painter does a painting. The more that the cinema moves away from being just an industry too much concerned with production and big profits, the more we will move to a personal expression of a point of view and a situation of life.'

Bergman's objection to many of the pictures being made today is that they are sloppily done. He said there is more to film making than going out on the streets with a shaky camera. 'But remember that the cinema is only sixty years old. Now it is starting to grow up and behave in a grown-up way. I have been in the cinema for twenty years and was fortunate to be present at the very beginning of the growing up. This is not so much a renaissance of films as a process of maturation. Of course, we have to educate the audience. It is our duty. At first you give the audience a pill that tastes good, and then you give them some more pills with vitamins but with some poison too. Very slowly you give them stronger and stronger doses. It is also my duty to entertain. You can never educate anybody by boring him. He must feel he is being entertained, and then when he is looking at the screen he must feel in his subconscious that "this speaks to me." I find that the younger generation is more receptive to good films now. It is a very slow process but it is a wonderful time to make pictures.'

A lot of people have found Bergman's pills, with or without poison, hard to swallow. They have seemed so heavy with symbolism, so befogging with misty messages of good and evil, so despairing with their questioning of belief in belief, that many a moviegoer has walked out in the middle of a film. Swedish pastors have denounced him from their pulpits. He has been accused of everything from puritanism to pornography. One critic cuttingly labeled him 'the best German director of the postwar cinema.' He has delved into the psychology of the female with rare insight and understanding, yet he has been labeled a misogynist. No film has ever captured the bittersweetness of young love better than *Summer Interlude*, but, like Strindberg, Bergman speaks of love as a kind of agony without end, just as life is without hope. Even when enlightenment and compassion finally come to the living dead, as they did to the old professor in *Wild Straw-berries* (played, incidentally, by elderly director Victor Sjöstrom), it doesn't do any good. 'He can't change,' Bergman says. 'I don't believe that people *can* change, not really, not fundamentally.'

So much of Bergman's films seem autobiographical that he has been accused of using the screen as his personal wailing wall, or confessional, so that the poor moviegoer gets nothing more out of it than one man's combat with his own wracked insides. But others, like Penelope Houston, say that 'he has taken us on a tour of the Swedish soul, so that no article purporting to explain that enigmatic country is now complete without its set of Bergman references.'

The Communicator

Ernst Ingmar Bergman was born in 1918 in the university town of Uppsala as the son of an Evangelical Lutheran parson who became the chaplain to Sweden's royal family. It was not only a sternly Swedish middle-class life, but also one of rigid moral rectitude which Bergman remembers with a heavy heart. But it was also a time of discovery of ways to escape the strait-jacketed life.

'When one is born and reared in the home of a minister,' Bergman has said, 'one has a chance at an early age to catch a glimpse behind the scenes of life and death. Father conducts a funeral, father officiates at a wedding, father performs a baptism, acts as a mediator, writes a sermon. The devil became an early acquaintance, and, in the way of a child, it was necessary to render him concrete. It was here the magic lantern came in, a little tin box with a kerosene lamp (I can still remember the smell of hot sheet metal) and the gaily colored glass slides. Little Red Riding Hood and the Wolf, among others. And the wolf was the devil, a devil without horns, but with a tail and wide, red jaws, strangely tangible, but still impalpable, the representation of evil and seduction on the nursery's flowery wallpaper.'

In spite of, or because of, this kind of environment, Bergman became a communicator—in written works, radio, television, and on stage and screen—who has grappled throughout his career with the Swedish difficulty of communicating emotion. In many of his films, Bergman attempts to cut through the barriers of silence and reach out to others with some faint words of love— some feeble transmission of human feeling and compassion. The thing to watch for in a Bergman film is that moment of awareness, that crucial instant when contact between two persons has finally been made.

Bergman attended Stockholm University, went into the theater, became a stage director at an early age and began his film career in 1944. He burst on the international scene a decade later with the release of such striking films as *Smiles of a Summer Night*, *The Seventh Seal*, *Wild Strawberries* and *Brink of Life*. And after them, *The Magician*, *The Virgin Spring*, *The Devil's Eye*, *Through a Glass Darkly*, *Winter Light*, *The Silence*, and *To Say Nothing of All These Women*. Anyone examining the whole of his career, including the fifteen other Bergman films, can only be astonished at his productivity and versatility. He has had his 'rose' and 'black' films, his psychological dramas and erotic comedies, his dream plays and matrimonial farces. All the talk about Bergman's soul searching has obscured his wit and puckish humor. His last film had as its theme song, *Yes, We Have No Bananas*.

Bergman has also pursued a second career in the theater, most prominently in the 1950s at the Malmö City Theater, one of the largest and most modern in all Europe, and from 1959 to 1966 at the Royal Dramatic Theater in Stockholm. Film Director Jörn Donner, author of *The Personal Vision of Ingmar Bergman*, calculates that between 1938 and 1962, in addition to his two dozen films, Bergman staged about seventy theatrical productions, some thirty radio drama productions and five television presentations. In short, as a colleague of Bergman's said, 'he has an enormous working capacity.' As Sweden's foremost film director and, simultaneously, chief of the leading theater in a country with a great stage tradition, Bergman has stood at the commanding heights of both stage and screen in Sweden, thus playing a cultural role which is unique in the world.

The New Breed

Ingmar Bergman's old-fashioned concern with metaphysical problems puts him in a class by himself, but it is striking how few Swedish directors have managed to deal with the more immediate problems of the contemporary society. The phenomenal changes in Scandinavian life during the last three or four decades, the whole development of a highly industrialized and urbanized society of increasing affluence, the celebrated welfare state itself—all these, and their impact on the human condition, would seem to be ripe topics for moviemakers, but, as one director confessed, it is hard to be passionately for or against the new society. The welfare state has simply become part of the Scandinavian scenery, accepted by almost everyone. It does not lend itself to extravagant praise or bitter denunciation. Alf Sjöberg once said that he envies the Italians for their social problems, the kind that gave life to such protest films as *Open City* and *Bicycle Thief.* The only stark social problem that the Swedes have been able to make something of is the wildness of some young people in a country which appears to be too secure and wealthy for their own good. Hence, there has been a rash of films, like *Raggare, Chance* and *491,* on Sweden's wayward youth.

The new breed of Swedish film directors—most notably Bo Widerberg, Jörn Donner and Vilgot Sjöman—edge into the larger issues of the wealthy welfare society by focusing on human relationships in an intensely personal way, with no holds barred on subject or treatment. The general impression that their movies give is of a way of life which is culturally and emotionally arid in the midst of an outpouring of material goods. Sexual matters are approached with such frankness that some of the films have brushed the border line of pornography. Unhappily, it often looks less like artistic courage than artistic poverty as sex becomes a substitute for ideas. Sjöman's film *491,* for example, is supposed to be a study of Stockholm juvenile delinquents and the ineptitude of the social workers who try to deal with them, but whatever message the film has is obscured by a blatant homosexual scene and by the versatility of a ripe little prostitute who is variously coupled with some drunken foreign sailors, assorted delinquents and a large dog. Most of the action in numerous other Swedish films is confined to bedrooms. An article on the subject in an English-language Swedish publication was aptly titled, 'Bed and Bored.'

So far, for reasons of size, resources and history, Sweden is the only Scandinavian country with a motion-picture industry of international importance. The Swedes thus perform, to some degree, as representatives on film of the Scandinavian world and the Scandinavian way of life. With the Swedish Film Institute in being, with all of its incentives for excellence, the new directors are likely to move up from the most obvious of Nordic clichés. The matter was succinctly stated in a Swedish cultural advertisement in the *International Film Guide, 1965*: 'Not all Swedish films are about sex and sin! Other aspects of Swedish life can be equally interesting!'

Part Five

Finland

Chapter 27

THE FATALISTS

We are only one jump from being a primitive people.
—FINNISH POLITICIAN

The Finns' tendency to live, financially and otherwise, with a certain confident recklessness has always been one of their most conspicuous and, to many people, attractive national characteristics. In addition, it is the trait that most noticeably sets them apart from their Nordic neighbors.
—JOHN BAINBRIDGE

Finland is Europe's odd man out. Its real name is Suomi. It is neither a member of the Western alliance nor a Soviet satellite. It is part of the Scandinavian community, but with certain qualifications. It is neutral like Sweden, but it is prevented from being a strongly armed neutral. Finland is a fiercely independent country, but its independence is compromised by the facts of life in its relationship with the Soviet Union. Although it has had democratic traditions for centuries, a fifth of the electorate votes Communist. Lodged in the cold northeastern corner of Europe, it is far removed from the mainstream of world affairs, yet it is peculiarly affected by the slightest changes in the political and economic policies of the great powers. It is the least advanced of the Scandinavian welfare states, yet it hums with prosperity and enjoys one of the ten best standards of living in the world. Above all, it is a stubborn, individualistic, indomitable, resilient, resourceful and courageous nation, magnificent in its loneliness.

The wonder is that there is a Finland at all. It has fought forty-two wars against Russia and lost every one. Time and again it has plucked survival from the jaws of defeat. It has been a completely independent nation for less than fifty years, but the Finns act as if they have always been free—and in many ways they have been. The Finnish nation endured during the more than six hundred years when it was a part of Sweden and during the century when it was a grand duchy of Russia. The Finns survived their own bitter civil war which came on the heels of the Soviet Revolution. They came out alive from the lopsided struggle in the Winter War with Russia in 1939–40. And somehow they emerged as free men from the hell of World War II, when they fell into an alliance with Nazi Germany, again fought the Russians and, at the end, suffered in Lapland the scorched-earth tactics of the Germans. Yet, strangely enough, Finland, apart from Russia and Great Britain, was the only European nation engaged in World War II which did not suffer occupation. Being on the losing side, however, cost Finland its second-biggest city and 12 per cent of its territory, and gave it the twin headaches of resettling 420,000 refugees and paying a staggering 500-million-dollar reparations bill from Moscow. Once again, the Finns persevered. They even turned adversity into advantage. The immense task of building up the nation's industrial plant to make the reparations material for Russia gave Finland equipment for a stronger, more diversified economy than it had ever known before.

Today Finland is the most prosperous and democratic of all the nations, from Poland and Czechoslovakia to Mongolia and North Korea, which live precariously on the borders of the Soviet Union. It is a glittering showcase for the free world. The brightness and vitality of Helsinki with its beautiful women, gleaming new buildings and bulging shop windows make a stunning rebuke to the drab conformity and sterile spirit of the neighboring Communist world. Finland is like a modern supermarket perched at the edge of a tired old neighborhood. Even those areas which still have a frontier flavor are impressive for their vitality. Leningrad, only a few hundred miles east of Helsinki, is a strange city, half museumlike and half built in Soviet obsolete-modern style. In contrast, Helsinki, although it has more of an Eastern flavor than the other Nordic capitals, is a thoroughly Scandinavian city.

Visit the parliament, call on the prime minister, shop at a cooperative store, eat at a roof-top restaurant, examine the inspired architecture, ogle the lovely girls lifting their faces to the sun—it is all Scandinavian. So is the industrial design, the trade-union movement, the employers' confederation, the housing subsidies, and the arguments about welfarism. Furthermore, there are high taxes, family allowances, athletics, abortions, equality, women's rights, cleanliness, honesty, a zeal for learning and a longing for summer. It is all Scandinavian, but with such a Finnish difference that it is an almost separate, unclassifiable society.

Scandinavia—With a Difference

Every assumption about the Nordic world must be re-examined in Finland. The Finns are a special people, and their singularity gives them an extraordinary presence on the Scandinavian scene. The Finns look a touch more Russian than the other northern peoples. Their cheekbones are set higher. They speak a language so different from the other Scandinavian tongues that it might as well be Uzbek or Gaelic. The fact that few people in the world outside Finland can understand what they say is a powerful factor in the sense of isolation that the Finns feel so deeply. And it helps account for the Finn's reputation as a man of few words. 'He doesn't say much because nobody understands what he has to say,' I was told by a foreign observer in Helsinki. Seven per cent of the Finnish population, however, is 'Swedish,' or Swedish-speaking, and Swedish is one of the country's two official languages.

Bilingualism is only one indication that Finland is a more divided and less harmonious society than the other Scandinavian nations. Not only is there a measure of antagonism between the Finns and the Swedish-Finns—largely because the latter have had a disproportionate amount of power and wealth—but between north and south, Left and Right, workers and capitalists, and between leaders in the same political parties, trade unions and even sporting organizations. The Finns are more combative, uncooperative and violent than their fellow Scandinavians. As already noted, their suicide rate in recent years has been the highest in Scandinavia. But perhaps the most startling statistics in the Nordic world are those which show that the Finns commit not only more murders and manslaughters than any other Scandinavians, but even more homicides, per capita, than any other Europeans.

According to United Nations statistics for 1962, there were only 16 homicides in Norway, 23 in Denmark, 43 in Sweden and 121 in Finland. Consequently, the homicide rates, on the basis of the number of homicides per 100,000 of population, were: Norway 0·4, Denmark 0·5, Sweden 0·6 and Finland 2·7. For purposes of comparison, some other rates were: The Netherlands 0·3, England and Wales 0·7, Japan 1·5, Australia 1·7, United States 4·8, Mexico 31·9 (1960 figure).

Every authority consulted says that there is an inescapable connection between the excessive consumption of hard liquor by some Finns and the high homicide rate, particularly because the country Finn has traditionally been as attached to his sheath knife, or *puukko*, as the Texan has been to his six-shooter. It is a combination tool and weapon, still widely used—and used in sudden moments of alcoholic anger. 'Even in our modern clothes,' said a Finnish sociologist, 'we are still an impulsive people.'

It is no surprise, then, that the Finns have more frequent economic crises, more strikes, and more passionate political controversies, than the Danes, Swedes or Norwegians. And yet in time of trouble they are almost fanatical in their patriotic togetherness. 'It is true of the Finns,' said the governor of Finnish Lapland, 'that when they have difficulties they grow strong, and when they have it easy they get quarrelsome.'

A Helsinki editor said that 'our politicians spend most of their time solving problems they have created themselves.' More succinctly, another Finn stated, 'We are good in peril, bad in peace.' Even in peril, the Finnish soldier has been described as the world's least disciplined and the least respectful of his superiors. The great Finnish World War II novel, *The Unknown Soldier,* is a candid chronicle of magnificent indiscipline by men who fought with stunning bravery, but not because they were told to. One passage in the book puts it this way: 'It is often said of an officer that he has "the unbounded admiration of his men," but actually it is never really true. The officer whom a Finnish soldier would boundlessly admire has yet to be born.' One foreign correspondent has noted that the Finns 'boast of indiscipline in their ranks. They are, like the Poles, the sort of people to use cavalry against tanks but, unlike the Poles, they would not expect to win.'

The differentness of the Finns on the Scandinavian scene is most immediately apparent in the fact that theirs is the only one of the four countries without a monarchy. Finland has a president instead, and he is the only Nordic head of state with real power in the day-to-day affairs of his country. Urho K. Kekkonen, in fact, is such a powerful figure that he is frequently described as a Nordic de Gaulle or Tito. Far from remaining above the political battle and letting the prime minister run the show, President Kekkonen masterminds the Agrarian Party, which until recently was the leading political group in the country and which now prefers to be known as the Center Party. He conducts the nation's foreign policy almost singlehandedly, and as a political wheeler-dealer he arouses the kind of emotional support and antagonism which Franklin D. Roosevelt once attracted in the United States.

As indicated, Finland, unlike the other Scandinavian countries, is not dominated by a Labor Party or a Social Democratic Party. It was, until 1966, the last nation in Europe to be led by an Agrarian Party, and yet the Social Democrats and the Communists together—the so-called socialist or nonbourgeois parties—draw half the votes in Finland. The anachronism of Agrarian leadership has become only too apparent in a rapidly urbanizing and industrializing country, and the political tide is running strongly in favor of the Social Democrats.

Although Finland is the least socialized of the Nordic countries in terms of lavish welfare programs and well-established economic planning, the state has taken a much greater portion of industry under its wing than in Sweden or Denmark. There is also a greater control of prices and a more feverish tinkering with the loudly backfiring economic engine. Finland's constant flirtation with financial disaster is largely due to a national propensity for living beyond its means. The Finns have had a larger appetite for social services, new industry and all manner of benefits and luxuries than they can afford. It is just such a daring and lighthearted approach to life, however, which sets the Finns apart from the more stolid Swedes, and even from the Danes and Norwegians. They live more dangerously. It is a kind of eat-drink-and-be-merry attitude of a people who know, from rueful experience, that tomorrow means trouble. When they drink, the Finns drink even more heartily and compulsively than the Norwegians. When they work, it is with a concentrated will. When they play, it is with a gay abandon. The Finns who go abroad—and tens of thousands now fly off to the Mediterranean or Canary Islands every winter in search of sunshine—act like millionaires and return home flat broke, but happy. 'This craziness is part of the Finnish character,' said H. O. Gummerus, the highly respected head of the Finnish Society of Crafts and Design. 'The Finn throws away a whole month's income on a single night's binge. In contrast, the Swede, if he's taking his girl out for the evening, knows exactly how much he can and will spend down to the last bus fare. The Swede always plans everything. The Finn seldom plans anything.'

Spartan Sophistication

The Finns are fascinating for their strange combination of primitiveness and sophistication. 'They are closer to the soil than any other people in Europe,' said a Helsinki businessman. 'The President himself is only one jump off the farm. At the drop of a hat every Finn in the city will go off to the country to live in a shack or ski all alone in the forests.' They often seem to be in revolt against the comforts of modern civilization. They put a high premium on all manner of Spartan virtues. They love to pit themselves against the elements and endure the worst that winter can offer. They bake like lobsters in the sauna and then plunge naked through a hole in the surface of a frozen lake. Their capacity for endurance was spectacularly demonstrated by 'the Flying

Finn,' Paavo Nurmi, now a successful businessman in his late sixties, who was the world's greatest medium and long-distance runner during the 1920s. He was a one-man show at the Olympics in Antwerp, Paris and Amsterdam, and held twenty-four official world records at distances ranging from the mile to the marathon.

Skiing, above all, is the national passion, even though Finland is notably short on hills. An American teacher in northern Finland said that 'skiing to the Finns is apple pie, mother and baseball. When the snow gives out they do it on pine needles.' Every year more than a million Finns participate in the ski competitions between towns or provinces and in the all-Nordic battles, which invariably see the Finns beating the Swedes and Norwegians. The object is to determine who, and which areas, can ski the greatest number of miles during a month or so. Some enthusiasts ski five hundred to a thousand miles in a winter. I was told that the participants at a recent competition in Kemi included 'five pregnant women, hundreds of children six years old and up, several eighty-year-old men, and a war veteran on one leg.'

Finland is, man for man, the greatest cross-country skiing country in the world. For skiers who are used to going uphill by some mechanical tow and then rushing swiftly downhill, cross-country seems at first too slow and arduous—the skier scuttles along on light, thin skis, working his legs like a pair of scissors—but in the mute forests there are immeasurable rewards in beauty and solitude. At present, Finland's greatest cross-country skier is Eero Mäntyranta, a Lapland border guard by profession, who won two gold medals in the 1964 winter Olympics at Innsbruck. Finland in all the Olympics since 1906 has won 101 gold medals, 92 silver and 108 bronze, an astonishing total for a small country.

But for all this concentration on robust disciplines, the Finns have a literacy rate which is among the very highest in the world, and they have such a reverence for books that it is not uncommon for a man to quietly boast that 'my grandfather was a peasant, but he had his own library.' There is an amazing addiction to newspapers. If all the newspapers which appear more than once a week are counted, then Finland has nearly 110 of them for a total circulation of two million, an impressive figure for a nation of

4·6 million persons. Finland's long history of popular education began in the seventeenth century, when the official Lutheran Church, anxious to have everyone understand the Bible, made a law of its own which practically forced everyone to learn to read and write. The penalty was loss of civil rights. Today there is a greater percentage of people receiving higher education in Finland than in any other Scandinavian country. The number of students has more than doubled since 1950 to more than 30,000, and Helsinki University, 325 years old, is the biggest in the North.

The Finnish thirst for education was wisely recognized by the United States government when it established the 'ASLA' scholarships to enable young Finns to continue their studies in America. The unusual program is an outgrowth of Finland's gilt-edged reputation as 'the country which pays its debts.' The United States lent Finland over nine million dollars immediately after World War I, and the Finns have been paying it off for more than forty years. Conceivably they could have settled the account long before this, but by making small annual payments they established Finland in the American mind as the only World War I debtor to consistently meet its obligations. In 1949 President Truman signed a bill which has made it possible for all the repayments and interest payments on the loan, which are to continue until the debt has been paid off in 1984, to be used to provide some sixty to seventy American scholarships to Finnish students each year and finance other Finnish-American cultural activities.

Finland has a host of outstanding writers, architects and composers to match its gallery of sports heroes. Finnish architecture and design is the most colorful and ingenious in Scandinavia, often with Italianesque flights of fancy of a kind rarely seen in Stockholm or Oslo. The Finnish theater is one of the best in Europe, and it goes deeply into the Finnish soul. Finland's social enlightenment is shown in its outstanding hospitals and housing projects, and in the increasing excellence of its medicine, which has reduced the number of infant deaths from 68 out of every 1,000 live births in 1938 to only 18 today. There is also an extraordinary degree of female emancipation in this land of rugged, forceful men : Finland was the second nation in the world after New Zealand, and thus the first in Europe, to give women full voting rights. Today women play a far more important role in public life than their counterparts in Scandinavia or in the rest of Western Europe.

If Finnish political life is marked by an unseemly rowdiness, the nation has achieved a praiseworthy and generally unrecognized level of subtlety and astuteness in its brittle relationship with the Soviet Union. It is the cool and nerveless approach of the soldier who has miraculously survived a long and bloody war against a vastly superior enemy. Such a soldier is no longer interested in hate or heroics; his capacity to endure is such that he can afford to try to understand what it is that motivates the enemy.

The Finns have a strong sense of separateness, of being at the end of the line, of knowing that they will have to stand alone if attacked. The conviction that no one will come to their rescue— as no one did during the Winter War—is at the root of a foreign policy which seeks to keep Russia at arm's length with one hand while offering a friendly handshake with the other. Despite the patently pro-Western inclinations of most Finns, the somewhat Eastward-leaning style of Finnish foreign policy as it walks a slippery tightrope has led some foreign editors to label Finland a Soviet satellite on their Cold War maps. A British headline in 1964 asked: 'Is Moscow the Capital of Finland?' All of which simply makes the Finns feel more lonely and misunderstood than ever. 'This is the forgotten country of Europe,' wrote one Helsinki journalist.

His exposed, isolated position has made the Finn the ultimate realist. He is a hard-shell fatalist. What will be, will be. 'It is ordered,' they say. A lot of idle chatter won't change conditions, so they have the habit of silence. Their silence is never more eloquent than on Independence Day every December, when thousands of students bearing torches march behind a wall of blue-crossed white flags through the streets of Helsinki. They stride by in absolute silence, their shoes and boots muffled in the snow. There are no bands, no blaring bugles or rolling drums. Just quiet marchers and grim-faced crowds on the sidewalks remembering all the pains of nationhood.

'These are a complicated and extraordinary people,' wrote Patrick O'Donovan in *The Observer* of London, 'who achieved independence only in 1917 and yet have a character and an identity and a history so different from their neighbors that it hurts. Not for them the somewhat bovine good order of their fellow Scandinavians. The best in Finland emerges not in adversity or in danger, but only when utter, irremediable and final disaster threatens. This is probably just as well, because few countries have been so tricked, betrayed, bullied, sold, deserted, exploited in recent times. And none have so wonderfully survived it all.'

Sisu

The quality which has made this possible is *sisu*. That is, guts, intestinal fortitude, the refusal to accept defeat. So much has been written about Finnish *sisu* that even the Finns are tired of the whole thing. Not every Frenchman is a lover, not every Englishman is a gentleman, and not every Finn is a hero on skis. Nonetheless, *sisu* is unavoidable when talking about the Finns. It is said that the Finns, when they learned in 1939 that they were at war with the Russians, who had fifty times their population, were so worried that they asked: 'Where will we be able to bury them all?'

A Finn told John Bainbridge of *The New Yorker* that 'if somebody knocks you down, and you know if you get up he'll knock you down again but you get up anyway, that's *sisu*.' A well-educated and entirely sane secretary in Helsinki told me about the time she met a young Swede. He teased her about *sisu* and said he doubted that the Finns had more courage or stamina than anyone else. 'If I put this lighted cigarette on your finger you would scream soon enough,' he said. She silently offered her finger. He slowly pressed the hot end of the cigarette on it, expecting her to draw it away. She didn't flinch or cry as her flesh sizzled. He raised the cigarette and muttered that 'anybody can do it once.' She turned her hand over and offered the other side of the same finger. He burned her again; still she showed no reaction. He finally admitted that there must be something to *sisu*.

She told me the story reluctantly and I believed it. The scars were still visible on her fingers; she had had to wear a bandage for some time. I said that I thought she was foolish and that he was no gentleman. 'Don't worry,' she said jovially, 'I told him that it was his turn. He wasn't happy about it but I touched him with the cigarette.' I asked how he had reacted. 'Well,' she said with satisfaction, 'he didn't scream but there were tears in his eyes.'

The story fits in neatly with the Finn's inclination to think of the Swedes as a little effete, not to mention stuffy, selfish and snobbish. The Finns love nothing better than getting one up on the Swedes. They still write about 'the famous Finland-Sweden Walking Contest in the spring of 1941, when everybody (including some hundred-year-olds and mothers with their seven or eight children) went out walking, and Sweden was overwhelmingly beaten.' The Finns go to great lengths—and successfully too —in order to come out ahead of the Swedes in the annual Nordic skiing competitions. But of course these flashes of superiority are dampened by a nagging feeling of inferiority. The Finns know Sweden is a richer, more accomplished and more mature nation. It hurts the national pride to know that in this era of a free labor market in Scandinavia, some 60,000 Finns have trooped over to Sweden to get better-paying jobs. At the same time, the Finn feels superior to the Russians, whom he is apt to think of as a bunch of unsanitary peasants, but he knows that Finland is greatly at the mercy of the Russians. It is no wonder that the Finns are schizophrenic. They are as moody and irascible as they are warm and generous. A gruff, blunt manner serves as a protective coating when they are in fear of seeming inadequate or ridiculous, or when they are just plain embarrassed, but it soon melts away.

The Existentialists

There is something enormously appealing about nations which have succeeded in preserving their identity after centuries of being menaced by more powerful neighbors. The Irish and the Koreans, for example, have a number of Finnish qualities, including a cheerful fatalism, sardonic good humor, love of a good time, and reckless stubbornness. They are all capable of wide swings from moroseness to gaiety and from the violent to the poetic. A sympathetic visitor to Finland is swept up in a round of drinking and gregarious conversation into the small hours of the morning. His host may have spent half of his month's pay on the festivities and will have to work twice as hard to make up for the loss of time and money, but that is a problem for tomorrow, not for the present. The friendliness and hospitality, once the ice is broken, can be so compelling that a visitor feels drawn into the emotional life of the Finns much more than in the rest of Scandinavia.

Like other beleaguered, unorthodox people, the Finns are fascinated with themselves. They delight in their own stories about their own special characteristics: stories which reinforce their strong sense of national pride; stories which help preserve the image of the phlegmatic Finn who finds fortitude in solitude. They tell, in many variations, the tale of the Finn who went north to stake out a piece of land for himself at the edge of the endless forest. One day he saw a piece of chopped wood floating down a river. Perceiving that a stranger had moved in, he picked up his axe, marched fifty miles until he found the intruder and killed him. He explained afterward that he didn't like to be crowded.

The legend of the silent Finn is preserved in the story of the farmer who was convinced that his son had been born deaf and dumb. Not a sound had escaped the boy's lips in twenty years. One day while they were working the fields together the young man broke his plow on a rock. 'Damn!' he said. The amazed father asked him why he hadn't spoken before. The son replied, 'I was waiting until I had something to say.'

The silent Finn is also the drinking Finn. A man who had gone off to America for forty years returned to his native village in Finland. He looked up a boyhood friend and took him off for a reunion over a bottle of cognac. An hour later, when they were working on their second bottle, the visitor asked, 'How's everything?' His home-town friend groaned, 'Hell, I thought we were going to drink, not make a lot of conversation.'

Although the dour, reserved Finn of great silence can be found all over the country, there are some notable regional variations. Along the west coast, for example, the Ostrobothnians are livelier and not so provincial as many of their countrymen. And in the east the people of Savo are cheerful and chatty while the Karelians, physically and temperamentally closer to the Russians, are dreamier, more poetic and more combustible. Within all Finns, however, there is, like a campfire in a cold forest, a glow of good humor even in the midst of adversity. 'We have seen that human life is not guaranteed,' said a Finnish professor, 'so we think perhaps it is better to take things with a more humorous attitude. We are not pessimists, but we do not have many illusions.' The story is told of the Savo man who was drunk at the reins and crashed his wagon into a ditch. His horse had disappeared by the time he finally woke up. 'If I am myself,' he muttered, 'I have lost a horse, but if I am somebody else, than I have found a darn good wagon.'

Chapter 28

GREEN GOLD

There is no fat in this country, nothing to spare.
—HELSINKI JOURNALIST

There is a summer life in Finland and a winter life. They are very different worlds.
—KAJ FRANCK

Finland, after Iceland, is the northernmost country in the world. President Kekkonen once told a group of visiting British business-men that the Finns only comprised 0·15 per cent of the world's population, yet of all the people living north of the 60th parallel (which runs just under Finland and Greenland), nearly 40 per cent are Finns.

It is one of the largest countries in Europe—bigger than Britain, West Germany or Poland—and almost exactly the size of Italy. From Helsinki on the southern shore to the northern border which meets the topmost knob of Norway, it is a stretch of more than seven hundred miles. Finland's frontier with the Soviet Union is nearly eight hundred miles long, more than any other nation except China and Mongolia. It is a forbidding, closely watched frontier, seldom crossed except in the summer, in the most remote corner of the Continent. For much of the year it is a silent world of snow and trees, the hush broken only by the swish of the border patrols on skis and the almost soundless movements of elk, bears, wolves and other forest animals. The rest of Finland's land frontier is friendly territory, shared with Norway and Sweden. The seacoast of almost seven hundred miles is washed by the Gulf of Finland and the Gulf of Bothnia. These are the waters of the Baltic Sea, the escape route to the Atlantic and Central Europe. Finland used to be locked in ice during the worst of a severe winter, but it has become the world's specialist in making powerful icebreakers which keep the sea lanes open.

In contrast to Norway and western Sweden, Finland is a flat, wet land with 60,000 lakes and some of the biggest marshes in Europe. The lakes, 'the blue eyes of Finland,' take up 9 per cent of the entire area. The rest seems to be nothing but outbursts of gray granite and 'green gold,' the vivid term for Finland's billions of trees. They are the country's greatest natural resource, accounting for nearly three quarters of its exports. The 54 million acres of forest cover more than two thirds of the entire territory. It is as natural to drive for hours through Finland and see nothing but trees and more trees as it is to see nothing but sand on a journey across the Sahara.

The 4·6 million Finns dwell in what is one of the most sparsely populated nations on earth. Most of them still live in the country, or in rural areas close to the towns. Only a third of the Finns are true city dwellers. Although Helsinki has half a million people, and Tampere and Turku are the only other cities with more than 100,000 inhabitants. And yet it is the cities of Finland which are most memorable of all to an outsider, once he gets used to the constant backdrop of forests and lakes. The cities gleam like rare white stones on green felt. Before the First World War many Finnish towns, with their rough wooden buildings, unpaved streets, and clouds of dust raised by the horse carts, looked like Siberian villages. Their drinking water was transported in barrels. Today those same towns are showplaces of modern Finnish design. Finland still shows traces of its old way of life, however. While few real slums can be seen, there are greater ramshackle sections in the less-developed cities of Finland than elsewhere in Scandinavia. Crude log cabins, often not much larger than the huts used for fodder, are scattered about the countryside, and gnarled old peasants in black boots walk about in the market places of the larger cities.

The New Look

The old Finnish way of life is fast disappearing, under the impact of new apartments, factories, office buildings, bridges, schools, sports palaces, theaters, observation towers, hydroelectric dams, and the new highways built under a road construction program which consumes a tenth of all public expenditures. Finland is a country of bold city planning, forceful architecture, and a fondness for monumental expression. The wartime razing of northern Finland permitted towns like Rovaniemi to rise up brightly as entirely postwar cities, while other places, like Vaasa and Kuopio, are full of stunning new buildings which seem to have come straight from the pages of an architectural magazine. Leading Finnish architects, particularly Alvar Aalto, have been given tremendous opportunities to change the face of the nation and make it as modern as any in the world. A city like Lahti is so up-to-date and pulsing with activity that it is known as 'the most American' town in Finland. Tapiola, the famous suburban community outside Helsinki, is possibly the most intelligent and attractive project of its kind in the world. Finnish apartment buildings and shopping centers are clever and cheerful. The great paper mills, pulp plants and engineering factories are well designed, and their equipment is strikingly up-to-the-minute. One paper mill I visited in Imatra, close to the Soviet border, used remote television cameras to keep track of production, while IBM computers hummed and clicked in an inner sanctum.

The Finns live in a cold and distant attic of Europe, and even their Scandinavian neighbors are inclined to think of them as only half-civilized. (An American sociologist who spent a year teaching in Denmark said that a number of Danes had insisted to him that the Finns, when they run out of potato alcohol, drink shoe polish.) The Finns understandably grumble about their reputation for primitiveness. As William Sansom wrote in *The Icicle and the Sun*:

Finland has long been thought too remote. Too easily it is thought of as a vague sort of shadow-place where there are endless forests and people playing dangerous games with knives and keeping endless silence between long vodka-bouts and longer Karelian bear-hunts . . . and only nowadays, with the established prevalence of air-travel, may the grumble at last be allowed to fade, and a delightful and progressive country permitted no longer to be remote, a whole peculiar people cease to be a geographical phantom.

It was air travel which first took me to Helsinki to report on an international Lutheran conference. My second visit took me by train and car to Lapland in the dead of winter to spend a week trailing Finland's cross-country skiers as they prepared for the Winter Olympics of 1964. I have since entered Finland by car at the very top of the country and by ship from Sweden in order to explore the west coast. It takes a lot of movement about the generally unchanging Finnish landscape to realize how many regional differences there are, and how the ultramodern lives check by jowl with the charmingly old-fashioned. Many Finns are intensely Nordic blue-eyed blonds, but there are a startling number of dark-haired people who are less tall and handsome than their Scandinavian neighbors.

The great bulk of the population lives in the south, where most of the industry is located and where the climate is more agreeable. The north, although lightly populated, is still plagued with unemployment problems, and the Communist Party has widespread support. Finns in general, with memories of real poverty still fresh, are living better than ever. The farmers have tractors and have made the country agriculturally self-supporting. Television has spread across the land, and Finns are beginning to buy automobiles at an ever faster pace. There are few luxuries, yet the Finns have learned the art of living comfortably. Their homes, often full of books and splendidly designed furnishings and kitchenware, are sturdy and warm.

It is just as well. Finland is not a warm country. On the other hand, it is not so buried in snow as some people imagine. Helsinki is only four or five degrees colder than Oslo and Stockholm during the winter, and just as warm in the summer. The Gulf Stream spreads its influence to Finland as it warms up Norway, and there are some helpful air currents to lessen the chill. Nonetheless, northern Finland is colder than the stretch of Norway which lies above it. Although it is possible for Helsinki not to have a white Christmas, most of Finland is laden with snow five months of the year, and for seven months in the north. Everyone, needless to say, skis. Boys ride their bicycles to school across frozen rivers and lakes. Housewives and grandmothers go shopping by pushing a simple snow scooter which looks like a kitchen chair on thin steel runners. Car and bus drivers, scorning chains, speed expertly on hard snow roads. It can get so cold in some places, as a luckless foreign scholar in Kemi said, 'that your engine can freeze solid in mid-stroke.'

Finland has a 'snow-forest climate,' and in the north the big freeze can last from October to May. It was a German visitor who is supposed to have said that 'the year in Lapland has nine months of winter, and for three months people wait for summer.' But summer does come, in time, to all parts of Finland, and it is greeted with all the joy of prisoners being released on parole. People rush to the steps of the Great Church in Helsinki to bask in the first rays of the spring sun. Finnish girls, who have been buried in their fur coats all winter, emerge like butterflies from cocoons.

Kaj Franck, a foremost Finnish designer, in noting the day-and-night difference between the summer life and the winter life of Finland, said 'Maine and Vermont may have the same climate as we have, but at least they have some variations in the light conditions. Many people like myself hate the endless grayness of winter. When the snow comes, you feel it will never go away. We go into hibernation. There is a terrible feeling of finality.'

Lapland

It is in that third of the nation known as Lapland that the winter bears down hardest and longest. The darkness lasts for almost two months. A pale moon stands at attention in the sky and the Northern Lights play a bit of magic. Eventually, the sun appears. It shines almost horizontally on the snow, which seems to murmur with assorted colors instead of shining whitely. Finally, there is nothing *but* sun, and a 1,752-hour day (73 days of ceaseless sun). 'We sleep about ten hours a night during the winter,' an engineer at the Arctic Circle said, 'and about six hours in the summer.' When the weather turns warm the mosquitoes and gnats appear. Hundreds of millions of logs drift south on the thawed-out rivers.

Lapland is a wilderness of trees, lakes and swamps; it easily absorbs the 200,000 Finns who live there. It is Finland's Wild West, or Wild North, with less than 5 per cent of the nation's population and an area larger than Belgium, Holland and Switzerland together. One dark October evening, after having spent a month bouncing along Norwegian roads, I drove into Finnish Lapland at Utsjoki. A lonely ferryman moved my car across a river in the blackness, muttering to himself about fool foreign motorists who drive about in the night. The border ceremony was a simple wave of the hand. Suddenly I was in Finland and driving on a smooth road which ran straight south through menacing forests. The road was covered by an inch of snow but there were no tire tracks to be seen. It was not the busiest highway in Europe. Like an ant making its way alone through a deep-pile rug, I drove for an hour and a half through an endless forest without seeing another automobile or any sign of life save a frightened hare which leaped before my headlights. Eventually there were a few other cars and an occasional cabin, and it was with considerable relief that I came to a rest house in the Lapp town of Inari. The snow was deepening and I was down to my last few drops of gasoline. A café adjoining the inn was throbbing with life as the local Lapps, small, coarse-skinned and bandy-legged, sat around tables telling stories and drinking great quantities of beer.

The next day's long drive to Rovaniemi just south of the Arctic Circle was a passage through a somber countryside of steel-blue lakes, purple bogs, wet reindeer moss and birch trees. Here and there, like dying embers, the final colors of autumn flashed in the green depths. Lapland seemed as moody as a symphony by Sibelius. It ached with loneliness. This was Finland as old as time, but then came Rovaniemi, the capital of Finnish Lapland, which was newness itself.

Rovaniemi

The all-modern, totally planned city just below the Arctic Circle springs out of the natural wildness of the north like a white bird in a thicket flapping its wings for take-off. One writer called it 'a great gleaming phoenix with concrete feathers.' As you drive across the new bridge into the new business center, you can feel the city growing on all sides. Rovaniemi used to be a simple market town where the Lapps brought their reindeer skin, dried fish and assorted homemade goods to trade for food and manufactured articles. By World War II it had about 8,000 inhabitants living mostly in wooden buildings. Then, as the Germans retreated from Finland in 1944 and scorched the earth behind them, Rovaniemi was all but erased from the map. 'The Germans were, as usual, thorough,' said a Rovaniemi official. 'They destroyed everything, even the sewing machines.'

The Finns who had been driven out of Lapland by the fighting returned. They picked their way through the rubble and built anew. Rovaniemi recruited Alvar Aalto to draw up a master plan for the city. Within seven years Rovaniemi was restored to its former size, but it had an entirely new look of broad avenues and solidly constructed buildings. The town just kept on growing, and today it has 25,000 persons. As a service and administrative center for Lapland, Rovaniemi has had a magnetic attraction. Aalto's original city plan was soon out of date. 'He had no way of knowing that we would have three times the population and a big traffic problem,' said a city architect. The planners are now figuring on a growth of another 10,000 persons in the next decade, and 300 automobiles for every 1,000 persons. Even if Rovaniemi took in no new settlers, it would still expand. The birth rate in the north of Finland is about double that of the south. One visitor asked a local official, 'What do you do in the summer in Lapland?' He was told, 'We fish and make babies.' The visitor then asked, 'What do you do in the winter?' Answer: 'Well, we don't fish.'

The energetic, bald-headed Governor of Lapland, Martti Miettunen, a former prime minister, has been head man in northern

Finland since 1958. 'No one dared imagine that it would go so well, that we would make such rapid development,' he said. The fact that three of the nine members of parliament from Lapland are Communists is a sign that all is not contentment, but there is no doubting the large-scale effort to give the north a better living standard. It is an uphill struggle because of the limited job possibilities and the highly seasonal character of employment. There are only a few months for a small farmer to make something grow in the stubborn soil, and then he turns into a lumberjack in the winter. In the days before the war the development of northern Finland was thought of largely in terms of the Arctic Highway which ran from Rovaniemi through a corridor between Norway and Russia to Petsamo, an ice-free port west of Murmansk on the Arctic Ocean. This large piece of northern territory was lost to the Russians. With it went Finland's outlet to the northern waters, a fledgling fishing industry, an important power station, a valuable mine, much of the Arctic Highway, and a number of settlements. The development aim today is to give the north a more diversified economy so that settlers will not be so totally dependent on the timber trade. It is subject to severe fluctuations as the international demand for paper and pulp products rises and falls. Another aim is to exploit the area's natural resources of minerals and water power.

Turku

Finland's major ports on the Bay of Bothnia—Kemi, Oulu, Vaasa, Pori—become ice-bound during the winter. At Turku in the southeast corner of Finland a fleet of seagoing bulldozers labors valiantly to keep open a sea lane through the spectacular archipelago which fans out toward the Åland Islands and Stockholm.

The Swedish name for Turku is Åbo, and it is a city heavily influenced by Sweden even though Swedish-speaking Finns are now just 8 per cent of its 135,000 population. It was Finland's capital during the centuries of Swedish rule. The famous castle in Turku, almost seven hundred years old, is bloody with history, including the time in the sixteenth century when its chief prisoner was Sweden's insane King Erik XIV. The castle is an imposing but hardly beautiful building. Its blank-faced stone exterior led one writer to compare it to 'an enormous block of flats or a badly maintained corn store.' It has survived repeated guttings, however, including a Russian air raid in 1941, and has been ingeniously restored to a 'living castle' which is alive with parties, banquets and music festivals. There is not much else of the past in Turku. Time and again the city suffered great fires and then was almost totally destroyed by the 1827 fire which probably was the worst in Scandinavian history. It caused the removal of Turku's university to Helsinki, and with it went the focal point of the nation's cultural life. Turku had already ceased to be Finland's capital in 1812. Sweden had surrendered Finland to Russia three years earlier, in the aftermath of the Napoleonic Wars, and the Tsar wanted to move the Finnish capital closer to St. Petersburg. Turku is now Finland's third-largest city, busily making everything from ships and textiles to ceramics and candy. Two outstanding universities, a great concert hall and a stunningly modern theater give the city a deep cultural tone.

Tampere

The tone in Tampere, about a hundred miles northeast of Turku, is much more industrial. With a population of 150,000, the city is now almost double its prewar size. A number of unusually tall factory chimneys soaring above Tampere seem to confirm that this is 'the Manchester of Finland,' but it is a wildly inaccurate comparison. It may make metal products, shoes, textiles, paper and scores of other goods in 420 industrial plants, but it is a working city amazingly free of grime and ugliness. It sits between a pair of lakes in an area bounded by forest. It is a clean-lined city with a new ice-skating 'palace,' new housing projects sprouting all around, and a striking new central hospital, the biggest in Finland.

Tampere started to become one of the biggest textile centers in northern Europe in 1828, when a Scotsman opened the first cotton mill. As a working-class city it gives most of its votes to the

Social Democrats and the Communists, but it is hard to tell a factory hand from a financier on the elegant downtown streets. In any event, Tampere citizens of all kinds flock to the city's five professional theaters. In the Tampereen Teatteri I saw *West Side Story*, a skillful, highly professional piece of work despite the built-in difficulty of turning husky blond Finns into dark and wiry Puerto Ricans. The theater was full of nicely dressed factory workers and their wives and husbands. Their employer had bought up all the seats for the evening and arranged to transport them from their homes in buses.

The most unusual theater in Tampere, however, is the famous Pyynikki Open Air Theater. It is beautifully sited at the side of a lake where the trees and water make a natural backdrop to the performances. Its most celebrated attraction is a revolving auditorium, an elliptical bowl which swings its 800 seated occupants around to face a variety of scenes on its perimeter. As a kind of reverse theater-in-the-round, with the audience moving around en masse in the center, it was a sudden, fantastic success when it opened in 1959. Thousands of Finns from all over the country, and then a tide of foreigners, went to Tampere for the short mid-June–to-mid-August theater season. The outstanding hit, repeatedly performed, has been a dramatization of *The Unknown Soldier,* whose author is a native of Tampere. It is the perfect subject for the open-air theatre since the action—the war with the Russians in the Karelian forests—is almost entirely outdoors. It is surely the only play in the world which has used a real airplane to conduct an air raid on the actors.

Land of Lakes

Finland is a watery world unlike anything I have ever seen. The Finns see it from their sailboats and skiffs or from the deck of those tubby white steamboats which chug about Saimaa Lake near the Soviet border. There are now a few hydrofoil passenger boats which flash about what has been described as 'the most optical landscape in the world.' In the winter the lakes freeze and offer themselves as icy roads strong enough to hold a truck, a tank or a regiment. Although 60,000 is the figure given for the number of lakes in Finland, they are not easy to count. The British geographer Roy Millward observed that 'they possess some of the most intricate shorelines on the face of the earth, with deep penetrating inlets and hundreds of forest-clad peninsulas.' The maze of lakes, some of them heavily sprinkled with islands like confetti in a puddle, is most outstanding in the southeast. It holds in its wet embrace the basic peasant culture of Finland, comparable to the folk culture of the central Norwegian valleys and the Dalarna region of Sweden. In his *Scandinavian Lands*, Millward wrote:

> Here, amid the quiet forests, a peasant culture survived into the twentieth century, practising methods of farming and forest burning that were much more widespread in Europe a millennium ago. For centuries this region has stood for the other half of the nation, a part different from the coastal plain with its Swedish-speaking towns and its outlook across the surrounding seas. The peasant culture of the lakes plateau helped to preserve Finnish as a living language, and deeper still, its folk tales, gathered together in the great legend of the *Kalevala*, represent the prehistoric roots of the modern Finnish nation.

During my first visit to this area, my Finnish companion remarked: 'Just think of the poor Russians trying to attack in this place. It's nothing but swamps and hills. They would have to use the roads, and we would be waiting.' It was in this same area that a Danish writer on a train between Lappeenranta and Savonlinna asked a Finn to tell him when they came to the border. 'Now,' said the Finn, 'now we are so close to the frontier that one could spit into the Soviet.' He quickly added, 'Which one doesn't, of course.'

Helsinki

In the heart of Helsinki an assertively modern building called the Marski announces that it is a *hotell* (in Swedish) and a *hotelli* (in Finnish). Its dimly lighted lobby is hushed and elegant. The clink of glasses can be heard in the cocktail lounge, and expensively dressed Finns and foreign guests make their way downstairs, past the frowning doorman, to the M Club, an after-hours gathering place for the well-heeled and well-employed of Helsinki (a leading banker said that '90 per cent of the M Club members are on expense accounts'). Breathtakingly beautiful women, suave diplomats and tired tycoons dance into the small morning hours or sink into the black-leather womb chairs as the band plays the mambo. This is what a tourist folder must have meant when it denied that Helsinki was dead after midnight: 'You can carouse till cockcrow, if you can keep going that long!' It is *la dolce vita* with a Finnish accent, an upholstered refuge for the sophisticated in a land of lumberjacks. But what is it that covers an entire wall of the M Club? Nothing less than a colossal photographic mural showing logs careening along a rapid which surges through the inevitable, inescapable Finnish forest.

It is one more demonstration that the Finn is determined to remain himself the more he prospers and mingles with the outside world. Helsinki is today one of the most attractive and affluent capitals in Europe, but it is still delightfully and unmistakably Finnish. In the morning, the market place by the sea front is full of farmers and fishwives selling their produce, but by early afternoon it is magically emptied out and swept up with not a fish scale or a potato eye in sight. The Helsinki restaurants, which run the international gamut from French to Indonesian, serve such Finnish delicacies as reindeer steak, pancakes with cloudberry jam, Karelian rice pie, and, in season, delicious heaps of crayfish.

Helsinki has many public parks and its ball-game fields are often used for *pesäpallo*, a Finnish variation of baseball. It has been described as a game in which the catcher pitches, the batter is 'wounded' if his fly ball is caught, and out if he hits a home run. Despite the overwhelming Finnish preference for Western products, about half the taxis in Helsinki are Russian-made.

Helsinki is a place where a summer or winter weekend will see the city emptied out, as if struck by the plague, as tens of thousands of families go off to hike or ski in the surrounding countryside. Many people simply strap on their skis at the front doors of their apartment houses and go off through the city streets. In midsummer the wives and children disappear to set up housekeeping in a lakeside hut while the husbands stay in Helsinki and fight off the temptation (often unsuccessfully) to amuse themselves with girl friends. There are something like 1,360 women to every 1,000 men in Helsinki, a fact of life which gives it a certain spontaneous combustion. Most of the barbers are girls, and in scores of saunas throughout the city, muscular middle-aged ladies in white smocks busily massage the kinks out of tired businessmen.

If Copenhagen is gay, Oslo wholesome and Stockholm dignified, then Helsinki is a mixture of all three, even though it is a small city as European capitals go. It behaves, however, like a big city. It is the country's biggest manufacturing center and the heart of almost everything else. It has no fewer than twelve theaters, and at the time of writing work is under way on what is likely to be the most original and radically designed theater in the world. There are dozens of shops in Helsinki which could easily hold their own on Fifth Avenue or Bond Street. Stockmann's, for example, is one of the truly great department stores in the world, a century-old institution in the center of Helsinki. Its massive reddish-brown building looks as solid as Fort Knox, and its 'Academic Book Store', with twelve miles of bookshelves, probably has the greatest offering of foreign books of any store anywhere. Stockmann's not only opens its doors to one tenth of Helsinki's population on its busier days, but also supplies the diplomatic and foreign press corps in Moscow with everything from baby carriages and transistor radios to pianos and Christmas trees.

An ambitious Aalto design for an ultramodern civic center will go far to make Helsinki a mecca for city planners. There are even plans for a subway. Almost surely, the city is trying to live beyond its means. If so, it is in character for Finland. It has an appealing bravado. Despite the troubles it has known, it is a spirited, optimistic and fast-growing metropolis.

Helsinki, or Helsingfors, to use its Swedish name, was ruthlessly founded more than four centuries ago, in 1550. In that year, King Gustavus Vasa of Sweden ordered the citizens of four towns to pack up and move to a new place on the rapids of the Vantaa river, where he wanted a port. He hoped to attract trade from Tallin just across the Gulf and thus break the grip of the Hanseatic League. (Helsinki and Tallin, capital of Estonia in the Soviet Union, have had little contact in recent years, but it is now pos- sible for them to pick up each other's television programs, and a ferry service opened in 1965.) Helsinki grew up in the shadow of Turku (Åbo) until Finland became a grand duchy of the Russian empire and Tsar Alexander I made it the capital in 1812. A devastating fire in 1808 had destroyed so much of the old wooden city that it was possible to start fresh on a grand scale. A young German architect, Ludvig Engel, created the Great Square and its surrounding buildings in the neoclassical style which sets Helsinki apart from the other Scandinavian capitals. And then the Turku fire in 1827 shifted the cultural center of Finland to Helsinki.

Those were the days when wolves roamed by the thousands in the eastern regions and during the winter bears invaded the forests at the fringe of the city. Despite its new importance, Helsinki had only 100,000 inhabitants by 1900. It led a nation still poor, still largely primitive, still smarting under Russian authority despite the large measure of self-government. But there has been a great population growth in the last half century. There were 320,000 residents at the outbreak of World War II, and today the popula- tion is 500,000. The city has growing pains. There is a housing shortage, but it is not so severe as Stockholm's. Somehow the city has found the resources to build the outstanding suburban communities and new schools which have attracted world atten- tion.

It is a sea city, with a pleasing body of water at every turn and a harbor bright with white liners, merchant ships and billowing sailboats. Visitors who arrive by ship are often awed at the white- ness of the 'White City of the North.' The skyline is dominated by the green-and-gold dome of the Lutheran Cathedral, which Engel designed. To one side, close to the Aalto-designed head- quarters of the Enso-Gutzeit company, the onion domes of an Orthodox church are reminders of Finland's Russian past. The charming town hall close to the water's edge has more in common with an aristocrat's manor house than with any of the tall, red-brick town halls of the other Scandinavian capitals. The massive President's Palace, for all its imposing lines, is memorable mainly for the sentries, whose gray uniforms, black boots and coal-scuttle helmets have a disturbing resemblance to those worn by the armies of Nazi Germany. The whole Engel-designed area around the Great Church—Senate Square, the library, the university and government buildings—has a classical dignity and a unity which one writer, Edward Maze, has rightly called 'a stupendous architectural achievement without counterpart in the North—it's hard to believe that it existed, in such mammoth proportions, when Helsinki was a mere wisp of a town.' Helsinki, therefore, is like Dublin, whose gracious Georgian squares and stately buildings are surprising to find in a small country's small capital.

What is missing, yet hardly missed, in this Scandinavian metropolis are the palaces, royal institutions, royal guards and other signs of monarchy. Instead, Helsinki has raised statues in honor of generals, athletes and ordinary workers, and it has done its parliament, post office, national museum and other public buildings on a monumental scale. The most famous Helsinki building is Eliel Saarinen's great brick railway station, in the dramatic arches and fluted lines of pre–World War I national romanticism. And the best-known modern work in spare, functional lines is the Helsinki Stadium, built for the 1940 Olympic Games, which had to be canceled because of the war. The stadium was finally used in the 1952 games. Like the Tokyo Olympics of 1964, which were so meaningful to the Japanese, those games were important events in the life of the country, because they marked the return of Finland to full membership in the international family of nations. The burden of reparations had finally been overcome, the early postwar austerity was relaxing, and better times were clearly on their way.

Chapter 29

SUBLIME FINLAND

The frontier opens like a rift in the ice,
Before us Asia, the East,
Behind, the West and Europe,
I, the guard, protect it.

           —UUNO KAILAS

Finland alone—in danger of death, superb, sublime Finland!—
shows what free men can do.

           —WINSTON CHURCHILL

The weapon brandished by the lion on Finland's coat of arms is, as a Finnish editor explained, 'the straight sword of the West as he tramples upon the scimitar of the East. The arms are thus symbolic of outpost Finland, standing against the might of Novgorod and Moscow.'

The history of Finland is a long and anguished one, beginning in the heart of pre–Tsarist Russia and continuing today at the nervous shoulder of Soviet Russia. The Finnish-Russian relationship has been a breathtaking cat-and-mouse rivalry, with the mouse always losing the chase and ending up in the cat's jaw, but somehow never quite getting swallowed. 'There are similarities in our history and also differences,' said President Kekkonen to visiting British Prime Minister Harold Macmillan in 1963. 'Whereas Britain is known to lose every battle but the last, Finland has followed the opposite method. It seems that for a nation with vitality either way is possible.'

The Finns were originally part of a nomadic tribal culture roaming about the Volga river territory west of Russia's Ural

471

mountains. These hunters, trappers and fishermen migrated westward and then split up. One group moved toward the warmer and more bountiful lands of the Hungarian plain, emerging in recorded history as the Magyars, or Hungarians. The other group selected the harder conditions around the eastern end of the Baltic Sea. Some stayed below the Gulf of Finland and became the Estonians. The rest pressed northward, past Lake Ladoga, the greatest lake in all Europe, and into what they called Suomi, or Finland. As they settled down several centuries after the birth of Christ, they forced the native Lapps farther to the north.

This exodus from the Russian interior placed in Finland a people speaking a language wholly separate from the tongues of the Slavs, Teutons and Norsemen who surrounded them. Finnish today is identified as a member of the Finno-Ugrian family, totaling about 18 million people, who include the Hungarians, Estonians and scattered minorities in Russia. The Soviet Union's absorption of Estonia and its crushing of the 1956 revolution in Hungary were events which the Finns took personally, and which made them more wary than ever of Russian intentions.

The awareness of being a distinct and separate race is the key to the survival of the Finns in the thousand years and more of rivalry in the Baltic lands. The Russians in their early years of statehood repeatedly attacked the Finns in order to get a greater foothold on the Baltic shores. The Swedes were ambitious as well, and more successful. Erik IX, Sweden's patron saint, moved into Finland in 1157 to convert the pagan Finns to Christianity and expand Swedish territory. An Englishman, Bishop Henry, helped to lead the Christian mission, but this energetic apostle, according to one account, 'was cut down by an irritated and pagan peasant called Lalli, who took an axe to him when he was crossing a frozen lake.' Tacitus had already written that 'the Finns are extremely wild.' Bishop Henry, as the first martyr in Finland, was made the patron saint of the Finns. It is hardly surprising that it took a while to make good Christians of the Finns, much less loyal subjects of Greater Sweden.

Swedish Rule

The Swedes only slowly, and never in great numbers, colonized Finland. Even then they stuck to the coastal areas closest to Sweden. Finland became one of the provinces of Sweden in 1362, an unusual distinction for a captured land and one which gave it the right to take part in Swedish royal elections. In 1556 Gustavus Vasa made Finland a grand duchy and installed his son John as the first grand duke. Over the six and a half centuries of Swedish rule, Finland took on a coating of Swedish culture and the super-structure of Scandinavianism. The Swedish legal system, the idea of constitutional government, and innumerable social and political institutions turned Finland into a Nordic nation with democratic and humanistic attitudes practically identical with those of the Danes, Norwegians and Swedes. Since Finland as a political vacuum almost necessarily had to come under the control of one of the larger Baltic nations, the Finns were fortunate to have Swedish rulers. They were never serfs, not even in the dark days of European feudalism, and they benefited from the economic development initiated by the Swedes. It is true, as one account puts it, that 'the country was ruled almost entirely by a privileged, overbearing, arbitrary Swedish nobility,' but in time many of the colonizers turned into Swedish-Finns, more at home in Finland than in Sweden.

Like the Englishmen who settled in the American colonies, they began to resent dictation from across the water and turned their thoughts toward independence. Henrik Gabriel Porthan, an Åbo Academy professor, wrote the first Finnish-language grammar and argued that Finland was a separate historical entity. Johan Ludvig Runeberg became Finland's great patriotic poet. Philosopher-statesman Johan Wilhelm Snellman championed Finnish national-ism. And Adolf Ivan Arwidsson, a poet and historian, cried out: 'Swedes we are no longer. Russians we cannot become. We must be Finns.'

During the centuries of rule by Stockholm, the Finns spent one sixth of their time fighting the Russians. The Karelian territory north and east of what is now Leningrad was a veritable revolving door for armies coming and going. The Finnish-speaking population of Karelia was cut in two as early as 1323, and it has been split almost all the time since then. The five wars between Sweden and Russia between 1570 and 1809 not only made Finland a battleground, but also drew on Finland's young manhood to serve as troops in the Swedish armies. Finland was worst hit during the Great Northern War of 1697-1718—the Finns called it 'The Great Wrath'—when the Cossacks of Peter the Great swept across the country and left it soaked in blood. The horror was so great, and famine and pestilence so widespread, that Finland lost more than 100,000 people, or a quarter of its population. Even so, the Russians settled for just a slice of Finland's southeastern territory. Sweden still ruled Finland, but the end was in sight for the Swedish empire.

Russian Rule

In 1807, Tsar Alexander I and Napoleon signed a secret agreement which gave Imperial Russia a free hand to annex Finland. It was a precursor of the Nazi-Soviet Pact of 1939, which gave Stalin the assurance that he could assert control over Finland without interference from Hitler. Alexander found an excuse to invade Finland. The war lasted for a year and a half and ended in September 1809, after Swedish forces had been driven into the northern wilderness. Sweden signed away the whole of Finland and the Åland Islands. Even before the end of the fighting, Tsar Alexander took some surprising steps to convince the Finns that life would be better under Russian rule. In a fit of generosity, he swore that they would have more rights, privileges and self-government as citizens of a Russian grand duchy than they had had under Swedish rule. He would reign as the constitutional Grand Duke of Finland. The Lutheran Church, the Swedish-based legal system, and the established rights and privileges—all would continue and be safeguarded. The Tsar even appeared in person before the Finnish Diet to grant a charter to the Finnish people and repeat his promises to give them virtual self-government. The benign policies of Alexander led to wholesale tax reduction, exemption from service in the imperial army, and the return to Finland of its southeastern territory, including the important city of Viipuri (Vyborg). The Finns were granted a special kind of citizenship unknown elsewhere in the sprawling Russian empire. It was a tribute to the relatively high stage of development achieved in Finland. As the Tsar said himself, the intention was 'to give this people political conditions such as will cause them to consider that they have not been conquered by Russia but have allied themselves with her for their own obvious advantage.'

The actual amount of self-government and special privileges permitted the Finns during the nineteenth century depended on which tsar was in power, but on the whole it was unusually liberal treatment by the autocrats of St. Petersburg. The Finns were allowed to have a separate currency, to use Finnish and Swedish, instead of Russian, as the national tongues, and to initiate legislation in the Diet in Helsinki. But even these favors were not enough to dampen the rising fever of nationalism. The publication in 1835 of the folk epic, the *Kalevala*, went far to make the Finns conscious of their national heritage and to inspire them to agitate for greater independence.

Toward the end of the nineteenth century the Russians became alarmed about the boiling up of Finnish nationalism and set in motion a policy of Russification. Russian was declared the official language in some branches of government and Russian-born civil servants were fitted into key posts in Finland. A new tsar, Nicholas II, gave the orders for a period of reaction which wiped out most of the special privileges Finland had enjoyed. In 1898 he assigned a hard-boiled character named Nikolai Ivanovich Bobrikov to deal with the Finns as Governor General. He was a ruthless, insensitive and inflexible colonial administrator. The Finns lost their exemption from being conscripted into the imperial forces when the orders were given to merge the Finnish and Russian armed services. The Diet was stripped of almost all its legislative functions. Freedom of speech, assembly and the press were struck down. The angry Finns turned to passive resistance, and then to more active resistance. The Finnish labor movement was just beginning, and Finns looked enviously at the reforms and new freedoms being gained in the Scandinavian lands to the west. One day in 1904 a Finnish civil servant named Eugen Schauman loaded a revolver, went to the Senate building and sought out the sixty-five-year-old Governor General. He met him on a staircase and fired at him three times before turning the gun on himself and committing suicide. Bobrikov continued on his way to the Senate chamber, took his usual seat, and then fell over unconscious. He was dead the next morning. Schauman became a legend.

At first the Russians cracked down harder than ever, but they were badly shaken by their defeat by Japan in the Far East and by the abortive 1905 uprising in St. Petersburg. The Finns were allowed to have a new constitution and a new single-chamber legislature based on universal suffrage. It was the most democratically elected parliament in Europe. Furthermore, the fact that the Social Democratic Party held 80 of the 200 seats gave it the greatest socialist representation yet to be seen in a national legislature anywhere. But then the Russians reversed themselves again. They made it clear that they were still the masters of Finland and kept a tight rein until the outbreak of World War I. Even then, as historian Bertram D. Wolfe has noted, the Tsarist government 'showed enormously more respect for the autonomy of Finland than would today be conceivable for the "autonomous republics" of the Soviet Union . . .'

The Finns were uncertain where they could find their best advantage in the war. Many believed that the defeat of Russia by Germany would give them their freedom. Hundreds of young Finns fled to Germany to form a special battalion to fight with the Germans. Others were planning to throw over Russian rule in Finland itself. The left-wing forces were spurred on by the revolutionary changes in Russia early in 1917 when the Romanovs were overthrown. Finland had served the Bolsheviks as a handy hideout and rendezvous. In Tampere, for example, Lenin first met Stalin, and one of the city's minor attractions today is a Lenin museum.

Freedom and Civil War

Finnish freedom was finally achieved in the wake of the Bolshevik *coup d'état* of November 7, 1917. On December 6, the Diet ratified a proclamation of independence, but it took a civil war—the Finnish 'War of Independence'—to decide whether Finland would be a Communist dictatorship or a Scandinavian-style democracy. Soviet Russia was the first power to recognize independent Finland (just as it was the first to recognize, but later consume, the Ukrainian Republic), but the Bolsheviks clearly were hoping that it would fall into their hands. They urged the Finnish Reds to seize power while the time was ripe. 'Rise, rise instantly,' cried Lenin to the Finnish workers, 'and take over the government in the hands of organized labor.' Stalin went personally to Finland to attend a Social Democratic Party conference. He said, 'If you need our help, we will give it to you, fraternally offering our hand.'

Most Social Democrats were still thinking of leading Finland to socialism through parliamentary means, but left-wing extremists were not that patient or democratic. In late January 1918, with about 30,000 members of the 'Red Guard' at their command, and counting on support from the 40,000 Russian troops in Finland, they overran the government buildings in Helsinki and proclaimed the establishment of a Socialist Workers' Republic. It was the ideal time for the new Soviet government in Russia to back up the *coup* in Helsinki with armed strength, but Lenin had his hands full with the seething domestic problems in Russia, a fact which saved Finland from becoming a Soviet colony. Moreover, the Russian troops inside Finland turned out to be of little help to the Finnish Reds. They were an undisciplined rabble, who had chased away their officers and could not effectively command themselves. With unexpected ease the 'White Guard' of the legal Finnish government disarmed them. The government had escaped from Helsinki and set up a temporary capital at Vaasa.

General Baron Gustaf Mannerheim, the brilliant Finnish-born, Russian-trained military leader, then fifty-one years old, had been put in charge of the counterrevolutionary armed forces.

He had little to work with, except raw farm boys and villagers, and some Swedish volunteers, until the arrival of the Finnish troops who had been training in Germany. With these seasoned soldiers, who numbered only two thousand, and with the experienced military leadership of the White command, the Mannerheim forces were more than a match for the Reds, who now had 100,000 troops and controlled the southern third of the country. The Whites shattered left-wing morale by winning a bloody battle at Tampere, a key workers' stronghold. Mannerheim was convinced that no outside help was needed; but, despite his objections, the government asked Germany to send troops. The German force of 12,000 men captured Helsinki and backed up the White Army in the swift mop-up of the fleeing Red Guards.

The fighting was over by the middle of May. It had lasted three and a half months. Finland was saved from communism, and Mannerheim was the national hero. But a savage civil war, of a kind unknown to the rest of Scandinavia, had taken place, and it is this which still scars Finnish political life and sets Finland apart on the Nordic political landscape. It helps explain why a quarter of the Finns still vote Communist despite the Winter War and the 'Continuation War' with Russia, why labor-management relations are more acrimonious than elsewhere in Scandinavia, and why a patriotic Finnish worker is as likely to denounce Mannerheim as a 'bloody reactionary' as he is to praise him for saving the country from its enemies.

Some 24,000 Finns of both sides were killed during the actual fighting, but it was the 'Red Terror' followed by the 'White Terror' that led foreign journalists to call it one of the most bloodthirsty civil wars in history. The forces of the Left had been ruthless enough but then the Whites, seeing the Reds as traitors, exacted punishment on a scale which still haunts the Finns. One historian, Anatole G. Mazour, wrote:

The Red fighters and their sympathizers were quickly rounded up to face severe judgment. Thousands of others, fearful of merciless vindictiveness, fled whenever opportunity permitted to the countryside, while a few managed to find a haven in Soviet Russia. . . . By the middle of the summer of 1918 reliable estimates cite 73,915 persons, including 4,600 women, who were corralled into internment camps. How many of these perished before the firing squads and how many more met slow death from starvation during their detention, particularly in the dreadful Suomenlinna (Sveaborg) fortress, will never be known with certainty; estimates run into figures as high as a fourth of the detained persons.

The unhappy situation was compounded by the way the victorious right-wing politicians, led by the pro-German prime minister, Pehr Evind Svinhufvud, threw out the Social Democrats (who held 40 per cent of the seats) when the parliament finally reassembled in Helsinki and then sought to turn Finland into a monarchy—a monarchy, moreover, which would put great authority in the hands of the king. Svinhufvud, after being named regent and endowed with supreme powers, asked Kaiser Wilhelm II of Germany to supply one of his sons to be King of Finland. The Kaiser suggested his brother-in-law instead, and in October 1918 the Finnish parliament elected Prince Friedrich Karl of Hesse as Finland's new ruler. World War I came to a climax shortly afterward. Germany collapsed, and in the circumstances the Prince decided it would be better not to be king after all. The Finnish leaders were also having second thoughts. Svinhufvud resigned, and General Mannerheim, who had opposed the whole arrangement with Germany and had left Finland, was called back to become regent and preside over the overhaul of Finnish political life. There were new elections in 1919 (the Social Democrats emerging as the largest party with 80 out of 200 seats) which produced a majority in favor of a republic. A new constitution was proclaimed which established a single-house parliament and a president elected by a popularly chosen electoral college for a six-year term. The law professor who drafted the constitution, Kaarlo Juho Ståhlberg, became the first president. Mannerheim, the loser in the election, went into retirement.

Communism and Fascism

In the two decades between the two world wars, Finland somehow managed to take some long social and economic strides despite the endless battling between the language groups and between the bourgeois and socialist political forces. To prove their loyalty the Social Democrats had cleansed themselves of their extreme leftists. These politicians, still bent on revolution, went into the Communist Party. The Communists grew in strength, both in the parliament and in the trade-union movement. They began holding mass rallies. One such meeting was staged in November 1929 in Lapua, a town in western Finland which had been a rallying point for the White forces in the civil war. It was also known for its militantly religious pietists, who were calling for a crusade against communism. The Lapua peasants, spurred on by clergymen, stormed the meeting of the Young Communist League, ripped off the red shirts of the Reds, beat them up and drove them out of town. That was the beginning of such a virulent anti-communist campaign that it turned into a reign of terror, which first struck at the Communists and then took on the Social Democrats. Many Reds, after their several regional headquarters were sacked and their printing presses were smashed, were driven across the border into Soviet Russia. Ironically enough, they often were seized by the Russians and sent on to Siberia.

The Lapua movement sent 12,000 peasants en masse to Helsinki in July 1930, to demand the suppression of communism in Finland. A new government of antisocialist parties, now led by Svinhufvud, responded heartily by arresting the twenty-three Communist members of parliament and arranging for new elections in order to have the two-thirds strength needed to amend the constitution and outlaw the Communist Party. The Finnish voters supplied the two-thirds majority needed. Communism was officially banned in Finland (and so it remained until the close of World War II), but the party members, of course, found other means to advance their cause. In the meantime the Lapuans, dizzy with success, moved on to new extremes and for a time gave Finland a fascist threat comparable to what was appearing in Italy and Germany. One group went so far as to kidnap former President Ståhlberg and his wife. And then, early in 1932, the Lapuans prepared for an armed *coup d'état* which would have destroyed Finnish democracy. The government was alerted and ringed Helsinki with troops. Svinhufvud, still pro-German and ultraconservative but no fascist, was now president, and he made a personal appeal to members of the Lapua movement to put down their arms. Most of them did. The crisis was brought to a close when legislation was passed to restrict the Lapuans and forbid the formation of paramilitary organizations. Right-wing extremists managed to get into the parliament through other means, but never achieved significant strength.

Soviet Pressure

Needless to say, Finland in those days of anticommunism was no friend of the Soviet Union, but it sought to be no enemy either. It signed a nonaggression treaty with Russia in 1932 and announced to the world that it had a neutral foreign policy, one that was in line with the rest of Scandinavia. But this was not enough for the Russians as they watched the rise of Nazism in Germany and feared that Hitler might one day use Finland as a stepping stone for moving into northwestern Russia. The political events in Finland led Moscow to believe that the Finnish leaders might willingly ally themselves with the Germans. As early as 1938 the Russians began to pressure the Finns to give guarantees that Finland would not allow itself to be used as a base for an attack against the Soviet Union. The Finns were willing to pledge that much, but the Russians wanted more evidence that the Finns understood Russia's security problem. They asked for a Soviet base on Finnish territory in order to guard the Gulf of Finland approach to Leningrad and a military treaty which would allow Russia to step in if Finland were invaded by another power.

It is easy to conclude that Stalin was simply seeking to grab Finnish territory through these security arguments, but Russian concern about defending Leningrad had begun long before the rise of communism. One glance at the map shows what an exposed capital Peter the Great had built only a few miles to the southeast of Finland. He once explained his conquest of nearby Finnish territory by writing: 'The ladies of St. Petersburg could not sleep peacefully as long as the Finnish frontier ran so close to our capital.' As the border stood in 1938, Leningrad was practically within artillery range of Finnish soil. It was so close that the tough Red boss of Leningrad, Andrei Zhdanov, told the Eighth Soviet Congress that through the windows of his 'advanced outpost' of Soviet Russia he could 'hear, ever more loudly, the howling of the fascist beasts and the snapping of their jaws.' For a long time the Russians openly accused the Finns of plotting adventures with the anti-communist powers; and, indeed, there were some groups in Finland agitating for a Greater Karelia. But Moscow began to regard the Finns more cordially when the series of Conservative governments gave way to a coalition of Agrarians, Liberals and Social Democrats. Pehr Svinhufvud, the veteran anti-communist, had been defeated as president by a milder man of the Agrarian Party whose main interest was agriculture. The new leadership in Finland went far to be conciliatory to the Russians, but the Russians were asking too much. It is argued today that all might have been well, and that the Winter War might never have happened, if only the Finns had agreed to let the Russians have the base off the Finnish coast and the guarantees they were seeking. But one answer is that Estonia, Latvia and Lithuania all tried to appease the Soviet Union by signing treaties of mutual assistance which gave the Russians military bases on their territory—and then were swallowed by the Soviet Union.

Finland's fate was sealed by the Nazi-Soviet pact of 1939, which assigned it to the Russian sphere of influence. Up to then Soviet diplomacy had pressured the Finns in secret talks, but now far greater demands were made in open negotiations. The Russians wanted a long-term lease on Hanko Peninsula at the mouth of the Gulf of Finland, other portions of Finnish territory, and the demolition of the Finnish fortifications near Leningrad. The Finnish government refused. Perhaps no government could have survived if it had made such large concessions to the historic enemy.

Even so, the Finns did attempt to meet the Russians part way by agreeing to give up some territory around Leningrad and in the north.

Interestingly enough, it was Marshal Mannerheim, 'the butcher of the working class' to the Reds, who understood that the Russians had some genuine defense problems concerning Leningrad, a city with a population almost as large as the whole of Finland. He advocated giving up Finnish islands at the entrance to the Gulf of Finland, though not mainland territory. This was even more than the Finnish political leaders were willing to concede. They were stubborn in the face of Stalin's demands and were sure that Stalin was bluffing about resorting to war if his demands were not met. One of the negotiators, Juho Kusti Paasikivi, who was to become Finland's great postwar president, later wrote in his memoirs that the Finnish cabinet had been too intransigent. So did Väinö Tanner, then the finance minister and the leading Social Democrat, and yet Tanner was later singled out by the Russians as the man who had blocked the Soviet-Finnish agreement. Both men (and Mannerheim) felt that Finland was alone in this situation and could not rely on any other nation to back up its stubbornness. Sweden, for example, sympathized with Finland's problem, but would not agree to provide military assistance in case Finland were attacked—not even after Tanner, as one Social Democrat to another, made a personal appeal to Swedish Prime Minister Per Albin Hansson. A leading Finnish diplomat, Max Jakobson, has since written that 'the Swedish government was treating Finland the way a man might treat a mistress whom he wishes to discard as gently as possible.'

Jakobson's excellent step-by-step account of *The Diplomacy of the Winter War* leaves the impression that the Finns were being too clever and unyielding for their own good: that they misjudged the determination of the Russians to tidy up their security situation.

The astonishment and disappointment that Stalin and Molotov had expressed in the course of their talks with the Finns must have been perfectly genuine. They could hardly have imagined that Finland would so stubbornly refuse to accept the role assigned to her during the August night Stalin and Ribbentrop had spent together redrawing the map of Eastern Europe. Probably they sincerely believed they had asked of Finland only what was their due, and the rejection of their demands must have seemed to them an incomprehensible, almost perverse, act of defiance; after all, even most Western observers thought the Finns were behaving in a most quixotic manner—bravely, perhaps, but quite unrealistically.

The Winter War

After those several months of agonizing negotiations in the fall of 1939 (the whole dialogue, beginning secretly in March 1938, had taken twenty months), the Russians manufactured an excuse to break diplomatic relations and launched the Winter War with assaults and air raids on November 30, 1939. There was no declaration of war—just an attack which had been in preparation during the final weeks of negotiations. 'RED ARMY HURLS BACK INVADING FINNISH TROOPS,' headlined the *Daily Worker* in New York.

The Russians expected to crush Finland like a hammer coming down on a walnut, but the country proved to be so difficult to crack that they eventually gave it up as a bad job and settled for a partial 'victory.' The Winter War, which lasted just three and a half months (to March 13, 1940), produced the first total warfare of World War II and ended with both sides as winners, and both as losers. The Finns were awesome in their defiance of seemingly overwhelming Russian forces. At one time, for example, there were 40 Finnish tanks facing 2,000 Russian tanks. The Russians controlled the skies and had an endless supply of ammunition while the Finns were so short that they often had to rely on what they could seize from the enemy. But the Finns were fighting for their own soil on their own soil. They were led by the brilliant Marshal Mannerheim, then in his seventies, who had come out of retirement. Whatever the soldiers lacked in discipline they made up for in courageous resourcefulness. The so-called Mannerheim Line, often thought to be some kind of heavily fortified bastion like the Maginot or Siegfried Line, was nothing of the sort. It consisted of a number of outdated concrete nests, tank traps, and a network of trenches hastily dug to meet the emergency. Most of all, it was manned by indomitable Finnish troops. It was the Russians who built up the idea of the impregnable Mannerheim Line to explain away their inability to break through the Finnish front during more than three months of battle.

Apart from the sheer fighting ability of the Finns, the Russians were halted by deep snow and freezing temperatures, which sometimes plunged to 40 degrees below zero. Finns on skis, all but invisible in their white uniforms, were able to encircle large Russian units, cut off their supply lines and eliminate the enemy one by one. The Russian tanks often proved ineffective since they had to operate on the vulnerable forest roads. A single Finn sneaking up to the lead tank and destroying it with a mine or Molotov cocktail could halt the whole armored parade.

Inevitably, of course, the Russian giant broke through the Finnish defenses. By that time Finland's desperate efforts to get military help from other countries had produced little more than a force of Swedish volunteers, much sympathy and promises of help which never materialized. The Germans would not help because of their agreement with Stalin, and they even prevented the Italians from sending a fleet of planes; Mussolini had seen it as a fine chance to hurt the Russian Communists and weaken Russia's ability to expand in the Balkans. The United States was full of admiration for the Finns, but it was not anxious to get involved in European quarrels. The French and British prepared plans to send help to the Finns across Norway and Sweden, but both Nordic nations refused to permit it, since it would be a breach of neutrality. They also correctly suspected that the real Anglo-French purpose was to gain control of the iron-ore mines in Swedish Lapland and the ports of Narvik and Luleå, where the ore was being shipped to Germany.

If the British and French had succeeded in giving military aid to the Finns it would have altered the whole shape of World War II; the alliance of Russia and the Western democracies against Germany could hardly have taken place. As it was, the poor showing by the Russian forces against Finland led Hitler to make the mistake of underrating Soviet power. He was inspired to attack the U.S.S.R., even though he already had a western front, and thus Nazi Germany was lured to its eventual destruction.

Victory in Defeat

When the Winter War had first begun, the Russians, counting on a quick victory, made plans for a Communist government of Finland. The man they selected to be the prime minister was a leading Finnish Communist, Arvo Tuominen, who had undergone ten years of imprisonment and seven years of exile for Communist activities in Finland. But when the Russians summoned him to go from Stockholm to Moscow to prepare the new satellite government, he twice refused, after much soul searching, because he knew it would mean the sellout of his own country. The Russians had to turn to Otto V. Kuusinen to be their Quisling in Finland. He was an old Finnish Red who had spent most of his career in Russia and eventually became one of the top figures in the Soviet hierarchy. Immediately after starting the Winter War the Russians announced that the true 'people's government' of Finland was the one which they said existed under Kuusinen. Finland's refusal to be defeated left this phony government high and dry. The Russians finally made believe it had never happened and agreed to speak again to Finland's legitimate government in order to negotiate an end to the Winter War.

'The Finnish campaign,' wrote Max Jakobson, 'far from being a painless local operation, had developed into a major war which had become a serious drain on Soviet resources, caused uneasiness among the population, and tied down the Red Army in a secondary direction at a time when the European war might at any moment present the Soviet Union with fresh dangers.' The Russians decided to let the war come to an end without a real conquest of Finland, and without a puppet Red government in Helsinki, but under terms which would convince the world that the Russians had won. The Russians demanded so much territory, more than a tenth of Finland, that they were in the remarkable position of asking for land that their own soldiers had not yet been able to win. The harshness of the Russian terms caused the Finns to back off and try again for outside military help. But it became clear that there would not be enough help, and that even if fair-sized forces should arrive, little Finland would be turned into a battleground for great-power armies. The Finnish army, now being filled out with half-trained schoolboys, was at the point of exhaustion. To go on fighting the Russians would be suicide; to accept the Soviet terms would be mutilation, but Finland would still live. It was one of the most heartbreaking moments in the nation's history. A distressed cabinet made the crucial decision and the President, Kyösti Kallio, as he signed the authorization, cursed, 'Let the hand wither that is forced to sign such a paper.' Within the year Kallio suffered a stroke which paralyzed his right arm.

The Finns had won the admiration of the world, but the war cost them 25,000 dead or missing and nearly 44,000 wounded. On the other hand, more than 100,000 Russian troops had been killed (Mannerheim estimated 200,000) and several hundred thousand were wounded. The Soviet Union had also lost tremendous face, as well as its claim to be the defender of small nations.

'The Continuation War'

The Finns had little more than fifteen months to patch up their Winter War wounds before they were plunged into another, directly related war, which lasted for three years. The peace agreement had forced Finland to lease its Hanko Peninsula to Russia and to give up Viipuri and its land in Karelia to the southeast which was home for one eighth of the Finnish population. Almost all the 450,000 Karelians in the ceded areas chose to give up their property and live in free Finland rather than submit themselves to Soviet rule, but it created a tremendous refugee problem for the exhausted Finnish nation.

Even after the peace had been concluded, the Russians

continued to put pressure on the Finns. They demanded further concessions, including the valuable nickel mines at Petsamo in the north. Russian fighters shot down a Finnish passenger plane over the Baltic. The Soviet annexation of Estonia, Latvia and Lithuania in June 1940, persuaded the Finns that the Russians had similar plans for them. And they did. Molotov said as much to the Germans the following November. The German conquest of Denmark and Norway had left Finland isolated from any Allied help in case of trouble. They felt at the mercy of the Russians. It was an unhappy thought, but Nazi Germany looked like the only power which might be able to deter the Russians from a new assault on Finland. The Finns therefore agreed to a transit agreement which the Germans requested in order to supply and rotate their occupation troops in northern Norway.

Like Sweden, which had just signed a similar transit agreement with the Germans, Finland, although desperate to remain neutral in the great war, felt it could not afford to refuse the Germans. The Finns were drawn by force of circumstance to the German side. The Soviet cancellation of its trade agreement with Finland, for example, forced it to depend ever more on the Germans for supplies. The Germans, now plotting to attack Russia, worked to draw Finland into their net. The fact that a Finnish military delegation visited Germany helped convince the Russians that the Finns were conspiring with the Germans to attack the U.S.S.R. Some Finns undoubtedly were looking forward to a German-Russian clash as a chance to recover the lost territories, but the official Finnish version insists that Finland had no intention of joining Germany in an attack on Russia. Nonetheless, the transit agreement gave the Germans the right to put troops on Finnish soil, and Hitler had poured thousands of men into northern Finland just before launching his attack on Russia in June 1941.

Only a handful of Finnish leaders, notably President Risto Ryti and a few others later identified as 'war criminals,' had authorized the transit agreement. It was not an act of the full government or the parliament. In his work *Finland Between East and West*, Anatole G. Mazour called the transit agreement 'the Pandora's box for Finland.' He wrote:

The consequences were truly catastrophic. It enabled Germany to become eventually virtual master in the northern portion of Finland. It tendered the Soviet government a pretext to open military action against German forces on Finnish soil immediately after June 22, 1941, and to Finland's entry in the war again. It placed Finland on the list of aggressor nations and led to diplomatic rupture with Great Britain and finally to a declaration of war. It caused relations between Finland and the United States to undergo the severest test and destroyed the reservoir of good will the Finnish people enjoyed in America. No matter how desperately the Finnish government tried to explain its relationship with Berlin, vigorously refuting the idea of an alliance, the cold fact remained that the nation was fighting on the side of Germany against a member of the Allied free nations. Almost overnight Finland lost her reputation of being 'the only nation that paid her debts,' and was pilloried as an Axis member totally subservient to the Nazi cause. By the time the Finnish nation awoke to the fact that it was on the wrong side of the fence, it was so enmeshed that it came to the brink of the abyss.

Although Finland announced that it was neutral in the German-Russian conflict, a round of Soviet bombing attacks on Finnish cities wiped out the brief hope that the nation could stay on the sidelines. The parliament declared that a state of war existed with the U.S.S.R. The Finnish forces, again with Mannerheim in command, swept into Karelia, and took back the lost lands where a multitude of soldiers had only recently fallen. For strategic reasons, and perhaps to have something to bargain with at the end of the war, they were ordered to penetrate into Soviet Karelia to a point just north of Leningrad. There they stopped and stayed put for a 'sitzkrieg' which lasted two and a half years. There was a lot of trench warfare, patrol activity and artillery clashes, but, as in France during World War I, little actual movement backwards or forwards. What is most important, the Finns repeatedly refused the German demands that they join the attack on Leningrad, help seize the Murmansk railway, and otherwise assist the German war effort.

It was Finland's contention that it was fighting a 'Continuation

War'—a sequel to the Winter War—and not as an ally of the Germans. Nonetheless, Britain declared war on Finland (but the United States did not). The Finns, once again, were caught in an intolerable situation. Theirs was a democracy fighting on the side of the Nazis, and thus against the democracies. Except for a few of the far Right, they did not want Nazism to triumph in Europe, but if the Germans failed to defeat the Russians, then Finland would again be menaced by Moscow. Finnish friends have told me how humiliating it was for Finland to have to entertain Adolf Hitler when he visited the country. But then it was more painful still when it became apparent, after Stalingrad, that Hitler was going to lose the war.

The Finns, still insisting that they were fighting a separate war, now sought to make a separate peace. The first Russian terms offered in March 1944 were impossible to fulfill. They included a demand for 600 million dollars in war reparations and the expulsion of German forces from Finnish soil in a single month. In early June 1944, just as the Allies were landing in Normandy to create a second front, more than twenty Soviet divisions launched an offensive against the Finnish lines in that blood-soaked neck of land known as the Karelian Isthmus. It was preceded by one of the greatest artillery barrages in the history of warfare, and by an attack of more than four hundred Soviet bombers. This was a far mightier offensive than anything the Finns had had to cope with in the Winter War. The Finns were once again forced to give ground, but only after a terrible toll on both sides. The Russians were now demanding nothing less than unconditional surrender, and there was every prospect that they would soon sweep over the whole of Finland.

At this point the Germans promised to supply arms, planes and troops if the Finns would agree not to make a separate peace. Desperately, the Finns found the answer to this latest of many dilemmas when President Risto Ryti gave the Germans that assurance in a personal letter to Hitler. Since it was unconstitutional for him to commit the nation in that manner, the Finns reasoned that the guarantee would be binding only so long as Ryti remained president. After the Finnish forces succeeded in halting the Russian advance (just short of the 1940 border), Ryti resigned ostensibly for reasons of health, and Mannerheim was elected in his place in August 1944. The way was now clear to an armistice with the Russians, although once again Finnish negotiators had to face and then succumb to onerous terms dictated by Stalin. By having signed the letter to Hitler in order to head off the Soviet devastation of Finland, President Ryti had willingly made himself the sacrificial goat. He was soon to be jailed as a war criminal in order to appease the Russians but, as Mannerheim stated at his trial, he had performed 'a meritorious civic act.' One writer has said that 'this act of personal courage has few parallels in the annals of world statesmanship.'

Aftermath

But the armistice with Russia did not end the horror for Finland. Under the terms of their agreement with Moscow they had to drive out the 200,000 German troops from northern Finland. It took them from September 1944 to March 1945 to do it. Nearly 4,000 more soldiers were killed and, as already related, the Germans destroyed every piece of property in sight, about 300 million dollars' worth, as they retreated from Finnish Lapland. In the Continuation War with Russia, some 85,000 Finnish lives were lost, an appalling number for a nation which then had little more than four million population.

The armistice terms called for the Finns again to clear out of Karelia—many of the Winter War refugees had returned in the wake of the Finnish troops—and to give up Petsamo in the north and other chunks of territory. Porkkala peninsula, only a few miles west of Helsinki, had to be leased to Russia. It became a dagger permanently poised an inch from the Finnish heart. And over 300 million dollars' worth of goods were to be delivered to Russia over a six-year period. It later developed that the Russians were talking about prewar, not current, prices, and the reparations bill, as finally ironed out, was actually about 500 million dollars. Some outside experts have calculated that the 'total cost' to the Finns of having to produce and deliver the materials on time was perhaps as much as 900 million dollars. Whatever it was, the burden was staggering. It was bravely borne and was worked off in just eight years. It meant a wholesale regearing of the Finnish economy. Although the nation's economic machinery had not been destroyed like that of so many other nations in war, it was old and exhausted. Finland lost not only 10 per cent of its land area in the cession of territory but also a great part of its industrial capacity. Its merchant fleet was mostly in Allied hands. There was a desperate shortage of capital to perform the horrendous reparations task. In a multitude of other ways, Finland was dangerously tied to the Soviet Union as the guns fell silent at the end of World War II.

The Finns had lost the war. By their participation on the side of the Germans, they had lost most of the high regard and sympathy they had enjoyed in the democratic world. The freedom of the Finns to conduct their own affairs was so proscribed by the Russian armistice conditions, and then by the peace treaty signed in 1947, that Finland was virtually a satellite of the Soviet Union. It was even less the master of its own house than it had been in the best years under the tsars. And yet, it was still a democracy, and it still had a chance to achieve full independence. It was the only loser in the war not to suffer occupation and a sweeping revision of its political system. Once again the Finns had survived.

Chapter 30

LIFE UNDER PRESSURE

We Finns tend to go to extremes. We used to hate the Russians to the point of absurdity. Now perhaps we are dangerously indifferent.

—HELSINKI BUSINESSMAN

Whatever happens, we will be on the wrong side.

—FINNISH CITIZEN

It has been said that 'in Finland bitter fights are fought over matters on which everybody desperately agrees.' The welfare state, pension programs, the spending of government money on farm subsidies or northern development, all these are heatedly debated as if the nation were divided between inhuman reactionaries and wild-eyed radicals, and yet almost all Finns are in agreement on the objective of creating a typically Scandinavian society. In the even more sensitive realm of foreign affairs the agreement on the wisdom of Finland's conciliatory approach to the Soviet Union is so widespread that one Finn claimed that 'we have the most universally supported foreign policy in the world.' There are fierce arguments, however, about precisely how that foreign policy should be carried out. The forces of Left and Right, both among the political parties and within the parties, are deeply suspicious of each other.

Trying to describe Finnish politics is a little like counting the arms of a squid while swimming through a cloud of black ink. When I was making my inquiries in Helsinki I had the uncomfortable feeling of being drawn deeper and deeper into a bottomless black sea. There was something Oriental about the rumors, alarms and intrigues which swirled around political circles in the capital. It was hard to find anyone who could speak dispassionately about the issues and personalities. Politicians did not hesitate to describe other politicians to me, a foreigner, in the most scurrilous terms. By the simple act of making appointments and asking questions I became involved in the political merry-go-round. One leading Social Democrat refused to see me when he discovered that I had committed the sin of having spoken to another leading Social Democrat first. It became clear that personalities often meant more than policies. One foreign commentator wrote: 'To analyze accurately the nature and causes of the tragic split in Finland's labor movement would require the services of a top-notch psychiatrist.'

According to a diplomat in Helsinki, 'All these politicians have known each other and fought each other for years. They've been rubbing each other the wrong way for a long time. They know one another's tricks. It's like small-town politics.' The politicians spend most of their time, it seems, turning little molehills into mighty mountains. Finnish *sisu*, for all its courageous individualism, has its dark side in the unreasoning stubbornness and everyman-for-himself attitude of many political figures. Since there are few differences on the broad lines of domestic and foreign policy, the argument about details gets so clamorous that Finnish governments have a life expectancy of less than one year. There have been more than twenty governments since the end of World War II and about fifty since Finland became independent in 1917. The politicians are engaged in a constant game of musical chairs, with the same faces reappearing in different cabinet posts in different coalition governments. And yet at various times over long stretches of years, three of the most important parties, the Communists, Conservatives and Social Democrats, have been frozen out of the government altogether.

A foreign observer is naturally reminded of the instability of politics in France during the postwar years before General de Gaulle returned to power and converted the French presidency into a position of genuine authority. But it is a misleading comparison. What Finland has is a combination of unstable governments *and* a de Gaulle. The fact that the Finnish president has great powers and carries on for a six-year term despite the rise and fall of governments means that the administration of the nation is not nearly so shaky as it seems. Since he is empowered to direct the nation's foreign policy, there is continuity in that critical sphere. The civil servants carry on as usual, whatever the politicians are up to. Every so often they even occupy the cabinet seats themselves when the parties find it impossible to form a government.

There is, in fact, a basic stability in the Finnish government amid the tumult and shouting. The play goes on despite the constant changes of actors. Finland has a multiparty system of government with about eight political parties represented in parliament at any one time. The members of parliament are elected by proportional representation. Unlike the other Scandinavian countries, no one party in Finland can even come close to having a majority of the seats in the parliament. Inevitably, a government is a coalition of several parties. In practice, these have been the parties close to the center of the political spectrum, most notably the Agrarian (or Center) Party. When governments collapse after losing a vote of confidence, or for other reasons, nothing really changes when new governments take over. The country is simply presented with a new combination of politicians. The faces are familiar. Urho Kekkonen, for example, in the years before he became president, was the prime minister of five out of seven governments formed in 1950–54, four of them in succession.

Three major parties have each held about a quarter of the two hundred seats in the parliament during most of the postwar years. They are the Agrarians, the Social Democrats, and the Communists, who call themselves the Democratic League of the People, or S.K.D.L. The Conservatives, or National Coalition Party, have generally had about thirty seats. Three or four other parties, including one representing the Swedish-Finns, have together held the remaining twenty or so seats. The situation became further complicated after 1958 with the creation of a rebel, and more radical, Social Democratic group, which has taken seats from the parent party.

From 1948 (when the Communists were first excluded from a Finnish cabinet) to 1958, the Agrarians and Social Democrats, with the help of a couple of minor parties, formed most of the governments. Then came the 'night frost' of 1958, when the Russians blatantly interfered in Finnish domestic politics, with the result that the Social Democrats, for all their one quarter of the parliamentary seats, were denied a place in the coalition governments until their electoral triumph in 1966.

Life with the Russians

To understand how Moscow looms large in Finland's political affairs, it is necessary to examine the highly involved, hot-and-cold Soviet-Finnish relationship since the end of World War II. Although it is not a particularly glorious chapter in Finnish history, the traditionally impulsive Finns earn high marks for political finesse under stress. When I asked an ambassador in Helsinki what had surprised him most about the Finns once he had come to know them, he said, 'Their sophistication. They are a far more subtle people than I had expected.'

The most important fact of Finnish life today is that it is an independent democratic state instead of the Communist-led Soviet satellite or Soviet province that it could easily have become. The scale of the Finnish achievement in eluding the fatal Russian bear hug can be seen by a glance at the map. With the exception of the bit of Norway above the Arctic Circle, Finland is the only non-Communist European nation on Russia's borders. It managed to fend off Russian control by its own wits, and with no direct outside help, whereas it took American military aid to save Greece and Turkey from Communist rule, and massive doses of economic assistance to keep Italy and France from being taken over by their Communist parties. Western military aid to Finland was unthinkable, in light of Russia's concern for the security of its borders, and the Finns, because of Soviet objections, were not even able to accept Marshall Plan help in their gigantic reparations and postwar rebuilding task.

A leading Finnish businessman, however, said that the United

States had inadvertently given Finland invaluable aid on two important occasions. 'We knew two years before the war ended,' he said, 'that we were on the losing side. When the Russians finally attacked our lines they came in like hell. We had to run back about fifty kilometers before we could stop them. They were about to smash us again, when they saw that the Americans were racing to Berlin. They didn't want them to get there first, so they pulled a great many of their troops out of Finland in order to strengthen the forces in Central Europe. At that moment we made the armistice agreement.' He and other Finns made it clear that the competition between the Anglo-American forces and the Russians for control of Germany saved Finland from being occupied and absorbed by the Soviet Union. 'And then when you fought the Korean War,' he continued, 'it gave a big boost to our economy. We were still paying off the Russian reparations. The Korean War brought us high prices for our pulp and paper at just the right time.'

For a number of years after the war Finland was widely believed to be more a Russian satellite than a free state, and for good reason. Few Russians can be seen in Finland today, but they were all too visible in the early years after the armistice of 1944. They took over Karelia in the southeast, Petsamo in the north and Porkkala peninsula near Helsinki. As stipulated in the armistice agreement, an Allied—actually a Soviet—control commission set up operations in Helsinki's Torni Hotel to see that the Finns lived up to the armistice terms. It numbered more than seventy Russians and was headed by a tough Soviet general, Andrei A. Zhdanov. They insisted on the swift reduction of Finland's armed forces, despite the great effort needed to drive the Germans out of Lapland.

There was a two-and-a-half-year armistice period, during which Finland was on probation. Russia's wartime allies had virtually turned the Finns over to Moscow's supervision. It meant not only the re-emergence in public of the Finnish Communist Party but also the taking over of vital security and police posts by Communists. With Justice Minister (now President) Kekkonen much in the foreground, the Finnish government set out to prove its desire for friendship with Russia by dissolving and banning all manner of right-wing and patriotic organizations and by bringing a number of scapegoat 'war criminals' to trial. It was one of the more ignominious episodes in Finnish history. The government proposed a bill to provide punishment for those Finnish leaders who 'in a decisive way contributed to Finland's joining with Germany in the war of 1941 against the U.S.S.R. and the United Kingdom of Great Britain and Northern Ireland, and who, during the course of the war, had prevented the conclusion of peace.'

It was post-factum legislation and not entirely constitutional, but right-wing as well as left-wing votes got it through the parliament. At least it gave the president the right to grant an amnesty, and it provided that a prisoner could be released on probation after serving half of his term. A trial lasting more than three months ended with the convictions of former President Ryti, two prime ministers, four other wartime cabinet members and the ex-minister to Berlin. All eight men were found guilty and were sentenced to varying terms of imprisonment. Ryti got the stiffest sentence—ten years at hard labor—but he was released in half that time, and the others served only a few years. As sacrificial goats, they accepted their fate philosophically. The leading personality of the 'war criminals,' Väinö Tanner, the veteran chief of the Social Democratic Party, said that the proceedings 'can hardly avoid leaving an ugly spot on the history of Finnish jurisprudence,' but he added that one could serve the nation 'as well in prison as in the President's Palace.' Tanner wrote his memoirs in prison and as soon as he was released received a huge vote which returned him to his old place in the parliament.

The humiliating armistice period ended in the fall of 1947, when the Russians, after stalling seven long months, ratified the peace treaty which had been signed in Paris in February by the Finns and the World War II victors. Finland was once again a free nation, but one of the most important portions of the treaty imposed strict limitations on the Finnish armed forces. They were restricted to fewer than 42,000 men and could undertake duties only of an internal character and the defense of the frontier. The air force, which today uses both Russian and British aircraft, was forbidden to possess any planes designed primarily as bombers, and a number of offensive weapons from missiles to submarines were banned. (The Finns later managed to win approval for their use of strictly defensive missiles.) Finland is, therefore, militarily weak in everything but the character and combat training of its fighting men. It has been spared, however, from spending a great part of its wealth on armaments.

Uneasy Friendship

Treaty or no treaty, the Finns would not consider it prudent to arm themselves too heavily in the face of Russian displeasure. The basic foreign-policy approach, known as the 'Paasikivi Line' after President (1946–56) Juho Paasikivi, was laid down in December 1944, when he pledged Finland to 'do nothing in conflict with the interests of the Soviet Union.' As one Finn explained, 'It doesn't cost anything to smile.'

The smile was painfully forced in February 1948 when Stalin, only three days after engineering the *coup* in Czechoslovakia, wrote to Paasikivi to propose that Finland and Russia negotiate a treaty of friendship and mutual assistance. Russia had only recently concluded the signing of such 'friendship' pacts with its Eastern European satellites. Was it now Finland's turn to be drawn into the Soviet web? There was no choice but to send a delegation to Moscow. What was finally agreed on was not something the Finns would have preferred, but it was better than they had feared. It was even regarded as a triumph for Finnish diplomacy. The Soviet-Finnish Mutual Assistance Treaty differed in several important respects from those signed by Russia and its satellites. Finland promised to fight any attacker who sought to invade the U.S.S.R. through Finnish territory, but it was not obliged to help Russia in other circumstances, and Russian help to Finland would be 'subject to mutual agreement' (unlike the satellite pacts).

The agreement was not a political alliance which tied Helsinki to Moscow but it committed Finland more firmly than ever to its nonalignment policy. Finland could not, for example, join

NATO, even if it desired to do so. Russia and Finland pledged in both the Peace Treaty and the Mutual Assistance Treaty 'not to conclude any alliance or join any coalition' directed against the other. The new pact was for a ten-year period, but it was extended for another twenty years in 1955; and as a reward the Finns were given back the Porkkala naval base which the Russians had leased for fifty years. It had been one of the major irritants in the Finnish-Russian relationship. The inland end of the peninsula was practically in the suburbs of Helsinki and was crossed by the Turku–Helsinki railroad line. The Finnish passengers called the crossing 'the longest tunnel in the world,' for they were locked in the coaches and steel blinds were placed over the windows when the trains, pulled by Russian engines, traversed the Russian Zone.

The return of Porkkala, and the Russian agreement to lease its portion of the Saimaa Canal to Finland a few years later, were taken as signs of the success of the Paasikivi foreign policy. But it was an outstretched-hand attitude which had to be maintained in the face of an internal Communist threat and the Russian flouting of Article 6 of the 1948 agreement which pledged 'non-interference in the internal affairs of the other state.'

In 1948 Finland almost went the way of Czechoslovakia when the Communists were on the verge of staging a *coup d'état*. A leading Communist, Yrjö Leino, held the vital post of minister of the interior, and several key security forces had been virtually taken over by the Reds. The State Police in particular were so abusing their authority that the parliament passed a vote of 'no confidence' in the Interior Minister. The army and regular police were alerted to protect the capital and keep weapons out of the hands of the special police forces. These forces were purged of their Communist members and reorganized. In the elections of 1948, which were marked by a rash of Communist demonstrations and acts of violence, the voters reduced the S.K.D.L. (Communist) representation in parliament from fifty-one seats to thirty-eight. In the years following the Communists regained most of their old strength but were excluded from the many coalition Governments until the spring of 1966.

An intriguing footnote to this critical time in Finnish postwar history is that Yrjö Leino himself is believed to have tipped off the authorities to the danger of a Red *coup* when his patriotic impulses overrode his Communist training. His memoirs were suppressed by the Finnish government as likely to prove too provoking to the Russians, but the autobiography of a onetime colleague tells of how Leino had gone to the commander of the defense forces to say that 'disturbances from the Left' were to be expected. Leino bowed out of political life as a broken man. He was expelled from the Communist Party and divorced by his wife, Hertta Kuusinen. As the tough, Russian-educated daughter of an old Finnish Bolshevik, Otto Kuusinen, she has been an important Communist boss in her own right. Today she leads the Finnish Reds as head of the S.K.D.L. and is the world's leading female Communist outside the Soviet Union.

Communists

The greatest Finnish paradox is that the nation which has spent most of the last half century warding off the Soviet threat to its national life gives large support to the Communists. In the 1966 parliamentary elections, the Communists, parading as the Democratic League of the People, won over a fifth of the total votes cast even though the number of their seats dropped from 47 to 41. The Moderate Social Democrats achieved a landslide victory by increasing their seats to 55, or six more than the formally supreme Agrarian Party. The Finns appear to be moving away from political extremism, and yet communist sympathies remain deep-rooted.

There are two main reasons for so many votes for Communists. First, there is the residue of feeling from the bitter civil-war days when the Communists seemed to be the champions of the working class against the reactionary Whites. Second, the Communists still present themselves as the true spokesmen of the workers, especially those who feel they have not received their fair share of the new prosperity in Finland, and their supporters regard them as nationalists, not agents of Soviet Russia. In areas of serious employment problems, the Communists have successfully exploited grievances and promised even more radical and expensive solutions to social problems. They are known as 'bread-and-butter Communists.' Many Finnish Reds fought against Russia in the Winter War and its aftermath, and there was no fifth column of any consequence which hurt the war effort. The party ranks include many persons who were driven from their Karelian homes by the Russian army.

It should also be added that the Communists have been strong because the Social Democrats, relative to the rest of Scandinavia, have been weak. Their weakness is due to their own feuding in the ranks, and their recent exclusion from a share in the government can be credited largely to the Russians—and to President Kekkonen.

For decades the Communists and Social Democrats have struggled for support of the workers and for command of the trade-union movement. As in the other Nordic countries, the Social Democrats saw themselves as the political arm of a democratic labor movement. The trade-union federation was successfully infiltrated by the Reds in the 1920s, however, and the Social Democrats were obliged to set up a rival federation. Ever since then, there has been such constant rivalry within the labor movement that it has fallen short of the goals already reached by the movements elsewhere in Scandinavia. Today there is such confusion in the Finnish Left that there are two major labor federations, a split in the Social Democratic party, and similar divisions in some other national institutions.

The Russian Communists have always looked upon the Finnish Social Democrats with acute disgust, and their displeasure was made most dramatically evident in 1958. The elections that year increased the Communist seats from forty-three to fifty and gave the Reds the plurality for the first time. A veteran Social Democrat, K. A. Fagerholm, put together a government which represented all parties except the Communists and radical Social Democrats. Since it included Conservative members for the first time since the war, as well as two Social Democrats who were noted for taking a hard line with the Finnish Communists, the Russians were enraged.

'The Night Frost'

Soviet newspapers and other propaganda organs went into action to denounce the 'rightist' government which had been formed. They detected other manifestations of unfriendly, reactionary activity in Finland. When the Finns did not immediately panic and replace the Fagerholm government with something more pleasing to them, the Russians proceeded to give a frightening demonstration of their ability to put the squeeze on Finland. 'The neighbor,' as Finns refer to the U.S.S.R. suddenly withdrew its ambassador from Helsinki, suspended talks about a ruble loan and the lease of the Saimaa Canal, refused to go ahead with joint arrangements about fishing grounds and a power plant, postponed some scheduled scientific and trade meetings, and, the most serious of all, suspended trade with Finland. Moscow refused to pay for goods which had already been delivered and to accept goods already ordered. Although Russia was no longer Finland's chief trading partner, having been replaced by Great Britain some years earlier, Soviet trade was still critically important to Finland. An extended postponement would seriously worsen the unemployment problem.

It was a blatant Russian attempt to tell the Finns that certain parties and certain individuals should not be permitted to participate in the government. A number of Finnish politicians were prepared to stand up to Russians at this time, but others felt that the facts of life demanded that the U.S.S.R. be appeased. It was the Agrarian Party, still primarily influenced by Urho Kekkonen, who had been elected President in 1956, that moved first to bring down the Fagerholm government. Johannes Virolainen, then the foreign minister (he later became Finland's prime minister in 1964), led the walkout of the Agrarians from the government. It took six weeks of agonizing negotiations to form a new minority government, and then it lasted for only half a year. But the Conservatives and the Social Democrats blacklisted by the Kremlin were now out of the picture. Trade and other relationships were resumed and all was smiles when President Kekkonen met Khrushchev during a private visit to

Leningrad and heard him express his approval of the new look in Finland.

The Finns were still feeling unsettled by the 1958 display of Soviet pressure, when they were jarred in October 1961 by a sudden Russian demand for immediate defense talks. This invoking of the Mutual Assistance Treaty raised fears that Moscow might force Finland to accept Soviet armed forces for vague purposes of joint security. Memories of Soviet troops in Hungary were still warm. The Berlin situation was more explosive than usual. The Cold War was going through an ugly phase. In this atmosphere, ordinary Finns feared the worst. A doctor in Helsinki telephoned a foreign resident to ask advice on whether he ought to move his family out of the country. The Russian demand for military talks was ostensibly inspired by the announcement that a new NATO Baltic Command, in which West Germany would participate, was to be formed. As a British journalist put it, 'Experience shows that Russia's attitude to Finland hardens or softens as she sees German strength and influence in the Baltic waxing or waning.'

Nonetheless, it eventually became clear to many Finns that a deeper reason for the abrupt Russian call for defense talks was Moscow's desire to see Urho Kekkonen kept in office as President of Finland. For a time it had appeared that Kekkonen would have no trouble winning a second six-year term in the 1962 elections, but then the moderate Social Democrats, Conservatives and several smaller parties reached surprising unanimity in an effort to put up a nonpolitician, a former attorney general named Olavi Honka, as a dignified, unifying figure to replace the controversial Kekkonen. A national leader who was unable to 'stand above politics,' Kekkonen had become President in the first place only because heavy Communist strength had been added to his Agrarian votes. He had pleased the Russians as a man who had gone all out to make the Paasikivi Line work. Now he was in danger of being succeeded by a man who had the support of elements which had been banned from the Finnish government in the 1958 political crisis. The new crisis provoked by the Russians conveniently coincided with the political campaign under way in Finland, a campaign in which the Agrarians and left-wing forces combined to depict their opponents, the opponents of Kekkonen, as reckless adventurers who were trying to upset Finland's carefully cultivated good relations with the U.S.S.R.

President Kekkonen happened to be in far-off Hawaii on that October day when the Russians called for defense talks. He was on an official visit to the United States. His reaction was magnificently calm. He explained to the press that Finland was not being threatened by Russia and he saw no need to hurry home to his nervous capital. He proceeded to Helsinki only after completing his American tour. A few weeks later, at the same leisurely pace, he flew off to the Siberian city of Novosibirsk to meet Khrushchev for a two-hour private chat. It apparently did not involve weighty military matters since no Finnish military expert was at hand. The result was that the Russian demand for military consultations was withdrawn. Somehow it didn't seem very important any more. What was important was the way opposition to Kekkonen's re-election gave way in face of the Russian show of interest. The coalition behind Honka crumbled. He stepped out of the presidential campaign, and Kekkonen was left without opposition. 'The election was decided in Novosibirsk,' one disheartened Finn told me.

It is no wonder that Urho Kekkonen is a man who attracts political lightning. He has been the dominant figure in Finnish politics during the past decade. He has single-mindedly imposed his will with such success that even those who claim to hate him admit that they vote for him. 'He's a terrible man,' said a Helsinki businessman, 'but I don't know anyone else who can fill his shoes. He may be just a clever opportunist, but we have become extremely dependent on him.' A Danish observer wrote: 'There is hardly any other non-Communist statesman who must steer his ship along a narrower path than the one Finland now has to navigate. Yet in all these years Finland has kept clear of the rocks on which so many political shipwrecks have occurred.'

Finland has a habit of thrusting up big men to suit the occasion. The three presidents since the end of World War II have been among the biggest men of all: Mannerheim, Paasikivi and Kekkonen.

Mannerheim

Marshal Mannerheim held office for less than two years in the agonizing days of 1944-46, but it was a time of great trial and, for Mannerheim, the last great chore of an unbelievably long, active and heroic career. In every sense of the old cliché, he was a man of destiny, and one of the greatest personalities ever to emerge in Scandinavia. He was repeatedly called upon to save the nation from almost certain disaster. Like Winston Churchill, he was an aristocrat, conservative and warrior-statesman whose long life (1867-1951) and multiple talents enabled him to enjoy high adventure in foreign fields in his youth and the highest positions in his nation's life in his later years.

Baron Gustaf Mannerheim was born in Finland of Swedish-speaking parents and served for some thirty years as a dashing officer in an exclusive cavalry regiment of the imperial Russian army. He explored Central Asia and China, fought for the Russians in the 1904-5 war with Japan and in World War I, and learned at least six languages. Although he was one of many Tsarist generals who suddenly became obsolete and imperiled when their forces rebelled during the Revolution in 1917, he defiantly returned through Russia to Helsinki in full uniform.

At age fifty-one, having played no part in Finland's nationalist movement, he was suddenly put in command of the White Army, which beat down the Reds in the 1918 civil war. He opposed the plan to install a German prince as king of Finland and went into retirement abroad. He soon returned to become Regent. Years later he served as commander in chief of the Finnish forces in the Winter War and the 1941-44 war, and as the first postwar president. Marshal Mannerheim was a stern, commanding, aloof figure who was much more of an awe-inspiring George Washington than a down-to-earth Abraham Lincoln. Even though many Finns could not help but think of him as a pillar of a reactionary establishment, he became a living legend, famous for his courage in five wars, his perfectionism and his amazing memory. His death in Switzerland in 1951 led to the greatest state funeral in Finland's history.

Paasikivi

Juho Kusti Paasikivi (1870–1956), who succeeded Mannerheim as president in 1946, was another man whose early associations with the Russians and full lifetime enabled him to provide outstanding service to his nation in his old age. He had a strange career in public life, since it was active only in his young manhood and in his old age. As a student at St. Petersburg he became fluent in Russian and developed into an authority on Russian history. After a brief academic career he became Finland's Paymaster General and entered parliament in 1907. Although he was a strong conservative he was not a rightist of fixed anti-Russian prejudices. According to Max Jakobson, he had always advocated, 'even in the days of Tsarist oppression, prior to World War I, a policy of conciliation with Russia, recognition of her strategic interests along the Gulf of Finland, and avoidance of such provocative attitudes as might challenge Russian prestige.'

Paasikivi was briefly prime minister in 1918, heading the first cabinet after the civil war, but his political career suddenly stopped short, partly because he was a leader in the abortive effort to make Finland a monarchy headed by a German prince. Although he led the Finnish delegation to the Tartu peace conference in Russia in 1920, which finally and officially separated Finland from Russia, Paasikivi stepped out of public life for almost two decades. He concentrated on the management of Finland's largest commercial bank. Then in 1939, after serving for a few years as ambassador in Stockholm, he was suddenly called on to undertake the painful job of heading the Finnish delegation to Moscow when the Russians made their demands for bases and territory which finally led to the Winter War.

Max Jakobson wrote:

The choice was one of the rare, intuitive, or perhaps accidental, strokes of genius that may change a nation's history. For Paasikivi personally, who then was 69 years of age and had retired from active politics years earlier, it meant the beginning of an astonishing career in statesmanship that was to last until his 85th year and secure him a permanent place in Finnish history. For Finland, it produced a leader to whom the nation turned in 1944 in the despondency and despair of defeat as the man who could be trusted to make and keep peace with Russia without sacrificing freedom and independence. Paasikivi came to mean to Finland what Churchill meant to Britain, with the difference that his task was not winning the war, but winning the peace after the war had been lost.

Paasikivi was a strong-willed, blunt-spoken man with a flaming temper. He is known to have thrown inkwells at subordinates who infuriated him and to have once pounded his fist so hard on a table that his false teeth fell out. Finns who believe that President Kekkonen has been too conciliatory with the Russians will tell about the time the Russian ambassador in Helsinki called on Paasikivi to express some misgiving about the approaching presidential elections. Paasikivi is supposed to have said: 'Mr. Ambassador, who is elected or re-elected president in Finland is Finland's own business. Good morning!' Nonetheless, it was Paasikivi as negotiator in 1944 and Paasikivi as prime minister and then as president during the first dozen postwar years who set Finland on its self-disciplined course of seeking to make close friends with Russia while preserving Finnish democracy and sovereignty.

Kekkonen

During the years when President Paasikivi dictated Finland's foreign policy, Urho Kaleva Kekkonen served as either prime minister or foreign minister. The two men, who saw eye to eye on almost every aspect of foreign policy, made a powerful team. Kekkonen, born in 1900, entered parliament in 1936 as an Agrarian. He served as minister of justice and as minister of the interior, and he headed the organization for assisting displaced persons during the war. Although he was one of three ministers who had voted against ending the Winter War, and later favored an advance into Russia in the Continuation War, he then switched from being a 'hawk' to a 'dove' and argued strenuously for an all-out effort to show good will toward Russia despite all the wrongs that the Finns had suffered. His personal standing with Moscow rose when he took the lead in bringing the so-called war criminals to trial when the Russians insisted that action be taken. Kekkonen has been much criticized for it, but at least one of the convicted men said that he would have done the same thing in Kekkonen's shoes. It was necessary, it seemed, to wipe the slate clean if a new friendship were ever to develop between the two countries.

The success of the Paasikivi-Kekkonen policy seemed assured in September 1955, when the two men were invited to Moscow for talks. A Russian call for negotiations usually meant trouble, but this time it was good news. International tensions had eased, explained Prime Minister Bulganin, and the Soviet Union was therefore ready to give up its base at Porkkala peninsula, which it had leased for fifty years. Of course, in the jet and nuclear age the base no longer had its former strategic significance, and by relinquishing it the Russians could embarrass the West by claiming that they, at least, had no bases on foreign soil. It looked like a magnanimous gesture, with only the price tag of a twenty-year extension of the Mutual Assistance Treaty. Paasikivi said that it was the first time in seven negotiations in Moscow that he was able to go home satisfied. As for Kekkonen, who said that the Russians had 'filled the hearts of the Finnish people with joy,' the action was nicely timed. It gave him a talking point for the presidential election just five months later, in February 1956, which he narrowly won, mainly with Agrarian and Communist support, by 151 parliamentary votes as against 149 for Fagerholm of the Social Democrats.

As a president who revels in political maneuvers, Kekkonen stirs great emotions in Finland. He has his passionate defenders, and he has opponents who are almost apoplectic in their antagonism. His detractors say that the President's left-wing domestic politics are turning Finland into 'Kekkoslovakia.' One Kekkonen critic asked: 'Where in the world is there anything like the personality cult that Kekkonen has set up?' A leading editor explained: 'Kekkonen's trouble is his very Finnish traits; his inability to forget a hurt or criticism for years back. This keeps him from being a great man. He has a kind of pettiness which keeps coming to the surface. He is so stubborn and so convinced he is right that he disparages the views of others. He personalizes everything. And now one can see his increasing isolation. He is reducing the circle around him. It was already small and full of yes-men. There is no doubt that we must support the policy of friendliness with the Russians, but he has leaned so far backward that he is unable to stand upright again. He has become a prisoner of the policy, and that makes it all the harder to change it if we have to.'

Sporting President

What everyone can agree on is that Kekkonen, as a private individual and a public person, is a formidable figure, perhaps the most formidable in Scandinavia. He confidently wields the greatest amount of political authority in the Nordic countries. A muscular, bald-headed six-footer, and every inch a Finn, he is now in his late sixties, but looks ten years younger. He ardently practices the physical fitness he preaches. As a young man he was twice Finland's high-jump champion. He has been the foremost leader of the Finnish Gymnastics and Sports Federation, serving as its chairman for eighteen years. He led the Finnish teams in the Los Angeles and Berlin Olympic Games in the 1930s and in a score of other international competitions during the great prewar days of Finnish sport.

For years Kekkonen has been in the habit of taking a regular daily walk through the woods, sometimes for as long as ten or fifteen miles. He goes off on frequent hunting and fishing trips. He skis regularly in the winter, sometimes for more than fifty miles in a day, and makes an annual journey to Lapland to live under the rigorously spartan conditions of the complete outdoors man. In speeches he cries out against the danger of people going soft in the age of automatic machines. He urges Finns—already about as athletic as any people anywhere—to get out and exercise. He bakes in the sauna two or three times a week. Some Finns believe that Finnish-Russian relations reached new heights when Kekkonen and Khrushchev sat naked and sweating together in a sauna.

When I called on President Kekkonen at his residence in a woodland at the outskirts of Helsinki, I was struck by the quantity of books which he kept readily at hand, and by his top-floor sportsman's retreat, his 'holy of holies,' where he can relax in what one woman visitor described as 'the most masculine room I have ever seen.'

The President of Finland has the use of the President's Palace in the heart of the capital, but it is too much of a monument for comfortable living. 'It is like an old hotel with nothing but corridors,' said Mrs. Kekkonen, 'and impossible to be happy in.' The villa at Tamminiemi (Oak Cape) is more to their taste. It is a large but unpretentious cream-colored house with a tile roof, which commands a view of water and birch woods. Imposing moose horns hang in the front hall. A deep-pile *ryijy* rug stretches like a great abstract painting on one living-room wall. During my visit, sunlight streamed in through huge picture windows. The President appeared immediately, and we sat down on a long, curved sofa behind a coffee table, which held a giant jar of peanuts. Kekkonen has the naturally authoritative presence of a general in a businessman's suit. His bullet head glowed faintly in the sun-drenched room and he gazed noncommittally from behind half-horn-rimmed glasses.

Kekkonen's responses to questions about social and economic affairs could as well have come from Tage Erlander or any other Scandinavian Social Democrat. 'We are pragmatists,' he said. As a man who had long commanded the Agrarian Party, he gave the impression that there were few real differences between Finnish Agrarians and Social Democrats. Years ago they were able to join forces in 'red-green' coalition governments. Now, he suggested, Finnish politics could be stabilized if only the Social Democrats would patch up their internal quarrels and prepare to cooperate again with the Agrarians. (But Kekkonen's opponents insist that it is he who encourages and exploits the Social Democratic split.) On foreign policy, Kekkonen made a forceful case that nothing of any importance to Finnish sovereignty had been yielded to the Russians in the pursuit of friendly coexistence.

A flow of warmth came into the conversation when it turned to books and sports. He led the way to his ground-floor office, where his desk was piled high with books, and then up to his bedroom, which had a single bed, two oversized pillows for comfortable reading, and a small table, which almost groaned from the weight of books. He said he was simultaneously reading Finnish and English works on Soviet military strategy, East German politics and Finnish foreign policy, as well as the Warren Report on the Kennedy assassination, some stories from Rabelais, and the newsmagazine *U.S. News & World Report*. Kekkonen has written several books himself and is known to writers and publishers as a man who enjoys the company of literary men. Every so often he invites a group of them to his home and encourages a lively intellectual argument. 'He doesn't say too much himself,' one writer said. 'He prefers to sit back and listen.' In this effort at keeping in touch with the world of ideas Kekkonen is greatly assisted by his wife, Mrs. Sylvi Kekkonen, a somewhat shy but energetic woman, who is as voracious a reader as her husband and the author of a number of books of her own.

When we climbed the staircase to the top floor of the villa we left behind the normal household furnishings and all the paraphernalia which come to a head of state—a vase from Khrushchev, a rococo pendulum clock from de Gaulle, a modern painting from Tito—and entered the small retreat where Kekkonen can get away from it all. There is a radio, but no telephone. The sloping pine walls and large dark beams suggest a cabin in the forest. The array of rifles, shotguns and fishing rods exude masculinity. A broad and fluffy white lamb's-wool Kazakhstan hat, another gift from Khrushchev, rests in a cabinet, and black boots stand on the floor. The room makes it plain that Kekkonen's heart is still deep in the Finnish countryside where he was born.

His father was a tenant farmer and forest worker who eventually rose to become a forest foreman for an important woodworking company. Urho Kekkonen, the eldest son in the family, grew up in a poor district of north-central Finland. He was a political activist from his boyhood days. As a young law student he was an uncompromising nationalist, rabidly anti-Swedish in the language battle which raged in Finland after independence. He became a leader in the right-wing, intensely nationalistic Academic Karelian Society which sought a Greater Finland by somehow bringing the Finnish-speaking people of Soviet Karelia within Finland's boundaries. He worked for the State Security Police, which was mainly engaged in anti-Communist work. As a student in Germany in 1931, however, he saw the beginnings of Nazism and wrote some warning articles about the threat to democracy if Germany went fascist.

Appointed a cabinet minister in an Agrarian government in 1936 after being elected to parliament for the first time, Kekkonen condemned the right-wing Lapua movement when it threatened to take over the government. As minister of the interior in 1938, he suspended many of the activities of the fascist-flavored Patriotic Peoples' Movement. From then on, through a succession of ministerial jobs, the prime ministership five times and the presidency, Kekkonen became Finland's most controversial figure. There was an interesting gap in his political career during the Continuation War of 1941–44. He had been one of those who vehemently opposed making any concessions of territory to Russia before the Winter War, and he had refused to go along with the acceptance of peace terms at the end of that war. 'My position has been that a peace dictated by Moscow should not be suffered,' he told the parliament, 'but that the fight for independence should still go on.' From this extreme position, Kekkonen a few years later swung to the opposite extreme of urging Finland to pull out of World War II, even at unfavorable terms. Cold analysis of the war situation had convinced him that Germany was bound to lose and that Russia would eventually have its way with Finland.

The combative politician who had been known to be particularly hostile to the Soviet Union, now became a leading advocate of concessions, cooperation and peaceful coexistence. According to a British expert on Finland, 'the change was a bigger one for a Finn to make than for an English Conservative who crosses the floor of the House of Commons and ranges himself with Labour. His apologists say he had matured. His detractors say that he was intelligent enough to look ahead and saw that only this way lay opportunity for advancement in the future.'

One of Kekkonen's severest opponents said that 'he has always had a partiality for extreme causes. He used to be far on the right and now he's a left-leaning Agrarian, even though he's supposed to be a nonparty president. He has always been a dividing force, not a uniting one. Paasikivi was not a mild man, but he was a statesman. Kekkonen is a politician.' He is charged with using foreign policy as an instrument to enhance the fortunes of the Agrarian Party and to consolidate his personal power under the theme 'Après moi les Russes.'

Foreign Policy

The most serious and most persistent charge against Kekkonen is that he has leaned so far backward in assuring the Russians of Finland's 'sincerity' that Churchill's sublime Finland has become supine Finland. Kekkonen is sure that he knows how to handle the Kremlin, but a good many Finns believe that he is playing a dangerous game of Russian roulette. They feel that there has been something undignified or oversolicitous about the way he traveled repeatedly to the Soviet Union to visit his friend Nikita Khrushchev, and then 'acted as the Kremlin's errand boy' in promoting a Moscow-supported plan for a nuclear-free Scandinavia. He was, of course, the first chief of state to visit the new Soviet leaders after Khrushchev's overthrow. On the home front, Kekkonen cracked down hard on the Finnish student organizations whose members were involved in anti-communist demonstrations during the Communist-backed Eighth World Youth and Student Festival in Helsinki in 1962. Although no one seriously suggests that Kekkonen is pro-Communist, there are objections when he speaks effusively about Lenin in an address in Moscow, or when he proposes for Finland an 'all-party government' which by definition would have to include the Communists.

Kekkonen's critics say that by brainwashing the nation in

favor of a ultrafriendly attitude toward the U.S.S.R. he is gravely weakening the Finnish will to resist the Russians in case they once again try to overwhelm Finland. They think it strange that the Finns should keep on acting like 'the kidnaped children of Scandinavia,' when the Yugoslavs, Albanians, Hungarians, Rumanians and others have repeatedly thumbed their noses at Moscow and gotten away with it.

Although several aspects of Finland's foreign policy are puzzling, not to say disturbing, there is no doubt that it makes sense for the Finns to try to get along with the Russians as best they can. They will fight if they must, but they have become mature enough to know that their traditionally belligerent approach cannot get them very far against the might of the Soviet Union. A popular story in Finland tells of the Finn who informs another that one Finn is worth ten Russians. 'Of course,' says the other, 'but what do we do when the eleventh Russian arrives?'

To a greater extent than would have seemed possible, the Finns are submerging their deeper passions about the traditional enemy and are disciplining themselves not to appear anti-Russian. Sometimes it goes too far. The Finnish press as a whole practices great restraint in not giving offense to the Russians, but the left-wing newspapers pull no punches in denouncing American and West European policies. More important, however, is the over-all attitude of the Finns who clearly consider themselves Scandinavians, West Europeans and residents of the Free World. Russia may be the next-door neighbor, but few Finns have any interest in learning Russian. The nation's economic and cultural interests are predominantly geared to Western Europe. The Paasikivi-Kekkonen policy has sufficiently pacified the Soviet Union to permit the Finns to emerge from their pillbox at the rim of Europe and move freely in the outside world. They are members of the Nordic Council and, with certain reservations, of the European Free Trade Association. The appointment of the late Sakari S. Tuomioja, a onetime prime minister, as United Nations mediator in Cyprus in 1964 was a sign that Finland, never behind the Iron Curtain, had come out from behind the special veil of its foreign policy.

Pekka Kuusi, a prominent Finnish social thinker and Social Democrat, put it this way: 'For centuries our nation has been an outpost of the West; in the last few decades it has been an ideological outpost of the West. But now that East and West are approaching one another, a new phase seems to be dawning for our nation. Finland is about to be freed from its heavy duty of serving as an outpost.'

Chapter 31

FINNISH SPECIALTIES

We always seem to be in some kind of financial crisis. We are too extravagant in the first place, and then the effort to catch up with the rest of Scandinavia has put too great a strain on our resources.
— LAHTI BUSINESSMAN

Yes, some people drink too much at a time, and our traffic accidents are high. The car is the modern form of the knife.
— FINNISH SOCIOLOGIST

'They speak about the German miracle. *This* is the miracle!'

The proud words came from Kauko Uusitalo, the large and ebullient chief of Metex, Finland's big export combine for the metals and engineering industries. Other Finns said much the same thing. Their case is simply put. Finland had staggered out of the war as a defeated and decimated nation. Some 130,000 men had been killed or permanently disabled. A great portion of the land area was lost to the Russians, the northern third of the country lay in ruins, and 13 per cent of the total population had to be resettled at great cost. The industrial machinery, although generally spared from the bombs which rained on Europe, was old and exhausted. A third of Finland's hydroelectric capacity, a fifth of the railways, the outlet to the Arctic, and a number of valuable mines and factories were lost to the Russians.

The Soviet Union demanded about 500 million dollars' worth of reparations goods, which had to be delivered quickly, otherwise ruinous penalties would be applied. Many of the materials required had never before been manufactured by a nation more accustomed to sawing wood than making sophisticated machinery. Tremendous amounts of capital for new equipment were needed, but the Russians prevented Finland from receiving Marshall Plan assistance. Even if all obstacles could be overcome, and all deliveries to Russia made on time, there loomed the dismaying prospect that Finland would find its economy irrevocably tied to the Soviet Union's. It could well become a captive of the Communist bloc.

The miracle is that Finland worked itself out of this tight squeeze in less than a decade. It then went on to its present high level of prosperity and an over-all living standard equal to that of West Europeans in general. Eighty per cent of Finnish trade today is with the non-Communist world, and the very chore of producing reparations goods has given Finland a wider and more diversified industrial base. Although some nagging problems remain and financial crises are almost a way of life, the central fact is that Finland now has a thriving economy. It is not so opulent as Sweden's, but it is astonishingly robust for a cornered country with few natural advantages beyond its trees.

A century ago, most Finns were dirt poor. 'In the poorest districts,' wrote historian Eino Jutikkala, 'pine bark was regularly used to eke out the flour used in breadmaking.' Industry for the home market was practically nonexistent, since the scattered population, the poor communications, and the poverty of the peasantry—which tried to produce all its own consumer goods at home—made the market for factory products so small that no large-scale manufacturing enterprise would have had any chance of success. Finland was then a primitive agricultural country, and it remained so until well into the present century. Half the working population was still engaged in agriculture and forestry by World War II; today it is a bit more than a quarter. Manufacturing, commerce, construction and communications have been forging ahead.

It is the tree which was and still is at the root of the modern Finnish economy. Finland is the most heavily forested country in Europe, but this fact of life could not be turned into an asset until a combination of events in the 1860s and '70s suddenly created a great demand for timber in Western Europe and provided Finland with the means to export its green gold. New railroads and canals connected Finland's secluded forest interior with the outside world. New industrial techniques took the nation well beyond the simple products of sawmills to the more refined products of pulp and cellulose plants. The demand for timber made jobs in the forest, which in turn stimulated the development of Finland's backward agriculture. Farm productivity rose strikingly between the two world wars.

It is a hard country to cultivate, but then the Finns are a hard people; the 350,000 who went to America during the decades of the great Scandinavian migration chose to live in north-central states, where the winter can be as severe as anything known in Finland. The Finnish soil is frozen and draped with snow most of the year. Cattle must be kept indoors for six to eight months. Farms are small, mechanization is difficult to apply, and incomes are low. Nonetheless, Finland in recent times has just about reached agricultural self-sufficiency. There has even been overproduction in farming, a noteworthy feat for a subarctic country.

Years of Sacrifice

Knowing how vulnerable they are when war breaks out in Europe, the Finns are desperately anxious to make sure that they can survive on their own resources. They were all but left on their own during the war, and in the aftermath they had to look to themselves to solve their own problems. It was a tremendous achievement in self-sacrifice. As Finns now describe those early postwar years, they are themselves awed about the way they managed to put aside their usual bickerings and pull together in the time of emergency. 'It just had to be done,' one Finn said. It meant that five years of wartime austerity had to be extended into about eight peacetime years. It was not until the end of the reparations period in 1952, the bright year of the Helsinki Olympics, that the Finns finally emerged from their dark tunnel of privation.

They had virtually been living on the bark of their trees, like the poverty-stricken peasants of the last century. They fed their cattle on cellulose hay and used wood products for their clothing and bedding. Food was severely rationed. In fact, just about everything was rationed. The housing shortage was overwhelming, because shelter had to be found for 425,000 refugees from the areas which had been given up to the Russians. Thousands of ex-servicemen, widows and orphans also had to be resettled. Millions of dollars' worth of bonds and trust certificates were paid to displaced persons for the property they had lost. Overall, they received a 40 per cent compensation. In a blitz of land reform, nearly 2,700,000 acres owned by the state, communities, wealthy families, land speculators and others were turned over to refugee farm families. In many cases the refugees had to settle down like pioneers on raw land in a re-enactment of Finnish ancient history, but they built their saunas, and then their homes, and prevailed.

The over-all cost of the resettlement program has been described as astronomic, at least in relation to Finland's resources, but the Finnish sense of social justice insisted that the program be carried out. There would have been serious political problems, of course, if this uprooted tenth of the nation had not been cared for. Nonetheless, one unhappy consequence was the further fragmentation of Finnish farm land in an age when high productivity requires more than a crazy quilt of 285,000 separate holdings of about twenty-two acres each. The 'little farmer' in Finland has had to be propped up with agricultural subsidies, and these have been at the heart of Finland's continuing argument about how to put the economy on a sound fiscal basis. The situation helps explain the fact that the Agrarians still get the most votes in Finland, and that the Communists win heavy support among the small farmers.

Finland's war indemnity had to be paid in a few short years, and two thirds of the items required were for non–forestry products. It required a crash program of industrial expansion, which the Finns somehow accomplished with little more than 100 million dollars in foreign loans during the whole indemnity period. Deliveries were originally demanded in six years, but the Russians in 1945 extended the deadline to eight years. To their credit, they made several other concessions when it became clear how enormous a burden the Finns were trying to carry, and they canceled many of the fines levied on late deliveries. Finnish workers often put in long overtime hours in order to get equipment to the Russians before heavy penalties could be imposed. They produced whole factories and power stations, 80 turbogenerators, 700 locomotives, more than 50,000 motors and engines, 35,000 tons of cable, more than 600 ships of every kind from tugboats to icebreakers, and a mountain-sized ransom of raw materials, metals, machinery, timber, paper, pulp, and other products.

Sheer resourcefulness did the job, but Finland benefited by the fact that there was a huge world demand for the very forest products which the Finns were notably qualified to supply. As a result, Finland found the means to pay for the overnight expansion of its shipbuilding and metallurgical industries. In the process it restored its trade to the predominantly Western pattern of the prewar days. But the nation faced a serious problem: at great expense it had built up shipyards and engineering plants to supply reparations goods to Russia, but because of their high costs of production they would find it difficult to compete in the non-Communist world with similar products from Western industries. Fortunately, the Soviet Union still had an enormous need for Finnish ships and machines and was glad to enter into long-term trade agreements with Finland to get them.

Mixed Economy

The fact that tree-saturated Finland imports timber from Russia shows how big and gluttonous its woodworking enterprises are. It is true that the metals industry has grown to four times its prewar size and accounts for a fifth of all exports, but the sawmills, pulp, paper and cellulose plants still stand supreme. The world buys 900,000 tons of Finnish newsprint every year. The Enso-Gutzeit company, the biggest industrial enterprise in Finland, is primarily a wood-processing concern, which runs Europe's largest pulp-and-paper production center in the very southeastern corner of Finland. There, the workers can look across the Soviet border and see the smokestacks of the old, confiscated Enso-Gutzeit factories.

State institutions own three quarters of the Enso-Gutzeit shares; the rest are in private hands. Nearly a third of Finland's 54 million acres of forested land are state-owned, but 60 per cent are owned by private farmers and the rest by private organizations. The same kind of state-and-private mixture can be found throughout the Finnish economy. It is overwhelmingly a free-enterprise system, but the government nonetheless has heavy influence in a number of the larger industries, and it is dominant in power, transportation, communications, and mining. There is also greater government regulation of prices than elsewhere in Scandinavia. Thus Finland would seem to have a large measure of socialism; but in actuality Finland's 'socialism' has been relatively restrained—largely because of the split in the trade-union movement and the inability of the Social Democrats to win a majority—or even a near majority—of the popular vote.

As in the rest of Scandinavia, the trade unions and the employers in Finland first formed national federations soon after the turn of the century, but it has been a long passage through stormy waters to reach a smooth system of collective bargaining. The industrial community was small until World War I, but what there was tended to be anti-union. By all accounts, the Finnish capitalists were more reactionary than their Nordic counterparts, and the workers were much more left-wing, if not outrightly Communist. World War II, however, compelled labor and management to move closer together, and the first general agreement between the employer and union organizations was reached in 1944.

The machinery for collective bargaining resembles the tested equipment in the other Nordic countries, but Finland still lags well behind them in achieving labor harmony. Although some branches of industry, and certainly a good many individual companies, are as advanced and enlightened in these matters as human institutions can be, there is a ragged look about the general scene which contrasts with the rest of Scandinavia. The employers' confederation embraces companies which account for 60 per cent of the industrial labor force, but that still leaves out 40 per cent. The trade-union movement, which has organized not quite half the total work force in Finland, is tragically divided into two bitterly competing forces (with the Communists forming a third force)—which makes it extraordinarily difficult for union representatives to bargain dispassionately with management. Strikes are more frequent than in the rest of the North.

The cooperative movement also has a history of discord, even though the co-ops in many ways play a larger role in Finland than in the other Scandinavian countries. The membership figures are so high that virtually every family belongs to at least one cooperative. In recent years the cooperatives have accounted for a quarter of all savings deposits in Finland and more than a third of all wholesale and retail trade of consumer goods, and they have thoroughly dominated the food manufacturing industry.

The Finnish cooperative movement began in typical Scandinavian fashion, but it split into two in 1916 over the issue of whether it should stick to its basic task of winning economic advantages for its members or should engage in politics under the banner of Social Democracy. The parent group carried on as the 'neutral' S.O.K. organization, while the rebels set themselves up as the 'progressive' K.K. co-ops. There is even a third but much smaller collection of 'Swedish-speaking co-ops.' An indication of the size and scope of the two major groupings—each has about half a million members—is given in the figures for S.O.K. in 1964: 356 cooperative associations encompassing 5,000 shops, 386 cafés and restaurants, 44 hotels and 35 department stores, with total sales of about 500 million dollars.

Perpetual Crisis

Finland's net national income per person in 1965 reached $1,250. It was still well behind the figures for the United States. Canada and Sweden, but respectably close to Norway, Denmark and all of the leading nations of Western Europe. The net national product was just about twice as high as it was before World War II. There were about 400,000 private cars on the roads, a stunning leap from the 19,000 of 1948 or even the 139,000 of 1958. The Finns owned half a million television sets, and they were beginning to travel abroad as eagerly as the Swedes. The whole look of Finland was of a dynamic society energetically modernizing itself in every way. And yet, in many important ways, it was a financial mess.

'By any reasonable standards,' said a Helsinki newspaperman, 'this country should be bankrupt. Successive governments move from crisis to crisis, always living beyond their means. There's no national economic planning. The Social Democrats bargain with the Agrarians for more social benefits in return for more farm subsidies. Two groups of voters are pleased, but the taxpayer screams. It is hand-to-mouth living. The governments have simply mortgaged the future.' A leading Finnish economist said that 'in Finland there is no economics, only politics.' This is putting it too bluntly. There are many exceptionally able financiers and administrators who are trying to put things right, but they have a long uphill battle.

To some degree they have an impossible task, because they are dealing with basic national psychology—the tendency of the Finns to make the spontaneous, extravagant gesture today and face the consequences tomorrow. Having met their great challenge in the early postwar days, the Finns seemed to become giddy with success in the boom times which followed. The annual rate of growth was often spectacular, but when it suddenly slackened, as it did after 1961, the country realized that spendthrift governments which had committed the state to ever-greater annual expenditures had left nothing in the till for the lean years. Finland has had one of the worst inflationary problems in Europe. The wholesale-price index rose 800 per cent between 1944 and 1963. Currency devaluations have been required. Price controls have had to be maintained or brought back on a number of key items. The cost of living has soared in recent years, making Finland a notably expensive country to live in. Housing costs in particular are high. Taxes on individuals are steep, and companies bear a heavy burden of state and local taxes, as well as large social-welfare contributions. The dizzying wage-price spiral is largely due to what one leading banker calls 'this curious incomes-linkage system.' It simply means that when the cost of living goes up, industrial wages automatically go up, and, in turn, farm incomes go up. What goes down, inevitably, is Finland's ability to remain competitive in Western Europe.

Welfare State

Finland's financial headaches stem in part from its proximity to the other Scandinavian countries. The ordinary Finn is aware of how much social-security progress has been made in Sweden, in particular, and he is anxious to have the same. It is a keeping-up-with-the-Olsens attitude, which has the unions and the citizenry in general pressing for welfare measures and fringe benefits that the nation cannot afford. The Finns spend about 12 per cent of their national income on social services, double the outlay of the early postwar days. In the 1960s the expansion of pensions, family allowances, national insurance and other benefits have brought Finland much closer to the welfare standards being set by Sweden and Denmark. One important step forward was the passage of a general Health Insurance Act, to be fully operative in 1967. It gives Scandinavian-style medical protection to everyone; but, once again, it is not 'free.' The average man makes his regular contribution to the program, and the state and private employers finance the rest of it.

As elsewhere in Scandinavia, there is much grumbling about all the welfare-state queues, shortages and inadequacies, but there is no doubting that Finns today are healthier and more socially secure than ever before in their history. The shortage of doctors and dentists is serious, but something is being done about it. The number of hospital beds in Finland has doubled since the war, and so has the number of physicians. There is still a clamor for more housing; but the tremendous postwar demand has largely been satisfied, thanks in part to the state's ARAVA home-loan system, which was set up soon after the war as a means of helping organizations and individuals to build homes. In a typical case a Finn gets 35 per cent of the money he needs from a low-interest (1 to 3 per cent) ARAVA loan, raises another 35 per cent from a private bank, and provides the rest himself.

Women: The Single Standard

One of the more arresting facts of Finnish life is the special importance of women in the workings of the nation and their confident sense of equality. They are more than just mothers and wives; they have an acute sense of their own worth and see no reason why they shouldn't be able to compete with men wherever they feel like it. Even in matters of sex they seem particularly self-reliant. According to one delighted bachelor in the Helsinki diplomatic corps, 'This is a single-standard country. The girls make up their own minds about sex. It's the only place I know of where you will get from a girl the same look of frank appraisal that a man will give to the woman who attracts him. There are some wonderful free spirits among them.'

A straightforward, every-girl-for-herself approach to sexual relations may be dictated in part by the cold statistics which show a considerable surplus of women in Finland. In 1962, for example, there were 2,341,000 females of all ages and 2,182,000 males. It was my impression in Helsinki that Finnish men, married or otherwise, do very well indeed when they are looking for instant romance. It is not uncommon for prominent men to have mistresses. And yet, despite (or because of) the extremely sophisticated attitude to sex, it is not a sex-drenched society. Unlike Americans and Englishmen, the Finns are not subjected to the same saturation of sex in advertisements, newspapers, magazines and books; indeed, many of the semipornographic films and novels available in other nations are not permitted in Finland.

As the first women in Europe to get the vote in national elections, the ladies of Finland went on to secure other important rights, including the equality of husband and wife before the law. They fill half the places in the universities, and it is said that there is a higher proportion of women with an academic education in Finland than in any other country. A great many of the professors are female. Women are well represented in the parliament, and it has become customary for one or two women to be given cabinet posts. The leading Communist in Finland is a female, and a woman police official is a representative of Finland in Interpol, the International Criminal Police Organization. (She once said that a good memory had helped get her the job: 'I know who are in prison in Finland. I know who have been in prison in Finland. And I know some people who should be in prison in Finland.')

Except for the Soviet Union, Finnish women hold more jobs outside the home than any other in Europe, and they are particularly important in the professions. They account for 24 per cent of the doctors, 83 per cent of the dentists, 90 per cent of the pharmacists, and for most of the teachers, barbers and bank employees. They hold nearly 90 per cent of all the jobs in cafés, restaurants, and hotels. Every big industrial plant I visited in Finland had a high proportion of women employees, including sawmills, where women have a third of the jobs, despite the amount of rough work involved. As in Russia, women labor in the fields and can be seen working in garages, driving trucks, sweeping the streets, hauling bricks at construction projects, and operating heavy equipment in factories. During the war the members of the Lotta Svärd women's auxiliary performed outstanding services, often under hazardous conditions. At war's end it was one of the national organizations of a paramilitary character which had to be disbanded at the insistence of the Russians.

Despite the tremendously important role of women there, Finland is anything but a matriarchy. The young unmarried girl may be a fairly free spirit, but marriage is another story. Finnish working wives are expected to carry out all the usual household chores and care for the children in addition to attending to their jobs. It is probable that they are the hardest-working women in Europe. The Finnish male, who sees himself as a two-fisted man's man, may help his wife in the kitchen but hates to admit it. One American educator in Finland, after visiting a number of Finnish families, said that 'this is one of the last remaining patriarchies in the world. The husband is the boss, even if his wife does go out and work.'

The Two-Language Problem

Finland is a signmaker's paradise. Not only are Finnish words as long as the names of Welsh villages, but in much of the country everything has to be written twice—in Swedish as well as Finnish. The two-language Helsinki telephone directory is more than twice as large as one expects for a city of its size, and the neon signs all over the country stretch out to heroic lengths. The Swedish name for the town of Kristinestad, to take one example, is long enough, but in Finnish it comes out as Kristiinankaupunki. Finnish is a tongue-twisting language full of double consonants and double vowels, and it is not surprising that the longest reversible word in any language is the Finnish term for soapmaker: *saippuakauppias*. The main street in Helsinki is Mannerheimintie, a leading restaurant is Kalastajatorppa, and a typical company is Teollisuusmarkkinointi Oy. The Finns seem to have no trouble rolling the words off their tongues, but an outsider feels that he has come upon a wholly disconnected race of humans.

The Finns have had some kind of language problem for at least a thousand years. In all that time Finnish has survived, like the Finns themselves, but as an orphan in a storm of other languages. When Finns went abroad it did no good to speak Finnish; no one except the Estonians and Hungarians had ever heard of it. It was necessary to learn a more widely known language, and today it is more necessary than ever. Even for Finns who had no interest in going abroad, the colonization of the country by the Swedes, and their succession by the Russians, often meant that Swedish and Russian had to be learned in order to get ahead. Before and during the last war there was a strong pull from the German language. Today it is English which most Finns learn first after Swedish. The impact of American and British films, not to mention television serials, has been great; but, according to one Helsinki resident, 'with subtitles in both Finnish and Swedish there isn't much space left for the picture.'

Finland's Swedish-speaking population was 13 per cent of the total in 1900; today it is down to 7 per cent. Emigration has been partly responsible. The remaining Swedish-Finns are becoming more Finnish all the time, thanks to intermarriage and their over-all absorption by the majority. 'Besides,' I was told, 'the Finns breed faster than the Swedes. They've always gone in for bigger families.' Even though the 'Swedes' have always been a minority, they used to hold most of the political and economic power. They still have more than their share, but it becomes less noticeable all the time. Education and a general leveling-out of incomes have helped to blur the differences between the once superior Swedes and the inferior mass of Finns. Between the two world wars there was a raging language controversy as the ultranationalists sought to reduce the influence of the Swedes, whom they deeply resented. To Finns like Urho Kekkonen, when he was a younger man, the Swedes were still intruders on Finnish soil and their patriotism was seriously questioned. It was argued that Swedish should not con-tinue to have equal status with Finnish. The wartime years served to take the fire out of the language argument. The Swedish-speak-ing community proved itself to be every bit as loyal as the rest of the Finns. It also began to be realized that Finland's knowledge of Swedish was an asset in the nation's effort to keep Russia at arms' length and to become more integrated with the other Scandinavian states. A wholesale rejection of Swedish would have been a classic case of a nation cutting off its nose to spite its face.

Today there is general support for the two-language system, which is protected by the constitution. Swedish is taught in the Finnish schools, and Finnish is taught in the smaller number of schools which teach in Swedish. Because the Swedish-speaking Finns are concentrated mainly in the southern and western regions of the country (they also account for nearly 100 per cent of the residents of the Åland Islands), it is only in these areas that signs come in two languages and officials are expected to know Swedish as well as Finnish. A law in 1922 set up a system of unilingual and bilingual communities, depending on whether the lingual minority had less or more than 10 per cent of the population. Swedish-Finns later became alarmed at the way they were losing ground as their numbers fell below 10 per cent even in com-munities in the south and west. It became apparent that even in such old strongholds as Vaasa, Turku and Helsinki, they would eventually fall below the line. As a result a new law was passed only a few years ago, which obliged a city to continue being a bilingual community so long as there were at least 5,000 resident members of the Swedish minority.

The language conflict has, to a large degree, been a class conflict, and the Swedish-Finns, four fifths of them, support their own Swedish National Party, which has fourteen seats in the parliament. Its coloration is mostly conservative. Many leading landlords, financiers and other men of influence are Swedish. There are Swedish newspapers, a Swedish university in Turku (Åbo) and other institutions which serve to resist the blending process. There is even a House of Nobles in the capital, which carries on, in its anachronistic way, a number of the old traditions of the Swedish aristocracy.

The Serious Drinkers

There is a saying that the Norwegians eat to live, the Danes live to eat, and the Finns eat to drink. Like all national characterizations, this hardly tells the whole story, but there is no denying the Finn's reputation as a dedicated, no-nonsense drinker. He will tell you himself about the Finn who went to Texas, heard a cowboy order a drink and saw him keel over, dead drunk, after gulping it down. 'I'll have what that fellow had,' said the Finn to the bartender, 'only make it a double.'

There is no escaping the alcohol issue in Finland. A traveler arriving at Helsinki's international airport will be asked by his Finnish friend, 'How was the landing?' not 'How was the flight?' If the visitor wonders why there should be special interest in the landing, the Finn will cheerfully explain: 'Well, I thought you might find the runway a little bumpy. It was built by some of our most distinguished citizens.' The customary penalty for anyone caught driving a car after consuming anything more than a single beer is a three-month stretch with the airport's pick-and-shovel brigade. A good many persons of standing, including members of parliament, businessmen, scholars and police officers, have qualified for the construction gang. 'Pretty soon we will have the longest runways in the world,' said one Finn.

The statistics, of course, show that the alcoholic intake of the Finns, per capita, is actually the lowest in Europe: about half that of the Swedes, Danes and English, and an eighth of the French. But those Finns who do drink have the habit of saving themselves for a once-a-week or once-a-month all-out binge with the most potent kind of alcohol. And all too often the inebriated Finn becomes violent—and uses his knife. Even among more temperate persons, drinking in the land of silent people has a special social importance as an icebreaker. Foreign businessmen who visit Finland find that there is an almost Oriental flavor to the pattern of ritualistic eating, drinking and bathing (in the sauna, of course) which accompanies business deals.

Finland's history of alcoholism, and the impact of the temperance movement, is much like Sweden's. People consumed so much alcohol during the first half of the nineteenth century that perhaps a fourth or fifth of the entire grain crop went into drink. The reformers began their work at the same time, with the result that the state finally assumed total command of production and distribution. Consumption was cut drastically, and total prohibition was imposed in 1919. It didn't succeed, of course, and was abandoned in 1932. Today, a state of semiprohibition exists, which in practice means that it is possible to get a drink, but with difficulty, especially for country people who live a good distance from the government retail shops. Customers are obliged to produce a purchasing license for hard liquor.

The Finnish workingman's favorite drink is *viina*, a potent potato alcohol, but on payday he is liable to part with $11 for a fifth of Scotch or turn to another expensive favorite, French cognac. Finland imports more of it than any other country except the United States and Great Britain. The importer, of course, is the inevitable government liquor monopoly, which works closely with the hundreds of temperance organizations to discourage people from drinking. Its name is Alkoholiliike Oy. This has been freely translated into English as 'Alcohol I Like. Oh Why?' Why indeed.

Chapter 32

DESIGN FOR LIVING

*Finland is the only place in the world where people will sit out-
doors in the rain watching a play about how their country lost
the war.*
　　　　　　　　　　　　　　　—AMERICAN EDUCATOR

The sauna is like a confession. It sweats out all your sins.
　　　　　　　　　　　　　　　—FINNISH BUSINESSMAN

A Finnish author, visiting the United States for the first time, told
a gathering of publishers in New York: 'You don't know our
best books, but in Finland we are familiar even with some of your
trash.'

More than the Swedes, Danes or Norwegians, the Finns live a
life of cultural isolation. Jean Sibelius, who died only as recently
as 1957, is an international name, and a few other Finns, like
architect Alvar Aalto and author Mika Waltari (best known for
The Egyptian), have large reputations in the world, but problems
of language and sheer remoteness have put the richness of Finnish
culture out of sight and out of mind. Only now, through the
incredible beauty and originality of Finnish design, is the outside
world beginning to get more than a glimpse of the peculiar intensity of the creative arts of Finland.

Once again, like Finnish behavior in general, it is Scandinavianism with a difference. The arts run to more emotional extremes
than in the more settled Nordic countries. The music goes deeper,
the poetry is more passionate, the artists and designers are more
flamboyant, the architects are more daring, and the typical

532

literary controversy is like a sideshow next to the main tent of the political circus. People argue about books as if Finland's very existence were at stake. It is right that they should, because the works of several authors have had an extraordinary importance in the making of modern Finland.

An indefatigable scholar named Elias Lönnrot early in the nineteenth century went about the country collecting folk poetry and ballads which were published as the *Kalevala* in 1835. It had an explosive effect on Finnish national pride. Suddenly the Finns realized that they had a cultural heritage and a poetic language worth fighting for. Eventually the *Kalevala* was recognized by scholars around the world as one of the all-time-great works of epic poetry, a Finnish *Iliad* or *Odyssey*.

The golden age of Finnish literature began in the 1860s with the publication of works by an ill-fated tailor's son, Aleksis Kivi, who lost his sanity and died at age thirty-six. His earthy, humorous novel, *The Seven Brothers*, became a Finnish masterpiece. Often called Finland's greatest author, his major role was to inspire other Finns to produce bold and realistic works in their own tongue.

Väinö Linna

One of Finland's great writers of this century was F. E. Sillanpää whose poetic but fatalistic accounts of simple, instinctive country people won him the Nobel Prize in Literature in 1939. No Scandinavian writer in modern times, however, has enjoyed anything quite like the explosive success which has come to Finland's Väinö Linna. He was born in 1920, the son of a poor peasant. While he was serving as an ordinary soldier on the Russian front during the 1941–44 war, he took notes about the dirt and degradation, and the magnificence of heroes who scorned all talk of heroism. Hoping to earn a little leave money, he wrote a modest novel about the war as he knew it and sent it to a publisher. 'They said it was clumsy and no good,' Linna told me. 'They wouldn't publish it. Thank God for that! But they said the way you see things is good. They told me to learn to write. I'm still learning.'

After the war, Linna went to work as a mechanic in a textile plant. In his spare time he took up the men-at-war theme again and wrote a long work of carthy realism called *The Unknown Soldier*. It was published late in 1954. Finland went wild. Within a year of publication, 200,000 Finns had bought copies. (A sale of similar proportion in the United States would have been eight and a half million.) In the decade since its appearance, the book has sold more copies than any other in Finnish history except for the Bible and the standard hymn book. It was translated around the world (in some countries under the title *Crosses in Karelia*) and acclaimed as the Finnish version of *All Quiet on the Western Front* and *The Naked and the Dead*. The film and the play based on *The Unknown Soldier* had an equally electrifying effect on the Finns and have reached an international audience. In the midst of all the excitement, Linna went on to prove that he had more in him than a single novel by writing three successive works for a trilogy on Finnish life since Tsarist times. They too were best sellers and touched off a great national controversy. They have been described as 'the confession of the Finnish soul.'

When Linna received the Nordic Literature Prize in 1963, the then prime minister of Finland, Ahti Karjalainen, stated to the Nordic Council: 'He has said much that Finnish authors have not dared to express. . . .' That is the heart of the matter. The Finns had so gloried in their brave resistance to the overwhelming Russian forces that it seemed blasphemous for Linna to suggest that it had been a dirty war, as all wars are dirty, fought by foul-mouthed and brutalized soldiers whose sardonic attitude to the struggle sounded downright unpatriotic. They were men who got drunk, disobeyed orders, jeered at Marshal Mannerheim's Orders of the Day, and went about stealing food. But against hopeless odds and knowing that defeat was inevitable, such men also fought and bled with a splendor unsurpassed in the history of warfare.

Linna, in short, described war in the raw. Then his trilogy, *Here Under the North Star*, opened up fresh wounds by describing, from the viewpoint of ordinary peasants in central Finland, the nation's suffering and stumbling progress from its last decades as a grand duchy to independence, and then through the suicidal civil war, the struggle with Russia, and the present-day search for national equilibrium. By rejecting the easy answer that the Whites were right in the civil war, and making it clear why conservative Finnish villagers came to support the Reds, Linna exposed himself to the assault of superpatriots. 'It was like writing in a glass box,' he said, but he wrote on in the midst of the furor and staked his place firmly in Finnish literary history.

When I called on Linna in Tampere, he was in the midst of a 'creative pause'—charging his batteries before the next book. In that relaxed mood he looked for all the world like a benign, middle-aged storekeeper who had made enough money to live a sumptuous life. He is a slight, dark Finn, with a battered face and fast-receding hairline. His horn-rimmed glasses, furrowed brow and intense expression gave him a certain intellectual mien, but the over-all surface impression was that of a very ordinary though unusually successful man. 'I spent my first seventeen years in very primitive country life,' Linna said. 'I am a self-educated man. All I know is what I read.' He has been an omnivorous reader all his life and was strongly influenced by Tolstoy and the other authors of Russian classics. He writes as a working-man and his opinions are inevitably left of center, but I found him to be anything but a doctrinaire champion of the great unwashed. He is simply aware of all that has been wrong with Finnish life. 'The old society had many nondemocratic values,' he said; and he welcomes the more reasonable and humane society which has come about. 'The conservative mind sees the golden age as behind us,' he said. 'But there was much suffering in the old Finnish society. Nothing much was said about it. People just endured.'

An important contemporary of Linna's, although eight years younger, is Veijo Meri, whom several authorities described as the most talented of the younger generation of writers. His novels reveal a grotesque sense of humor. A leading literary figure said that 'Meri has a special conception of war. Linna feels that war is absurd but that the people in a war are sensible. Meri feels that both war and the people are absurd, and yet the people somehow survive. He leads our young authors who do not have the strong beliefs of the old schools. They deal dispassionately with issues.'

Like Linna, Veijo Meri is a quiet, serious, ordinary-looking Finn, who lives an orderly life in an ordinary Helsinki apartment. While his wife supplied us with a vast amount of sandwiches and cakes, Meri said that 'there is no taboo-thinking in the young,' but a writer must nonetheless hurdle a great many taboos in order to have his say. The combination of a rigid bureaucratic tradition from the Russian days, and the powerful influence of the Church on the written word, has served to inhibit Finnish authors. 'One hundred years ago we had only the Bible. All our literature has developed since then, but there is still Bible-thinking.'

Although most Finns are indifferent to religion, the official Lutheran Church is still influential in Finland; and in some parts, especially in the central villages, there is still an important and uncompromising core of austere Lutheranism. President Kekkonen once said that 'the rugged individuality of Martin Luther's movement seemed as if made to order for the way of life that was growing up here amidst the dark forests.' Another Finn said that 'we have as many religious extremists as we have Communists, and they both make too much trouble.'

Stage-Struck

Literature is vital in Finland, but it is the theater that evokes the most passionate popular response. Finland is possibly the most stage-struck country in the world, and yet a great many Finns are so silent and remote so much of the time that they hardly seem likely candidates for amateur dramatics. The theater, of course, serves in an almost alcoholic way to release the personality from its cage and set it free for a while. Finnish author Matti Kurjensaari has written that 'every Finn has appeared on an amateur stage at least once in his life. In the imaginary world of the theater the Finn dares to unburden himself, to reveal his innermost soul. He thinks that he is acting. But the truth is probably that when he believes he is acting he is in reality living his truest life.'

The Finnish theater began only a century ago, at the time of

Finland's great national awakening. Often the same men who broke new literary trails, Aleksis Kivi in particular, wrote the early works of the national theater. Kivi's *Cobblers on the Heath*, published in 1864, is the premier Finnish comedy and undoubtedly deserves greater international recognition as a comic masterpiece. Generally speaking, however, the strength of the Finnish theater is more in its performers than in its playwrights. About 60 per cent of the works produced in Finnish theaters are foreign, with English, French, Russian and Scandinavian plays predominating, but with modern American works achieving ever more popularity. Although there is a solid comic tradition, the average Finn goes to the theater in a serious mood. He is seeking culture and enlightenment, and apparently he prefers meaty and woeful drama which confirms his view that life is a long travail, with little joy or justice to be found. The theater is not an escape from reality. 'We want something to think about,' said one Finn. They are thoughtful, phlegmatic theatergoers. Finnish audiences, in my experience, do not vigorously show their appreciation of a good, entertaining performance. Their applause is so light and perfunctory that foreign artists visiting Finland have been unnerved about the audience reaction and have had to be reassured over and over that the people really loved the show.

The theater has been an educational institution and an instrument of social advance in Finland, which is one reason why it is rooted as deeply in the farming and working communities as in the better-off and better-educated classes. There are some famous 'workers theaters' in the country, which were born in the labor movement and have gone in for social realism without the heavy-handedness of the Russians.

The Finns, according to Swedish author Vilhelm Moberg, have a 'lyrical-dramatic side, which makes them especially susceptible to dramatic arts.' There are some eight thousand amateur theaters and dramatic clubs, in addition to the forty professional theaters, five of which put on performances in the Swedish language. The state and municipalities have been giving financial support to theaters ever since 1860. About 60 per cent of the revenue of the professional theaters comes from such funds, with the result that ticket prices are low and almost every Finn can afford to be a theatergoer. Finland is also one of the few countries which turn regularly to amateur performers to put on television dramas.

The Architects

My own first acquaintance with the splendors and traditions of Finnish architecture and design came in Bloomfield Hills, Michigan, in 1956, when I spent several weeks on a *Time* cover-story assignment with an immensely gifted architect, the late Eero Saarinen. As the son of Eliel Saarinen, one of Finland's great modern architects, Eero Saarinen spent the first twelve years of his life in a rustic, thirty-eight-room country home and architect's studio eighteen miles outside Helsinki. The house was often full of celebrities—everyone from Sibelius to Russian author Maxim Gorky.

Eliel Saarinen was the foremost architect and city planner during Finland's turn-of-the-century period of National Romanticism. He moved his office and family to America in 1923, after winning a $20,000 second prize in a competition for the design of a skyscraper tower for the Chicago Tribune. His design won more acclaim than the winning entry. He lived the rest of his life in America, working in close association at Cranbrook Academy, which he designed, with Swedish sculptor Carl Milles. Eero, who was clearly born to be an architect, worked under his father at first, but eventually escaped the old man's shadow and went on to a meteoric career as the most exciting and versatile American architect of his time. Tragically, he died in his prime in 1961, leaving behind a landscape of works which are much in the public eye: the CBS Building in Manhattan, the T.W.A. Flight Center at New York's Kennedy Airport, the Dulles International Airport Terminal outside Washington, the General Motors Technical Center near Detroit, the St. Louis Memorial Arch, the American Embassy buildings in London and Oslo, and dozens of remarkable business, university and church buildings.

Although he was an American citizen, Saarinen's moods and methods were Finnish. He told me that his 'exhaustive approach' to an architectural challenge—an all-out, almost savage drive to get the job done—probably came out of Finland's *sisu* heritage. 'It means elongated guts; that's why Finland produces long-distance runners.' But he also described Finland as a small country with a massive inferiority complex: 'It is terribly aware that it has to make its mark in the world in order to survive. That's why the Finns made such a point about paying off their war debt. A man becomes a great hero and a national asset when his work gets known outside Finland. The Finns knew Alvar Aalto's roofs leaked and my father's too, but boy!—when the outside world recognized them they could do no wrong. The Finnish kids read that all the important things happen outside their country, so they make the most out of what they've got. I remember visiting the middle of Finland when I was a boy and being told that a certain building was 'the world's largest spool factory.' It probably wasn't true. It was probably the biggest spool factory in Scandinavia, or in Europe, or in the world twenty years before. But the Finns long to be first in something. They don't want to be forgotten and just swallowed up by Russia.'

It is in design, architecture and city planning that the Finns can claim to be first in something. Oddly enough, it was poverty and politics that led to Finland's ultramodern look. Other nations may boast of buildings dating back centuries or even thousands of years. Finland is all relatively new. Only an odd castle or church here and there suggests any sort of history, architectural or otherwise. Finland was the most remote and empty pocket of Europe. With few exceptions, all of the buildings in the land of a trillion trees were made of wood, and in time almost all of them burned down. By the time Finland had developed enough to build more permanently, it was the nineteenth century and a time of growing national reaction to what the Finns describe as 'Russian repression.' With few traditions to hamper them, and with every reason to build in an assertive national style, the architects created distinctively Finnish buildings—first decorative and romantic, taking their themes from nature, and then ever more clean-cut and functional. As one expert put it: 'Patriotism made avant-gardes out of the artists of Finland.' Architects as well as poets, authors, dramatists

and musicians, were national heroes. A famous Finnish headline
of several decades ago said:

> 'PROFESSOR SAARINEN ARRIVES FROM AMERICA;
> GRETA GARBO ON SAME BOAT'

The wartime devastation of northern Finland, the postwar need
to rebuild exhausted towns, and the galloping urbanization of
Finland have presented modern Finnish architects a silver platter of
assignments. I know of no country, except perhaps Sweden,
which has gone in for city planning so enthusiastically as Finland,
or where small towns and large cities feel incomplete if they cannot
boast a dramatic city hall, hospital, school, factory or apartment
project by a leading architect.

Alvar Aalto

Although there are outstanding younger architects like Aarne
Ervi, Jorma Järvi and Reima Pietilä (the late Viljo Revell's Toronto
City Hall is one of Canada's boldest works), the lion's share of the
architectural plums have gone to Alvar Aalto, the greatest name in
modern Finnish architecture. He was born in 1898 and swept
into the forefront of the modern movement thirty years later
with such strikingly original buildings as the Paimio sanatorium
and the Viipuri municipal library. He resisted the starkness of
conventional functionalism, however, by rich use of wood and
native materials, often formed in senuous, curving lines, and by an
instinctive feeling for natural surroundings. Much of his work was
criticized as out of step with the geometric Bauhaus-style architecture which eventually covered the world with rectangular
glass boxes. Aalto stuck to his guns and watched amusedly as
architectural thinking swung around again to his views. Even
though most authorities do not put him in the select front row of
creators like Frank Lloyd Wright, Le Corbusier and Mies van
der Rohe, his place is secure as one of the great architects of the
past half century.

Aalto and his associates in his Helsinki studio have been working
at a breathtaking pace since the war. Apart from a few foreign

projects, like an undulating brick dormitory at Massachusetts Institute of Technology, his work has been concentrated in Finland. He did the basic town planning for Rovaniemi, Oulu, Imatra and several other small cities, the National Pensions Institute and House of Culture in Helsinki, a complex of buildings for the new university at his home town of Jyväskylä, and so many other buildings all over Finland that it is fair to say that no other architect anywhere has shaped the urban face of his country more thoroughly than Aalto. He has done so many works for the state-owned Enso-Gutzeit company that a Helsinki newspaperman said 'his relationship to the company has been something like that of the Medici sponsorship of art in the Middle Ages.'

For several years now Aalto has been at work on the greatest architectural project of all: a dramatic new city center for Helsinki, with a five-lane superhighway (built on top of the railroad) sweeping into the downtown area, a cultural center clinging to the shores of a bay in the middle of the city, and a central plaza with pedestrian areas lifted well away from traffic. It is costly, ambitious and visionary, and it will be some years in the building, but its boldness and extravagance are characteristically Finnish.

Aalto is in his late sixties now, but he told me that he is busier than ever. He rattled off an awesome list of projects which his private studio, staffed by twenty-eight architects, was handling at the time. They ranged from an opera house for Essen, Germany, to a radically designed library for Seinäjoki, a small town in western Finland which Aalto is almost completely face-lifting with a church, theater, city hall, other public buildings and, in time, a university.

I found his enthusiasm infectious and marveled at his versatility. He has a weathered, somewhat flushed face, thinning gray hair, and blue eyes behind horn-rimmed glasses. Most architects are hopeless egotists, and savagely quick to criticize their colleagues (Eliel Saarinen used to speak about 'Frank Lloyd Wrong'); but Aalto, on this occasion at least, was more than modest, and he wouldn't speak a word of criticism against other architects. He preferred to talk about his experiments with clusters of thin birch rods which could be bent in any direction to make free-form furniture. Aalto is accustomed to designing all the furniture, lamps and other fittings for his major buildings, and his 'potato-chip' chair of thin, molded, laminated wood has become familiar around the world.

The Designers

This kind of versatility can be found even more emphatically in the flourishing world of Finnish design. In the early 1950s, thanks to the work that Finnish artists put on display at important exhibitions in Milan, Finnish industrial art or domestic design 'blossomed out of the gray poverty of the postwar years,' as one authority, Benedict Zilliacus, said. 'It was a sudden out-burst of unrestrained imagination and unrestricted experiment, marked by a combination of robust vigor, brashness, and sensi-tivity.' What the Finns were creating in ceramics, glassware, textiles, furniture, lamps, rugs and so forth seemed to have all the Scandinavian virtues, but without the coldness or starkness which is often mentioned by way of criticism. They had something extra: a richness, intensity and deeper feeling for warm colors. Perhaps it flows from that touch of the Russian in every Finn, or perhaps the fact that Finland, in the century before independence, was strongly influenced by St. Petersburg, a Russian city built and beautified by Mediterranean artists.

Zilliacus in an art volume, *Scandinavian Domestic Design*, has written that the Finns 'have a faintly oriental weakness for the extravagant, for luxury for its own sake, which sometimes amazes casual visitors. . . . Finns to some extent can see beyond the "more beautiful useful things" of the rest of Scandinavia to the enjoyment of irresponsible "more beautiful things for pleasure."'

This characteristic is nowhere better illustrated than in the fantastic birds of ceramic beads on steel frames by Birger Kai-piainen, an artist of bizarre and Byzantine imagination. The daring uses of color are most forcefully shown in the deep-pile *ryijy* rugs which had their origins in rural Finland of several centuries ago and are being created today by abstract artists. Finnish painting is so-so; the *ryijy* rugs are magnificent. It follows that the rugs, some of them as glowing and warm as a log fire, are as often hung on walls as they are placed on the floor. Long ago they were used as traveling rugs when Finns moved by small boat or sledge. The modern furniture, glassware, pottery and other everyday objects of Finland also echo the old peasant culture. The earthenware pots and seemingly petrified glassware look as though they had come directly out of the ground instead of from the back door of a factory. As a people so often forced to fall back on their own resources, the Finns have had a kind of folk revival without being folksy. It is by no means an imitation of the past, but a reflection of the nation's original simple values and an instinctive feeling for Finland's natural surroundings.

Although several important design and handicraft institutions were founded in Finland as long ago as the 1870s, the work in the decorative or industrial arts was uncertain until the Milan Triennial Exhibition of 1951, when Finnish designers stole the show. During the twelve-year period beginning in 1951, the Finns won a fifth of all the big prizes, with only the Italians having anything like the same success. Finland, in short, had finally found itself. In glassware, ceramics and textiles in particular, it was the most inspired of the Scandinavian countries. Alvar Aalto's name still loomed large for his furniture, lamps and other works, but younger artists came to the fore with much more exciting work— Kaj Franck, Tapio Wirkkala, Timo Sarpaneva, Birger Kaipiainen, Dora Jung and a score of others. The almost overnight world reputation of Finnish design was spurred on by the commercial success of firms like Marimekko, whose colorful fashions, particularly a dress which has the look of an elegant beach shift, are sold all over Europe and America. Finns themselves suddenly realized that their designers were great national assets now that Sibelius was dead and Paavo Nurmi had stopped running. They were more generously supported and promoted than ever. It is a rare Finnish company today which is not design-conscious. Some major firms have all but elevated the designer to the rank of high priest.

Arabia

A writer for *The Times* of London, deploring the low level of British design, said: 'It is different in Scandinavia. There one will not hear the aesthete deriding the industrialist, nor vice versa. Neither could survive without the other. It might be a marriage of convenience, but it works, particularly in Finland.' The most celebrated of the Finnish design companies has the misplaced name Arabia. It is an old ceramics factory at the fringe of Helsinki. It is now so renowned that it has become a major tourist attraction. The plant was built in 1874 on a portion of a baronial estate which had been named Arabia long ago by owners who identified their property by means of Biblical lore. It employs 1,700 workers today and is said to be the largest ceramics plant of its kind in Europe. Even so, it is just a fragment of Finland's Wärtsilä industrial giant, which makes icebreakers and all manner of heavy equipment and machinery, and operates a leading glassware plant, as well as the ceramics factory. Arabia devotes most of its production to such prosaic items as bathroom fixtures and ceramic-coated skillets, but its fame rests primarily on the beauty of its pottery for everyday household use and the remarkable relationship it has with about ten of Finland's leading ceramic artists. The hardheaded businessmen of Arabia pay them well and turn them loose on the ninth floor of the factory to concoct what they want, whether it makes commercial sense or not. The result, as one observer said, may be rubbish, or 'it may grow into a mosaic for a millionaire or a frying pan for the millions. Arabia markets both.' Artists like Kaipiainen and Toini Muona not only are given carte blanche to be original in the company's service but are permitted to engage in international competitions as if they were free-lance artists.

Kaj Franck, a slight but dynamic man in his late fifties, probably did more than anyone else to build Arabia's reputation as a patron of the arts and as a manufacturer of handsome practical ware for Finnish homes. 'I was asked to come to Arabia soon after the war,' he said. 'I was a furniture designer. I knew nothing about ceramics.' As it turned out, he became a foremost ceramist and a brilliant glass designer, as well as Arabia's production planner for the practical ware which has radically improved the look and utility of the Finnish household. It is this kind of versatility which I felt was even more pronounced in Finland than in the rest of Scandinavia. Franck says it is due in part to the more generalized character of training in the Finnish arts and crafts schools—'the secret weapon of Finnish design.'

Tapiola

All of the wondrous Finnish talents for shaping their homes and things, and themselves, to live in the greatest harmony with nature, come to a stirring crescendo in the garden city of Tapiola, seven miles from the heart of Helsinki. It may be the finest modern planned community in the world. Tapiola was begun fifteen years ago, and the first families moved into the project in 1953. The ambitious plans were to create an entirely new city for 17,000 people, with three separate neighborhoods of five to six thousand persons each, and each with its own schools and shopping center. There would be a variety of dwellings for a variety of ages and incomes. Twelve leading architects were chosen for the dream assignment. The administrator of the project, Heikki von Hertzen explained: 'We were not interested in just creating housing. We wanted to keep the nearness and beauty of nature. More than just dwellings, we were looking for an optimum environment for modern man.'

To an extent which has made Tapiola a mecca for architects and city planners, the creators of the garden city have succeeded. The white clusters of apartment towers, the red- or yellow-brick row houses, individual homes and shops and schools, are thoughtfully set down on a varied landscape so rich in trees and flowers that it seems to have hardly noticed the invasion of people. From the roof-top restaurant of the central office tower, diners can look down on a forest of birch trees, rocky slopes, fountains and a great blue lagoon, as well as the variety of homes. 'Tapiola,' said *The New York Times*, 'can only awaken a frustrating combination of heartache and anger in any observer who has watched the destructive march of developers' housing across the American landscape. . . . It is an example and a rebuke.'

The Sauna

At the end of it all, of course, we come to the sauna, and for reasons as much cultural as religious, philosophic and hygienic. Although the Swedes indulge to some extent and it has become a fad in America, it is a peculiarly Finnish institution. To the Finns the sauna is a personal kind of dry cleaning, a recuperative, a ritual, a luxury and a necessity. 'HOLINESS IS A HOT BATH' said the headline on an article in a Finnish magazine.

There are more than half a million saunas in Finland. They can be found in private homes, hotels, companies, public baths, in the basements or top floors of almost every apartment building, and, best of all, on the shores of Finland's thousands of lakes. Home builders put up the sauna first and add the rest of the house later. Soldiers at the front are either supplied with portable saunas or they build their own. Finnair apologizes for not having figured how to provide a sauna on its airplanes. In its ideal form, the sauna should be close to water, so that the naked bather, after having achieved the glow of a baked lobster, can douse himself by leaping off the end of a dock. Most exhilarating of all is a midwinter plunge through a hole carved in the ice of a frozen lake.

Inside the sauna itself, a fire blazing away underneath a pile of hot rocks raises the temperature to about 200 degrees Fahrenheit, although a few devotees like it as hot as 250 or 280 degrees. The object is to induce perspiration, but unlike a Turkish bath it is basically a dry heat. Consequently, the temperature can be higher. The birch walls and ceiling absorb much of the moisture. Bathers sit or lie on a slatted wooden platform facing the furnace. They beat themselves now and then with a whisk of fragrant birch leaves to stimulate the skin. It obviously makes sense to go naked into the sauna with family or friends. Like the Japanese bath, it makes for sociability as well as efficient perspiration. The most horrified Finn I have ever met was the man who had just learned that Americans were 'sitting in the sauna in their bathing suits!'

Perhaps most Finns go to the sauna once a week, especially on Saturday, but many indulge two or three times a week. I was told of an American woman in Helsinki who wanted to live as the Finns live and thought this meant a daily sauna. She was a physical wreck by the time someone mentioned that a weekly bath, Finnish-style, was quite sufficient. Some visitors have been known to carry a raw egg into the sauna just for the fun of having it hard-boil in their hand while they sit sweating. The most anxious moments in a sauna come when one's Finnish companions start tossing water on the hot stones. Cruel clouds of steam hit like shock waves. But when it is all over, there is a sense of having been cleansed to the core, and a powerful feeling of bliss and well-being.

The sauna is Finland's oldest national institution and in no way can it be improved by modern plumbing, machinery or mass production. Its present-day popularity in its traditional form symbolizes the endurance of the best of the old in modern Scandinavia. If any single Nordic characteristic explains the high level of civilization which has been achieved in a rigorous section of the globe, it is this instinct for blending the most valued customs and institutions of the past with the new manners and methods of the present. Just as the builder of a new factory or housing project takes care to save the trees and the contours of the land, so the lawmakers and social planners of Scandinavia build up the new society from the roots of the old. There is no natural conflict between the traditionalist and the modernist. The conservative welcomes progress, and the progressive is concerned with heritage. 'The art of progress,' said Alfred North Whitehead, 'is to preserve order amid change, and to preserve change amid order.' The instinctive understanding of this by the Danes, Norwegians, Swedes and Finns has meant the creation of a humane society of luminous integrity.

Postscript

Iceland

Chapter 33

THE ULTIMATE VIKINGS

Iceland is a scale model of Scandinavia anchored in the North Atlantic. Not only are there the predictable welfare institutions, cooperatives, empty Lutheran churches, and candles glowing on the tables of severely modern apartments, but the Icelandic eyes seem bluer and the blonds fairer than in the rest of the North. It is a Viking civilization in modern dress, an ancient society whose recovery of independence and outburst of prosperity have happened so recently that it has been called 'the newest of the old nations and the oldest of the new nations.'

The Icelanders are even more determinedly egalitarian than the Danes, Swedes, Finns and Norwegians. The only persons who are addressed by their titles are the president and the solitary bishop. There is a more nearly absolute equality of income, education and social status than anywhere else in the civilized world. There is no monarchy, no aristocracy, and a fisherman or a carpenter can easily earn as much as a doctor or a professor. Iceland is such a first-name community that the national telephone directory lists subscribers in alphabetical order by their Christian names instead of their last names. Because so many common names like Jón Jónsson and Inga Snorradóttir are held by so many people at the same time, the Icelanders must identify themselves in the directory as 'teacher,' 'hairdresser,' and so forth.

The custom of giving children the *first* name instead of the *last* name of the father persists. Consequently, Bjarni, the son of Björn, becomes Bjarni Björnsson, and Lára, the daughter of Jón, becomes Lára Jonsdóttir. Married women keep their maiden names instead of taking their husbands', a fact which caused embarrassment at foreign hotels until the ladies decided to become

'Mrs.' when they went abroad. No wonder Richard F. Tomasson, an American sociologist, wrote that 'many of the culture forms here are closer to the proto-Scandinavian culture of the pre-Viking era than elsewhere in present-day Scandinavia.'

If the rest of Scandinavia is passionate for the printed word, Iceland is even more so. It has had the nearest thing in the world to a hundred per cent literacy for a long time. Centuries ago, when Europe was still in the Dark Ages, the 'Land of the Sagas' was producing works which have been described as the first master-pieces of Western prose narrative since the fall of Greece and Rome. For the size of its population, Iceland publishes and reads more books than any other nation. A successful work of poetry may well be purchased by a tenth of the entire population. The fact that there are at least forty shops selling books in Reykjavik is almost the most impressive thing about the busy little capital. Reykjavik is a city of merely 80,000 people, or half the total population, yet it produces five daily newspapers. Suitably enough, the best-known Icelander is a winner of the Nobel Prize in Literature: Halldór Laxness.

There is, of course, a University of Iceland which is free to all who qualify, a national theater, and the kind of health conditions which put the Icelanders next to the Swedes as the people who live longer than all others on earth. If Scandinavians live more to the north than Europeans in general, then the Icelanders live still farther north: their rugged island hangs like a pendant from the Arctic Circle. If the other Scandinavians pursue a thoroughly contemporary life, then the Icelanders are yet more contemporary. Despite the nation's 1,100-year history there is hardly a trace of the old days to be seen. There are no ancient castles, crumbling fortresses or skeletons of Viking ships. Even the fishing villages look more functional than picturesque. Almost all of Iceland's homes and buildings have been constructed during the past thirty years and the postwar building boom still goes on at such a pace that Reykjavik is surrounded by half-finished concrete structures. It is a neat and well-ordered miniature metropolis with straight, wide streets, but it has all the charm of a mass-produced housing development.

Fire and Ice

All in all, the Icelanders appear at first glance to be expatriate Scandinavians on a distant island whose version of Nordic life seems even more authentic than the original on the mainland. And yet, how astonishingly different their life is, and how singularly Icelandic their behavior. They have lived so closely together for so long under such rigorous circumstances that they are like a great family which squabbles constantly about minor matters but which is single-minded on matters of national pride. In this respect, if not in geography or racial ties, the Icelanders are much like the Finns. Labor-management relations, for example, are more turbulent in Iceland than one expects. In the midst of such economic well-being it is strange to see how firm a grip the local Communists have on the trade unions. They have helped fuel the inflation which has bedeviled Iceland since the war. As for politics, it seems to be the national blood sport. The personality clashes are appropriately volcanic for an island with a hundred volcanoes. The governments have usually been more conservative in their thinking than are those in the rest of Scandinavia, but the left-wing parties are influential and their more vocal members are always able to point to the big NATO base at Keflavik, thirty miles east of the capital, and shout that Iceland is under the thumb of the 'American occupiers.'

Even with my interest in Scandinavian affairs I had no strong desire to visit Iceland until the day that a prominent Norwegian told me that 'the Icelanders are the most difficult people in Europe. They are isolated, inbred and impossible. But what else can you expect when you cross a Viking with an Irishman?' When I finally met the Icelanders, they were not at all impossible—just different. They could not have been more friendly. It is true that a foreigner on the scene said that 'this country is as incestuous as Peyton Place'; but my inquiries revealed that the population, though smaller than that of Kalamazoo or Coventry, is large enough to enable the Icelanders to escape the worst effects of a tight little island. Far from showing signs of deterioration, they are a stunningly vital people who think that the rest of the Nordic world has gone soft.

I flew from New York to Reykjavik on Icelandic Airlines, an efficient but almost quaint operation which still relies on propeller-driven aircraft to cross the ocean. As an outlaw of the International Air Transport Association, which sets the fares and standards for all the other transatlantic airlines, Icelandic has built up a tidy business by offering the cheapest flights between America and Europe. They are also the slowest flights, and a stop in Iceland is obligatory. Amazingly enough, Iceland has not one but two international airlines, and both of them are private concerns. Icelandair, which calls itself 'the biggest little airline in the world,' not only flies to four cities in Europe but operates numerous domestic services for a people who seem as nonchalant about taking the airplane as catching the local bus. Not that they have much choice; there are no railroads in Iceland and a cross-country drive is still an adventure.

The foreigner arriving at Keflavik Airport has the impression that he has landed on another planet. The drive into Reykjavik takes him across a bleak wilderness of black lava garnished with green mold. I was not surprised to learn that during the past summer ten American astronauts had flown to Iceland to spend a week familiarizing themselves with the kind of terrain they are likely to find on the moon. Iceland is nearly as large as England and almost exactly the size of Kentucky, yet most of it is so unfit for habitation that its people must cling like barnacles to the shoreline. Only one per cent of the total area is farmed. Inevitably, it is one of the least crowded of all countries. Most of the island is overlaid with volcanic mountains, vast glaciers and a treeless black desert. One glacier is as large as Corsica. There are no snakes or frogs—not even penguins or polar bears.

In the Middle Ages, Europeans had the notion that the Devil had set up business in the far-off land where the collision of fire and ice is a daily occurrence. Mount Hekla was known as the Abode of the Damned and the doorway to Hell was said to be placed in its fiery innards. In 1783 the eruption of Mount Lakagígir was so stupendous that it covered all Europe with a blue haze and nearly wiped out the Icelandic nation. Geologically, Iceland is an angry young country still in the exciting process of growth. In 1963 a volcano erupted beneath the ocean just off the southern shore and a new island (Surtsey) was spectacularly formed by the rising mountain of cooling lava.

Iceland is not nearly so icy as it sounds. It was named, or mis-named, by accident. A thousand and more years ago it was variously known as Thule, Snaeland and Gardars-Holmi. Then one day a Norwegian visitor climbed to a mountain top and saw the once-in-a-lifetime phenomenon of icebergs drifting in the fjord below. Back home, he went about describing the place as Iceland, and the name stuck. Far from being oppressed by the cold, the Icelanders sometimes feel as though they are living on the spout of a tea-kettle. The island is huffing and puffing with hot springs. The Great Geysir, which hurls its boiling water and steam 175 feet into the air, gave the word 'geyser' to the world. The wonder of natural hot water has been turned to advantage by the Icelanders who long ago learned to make the most of the island's meager natural resources. It permits bananas, tomatoes and various semi-tropical foods and plants to be grown in greenhouses even in the day-long darkness of mid-winter. Nearly every home in Reykjavik is heated by nationalized hot-spring water and a bath smells vaguely of rotten eggs. The capital has a number of large thermal swimming pools where bathers in wintertime splash about in comfort while a crust of ice forms on their heads. The ordinary citizen who wishes to have a word with Ásgeir Ásgeirs-son, the elderly president of Iceland, can find him easily enough any morning of the week at one of the city's public pools.

The Hard Life

It was the Norsemen fleeing the tyrannical rule of King Harald the Fair-haired in the ninth century who established the first per-manent settlements on Iceland. They and their Irish slaves, not to mention the Scandinavian and Celtic voyagers who came along later, could hardly have chosen a more difficult place to live in, yet they did more than survive: they governed themselves with the kind of institutions which enable Iceland to claim to be the oldest democracy in Europe. The Althing or parliament was founded in 930 A.D. The Norwegian (and later Danish) overlordship which was imposed more than three centuries later did little to affect the independent ways of the hardy Icelanders. Self-government was recovered in 1918 and the formal connection with the Danish crown was severed in 1944.

Life on the bleak and pitiless island was incredibly hard going. Even in today's welfare state an Icelandic writer can say that 'we are a people who live on the edge of disaster.' The sheep herders, farmers and fishermen endure some of the most arduous working conditions of any people anywhere. In the Westman Islands off the southern coast the egg-pickers have a particularly perilous occupation. As they dangle from ropes attached to crude winches at the top of the cliffs, they rob the nests of sea birds that live on the jagged ledges. For Iceland's more than 6,000 fishermen, life at sea is so tough that they usually retire before they reach their fiftieth year. The fish they haul in account for 95 per cent of the country's exports, a figure which explains why the Icelanders fear the day when the fish swim off to other waters, as they did in recent years along the Norwegian coast.

Fishing is a deadly serious business in Iceland. During the 'cod war' in the 1950s when the British objected to their imposition of a twelve-mile territorial fishing limit, the Icelanders became so incensed that they came close to attacking the Royal Navy with their trawlers. Even a brief exchange of gunfire would have soiled Iceland's proud record as the most peaceful of all nations. Never in its long history has it fought a war with another nation. Even today, though a charter member of the North Atlantic Treaty Organization, Iceland has no army, navy or air force. There is no such thing as an Icelandic soldier. The country is protected, of course, by the United States, which operates, under agreement, the huge NATO base at Keflavik. It was World War II and then the Cold War which brought about the radical change in Icelandic life. The island served as an unsinkable aircraft carrier for the United States during the war. Today it serves both as an armed sentinel keeping watch over the ships crossing the

North Atlantic, both above and below the water, and as a link in the United States radar chain which stretches across North America and the ocean.

In 1940, just a month after the Germans invaded Denmark, a force of British marines landed on Iceland to make sure that the highly strategic territory did not fall into enemy hands. The Americans took over as protectors the following year and promised to leave at the end of the war. The island was so eminently useful to the United States that the male population of Iceland suddenly doubled. The tidal wave of Americans receded at the end of the war and then reappeared, though in not quite the same quantity, several years later, when the Cold War made Iceland a strategic prize once again.

The Icelanders are determined that their little country will not become a mere appendage of the United States. 'We are not the fifty-first state!' they insist. Inevitably, there has been friction from time to time between the United States forces and the local populace, and the 'Opponents of the Occupation' stage an occasional demonstration outside the base. In 1956, under a new left-wing government, the Icelanders were on the verge of officially asking the United States to clear out of the 150-million-dollar base when the Soviet Union's ruthless crushing of the Hungarian revolution shocked them into changing their minds.

The good relations of recent years, a kind of peaceful coexistence between the natives and the U.S. forces, have been reached through a policy of voluntary separation. 'Good fences make good neighbors' seems to be the theme. Keflavik, which is now the responsibility of the United States Navy after many years of Air Force command, has been turned into a veritable Little America, complete with its own shops, schools, clubs, theaters, snack bars, launderettes, youth center, tennis courts, softball park and golf range. Although it is about as dreary a military outpost as the mind of man can conceive, Keflavik's comforts and conveniences succeed in keeping the servicemen and their dependents on the reservation almost all the time. Many a sailor, airman or wife never sets foot on the rest of Iceland. A quota system which limits the number of Americans who can leave the base at any one time seldom needs to be applied. As one navy man told me, 'Reykjavik is not exactly Naples.' A further deterrent to revelry in the capital is the ten-o'clock curfew which is enforced every night except Wednesday, when the deadline for clearing out of town is midnight. By no coincidence, Wednesday is the very night when the law forbids the sale of hard liquor.

Super-Prosperity

The American presence on Iceland during the last quarter century has poured millions of dollars into the economy and has given the country a crash course in modern technology. The modernization of the fishing industry in particular has led to such good times that Icelanders are now buying imported appliances and luxuries at a feverish pace, even though they cost more than twice as much as in America or on the Continent. Iceland has made a stupendous leap from the pinched economy of an underdeveloped country twenty-five years ago to the status of an affluent society today. Global measurements of living standards usually place it within the top ten or twelve nations, along with its larger Scandinavian brethren. One survey puts Iceland eighth in the world for national product per head of population. An Icelander is likely to fly off to London, Edinburgh or Copenhagen to do his shopping. Before the war Reykjavik was a small frontier town of log and corrugated-iron houses, battered fishing boats and little else. Today its towering apartment buildings, crowded shops and traffic jams have inspired one writer to call it a suburban Klondike.

Super-prosperity has not only meant jobs for everyone but has caused such a labor shortage that a man customarily holds two jobs at once, and over the years he will be a jack-of-all-trades. A businessman will be an airline executive one day and a police chief the next. A teacher will double his or her money in a fish cannery. Since there are ten ministries of government and only seven ministers to go around, the head of Commerce must worry about Education as well. Iceland's world-wide diplomatic corps is thinly spread; all of its ambassadors could fit into a single limousine. The ambassador in West Germany, for example, is responsible for Switzerland, Greece and Japan as well. The Icelandic worker who has only one job is sure to demand plenty of overtime—a sixty-hour work week is common—and then in his spare time he helps build his own or his neighbor's house. It has been called a do-it-yourself society. The clue to its happiness may be found in the observation that it is just small enough to make everyone feel indispensable.

Icelandic women, who won their battle for equal rights long ago, work outside the home, and children of an extremely tender age are depended on for man-sized labor. Inasmuch as a third of the population is less than fourteen years old, a wholesale defection of the children to the playgrounds would probably cripple the economy. As it is, they are bright and sturdy creatures who seem to enjoy being treated as little adults. A four-month school vacation makes it possible for them to work full-time on the trawlers or in the fields and factories. While I was in Iceland the beginning of the school year had just been put off for two weeks in a number of communities because the teen-agers were needed to help get all the fish in. During his few months on a herring boat a youth may well earn several thousand dollars, a circumstance which tends to undercut parental authority. The government has felt obliged to institute a compulsory savings program for the rich unmarried youngsters.

Marriage is something which numerous young people get around to only after they have been living together for some time. 'Many couples,' according to one official, 'see marriage as adding little to social status.' Iceland has not only the highest illegitimacy rate of any advanced nation but also the highest fertility rate. Its population is increasing three times as fast as Sweden's. I have yet to meet an Icelander who is at all embarrassed by the casual attitude toward early sexual relations. Yes, they will say, there may be a few thirty-year-old grandmothers who are not exactly married, but in comparison with other nations Iceland has few divorces, few suicides and hardly any violence. At the most, Iceland has one murder a year; New York City—with many more people, of course—has nearly two a day.

So far, the Icelanders have been spared many of the disorders that plague nations when they finally achieve a winning combination of wealth and social security. There is an old Icelandic saying, however, that 'character is always corrupted by prosperity,' and the English poet, W. H. Auden, wrote after a visit to Iceland:

> Fortunate island,
> Where all men are equal
> But not vulgar—not yet.

Iceland has come upon good times so suddenly that it tends to react like a small boy at the toy store window who discovers that his pockets are miraculously full of money. I have heard the Icelanders described as 'gadget crazy.' A visitor certainly has the impression of galloping materialism which is in no way restrained by any religious force. The automobile, despite its incredible price tag, is now the most sought after gadget on the island. The Icelanders now own more cars per capita than almost all of Western Europe. Just why they feel they need an automobile in the first place is not altogether clear. They cannot drive far without encountering the ocean or a glacier. People insist that they need to drive to work, even though work may be a ten-minute walk from home, or they say that a car makes it convenient for them to visit their relatives. Since everyone on Iceland is related to everyone else, this has the ring of truth. As the automobiles thump along the cinder roads their engines complain loudly about the low-octane gasoline which they are fed. The Icelanders are apologetic about the fact that the Esso and Shell service stations dispense Russian gasoline instead of American or British. They say that because the Russians buy great quantities of their fish they are obliged to buy Soviet oil.

Pursuit of Pleasure

After working long hours at their several jobs, the Icelanders relax strenuously. Because there is 'nothing to do' and few places to go in Iceland, there is an almost desperate search for diversion and amusement. The dances at the Saga Hotel are unbelievably crowded and the bouncers must keep a sharp eye out for the hard-drinking couples who became much too boisterous. I was reminded of the young Russians I had once seen in a Siberian city who were delirious with joy when a Moscow jazz band appeared at the antiseptic airport restaurant. A party which begins soberly at a private home in Iceland can easily go wild and carry on all weekend. The Icelanders have an extraordinary addiction to snuff and Coca-Cola, but in their more adventurous moments they drink a kind of akvavit known as The Black Death.

As in the rest of Scandinavia, the consumption of alcohol per person is low, but the dedicated drinkers go at it with a vengeance. Significantly, the alcohol monopoly controls the sale of hair tonic and perfume as well as liquor. This may be a throwback to prohibition days, when sailors would break open the captain's compass to get at the alcohol within. The strangest quirk in the multiplicity of drinking restrictions is the fact that Iceland manufactures an admirable product called Polar Beer, but it is sold only to American servicemen, foreign diplomats and travelers on Icelandic ships and planes. The locals have to get along with a weak 'near-beer.' There is, predictably, a fair amount of smuggling and home brewing.

It is bootleg television, however, which is the cause of much more alarm. Some years ago, when the American forces at Keflavik erected a television station and began broadcasting canned programs from the United States—everything from *Gunsmoke* to *Perry Mason*—they were obviously intended solely for the servicemen and their families. There were no television sets anywhere else on Iceland. It did not take the Icelanders long to discover that they too could enjoy seven hours a day of free entertainment if they had the right equipment. Some enterprising businessmen went to work and soon were selling imported television sets for $300 and up to their eager customers. Now 7,000 families or 30,000 persons watch United States television on Iceland. The development has caused great controversy. A group of sixty cultural figures protested that the Icelandic way of life was being undermined by American television but the country's leading newspaper, *Morgunbladid*, took the calmer view that 'Ed

Sullivan will never be put down as the death of Icelandic culture.' The government's response is to fight fire with fire. It began a national television service in 1966.

There is no doubt that the country is undergoing the kind of rapid social change that worries a good many people. It is even said that the Icelanders no longer burst out in song during bus journeys the way they used to. For centuries parents made a ritual of reading the Sagas to their children in the evening, but in these modern days the Sagas are heard as interminable Norse operas on the radio, and such figures as Guthmund the Powerful and Björn the Butter-Carrier appear as comic strip characters. 'Young people,' complained a middle-aged teacher, 'are losing their uniqueness about being Icelanders. All they care about are American films and British pop singers. They even dress like the Beatles.'

American television, British pop music, Russian oil—the outside world is crowding in as never before. The Icelanders want all the things which add up to a prosperous modern society but they want to preserve the integrity of their unique civilization as well. It calls for vigilant efforts. Parents, for example, are forbidden to give their children anything but Icelandic names like Haraldur and Ólafur. Those few foreigners who are permitted to become citizens must adopt local names. I was told of a man named Max Keil who came out of the national whitewash as Magnús Teitsson. The Icelandic language is so stubbornly protected from foreign intrusions that such terms as electricity and the military tank are turned into 'amber power' and 'creeping dragon.'

The national pride is intense, but the trouble is that the Icelandic society is so cramped and personal that many people come to feel an overwhelming urge to get away from it all. A young man told me that 'it is such a relief to go to a place where no one knows you.' These days the Icelanders travel abroad by the thousands— a tenth of the population each year in fact. They escape to anonymity. They bask for a while in the glitter and ease of more fortunate lands. But only for a while. Then they return eagerly to their stark island where there is fire under the ice and a challenge to everyday life. The Viking heart still beats strongly.

Acknowledgments
Bibliography
Index

ACKNOWLEDGMENTS

A book of this kind, relying as it does on personal observations, conversations and on-the-scene research, would be impossible to write without the generous help and guidance of many hundreds of officials, experts, average citizens, old friends and new acquaintances in Denmark, Norway, Sweden, Finland and Iceland. For their hospitality and innumerable kindnesses, they have my gratitude and affection.

During almost every discussion of length, particularly on sensitive social and political subjects, I took careful notes, filling more than fifty tightly inscribed notebooks; no one should have been in doubt that I was a reporter seeking material and opinions for publication. I have not, however, considered the candor of my sources to be an invitation to quote them by name to their embarrassment. I have, in many instances, identified them, particularly in the case of public personalities, but more often it has seemed to me sufficient, and more proper, to simply refer to a 'Danish businessman' or 'Swedish diplomat.' Whether directly or indirectly attributed, the comments and factual material are set down as accurately as humanly possible. Any mistakes or misjudgments are my fault entirely.

To list only those persons who gave me an extraordinary amount of their time during the preparation of this book, and who went out of their way to open doors for me, would occupy many pages, and even then I would risk omitting those names which should be included. Perhaps it is enough to record that in my passage through the Scandinavian countries there were always wise and kind editors and reporters, government officials and embassy officers, professionals of every kind, spokesmen for

565

companies and institutions, and many private persons who smoothed the way for me and patiently submitted to what was a shameless exercise in brain-picking.

For interviews with high government officials, and for all manner of appointments and arrangements, I was enormously assisted by the chiefs of the press departments of the four foreign ministries and their associates: Kai Johansen and Bengt Petersen of Denmark, Tor Myklebost (now the ambassador to Iceland) and Christopher Prebenson of Norway, Sten Sundfeldt and Mrs. Gunvor Hildén of Sweden, and Matti Tuovinen and Paavo Laitinen of Finland. Four particularly close journalist friends and their wives were always prepared to steer me in the right direction or provide a home-cooked meal: Mr. and Mrs. Knud Meister in Copenhagen, Mr. and Mrs. Arne Bonde in Oslo, Mr. and Mrs. Alan Simon in Stockholm, and Mr. and Mrs. Lance Keyworth in Helsinki. And in Iceland: Mr. and Mrs. Thordur Einarsson. Similarly, such friends as Mr. and Mrs. Toivo Sibirzeff and Mrs. Anne-Marie Rådström in Sweden were imposed upon more often than I dare admit. Most of my Scandinavian acquaintances first became known to me during my days as a *Time* and *Life* correspondent, and thanks are due to Time Inc.—and more directly to Richard Clurman, Chief of Correspondents, and Robert Elson, formerly the London Bureau Chief—for frequent assignments in the Nordic countries and support for the idea of producing a book on contemporary Scandinavia.

My wife Leslie shared this enterprise with me from beginning to end, giving cheerful encouragement and astute counsel throughout, holding down the home front while I journeyed through the North and assisting in all the mechanics of preparing the manuscript.

BIBLIOGRAPHY

I have, of course, read as widely as time permitted on the whole subject of the Scandinavian civilization, and I have made use of a wide variety of documentation. I have had assistance in translating material in the Scandinavian languages, but for the most part it was not necessary. English is the most universally used foreign language in the Nordic world, and a remarkable amount of essential information is printed in English as fast as it appears in the local tongues.

The governments of each of the four countries publish invaluable books and pamphlets in English on political, economic and social affairs, while such institutions as Det Danske Selskab in Denmark, the Norwegian Joint Committee on International Social Policy, and the Swedish Institute turn out scores of excellent publications on cultural and other matters. The corporations, employers' associations, trade-union organizations and cooperatives produce excellent reports, and the leading banks publish economic surveys and statistical material which are gold mines for an inquiring reporter or scholar. I made particular use of the national statistics and corporation information compiled by the Stockholms Enskilda Bank. I learned much from the annual English-language volumes of *Industria,* published by the Swedish Employers' Confederation; the reports of the American-Swedish News Exchange; the booklet *20,500,000 New Customers,* published by AB Svenska Telegrambyrån; and *The Intellectual Face of Sweden,* by the Uppsala Students' Union. For a regular summary of developments in the North, the newsmagazine *The Scandinavian Times* was frequently consulted and borrowed from, and the books and pamphlets of the Nordic Council provided data on

Scandinavia in general. Such United Nations publications as the *Statistical Yearbook* and the *Demographic Yearbook* were used to measure Scandinavia's performance in the international context.

Some especially helpful books on aspects of Scandinavian life are these:

Scandinavia in General

BREINHOLST, WILLY, *The North from A to Z.* Privately printed in Copenhagen.

——, *Scandinavians—That's Us!* Privately printed in Copenhagen.

BRØNSTED, JOHANNES, *The Vikings.* Harmondsworth: Penguin Books, 1965.

FODOR, EUGENE, ed., *Scandinavia*, Fodor's Modern Guides. The Hague: MacGibbon & Kee, n.d.

HENDIN, HERBERT, *Suicide and Scandinavia.* New York: Grune and Stratton, 1964.

INNES, HAMMOND, and the Editors of *Life* Magazine, *Scandinavia*, Life World Library. New York: Time Inc., 1963.

MAZE, EDWARD, *The Traveler's Guide to the Northern Capitals.* Stockholm: Almqvist & Wiksell/Gebers Förlag, 1964.

MILLWARD, ROY, *Scandinavian Lands.* London: Macmillan Company, 1964.

RUGE, HERMAN, *Educational Systems in Scandinavia.* Oslo and Bergen: Norwegian Universities Press, 1962.

SANSOM, WILLIAM, *The Icicle and the Sun.* London: Hogarth Press, 1958.

SHIRER, WILLIAM L., *The Challenge of Scandinavia.* Boston: Little, Brown and Company, 1955.

ZAHLE, ERIK, ed., *Scandinavian Domestic Design.* London: Methuen and Company, 1963.

Denmark

BAILHACHE, JEAN, *Denmark.* London: Vista Books, 1961.

Denmark. Copenhagen: Royal Danish Ministry of Foreign Affairs, 1964.

Facts about Denmark. Copenhagen: Royal Danish Ministry of Foreign Affairs and Politikens Forlag, 1965.

LAURING, PALLE, *A History of the Kingdom of Denmark.* Copenhagen: Høst and Son, 1963.

Norway

BOARDMAN, PHILIP, *How to Feel at Home in Norway.* Oslo: H. Aschehoug and Company, 1960.

———, *Northern Paradise.* Oslo: H. Aschehoug and Company, 1963.

ERICHSEN, EIVIND, *Norway in a Nutshell.* Bergen: John Griegs Forlag, n.d.

LUNDEVALL, ELIZABETH, and HAGEN, PER, eds., *Facts about Norway.* Oslo: Chr. Schibsteds Forlag, 1963.

MIDGAARD, JOHN, *A Brief History of Norway.* Oslo: Johan Grundt Tanum Forlag, 1963.

MORTENSEN, SVERRE, ed., *The Norway Year Book.* Oslo: Johan Grundt Tanum Forlag, 1962.

NESHEIM, ASBJÖRN, *Introducing the Lapps.* Oslo: Johan Grundt Tanum Forlag, 1963.

Sweden

ANDERSSON, INGVAR, *A History of Sweden.* Stockholm: Natur och Kultur, 1962.

BASTIDE, FRANÇOIS-REGIS, *Sweden.* London: Vista Books, 1962.

CHILDS, MARQUIS W., *Sweden, The Middle Way.* New York: Penguin Books, 1948.

DONNER, JÖRN, *The Personal Vision of Ingmar Bergman.* Bloomington: Indiana University Press, 1964.

GULLERS, K. W., and LINKLATER, ERIC, *Gullers Sweden.* Stockholm: Almqvist & Wiksell/Gebers Förlag, 1964.

GUSTAFSSON, LARS, *The Public Dialogue in Sweden.* Stockholm: P. A. Norstedt & Söners Förlag, 1964.

HECKSCHER, ELI F., *An Economic History of Sweden.* Cambridge, Mass.: Harvard University Press, 1954.

570   BIBLIOGRAPHY

HUGHES, DAVID, *The Road to Stockholm and Lapland.* London: Eyre and Spottiswoode, 1964.

NOTT, KATHLEEN, *A Clean, Well-Lighted Place.* London: Heinemann, 1961.

SHAPLEN, ROBERT, *Kreuger, Genius and Swindler.* London: André Deutsch, 1961.

Finland

DESNEIGES, GEORGES, *Finland.* London: Vista Books, 1964.

Facts about Finland. Helsinki: Otava Publishing Company, 1964.

GOODRICH, AUSTIN, *Study in Sisu.* New York: Ballantine Books, 1960.

JAKOBSON, MAX, *The Diplomacy of the Winter War.* Cambridge, Mass.: Harvard University Press, 1961.

MAZOUR, ANATOLE G., *Finland Between East and West.* Princeton, N. J.: D. Van Nostrand Company, 1956.

STENIUS, GÖRAN, ed., *Introduction to Finland 1963.* Porvoo and Helsinki: Werner Söderström, 1963.

TOIVOLA, URHO, ed., *Introduction to Finland, 1960.* Porvoo and Helsinki: Werner Söderström, 1960.

INDEX

571